ASIAN DEVELOPMENT OUTLOOK 2020

WHAT DRIVES INNOVATION IN ASIA?

Special Topic: The Impact of the Coronavirus Outbreak—An Update

APRIL 2020

ASIAN DEVELOPMENT BANK

ADB

© 2020 Asian Development Bank
6 ADB Avenue, Mandaluyong City, 1550 Metro Manila, Philippines
Tel +63 2 8632 4444; Fax +63 2 8636 2444
www.adb.org

Some rights reserved. Published in 2020.

ISBN 978-92-9262-155-1 (print); 978-92-9262-156-8 (electronic); 978-92-9262-157-5 (e-book)
ISSN 0117-0481 (print), 1996-725X (electronic)
Publication Stock No. FLS200119-3
http://dx.doi.org/10.22617/FLS200119-3

The views expressed in this publication are those of the authors and do not necessarily reflect the views and policies of the Asian Development Bank (ADB) or its Board of Governors or the governments they represent.

ADB does not guarantee the accuracy of the data included in this publication and accepts no responsibility for any consequence of their use. The mention of specific companies or products of manufacturers does not imply that they are endorsed or recommended by ADB in preference to others of a similar nature that are not mentioned.

By making any designation of or reference to a particular territory or geographic area, or by using the term "country" in this document, ADB does not intend to make any judgments as to the legal or other status of any territory or area.

Corrigenda to ADB publications may be found at http://www.adb.org/publications/corrigenda.

Notes:
In this publication, "$" refers to US dollars.
ADB recognizes "Hong Kong" as Hong Kong, China; "China" as the People's Republic of China; "Korea" and "South Korea" as the Republic of Korea; and "Vietnam" as Viet Nam.

Cover design by Anthony Victoria.

Cover artwork by Atsuko Yamagata/2020.

Contents

Foreword

We face extraordinarily challenging times. The outbreak of coronavirus 2019 (COVID-19) is disrupting people's lives and interrupting business and other economic activities around the world. Developing Asia will weaken tremendously due to the pandemic, considering the region's deep integration with the global economy through tourism, trade, and remittances. Plummeting commodity prices are also placing a severe burden on some countries.

As the disease spreads and strict measures are imposed to contain it, rapidly undermining domestic demand and the external environment, we forecast regional growth declining from 5.2% last year to 2.2% in 2020. Growth will rebound to 6.2% in 2021, assuming that the pandemic ends this year and activity promptly normalizes. Excluding Asia's high-income newly industrialized economies—Hong Kong, China; the Republic of Korea; Singapore; and Taipei,China—growth will drop from 5.7% to 2.4% this year before recovering to 6.7% next year.

Growth could underperform these already lowered forecasts, as the pandemic poses downside risks. Outbreaks could worsen in more countries, and containing them could take longer than currently projected. Our research sees global losses from COVID-19 ranging from $2.0 trillion to $4.1 trillion, equal to 2.3%–4.8% of global GDP. It should be noted that the estimate does not take into account such factors as supply disruptions, interrupted remittances, urgent health-care costs, and potential financial disruptions, as well as long-term effects on education and the economy.

To mitigate these losses, effective response requires decisiveness, agility, coordination, and vigilance from policy makers and institutions throughout the region and around the world. The Asian Development Bank has been supporting our clients, both governments and the private sector, from the early stages of the crisis and stands ready to provide further support in collaboration with other international organizations such as the International Monetary Fund and the World Bank.

In the midst of such unprecedented economic disruption, innovative thinking is vital to overcome the current difficulties and rebound quickly. The ability to think up new solutions is necessary to restore developing Asia to its impressive growth path over the past decade. With this in mind, our theme chapter discusses the strong progress Asia has already made in fostering innovation. It argues for even greater efforts to advance the region's transformation from middle income to high income, while achieving more inclusive and sustainable growth. It highlights and explicates the crucial roles of sound education, innovative entrepreneurship, strong institutions, well-developed financial markets, and dynamic cities in fostering innovation.

I sincerely hope that *Asian Development Outlook 2020*, with its near-term economic perspective and medium- to long-term policy recommendations, will be useful for policy makers in Asia and the Pacific toward developing economic and social policies to overcome the crisis, and to make each country even more resilient, innovative, and inclusive.

MASATSUGU ASAKAWA
President
Asian Development Bank

Acknowledgments

Asian Development Outlook 2020 was prepared by staff of Asian Development Bank (ADB) regional departments and resident missions under the guidance of the Economic Research and Regional Cooperation Department (ERCD). Representatives of these departments met regularly as the Regional Economic Outlook Task Force to coordinate and develop consistent forecasts for the region.

Economists in ERCD, led by Abdul Abiad, director of the Macroeconomics Research Division, coordinated the production of the publication, assisted by Edith Laviña. Technical and research support was provided by Shiela Camingue-Romance, Cindy Castillejos-Petalcorin, Rhea Manguiat Molato, Nedelyn Magtibay-Ramos, Pilipinas Quising, Dennis Sorino, Priscille Villanueva, and Mai Lin Villaruel. Additional research support was provided by Emmanuel Alano, Rosa Mia Lasam Arao, Donald Jay Bertulfo, Nina Ashley O. Dela Cruz, Christian Regie Jabagat, Jesson Pagaduan, Reizle Jade Platitas, Rene Cris Rivera, and Michael Timbang. The support provided by Mahinthan J. Mariasingham and Aiko Kikkawa Takenaka is much appreciated. The economic editorial advisors Robert Boumphrey, Eric Clifton, Joshua Greene, Henry Ma, Srinivasa Madhur, Richard Niebuhr, and Reza Vaez-Zadeh made substantive contributions to the country chapters and regional outlook.

The support and guidance of Yasuyuki Sawada, Joseph E. Zveglich, Jr., Edimon Ginting, Juzhong Zhuang throughout production is gratefully acknowledged. Margarita Debuque-Gonzales provided editorial advice on the theme chapter and the regional outlook.

Authors who contributed the sections are bylined in each chapter. The subregional coordinators were Kenji Takamiya, Lilia Aleksanyan, and Fatima Catacutan for Central Asia; Akiko Terada-Hagiwara for East Asia; Lei Lei Song and Lani Garnace for South Asia; Thiam Hee Ng and Dulce Zara for Southeast Asia; and Rommel Rabanal for the Pacific.

Peter Fredenburg advised on ADB style and English usage. Alvin Tubio handled typesetting and graphics generation, in which he was assisted by Heili Ann Bravo, Elenita Pura, and Angel Love Roque. Art direction for the cover was by Anthony Victoria, with artwork from Atsuko Yamagata. Critical support for printing and publishing the report was provided by the Printing Services Unit of the ADB Office of Administrative Services and by the publications and web teams of the ADB Department of Communications. Fermirelyn Cruz and Rhia Bautista-Piamonte provided administrative and secretarial support. The Department of Communications, led by Vicky Tan and Karen Lane, planned and coordinated the dissemination of *Asian Development Outlook 2020.*

Definitions and assumptions

The economies discussed in *Asian Development Outlook 2020* are classified by major analytic or geographic group. For the purposes of this publication, the following apply:

- **Association of Southeast Asian Nations** (ASEAN) comprises Brunei Darussalam, Cambodia, Indonesia, the Lao People's Democratic Republic, Malaysia, Myanmar, the Philippines, Singapore, Thailand, and Viet Nam. In this report, the ASEAN-5 are Indonesia, Malaysia, the Philippines, Thailand, and Viet Nam.
- **Developing Asia** comprises the 46 members of the Asian Development Bank listed below.
- **Newly industrialized economies** comprise Hong Kong, China; the Republic of Korea; Singapore; and Taipei,China.
- **Central Asia** comprises Armenia, Azerbaijan, Georgia, Kazakhstan, the Kyrgyz Republic, Tajikistan, Turkmenistan, and Uzbekistan.
- **East Asia** comprises Hong Kong, China; Mongolia; the People's Republic of China; the Republic of Korea; and Taipei,China.
- **South Asia** comprises Afghanistan, Bangladesh, Bhutan, India, Maldives, Nepal, Pakistan, and Sri Lanka.
- **Southeast Asia** comprises Brunei Darussalam, Cambodia, Indonesia, the Lao People's Democratic Republic, Malaysia, Myanmar, the Philippines, Singapore, Thailand, Timor-Leste, and Viet Nam.
- **The Pacific** comprises the Cook Islands, the Federated States of Micronesia, Fiji, Kiribati, the Marshall Islands, Nauru, Niue, Palau, Papua New Guinea, Samoa, Solomon Islands, Tonga, Tuvalu, and Vanuatu.

Unless otherwise specified, the symbol "$" and the word "dollar" refer to US dollars.

A number of assumptions have been adopted for the projections presented in the *Asian Development Outlook 2020*: The established policies of national authorities are maintained. Real effective exchange rates remain constant at their average from 7 February to 17 March 2020. The average price of oil is $35/barrel in 2020 and $55/barrel in 2021. The 6-month London interbank offered rate (Libor) for US dollar deposits averages 0.4% in 2020 and 0.1% in 2021, the European Central Bank refinancing rate averages 0.0% in both years, and the Bank of Japan overnight call rate averages –0.1% in both years.

Asian Development Outlook 2020 is generally based on information available to **20 March 2020**.

Abbreviations

ADB	Asian Development Bank
ADO	Asian Development Outlook
ASEAN	Association of Southeast Asian Nations
BISP	Benazir Income Support Program in Pakistan
CIF	Consolidated Investment Fund in Tuvalu
COVID-19	coronavirus disease 2019
CSPP	Civil Service Pension Plan of Palau
FDI	foreign direct investment
FSM	Federated States of Micronesia
FY	fiscal year
GDP	gross domestic product
GFC	global financial crisis of 2008–2009
GHG	greenhouse gas
GST	goods and services tax
GVC	global value chain
HFC	housing finance company
ICT	information and communication technology
IMF	International Monetary Fund
IPR	intellectual property right
IT	information technology
Lao PDR	Lao People's Democratic Republic
Libor	London interbank offered rate
LNG	liquefied natural gas
M1	money that includes cash and checking accounts
M2	broad money that adds highly liquid accounts to M1
M3	broad money that adds time accounts to M2
mbd	million barrels per day
MSME	micro, small, or medium-sized enterprise
NBFC	nonbanking financial company
NBFC-D	nonbanking financial company that takes deposits
NBFC-ND	nonbanking financial company that does not take deposits
NBFC-SI	systemically important nonbanking financial company
NFRK	National Fund of the Republic of Kazakhstan
NGO	nongovernment organization
NIE	newly industrialized economy
NPL	nonperforming loan
OECD	Organisation for Economic Co-operation and Development
OPEC	Organization of the Petroleum Exporting Countries
PMI	purchasing managers' index
PNG	Papua New Guinea
PRC	People's Republic of China
Q	quarter
R&D	research and development
ROK	Republic of Korea
RPC	Regional Processing Centre in Nauru

SEZ	special economic zone
SME	small or medium-sized enterprise
SOE	state-owned enterprise
SOFAZ	State Oil Fund of Azerbaijan
SSRF	Social Security Retirement Fund
STEM	science, technology, engineering, and math
TTF	Tuvalu Trust Fund
TVET	technical and vocational education and technical training
UDIP	Universal Declaration of Income and Property
UN	United Nations
US	United States
VAT	value-added tax
WTO	World Trade Organization

ADO 2020—Highlights

After a disappointing 2019, growth in the region is expected to slow sharply to 2.2% in 2020 under the effects of the current health emergency and then rebound to 6.2% in 2021. Excluding Asia's high-income newly industrialized economies, growth will drop from 5.7% to 2.4% this year before recovering to 6.7% next year.

Headline inflation accelerated in 2019 as food prices edged up but remained low by historical standards. Inflation will climb further to 3.2% in 2020, but declining food prices in the latter half of the year will set the stage for easing inflation in 2021.

Downside risks to the outlook are severe, most notably from coronavirus disease 2019 (COVID-19). No one can say how widely the COVID-19 pandemic may spread, and containment may take longer than currently projected. The possibility of severe financial turmoil and financial crises cannot be discounted. Sharp and protracted declines in commodity prices and tourist arrivals will challenge dependent economies across the region.

In these difficult times, when challenges to growth abound, innovation is critical to inclusive and environmentally sustainable growth. While some economies in developing Asia are near or at the global innovation frontier, many others lag behind. The theme chapter in this report identifies five key drivers of innovation that should inform policy: sound education systems, innovative entrepreneurship, conducive institutions, deeper capital markets, and dynamic cities that bring together top universities and forward-thinking firms. Asian countries must first get the basics right because there are no shortcuts to an innovation society. Strikingly, one in three 10-year-old Asians cannot read adequately. This suggests that the education systems of lagging countries must be strengthened and reformed. The journey toward a more innovative Asia thus requires long-term commitment and a lot of hard work.

Yasuyuki Sawada
Chief Economist
Asian Development Bank

Asia reels from the COVID-19 outbreak

After a difficult 2019, challenges mount

- **Following a lackluster 2019, an incipient recovery is upended by COVID-19.** Growth in developing Asia slowed from 5.9% in 2018 to 5.2% in 2019, handicapped by trade tensions, a downturn in electronics, and weak domestic investment. Just as recovery in the electronics industry and progress toward what would become the "phase one trade agreement" between the United States and the People's Republic of China (PRC) began to lift the region's prospects in late 2019, momentum was halted by an outbreak of coronavirus disease 2019 (COVID-19). The outbreak emerged in January 2020, severely affecting the PRC and rapidly spreading around the world. The evolution of the outbreak, and hence this outlook, remain highly uncertain, but the baseline forecast is that regional growth will slow steeply to 2.2% in 2020 before recovering to 6.2% in 2021. Excluding the newly industrialized economies, growth is seen to slow from 5.7% in 2019 to 2.4% in 2020 and then to pick up to 6.7% in 2021.

- **The external environment is worsening as the outbreak spreads.** Growth in the major industrial economies of the US, the euro area, and Japan had already decelerated from 2.2% in 2018 to 1.7% in 2019. Signs of revival emerged in November 2019 as global trade and manufacturing trended upward for the first time in several months. But, with the COVID-19 outbreak increasingly overwhelming Europe and the US, economic activity in those economies is expected to fall sharply as they undertake containment. Growth in the major industrial economies is expected to contract by 0.3% in 2020 before recovering to 1.8% in 2021.

- **Growth will fall substantially in the PRC this year.** In 2019, US–PRC trade tensions weighed on both exports and domestic demand in the PRC. GDP growth slowed from 6.7% in 2018 to 6.1% in 2019. The shock from the COVID-19 outbreak this year is much greater. Data for the first 2 months of the year indicate double-digit contractions in industry, services, retail sales, and investment. As a result, growth in the PRC is forecast to slow to 2.3% in 2020 before rebounding to 7.3% in 2021.

- **Growth in India will remain subdued after a disappointing 2019.** India suffered a sharp slowdown last year, from 6.1% in fiscal 2018 to 5.0%, as a credit crunch that originated in nonbanking financial companies severely hampered bank lending. COVID-19 has not yet spread extensively in India, but measures to contain the virus and a weaker global environment will whip up headwinds, offsetting support from corporate and personal income tax cuts as well as financial sector reform meant to revive credit flows. GDP growth in India is forecast to slow further to 4.0% this year before strengthening to 6.2% in fiscal 2021.

■ **All of developing Asia's subregions will see growth weaken in 2020.** Global demand curtailed by the pandemic will weigh on the 2020 outlook, particularly in the more open subregions and tourism-dependent economies like those in the Pacific. Growth in East Asia will dip from 5.4% in 2019 to 2.0% in 2020 before reaccelerating to 6.5% in 2021. As the larger Southeast Asian economies wrestle with COVID-19, growth in the subregion is forecast to drop to 1.0% in 2020 before recovering to 4.7% in 2021. Growth in Central Asia will also slow, to 2.8% this year with lower oil prices, and the Pacific will contract by 0.3% with declining tourism, before rebounding in 2021. South Asia's growth rate is forecast to slow from 5.1% in fiscal 2019 to 4.1% in fiscal 2020 and reaccelerate to 6.0% in fiscal 2021, largely tracking recovery in India. Across Asia and the Pacific, the authorities have introduced stimulus packages to support economic activity.

■ **Inflation will tick up on increased food prices before easing in 2021.** Regional inflation increased from 2.5% in 2018 to 2.9% in 2019, driven mainly by rising food prices, particularly pork prices in the PRC and vegetable prices in India. However, inflation has remained under control, below the 3.3% average in the past 10 years, which has allowed many central banks across developing Asia to cut policy rates to stimulate growth. Regional inflation is projected to increase to 3.2% in 2020, driven by pork prices in the PRC, before easing again to 2.3% in 2021. Weakening economic activity and softening commodity prices will partly offset the effect of food prices.

■ **A widening current account surplus in 2019 and 2020 will narrow in 2021.** Global trade tensions kept developing Asia's exports and imports similarly in the doldrums in 2019, but imports fell more sharply, reflecting in part lower investment growth in the region. Trade growth will likely weaken even further this year as domestic demand wanes, and as trade and supply are disrupted by the COVID-19 outbreak. Thus, the regional current account surplus for the whole of developing Asia will expand only slightly from the equivalent of 1.5% of GDP in 2019 to 1.6% in 2020, before falling back to 1.4% in 2021.

■ **COVID-19 poses a grave threat to regional and global outlooks.** The forecast assumes the outbreak contained within this year and a return to normal next year. But even as the epicenter of the disease has shifted to Europe and the US, the potential for additional outbreaks in the region and worldwide remains, leaving vast uncertainty about the duration and severity of the pandemic. Outcomes can thus be worse than forecast and growth may not recover as quickly. The *Special Topic* in this report is an updated assessment of the regional and global impacts of the outbreak, indicating substantial downside risks if it spreads further in the region's economies. The possibility of a financial crises cannot be discounted, and the pandemic could bring about fundamental changes to the global economy over the long term.

The impact of COVID-19 on developing Asia—an update

■ **The rapid spread of COVID-19 makes it the worst pandemic in a century.**
The outbreak was still concentrated primarily in the PRC when ADB released
initial estimates of its economic impact on 6 March. Since then the outbreak
has expanded significantly, with its epicenter shifting to Europe and the
United States. The use of containment measures such as travel bans and
community quarantines has expanded greatly. Data from the PRC indicate that
the outbreak caused a double-digit decline in economic activity in the first
quarter of 2020.

■ **Updated scenarios suggest a much larger impact than earlier envisioned.**
The range of scenarios reflecting new realities and explored in this update
suggest a global cost of $2.0 to $4.1 trillion, equal to 2.3% to 4.8% of global GDP.
The much higher estimate reflects its spread to Europe, the US, and other major
economies. Developing Asia including the PRC accounts for just 22% to 36%
of the total. Nevertheless, regional economies will be hit hard, with impact on
the PRC approaching 5% of GDP. The loss to the rest of developing Asia will be
1.0% to 2.2% of GDP. These estimated impacts could be underestimates, as
additional channels such as supply disruptions, interrupted remittances, possible
social and financial crises, and long-term effects on health care and education
are excluded from consideration. The analysis provides estimates of the impact
on individual economies in developing Asia, and on sectors within them,
including the additional impact on an economy if it experiences a significant
outbreak of its own.

Estimated global and regional impact of the COVID-19 outbreak, under different scenarios

	Shorter containment, smaller demand shocks		Longer containment, larger demand shocks	
	% of GDP	Losses, $ billion	% of GDP	Losses, $ billion
World	−2.3	2,013.0	−4.8	4,090.8
People's Republic of China	−4.6	628.0	−5.1	691.6
Developing Asia excluding the PRC	−1.0	93.3	−2.2	200.1
Rest of the world	−2.0	1,291.6	−5.1	3,199.1

GDP = gross domestic product, PRC = People's Republic of China.
Source: ADB estimates.

Outlook by subregion

■ **Developing Asia will slow sharply in 2020 as it strives to contain COVID-19.** Growth will slow in most regional economies this year, with output in 9 of 46 ADB developing member countries expected to shrink. Aggregate economic growth will decelerate to 2.2% in 2020 but reaccelerate to 6.2% in 2021. By subregion, deceleration will be mildest in South Asia and steepest in the Pacific.

■ **East Asia will weaken but can expect to bounce back.** The slowdown is most prominent in the PRC, where the global health crisis first emerged. Recession in Hong Kong, China caused by separate stresses at home and abroad in 2019 will deepen in 2020 but begin to ease as fiscal responses and stronger exports bring recovery, probably beginning in 2021. Growth in the Republic of Korea (ROK) and Taipei,China will dip this year before rising next year on public spending and resurgent exports. Similarly, growth in Mongolia will decline this year as foreign direct investment inflow ebbs but will climb next year as mining and investment pick up. Despite the growth slowdown this year, inflation in the subregion will accelerate to 3.2% on temporarily higher prices for food, especially pork, in the heavily weighted PRC, and as inflation inches up in the ROK. In the rest of the subregion, inflation will slow in 2020 as demand wanes and then quicken in 2021 as economic activity revives.

■ **South Asia will face a milder slowdown.** Growth in South Asia will decelerate to 4.1% in 2020 and then recover to 6.0% in 2021, largely tracking the trend in the dominant Indian economy. GDP performance will remain strong in Bangladesh, which is forecast to grow by 7.8% this year even as global demand pulls back, and continue to accelerate in Bhutan both this year and next as a new 5-year plan strengthens government spending, and despite lower tourist arrivals. Maldives and Sri Lanka are less sheltered from global efforts to limit the spread of COVID-19, which are forecast to cause the tourism-dominated economy of Maldives to contract by 3.0% in 2020 before surging back in 2021. Leaving aside external upheaval, growth in Pakistan will slow as agriculture stagnates, notably affecting cotton output, and as stabilization efforts constrain domestic demand. The intended correction of macroeconomic imbalances in Pakistan should restore confidence in the economy and bring later benefits. Inflation in the subregion will soften to 4.1% in 2020 as food inflation eases in India with improved agriculture. Unusually low inflation will continue in Maldives with subsidies and price controls on basic goods joined by anticipated deterioration in demand. Pakistan, by contrast, will struggle this year with double-digit inflation fueled by escalating food prices, scheduled hikes to utility rates, and domestic currency depreciation.

■ **Southeast Asia will track the PRC and decelerate to 1.0% growth in 2020.** All economies in the subregion will endure a growth slowdown in 2020 because of COVID-19 and a consequent global slump, especially given their strong trade and investment ties with a slowing PRC. Thailand, the second-largest economy in the subregion, will likely contract by 4.8% this year, continuing a steady slide in recent years. Growth in the closely intertwined economies of Malaysia and Singapore will plummet nearly to zero in 2020, with only Malaysia enjoying a strong rebound next year. Cambodia and Indonesia will see sharp deceleration, as will the Philippines despite expansionary government policies, which should facilitate an upturn in 2021. Growth in Viet Nam is forecast to decelerate significantly but remain uniquely robust in the subregion. With most economies weakening and global oil prices softening, subregional inflation should stay tame at just 1.9% in 2020 and 2.2% in 2021. Counting mitigated deflation in Brunei Darussalam, 8 of the 11 economies will see somewhat higher inflation this year because of continued food price pressure, but inflation will slow in Myanmar and the Philippines and reverse to deflation in Thailand.

- **Central Asia will decelerate, reversing steady acceleration in recent years.** Under COVID-19, growth in the subregion will drop to 2.8% in 2020 as economies falter worldwide and drag down global commodity prices. Lower petroleum prices and sluggish production will weaken oil exporters, with growth slowing to 0.5% in Azerbaijan and 1.8% in Kazakhstan, the largest economy in the subregion, slowed as well by reduced public investment. Fiscal consolidation and lower remittances from the Russian Federation will weaken growth in Tajikistan. Georgia's highly tourism- and trade-dependent economy will be particularly vulnerable to COVID-19 as closed borders and monetary tightening grind growth to a halt in 2020. Growth in Armenia, a metal producer notable for its sales to the PRC, will fall sharply this year, and slower mineral exports to the PRC will slow growth less dramatically in the Kyrgyz Republic and Uzbekistan. Subregional inflation at 7.6% this year will be little changed as mixed projections balance out. Monetary tightening is expected to lower inflation in Georgia and Uzbekistan in both years and in Kazakhstan in 2021.

- **The Pacific will be hard hit by the pandemic and resulting global slowdown.** Combined output in the subregion is forecast to decline by 0.3% in 2020 as 5 of its 14 economies contract. Countries that rely heavily on tourism and commodity exports will be particularly vulnerable. Fiji's dependence on both will cause the steepest decline, with GDP contracting by 4.9%. The Cook Islands, Palau, Samoa, and Vanuatu, which also have large tourist industries, will see output shrink this year. As restrictions on the movement of labor and capital equipment delay infrastructure projects, growth will suffer in smaller economies. With only subdued recovery in 2021, growth in the subregion will remain below average in developing Asia next year. Inflation will edge down to 2.7% this year with fading demand but rebound to 3.8% in 2021 on expected currency depreciation in Papua New Guinea, the largest economy in the subregion, and growth recovery in Fiji, the second largest.

What drives innovation in Asia?

Innovating for inclusive and sustainable growth

■ **Innovation is a complex, diverse, and multifaceted process.** The term refers to new, significantly different products and processes that improve productivity and benefit users. Innovation occurs through a wide range of activities carried out by a variety of actors. Some innovations are game changers, such as the mobile phones that left landline phones to gather dust. Much more common are incremental innovations, such as those that create more and better features in mobile phones. While first-in-the-world frontier innovations like driverless cars grab most of the headlines, developing Asia receives more impetus from a steady stream of first-in-your-market catch-up innovations.

■ **Asia's emergence as a middle-income region argues for more innovation.** The region owes its transition from low to middle income to the accumulation of production factors such as capital and skilled workers and to productivity growth—the latter assuming a larger role in growth as economies mature and become heavily dependent on innovation. Middle-income countries that successfully graduate to high income invest three times more on research and development (R&D) than do countries mired in the middle-income trap, and they file four times more patent applications. The ROK and Asia's other three newly industrialized economies are examples of economies innovating their way to high income.

■ **Innovation can promote more inclusive and sustainable growth.** Innovation sustains regional growth and improves its quality in an inclusive manner. Many basic innovations—notable examples being insecticide-treated bed nets, cost-effective water filters, and payments transacted through mobile phones— can improve the quality of life for the most disadvantaged and are often the brainchildren of impoverished innovators with the keenest insights into the needs of these communities. Similarly, green innovations in energy, transport, and other areas promote a cleaner environment.

Landscape of innovation in Asia

■ **The innovation gap is narrowing, but unevenly.** While advanced economies invest on average 2.5% of their GDP in R&D, developing Asia is close behind at 2.1%, up from 0.9% in the late 1990s. Excluding the four newly industrialized economies, investment in developing Asia equals 1.9% of GDP, well ahead of 0.8% in Latin America. However, Asia's high average masks wide variation across countries, with lower-income countries more likely to undertake catch-up adaptation than innovate at the global technology frontier.

■ **Evidence from firms shows that Asia already innovates a lot.** Analysis of almost 27,000 firms in developing Asia finds that 53% of them innovate to produce new products, processes, or both. However, most innovation by firms improves existing products or processes incrementally, at some distance from the global technology frontier. This explains why reported innovation rates are higher among firms in low-income countries with greater scope for incremental, catch-up innovation. In the region as a whole, firms that are relatively innovative are usually larger, older, active exporters, or engaged in information and communication technology (ICT) or high-tech manufacturing.

■ **Research highlights the role of R&D, human capital, and infrastructure.** Cross-country analysis finds a positive relationship between innovation and economic growth across countries and, in developing Asia, between innovation and spending on R&D and human capital. The effect of human capital is more pronounced and robust. A 1% increase in secondary school enrollment is associated with a 2% increase in innovation, proxied by patent flows. The coverage and quality of energy, transport, and ICT infrastructure also correlate positively with innovation. The effect of human capital investment is especially robust, as detailed below.

Fostering innovators and an innovative culture

■ **Evidence from firms strongly links human capital and innovation.** Intuitively, a workforce that is highly skilled and educated, especially to the tertiary level, powers a more innovative economy. Many innovators who achieve technological breakthroughs are, after all, scientists and engineers. Analysis of firms in Asia that considered three indicators of human capital—workers' formal educational attainment, managerial experience, and training provided by firms—found a robust positive association between human capital and innovation. Firms that trained their employees, for example, were more likely to innovate than were firms that did not, by as much as 12.4 percentage points.

■ **Sound education systems can help create a larger pool of innovators.** However, the link between education and innovation is not automatic. A prerequisite for a well-educated workforce that can innovate is high-quality schooling in literacy, numeracy, and other basic skills. Where education systems fail to deliver, they must be reformed thoroughly to improve the quality of education in basic skills. More student-centered teaching can foster creative and innovative thinking. Finally, a mix of skills is needed to drive innovation. While the STEM quartet of science, technology, engineering, and math clearly provide key competencies that promote innovation, other qualities critical to innovation—such as creativity, critical thinking, collaboration, and grit—must also be nurtured.

■ **Strong institutions enable innovative entrepreneurs.** The quality of entrepreneurship in an economy is more important for innovation than its quantity. A very small minority of entrepreneurs, known in the business world as "gazelles," account for the bulk of innovation and job growth, while most entrepreneurs neither innovate nor create jobs. A country's ability to foster gazelles depends largely on its institutional conditions. Analysis of more than 36,000 businesses in 17 Asian economies reveals that strong property rights and rule of law encourage entrepreneurs to formalize their businesses, and that growth in formalized businesses is associated with greater innovation.

■ **Rapid advances in ICT have revolutionized the entrepreneurial ecosystem.** Technological developments have sharply reduced the cost of innovative entrepreneurship. They have spawned new business models that use frontier technology platforms such as the Global Positioning System, as exemplified by the ride-sharing and delivery services Gojek and Grab. As a result, entrepreneurial ecosystems have emerged and multiplied all over the world to exploit entrepreneurial opportunities opened up by the global digital transformation. This transformation is driven by relentless advances in digital technology and infrastructure, notably the internet. The transformation of Alibaba and Amazon into global tech giants illustrate the huge potential of digital entrepreneurship.

Conducive institutions and environment for innovators

■ **Intellectual protection should reflect the stage of economic development.** Patents and industrial design are critical for frontier innovations and in higher-income economies. Other types of intellectual property rights such as utility models or petty patents are better suited to the incremental catch-up innovations that are important in less-developed countries. Analysis of more than 7,000 firms in the ROK from 1970 to 2010 indicates that petty patents and trademarks facilitated firms' growth during the country's earliest stage of modern development. Design protection assumed a bigger role during the subsequent catch-up phase of ROK development, and patents became prominent during the most recent globalized phase. Thus, property rights cannot be judged solely on whether they are strong or weak. It is more important to offer the right type of intellectual property protection for a country's stage of development.

■ **Equity and other capital markets are key to financing innovation.** Analysis of patent data by industry in 47 countries from 1997 to 2016 reveals that financial markets matter greatly to innovation in an economy. The vitality of both the equity market and the debt market have positive and significant effects on R&D efficiency, as measured by the number of patents granted. Equity and debt markets also have positive and significant effects on innovation quality, as measured by citations in research papers. The effect is more pronounced for equity markets. The implication for Asian countries is that they should continue to develop their capital markets.

■ **Evidence confirms the importance of cities as engines of innovation.** Innovation tends to be concentrated in a few urban innovation hubs able to generate strong agglomeration economies. Across Asia, such concentration of innovation can be seen in product innovation, process innovation, and R&D. The 10 most innovative cities in the PRC account for 72% of product innovation but only 55% of the urban population. In India, the corresponding figures are 76% of innovation but only 43% of the urban population. Evidence shows that city size has a significant effect on innovative activity, with firms in larger cities tending to be more innovative, as does the presence of top-tier universities. However, haphazard urbanization that causes traffic congestion and other urban ills can undermine a city's potential as an engine of innovation and growth.

Toward a more innovative Asia

■ **Asian governments can and should become catalysts for innovation.**
Governments play a major direct role in innovative activity and sponsor a
substantial share of R&D. From 1996 to 2017, government shares of R&D
were 23% in the PRC, 24% in the ROK, and 42% in Viet Nam. While private
R&D typically concentrates on immediately practical commercial applications,
governments tend to support basic research that can spill over in multiple
directions. Plenty of scope exists, however, for government-supported innovation
to improve products and processes directly. Public sector innovation labs like
those in Armenia and Sri Lanka can promote experimentation and openness to
new approaches.

■ **The policy environment for innovators must evolve with the economy.**
Each country has a unique national innovation system to address market failures,
which are inherent in innovation. Governments should play direct and leading
roles in developing these systems at their early stages but shift to less direct,
supportive functions after the private sector has stepped up and assumed a
bigger role. Meanwhile, the evidence is mixed on how effective active innovation
policies are. Subsidies paid by Innofund, for example, through which the
Government of the PRC supports R&D by smaller tech companies, seem to offer
only limited increments in innovative output. This observation highlights the
need for nuance in government interventions.

■ **Local policies must complement national policies to foster innovation.**
To facilitate local entrepreneurial ecosystems, local policies should
adhere to key principles: (i) adopting a bottom–up approach to facilitate
entrepreneurship, which can achieve more than a top–down hierarchical
approach; (ii) engaging closely with all stakeholders; (iii) nurturing communities
of entrepreneurs, accelerators, financiers, large businesses, mentors, public
agencies, educational institutions, and regional agencies by serving as their
secretariat; (iv) enabling entrepreneurs to share their knowledge gleaned from
business model experiments by promoting networking events and platforms;
and (v) encouraging active public–private interaction though systematic and
institutionalized dialogue. Local policies can thus help cities and other localities
realize their potential to apply new technologies to incubate innovation and new
business models.

GDP growth rate and inflation, % per year

	GDP growth				Inflation			
	2018	2019	2020	2021	2018	2019	2020	2021
Central Asia	**4.4**	**4.9**	**2.8**	**4.2**	**8.2**	**7.5**	**7.6**	**6.3**
Armenia	5.2	7.6	2.2	4.5	2.5	1.4	2.8	2.2
Azerbaijan	1.4	2.2	0.5	1.5	2.3	2.6	2.5	3.5
Georgia	4.8	5.1	0.0	4.5	2.6	4.9	4.5	3.0
Kazakhstan	4.1	4.5	1.8	3.6	6.0	5.3	6.0	5.7
Kyrgyz Republic	3.8	4.5	4.0	4.5	1.5	1.1	3.5	3.0
Tajikistan	7.3	7.5	5.5	5.0	5.4	8.0	9.0	8.0
Turkmenistan	6.2	6.3	6.0	5.8	13.2	13.4	13.0	8.0
Uzbekistan	5.4	5.6	4.7	5.8	17.5	14.6	13.0	10.0
East Asia	**6.1**	**5.4**	**2.0**	**6.5**	**2.0**	**2.6**	**3.2**	**1.8**
Hong Kong, China	2.9	-1.2	-3.3	3.5	2.4	2.9	2.0	2.5
Mongolia	7.2	5.1	2.1	4.6	6.8	7.3	6.6	7.9
People's Republic of China	6.7	6.1	2.3	7.3	2.1	2.9	3.6	1.9
Republic of Korea	2.7	2.0	1.3	2.3	1.5	0.4	0.9	1.3
Taipei,China	2.7	2.7	1.8	2.5	1.3	0.6	0.4	0.8
South Asia	**6.1**	**5.1**	**4.1**	**6.0**	**3.7**	**4.9**	**4.1**	**4.4**
Afghanistan	2.7	3.0	3.0	4.0	0.6	2.3	2.3	3.5
Bangladesh	7.9	8.2	7.8	8.0	5.8	5.5	5.6	5.5
Bhutan	3.8	4.4	5.2	5.8	3.7	2.8	3.8	4.0
India	6.1	5.0	4.0	6.2	3.4	4.7	3.0	3.8
Maldives	6.9	5.7	-3.0	7.5	-0.1	0.2	1.0	1.2
Nepal	6.7	7.1	5.3	6.4	4.2	4.6	6.0	5.5
Pakistan	5.5	3.3	2.6	3.2	4.7	6.8	11.5	8.3
Sri Lanka	3.2	2.6	2.2	3.5	4.3	4.3	5.0	4.8
Southeast Asia	**5.1**	**4.4**	**1.0**	**4.7**	**2.6**	**2.1**	**1.9**	**2.2**
Brunei Darussalam	0.1	3.9	2.0	3.0	1.0	-0.4	-0.2	0.1
Cambodia	7.5	7.1	2.3	5.7	2.5	1.9	2.1	1.8
Indonesia	5.2	5.0	2.5	5.0	3.2	2.8	3.0	2.8
Lao People's Dem. Rep.	6.2	5.0	3.5	6.0	2.0	3.3	4.0	4.5
Malaysia	4.7	4.3	0.5	5.5	1.0	0.7	1.0	1.3
Myanmar	6.4	6.8	4.2	6.8	5.9	8.6	7.5	7.5
Philippines	6.2	5.9	2.0	6.5	5.2	2.5	2.2	2.4
Singapore	3.4	0.7	0.2	2.0	0.4	0.6	0.7	1.3
Thailand	4.2	2.4	-4.8	2.5	1.1	0.7	-0.9	0.4
Timor-Leste	-0.6	3.4	-2.0	4.0	2.3	0.9	1.3	1.8
Viet Nam	7.1	7.0	4.8	6.8	3.5	2.8	3.3	3.5
The Pacific	**0.4**	**3.8**	**-0.3**	**2.7**	**4.3**	**3.0**	**2.7**	**3.8**
Cook Islands	8.9	5.3	-2.2	1.0	0.1	0.8	1.5	1.7
Federated States of Micronesia	0.2	3.0	1.6	3.0	1.4	1.0	0.5	1.0
Fiji	3.5	0.7	-4.9	3.0	4.1	1.8	1.5	3.5
Kiribati	2.3	2.4	1.6	1.8	2.1	-1.8	1.0	1.1
Marshall Islands	3.6	3.8	2.5	3.7	0.8	0.1	0.3	0.5
Nauru	5.7	1.0	0.4	1.1	0.5	3.9	2.8	2.3
Niue	6.5	...	...	...	10.1	...	...	...
Palau	1.5	-3.1	-4.5	1.2	2.0	0.6	0.4	0.8
Papua New Guinea	-0.8	4.8	0.8	2.8	4.7	3.6	3.3	4.4
Samoa	-2.2	3.5	-3.0	0.8	3.6	2.2	2.0	2.5
Solomon Islands	3.9	2.6	1.5	2.7	3.5	1.6	2.0	2.3
Tonga	0.2	3.0	0.0	2.5	7.0	4.1	1.3	2.2
Tuvalu	4.3	4.1	2.7	3.2	1.8	3.3	3.5	3.5
Vanuatu	2.8	2.8	-1.0	2.5	2.3	2.4	1.5	2.0
Developing Asia	**5.9**	**5.2**	**2.2**	**6.2**	**2.5**	**2.9**	**3.2**	**2.3**
Developing Asia excluding the NIEs	**6.4**	**5.7**	**2.4**	**6.7**	**2.6**	**3.3**	**3.6**	**2.5**

... = not available, GDP = gross domestic product, NIEs = newly industrialized economies of Hong Kong, China; the Republic of Korea; Singapore; and Taipei,China.

1

ASIA REELS FROM THE COVID-19 OUTBREAK

Asia reels from the COVID-19 outbreak

With gross domestic product (GDP) growth already downshifted in 2019, prospects in developing Asia appear bleak in light of the colossal economic impact of the current health crisis. Growth decelerated from 5.9% in 2018 to 5.2% in 2019 as global activity softened and trade tensions mounted, the electronics industry endured a global downcycle, and domestic investment weakened (Figure 1.0.1). Economic activity showed signs of recovery toward the turn of 2020, but hopes were quickly dashed by coronavirus disease 2019 (COVID-19), which broke out in January in the People's Republic of China (PRC) and has since expanded into a worldwide pandemic. Disruption to regional and global supply chains, trade, and tourism, and the continued spread of the outbreak, have the region reeling under massive economic shocks and financial turmoil.

How the pandemic will evolve is unknown, leaving the outlook highly uncertain as the situation remains fluid. Based on information available to 20 March, economic growth in the region is forecast to slow to 2.2% in 2020, with all subregions weakening. Assuming that the outbreak ends within this year, growth will recover to 6.2% in 2021. Much of the expected decline in regional growth stems from a slowdown in the PRC, where growth is projected to plunge from 6.1% in 2019 to 2.3% in 2020 before rebounding above normal to 7.3% in 2021. Growth in India is expected to decline further to 4.0% in 2020 before strengthening to 6.2% in 2021.

The gravest threat to the outlook is the global pandemic. The forecast assumes containment within this year and a return to normal next year, but outcomes could well be worse than forecast. The outbreak could spread more widely, and containing it may take longer than currently projected. The possibility of financial turmoil and financial crises cannot be discounted. Further, the global pandemic could leave permanent scars that force fundamental changes to the global economy over the long term.

Figure 1.0.1 GDP growth outlook in developing Asia

The COVID-19 outbreak has Asia reeling.

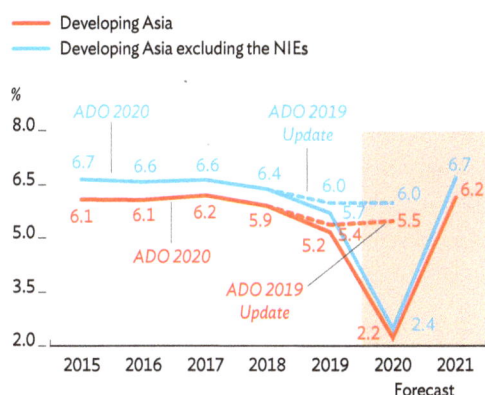

GDP = gross domestic product, NIEs = newly industrialized economies of Hong Kong, China; the Republic of Korea; Singapore; and Taipei,China.

Source: *Asian Development Outlook* database.

This section was written by Abdul Abiad, Shiela Camingue-Romance, Matteo Lanzafame, Madhavi Pundit, Irfan Qureshi, Arief Ramayandi, Dennis Sorino, and Priscille Villanueva of the Economic Research and Regional Cooperation Department, ADB, Manila.

1.1 After a difficult 2019, challenges mount

This report comes at a very challenging time. The COVID-19 outbreak that started in the PRC in early January has become a global pandemic. Its epicenter has shifted to Europe and the US. The pandemic imposes a deep and extensive negative shock to the global economy, as wide-ranging containment measures enacted around the world constrain both supply and demand. The *Asian Development Outlook 2020* (*ADO 2020*) baseline assumes the COVID-19 shock will be very large but also temporary. However, the duration and severity of the pandemic are subject to such extreme uncertainty at this point that a scenario in which the world economy comes out of this crisis fundamentally changed cannot be excluded. Recognizing that any forecasts done in such a fluid environment will quickly become outdated, ADB will monitor the situation and update its forecasts with the release of *ADO Supplements* as needed.

1.1.1 Signs of recovery quickly overturned

COVID-19 has buried signs of improvement in the global economy that appeared at the beginning of 2020. After weak growth in 2019, the lowest since the global financial crisis of 2008–2009, this year opened with receding uncertainties over the US–PRC trade conflict, Brexit, and the tightening cycle of the US Federal Reserve. Output growth in the advanced economies of the US, the euro area, and Japan had decelerated from 2.2% in 2018 to 1.7% in 2019 (Figure 1.1.1), but toward the end of the year the downturn appeared to be bottoming out, with global growth on the cusp of a mild revival. Prospects for global manufacturing, as indicated by the purchasing managers' index (PMI), improved in November for the first time in 7 months, however marginally. By January of 2020, the global composite PMI had risen to 52.2, its highest since March 2019 (Figure 1.1.2). Growth in world trade volume crossed into positive territory in December 2019 in tandem with signs of the US and the PRC deescalating their trade conflict. The deep downturn in the global electronics cycle, which affected exports from many East and Southeast Asian economies, also recovered to show mild growth by December. But the latest data show COVID-19 halting that recovery in its tracks. Composite and manufacturing PMIs fell in February of this year—early indicators of disrupted supply chains and battered trade and tourism globally.

Figure 1.1.1 Growth in the major industrial economies

Growth in the major advanced economies decelerated from 2.2% in 2018 to 1.7% in 2019.

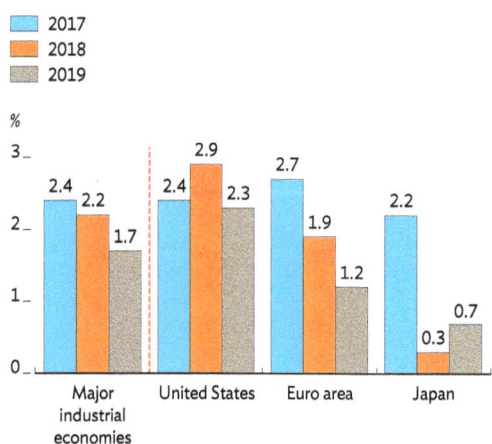

Note: Average growth rates in the major industrial economies of the US, the euro area, and Japan are weighted by gross national income, Atlas method (current $).

Sources: US Department of Commerce, Bureau of Economic Analysis, http://www.bea.gov; Eurostat, http://ec.europa.eu/eurostat; Economic and Social Research Institute of Japan, http://www.esri.cao.go.jp; Haver Analytics; ADB estimates.

GDP growth in developing Asia slowed in 2019 as trade and investment weakened against the backdrop of a global slowdown. The regional performance deteriorated from 5.9% in 2018 to 5.2% last year, with 23 of 45 Asian Development Bank (ADB) developing member economies recording slower growth (Figure 1.1.3). Growth in India declined from 6.1% in fiscal 2018 to 5.0% as domestic investment and consumption collapsed under stress on nonbanking financial companies and a sharp slowdown in credit growth more generally (Figure 1.1.4). Growth in the PRC decelerated from 6.7% to 6.1% in the same period, the ongoing slowdown caused by trade tensions and weakening domestic demand. Beyond the PRC, prolonged uncertainty from the trade conflict, weak global demand, and a downturn in the electronics cycle weighed on growth in the more open subregions of East and Southeast Asia. Among the newly industrialized economies (NIEs), Hong Kong, China actually contracted for the first time in a decade as domestic political tensions exacerbated a challenging external environment. The Republic of Korea (ROK) and Singapore also slowed considerably. The larger Southeast Asian economies slowed mildly, except Thailand, where growth fell substantially as major categories of merchandise exports continued to contract. The economically smaller subregions of Central Asia and the Pacific bucked the trend with rising growth in 2019.

Consumption remained the bulwark of growth in Asia in 2019, though its contribution declined in the four NIEs, especially in Hong Kong, China, and in the region's two largest economies, India and the PRC (Figure 1.1.5). It was mostly stable from 2018 to 2019 in five large Southeast Asian economies (ASEAN-5). The contribution of investment to GDP growth has declined across the board over the past couple of years in response to economic weakness and uncertain prospects. Net exports boosted growth in the NIEs, but this was only because import declines outpaced those of exports, reflecting weakening investment.

In the PRC, trade tensions weighed on exports in 2019, and domestic demand softened. Growth in the PRC slowed from 6.7% in 2018 to 6.1% in 2019. On the domestic front, consumption decelerated as both household disposable income and consumption expenditure softened, reflecting a rapid increase in food prices, which drove down consumers' purchasing power in real terms. The contribution of investment to growth fell with sharp deceleration in manufacturing investment as domestic demand softened, external demand deteriorated, profits declined, and overcapacity continued to be cut in some upstream industries. On the external front, imports of investment goods such as machinery and electrical equipment declined, while trade tensions with the US kept export growth marginal.

Figure 1.1.2 Global activity indicators

Signs of a global recovery in late 2019 were snuffed by the COVID-19 outbreak.

PMI = purchasing managers' index, sa = seasonally adjusted.
Sources: ADB estimates based on data from CEIC Data Company; CPB Netherlands Bureau for Economic Policy Analysis, https://www.cpb.nl/en/worldtrademonitor; World Semiconductor Trade Statistics (all accessed 23 March 2020).

Figure 1.1.3 Growth by subregion, 2017 to 2019

GDP growth decelerated in the larger subregions of developing Asia in 2019.

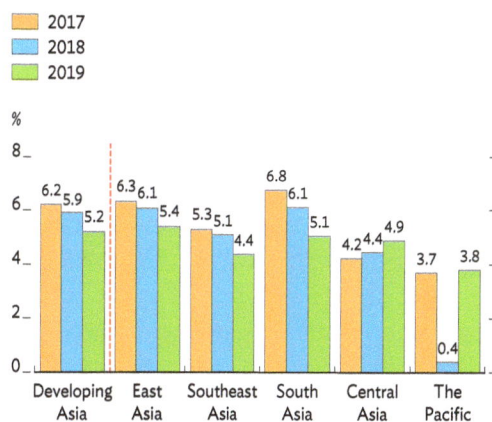

Source: *Asian Development Outlook* database.

Figure 1.1.4 Demand-side contributions to growth, selected economies

Domestic investment was a drag on many economies in 2019.

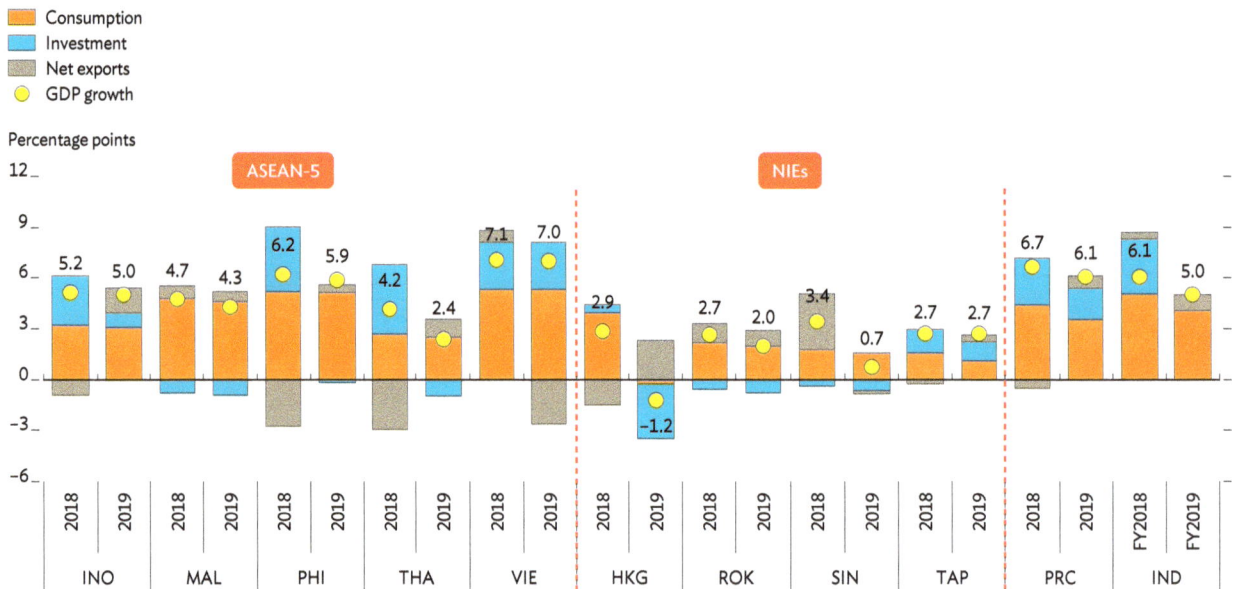

■ Consumption
■ Investment
■ Net exports
○ GDP growth

Percentage points

ASEAN-5   NIEs

INO: 2018 5.2, 2019 5.0
MAL: 2018 4.7, 2019 4.3
PHI: 2018 6.2, 2019 5.9
THA: 2018 4.2, 2019 2.4
VIE: 2018 7.1, 2019 7.0
HKG: 2018 2.9, 2019 −1.2
ROK: 2018 2.7, 2019 2.0
SIN: 2018 3.4, 2019 0.7
TAP: 2018 2.7, 2019 2.7
PRC: 2018 6.7, 2019 6.1
IND: FY2018 6.1, FY2019 5.0

ASEAN = Association of Southeast Asian Nations, FY = fiscal year, HKG = Hong Kong, China, IND = India, INO = Indonesia, MAL = Malaysia, NIE = newly industrialized economy, PHI = Philippines, PRC = People's Republic of China, ROK = Republic of Korea, SIN = Singapore, TAP = Taipei,China, THA = Thailand, VIE = Viet Nam.
Notes: Data for India are fiscal years ending 31 March of the next year. Components do not sum to GDP growth because statistical discrepancy is excluded.
Sources: Haver Analytics (accessed 23 March 2020); ADB estimates.

Monetary policy remained largely accommodative in 2019 with bolstered support for the real economy and for banks, including several rounds of cuts in reserve requirement ratios for various types of banks. The government cut taxes and fees for corporations and incurred a sizeable budget deficit as fiscal expenditure greatly outpaced revenue.

A slowdown in India further weighed down regional growth in 2019. GDP growth in India fell from 6.1% in fiscal 2018 to an estimated 5.0% in the fiscal year just finished, below its decade average of 7.0%. A steep deceleration in credit weighed heavily on private consumption and investment in 2019. Recent years had seen a sharp rise in loans from nonbanking financial companies, partly in response to lending constraints on public sector banks as they cleaned their balance sheets. Then, in September 2018, one such company defaulted, which, along with declining asset quality across this finance segment, triggered a slowdown in credit growth. This brought to the fore systemic problems in the financial sector. Growth in nonfood credit (which excludes public sector loans for procuring crops from farmers) slumped by half from a peak of 14.6% at the beginning of 2019 to 7.1% at year-end, undermining economic growth (Figure 1.1.6).

Figure 1.1.5 Changes in domestic demand contribution to growth from 2018 to 2019, selected economies

The investment contribution to growth declined from 2018 to 2019 across developing Asia, and the consumption contribution also fell in some large economies.

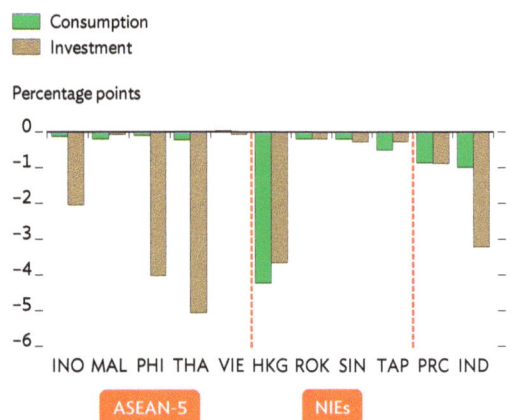

■ Consumption
■ Investment

Percentage points

INO MAL PHI THA VIE HKG ROK SIN TAP PRC IND

ASEAN-5   NIEs

ASEAN = Association of Southeast Asian Nations, HKG = Hong Kong, China, IND = India, INO = Indonesia, MAL = Malaysia; NIE = newly industrialized economy, PHI = Philippines, PRC = People's Republic of China, ROK = Republic of Korea, SIN = Singapore, TAP = Taipei,China, THA = Thailand, VIE = Viet Nam.
Sources: Haver Analytics (accessed 23 March 2020); ADB estimates.

Consumption, meanwhile, languished under other factors, notably subdued job and wage growth and continued rural distress. Domestic production and investment were further weighed down by inadequate infrastructure, low productivity in the absence of land and labor market reform, and tight fiscal space constrained by low tax revenue.

Some indicators suggested an uptick in regional economic activity around the turn of 2019. A decline in manufacturing that had begun in the latter part of 2018 continued through much of 2019 but appeared to turn a corner toward the end of the year. Industrial production in developing Asia inched up in December on incipient gains in India, the PRC, and the NIEs, though production continued to decline in the ASEAN-5 (Figure 1.1.7). Then COVID-19 squelched it. In January and February, PRC industrial output reversed 6.9% growth year on year in December by contracting dramatically by 13.5%, the weakest reading in over 3 decades.

Similarly, the forward-looking PMI had pointed in early January to expanding manufacturing in many Asian economies, only to be overtaken by the COVID-19 outbreak (Table 1.1.1). Subsequently, large and extended factory and service closures in the PRC induced unprecedented plunges in the country's PMI readings in February: in manufacturing, from 51.1 across the contraction threshold at 50 to 40.3, and in services, from 51.8 all the way down to 26.5. The ROK, which has suffered Asia's worst COVID-19 outbreak outside of the PRC, saw its manufacturing PMI fall further below the 50 threshold. In Southeast Asia, the index dipped slightly below 50 in Viet Nam and Thailand but stayed mostly stable and above 50 in Malaysia and the Philippines. Manufacturing in Indonesia strengthened in February after contracting for 7 consecutive months, with the PMI reaching 51.9 as elections dissipated uncertainty. Up to February, India's economy remained little affected by the outbreak. While its manufacturing PMI dropped from an 8-year high of 55.3 in January to 54.5 in February, its service index rose from 55.5 to 57.5.

Retail sales data in December showed stable consumption alongside a pickup in consumer confidence in East Asia (except in Hong Kong, China because of political turmoil) but not in Thailand and Indonesia, where economic strains kept sales subdued (Figure 1.1.8). In the Philippines, sentiment rebounded strongly in 2019 after consumption plummeted the previous year. In the PRC, retail sales shrank in January and February 2020 by 20.5% from the previous year, the first such decline on record as rattled consumers stayed away from shops, restaurants, and other commercial establishments in line with tough government containment restrictions. While the initial impact of virus containment on economic activity is clear in the PRC, disruption to both supply and demand in other regional economies is not yet evident in the monthly data.

Figure 1.1.6 Credit growth in India

A deceleration in credit undermined growth in 2019.

% change year on year

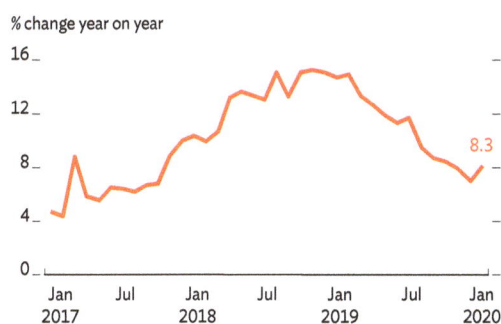

Note: Nonfood credit, which excludes public sector loans for procuring crops from farmers.
Source: Haver Analytics (accessed 24 March 2020).

Figure 1.1.7 Growth in industrial production, selected economies

Manufacturing in Asia turned a corner toward the end of 2019, before COVID-19 caused production in the PRC to contract in January and February, for the first time in modern history.

— Developing Asia
— ASEAN-5
— NIEs
— India
— People's Republic of China

% change year on year

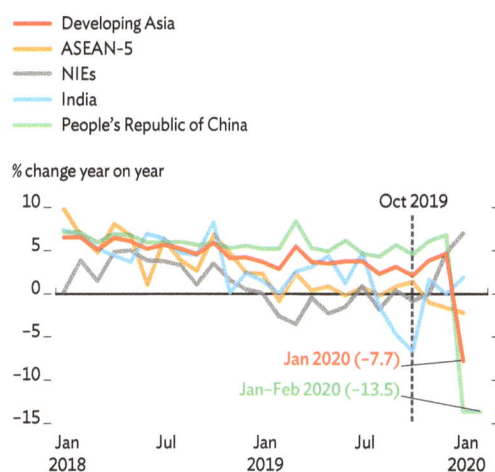

ASEAN-5 = five large economies in the Association of Southeast Asian Nations (Indonesia, Malaysia, the Philippines, Thailand, and Viet Nam), NIEs = newly industrialized economies of the Republic of Korea; Singapore; and Taipei,China.
Note: PRC data is combined for the months of January and February.
Sources: CEIC Data Company, National Bureau of Statistics (both accessed 20 March 2020); ADB estimates.

Table 1.1.1 Markit purchasing managers' index, selected economies

This leading indicator pointed in early January to manufacturing expansion in many Asian economies but then nosedived in the PRC after COVID-19 struck.

Manufacturing purchasing managers' index, seasonally adjusted

Economy	2018 Q1			2018 Q2			2018 Q3			2018 Q4			2019 Q1			2019 Q2			2019 Q3			2019 Q4			2020 Q1	
PRC	51.5	51.6	51.0	51.1	51.1	51.0	50.8	50.6	50.0	50.1	50.2	49.7	48.3	49.9	50.8	50.2	50.2	49.4	49.9	50.4	51.4	51.7	51.8	51.5	51.1	40.3
India	52.4	52.1	51.0	51.6	51.2	53.1	52.3	51.7	52.2	53.1	54.0	53.2	53.9	54.3	52.6	51.8	52.7	52.1	52.5	51.4	51.4	50.6	51.2	52.7	55.3	54.5
Indonesia	49.9	51.4	50.7	51.6	51.7	50.3	50.5	51.9	50.7	50.5	50.4	51.2	49.9	50.1	51.2	50.4	51.6	50.6	49.6	49.0	49.1	47.7	48.2	49.5	49.3	51.9
Malaysia[a]	53.5	52.9	52.5	51.6	50.6	52.5	52.7	54.2	54.5	52.2	51.2	49.8	50.9	50.6	50.2	52.4	51.8	50.8	50.6	50.4	50.9	52.3	52.5	53.0	51.8	51.5
Philippines	51.7	50.8	51.5	52.7	53.7	52.9	50.9	51.9	52.0	54.0	54.2	53.2	52.3	51.9	51.5	50.9	51.2	51.3	52.1	51.9	51.8	52.1	51.4	51.7	52.1	52.3
Rep. of Korea	50.7	50.3	49.1	48.4	48.9	49.8	48.3	49.9	51.3	51.0	48.6	49.8	48.3	47.2	48.8	50.2	48.4	47.5	47.3	49.0	48.0	48.4	49.4	50.1	49.8	48.7
Taipei,China	56.9	56.0	55.3	54.8	53.4	54.5	53.1	53.0	50.8	48.7	48.4	47.7	47.5	46.3	49.0	48.2	48.4	45.5	48.1	47.9	50.0	49.8	49.8	50.8	51.8	49.9
Thailand	50.6	50.9	49.1	49.5	51.1	50.2	50.1	49.9	50.0	48.9	49.8	50.3	50.2	49.9	50.3	51.0	50.7	50.6	50.3	50.0	50.6	50.0	49.3	50.1	49.9	49.5
Viet Nam	53.4	53.5	51.6	52.7	53.9	55.7	54.9	53.7	51.5	53.9	56.5	53.8	51.9	51.2	51.9	52.5	52.0	52.5	52.6	51.4	50.5	50.0	51.0	50.8	50.6	49.0

Service purchasing managers' index, seasonally adjusted

Economy	2018 Q1			2018 Q2			2018 Q3			2018 Q4			2019 Q1			2019 Q2			2019 Q3			2019 Q4			2020 Q1	
PRC	54.7	54.2	52.3	52.9	52.9	53.9	52.8	51.5	53.1	50.8	53.8	53.9	53.6	51.1	54.4	54.5	52.7	52.0	51.6	52.1	51.3	51.1	53.5	52.5	51.8	26.5
India	51.7	47.8	50.3	51.4	49.6	52.6	54.2	51.5	50.9	52.2	53.7	53.2	52.2	52.5	52.0	51.0	50.2	49.6	53.8	52.4	48.7	49.2	52.7	53.3	55.5	57.5

PRC = People's Republic of China, Q = quarter.

a For Malaysia, the series is adjusted by adding 3 points because historical experience suggests that values above 47 are consistent with expansion.

Note: Pink to red indicates contraction (<50), and white to green indicates expansion (>50).

Source: CEIC Data Company (accessed 5 March 2020).

Figure 1.1.8 Consumer confidence and retail sales, selected economies

Retail sales were stable in some parts of Asia but not in others at the end of 2019, and the crippling impact of the COVID-19 outbreak on PRC retail was already evident in January and February data.

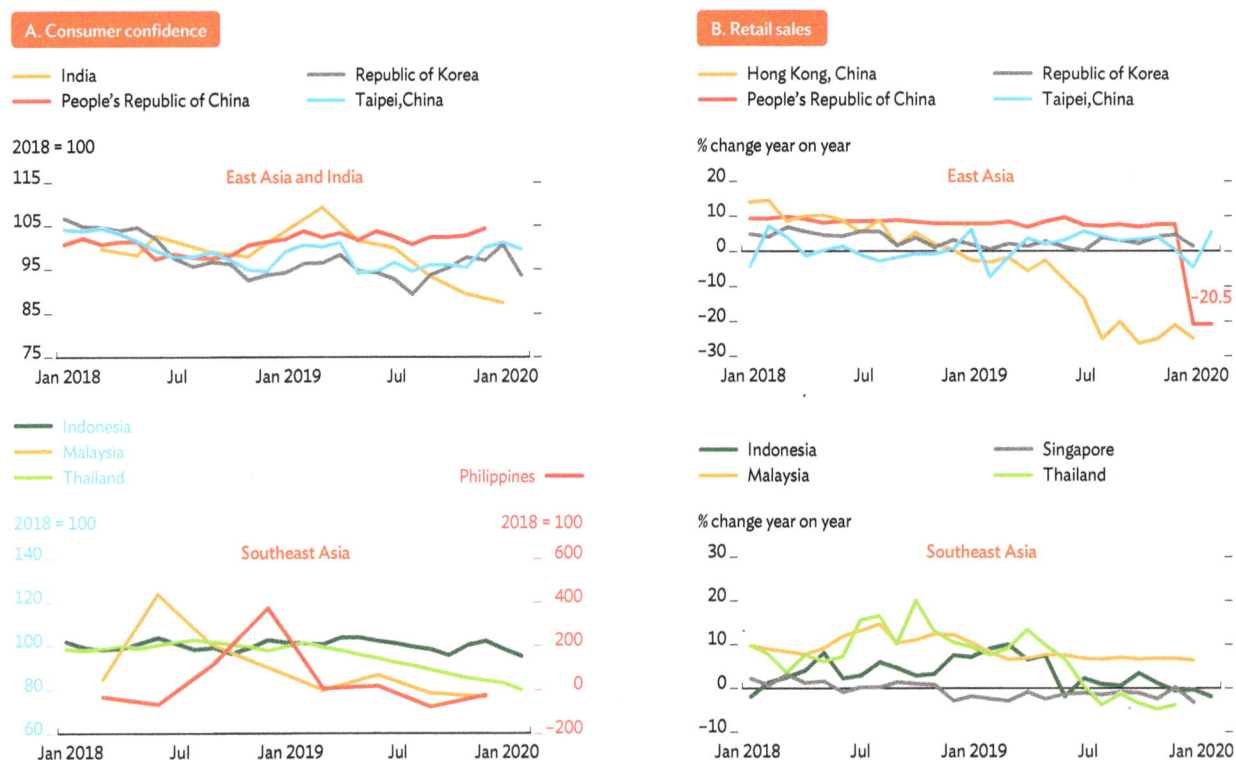

A. Consumer confidence

B. Retail sales

Notes: Data inconsistency or unavailability excludes Central Asia, the Pacific, and some other smaller economies from this analysis, as well as South Asia except for India's inclusion in consumer confidence. Data are quarterly for India, Malaysia, and the Philippines. The consumer confidence index measures positive or negative consumer household expectations.

Sources: CEIC Data Company, National Bureau of Statistics (both accessed 20 March 2020).

Headline inflation in developing Asia accelerated from 2.5% in 2018 to 2.9% in 2019 as food prices rose but remained below the regional 10-year average of 3.3%. South Asia recorded a sizable increase in annual inflation, from 3.7% in 2018 to 4.9% in 2019, and monthly inflation at 7.1% in February 2020 stood out as the highest among the five subregions. The spike was caused mainly by a surge in Indian prices for vegetables, particularly onions. Annual inflation in East Asia increased from 2.0% in 2018 to 2.6% in 2019, while monthly inflation rose further to 4.6% in February 2020. Much of the increase, especially in the PRC, was traceable to a surge in pork prices caused by an outbreak of African swine fever. Yet core inflation, which excludes fresh food and energy, remained low and stable (Figure 1.1.9).

Figure 1.1.9 Inflation in developing Asia

Headline inflation in developing Asia increased from 2.5% in 2018 to 2.9% in 2019 on higher prices for food: pork in the PRC and onions in India.

A. Annual inflation

Source: *Asian Development Outlook* database.

Higher inflation mainly reflected food price spikes as core inflation remained stable.

B. Monthly inflation

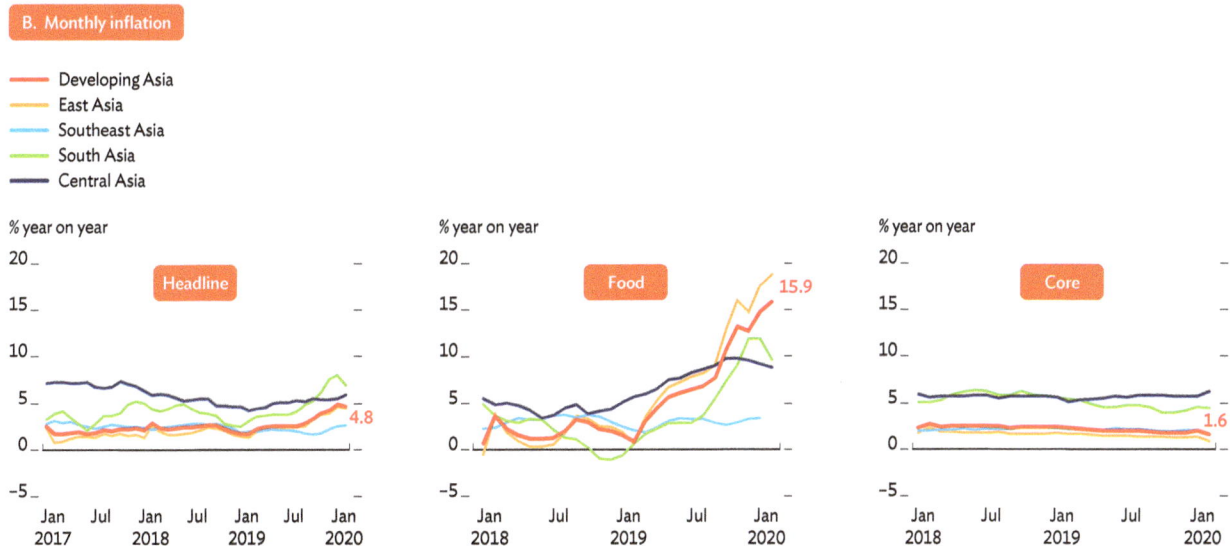

Note: The Pacific is excluded because data are not available.
Sources: CEIC Data Company (accessed 21 March 2020); ADB estimates.

1.1.2 Rising trade tensions and falling trade flows

Trade in developing Asia remained in the doldrums in 2019, with imports falling faster than exports. After moderating in 2018, external demand declined last year as tensions emanating from the US–PRC trade conflict reverberated across the region through depressed aggregate demand and disrupted global value chains. The ensuing fall in exports of primary products and other manufactures was compounded by a pronounced slowdown in the electronics cycle, which showed signs of bottoming out only in the second half of the year (Figures 1.1.10 and 1.1.11).

In line with softening global trade and economic activity, the value of developing Asia's exports and imports trended down (Figure 1.1.12). Data for January–November 2019 show this pattern determined by poor performance in East Asia, where all economies except Mongolia recorded negative export growth, and in Southeast Asia, where only countries with small regional export shares saw their exports increase, as did the Lao People's Democratic Republic and the Philippines, or soar, as did Cambodia. After booming in 2017 and 2018, Viet Nam's exports declined by 10.5% in 2019, dragged down by softer growth in developing Asia, the market for 40% of its exports. Buttressed by healthy demand for fuel and energy, export growth held up well in Central Asia, while it stagnated in South Asia and the Pacific.

The US–PRC trade conflict played a significant role in shaping trade dynamics. Conflict escalation reached a peak on 1 September 2019, when a new round of tariffs came into force on $125 billion in PRC exports to the US and $75 billion in US exports to the PRC. Soon after, however, the two parties agreed to fresh rounds of trade talks, and tensions reduced further when both countries announced tariff exemptions on various types of imports. By mid-October, intense negotiations brought an announcement of a "phase one trade agreement," to be finalized over several weeks, and the consequent postponement of an additional tariff hike by the US on $250 billion in PRC goods scheduled for 15 October. On 13 December, just before another scheduled tariff increase by the US, the two countries reached an agreement on the phase one deal, and the 15 January 2020 signing occurred 2 days after the US Treasury Department withdrew its designation of the PRC as a currency manipulator.

Figure 1.1.10 Exports by product category, developing Asia

Battered by trade tensions, exports fell through most of the year, showing signs of revival only in the last quarter.

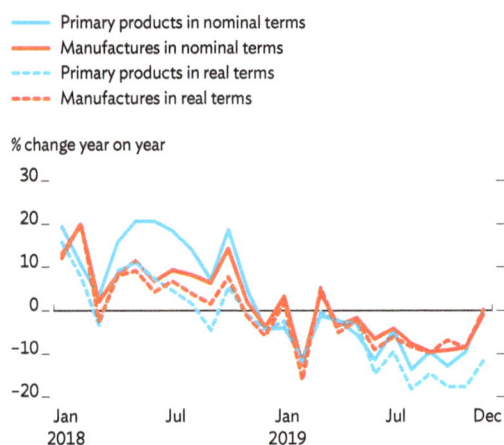

Notes: Developing Asia refers here to 10 economies that provide 90% of regional GDP. Real export and import data are estimated using monthly export and import price indexes except for India and the Philippines, which are estimated from annual data.
Source: ADB estimates using data from CEIC Data Company (accessed 4 March 2020).

Figure 1.1.11 Semiconductor billings

The electronics cycle slumped but at a decelerating rate in the second half of the year.

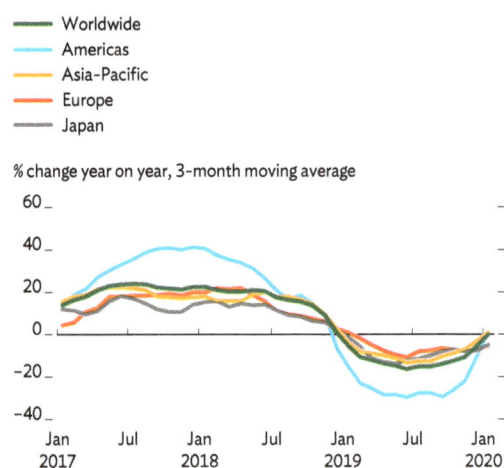

Source: World Semiconductor Trade Statistics (accessed 23 March 2020).

Figure 1.1.12 Growth in exports and imports, developing Asia

As spillover from the US–PRC trade conflict disrupted demand and global value chains, trade stagnated in all subregions except Central Asia.

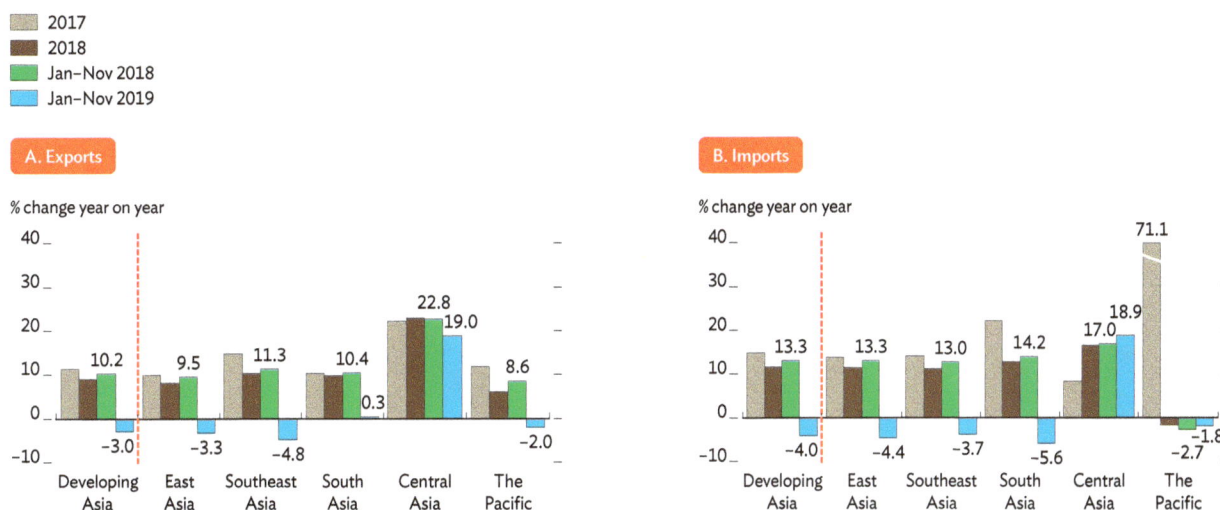

- 2017
- 2018
- Jan–Nov 2018
- Jan–Nov 2019

A. Exports

% change year on year

B. Imports

% change year on year

Source: International Monetary Fund Direction of Trade Statistics database in Haver Analytics (accessed 4 March 2020).

The key feature of the phase one deal is a commitment from the PRC to increase imports of US goods and services in 2020 and 2021 by $200 billion over 2017, pre-conflict values. From the outset, this overall target appeared to be ambitious, as did specific targets for imports of agricultural, manufacturing, and energy products and services. Moreover, while likely to prevent further tariff increases over the next 10 months, the deal left in place most of the tariffs imposed since 2018. As such, despite easing concerns of further escalation in the short term, the phase one deal did little to change the widely held view that US–PRC trade relations would remain jittery in the medium term.

Trade was therefore a tense topic for most of 2019, gradually becoming less so only in the last quarter of the year. PRC exports to the US in 2019 plunged by 21.3%, while PRC imports from the US dropped by a substantial 12.9%. PRC imports of tariff-affected goods fell for most of 2019 but recovered somewhat during the last quarter. The knock-on effect of trade tensions with the US, as well as a home-grown economic slowdown, reduced PRC imports from developing Asia by 1.6% in 2019, including a 3.6% fall from the 10 other largest economies in the region. Meanwhile, trade redirection away from the PRC boosted US imports from other countries in developing Asia by 8.5%, with the ASEAN-5 benefiting the most with 12.0% growth.

Figure 1.1.13 Current account balance

With falling exports and investment reducing import volumes, current account balances improved in every subregion except Central Asia.

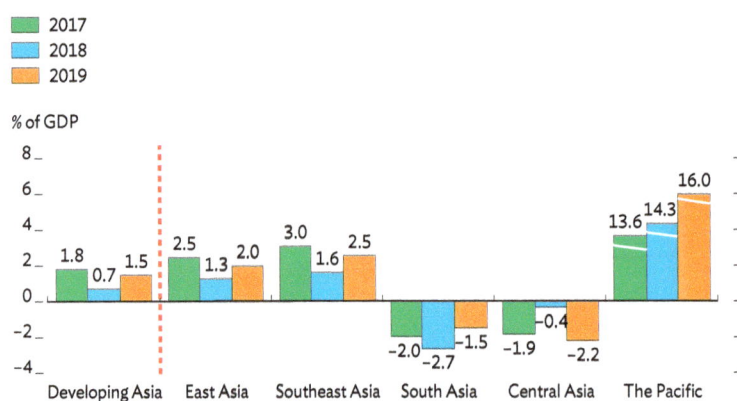

- 2017
- 2018
- 2019

% of GDP

Developing Asia: 1.8, 0.7, 1.5
East Asia: 2.5, 1.3, 2.0
Southeast Asia: 3.0, 1.6, 2.5
South Asia: -2.0, -2.7, -1.5
Central Asia: -1.9, -0.4, -2.2
The Pacific: 13.6, 14.3, 16.0

Source: *Asian Development Outlook* database.

Stagnant trade improved the regional current account surplus to the equivalent of 1.5% of GDP in 2019 as imports contracted more than exports (Figure 1.1.13). This pattern was largely determined by the impact of the US–PRC trade conflict on the most import-intensive components of aggregate demand: exports and investment. The fall in export volumes induced by rising trade tensions brought about a decline in imports of intermediate goods used in reexports. Together with softening economic activity, the export slump was reflected as well in lower demand for investment goods, further reducing imports. Current account balances consequently improved over 2019 in four of the five subregions as surpluses widened in East Asia to the equivalent of 2.0% of aggregate GDP, in Southeast Asia to 2.5%, and in the Pacific to 16.0%, and the deficit in South Asia narrowed to 1.5%. In Central Asia, by contrast, the deficit worsened to 2.2%.

1.1.3 Renewed financial turbulence in Asia

Exchange rate movements in 2019 reflected dynamics in capital flows and the US–PRC trade conflict. In the more open subregions, rates were affected primarily by changes in US–PRC trade relations in 2019. Major currencies in East Asia weakened with conflict escalation, while Southeast Asian currencies strengthened as production and trade were redirected to many of these economies (Figure 1.1.14). The Thai baht and Indonesian rupiah both posted gains greater than 4% during the period from 1 May 2019 to 17 January 2020. In South Asia, some swings were observed in the first half of 2019, but currencies stabilized from mid-August until January 2020. The Sri Lanka rupee appreciated strongly in the first half of 2019, while the Pakistan rupee endured the region's largest depreciation starting in mid-May, as the country continued to shift to a flexible exchange rate regime driven by the market.

Figure 1.1.14 Exchange rate against the US dollar, selected economies

Regional currencies weakened.

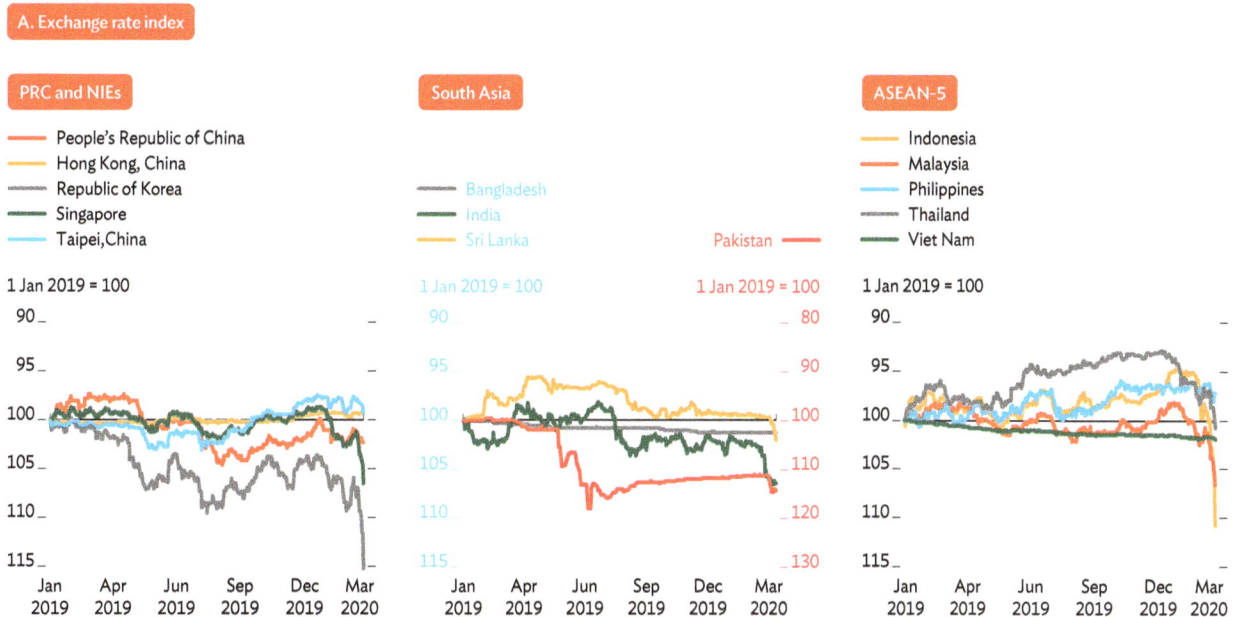

A. Exchange rate index

PRC and NIEs
— People's Republic of China
— Hong Kong, China
— Republic of Korea
— Singapore
— Taipei,China

South Asia
— Bangladesh
— India
— Sri Lanka
— Pakistan

ASEAN-5
— Indonesia
— Malaysia
— Philippines
— Thailand
— Viet Nam

B. Exchange rate index, comparison across various shocks

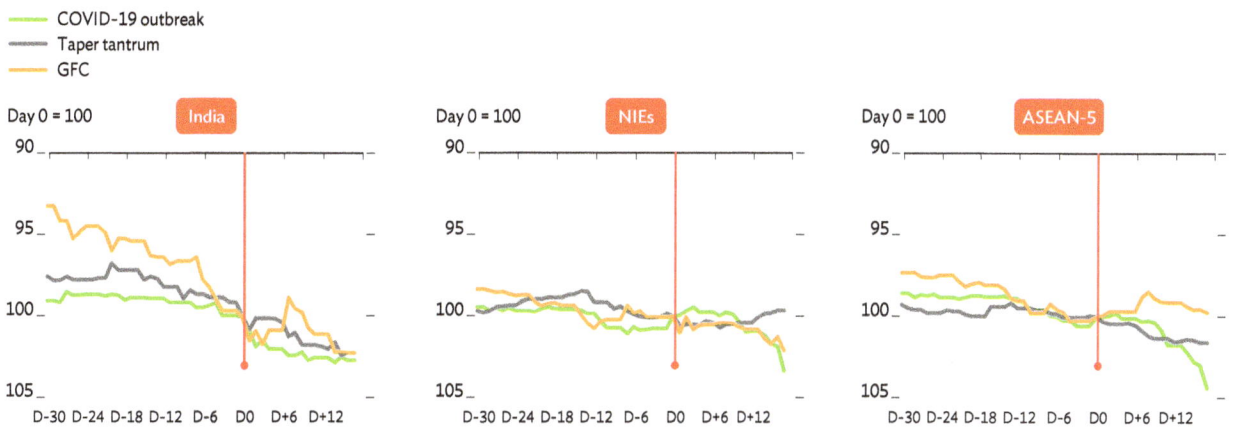

— COVID-19 outbreak
— Taper tantrum
— GFC

ASEAN-5 = five large economies in the Association of Southeast Asian Nations (Indonesia, Malaysia, the Philippines, Thailand, and Viet Nam), COVID-19 = coronavirus disease 2019, GFC = global financial crisis of 2008–2009, NIEs = newly industrialized economies of Hong Kong, China; the Republic of Korea; Singapore; and Taipei,China.

Notes: Day 0 for COVID-19 is 2 March 2020, when cases outside the PRC reached more than 10,000. Day 0 for the taper tantrum is 22 May 2013, when the chair of the US Federal Reserve appeared before Congress. Day 0 for the GFC is 15 September 2008, when Lehman Brothers collapsed. NIEs and ASEAN-5 aggregates are simple averages. Increase (decrease) in exchange rate index means depreciation (appreciation).

Source: CEIC Data Company (accessed 20 March 2020).

Most Asian currencies weakened against the US dollar in early 2020 with the onset and global expansion of the COVID-19 outbreak. As the ensuing pandemic spread first to Europe and then the US, stock markets around the world collapsed and global financial turbulence hit record highs.

In Asia, spillover from global financial jitters quickly translated into substantial capital outflow to safe havens. The pace at which regional currencies have depreciated so far has been faster than in recent shocks, either the global financial crisis of 2008–2009 or the taper tantrum in 2013, particularly in NIEs and Southeast Asia. Focusing on 2–19 March, during which the number of COVID-19 cases outside of the PRC topped 10,000 and the World Health Organization declared a global pandemic, the steepest depreciation has hit Indonesia, at 11.5%, and the ROK, at 7.7%. The Thai baht, Malaysian ringgit, and Singaporean dollar also depreciated by more than 4% each.

Worsening financial conditions reflect and aggravate ongoing economic turbulence. They had broadly improved in 2019 despite ups and downs in response to the trade conflict. In 2019, bond spreads in major Asian markets slightly widened in tandem as the trade conflict escalated in May and early August (Figure 1.1.15). But, more generally, spreads narrowed through the year and improved further toward the end, particularly in the PRC, as trade tensions eased. Asian equity markets also remained stable in 2019, though troubled by occasional jitters. With the phase one agreement between the US and the PRC in mid-December 2019 and the consequent softening of trade tensions, major Asian equity markets continued to post positive returns into the first 3 weeks of 2020.

Figure 1.1.15 JP Morgan EMBI stripped spreads, selected Asian economies

Bond spreads in major Asian markets, which narrowed with the phase one trade deal, widened significantly as the outbreak worsened.

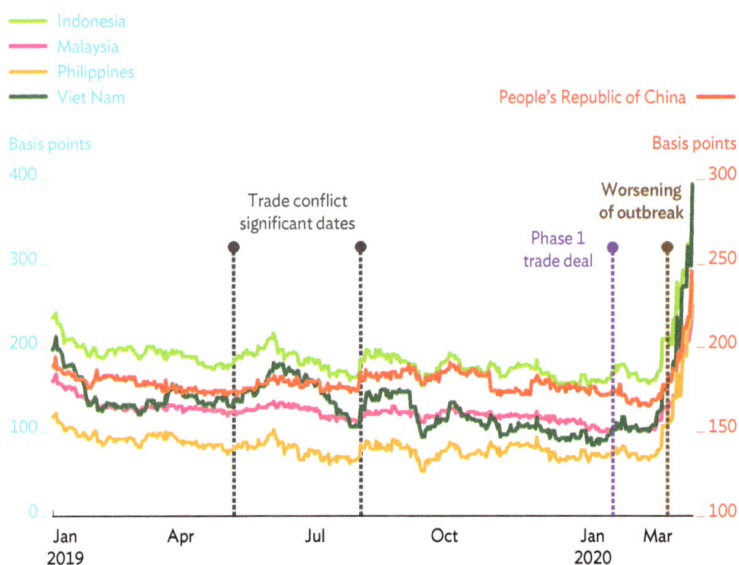

EMBI = emerging markets bond index.

Note: Stripped spreads capture yield differences between US and emerging market government debt securities.

Source: Bloomberg (accessed 20 March 2020).

The COVID-19 shock then caused equity markets to fall and bond spreads to widen significantly. After the outbreak became a global pandemic, the pace of stock market losses in Asia was faster than the declines during the initial phases of the global financial crisis (Figure 1.1.16). On 17 March, the Philippine Stock Exchange Index closed 31% lower than on 2 January, the first trading day of 2020, and trading was suspended amidst a lockdown. Similarly, markets in other ASEAN economies, NIEs, and India shed more than 20% to hit new lows amid dismal market sentiment.

Figure 1.1.16 Equity index, selected Asian economies

Equity markets were stable in 2019 until COVID-19 woes gripped investor sentiment in early 2020.

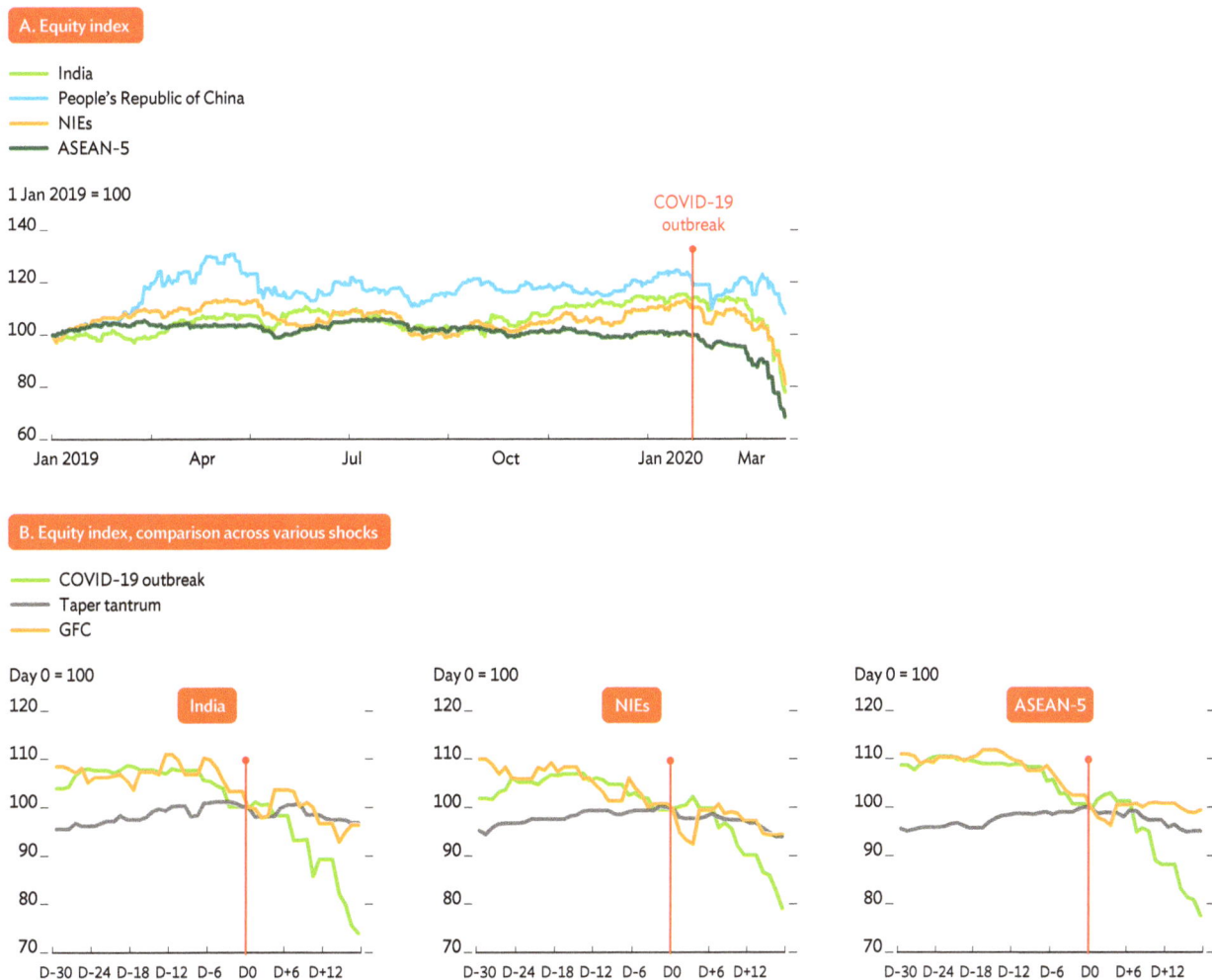

ASEAN-5 = five large economies in southeast Asia (Indonesia, Malaysia, the Philippines, Thailand, and Viet Nam), COVID-19 = coronavirus disease 2019, GFC = global financial crisis of 2008–2009, NIEs = newly industrialized economies of Hong Kong, China; the Republic of Korea; Singapore; and Taipei,China.

Notes: Day 0 for COVID-19 is 2 March 2020, when cases outside the PRC reached more than 10,000. Day 0 for the taper tantrum is 22 May 2013, when the chair of the US Federal Reserve appeared before Congress. Day 0 for the GFC is 15 September 2008, when Lehman Brothers collapsed. NIEs and ASEAN-5 averages are weighted using 2018 market capitalization data.

Source: CEIC Data Company (accessed 20 March 2020).

1.1.4 Asian governments respond with policies to support economies

With growth slow and inflation muted in 2019, monetary policy was loosened across Asia to spur economic activity, as shown in Table 1.1.2. Indonesia and India cut rates four times each last year to spur economic growth, Indonesia lowering its benchmark rate by a total of 100 basis points and India 135 points. Except for Taipei,China, which did not cut interest rates, and Kazakhstan, which cut and raised by equal amounts, other economies lowered rates, and many did so several times.

In 2020, monetary authorities were prompted to take further actions as their economies were hit by the COVID-19 outbreak. Central banks that have recently cut rates include Armenia; Hong Kong, China; Indonesia; Malaysia; the Philippines; the PRC; the ROK; Sri Lanka; Taipei,China; and Thailand. The People's Bank of China announced other instruments through which to ease liquidity: open market operations, the reserve requirement ratio, loan facilities, refinancing, and rediscount policies. Across Asia, central banks and financial institutions introduced financial support to extend credit to small businesses and households affected by the outbreak and to lower their financial costs. In contrast, Kazakhstan raised its policy rate in March to prop up the country's falling currency as inflation soared and oil prices collapsed.

Table 1.1.2 Monetary policy cuts, selected economies

Benchmark rates were lowered through 2019 to stimulate growth and continued to be eased in 2020 in response to the COVID-19 outbreak.

	Policy rates			Number of cuts		
	As of Jan 2019	As of 19 Mar 2020	Difference	2019	2020	Total
Hong Kong, China	2.75	0.86	1.89	3	2	5
Sri Lanka	8.00	6.50	1.50	2	1	3
Philippines	4.75	3.25	1.50	3	2	5
Indonesia	6.00	4.50	1.50	4	2	6
India	6.50	5.15	1.35	4	0	4
Papua New Guinea	6.25	5.00	1.25	3	0	3
Republic of Korea	1.75	0.75	1.00	2	1	3
Armenia	6.00	5.25	0.75	2	1	3
Malaysia	3.25	2.50	0.75	1	2	3
Thailand	1.75	1.00	0.75	2	1	3
People's Republic of China	4.35	4.05	0.30	3	1	4
Viet Nam	4.25	4.00	0.25	1	0	1
Taipei,China	1.38	1.13	0.25	0	1	1
Kazakhstan	9.25	12.00	-2.75	1↓, 1↑	1↑	0

Sources: Haver Analytics; Central bank rates, http://www.cbrates.com/decisions.htm (accessed 20 March 2020).

Fiscal packages are being rolled out to respond to the outbreak and protect economies from its impact. Since the onset of the COVID-19 pandemic, governments around the world have announced targeted and bold fiscal rescue packages, various Asian governments among them. Measures are being introduced first to slow the spread of infection and facilitate medical support and second to compensate vulnerable households and firms for lost income. Malaysia, for example, has so far rolled out a fiscal stimulus package worth about 17% of GDP to counter the economic impact of the COVID-19 pandemic on its hardest-hit residents and businesses. In Singapore, a stimulus package amounting to 11% of GDP was unveiled to deal with the likely impact on the economy, with allocation to ramp up existing job support schemes and support households with cash payouts based on family income. Many other economies are also rolling out fiscal responses.

1.1.5 A dire growth outlook

The growth outlook for developing Asia has dimmed considerably as the region staggers under the COVID-19 shock. Regional economic growth is expected to slow sharply from 5.2% in 2019 to 2.2% in 2020 before rebounding to 6.2% in 2021 (Figure 1.1.17). Excluding the NIEs, growth will drop from 5.7% in 2019 to 2.4% in 2020 before recovering to 6.7% in 2021.

COVID-19 is expected to weaken economic activity substantially this year, both globally and regionally. Baseline assumptions take into account confirmed COVID-19 cases to 20 March, with serious outbreaks across numerous countries, including the major economies of the US, Europe, and the PRC. The assumption is that these countries' outbreaks will come under control in 3 to 6 months and that activity will gradually return to normal (see the *Special Topic* that follows, which analyzes the impact of the COVID-19 outbreak under various scenario assumptions). In the meantime, economic activity is expected to fall sharply as countries undertake containment.

Aggregate growth in the advanced economies of the US, euro area, and Japan is expected to drop from 1.7% in 2019 and contract by 0.3% in 2020, before recovering to 1.8% in 2021 (Table 1.1.3). Japan is expected to slow sharply from 0.7% growth in 2019 to 1.5% contraction in 2020 as it reels from, first, a sales slump following a value-added tax hike in the fourth quarter of 2019 and then from the widening COVID-19 outbreak, before recovering to 0.9% growth in 2021.

Figure 1.1.17 GDP growth outlook in developing Asia

The outlook is for growth to stumble under COVID-19 as demand weakens and production stalls.

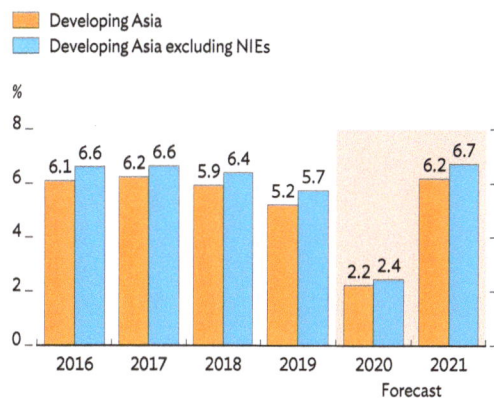

NIEs = newly industrialized economies of Hong Kong, China; the Republic of Korea; Singapore; and Taipei,China.
Source: *Asian Development Outlook* database.

Table 1.1.3 Baseline assumptions on the international economy

Major advanced economies are set to contract this year.

	2019		2020		
	ADO 2019 Update	ADO 2020	ADO 2019 Update	ADO 2020	2021
GDP growth (%)					
Major advanced economies	1.7	1.7	1.4	-0.3 ▼	1.8
United States	2.3	2.3	1.9	0.4 ▼	2.1
Euro area	1.0	1.2 ▲	1.0	-1.0 ▼	1.6
Japan	1.2	0.7 ▼	0.5	-1.5 ▼	0.9
Brent crude spot prices (average, $ per barrel)	65.00	64.03 ▼	63.00	35.00 ▼	55.00

▲ = upgraded forecast, ▼ = downgraded forecast, no sign = unchanged.

Note: Major industrial economies average growth rates are weighted by gross national income, Atlas method (current $).

Sources: US Department of Commerce, Bureau of Economic Analysis, http://www.bea.gov; Eurostat, http://epp.eurostat.ec.europa.eu; Economic and Social Research Institute of Japan, http://www.esri.cao.go.jp; Consensus Forecasts; Bloomberg; CEIC Data Company; Haver Analytics; World Bank, Global Commodity Markets, http://www.worldbank.org; ADB estimates.

Worsening public health conditions and resulting mobility restrictions in the US will substantially squelch economic activity, which is projected to slow from 2.3% in 2019 to 0.4% in 2020 (with contraction in the second quarter) before growth recovers to reach 2.1% in 2021, helped by a recently announced $2 trillion stimulus package. The euro area is expected to fall from 1.2% growth in 2019 to 1.0% contraction in 2020. The large negative impact of COVID-19 will be partly offset by policy responses, such as Germany's $610 billion lending program and the European Central Bank's €750 billion Pandemic Emergency Purchase Programme. Growth in the euro area is forecast to recover to 1.6% in 2021 with exports restored and able to spur a rebound in investment. Oil prices are expected to decline from $64/barrel in 2019 to $35/barrel in 2020 before rebounding to $55/barrel in 2021 as demand recovers. Across most advanced economies, monetary and fiscal policies are expected to remain supportive to shore up growth this year and next.

Much of the expected decline in regional growth stems from a slowdown in the PRC. Growth there is projected to fall from 6.1% in 2019 to 2.3% in 2020 before accelerating to 7.3% in 2021. The dip in economic activity in the PRC reflects both demand-side and supply-side domestic disruptions from COVID-19. Data for the first 2 months of 2020 indicate double-digit contraction in industrial production and retail sales (Figure 1.1.18), an outturn much worse than those witnessed during the Asian financial crisis of 1997–1998, the severe acute respiratory syndrome (SARS) epidemic of 2003, or the global financial crisis of 2008–2009.

Figure 1.1.18 People's Republic of China retail sales and industrial production

Double-digit contraction in industry and retail sales indicate a sizeable decline in PRC economic activity.

——— Asian financial crisis (time = July 1997)
——— Severe acute respiratory syndrome (time = February 2003)
——— Global financial crisis (time = September 2008)
——— COVID-19 outbreak (time = December 2019)

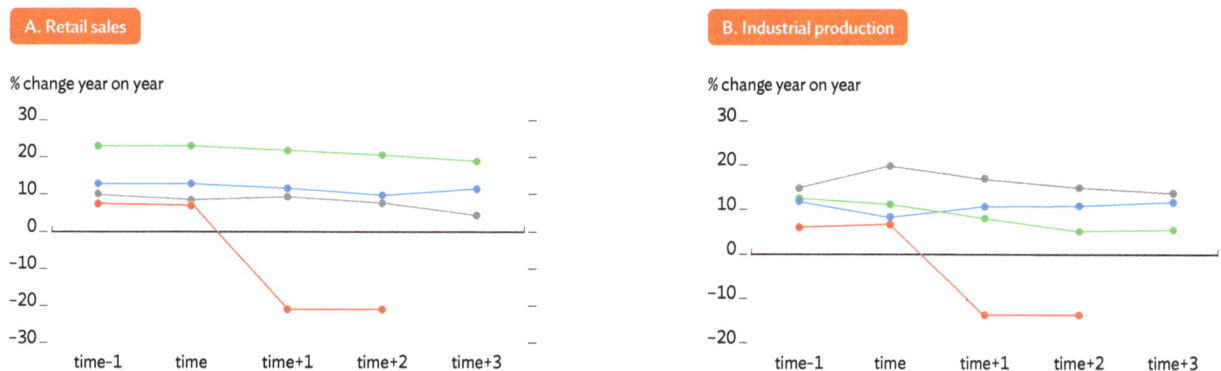

COVID-19 = coronavirus disease 2019, PRC = People's Republic of China.
Sources: CEIC Data Company, National Bureau of Statistics (both accessed 20 March 2020).

On the demand side, consumption in the PRC will remain a key driver of growth, but discretionary consumer spending is likely to be affected as growth in household income falters. Fiscal policy should become more supportive. Government spending, especially on health care, is expected to increase further this year. Infrastructure investment is expected to pick up from the second quarter with an increase in special bond issues by local governments, which were higher early in 2020 and are expected to stay high through 2021. Monetary policy in the PRC will likely remain accommodative this year and next through further cuts to the medium-term lending facility rate and the reserve requirement ratio, as well as a special onlending program for selected industries and smaller enterprises.

The outlook for India remains subdued, with growth slowing from 5.0% in fiscal 2019 to 4.0% this year and then strengthening to 6.2% next year. COVID-19 has not yet spread extensively in India, but containment measures including a national lockdown and a weaker global environment will whip up headwinds with demand depressed and supply disrupted. In late March, the government took immediate action to strengthen the health system and support the poor and vulnerable. The Reserve Bank of India has cut its policy rate to the lowest ever, undertaken unconventional measures, and committed to using all instruments to fight the pandemic. Both urban and rural consumption will rebound in 2021, supported by reduced personal income taxes and increased assistance to agriculture and rural areas.

Corporate tax cuts and increased public investment in infrastructure, including in the National Infrastructure Pipeline, will revive investment. The recapitalization of state-owned banks and financial sector reform to revive credit promise to help alleviate much of the financial stress that has undermined growth prospects in previous years.

The COVID-19 outbreak will take a substantial toll on growth in all economies in East Asia this year, driving subregional growth down to 2.0%. Higher growth at 6.5% is forecast for 2021 as the outbreak subsides. In Hong Kong, China, recession will continue on faltering domestic and external demand, but fiscal measures and higher exports will lead recovery at 3.5% in 2021. In Taipei,China, growth will dip this year to 1.8% before reviving to 2.5% on recovering exports and public outlays—as in the ROK, with growth at 1.3% in 2020 and 2.3% in 2021. In Mongolia, growth will fall sharply to 2.1% in 2020 on lower inflow of foreign direct investment but rebound to 4.6% in 2021 as mining and investment pick up.

Growth in Southeast Asia will decelerate from 4.4% in 2019 to 1.0% in 2020 before rebounding to 4.7% in 2021. All 11 economies in the subregion will post lower growth in 2020 than in 2019 because of COVID-19, especially considering the subregion's strong trade and investment ties with the PRC. Indonesia, the largest economy in the subregion, will decelerate from 5.0% in 2019 to 2.5% this year and bounce back to 5.0% in 2021. Tourism-dependent Thailand, the second largest economy in the subregion, is forecast to reverse 2.4% expansion in 2019 with 4.8% contraction before recovering to 2.5% in 2021. Similarly, GDP growth in the Philippines will decelerate to 2.0% this year, even as the impact of COVID-19 and the global slowdown are partly offset by government expansionary policies that will help lift growth to 6.5% in 2021. Growth in Viet Nam has stuck close to an annual pace of 7.0% in recent years but will decelerate to 4.8% in 2020 before recovering to 6.8% in 2021. Cambodia, which has strong economic ties with the PRC, will be unable to sustain average annual GDP growth above 7.0% in recent years, slumping to 2.3% this year and recovering somewhat to 5.7% in 2021. Singapore will continue its growth slowdown that began in 2018, expanding in 2020 by a paltry 0.2% before reviving to 2.0% in 2021.

Countries in South Asia are expected to be adversely affected to varying degrees by the economic impact of efforts to contain COVID-19 in 2020. Growth in South Asia is forecast to decelerate from 5.1% in 2019 to 4.1% in 2020 and rebound to 6.0% in 2021. In Bangladesh, growth will slip from 8.2% in 2019 to 7.8% this year as major markets pull back demand for its fast fashion garment exports. A growth advance to 8.0% in 2021 is expected as global consumer confidence improves. Growth in Pakistan will plummet to 2.6% in 2020 as economic stabilization constrains domestic demand, cotton output stagnates, and COVID-19 takes its toll, before edging up to 3.2% in 2021 as presumed successful correction of macro imbalances restore confidence.

In tourism-dependent Maldives, GDP will reverse 5.7% expansion in 2019 with contraction by 3.0% in 2020 as arrivals plummet. Growth is expected to bounce back to a high 7.5% in 2021 as pent-up demand is released. In Sri Lanka, ebbing global demand will stunt expansion in the tourism and garment industries, slowing growth to 2.2% in 2020 before expected recovery to 3.5% in 2021. In Nepal, growth is forecast to slip from 7.1% in 2019 to 5.3% in 2020 with weakness in both agriculture and tourism, then strengthen to 6.4% in 2021. Growth in Bhutan is forecast to strengthen to 5.2% in 2020 and 5.8% in 2021 on high government expenditure under a new 5-year plan, and despite depressed international tourist arrivals. In Afghanistan, growth is forecast unchanged in 2020 but picking up to 4.0% in 2021 on improving business and consumer confidence.

Growth will slow in Central Asia in 2020 as the impact of COVID-19 reverberates, before recovering in 2021. Having accelerated to 4.9% in 2019, subregional growth is projected to slow to 2.8% in 2020 as growth decelerates in all eight economies, recovering to 4.2% in 2021 as growth picks up in six of them. Expansion in Kazakhstan, the subregion's largest economy, is projected to slow to 1.8% in 2020 as oil and gas production stagnates, petroleum prices decline, and expansion in the economy aside from the large petroleum industry is enfeebled by cuts to public investment spending. An expected rise in oil production and government support for manufacturing are projected to boost growth to 3.6% in 2021.

In Azerbaijan, growth will slow to 0.5% as oil prices decline, but higher oil and gas production will lift growth to 1.5% in 2021. Slower expansion in hydrocarbon output and exports in Turkmenistan is projected to reduce growth to 6.0% in 2020 and 5.8% in 2021. In Uzbekistan, weaker demand and prices for copper and natural gas will, along with the effects of COVID-19, cut growth to 4.7% in 2020, with slightly higher expansion in services lifting growth to 5.8% in 2021. In Armenia, COVID-19 will slash growth from the unusually high rate of 7.6% achieved in 2019 to 2.2% in 2020, but the realization of structural reform promises to revive expansion to 4.5% in 2021. In Georgia, COVID-19 and monetary tightening are projected to slow growth to zero this year, picking up to 4.5% in 2021. Tajikistan will slow to 5.5% growth in 2020 and 5.0% in 2021 as fiscal consolidation squeezes growth in public investment and as remittances from the Russian Federation decline. With growth slowing in the PRC, the Kyrgyz Republic will decelerate to 4.0% growth in 2020 despite higher gold output, edging up to 4.5% in 2021.

The Pacific is projected to contract by 0.3% in 2020 as all economies slow and COVID-19 hammers in particular those with large tourism industries: the Cook Islands, Fiji, Palau, Samoa, Tonga, and Vanuatu. Commodity exports—mainly from Fiji, Papua New Guinea, and Solomon Islands—will also be adversely affected. In the smaller economies, restrictions on the movement of labor and imported capital equipment will delay critical infrastructure projects and undermine stimulus from construction. The outlook for 2021 is cautiously positive as recovery from COVID-19 restores aggregate growth to 2.7%, still well below recent average growth in the subregion but with all economies expected to grow.

1.1.6 Inflation outlook dictated by food price dynamics

Rising domestic food prices in some countries are lifting regional inflation in 2020, but it should ease in 2021. Headline inflation is expected to rise from 2.9% in 2019 to 3.2% in 2020, mainly as East Asia experiences a transitory rise in food prices, but will likely ebb in the latter half of 2020, setting the stage for inflation to decline to 2.3% in 2021 (Figure 1.1.19). Excluding NIEs yields inflation a bit higher, picking up to 3.6% in 2020 before falling to 2.5% in 2021.

Meanwhile, consumer price inflation in the advanced economies of the US, the euro area, and Japan will remain steady at 1.4% in 2020, held down by declining oil prices and waning demand. Inflation in these economies should rise to 1.7% in 2021 as oil prices and domestic demand recover (Table A1.1).

By subregion, East Asia will see inflation rise to 3.2% in 2020 and then moderate to 1.8% in 2021. In the PRC, higher pork prices will push inflation to 3.6% in 2020 before it retreats to 1.9% in 2021 as those prices normalize. In Hong Kong, China and in Taipei,China, inflation will decelerate in 2020 but reaccelerate in 2021 as economic activity rebounds. Inflation in the ROK will edge up to 0.9% this year and 1.3% next, while in Mongolia it will slow this year and quicken next year.

As growth slows in Southeast Asia, inflation should remain tame. Average inflation in the subregion is forecast to fall to 1.9% in 2020 before rising to 2.2% in 2021, but with significant differences by country across the subregion. Inflation in Indonesia will remain steady at 3.0% before declining to 2.8% in 2021. Thailand will experience deflation at 0.9% in 2020 before 0.4% inflation returns in 2021. Inflation in Cambodia, Malaysia, Singapore, and Viet Nam is expected to be higher this year than last year, with Viet Nam showing the most acceleration, rising from 2.8% last year to 3.3%.

Figure 1.1.19 Subregional contributions to inflation, developing Asia

Inflation will be affected mainly by higher food prices but remain low.

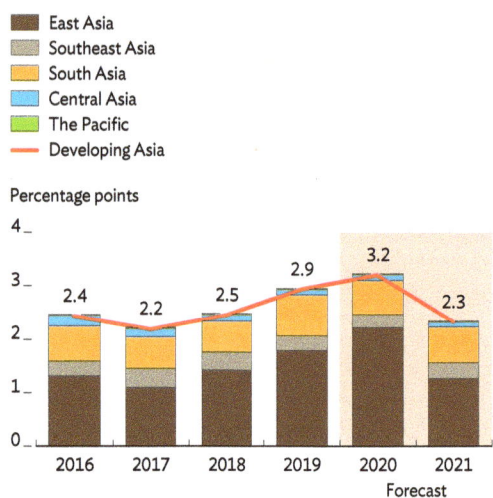

Source: *Asian Development Outlook* database.

In the Philippines, inflation will likely slow from 2.5% last year to 2.2%, staying within the central bank target range of 2.0%–4.0% as price pressures caused by African swine fever counter lower global oil prices.

Inflation will moderate in South Asia from 4.9% in 2019 to 4.1% in 2020, edging up in 2021 but remaining moderate at 4.4%, with little variation across countries, except in Maldives and Pakistan. Lower subregional inflation in 2020 largely reflects lower food inflation in India on improved agricultural production, while the slight hardening in 2021 mostly reflects strengthened domestic demand in India on the forecast growth revival. Inflation in Pakistan will remain in double digits in 2020 as food prices rise, planned utility price hikes take effect, and currency depreciation makes itself felt. Inflation in Pakistan will moderate to 8.3% in 2021 as food prices stabilize. Unusually low inflation in Maldives reflects subsidies and price controls on staples.

Inflation in Central Asia is projected to accelerate marginally to 7.6% in 2020 before slowing to 6.3% in 2021. The slight rise in 2020 will come as higher inflation in Armenia, Kazakhstan, the Kyrgyz Republic, and Tajikistan outweighs declines in the other four countries. Much of the decline in 2021 will come from Uzbekistan, where monetary tightening is expected to reduce credit sharply and slow inflation from 14.6% in 2019 to 13.0% this year and 10.0% in 2021. Monetary tightening is also projected to trim inflation in Georgia from 4.9% in 2019 to 4.5% this year and 3.0% in 2021.

Inflation is projected to slow in Turkmenistan from 13.4% in 2019 to 13.0% this year and 8.0% in 2021, and in Azerbaijan from 2.6% in 2019 to 2.5% this year with slower growth, but rising to 3.5% in 2021 as growth recovers somewhat. Kazakhstan will likely see inflation rise to 6.0% in 2020 as its currency depreciates but then ease to 5.7% in 2021 with monetary tightening and administrative limits on markups for key food staples. In the Kyrgyz Republic, inflation is projected to quicken from 1.1% in 2019 to 3.5% this year before relaxing to 3.0% in 2021, and in Tajikistan from 8.0% in 2019 to 9.0% this year as salaries increase before returning to 8.0% in 2021. Fiscal expansion should lift inflation in Armenia from 1.4% in 2019 to 2.8% this year before consolidation reduces it to 2.2% in 2021.

In the Pacific, inflation will likely ease from 3.0% in 2019 to 2.7% this year as demand wanes before rising to 3.8% in 2021. It is projected to moderate in 8 of 13 subregional economies with projections, excepting the Cook Islands, Kiribati, the Marshall Islands, Solomon Islands, and Tuvalu. Nauru and Tonga will experience the steepest falls in line with subdued global fuel prices and transport costs. In 2021, inflation in the subregion is projected to be substantially higher, largely reflecting higher inflation in the two largest economies, Fiji and Papua New Guinea, as growth accelerates.

1.1.7 Worsening before getting better: A subdued external outlook

The COVID-19 outbreak has clouded the outlook for the region's external sector in 2020. With many countries introducing progressively stricter lockdowns and mobility limitations, the global pandemic continues to upend production, trade, and tourism, both within the region and with the rest of the world. Aside from rapid deterioration in global PMIs, both composite and manufacturing, other leading indicators point to substantial suppression of global trade volume. The Services Trade Barometer of the World Trade Organization released on 11 March 2020 shows that growth in global trade in services continued to slow in late 2019 and the first quarter of 2020, with a reading of 98.4 in September sliding further away from 100, the threshold for trend growth, to 96.8 in the latest reading. Subcomponents in the aggregate index covered to January show passenger air travel falling to 93.5 and container shipping to 94.3, these largest declines indicating early disruption from COVID-19. Further, the Baltic Dry Index on shipping performance continued on a downward trajectory begun in the last quarter of 2019 to 411 in early February, its lowest reading in nearly 4 years, before recovering somewhat in March. Changes in container throughput year on year to January sketch a similar picture, with Hong Kong, China shrinking by 20.4%; the ROK by 2.5%; and Taipei,China by 7.1%.

Foreign direct investment (FDI) flows present a similarly gloomy outlook. In a special issue of *Investment Trends Monitor* published on 8 March, the United Nations Conference on Trade and Development forecasts that COVID-19 will put paid previous projections of marginal growth in trend FDI, bringing instead a decline in global FDI flows by 5% in 2020, assuming the global outbreak is brought under control in the first half of the year. A worse scenario that assumes the health crisis persisting throughout the year causes a 15% drop, with negative demand effects carrying over to 2021. While highlighting a likely global slowdown in market-seeking FDI and investment projects in extractive industries in response to negative demand shocks, the projections also point to significant drops in efficiency-seeking FDI in East and Southeast Asia, in particular the PRC, because of their high integration in global value chains.

The report also highlights a fall in profits for foreign affiliates of multinational enterprises as a further channel through which COVID-19 will affect the outlook for FDI, considering that reinvested earnings typically make up a large share of FDI flows. Data for the global top 5,000 multinationals as of 8 March show earnings forecasts for 2020 revised down by an average of 9% since 1 February, with the energy, automotive, travel, and tourism industries particularly affected (Table 1.1.4).

Table 1.1.4 Earnings revisions for the top 5,000 multinational enterprises and the relative importance of reinvested earnings in FDI, by region

The COVID-19 shock will affect FDI flows through a fall in the reinvested earnings of multinational enterprises.

Region/economy	Number of companies with earnings revision	Average earnings revision (%)	Share of reinvested earnings in FDI, 2018 (%)
Developed	2,334	−6	61
Developing economies	864	−16	40
Africa	42	−1	27
Developing Asia	730	−18	41
Singapore	16	−30	...
People's Republic of China	259	−26	...
Republic of Korea	121	−20	22
Malaysia	33	−20	...
Thailand	32	−15	72
Viet Nam	8	−10	...
Latin America and the Caribbean	92	−6	43
Transition economies	28	−10	93
Total	3,226	−9	52

... = data not available, FDI = foreign direct investment.

Source: Investment Trends Monitor, UNCTAD (March 2020), https://unctad.org/en/pages/publications/Global-Investment-Trends-Monitor-(Series).aspx.

The revision is much larger for developing countries, at 16% lower earnings, than for developed economies, at 6% less, and is particularly significant in Asia, where earnings expectations in some economies are slashed by 18%. As the reinvested earnings component of FDI in the region was 41% in 2018, these substantial downward revisions foretell sizeable effects on FDI from earnings losses.

The developing Asia current account surplus is projected to edge up slightly to the equivalent of 1.6% of aggregate GDP in 2020 and fall back to 1.4% in 2021. Because of supply disruption and waning global demand under COVID-19, trade flows will shrink further in 2020 but are projected to recover in 2021 as regional and global activity normalizes. Surpluses are expected to narrow in East Asia, Southeast Asia, and the Pacific to the forecast horizon. Meanwhile, South Asia's current account deficit is forecast to shrink marginally, and Central Asia's to widen (Figure 1.1.20). The outlook for developing Asia closely tracks expectations for current account dynamics in the PRC, which has a 60% weight in the total. As such, the positive change in the regional external balance in 2020 reflects primarily substantial contraction in imports to the PRC, where the sharp slowdown in growth will subdue investment, and also substantial shrinkage in the service deficit from devastated outbound tourism.

Figure 1.1.20 Current account in developing Asia

The current account surplus will increase in 2020 but fall back in 2021.

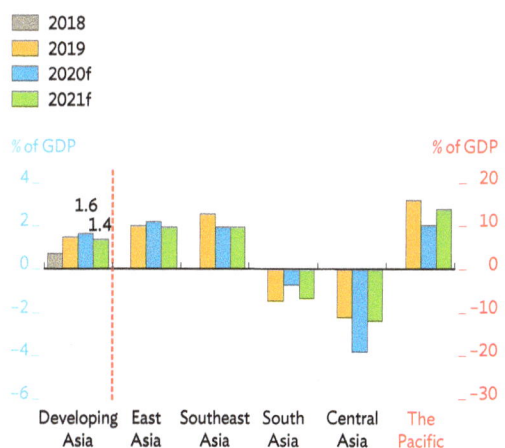

f = forecast.

Source: *Asian Development Outlook* database.

Similarly, the lower projected regional surplus in 2021 largely reflects the anticipated growth rebound in the PRC, sustained by rising investment and accompanied by revived tourism as COVID-19 mobility restrictions are gradually lifted.

1.1.8 COVID-19 poses an extreme risk to the outlook

Risks to the outlook are severe, emanate primarily from the pandemic, and tilt to the downside. Other risks still come from a range of issues, of course, from natural hazards to geopolitical events. Trade conflict remains an important risk. While the phase one deal eased trade tensions between the PRC and the US, it is only a fragile truce featuring import commitments that the PRC will find more difficult to meet in the current economic environment than when the deal was negotiated. By far the most pressing risk to the regional and global outlook comes, however, from the global COVID-19 pandemic. Forecasts here assume containment within this year and a return to normal next year. The future evolution and effects of the outbreak are highly uncertain, however, and the following are some of the many ways in which events could unfold that are worse than the baseline.

The pandemic could easily spread more widely. Just a month before this report went to press, the PRC still accounted for 93% of global cases and 97% of global fatalities. In just 1 month, the PRC share in the global total has fallen below 20%, with at least 25 countries having more than 2,000 cases each as of 27 March. The situation changes very rapidly, with case counts in some countries doubling every few days. Many countries for which these forecasts assume no domestic outbreak could see serious outbreaks occurring in the near future.

Country outbreaks could last much longer than assumed before containment. In the *Special Topic* that follows, the assumed range is 3–6 months, supported by experience in the PRC and the ROK. But outbreaks in other countries could last longer because governments differ in their ability to respond. Second-wave outbreaks cannot be ruled out. And, even after an outbreak ends, economic activity may take a long time to normalize. Even in the PRC, which has already started reporting days with no new local COVID-19 cases, activity has yet to return to normal.

Severe financial turmoil and financial crises cannot be discounted. Movements in equity markets, exchange rates, bond spreads, and volatility indexes have been sharp, reminiscent of the global financial crisis of 2008–2009 and in some cases exceeding it. March saw a surge in capital outflow from emerging markets in Asia (Figure 1.1.21).

Figure 1.1.21 Emerging Asia portfolio flows

Worsening prospects spurred substantial capital outflow from emerging Asia in March, raising concerns about financial stability.

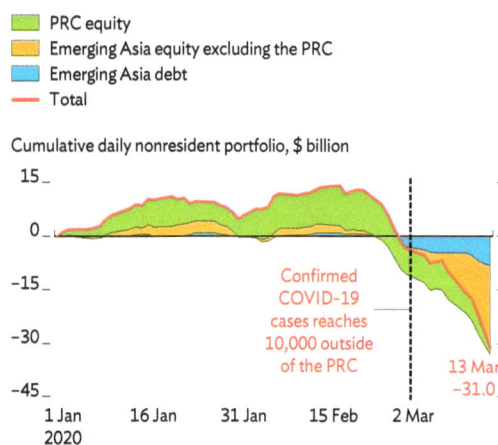

- PRC equity
- Emerging Asia equity excluding the PRC
- Emerging Asia debt
- Total

Cumulative daily nonresident portfolio, $ billion

PRC = People's Republic of China.

Notes: Emerging Asia debt data include India, Indonesia, and Thailand. Emerging Asia equity data excluding the PRC include India; Indonesia; Pakistan; the Philippines; the Republic of Korea; Sri Lanka; Taipei,China; Thailand; and Viet Nam. The total is the sum of emerging Asia debt plus emerging Asia equity, excluding the PRC.

Evidence suggests that heightened financial volatility and a sudden stop to capital flow into the region are distinct possibilities. This poses a danger, particularly in light of a decade-long rise in regional debt, primarily private but some of it public, that has been flagged in past issues of *ADO*. One segment that may be susceptible to tightening financial conditions and a worsening economic environment are small and medium-sized enterprises (Box 1.1.1).

Box 1.1.1 COVID-19 attacks corporate earnings and sustainability in the People's Republic of China

Firms in the People's Republic of China (PRC) have seen their earnings plunge as the COVID-19 epidemic spread across the country and crippled the economy. Retail and consumer spending remain heavily depressed, and production has struggled to restart after coming to a near standstill at the end of January this year. The areas most exposed are retail and consumer services, leisure and tourism, real estate, transportation, and utilities. Heavily affected as well are manufacturing firms that have suffered disruption along their supply chains, notably those in the automotive, electrical, and electronics industries. While most firms in affected industries suffer, earnings are a less stringent factor in determining the viability of the state-owned enterprises (SOEs). Of greater concern are small and medium-sized enterprises (SMEs), a growing share of which have seen their earnings drop to a point that they may soon be unable to service their debt.

To assess the vulnerability of SMEs in the PRC under two scenarios (which informed a broader economic impact assessment discussed elsewhere), a 50% reduction in affected firms' earnings is envisaged lasting for 3 months or, in a worse-case scenario, for 6 months.[a] Considering a continuing dearth of data about the impact of this crisis on specific areas in the PRC economy, keeping scenarios this simple allows easy interpretation and is best thought of as implicitly encompassing a range of plausible circumstances. These include possible impacts in excess of a 50% plunge but over a shorter period or a slow recovery with earnings less depressed but for a longer period, up to a year.

The proportion of a firm's earnings to its interest payment obligations—the interest coverage ratio (ICR)—is the metric for distinguishing firms deemed sustainable (ICR ≥1) from those that are not (ICR <1).[b] A ratio less than 1 signals a firm's impending liquidity shortage and difficulty making payments, and a risk that nonperforming loan status will ensue. Aggregating the debt outstanding of firms with ICRs less than 1 provides a measure of total debt at risk among affected firms and their economic segments.

Using the latest data available, from 2018, in the Orbis company database on PRC firms' earnings before interest and taxes, and their interest payments, the ICR was computed for a sample of 4,740 SMEs.[c] Included firms had financial statements, which excluded all companies that did not report as well as millions of small firms across the PRC industrial landscape that were not in the Orbis database. Thus, the sample likely underestimated the portion of debt at risk in the larger population of companies. This scenario analysis cannot be strictly accurate but is a rough indicator of orders of magnitude.

With this caveat in mind, analysis found 6.4% of reporting SMEs' total debt outstanding at risk in 2018, the baseline year (box figure). Halving firms' earnings for 3 months raised this share by 1.6 percentage points as a greater proportion of firms' ICRs fell below 1 and their leverage added to the pile of debt that might never be repaid. This relatively small increment suggests a certain resilience to a 3-month shock. However, should the earnings stay compressed for 3 months longer, 6 months in total, a significantly higher share of firms would have trouble paying interest. Debt at risk would rise by a further 10.4 percentage point to 18.5% of total debt, or nearly three times the baseline.[d]

While nearly a fifth of debt could thus end up jeopardized or at least problematic, most firms included in the sample seemed to be well cushioned against a temporary plunge in earnings. In the 2018 baseline, they were scattered well above the ICR = 1 line shown in the figure, with a median ICR equal to 10 and its interquartile range spanning about 4–53. The ICR distribution compresses somewhat as earnings shrink under the two scenarios, and the median falls to about 8 if the earnings ordeal lasts for 6 months, but most firms' debt appears to remain serviceable.

However, SME debt at risk above 18% would be of considerable concern to policy makers, inducing them to devise adequate support to struggling firms to avert systemic risk from a resulting sharp increase in nonperforming loans.

continued next page

Box 1.1.1 *Continued*

SME debt at risk in affected segments, % of all debt

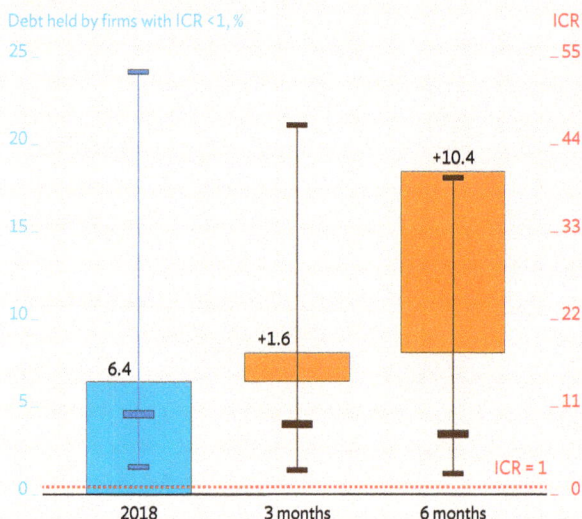

ICR = interest coverage ratio, PRC = People's Republic of China, SME = small or medium-sized enterprise.

Notes:

(i)   SMEs include firms with fewer than 2,000 employees.

(ii)   Debt at risk is that held by firms with ICRs <1.

(iii) Affected industries include utilities, construction, manufacturing, retail trade, transportation and warehousing, telecommunications, real estate, rental and leasing, accommodation, food services, and art, entertainment, and recreation.

(iv) Scenarios consider a 50% fall in earnings for 3 or 6 months.

(v)   Vertical lines represent the interquartile range of the ICR for each scenario, with the axis on the right-hand side. For each line, the bottom marker represents the first quartile, and the top marker indicates the third quartile. The middle horizontal line marker indicates the median.

Source: ADB calculations using data from the Bureau van Dijk Orbis database (accessed 25 February 2020).

This ratio could climb significantly higher if earnings fell by more than 50% and for a longer period than envisaged in these two scenarios, consuming the next tier of firms. Recognizing these risks, the PRC monetary and financial regulatory bodies took early steps in late February to support SMEs. They essentially instructed lenders to roll over SME loans falling due, not to downgrade loans with missed payments, and to defer by several months the reporting of any delinquencies to the country's credit-scoring system. These and other support measures for micro and small enterprises, such as a temporary waiver of social security contributions, are described in Box 3.11.1 on page 196.

While helping SME survival rates, these support measures are bound to weigh on the balance sheets of banks and providers of shadow finance, stressing a system already struggling with impaired profitability in SOE clients and itself. The ICR dataset shows SOE debt at risk more than doubling in the worse-case scenario, from 6.6% in the 2018 baseline to 15.6%. State financial and other support makes SOEs more resilient despite low earnings but applies pressure on national finances and the sovereign debt ratio. Ultimately, any fiscal rescue and recovery operation in the PRC will have to tackle at least some of the troubled debt of SOEs and SMEs, either directly or through state-owned banks.

a   ADB. 2020. The Economic Impact of the COVID-19 Outbreak in Developing Asia. *ADB Briefs*. Manila.

b   The ICR is the ratio of a company's earnings before interest and tax to its payments of interests on debt outstanding. It indicates a company's ability to pay interests in accordance with its debt service schedule and without experiencing financial distress or repayment difficulties.

c   In the PRC, the definition of SMEs varies by sector. This analysis used the upper limit of 2,000 employees, as in industry. For more information, see Liu, X. 2008. SME Development in China: A Policy Perspective on SME Clustering. In H. Lim (ed.), *SME in Asia and Globalization*. ERIA Research Project Report 2007–5 (http://www.eria.org/SME%20Development%20in%20China_A%20Policy%20Perspective%20on%20SME%20Industrial%20Clustering.pdf).

d   For comparison, S&P Global Ratings estimated that, before the COVID-19 outbreak, 6.5%–7.5% of all loans across the PRC economy were nonperforming or questionable, and that this ratio could grow to 10.5%–11.5% in the aftermath of the epidemic (https://www.spglobal.com/ratings/en/research/articles/200220-china-banks-and-coronavirus-forbearance-today-diminished-standards-tomorrow-11354815).

This box was written by Benno Ferrarini and Suzette Dagli of the Economic Research and Regional Cooperation Department, ADB, Manila, and Paul Mariano, consultant, Economic Research and Regional Cooperation Department, ADB, Manila.

Sharp and protracted declines in commodity prices and tourism will challenge economies in the region that depend heavily on one, the other, or both. A sharp fall in global demand has already depressed oil prices beyond the lows reached during the global financial crisis or the commodity price collapse in 2015. Travel bans around the world as of 25 March 2020 affect more than 550 million international travelers, more than 40% of the total.

Other adverse impacts may come through many channels. Disruption to production and trade are clearly extensive, but it is very difficult at present to evaluate how they will affect economies, both domestically and through global supply chains. Remittance-dependent economies may struggle as many migrant workers are unable to return to their countries of employment. In countries with inadequate social safety nets, large losses of jobs, wages, and wealth could trigger social unrest. And, if the scale of the outbreak increases to the extent that it infects a substantial portion of the global population, as some experts predict, the impact on public health will be significant. Even education has taken a hit as schools around the world have closed for extended periods.

Finally, the pandemic has the potential to change the world economy in fundamental ways. For starters, the rapid spread of the virus across countries has laid bare the downside of highly integrated global production processes and heavy specialization, vulnerable as they are to shutdowns on a global scale and for prolonged periods caused by massive disruption to transport and trade. The outbreak could thus leave permanent scars on globalization, which has underpinned the rise of developing Asia. In such an environment, countries will need to rely more on internally generated growth, including through domestic innovation activity such as research and development. The use of technology itself, such as technology that enables transactions at a distance, could also be forever changed. Such changes will become manifest only with the passage of time, but the COVID-19 crisis has already made clear the extent to which technological innovation will shape the way people do things and interact in the future. The challenge for developing Asia and the world as a whole is to foster innovation to promote and sustain a process of inclusive growth—the topic of this report's theme chapter.

The impact of COVID-19 on developing Asia—An update

The first ADB estimates of the economic impact of the outbreak were released in early March. Since then it has become a global pandemic, the use of containment policies and travel bans has proliferated, and data from the People's Republic of China (PRC) suggest a sharp economic contraction there in the first quarter of 2020. This updated analysis reflects these new realities and estimates a global cost of $2.0 trillion–$4.1 trillion, equal to 2.3%–4.8% of global GDP. This analysis estimates the impact on individual economies in developing Asia and on sectors within them.

The current pandemic is the most severe in a century. Coronavirus disease 2019 (COVID-19) was first identified in December 2019 in Wuhan, the capital of Hubei Province in the PRC. The virus that causes this disease is similar to the coronaviruses that caused severe acute respiratory syndrome (SARS) in 2003 and Middle East respiratory syndrome (MERS) in 2012. The mortality rate is currently estimated by the World Health Organization (WHO) at 3%–4% of those reported infected, but some studies put it as high as 5.7%. Both figures likely overestimate the true mortality rate, assuming that many victims recover from undiagnosed and unreported cases. The true mortality rate of COVID-19 is likely to be significantly lower than for SARS at 10% or MERS at 34% but higher than for seasonal flu at 0.1% (Table 1.2.1). What is important to the spread of the outbreak, however, is the COVID-19 infection rate, more precisely its reproduction number, or the average number of new infections generated by a single infectious person. Studies show that it could be high, with a top estimate more than double that of SARS and five times that of seasonal flu.

The epidemic was primarily concentrated in the PRC in January and February. Health officials there first alerted WHO of 41 unusual pneumonia cases in Wuhan on 31 December 2019. By 23 January, the number of confirmed cases had reached 571, prompting the PRC to place Wuhan, a metropolis of 11 million people, under quarantine.

Table 1.2.1 Mortality and infection rates of COVID-19 and other epidemics

COVID-19 has only a moderate mortality rate but is highly infectious.

	Mortality rate, % of cases causing death	Reproduction number, new infections generated per infected person
Ebola	50	1.5–2.5
MERS	34	0.4–0.9
SARS	10	3
COVID-19	3.0–5.7	1.4–6.5
Seasonal flu	0.1	1.3

COVID-19 = coronavirus disease 2019, MERS = Middle East respiratory syndrome, SARS = severe acute respiratory syndrome.

Sources: World Health Organization; Centers for Disease Control and Prevention; Althus 2014; Baud et al. 2020; Choi et al. 2018; Heymann and Shindo 2020; Liu et al. 2020; Wu and McGoogan 2020.

This section was written by Abdul Abiad of the Economic Research and Regional Cooperation Department, ADB, Manila, and Rosa Mia Arao, Reizle Platitas, Jesson Pagaduan, and Christian Jabagat, consultants, Economic Research and Regional Cooperation Department, ADB, Manila.

Figure 1.2.1 Global COVID-19 Cases

COVID-19 is now a global pandemic.

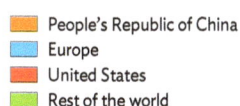

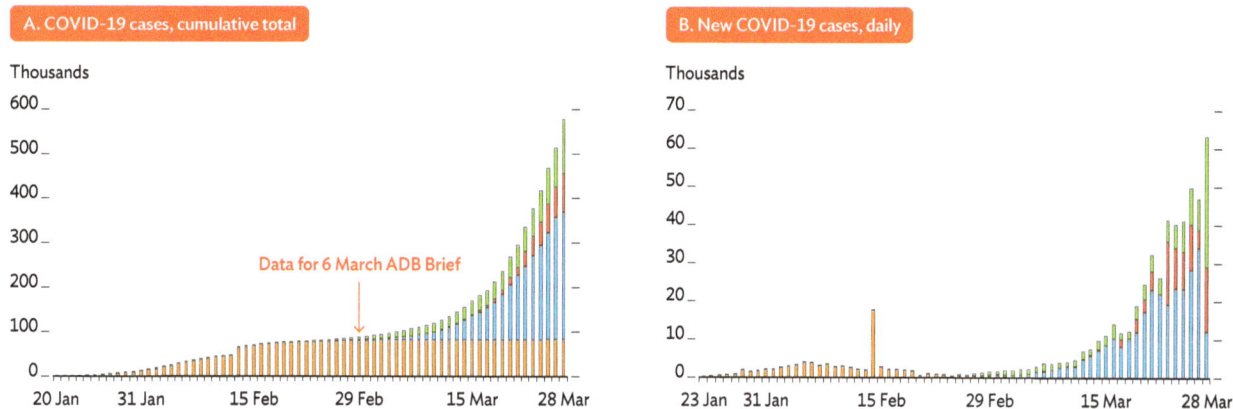

- People's Republic of China
- Europe
- United States
- Rest of the world

A. COVID-19 cases, cumulative total

B. New COVID-19 cases, daily

COVID-19 = coronavirus disease 2019.

Note: The discrete jump in the PRC in mid-February reflects a change in the diagnostic criterion applied to identify infections. Europe includes the 27 members of the European Union plus Switzerland and the United Kingdom.

Sources: CEIC Data Company; World Health Organization (accessed 29 March 2020).

The number of COVID-19 cases steadily rose through the remainder of January and throughout February, reaching close to 80,000 by the end of February (Figure 1.2.1, panel A). While there were cases outside of the PRC as early as 20 January in Thailand and 21 January in the US, at the end of February the epidemic was still primarily within the PRC, which had 93% of global cases and 97% of global fatalities. That was the data used in the *ADB Brief* released on 6 March 2020, when ADB did its initial estimate of the economic impact of the outbreak.[1]

The outbreak quickly became a global pandemic in March. COVID-19 cases started rising in Iran, Italy, and the ROK in the last few days of February and accelerated in March. Other countries that soon started seeing rapid increases in COVID-19 cases were France, Germany, Spain, and the US (Figure 1.2.1, panel B). On 11 March, WHO declared the COVID-19 outbreak a global pandemic. Cases steadily increased globally through March, crossing on 27 March the half-million mark. By 28 March, the US had surpassed Italy and the PRC in confirmed cases, with Europe as a whole accounting for 54% of global cases, the US 15%, the PRC 14%, and the rest of the world 17% (Figure 1.2.1, panel A).

This *ADO Special Topic* updates ADB estimates of the economic impact of COVID-19. Initial ADB estimates were presented in an *ADB Brief* released on 6 March. In the month since then, three important changes have occurred that necessitate an update. The first is the escalation of the outbreak into a global pandemic, as noted above. The second is the arrival of the first hard evidence, from the PRC, of how the outbreak and resulting containment policies negatively affected consumption and investment. The third change is the sharp rise in the deployment of containment policies such as travel bans, border closures, and quarantines. Scenario assumptions have been updated to reflect these developments. As in the 6 March *ADB Brief*, the analysis here describes the various channels through which economies can be affected. It explicitly lays out the assumptions underlying various scenarios regarding how the outbreak may play out. It then quantifies the likely magnitude of each scenario's economic impact. Finally, it provides details on how individual economies and sectors within them will be affected.

COVID-19 will affect economic activity through multiple quantifiable channels. The channels used in this analysis include declines in domestic consumption and investment from containment policies and precautionary behavior. The induced decline in domestic demand is likely to be the most important channel of economic impact in economies with serious outbreaks, or in those that implement strong containment policies preemptively, even before an outbreak becomes serious. Travel bans, border closures, and reduced demand for travel will affect tourism, transport, and trade. These effects will be important for more open and tourism-dependent economies. Weaker demand in one sector can spill over to others, both domestically or internationally, through production and trade links. As in the 6 March *ADB Brief*, the analysis accounts for and quantifies effects through these channels.

Many additional channels for effects on economic activity are not as easily analyzed or quantified. These channels include disrupted supply from production stoppages or border closures, which can affect other industries that use these intermediate inputs. Hard data is lacking on which sectors have seen significant supply disruptions, how long the disruptions will last, and whether other industries have sufficient inventories.

This analysis nevertheless captures part of the impact of the supply-side shock as disruptions reduce household incomes and corporate, suppressing domestic demand. Weaker global demand because of the pandemic has forced down prices for oil and other commodities, which will slow growth in economies that produce and export these products even as it lowers inflation in consuming economies. Hard data are lacking, but remittances can be affected in many ways, as the pandemic affects not only migrant workers' home countries but also the countries where they work. The scale of the economic shock has roiled financial markets and tightened financial conditions, heightening the risk of financial crises. Lastly, economic effects can flow directly from worsened disease incidence and mortality, as well as from forced shifts in health care spending.

ADB is working on quantifying impact through these channels and will present results in upcoming reports.

PRC consumption and investment fell substantially in the first 2 months of 2020. Combined data for January and February indicate that retail sales in those months fell by 20.5% from the same period in 2019 (Figure 1.2.2). Fixed asset investment fell by even more, contracting by 24.5%. Supply-side data on production in industry and services also showed double-digit declines. Because January was little affected by the nascent COVID-19 outbreak, most of the decline must have come in February, implying declines year on year in that month by about 40% for consumption and 50% for investment. If consumption and investment in March made up half the ground toward normalization from February's sharp decline, that would suggest declines in March year on year by about 20% in retail sales and 25% in investment. These figures are consistent with available high-frequency proxies for economic activity in the PRC, described below. If activity returns to normal in April, consumption in the year as a whole is estimated to be 5 percentage points below normal, and investment by 6.25 percentage points. These are the declines in consumption and investment growth used for the PRC in this analysis.

Since mid-March, many countries have declared states of emergency. As of 24 March, 50 countries that together provide 39% of global GDP had declared a state of emergency in response to COVID-19, and 174 countries had enacted some form of school closure (Figure 1.2.3). Many countries have instituted community quarantines and stay-at-home policies to slow virus transmission.

Travel bans and border closures spread in March, hurting tourism-dependent economies. One of the earliest travel bans was imposed on 24 January, when the PRC prohibited all outbound travel by tour groups, or 55% of all tourism outbound from the PRC. In late January and early February, many countries banned travel to the PRC. The use of travel bans accelerated in March as the pandemic spread to many other countries. Analysis using bilateral tourist arrivals data from past years suggests that current travel bans will affect more than 550 million international trips, or over 40% of the total in a typical year (Figure 1.2.4). Arrivals and tourism receipts in many economies in developing Asia are thus expected to decline sharply as a result of these travel bans and precautionary behavior. Tourism is an important revenue source in many economies in developing Asia. International tourism receipts provide more than 40% of GDP in Maldives and Palau, for example, and total travel and tourism receipts including domestic tourism exceed 10% of GDP in almost half of ADB developing member countries (DMCs).

Figure 1.2.2 Economic activity in the PRC

PRC data indicate sharp contraction in the first 2 months of 2020.

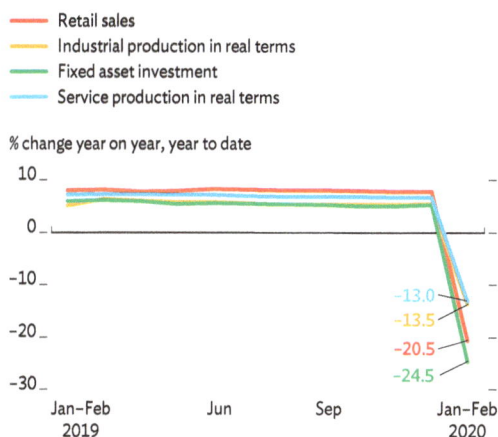

Source: CEIC Data Company.

Figure 1.2.3 Emergency declarations and school closures in response to COVID-19

Many countries have imposed a state of emergency and enacted containment policies.

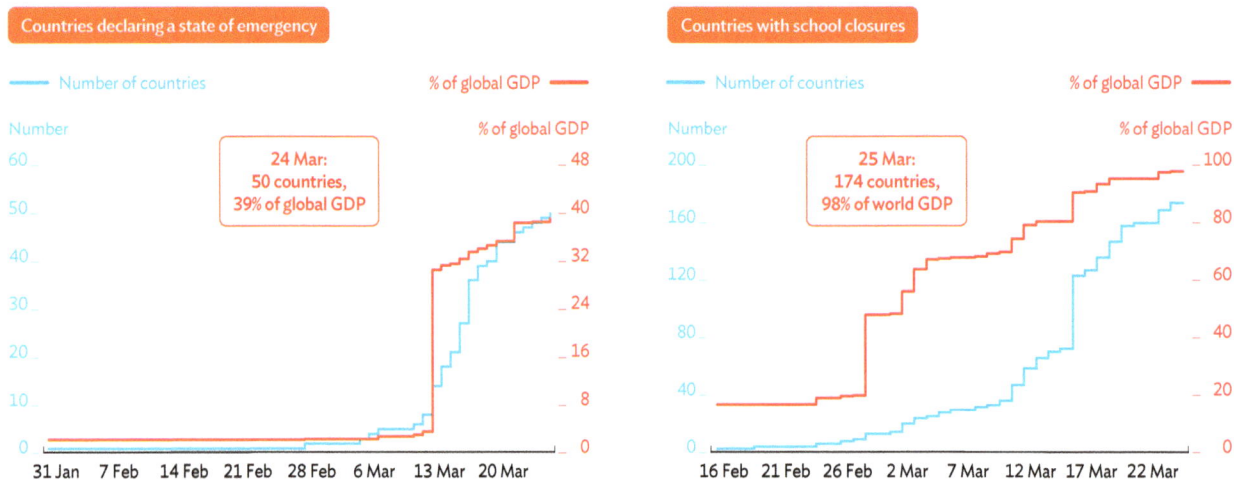

Countries declaring a state of emergency

— Number of countries   % of global GDP —

24 Mar:
50 countries,
39% of global GDP

Countries with school closures

— Number of countries   % of global GDP —

25 Mar:
174 countries,
98% of world GDP

Source: CICC Macro Research.

Lower demand will spill over to other areas through trade and production links. The analysis here uses the ADB 2018 Multiregional Input–Output Table (MRIOT) to incorporate spillover from demand shocks to other economies and sectors through trade and production links. It measures all links in 62 economies that together provide 95% of global GDP, with each economy disaggregated into 35 industries providing both goods and services. Shocks to final demand—in this case, to tourism and domestic consumption and investment—are transmitted across borders and industries through trade and production links, their knock-on effects traceable through the MRIOT.[2]

Figure 1.2.4 Number and share of international trips affected by travel bans

The use of travel bans has increased dramatically.

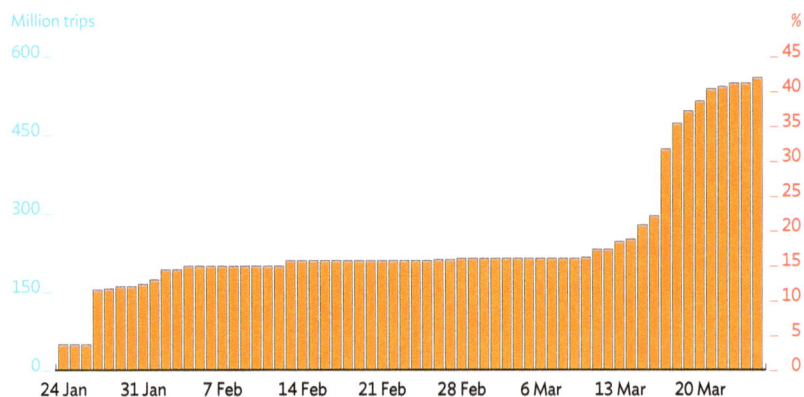

Note: Bars indicate the number of international trips affected by travel bans (left axis), with the top of the bar indicating the share of affected international trips in global tourism (right axis).

Sources: World Tourism Organization; International Air Transport Association 2020; New York Times 2020; Al Jazeera 2020; other international news sources; national sources; ADB estimates.

Production and trade disruption is evidenced in incomplete PRC normalization. High-frequency data indicate that PRC economic activity began to normalize in March but is not yet completely back to normal. One such daily activity tracker, by China International Capital Corporation, combines data on coal consumption, labor migration, freight logistics, and urban transport use. The tracker suggests that February activity averaged 53% below normal, and data to 26 March show March activity averaging about 21% below normal. Labor migration, coal consumption, and freight logistics indicators have returned to normal, but urban transportation is still far below normal (Figure 1.2.5).

The unpredictable COVID-19 outbreak trajectory requires the use of multiple scenarios. Huge uncertainties persist over how quickly affected economies can get outbreaks under control and normalize economic activity. While current evidence from the PRC suggests that outbreaks can be ended in 3 months, no guarantee exists that outbreak duration in other countries will be similar. Even in the PRC, activity has not yet fully normalized, as noted above. Many restrictions including some travel bans remain, and the possibility of a resurgence in COVID-19 cases cannot be ruled out. This argues for allowing in scenarios some variation in duration. This analysis assumes containment in 3 months in a better scenario, and in 6 months in a worse scenario. Outbreaks of even longer duration are possible, especially in less-developed economies where capacity to implement required policies is more limited and health systems are less developed.

There is also uncertainty about how deeply domestic demand will decline as a result of the outbreak and containment measures. The 6 March *ADB Brief* assumed declines in consumption and investment growth by 2 percentage points from normal, and that assumption is repeated here in the better scenario. In the ROK and Singapore, outbreaks have been held at bay through social distancing, extensive testing, and contact tracing, without resort to widespread quarantines or stay-at-home policies that are more deleterious to economic activity. At the other end, PRC data show that declines in consumption growth could be as large as 5 percentage points and in investment growth 6.25 percentage points. The analysis thus considers two scenarios, with assumptions detailed in Table 1.2.2:

(i)   First is a better scenario with shorter containment and smaller demand shocks. Economies suffering serious outbreaks take 3 months to contain them, with restrictive policies, travel bans, and precautionary behavior ending shortly after and economic activity normalizing.[3] These economies see declines in consumption and investment growth by 2 percentage points in 2020 relative to the scenario with no outbreak. The PRC is an exception, as data there indicate a steeper decline.

Figure 1.2.5 PRC daily economic activity tracker and production proxies

PRC activity gradually normalized in March but is not yet back to normal.

— 2020
— 2019
— 2018

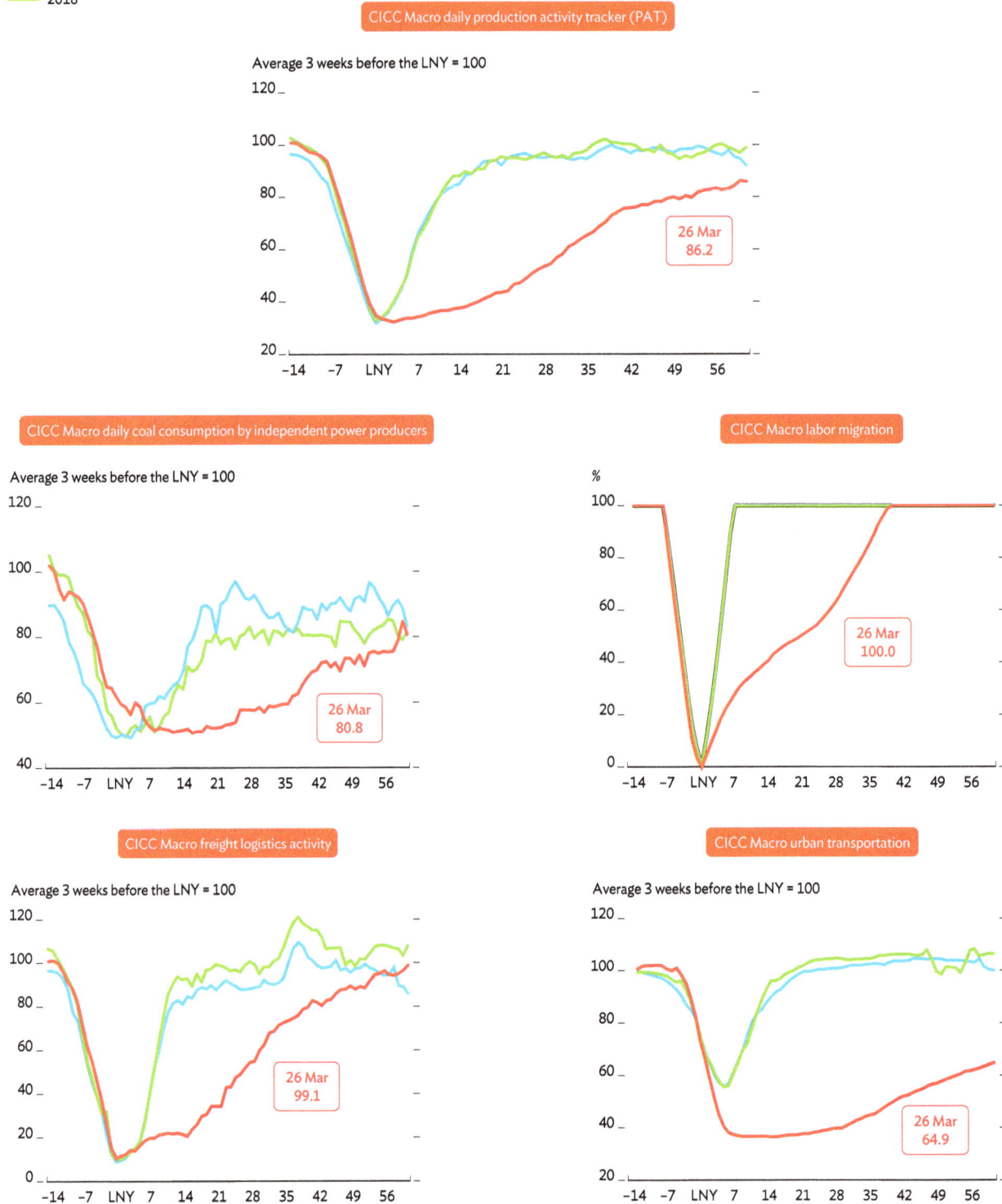

CICC Macro daily production activity tracker (PAT)

Average 3 weeks before the LNY = 100

26 Mar
86.2

CICC Macro daily coal consumption by independent power producers

Average 3 weeks before the LNY = 100

26 Mar
80.8

CICC Macro labor migration

%

26 Mar
100.0

CICC Macro freight logistics activity

Average 3 weeks before the LNY = 100

26 Mar
99.1

CICC Macro urban transportation

Average 3 weeks before the LNY = 100

26 Mar
64.9

LNY = Lunar New Year.
Note: The x-axis indicates days before or after the Lunar New Year. Activity normally falls sharply during and immediately after the Lunar New Year holiday, with 90% of activity typically restored 2 weeks after the new year and 100% restored just over a month later.
Source: CICC Macro Research.

Table 1.2.2 Scenario assumptions

	Shorter containment, smaller demand shocks	Longer containment, larger demand shocks
Tourism	• Outbound PRC tourism drops by 55% for 3 months. • Economies that impose travel bans on visitors from outbreak-affected economies earn no tourism receipts from these countries for 3 months. • Inbound tourism to outbreak-affected economies falls by 80% for 3 months. • Inbound tourism to Asia excluding the PRC, the ROK, and Japan falls by 40% for 3 months. • Inbound tourism to Europe excluding the European Union, Norway, Switzerland, and the United Kingdom falls by 30% for 3 months.	• Outbound PRC tourism drops by 55% for 6 months. • Economies that impose travel bans on visitors from outbreak-affected economies earn no tourism receipts from these countries for 6 months. • Inbound tourism to outbreak-affected economies falls by 80% for 6 months. • Inbound tourism to Asia excluding the PRC, the ROK, Japan falls by 40% for 6 months. • Inbound tourism to Europe excluding the European Union, Norway, Switzerland, and the United Kingdom falls by 30% for 6 months.
Consumption	• Growth in domestic consumption in the PRC slows by 5 percentage points. • Growth in domestic consumption in outbreak-affected economies excluding the PRC declines by 2 percentage points.	• Growth in domestic consumption in outbreak-affected economies declines by 5 percentage points.
Investment	• Growth in domestic investment in the PRC declines by 6.25 percentage points. • Growth in domestic investment in outbreak-affected economies excluding the PRC declines by 2 percentage points.	• Growth in domestic investment in outbreak-affected economies declines by 6.25 percentage points.

PRC = People's Republic of China, ROK = Republic of Korea.

Note: Outbreak-affected economies are Australia, Brazil, Canada, the European Union (treated as a bloc for simplicity as most of its large economies have serious outbreaks), Iran, Japan, Norway, the People's Republic of China, the Republic of Korea, Switzerland, Turkey, the United Kingdom, and the United States.

(ii)   Second is a worse scenario with longer containment and larger demand shocks. Economies suffering serious outbreaks take 6 months to contain them, with restrictive policies, travel bans, and precautionary behavior ending shortly after and economic activity normalizing. These economies see declines in consumption growth by 5 percentage points in 2020 and in investment growth by 6.25 percentage points relative the scenario with no outbreak, in line with recent data from the PRC.

An unknown is whether other DMCs will suffer serious outbreaks. Several DMCs already have more than 1,000 confirmed COVID-19 cases. Some have declared a state of emergency and instituted containment policies such as school closures, community quarantines, and stay-at-home policies and have shut down public transportation and nonessential businesses. These economies will likely see substantial declines in consumption and investment. In other DMCs, the number of cases remains in the hundreds or fewer, but the past 2 months have shown that the situation can change quickly, and outbreaks can spread rapidly. For this reason, the analysis calculates for all DMCs the additional impact of having a serious domestic outbreak. Here as well, two possibilities are considered: a scenario with shorter domestic outbreak containment and smaller demand shocks, and another with longer domestic outbreak containment and larger demand shocks.

Table 1.2.3 Estimated impact of the COVID-19 outbreak, two scenarios

	Shorter containment, smaller demand shocks		Longer containment, larger demand shocks	
	% of GDP	Losses, $ billion	% of GDP	Losses, $ billion
World	-2.3	2,013.0	-4.8	4,090.8
People's Republic of China	-4.6	628.0	-5.1	691.6
Developing Asia, excluding the PRC	-1.0	93.3	-2.2	200.1
Rest of the world	-2.0	1,291.6	-5.1	3,199.1

GDP = gross domestic product, PRC = People's Republic of China.

Source: ADB estimates.

Updated scenarios suggest global impact at $2.0 trillion–$4.1 trillion. This loss equals 2.3%–4.8% of global GDP, with most of the impact outside the region. Developing Asia will bear 22%–36% of the loss, depending on the scenario used. This does not mean that impact on DMCs will be small. In the PRC in particular, the estimated impact is close to 5% of GDP. In the rest of developing Asia in aggregate, the impact will be 1.0%–2.2% of combined GDP. Considering that world GDP growth was just 2.4% last year, the estimated global impact suggests that global recession is indeed possible unless policy makers respond swiftly and decisively.

Regional impact will be greatest in DMCs with domestic outbreaks or tourism dependence. Spillover from the global pandemic is greatest in Maldives, whose economy relies heavily on international tourism, receipts from which provide close to 60% of GDP. Travel bans and reluctance to travel will cost Maldives the equivalent of 7%–14% of GDP (Figure 1.2.6).

Figure 1.2.6 Impact on individual regional economies

DMCs will be affected by spillover from other countries, and they risk suffering additional losses from domestic outbreaks.

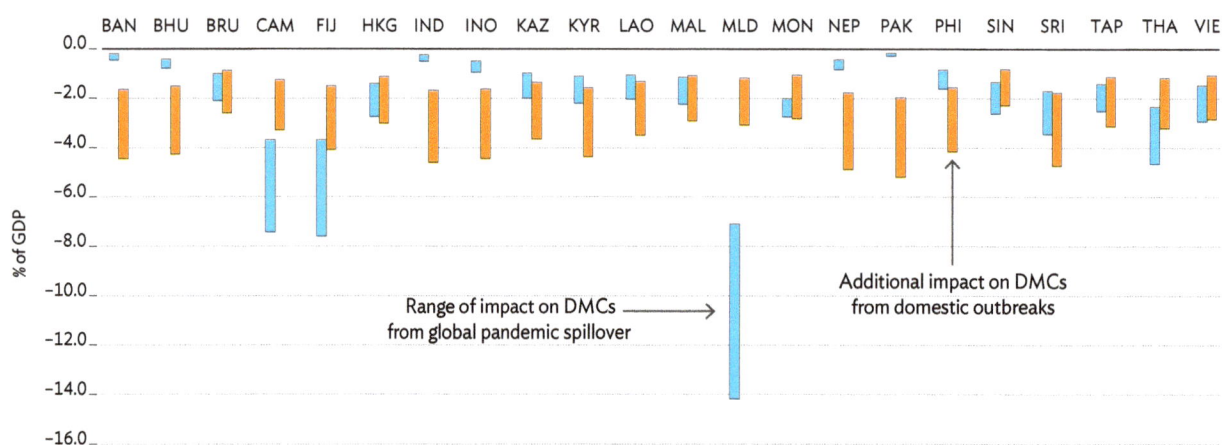

BAN = Bangladesh, BHU = Bhutan, BRU = Brunei Darussalam, CAM = Cambodia, DMC = developing member country, FIJ = Fiji, GDP = gross domestic product, HKG = Hong Kong, China, IND = India, INO = Indonesia, KAZ = Kazakhstan, KGZ = Kyrgyz Republic, LAO = Lao People's Democratic Republic, MAL = Malaysia, MLD = Maldives, MON = Mongolia, NEP = Nepal, PAK = Pakistan, PHI = Philippines, SIN = Singapore, SRI = Sri Lanka, TAP = Taipei,China, THA = Thailand, VIE = Viet Nam.

Notes: Blue bars indicate the range of estimated impact from global pandemic spillover. Orange bars are additional impact on DMCs that suffer their own outbreaks. The tops of bars indicate the shorter containment, smaller demand shock scenario, and bottoms of bars indicate the longer containment, larger demand shock scenario.

Source: ADB estimates.

Other DMCs significantly affected by the global pandemic are Cambodia, Fiji, and Thailand, all of which have significant tourism industries. In many other DMCs, the impact from global spillover will be smaller. But the risk—and for some economies the reality—is a domestic outbreak that further depresses economic activity. In these economies, the domestic outbreak imposes an additional impact, on top of the loss from spillover, equal to 2%–4% of GDP (Figure 1.2.6).

Within economies, tourism-related businesses will be hard hit by lower global demand. Detailed results showing the impact on individual economies and on sectors within them can be found on the ADB website dedicated to COVID-19.[4] In Thailand, for example, some 55% of spillover from the global pandemic falls on two service categories: hotels and restaurants and other personal services, which could suffer a temporary 23% employment loss under the longer scenario, and transport services, which could suffer a temporary 16% employment loss.

Limitations on this analysis may mean it underestimates impact on DMCs. Channels not accounted for in this analysis include disruption to production and trade, lower commodity and oil prices, interrupted remittances, possible social and financial crises, and long-term effects on health care and education. Each of these channels could substantially worsen the impact of the COVID-19 pandemic. In less-developed economies, inadequate capacity in the health system to cope or in the government to undertake necessary measures to contain the virus or ameliorate its economic effects could mean longer outbreaks with more severe economic disruption. ADB analysis is currently under way to shed light on these issues, including country studies that account for the unique characteristics of each country's health system and institutional capacity.

Endnotes

1   A. Abiad et al. 2020. The Economic Impact of the COVID-19 Outbreak on Developing Asia. *ADB Briefs* No. 128, 6 March. https://www.adb.org/sites/default/files/publication/571536/adb-brief-128-economic-impact-covid19-developing-asia.pdf.

2   The MRIOT allows the calculation of a *technical coefficients matrix A* that specifies how much inputs are needed from every sector in every country to produce one unit of output in sector i in country j. Given the vectors of gross outputs x and final demand f (covering all country sectors), one can show that $x = Ax + f$ and $x = (I - A)^{-1}f$, or $\Delta x = (I - A)^{-1}\Delta f$. That is, for a given exogenous change in final demand one can calculate the impact on gross output and on value-added or GDP, using the matrix $(I - A)^{-1}$, also known as the Leontief inverse. More sophisticated general equilibrium models are richer as they allow for substitution, prices adjustments, and policy responses.

3   This analysis defines economies with at least 2,000 cases as of 27 March as having serious outbreaks. The list includes Australia, Brazil, Canada, the European Union (treated as a bloc for simplicity as most of its large economies have serious outbreaks), Japan, Norway, Switzerland, Turkey, the United Kingdom, and the United States. Japan is included even though it had only 1,387 cases on 27 March as a sharp rise in recently confirmed infections suggests it will surpass 2,000 cases in a few days.

4   http://www.adb.org/covid-19.

References

Abiad, A. et al. 2020. The Economic Impact of the COVID-19 Outbreak on Developing Asia. *ADB Briefs* No. 128, 6 March. https://www.adb.org/sites/default/files/publication/571536/adb-brief-128-economic-impact-covid19-developing-asia.pdf.

Al Jazeera. 2020. *Coronavirus: Travel Restrictions, Border Shutdowns by Country.* https://www.aljazeera.com/news/2020/03/coronavirus-travel-restrictions-border-shutdowns-country-200318091505922.html (accessed 26 March 2020).

Althus, C. 2014. *Estimating the Reproduction Number of Ebola Virus (EBOV) during the 2014 Outbreak in West Africa.* https://doi.org/10.1371/currents.outbreaks.91afb5e0f279e7f29e7056095255b288.

Baud, D. et al. 2020. Real Estimates of Mortality Following COVID-19 Infection. *The Lancet.* https://doi.org/10.1016/S1473-3099(20)30195-X.

Centers for Disease Control and Prevention. 2020. *2019–2020 U.S. Flu Season: Preliminary Burden Estimates.* https://www.cdc.gov/flu/about/burden/preliminary-in-season-estimates.htm.

———. 2019. *MERS Clinical Features.* https://www.cdc.gov/coronavirus/mers/clinical-features.html.

———. 2017. *SARS Basics Fact Sheet.* https://www.cdc.gov/sars/about/fs-sars.html.

Choi, S. et al. 2018. High Reproduction Number of Middle East Respiratory Syndrome Coronavirus in Nosocomial Outbreaks: Mathematical Modelling in Saudi Arabia and South Korea. *Journal of Hospital Infection 99.*

Heymann, D. L. and N. Shindo. 2020. COVID-19: What is Next for Public Health? *The Lancet.* https://doi.org/10.1016/S0140-6736(20)30374-3.

IATA Travel Centre. 2020. *Coronavirus Outbreak—Update.* 27 March. https://www.iatatravelcentre.com/international-travel-document-news/1580226297.htm (accessed 26 March 2020).

Liu, Y. et al. 2020. The Reproductive Number of COVID-19 Is Higher Compared to SARS Coronavirus. *Journal of Travel Medicine* 27(2). https://doi.org/10.1093/jtm/taaa021.

New York Times. 2020. Coronavirus Travel Restrictions across the Globe. https://www.nytimes.com/article/coronavirus-travel-restrictions.html (accessed 26 March 2020).

Coronavirus: Places and Airlines Restricting China Transit. 18 February 2020. https://multimedia.scmp.com/infographics/news/world/article/3051149/coronavirus-travel-restrictions-on-china/index.html (accessed 26 March 2020).

World Health Organization. *Coronavirus Disease (COVID-19) Situation Reports.* https://www.who.int/emergencies/diseases/novel-coronavirus-2019/situation-reports/ (accessed 26 March 2020).

———. 2003. Consensus Document on the Epidemiology of Severe Acute Respiratory Syndrome (SARS). https://www.who.int/csr/sars/en/WHOconsensus.pdf.

———. 2020. Middle East Respiratory Syndrome. http://www.emro.who.int/health-topics/mers-cov/mers-outbreaks.html.

———. 2020. Ebola Virus Disease. https://www.who.int/news-room/fact-sheets/detail/ebola-virus-disease.

World Tourism Organization. 2019. *Guidelines for the Success in the Chinese Outbound Tourism Market.* https://doi.org/10.18111/9789284421138.

Wu, Z. and J. McGoogan. 2020. Characteristics of and Important Lessons from the Coronavirus Disease 2019 (COVID-19) Outbreak in China: Summary of a Report of 72,314 Cases from the Chinese Center for Disease Control and Prevention. *Journal of the American Medical Association* 395(10225). https://10.1001/jama.2020.2648.

Annex: Tumbling global growth in a time of COVID-19

The major advanced economies of the United States, the euro area, and Japan are expected to lose steam to the forecast horizon. Aggregate growth slowed to an estimated 1.7% in 2019 and is expected to contract by 0.3% in 2020 before returning to 1.8% in 2021. As coronavirus disease 2019 (COVID-19) spreads, it is dampening what was an incipient recovery in global activity and trade. As this report goes to press, growth in the US is expected to fall to 0.4%. The euro area and Japan are now expected to contract in 2020 before recovering in 2021.

Table A1.1 Baseline assumptions on the international economy

	2018	2019	2020	2021
	Actual		ADO 2020 *Projection*	
GDP growth (%)				
Major industrial economies[a]	2.2	1.7	-0.3	1.8
United States	2.9	2.3	0.4	2.1
Euro area	1.9	1.2	-1.0	1.6
Japan	0.3	0.7	-1.5	0.9
Prices and inflation				
Brent crude spot prices (average, $/barrel)	71.15	64.03	35.00	55.00
Food index (2010 = 100, % change)	0.3	-3.8	2.0	2.0
Consumer price index inflation (major industrial economies' average, %)	2.0	1.4	1.4	1.7
Interest rates				
United States federal funds rate (average, %)	1.8	2.2	0.4	0.1
European Central Bank refinancing rate (average, %)	0.0	0.0	0.0	0.0
Bank of Japan overnight call rate (average, %)	-0.1	-0.1	-0.1	-0.1
$ Libor[b] (%)	2.1	2.2	0.4	0.1

ADO = Asian Development Outlook, GDP = gross domestic product.

[a] Average growth rates are weighted by gross national income, Atlas method.

[b] Average London interbank offered rate quotations on 1-month loans.

Sources: US Department of Commerce, Bureau of Economic Analysis, http://www.bea.gov; Eurostat, http://ec.europa.eu/eurostat; Economic and Social Research Institute of Japan, http://www.esri.cao.go.jp; Consensus Forecasts; Bloomberg; CEIC Data Company; Haver Analytics; and the World Bank, Global Commodity Markets, http://www.worldbank.org; ADB estimates.

This annex was written by Matteo Lanzafame, Nedelyn Magtibay-Ramos, Madhavi Pundit, Pilipinas Quising, Arief Ramayandi, Dennis Sorino, and Priscille Villanueva of the Economic Research and Regional Cooperation Department, ADB, Manila, and Michael Timbang, consultant, Economic Research and Regional Cooperation Department, ADB, Manila.

Recent developments in the major advanced economies

United States

Growth in the US economy slowed to 2.3% in 2019, dragged down by weak external trade and investment. Exports picked up in the first quarter (Q1) in seasonally adjusted annualized terms (as assumed for all quarterly growth rates in this *Annex* unless otherwise stated). Meanwhile, imports fell as the effects of higher tariffs in the US trade conflict with the People's Republic of China (PRC) started to kick in, the two trends generating a positive contribution to GDP growth from net exports (Figure A1.1). Since then, GDP growth slowed as global trade uncertainty caused both investment and trade to slump. With prolonged uncertainty in the global economy, continuing trade tensions with the PRC, and a strong US dollar, exports steadied but remained weighed down in the second half after a 5.7% fall in Q2 (Figure A1.2). A large drop in goods imports in Q4 meant a substantial fall in imports for the whole year, leaving a positive trade balance that contributed 1.5 percentage points to 2.1% GDP growth in the quarter.

Consumption picked up and contributed strongly to overall GDP growth in Q2 and Q3 of 2019 but weakened in Q4. This is consistent with trends in indexes for consumer confidence and retail sales, both of which, supported by steady wage growth throughout the year, recovered rapidly in Q2 and Q3 (Figure A1.3). After a strong Q1 of 2019, private investment declined as nonresidential fixed investment dropped in the remainder of the year. Echoing the fall in investment, the purchasing managers' index (PMI) showed mostly a downward trend throughout the year (Figure A1.3). The PMI managed to stay above the 50 threshold, indicating future expansion, but did so mainly on continuous expansion outside of manufacturing, while the manufacturing component languished below 50 from August, indicating contraction in manufacturing (Figure A1.3).

Data releases in early 2020 suggested that the US economy was regaining momentum. The consumer confidence index hit 126.5 in February (2007 = 100), having increased since late 2019. This was consistent with improvement in the retail sales index. Economic deceleration suggested by PMI readings last year also reversed, with the manufacturing component bouncing back into expansionary territory in January and February. These rebounds suggested further expansion of the US economy, in line with a continued strong outturn in the labor market to February 2020. Job numbers consistently showed healthy increases in the first 2 months of the year,

Figure A1.1 Demand-side contributions to growth, United States

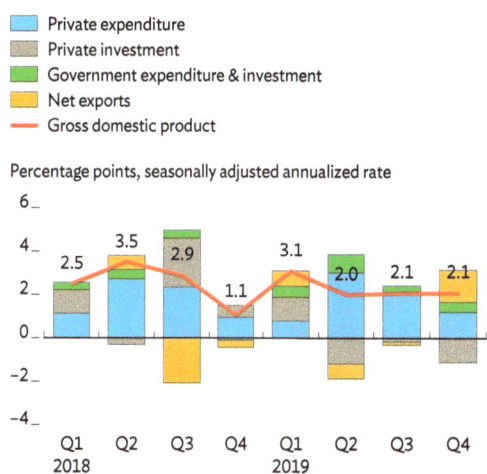

- Private expenditure
- Private investment
- Government expenditure & investment
- Net exports
- Gross domestic product

Percentage points, seasonally adjusted annualized rate

Q = quarter.
Sources: US Department of Commerce. Bureau of Economic Analysis. http://www.bea.gov; Haver Analytics (both accessed 14 March 2020).

Figure A1.2 Export and import growth, United States

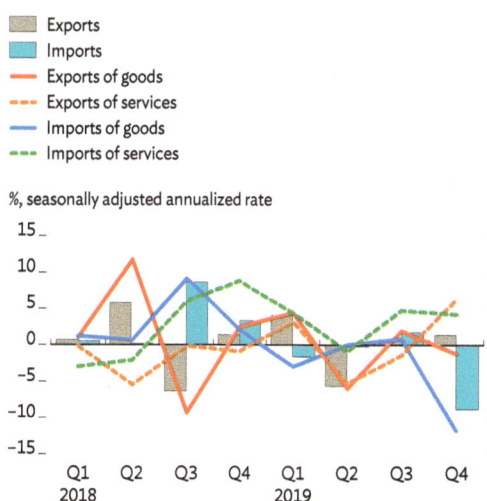

- Exports
- Imports
- Exports of goods
- Exports of services
- Imports of goods
- Imports of services

%, seasonally adjusted annualized rate

Q = quarter.
Sources: US Department of Commerce. Bureau of Economic Analysis. http://www.bea.gov; Haver Analytics (both accessed 14 March 2020).

holding down the unemployment rate at 3.5%, which suggested continuing income growth to support expansion in domestic spending.

Along with positive economic growth, headline inflation edged up to 2.5% in January but softened in February following a fall in oil prices in response to the COVID-19 outbreak globally. Core inflation edged up to 2.4% as higher prices for services continued to reflect the strong outturn in economic data up to February (Figure A1.4). However, headline inflation should ease further with oil prices lower following disagreement between Saudi Arabia and the Russian Federation over a proposed production cut to stabilize the market, and then weaker demand following the imposition of restrictions of people's movements to deal with COVID-19. Inflation is seen averaging 1.8% in 2020 before picking up to 2.1% in 2021.

A spike in reported COVID-19 cases in the US since early March was a game changer. Although available hard data to the time of writing still indicate economic strength, the risk is mounting that growth will be slower than expected in Q2 in the wake of pervasive disruption to business. The US Federal Reserve conducted two emergency rate cuts to preempt negative economic impact from COVID-19. On 3 March, the Fed slashed the federal funds rate by 50 basis points and, on 14 March, brought it down to the zero lower-bound, announcing as well that it would resume quantitative easing with the purchase of $500 billion in Treasury bills and $200 billion in mortgage-backed securities. All these moves came on top of a national emergency declaration on 13 March that allows the federal government to distribute up to $50 billion in aid to states, cities, and territories.

More recently, the US Federal Reserve extended the quantitative easing policy to buy an unlimited amount of bonds to suppress the cost of borrowing, and the Senate approved a historic $2 trillion stimulus package to deal with the negative economic impact of the pandemic. With these policies in place, and assuming a baseline scenario in which the virus is contained relatively quickly, GDP growth in the US is projected to slow to 0.4% this year before rebounding to 2.1% in 2021. Risks to the forecast tilt heavily to the downside. If the impact of COVID-19 turns out to be much more severe than anticipated, and activity stays stalled longer than currently expected, the economy may contract in 2020.

Euro area

Growth in the euro area slackened from 1.9% in 2018 to 1.2% in 2019 (Figure A1.5). Moreover, it slowed from 1.2% in Q3 to only 0.5% in Q4. Tepid external demand prolonged weakness in euro

Figure A1.3 Business activity and consumer confidence indicators, United States

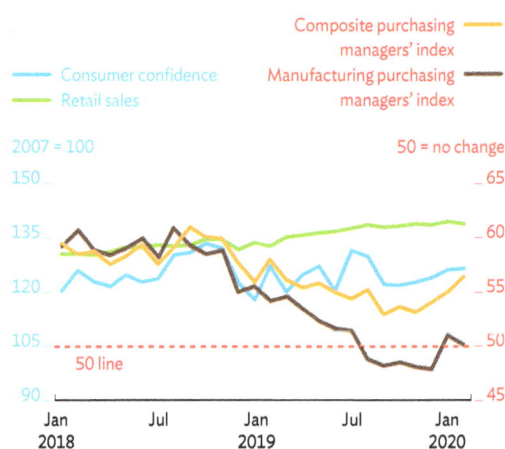

Note: A purchasing managers' index reading <50 signals deterioration, >50 improvement.
Source: Haver Analytics (accessed 14 March 2020).

Figure A1.4 Inflation and the US Federal Reserve rate, United States

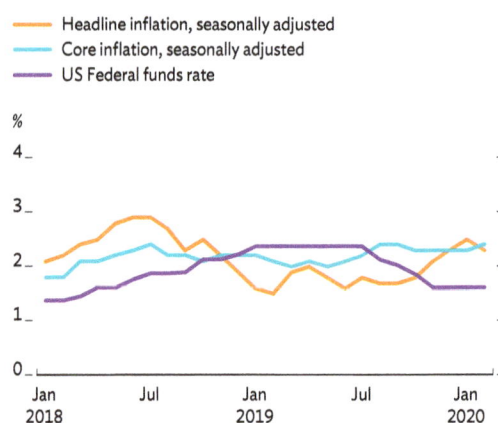

Source: Haver Analytics (accessed 14 March 2020).

area industry that impaired economic activity in Q4, causing net exports to subtract 3.1 percentage points from growth. Slower growth in private consumption, evidenced by a sharp decline in retail sales in December, further held down economic activity in the quarter, adding only 0.2 percentage points. The disappointing Q4 performance reflected contraction in the second and third largest economies in the currency bloc. In France, GDP dropped by 0.2% in Q4 as country-wide protests slowed consumer spending and inventories fell. Italy's GDP declined by 1.2% in the quarter as policy uncertainty, stifled credit, muted wage growth, and labor market slack dented domestic demand. In Germany, meanwhile, the area's largest economy ended 2019 on a sour note with scant 0.1% growth in Q4. On the upside, growth in Spain picked up from 1.6% in Q3 to 2.1% in Q4 on an upbeat external sector and despite disappointing domestic demand.

Early in the year, before the onset of COVID-19 in Europe, leading indicators suggested economic softness would persist at least in the first half of 2020. After hitting a nearly 5-year low of 100.9 in December, overall economic sentiment recovered to 102.6 in January and further to 103.5 in February, reflecting stronger confidence in industry and construction. However, the composite PMI failed to pick up, remaining broadly unchanged at 51.3 in January from 51.6 in February and still uncomfortably close to the threshold at 50 that separates growth from decline (Figure A1.6). The manufacturing PMI remained contractionary at 49.1 in February, but firms' expectations of future output strengthened, and the ratio of orders to inventory surged in January to its highest in nearly 18 months, indicating that the manufacturing slump was bottoming out. Meanwhile, the service sector remained resilient, albeit less positive than in 2019 at a PMI reading of 52.6 as growth was crimped by a fall in exports.

In early March, the rapid global spread of COVID-19 prompted the implementation of severe mobility restrictions and lockdown in Italy, where the number of infections has reached 53,600 as *Asian Development Outlook 2020* (*ADO 2020*) goes to press. By mid-March, the European Union decided to close its external borders for at least 30 days, and lockdown regulations were adopted in France and Spain, while Germany and the Netherlands also appear likely to tighten their currently lighter approach to containment. The baseline assumptions underpinning *ADO* forecasts factor in a substantial negative shock to economic activity in the first half of 2020 in these five countries, which collectively contribute about 80% of euro area GDP. In the absence of hard evidence on the future evolution of the outbreak, the baseline scenario assumes that the impact of the COVID-19 outbreak will be limited in other European countries.

Figure A1.5 Demand-side contributions to growth, euro area

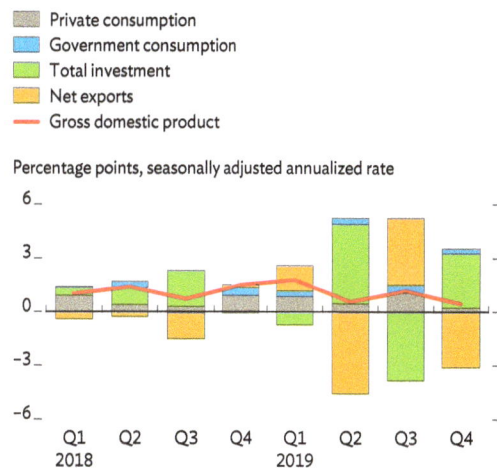

Private consumption
Government consumption
Total investment
Net exports
Gross domestic product

Percentage points, seasonally adjusted annualized rate

Q = quarter.
Source: Haver Analytics (accessed 14 March 2020).

Figure A1.6 Economic sentiment and purchasing managers' indexes, euro area

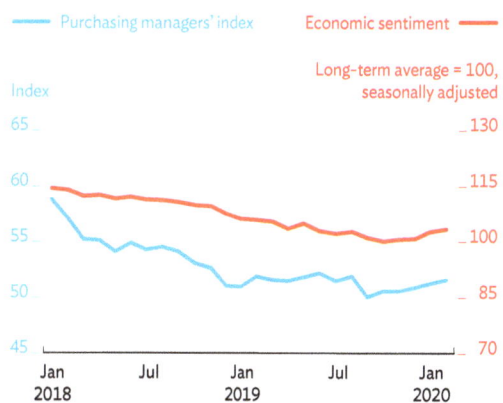

Purchasing managers' index   Economic sentiment

Long-term average = 100, seasonally adjusted

Index

Sources: Bloomberg and Haver Analytics (both accessed 14 March 2020).

The upshot is that growth in the euro area is forecast to contract by 1.0% in 2020 as challenging domestic and external conditions weigh heavily on the economy. Investment is expected to deteriorate significantly in response to anemic domestic and external demand, declining capacity utilization, and highly elevated uncertainty. Consumer spending is expected to take a hit in the coming months from lockdown measures, worsening consumer confidence, slow employment growth, and cooling wage inflation. On the external front, export growth is seen to be modest in line with a slowdown in global trade.

Assuming a gradual weakening of domestic and external headwinds and recovery in manufacturing, the currency bloc is poised to regain traction next year, buttressed by an ultra-accommodative monetary policy. Further support will likely come from more expansionary fiscal measures, as a widening structural budget deficit—which last December the European Central Bank projected rising from 1.0% in 2019 to 1.3% in 2020 and 1.5% in 2021—is likely to be complemented by additional transitory spending packages currently being formulated to deal with COVID-19. Exports are projected to recover, and investment to rebound, as firms expand production capacity, buoyed by improving financing conditions. Growth in private consumption should find support in low nominal bank lending rates and rising net worth, benefiting as well from modest inflation. Growth is thus forecast to pick up to 1.6% in 2021.

Headline inflation, having climbed to 1.4% in January 2020, edged down to 1.2% in February following a renewed fall in energy prices as a result of the COVID-19 outbreak. Core inflation, by contrast, ticked up from 1.3% in January to 1.4% in February (Figure A1.7). Consumer price inflation averaged 1.2% in 2019, well within the European Central Bank target of just below 2.0%. Meanwhile, in response to economic disruption caused by the COVID-19 outbreak, the central bank announced at its 12 March meeting a further expansion of its asset-purchasing program and additional liquidity facilities. In a surprise move, the central bank unveiled on 18 March its Pandemic Emergency Purchase Programme, endowed with €750 billion to purchase securities, both private and public. These recent actions follow a central bank decision in September to loosen policy for the first time since 2016, introducing a batch of new stimulus measures: cutting the deposit rate deeper into negative territory, restarting quantitative easing, and extending forward guidance. Policy is seen staying ultra-accommodative. In keeping with the expected recession and V-shaped recovery, inflation is forecast at 1.0% in 2020 and 1.4% in 2021.

Figure A1.7 Headline and core inflation, euro area

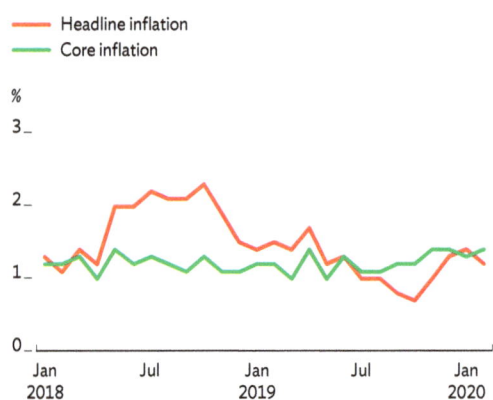

Source: Haver Analytics (accessed 14 March 2020).

Downside risks to the outlook stem primarily from a COVID-19 pandemic more widespread and prolonged than currently forecast, particularly in Germany but also in France, Spain, the United Kingdom and the US—all of which have, as *ADO 2020* goes to press, recorded significant and rapidly growing numbers of infections. Additional risks could arise from worsening trade tensions with the US, the US–PRC trade conflict, uncertainty surrounding a possible disorderly Brexit, a slowdown in the PRC that surprised on the downside, lingering weakness in manufacturing, and market concerns about debt sustainability in Italy.

Japan

With a strong performance in the first half of 2019 propelled mainly by domestic demand, Japan accelerated economic growth from 0.3% in 2018 to 0.7%. Trade tensions and soft global demand then cooled the economy considerably in the second half, with growth plunging by 7.1% in Q4 after a sales tax hike and a destructive Typhoon Hagibis, both in October. Private consumption, having boosted growth ahead of the tax increase, declined in Q4 by a sharp 10.6% from the previous quarter and dragged down GDP growth by 6.1 percentage points. The consumption drop was more severe than a 5.3% decrease after a 1997 tax hike but slightly less so than a 11.4% plunge after a 2014 tax hike. Private investment also dragged on growth, but net exports provided a boost if only because various headwinds drove down imports more sharply than exports (Figure A1.8).

Industrial production weakened throughout the second half of 2019 and declined further by 2.4% in January 2020 (Figure A1.9). Exports continued their weakening streak for 15 months, excepting a brief pickup in July last year, and fell by 0.6% in February 2020, mainly reflecting low global demand for machinery and transport equipment (Figure A1.10). Imports fell by a sharp 13.6% in the same month, reflecting weakness in investment. Going forward, production is likely to remain under pressure as the manufacturing PMI, which improved marginally around the turn of the year, deteriorated from 48.8 in January to a 7-year low of 47.6 in February with the COVID-19 outbreak disrupting supply chains and exports. The service sector was hard hit, possibly by a fall in tourism, and the PMI for services tumbled from 51.0 in January to 46.7 in February, below the 50 threshold indicating a contractionary trend. A slight 2.9% rise month on month in machinery orders in January, following on the heels of a massive 12.5% fall in December, suggested that business spending was recovering, albeit slowly, when COVID-19 hit and derailed activity in every way.

Figure A1.8 Demand-side contributions to growth, Japan

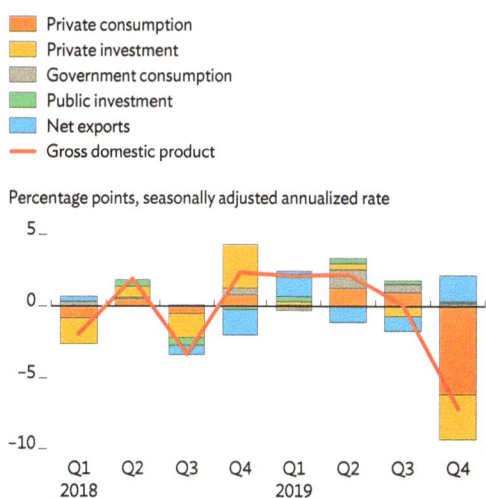

- Private consumption
- Private investment
- Government consumption
- Public investment
- Net exports
- Gross domestic product

Percentage points, seasonally adjusted annualized rate

Q = quarter.
Source: Economics and Social Research Institute, Cabinet Office, Government of Japan. http://www.esri.cao.go.jp (accessed 9 March 2020).

Figure A1.9 Consumption and business indicators, Japan

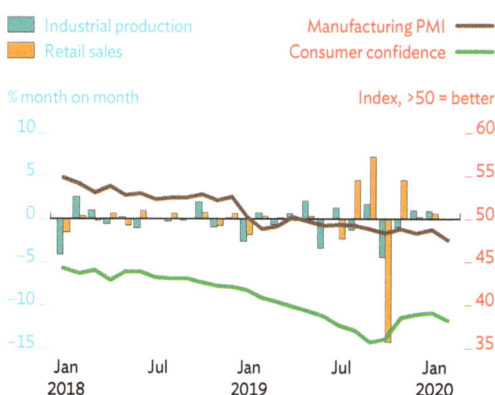

- Industrial production
- Retail sales
- Manufacturing PMI
- Consumer confidence

% month on month   Index, >50 = better

PMI = purchasing managers' index.
Notes: A purchasing managers' index reading <50 signals deterioration, >50 improvement. A consumer confidence reading >50 signals better conditions.
Sources: Haver Analytics; Bloomberg (both accessed 10 March 2020).

With production and exports weak, consumption was a key growth driver in most of 2019. Then, in October, a nationwide sales tax hike from 8% to 10% weighed heavily on domestic spending. Seasonally adjusted retail sales dived that month, as expected, but the 14.2% drop from the previous month was sharper than a decline in the previous tax hike episode. With sales picking up in the following 3 months amid improving consumer confidence and low unemployment, the expectation was for mild economic recovery in early 2020. Instead, the tax blow to consumption and activity was exacerbated by COVID-19. A plunge in the Economy Watcher's Survey indicates bleak sentiment about household activity, production, and employment. With 30% of international tourists coming from the PRC in 2019, sudden strong travel restrictions hammered Japan's booming tourism industry in Q1 of 2020, which will aggravate the domestic consumption slump.

Headline inflation accelerated to 0.8% year on year in December 2019, likely driven in part by the sales tax hike, before falling to 0.6% in January 2020. Core inflation, which excludes fuel and fresh food, also fell, from 0.6% to 0.4%. At its most recent meeting, the Bank of Japan kept monetary policy unchanged, including a short-term interest rate of –0.1%, purchases of Japanese government bonds to keep 10-year yields near zero, and forward guidance that it will lower interest rates further if prospects worsen for meeting the price stability target. Further, measures to inject additional liquidity and ease financial conditions have been initiated.

A positive start to 2020 emerged from accommodative policies to buffer the tax hike, and from receding trade uncertainty. But the virus outbreak has crimped economic activity as businesses deal with disrupted supply chains on the one hand and weaker demand from anxious consumers on the other. The rapid global spread of COVID-19 and the severity of the downturn in the PRC will weigh heavily on Japan's external sector, on top of domestic consumption constrained by outbreak containment measures, the tax burden, and tepid wage recovery. The postponement of the 2020 Summer Olympics dealt an additional blow to local businesses. The GDP forecast for 2020 is thus revised down to contraction by 1.5%. A major downside risk to the forecast would be a prolonged worldwide spread of COVID-19, dampening global demand. Once the outbreak is contained, additional government stimulus and liquidity easing from the Bank of Japan will support recovery. Growth is expected to pick up in the second half of 2020 and forecast at 0.9% in 2021. Inflation is projected to average 0.7% in 2020 and 2021.

Figure A1.10 Trade indicators, Japan

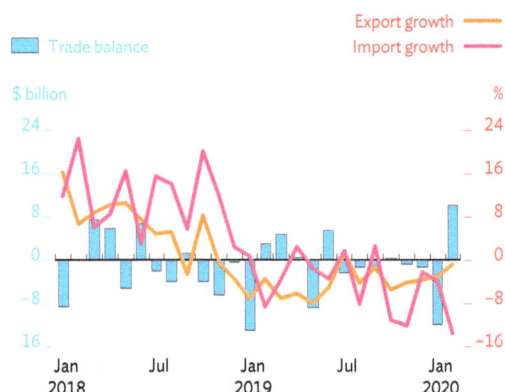

Sources: Haver Analytics; CEIC Data Company (both accessed 18 March 2020).

Recent developments and outlook in nearby economies

Australia

As weakening investment offset improved consumption, GDP growth slipped from 2.2% in Q3 to 2.1% in Q4. Consumption, mostly household, added 1.5 percentage points to growth, net exports 0.4 points, and change in inventories 0.7 points. Fixed investment contracted with declines in mining, manufacturing, and housing investment, subtracting 0.9 points (Figure A1.11).

Consumer and business sentiment improved but remained negative. Seasonally adjusted growth in retail sales fell from 2.6% in December to 2.0% in January. The consumer sentiment index improved from 93.4 in January to 95.5 in February but remained below the threshold at 100 dividing optimism from pessimism. The business confidence index, the percentage difference between optimists and pessimists, rose from –2.5 in December to –0.8 in January. The Australian Industry Group performance of manufacturing index declined from 45.4 in January to 44.3 in February, ebbing deeper into contractionary territory below 50. Unemployment fell marginally from 5.3% in January to 5.1% in February. Inflation ticked up from 1.7% in Q3 of 2019 to 1.8% in Q4, still below the target of 2.0%–3.0% set by Reserve Bank of Australia, the central bank.

On 18 March 2020, the central bank announced a comprehensive support package that cuts the cash rate to 0.25%, keeps the 3-year government bond yield at 0.25% through bond acquisition, establishes a 3-year funding facility for authorized deposit-taking institutions at a fixed rate of 0.25%, and newly remunerates exchange settlement balances at the central bank at 10 basis points. The government announced an A$17.6 billion stimulus package targeting jobs and small and medium-sized businesses, and a complementary program to support A$15 billion in lending to consumers and smaller businesses.

COVID-19 is expected to depress GDP growth in Q1 with declines in trade, tourism, and students from the PRC. If the outbreak intensifies in Australia, domestic demand will likely take a significant hit.

The growth forecast is revised down, first considering bushfires that lasted until January 2020, and now COVID-19. Growth will enjoy support, however, from accommodative monetary policy. On 23 March 2020, the Consensus Forecast was for GDP to contract by 0.6% in 2020 and grow by 3.8% in 2021.

Figure A1.11 Demand-side contributions to growth, Australia

■ Consumption
■ Gross fixed capital formation
■ Change in inventories
■ Net exports
— Gross domestic product

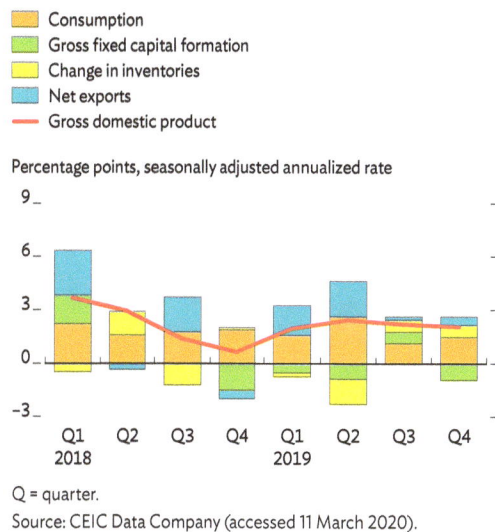

Percentage points, seasonally adjusted annualized rate

Q = quarter.
Source: CEIC Data Company (accessed 11 March 2020).

New Zealand

GDP growth slowed from 2.3% in Q3 of 2019 to 0.6% in Q4 as change in inventories subtracted 2.6 percentage points from growth, and fixed investment 0.1 points. Consumption contributed 2.4 percentage points, most of it government, and net exports 1.3 points (Figure A1.12).

Retail expansion slowed from 4.2% in Q3 to 3.4% in Q4. The consumer confidence index slipped slightly to 122.7 in January but remained above the 100 threshold signifying optimism. Business sentiment plunged from –19.4 in February to a dismal –53.3 in March, despite the manufacturing performance index improving from 49.8 in January across the expansion threshold to 53.2 in February. As food inflation jumped from 1.8% in Q3 to 2.5% to Q4, headline inflation accelerated from 1.5% to 1.9%, the middle of the Reserve Bank of New Zealand target range. The labor market remained robust as the seasonally adjusted unemployment rate improved from 4.1% in Q3 to 4.0% in Q4.

Under COVID-19, domestic production will be constricted by international and domestic plans to limit the spread of the virus and their severe effects on travel and trade, affecting both supply and demand.

While citing several areas of strength in the New Zealand economy, the Monetary Policy Committee agreed to cut the cash rate to 0.25% from 17 March 2020 to at least 12 months later. It noted that an asset purchase program of government bonds was on the table if needed.

To halt the spread of COVID-19, a nationwide lockdown from 25 March suspended schools and nonessential services for at least 4 weeks. To mitigate its economic impact, the government announced a NZ$12.1 billion stimulus package that includes wage subsidies, additional welfare payments, and business tax breaks. More stimulus may be announced in the annual budget meeting in May.

Growth will likely drop this year as exports and domestic demand continue to soften, but accommodating monetary and fiscal policies and a tight labor market should help. The 23 March 2020 Consensus Forecast was for GDP to grow by 0.7% in 2020 and 3.0% in 2021.

Russian Federation

A slump in exports slowed GDP growth from 2.5% in 2018 to 1.3% (Figure A1.13). As exports contracted by 2.1%, net exports subtracted 1.1 percentage points from growth. Slowing inflation supported real incomes, and the consumer confidence index, while languishing below the zero threshold dividing pessimism from optimism, improved slightly from –15 in Q2 of 2019 to –13 in Q3 and Q4.

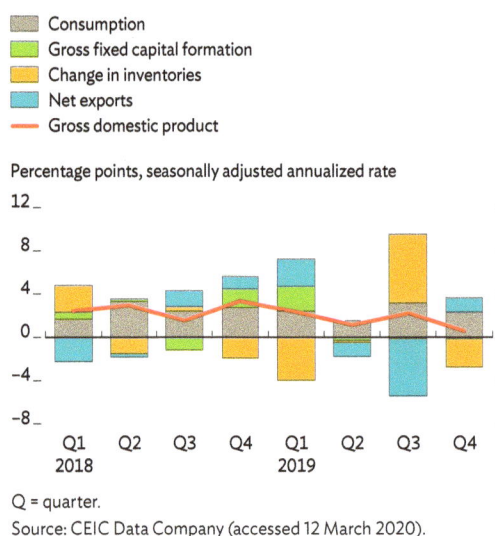

Figure A1.12 Demand-side contributions to growth, New Zealand

- Consumption
- Gross fixed capital formation
- Change in inventories
- Net exports
- Gross domestic product

Percentage points, seasonally adjusted annualized rate

Q = quarter.
Source: CEIC Data Company (accessed 12 March 2020).

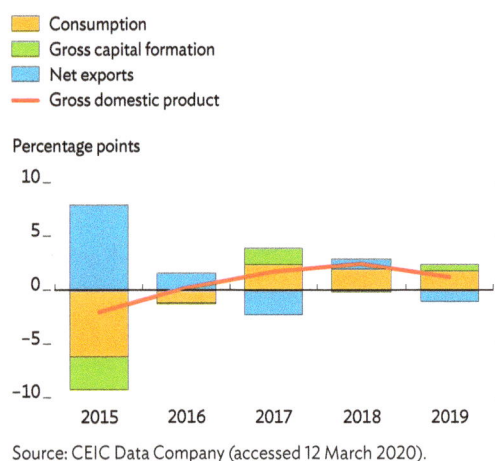

Figure A1.13 Demand-side contributions to growth, Russian Federation

- Consumption
- Gross capital formation
- Net exports
- Gross domestic product

Percentage points

Source: CEIC Data Company (accessed 12 March 2020).

This sustained private consumption growth in 2019 and allowed total consumption to contribute 1.8 points to growth. Retail trade turnover was similarly unchanged at 6.2%.

Gross capital formation reversed 0.5% contraction in 2018 to grow by 2.7% in 2019 and add 0.6 percentage points to growth. Industrial production expanded significantly, with the index rising by 9.6% from 108 in Q3 to 118 in Q4. The Markit manufacturing PMI rose from 47.9 in January to 48.2 in February, though still below the threshold of 50 indicating contraction. Unemployment improved from 4.8% in 2018 to 4.6%.

Though sustained, domestic demand was modest enough to slow inflation to 2.3% in February, a 2-year low and well below the target of 4.0% set by the Central Bank of the Russian Federation. On 20 March 2020, the central bank decided to keep its policy rate at 6% in light of the COVID-19 pandemic, a sharp decline in oil prices, and the resulting constraint on inflation.

COVID-19 and its consequences will slow growth in the coming quarters. The economy will benefit from a government response package and central bank measures. In January, the President announced a spending package worth the equivalent of 0.3%–0.5% of GDP to support lower-income families with children. Such social measures and the implementation of national projects as scheduled should boost domestic demand. Further, a $4 billion crisis fund unveiled on 16 March includes tax breaks for airlines and other firms in the tourism industry. Preferential loans for businesses will be expanded.

Risks to the outlook would be unanticipated severity in the COVID-19 pandemic, delays in carrying out government projects, commodity price volatility, and continuing global trade tensions. On 23 March 2020, the Consensus Forecast was for GDP to contract by 0.3% in 2020 and grow by 2.0% in 2021.

Commodity prices

Oil price movements and prospects

Brent crude finished 2019 at $66.42/barrel, the spot price up by $13.25/barrel from the end of 2018 on the expectation of better global conditions and deeper supply cuts by oil producers in 2020 (Figure A1.14). On 6 December 2019, member countries of the Organization of the Petroleum Exporting Countries (OPEC) and several allied oil producers agreed to rein in supply by an additional 500,000 barrels/day beyond what they had agreed in December 2018. On top of this, Saudi Arabia volunteered to reduce production further by 400,000 barrels/day, bringing old and new output cuts to more than 2 million barrels/day (mbd), or 2% of global oil demand. Following this new deal, oil prices averaged $66.74/barrel in the remaining days of December before escalated tension between the US and Iran pushed prices above $70 in January.

Figure A1.14 Brent crude spot prices

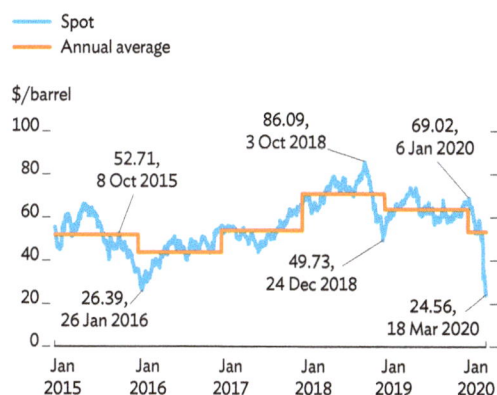

Source: Bloomberg (accessed 21 March 2020).

However, oil prices reversed course as concerns intensified about the impact of COVID-19 on the global economy. Brent crude slid into bear market territory on 3 February, its price falling by 23% from its January peak. It then hovered within the narrow range of $50–$59/barrel for a month before breaking below the $50 mark on 5 March, the day OPEC and its allies met to discuss oil production cuts. After the group failed to reach a consensus, and the resultant decision by Saudi Arabia to slash its export prices for crude and boost oil production, the Brent crude oil price dropped by as much as 31% to close on 9 March at $32.34/barrel. Then, as countries implement more restrictive containment measures, further curtailing global oil demand, prices dropped below $25/barrel on 18 March, the lowest in 17 years. The Brent crude average in the year to the third week of March was $53.69/barrel.

The International Energy Agency report *Oil 2020* forecasts oil supply remaining comfortable to 2025. Oil supply from outside OPEC is forecast to increase by 2.1 mbd in 2020 but only 1.3 mbd in 2021, the slowdown mainly from US production lacking incentive when oil prices are low. In its March report, the US Energy Information Administration forecast US crude oil production averaging 13.0 mbd in 2020 and then falling to 12.7 mbd in 2021, the first such annual decline in US crude oil production since 2016.

The global economic slowdown now expected from COVID-19 will weigh on petroleum demand. The International Energy Agency forecasts global oil demand falling sharply from estimated 1.0 mbd growth in 2019 to a decline of 90,000 barrels/day in 2020—the first contraction since 2009. However, as government policies continue to evolve, many analysts hesitate to predict how much global oil consumption will fall, made cautious by extreme uncertainty about how long it will be before COVID-19 is contained and the extent of its economic impact. Demand concerns and greater oversupply prospects are overpowering any remaining upward pressure on oil prices from agreed supply cuts, renewed supply disruption in Libya, geopolitical tensions in the Middle East, and the global implementation by the International Maritime Organization on 1 January 2020 of a 0.50% sulfur cap for marine fuel.

Evidence suggests that demand shocks are more persistent and have larger impacts on oil price movements than do supply shocks. As much as geopolitically induced supply shocks may appear to significantly move prices, historically they have failed to produce large and lasting price increases, especially in periods of weak demand and abundant spare capacity. Such shocks tend to be resolved in the short run by increased production elsewhere as higher prices induce the release of spare capacity. Barring further large and sharp changes in global oil supply and demand, Brent crude prices are forecast to average $35/barrel in 2020 and rise to $55/barrel in 2021 as global demand improves and oil inventories diminish.

Food price movements and prospects

The World Bank food price index dropped by 3.8% in 2019 following strong harvests (Figure A1.15). Prices for edible oil retreated as harvests exceeded expectations for soybeans in the US and South America and palm oil in Indonesia and Malaysia, demand for soybeans fell in the PRC, and African swine fever cut demand for animal feed. Poultry prices eased with increased production spurred mainly a decline in the "other food" price index. The grain price index, on the other hand, showed an uptrend in 2019 as weather disturbances, notably in Australia, the Russian Federation, and Ukraine, supported wheat prices and robust trade pushed up maize prices.

The increase in food prices has continued in 2020, with the index up by 5.7% in the first 2 months of the year. Upward pressure on global food prices has come from production difficulties, disrupted global supply chains, and high international demand for commodities like rice, sugar, and meat. These trends have been tempered, however, by fears of a slowdown in global demand following the outbreak of COVID-19.

The increase in food prices will continue this year, albeit at a slower rate. The March 2020 report of the US Department of Agriculture estimated global grain production in the crop year 2019/2020 increasing by 1.5% to reach 2,667 million tons. Global supply of the three main grains—wheat, maize, and rice—is projected to increase by 0.8% this cropping season. Similarly, global supply of the 17 major edible oils is estimated to increase by 1.7%. This favorable production outlook finds support from forecasts of neutral weather in the first half of 2020 and low input prices because of softer oil prices. However, consumption is expected to outpace production, leaving ratios of stock to use lower than in previous cropping seasons. The forecast lower ratios are comfortable but nevertheless exert upward pressure on prices, especially as disrupted global supply chains further tighten supply. On balance, the food commodity price index is forecast to rise slightly by 2.0% in both years to the forecast horizon.

Among several risks to these forecasts are severe worsening of the COVID-19 outbreak, trade friction, changes to domestic support policies, further depreciation of commodity exporter currencies, and the ever-present potential for oil price volatility and adverse weather.

Figure A1.15 Food commodity price indexes

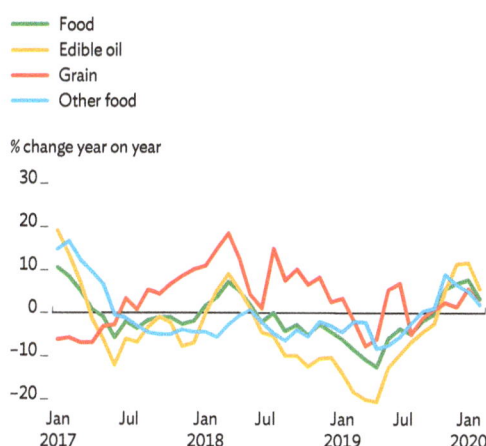

Source: World Bank. Commodity Price Data (Pink Sheet). http://www.worldbank.org (accessed 6 March 2020).

2

WHAT DRIVES INNOVATION IN ASIA?

What drives innovation in Asia?

Innovation is critical to growth and development. While some economies in developing Asia are near the forefront of innovation, many others lag behind. This theme chapter outlines what policy makers can do to foster greater innovation.

It identifies five key drivers of innovation. The first is education, which is hardly surprising since innovation is an intrinsically human enterprise. In a number of Asian economies, too many children lack even the most basic literacy and numeracy skills. Policy makers must therefore focus first on strengthening basic skills, but they must also shift to more learner-centered teaching practices while broadening and diversifying the skill mix.

The second driver is entrepreneurship. While people tend to link entrepreneurship with innovation, fewer than 1% of entrepreneurs create more than half of job growth and innovation. It is therefore crucially important to design policy that facilitates the potential of these productive entrepreneurial firms and thereby better harness them for economic development.

The final three drivers of innovation are high-quality institutions, robust financial systems, and big cities. High-quality institutions, including the rule of law and strong property rights, give innovative entrepreneurs the confidence they need to take risks and experiment with new ideas. The evolution of intellectual property rights in the Republic of Korea suggests that different institutions and kinds of protection may matter more at different stages of development.

A sound and efficient financial system can channel resources to innovators. Indeed, analysis suggests that the development of financial markets, for both equity and debt, has a positive effect on patents. Finally, cities can be powerful forces for promoting innovative activity because they facilitate knowledge spillover and dissemination. Innovation policy thus requires a nuanced, bottom-up approach geared toward enabling local innovators.

In the end, there are no shortcuts to creating an innovative society. The journey requires long-term commitment and a lot of hard work.

This chapter was written by Donghyun Park, Elisabetta Gentile, Abdul Abiad, Liming Chen, Sameer Khatiwada, Rhea Molato-Gayares, Kirsty Newman, Madhavi Pundit, Irfan Qureshi, and Shu Tian.

Innovating for inclusive and sustainable growth

Innovations, including social innovations such as work-from-home arrangements, can help Asian countries better cope with the economic repercussions of coronavirus disease 2019 (COVID-19), future shocks, and trends over the longer term. Despite a universal consensus that innovation is vital to sustained economic, social, and technological progress, the term is hard to define. Innovation exists along a continuum that stretches from incremental innovations that improve existing products or processes in small but material ways to, at the other extreme, radical innovation that spawns the rare inventions that destroy or supplant existing business models. It is not always easy to identify an innovation. The mapping of the human genome, for example, was hailed at the time as a radical innovation to provide new treatments for diseases, but it turned out to be only an incremental step in that direction. Using something already known—but in a different way or at a different time or place—is also an innovation. Finally, innovation encompasses a range of activities carried out by a wide variety of actors: firms, governments, nongovernment organizations, and individuals.

Because innovation is a complex, diverse, and multifaceted concept, it comes as no surprise that measuring it is also complicated. Survey respondents in different countries may have diverse understanding of innovation, with firms in developing countries perhaps considering a minor design change as a new or significantly improved product, though the same change would go all but unnoticed in more advanced economies (Cirera and Maloney 2017).

What is innovation?

The *Oslo Manual 2018* defines innovation as a "new or improved product or business process (or combination thereof) that differs significantly from the firm's previous products or business processes and that has been introduced on the market or brought into use by the firm."[1] This is a measurable definition that forms a solid basis for analysis at the level of the individual firm.

While a rich typology has been developed over the years to reflect the multifaceted nature of innovation, this chapter focuses on four key concepts that are particularly relevant to the Asian experience. First is the distinction between product and process innovation, which stems directly from the definition provided in the *Oslo Manual 2018*.

Product innovation refers to an improvement in the performance of a product or new features in a product, often visible to the customers. Process innovation refers to an improvement in how the product is produced, which can include changes all along the value chain but is often invisible to customers.

The distinction between frontier and catch-up innovation is particularly important in developing economies. Frontier innovation is defined as the first application of a specific innovation in the world. It can be either radical or incremental (but, as mentioned above, most innovation is incremental). Figure 2.1.1 shows that, when advanced countries push the frontier of innovation, they improve global technology. Catch-up innovation, on the other hand, is the first application in a specific context, perhaps a particular country or firm, of an innovation that already exists elsewhere in the world. Catch-up innovations are crucial to improving productivity in developing countries.

Figure 2.1.1 Catch-up versus frontier innovation

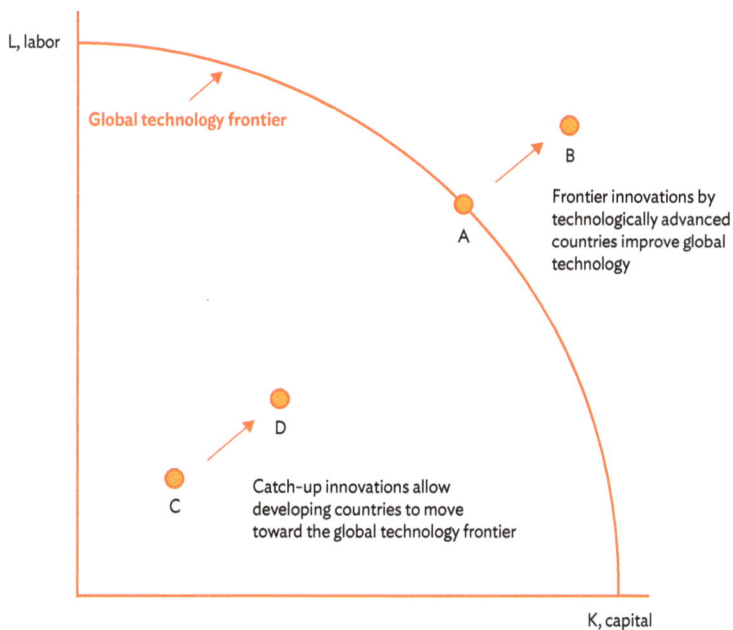

L, labor

Global technology frontier

B

Frontier innovations by technologically advanced countries improve global technology

A

D

C

Catch-up innovations allow developing countries to move toward the global technology frontier

K, capital

Source: Authors.

Although they differ slightly in their definitions, frugal innovation, inclusive innovation, and bottom-of-the-pyramid innovation all refer to solutions that address the needs of low-income populations. They can be high-tech, such as digital platforms that bring services to underserved communities, or low-tech, such as a terracotta clay refrigerator that keeps perishable food cool without electricity. They can emerge from the efforts of firms, governments, nongovernment organizations, or individuals.

Finally, sustainable innovation integrates consideration of how environmentally, socially, and financially appropriate an innovation is, from idea generation to research and development (R&D) and all the way to commercialization. Environmentally sustainable innovation includes techniques to reduce waste, use recycled inputs and alternative energy sources, and reduce, reuse, and sequester the greenhouse gas carbon dioxide. Jeepneys and *tuk-tuks* powered by electricity or liquefied petroleum gas that promote a cleaner environment and improve the quality of life for the poor are examples of innovations that are both sustainable and inclusive.

Innovation in Asia: past and present

Developing Asia has a rich tradition of innovation. In fact, mankind can thank the region for many innovations that have profoundly affected the course of world history. The four great inventions of ancient Chinese civilization—papermaking, printing, gunpowder, and the compass—are well-known examples. Another case in point is the mathematical concept of zero, which originated on the Indian subcontinent. Asia began to fall behind the West in the 15th century, however, and the gap widened further with Europe's industrial revolution. As a result, Asia needed to catch up technologically.

Over the past 50 years, rapid and sustained growth, development, and technological progress have moved Asia and the Pacific much closer to the global technology frontier. The region is no longer just an importer of advanced foreign innovations but has increasingly become a globally significant innovator. In line with its rising share of global income, the role of developing Asia in global innovation is clearly on the rise. While there are substantial differences across subregions and countries, the region as a whole is investing more in innovative activity and producing more innovative output.

One indication is that Asia's share of R&D investment rose from 22% in 1996 to 40% in 2017, according to the Global Innovation Index 2019. The shifting geography of innovation is evident in the swift rise of several Asian economies among the 129 economies chosen for comparison and listed in the index. In 2019, the Republic of Korea (ROK) and the People's Republic of China (PRC) edged closer toward inclusion in the world's top 10 innovators, performing especially well in the categories patents by origin, industrial designs, trademarks by origin, high-tech net exports, and creative goods exports. Other strong regional performers were India, Malaysia, the Philippines, Thailand, and Viet Nam, in addition to the more advanced economies of Singapore and Hong Kong, China.

The 2020 Bloomberg Innovation Index—which ranks the world's most innovative 95 countries based on R&D spending, manufacturing capability, and concentration of high-tech public companies—ranks the ROK at 2, Singapore at 3, Japan at 12, and the PRC at 15. In the *Nature* Index 2019, which tracks articles published in 82 high-quality journals in the natural sciences, the PRC ranked second, after the US. The PRC holds a similar position in Clarivate's 2019 Annual G20 Scorecard for the most highly cited researchers. Interestingly, the report found that, while Australia leads the pack in terms of research output, Indonesia achieved a threefold increase in a decade.

Innovation and economic growth and development: theory and evidence

Innovation can improve productivity by extracting greater output from the same inputs, thereby generating more goods and services and higher wages, profitability, and economic growth. Early studies that built on the seminal work of Solow (1956) concluded that long-run growth comes mainly from technical change, which can be continually renewed, rather than from labor and capital, which suffer decreasing marginal productivity.[2]

Two defining characteristics of technology are that its use by one firm or person in no way limits its use by another, yet it can be made exclusive by preventing access to those who have not paid for it. This provides private firms with a strong incentive to innovate. These two features of new ideas generate higher returns as the scale of production increases, and this is what sustains growth in the long run (Romer 1990).

To understand the nature of technical change and how it evolves over time, growth accounting exercises were augmented with an innovation component that found strong links between R&D capital, for example, and growth (Griliches 1980, Mansfield 1980).

The frontier in economic thinking was further pushed by endogenous growth models that included other representations of innovation such as R&D investment by private firms, learning by doing, human capital and knowledge accumulation, and public infrastructure (Romer 1986 and 1990, Lucas 1988, Aghion and Howitt 1992, Barro 1990, Grossman and Helpman 1994). These models suggest that innovation within an entity and positive spillover to the rest of the economy can drive sustainable, long-term economic growth, and that these factors are generated by economic incentives within the system. A branch of the literature focused on the interaction between competition and innovation, as well as the critical role played by private firms, which have implications for a country's industrial and technology policy (Aghion et al. 2005, Aghion, Carlin, and Schaffer 2002). The prescriptions and debates that ensued from these models accommodated the observed growth trajectories of Japan, Germany, and the US starting in the 1950s and, subsequently in the 1980s, of Hong Kong, China; the Republic of Korea; Singapore; and Taipei,China. They have become relevant more recently to the PRC. The general pattern of innovation in Asian economies is an initial phase of catch-up innovation with the adoption of technology to generate progress and growth, followed by a later phase of growth driven by their own innovation (ADB 2020).

However, inquiry found conventional assumptions and theories far removed from the experiences of other developing economies grappling with social and environmental problems and serious scarcity of resources. This called for a different alignment of innovation models driven by the needs of low-income and price-sensitive consumers in developing economies, and a strong discourse for inclusive and sustainable development. The consensus was that, if innovation is highly capital- and energy-intensive and requires superior infrastructure and other networks, skilled labor, abundant credit, and demand for complex products, the world's poor have little hope of benefiting from innovation and its impact on growth (Chataway, Hanlin, and Kaplinsky 2014). Given massive disparity in the needs and capabilities of different economies, even within a single region like Asia, one-size-fits-all policy prescriptions appear to be sorely inadequate.

As a result, links between innovation, capacity creation, and development emerged as a critical concern for policy makers. So too did complementarity in the innovation process between markets and players outside of them, such as the public sector and nongovernment organizations. Turning away from a focus on technological advance as the basis of growth, research explored alternate trajectories in the literature of economics and other fields. The existence of alternate trajectories contested long-established models and upended the belief that only advanced countries innovate. These trajectories feature instead strategies crafted to incorporate the strengths of developing countries toward answering their needs. Alternate strategies innovate in accordance with industry dynamics unique to economies with abundant natural resources (Andersen, Marìn, and Simensen 2018), grassroot community action for solutions that are inclusive and sensitive to context (Seyfang and Smith 2007), or efforts to build capacity for technology adaptation, development, and implementation, often through incremental and frugal innovations (Katz and Shapiro 1987, Wooldridge 2010). The incremental and frugal innovations deployed in the near term may be augmented over the longer term by institutional adjustments, targeted public investments, and education (ADB 2014, Calestous and Lee 2005).

Why does innovation matter for developing Asia?

The preceding discussion makes evident several clear theoretical and empirical links between innovation and economic development. At the same time, it has shown how developing Asia has revived as the center of global innovation. Why then does innovation matter so much for developing Asia right now?

First, rapid and sustained growth has transformed developing Asia into a region that is overwhelmingly middle income, at which stage innovation assumes a larger role in economic growth. Second, innovation can help improve the quality of growth and of life in the region by making growth more inclusive and environmentally sustainable. The following summarizes the importance of innovation to Asia at this stage in its development and the specific ways that innovation can support development in the region.

Innovation plays a larger role in growth as economies reach middle income. Rapid and sustained growth transformed developing Asia from a largely low-income region in 1991 to one overwhelmingly middle income by 2015 (ADB 2017). While labor and capital are still necessary for growth in middle-income economies, growth in total factor productivity becomes more important to economic success. Figure 2.1.2 shows that growth in Asia has relied increasingly on total factor productivity as it has become increasingly middle income. And innovation is a vital ingredient of productivity growth.

Figure 2.1.2 Contribution to growth by factor of production in Asia, % of total

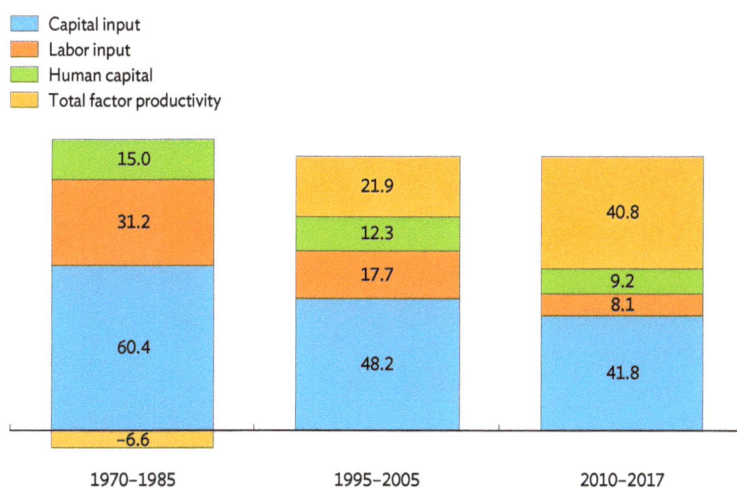

Legend:
- Capital input
- Labor input
- Human capital
- Total factor productivity

1970–1985:
- Human capital: 15.0
- Labor input: 31.2
- Capital input: 60.4
- Total factor productivity: −6.6

1995–2005:
- Total factor productivity: 21.9
- Human capital: 12.3
- Labor input: 17.7
- Capital input: 48.2

2010–2017:
- Total factor productivity: 40.8
- Human capital: 9.2
- Labor input: 8.1
- Capital input: 41.8

Notes: Central Asia is excluded in 1970–1985. The 21 economies in the first period are Bangladesh; Brunei Darussalam; Cambodia; Hong Kong, China; India; Indonesia; Japan; the Lao People's Democratic Republic; Malaysia; Mongolia; Myanmar; Nepal; Pakistan; the People's Republic of China; the Philippines; the Republic of Korea; Singapore; Sri Lanka; Taipei,China; Thailand; and Viet Nam. Added in the latter two periods are Armenia, Kazakhstan, the Kyrgyz Republic, and Tajikistan. In 2017, these 25 economies accounted for 99% of the combined GDP of Asian Development Bank developing member economies plus Japan.

Source: ADB 2020.

Middle-income economies that graduate to high income have R&D establishments three times bigger than economies mired in the middle-income trap, for example, and they file four times more patent applications (ADB 2017). The way forward for developing Asia is directed by the experience of Asian newly industrialized economies (NIEs) such as the ROK, which leveraged innovation to transition to high income after only 23 years in the middle-income category.

Innovation can make growth inclusive and environmentally sustainable. Recognition is growing in developing Asia that economic growth cannot be sustained in the long run if it manages to benefit only a small elite while degrading the environment. Innovation can make growth more broadly based and able to improve the quality of life and extend productive opportunities to the disadvantaged. As discussed above, while innovation tends to be associated with state-of-the-art technologies such as artificial intelligence or robotics, plenty of inexpensive, bottom-of-the-pyramid innovations are able to help the poor tackle the everyday challenges of life. Further, innovation to improve energy, transport, and other infrastructure can contribute to a cleaner environment.

Important at all stages of development, innovation will vary by stage. The potential gains from innovation are large in terms of supplying jobs and boosting productivity, incomes, and economic growth. Developing Asia as a region will reap large economic benefits from innovation. But a country's stage of economic and technological development determines the nature and scope of innovation available to it. Lower-income Asian countries that fall far short of the global technology frontier can best accelerate their development by tapping existing knowledge and know-how and adapting them to local needs (Figure 2.1.1). To enable themselves to do so effectively, they must nurture their capacity to absorb technology and ensure its adequacy. Upper-middle-income Asian countries, on the other hand, need to invest much more in frontier-pushing innovation because adopting existing technology and know-how offers them only diminishing returns, and they are able to push against the global technology frontier because they are closer to it—as illustrated by explosive growth in R&D investment in the PRC in recent years. Whether innovations push the frontier or are far from it, they serve as engines of technological, economic, and social progress.

New tech and value chains leapfrog to the global technology frontier. While the scope and nature of innovation depends on a country's stage of development, new technologies, particularly information and communication technology (ICT), can accelerate the catch-up process in lower-income countries.

Developing Asia is a global leader in the production and consumption of ICT, which has permeated every facet of life in the region and supported many innovations large and small, as it will continue to do. One notable example is how quickly the PRC is becoming a cashless society where you can use your mobile phone for every transaction, even giving alms to street beggars. Asia can foster innovation by leveraging its openness to trade and active participation in global value chains, which can be powerful channels for knowledge transfer to developing countries, accelerating their catch-up and advance to the global technology frontier.

Innovation is key to a better quality of life and more dynamic societies. While innovations make Asian firms more productive, they also enhance the well-being of Asian people. The advent of ICT is a powerful case in point. The internet and mobile phones have dramatically reduced communication costs for producers and consumers alike. An innovative economy is often the bounty of an innovative society that encourages the free and open exchange of ideas and knowledge. Further, innovation and technological progress can contribute to more dynamic and vibrant Asian societies, in which Asians are constantly asking new questions and seeking new solutions.

Landscape of innovation in Asia

This section examines in more detail the current landscape of innovation in Asia. It begins by looking at how aggregate innovation in the region stacks up against other parts of the world. Data at the level of the individual firm permits a deeper inquiry into the nature of innovation within the region. For example, do firm size and export orientation affect the propensity to innovate among Asian firms? Regression analysis empirically reveals the determinants of innovation in developing Asia. What is the effect on innovation in the region of human capital, for instance, or of R&D and other variables?

The current state of innovation in Asia: An aggregate perspective

In the past, developing Asia adopted innovations and superior technologies from advanced economies in Japan, the US, and Western Europe to power its industrialization and economic growth. The exact mechanism through which Asian economies imported foreign innovations differed from country to country. Singapore leveraged foreign direct investment by large multinational corporations, for example, while the ROK capitalized on domestic firms' licensing of foreign technology. Although the mechanism varied, the region imported and adapted more advanced foreign technology for its own needs. It remained far from the global technology frontier, and many of its innovations were incremental innovations. However, despite relative lack of indigenous innovation, the NIEs, the PRC, and other economies were able to absorb and use foreign innovations effectively, and this contributed to their rapid and sustained growth.

After a country reaches a certain stage of economic and technological development, it begins to invest in frontier innovation. The experience of the NIEs fits this established pattern of steady graduation from catch-up innovation to frontier innovation. The ROK, for example, has become one of the most innovative economies in the world, and other Asian economies, most notably the PRC, are following the path blazed by the ROK and other Asian NIEs. More broadly, rapid and sustained growth has transformed developing Asia into an overwhelmingly middle-income region that has achieved a lot of technological progress. It is therefore outdated to credit the stereotype of developing Asia as a region that innovates little on its own.

Figure 2.2.1 R&D expenditure as a share of GDP by region, 2016

% of GDP

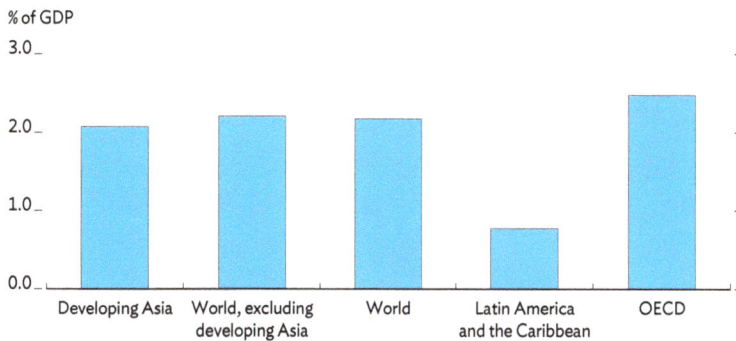

GDP = gross domestic product, OECD = Organisation for Economic Co-operation and Development, R&D = research and development.
Source: ADB estimates using data from the World Development Indicators database.

In fact, the data indicate that developing Asia is no longer at the periphery of the global innovation landscape but rapidly moving toward its center. It is informative to compare the region's performance with that of Latin America, another largely middle-income region that is broadly comparable to developing Asia in its stage of development. Figure 2.2.1 offers a snapshot of innovative activity, proxied by R&D, in developing Asia, Latin America, and advanced economies of the Organisation for Economic Co-operation and Development (OECD) in 2016. Developing Asia invests substantially more in innovation than does Latin America. It still innovates less than advanced economies, but the gap is small and narrowing. While developing Asia as a whole has become a major player in global innovation, substantial differences exist within the region, which divides it into two groups: the leading group of NIEs and the PRC, which invest a lot in innovation, and the rest of the region, which invests less (Figure 2.2.2).

According to R&D data, developing Asia is no longer a laggard in innovation but has become one of the global hubs of innovative activity. Further, trends for innovation indicators suggest that the region has become tangibly more innovative in recent years (Figure 2.2.3). The magnitude of regional innovation is sizable and growing rapidly. The region's transformation from an innovation laggard into a major innovation player is consistent with its emergence as one of the three centers of gravity in the world economy, along with North America and Western Europe. Technological progress has contributed to the industrialization and development of many economies, most notably the NIEs and the PRC, and has elevated their technological capacity to levels that enable indigenous innovation that pushes the global technology frontier.

Figure 2.2.2 R&D expenditure as a share of GDP in selected economies, 2016

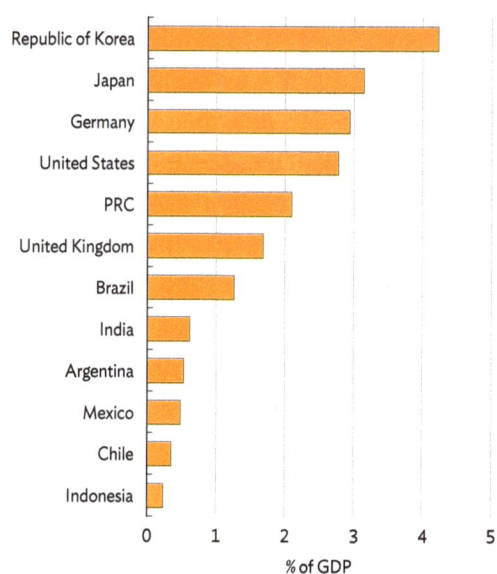

% of GDP

GDP = gross domestic product, PRC = People's Republic of China, R&D = research and development.
Note: Data for India is from 2015.
Source: ADB estimates using data from the World Development Indicators database.

Figure 2.2.3 R&D expenditure as a share of GDP, 1996–2017

- Newly industrialized economies
- People's Republic of China
- Other developing Asia
- Organisation for Economic Co-operation and Development

% of GDP

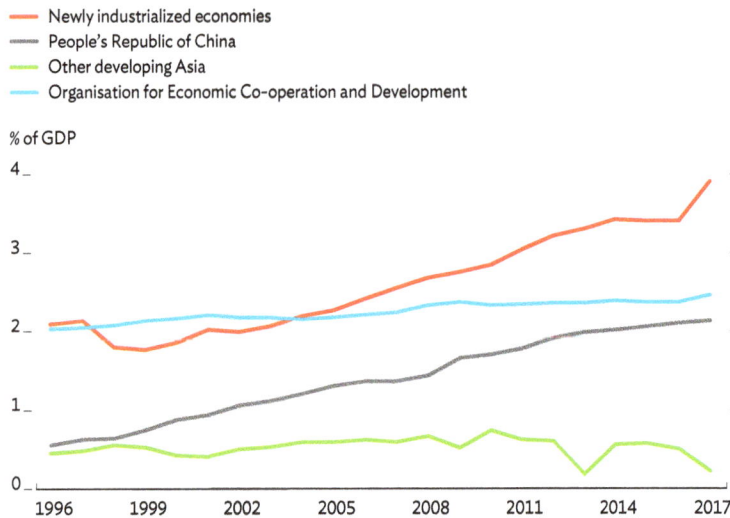

GDP = gross domestic product, R&D = research and development.
Source: ADB estimates using data from the World Development Indicators database.

Like R&D, other major indicators of innovation point to a growing footprint of developing Asia on the global innovation landscape. Figure 2.2.4 shows one major input indicator for frontier innovation (R&D workforce) and two major output indicators (patent applications by residents and scientific publications) for three distinct groups of economies in developing Asia, with the wealthy OECD as a comparator. The first column presents the indicators in absolute terms and documents the rise of the PRC as a player in global innovation. In the second column, the same indicators are weighted by population and show that Asia's NIEs are innovation powerhouses that outperform the OECD when population size is taken into account. The figure also documents substantial disparity across the region, with the rest of developing Asia performing far below the advanced economies in both absolute and relative terms.

Figure 2.2.5 presents productive capability in the same three groups of Asian economies and the OECD. In terms of economic complexity, the NIEs have outperformed the OECD since 2008, and the PRC is gradually catching up to it. While the PRC and the NIEs have long been major exporters of high-tech manufactures, outperforming the OECD, now the rest of developing Asia is catching up. Asia's participation in global production networks is undoubtedly one of the factors that explain this performance.

Figure 2.2.4 Innovation gaps as measured by other indicators

— Newly industrialized economies
— Organisation for Economic Co-operation and Development
— People's Republic of China
— Rest of developing Asia

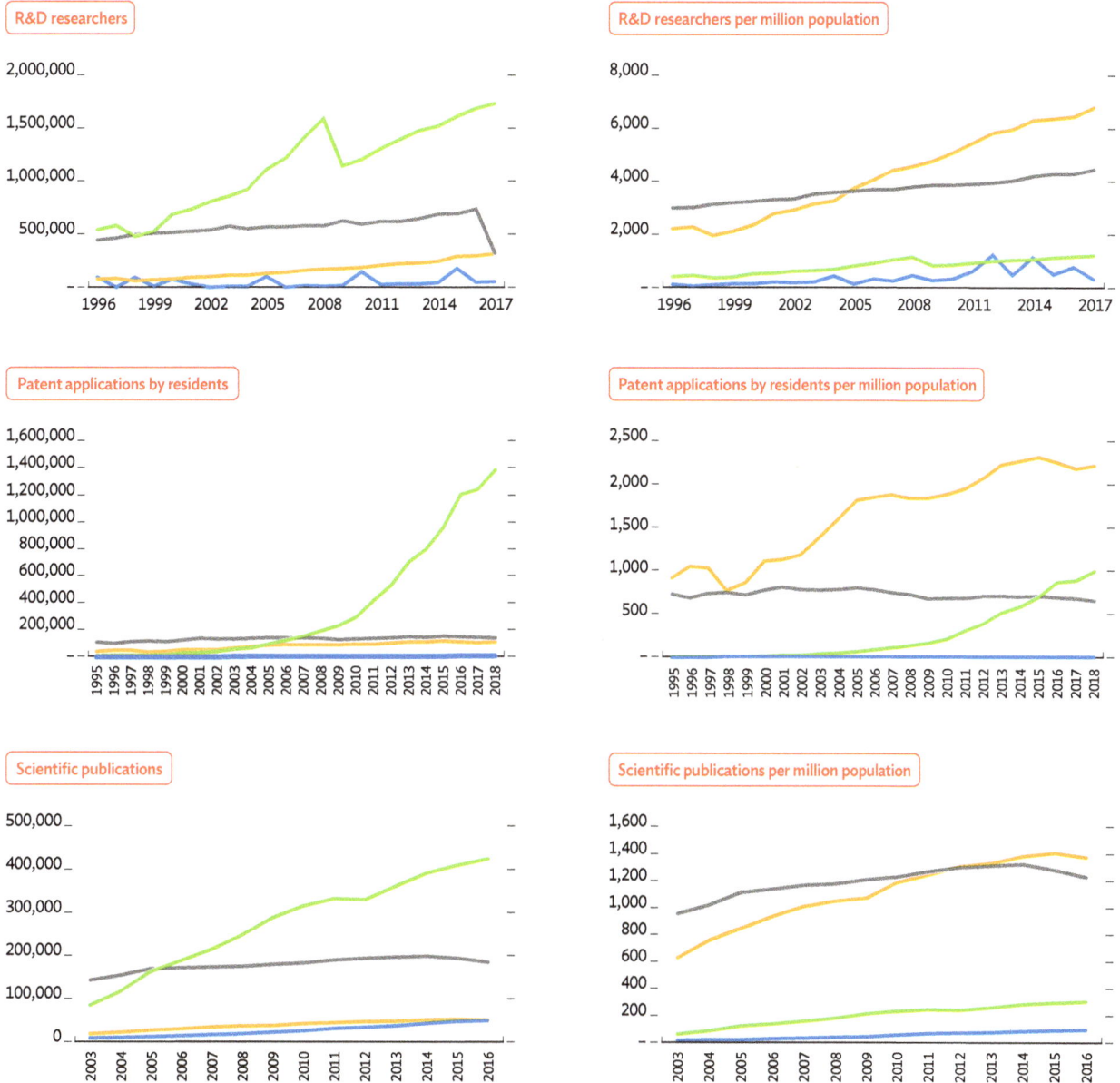

R&D = research and development.

Note: Regional averages are weighted by gross domestic product. Newly industrialized economies data exclude Taipei,China. Organisation for Economic Co-operation and Development data exclude the Republic of Korea.

Source: Qureshi et al., forthcoming.

Figure 2.2.5 Innovative capability as reflected in the structure of Asian economies

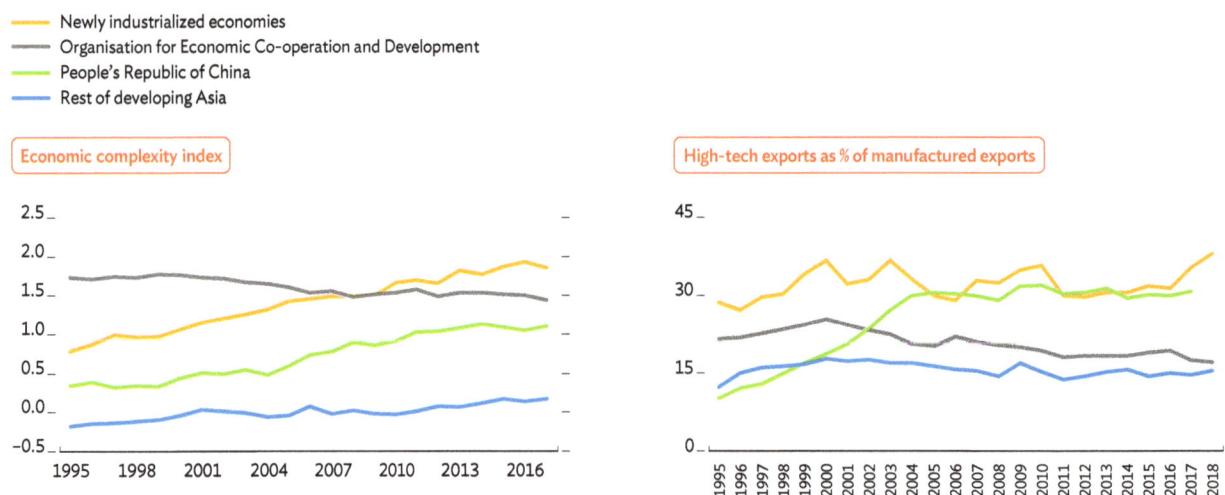

—— Newly industrialized economies
—— Organisation for Economic Co-operation and Development
—— People's Republic of China
—— Rest of developing Asia

Economic complexity index

High-tech exports as % of manufactured exports

Note: Regional averages are weighted by gross domestic product. Newly industrialized economies data exclude Taipei,China. Organisation for Economic Co-operation and Development data exclude the Republic of Korea.

Source: Qureshi et al., forthcoming.

The seemingly large discrepancy in innovation between developing Asia's innovation leaders such as PRC and the rest of the region is subject to one important caveat. As noted above, most innovation in developing economies occurs well inside the global technology frontier. Adapting advanced foreign technology to specific local requirements usually does not involve R&D or generate patents or licensing income. Such innovation nevertheless played a major role in the past industrialization and technological progress of the NIEs and the PRC. Therefore, conventional measures of innovation such as R&D and patents may significantly underestimate the extent of innovation in developing economies.

The current state of innovation in Asia: A firm-level perspective

An extensive empirical literature highlights the positive impact of innovation in individual firms, including R&D, on firm performance and productivity (Hall, Lotti, and Mairesse 2009, Harrison et al. 2008, Mairesse, Mohnen, and Kremp 2005, Raffo, L'huillery, and Miotti 2008). The literature shows that knowledge capital investments to boost productivity do not occur solely in advanced countries. However, the nature of innovation in developing countries is somewhat different and best characterized as piecemeal improvements to processes or products (Cirera and Maloney 2017). This is a process of technology adoption, imitation, and adaptation that takes place far from the technology frontier, where firms adopt incremental changes (Fagerberg, Srholec, and Verspagen 2010).

While innovation in developing countries often occurs at the margins and depends on implementing technologies and products already available elsewhere, this process can still enable the development of comparative advantage. However, little is known about the nature of activities and processes by which firms in developing Asia foster innovation. This section describes the extent and intensity of firm-level innovation in developing Asia. It explores where innovation is occurring in the region and examines firm characteristics associated with higher innovation rates. It also examines firms' activities such as R&D and technology use to reveal variation in innovation by industry and firm characteristics. This study aims to paint a picture of firms' innovative behavior in developing Asia and how their characteristics relate to innovation.

For each economy, analysis uses the latest available year of relatively strong World Bank Enterprise Surveys to describe the innovation behavior of firms in developing Asia (Table 2.2.1). The survey dataset is comparable across economies and available from 2004. It provides the density of new business registrations adjusted for population and compiles data primarily from face-to-face interviews with business owners and top managers, as well as correspondence with participating business registrars. The survey uses stratified random sampling organized by firm size, business sector, and geographic region within a country, defining innovation rates as the share of firms introducing product or process innovations.[3] It covers 27 countries in developing Asia, including 26,855 firms in manufacturing, retail, and other services (Table 2.2.1).[4]

Innovation data from the Enterprise Surveys suffer from subjectivity regarding what constitutes a new or significantly improved product or process. A lack of follow-up questions to provide detail on the accuracy of answers may thus give an inaccurate picture of firms' innovation activities and overestimate innovation rates (Cirera and Muzi 2016). Despite these limitations, the survey is the most useful option because it covers a wide set of countries in developing Asia and uses a standard survey questionnaire and similar sampling methodology and populations of inference, which allow cross-country comparisons of firms.

Deeper analysis of the survey data outlines the landscape of innovation in developing Asia. Outstanding features include relatively strong firm-level innovation in the region, a tendency for innovation rates to be higher in low-income countries, and a predominance of small improvements to existing products, as opposed to the introduction of new products in new markets. These and other findings are discussed below.

Table 2.2.1 Sample composition by region and country

| Region | Country (survey year) | Firm size | | | Total |
		Small (<20)	Medium (20–99)	Large (100+)	
Central and West Asia, n = 2,729	Armenia (2013)	179	135	46	360
	Azerbaijan (2013)	214	143	33	390
	Georgia (2013)	247	87	26	360
	Kazakhstan (2013)	308	219	73	600
	Kyrgyz Republic (2013)	114	119	37	270
	Tajikistan (2013)	199	124	36	359
	Uzbekistan (2013)	152	143	95	390
East Asia, n = 3,060	People's Republic of China (2012)	625	1,084	991	2,700
	Mongolia (2013)	200	126	34	360
South Asia, n = 13,725	Afghanistan (2014)	270	112	28	410
	Bangladesh (2013)	507	514	421	1,442
	Bhutan (2015)	156	82	15	253
	India (2014)	3,065	4,028	2,188	9,281
	Nepal (2013)	293	140	49	482
	Pakistan (2013)	536	451	260	1,247
	Sri Lanka (2011)	322	179	109	610
Southeast Asia, n = 6,999	Cambodia (2016)	194	118	61	373
	Indonesia (2015)	484	451	385	1,320
	Lao People's Democratic Republic (2016)	217	104	47	368
	Malaysia (2015)	347	343	310	1,000
	Myanmar (2016)	363	160	84	607
	Philippines (2015)	464	504	367	1,335
	Thailand (2016)	400	324	276	1,000
	Viet Nam (2015)	376	352	268	996
The Pacific, n = 342	Papua New Guinea (2015)	13	33	19	65
	Solomon Islands (2015)	64	67	20	151
	Timor-Leste (2015)	88	30	8	126
Total		10,397	10,172	6,286	26,855

Source: Khatiwada and Arao, forthcoming(a).

High innovation in firms in developing Asia

The first feature of innovation in developing Asia is its high number of firms that innovate. The average innovation rate in developing Asia—the share of firms that have introduced a new or significantly improved product or process in the past 3 years—is 52.7% (Figure 2.2.6). Innovation is highest in the Pacific, where fully 73.0% of firms report introducing a new or significantly improved product or process, followed by 64.8% of firms in South Asia, 59.6% in East Asia, 37.1% in Southeast Asia, and 21.2% in Central Asia.

Figure 2.2.6 Share of firms reporting a new product or process, by region

- Central Asia (n = 2,729)
- East Asia (n = 3,060)
- South Asia (n = 13,725)
- Southeast Asia (n = 6,999)
- The Pacific (n = 961)
- All firms

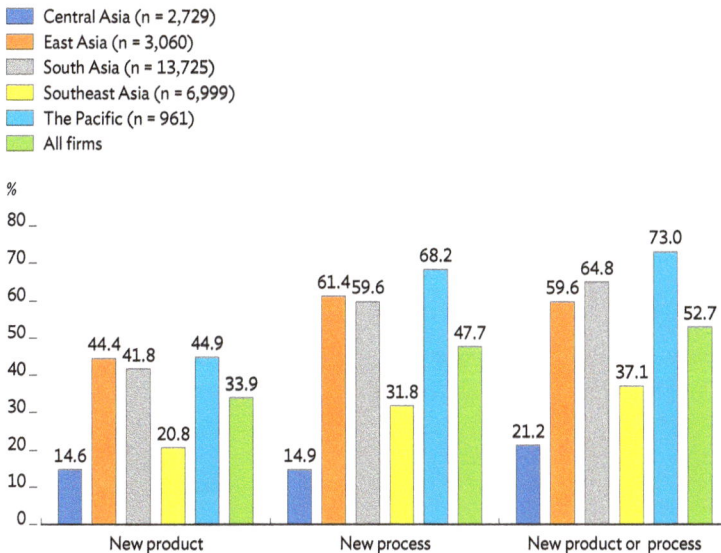

Notes: The Pacific regional average includes only Papua New Guinea, Solomon Islands, and Timor-Leste. Regional averages of innovation indicators are computed with a simple average of country estimates.

Source: Khatiwada and Arao, forthcoming(a).

Further, 33.9% of firms in developing Asia report introducing a new product. Product innovation is highest in the Pacific, East Asia, and South Asia at more than 40%. This figure is notably lower in Central Asia at 14.6% and Southeast Asia at 20.8%.

Compared with product innovation, the share of firms that report process innovation is higher, at 47.7% on average in developing Asia. At 60% or higher, this type of innovation is strongest in the Pacific, South Asia, and East Asia.

Higher innovation rates in low-income countries

The second feature is a higher rate of innovation in low-income countries. Looking at innovation rates by country reveals that firms in countries with lower income per capita report higher innovation rates (Figure 2.2.7). As firms that are further away from the technology frontier have lower productivity, small improvements in products or processes may be regarded as "innovation" much more readily than in more advanced economies. Moreover, making incremental improvements in products or processes is less expensive for firms further away from the technology frontier, which translates in the data to higher innovation activity.

Figure 2.2.7 Innovation and GDP per capita

- ● Product innovation
- ● Process innovation
- ⋯⋯⋯ Linear product innovation
- ⋯⋯⋯ Linear process innovation

Firms reporting product and/or process innovation, %

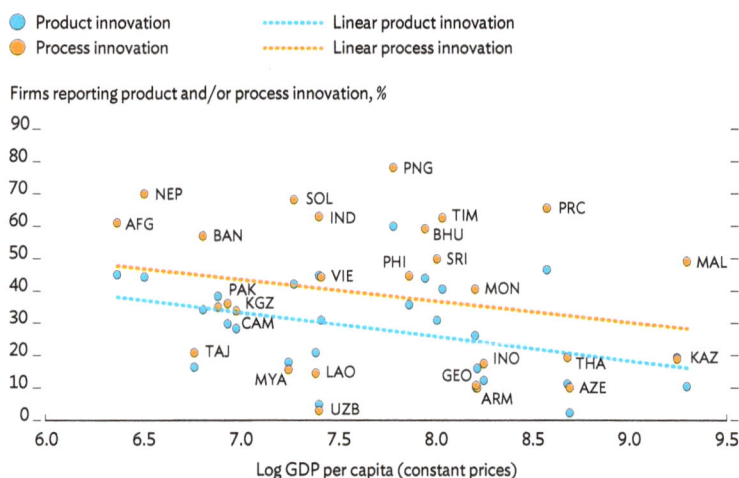

Log GDP per capita (constant prices)

AFG = Afghanistan, ARM = Armenia, AZE = Azerbaijan, BAN = Bangladesh, BHU = Bhutan, CAM = Cambodia, GDP = gross domestic product, GEO = Georgia, IND = India, INO = Indonesia, KAZ = Kazakhstan, KGZ = Kyrgyz Republic, LAO = Lao People's Democratic Republic, MAL = Malaysia, MON = Mongolia, MYA = Myanmar, NEP = Nepal, PAK = Pakistan, PNG = Papua New Guinea, PHI = Philippines, PRC = People's Republic of China, SOL = Solomon Islands, SRI = Sri Lanka, TAJ = Tajikistan, THA = Thailand, TIM = Timor-Leste, UZB = Uzbekistan, VIE = Viet Nam.

Source: Khatiwada and Arao, forthcoming(a).

Predominance of small improvements to existing products

A third feature, shown in Figure 2.2.8, is that, when including consideration of whether a product innovation is novel in a firm's main market, innovation rates fall substantially. On average, 33.9% of firms in developing Asia introduced a new product, but only 19.9% introduced a product that was also new to the market. This was true in all subregions of developing Asia but most apparent in South Asia, where 41.8% of firms reported introducing a new product, but only 28% introduced a new product that was new to the market.

Figure 2.2.8 Share of firms reporting a new product

- ☐ New product
- ☐ New product novel to the firm's main market

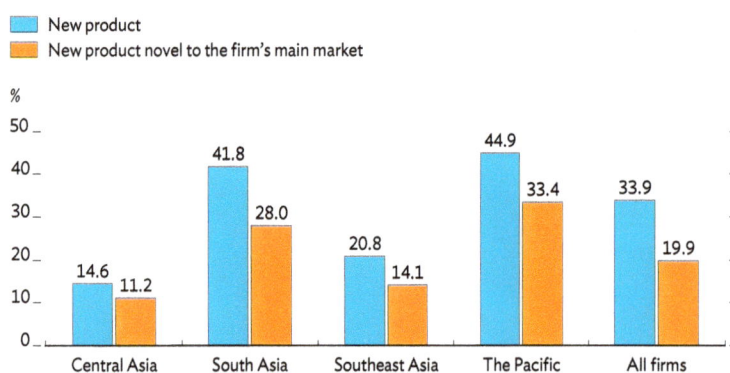

Notes: East Asia not included because data cover only Mongolia. The Pacific regional average includes only Papua New Guinea, Solomon Islands, and Timor-Leste.

Source: Khatiwada and Arao, forthcoming(a).

In line with the findings of Cirera and Maloney (2017), product innovation in developing Asia consists mainly of small improvements to existing products.

Relatively strong innovation in manufacturing

Fourth, a comparison of innovation patterns by industry shows innovation rates higher for firms in manufacturing, as 35.5% of them reported introducing a new product, 50.8% reported introducing a new process, and 56.0% reported introducing one or the other (Figure 2.2.9). The differences between manufacturers and other firms in retail or other services were statistically significant.

Strong innovation in information technology and high-tech manufacturing

Fifth, information technology and such high-tech manufacturing industries as machinery and equipment, electronics, and chemicals appear to have the highest share of firms engaged in innovation (Figure 2.2.10). Analysis similarly revealed a significantly bigger share of these firms than others innovating both products and processes.

Figure 2.2.9 Share of firms reporting a new product or process, by industry

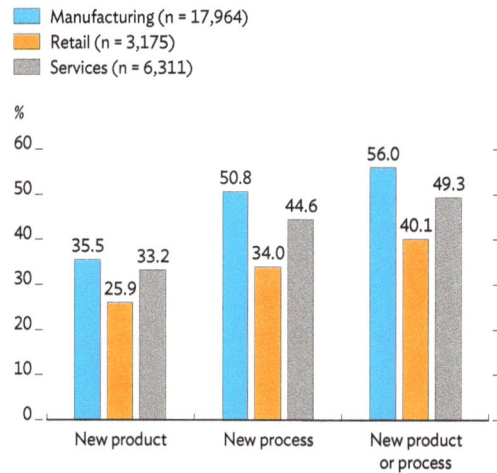

Source: Khatiwada and Arao, forthcoming(a).

Figure 2.2.10 Share of firms reporting a new product or process, by industry

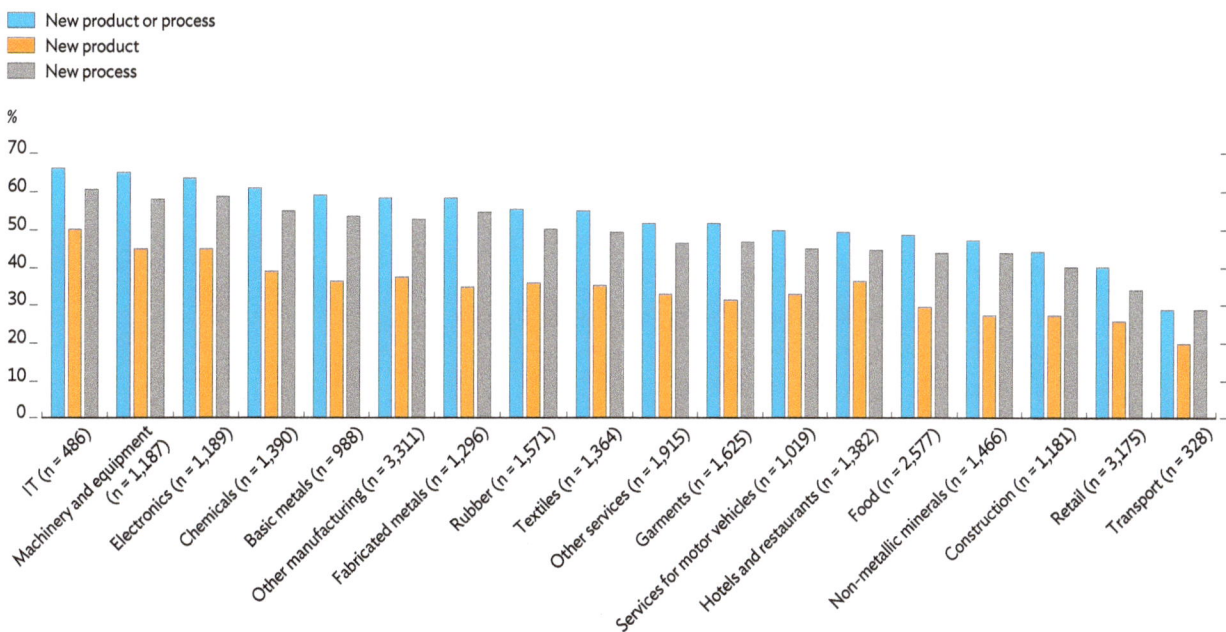

IT = Information technology.
Source: Khatiwada and Arao, forthcoming(a).

Figure 2.2.11 Share of firms reporting a new product or process, by firm size

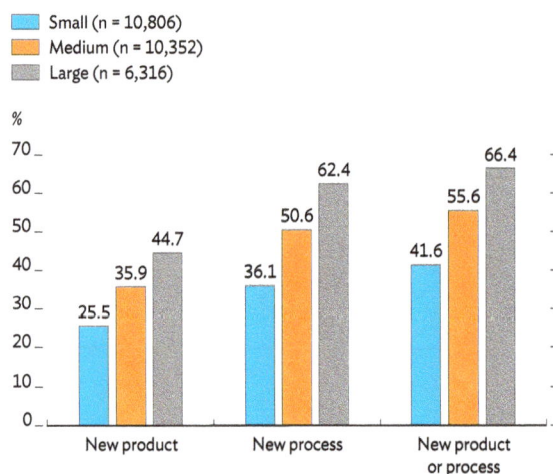

Note: Small firms had fewer than 20 employees, medium-sized firms 20–99 employees, and large firms more than 100.
Source: Khatiwada and Arao, forthcoming(a).

Figure 2.2.12 Share of firms reporting a new product or process, by firm age

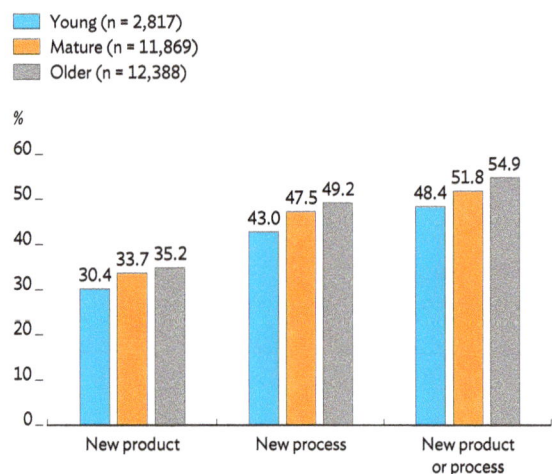

Note: Young firms had been in operation for up to 5 years, mature firms for 6–15 years, and older firms for 16 years or more.
Source: Khatiwada and Arao, forthcoming(a).

Higher innovation rates in larger firms

Sixth, two-thirds of large firms report introducing either product or process innovation, compared with 55.6% of medium-sized firms and 41.6% of small firms (Figure 2.2.11). Large firms were found to have statistically significant higher shares of both product and process innovation.

Process innovation rates were higher than product innovation rates for firms of all sizes: among large firms, 62.4% introduced a process innovation but only 44.7% a product innovation; among medium-sized firms, 50.6% over 35.9%; and among small firms 36.1% over 25.5%.

Higher innovation rates in older firms

Seventh, product and process innovation rates are higher for older firms that have been in business for 16 years or longer than for younger firms. This difference is also statistically significant (Figure 2.2.12).

Higher innovation rates in exporting firms

Eighth, product and process innovation rates were found to be higher in firms that export than in those that do not, with 67.1% of exporters having introduced either a product or a process innovation but only 50.7% of non-exporters (Figure 2.2.13). The difference in process innovation rates was considerably greater, at 62.4% for exporters but only 45.5% for others.

Figure 2.2.13 Share of firms reporting a new product or process, by exporting activity

Exporter (n = 3,596)
Non-exporter (n = 23,496)

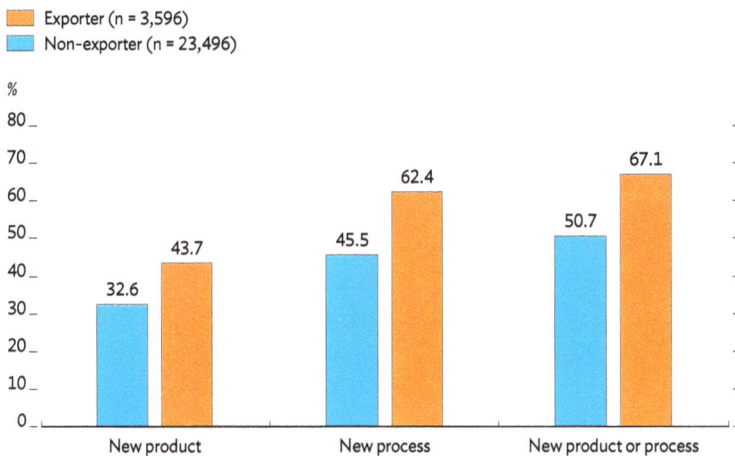

Source: Khatiwada and Arao, forthcoming(a).

Greater R&D spending by large firms, exporters, and foreign-owned companies

Ninth, R&D spending is greater in large firms, exporters, and foreign-owned companies in developing Asia. Fully 37.0% of large firms invested in R&D, almost three times the share of small firms doing so (Figure 2.2.14). Exporting firms in developing Asia are twice as likely to invest in R&D than non-exporters, at 39.3% to 20.0%. The higher shares of large firms, older firms, exporters, and foreign-owned firms that spend on R&D are statistically significant.

Figure 2.2.14 Share of firms reporting R&D spending, by selected characteristics

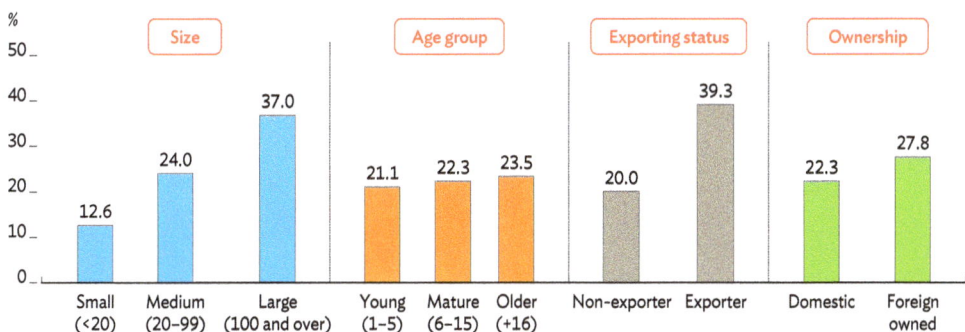

R&D = research and development.
Note: Firm size is by number of employees.
Source: Khatiwada and Arao, forthcoming(a).

Greater adoption of foreign technology by large and foreign-owned firms and exporters

Tenth, data show greater adoption of foreign technology by large firms, exporters, and foreign-owned companies. The share of firms that use technology licensed from foreign companies is 34.0% in the Pacific and 22.6% in East Asia (Figure 2.2.15). In Central and West Asia, South Asia, and Southeast Asia the use of licensed technology is lower, below 20%. As technology licensing is also lower in less-developed countries, the share of firms reporting their use of licensed technology increases with per capita GDP (Figure 2.2.16).

By firm size, the share of firms that report using technology licensed from foreign companies is 27.0% for large firms, 13.1% for medium-sized firms, and 7.5% for small firms (Figure 2.2.15). Exporting firms are twice as likely to use licensed technology as non-exporters, at 26.9% versus 12.7%, and foreign-owned firms almost three times as likely as domestic firms, at 37.3% versus 13.3%.

Figure 2.2.15 Percentage of firms licensing foreign technology, by region, size, and industry

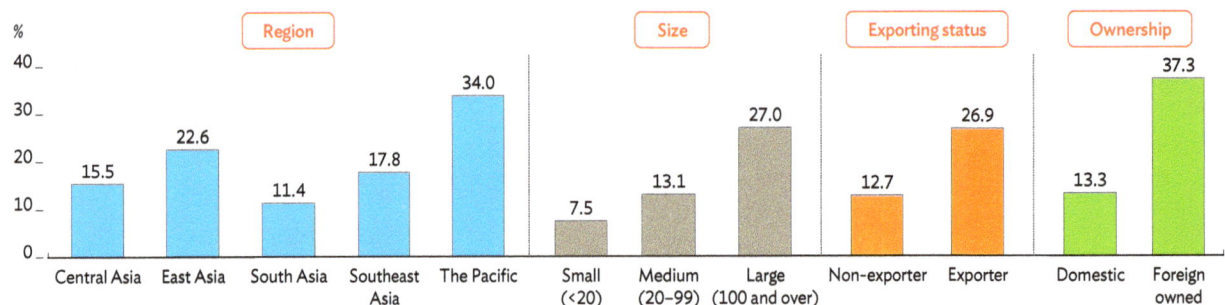

Source: Khatiwada and Arao, forthcoming(a).

Figure 2.2.16 Scatter plot of technology licensing, by GDP per capita

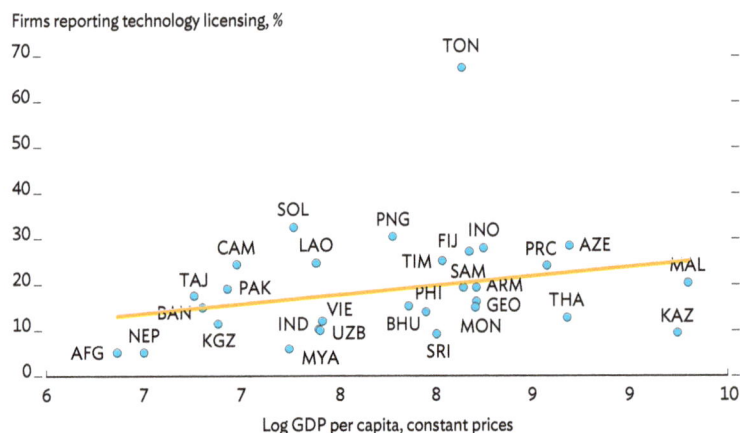

AFG = Afghanistan, ARM = Armenia, AZE = Azerbaijan, BAN = Bangladesh, BHU = Bhutan, CAM = Cambodia, FIJ = Fiji, GDP = gross domestic product, GEO = Georgia, IND = India, INO = Indonesia, KAZ = Kazakhstan, KGZ = Kyrgyz Republic, LAO = Lao People's Democratic Republic, MAL = Malaysia, MON = Mongolia, MYA = Myanmar, NEP = Nepal, PAK = Pakistan, PNG = Papua New Guinea, PHI = Philippines, PRC = People's Republic of China, SAM = Samoa, SOL = Solomon Islands, SRI = Sri Lanka, TAJ = Tajikistan, THA = Thailand, TIM = Timor-Leste, TON = Tonga, UZB = Uzbekistan, VIE = Viet Nam.

Source: Khatiwada and Arao, forthcoming(a).

Determinants of innovation in developing Asia: Country-level evidence

As seen above, developing Asia now invests substantially in innovation and produces a significant amount of innovative output. A wide array of factors can influence the environment for such activity, including a country's spending on R&D, investment in human capital and infrastructure, and openness to trade. Clearly, identifying these factors can be very useful for informing policy. This section reports the results of an empirical analysis that uses country-level data to identify the determinants of innovation in developing Asia (Box 2.2.1).

Box 2.2.1 Determinants of innovation: Empirical framework

Qureshi et al. (forthcoming) examined the determinants of innovation in developing Asia using a fixed-effects panel regression framework. Innovation was represented by patent flows, a commonly used measure that counts the number of patent applications by a country's residents. The analysis covered unbalanced panel data from 22 economies in the region annually from 2000 to 2016.

The regression equation takes the following form:

$$Innov_{it} = \alpha RD_{i,t-2} + X'_{it}\beta + u_i + v_i + \varepsilon_{it} \qquad (1)$$

in which the subscript i refers to the country and t to the year. *Innov* is innovation as measured by patent flows; *RD* is annual spending on R&D, the key explanatory variable; X is a vector of time-varying country-level control variables; u_i is the country fixed effect and v_i the time fixed effect; and ε_{it} is the well-behaved error term.[a] Note that country fixed effects can capture omissions at least partly (ADB 2020, Borensztein, De Gregorio, and Lee 1998, Sawada, Matsuda, and Kimura 2012, among others). Variables were normalized by either population or GDP to control for the size of the economy. All variables are in natural logs.[b]

Patent flows include only those applications filed by residents through the Patent Cooperation Treaty procedure or with a national patent office for exclusive rights to an invention.[c] Most studies and empirical evidence consider patents a reliable measure of innovation (Acs, Anselin, and Varga 2002). They are an important feature of innovation, as they protect the intellectual property of inventors. Bloom, Van Reenen, and Williams (2019) further showed that patent citations can be a measurable indicator of knowledge spillover, as firms benefited from existing patents to improve existing products or services.

R&D spending proxies for knowledge accumulated over time (knowledge stock) and human capital in R&D. Such data can be interpreted as inputs used in the innovation process, with patents representing innovation output. To construct R&D capital stocks, a 20% depreciation rate was adopted here following Ulku (2004), as recent studies suggest that the actual figure may be higher than the 15% traditionally assumed and may vary across industries.

Several other factors possibly influence innovation apart from R&D. Higher educational attainment, for instance, provides a base of highly skilled personnel that firms and other institutions can employ in R&D (Stern, Porter, and Furman 2000). The higher education needed for innovation can be reflected by secondary school enrollment, which measures the intensity of human capital investment. This variable was therefore included in the regression to capture, at a broader level, the effect of human capital on a country's innovation.

Country-level control variables in the empirical model were trade openness, the share of imports of manufactures in two-way trade in manufactures, the share of two-way trade with the US in national GDP, and measures of financial development and good governance.

Various studies have documented the role of trade in technology flows and innovation across countries (ADB 2020, Grossman and Helpman 1991, Romer 2010, among others). Trade openness is self-explanatory. The share of imports of manufactures in two-way trade in manufactures accounted for the "international technology spillover effect," which may increase developing countries' innovative capacity.

continued next page

Box 2.2.1 *Continued*

Meanwhile, the share of two-way trade with the US in national output controlled for the effect of economic alliance with the world's largest economy, given that most patent applications worldwide are also filed with the US Patent Office.

The International Monetary Fund's financial development index measures how developed financial institutions and markets are in terms of depth (size and liquidity), access (the ability of individuals and companies to tap financial services), and efficiency (the degree to which institutions and financial markets provide financial services at low cost and with sustainable revenue). A highly developed financial system has been shown to help small innovative firms find funding from venture capitalists (Morck and Yeung 2001). Moreover, evidence shows that financial constraints or funding gaps frequently mean costly R&D capital, which holds back innovation (Hall and Lerner 2010, Kerr, Nanda, and Rhodes-Kropf 2014).

The good governance variable is a normalized score using index scores from the World Bank's Worldwide Governance Indicators to measure institutional quality. The score from 1 (worst) to 6 (best) was calculated from the normalized summation of the six dimensions of governance: (i) voice and accountability, (ii) political stability and absence of violence, (iii) government effectiveness, (iv) regulatory quality, (v) rule of law, and (vi) control of corruption (ADB 2018).

The box table reports the result of the empirical analysis of determinants of innovation, which are proxied by patent flows.

[a] This innovation function is adapted from Ulku (2004), using a log linearized version.

[b] Country and year dummies have been included to control for the time trend and idiosyncratic shocks. Robust standard errors are clustered at the country level.

[c] Patent applications are preferable to patents granted to eliminate the considerable lag between them and make readily available longer time series.

Empirical results: determinants of patent flows

	Developing Asia	Developing Asia excluding the PRC
R&D stock	0.215** (0.101)	0.174** (0.079)
Secondary school enrollment	2.001*** (0.682)	1.096** (0.446)
Trade openness	−0.305 (0.353)	−0.070 (0.287)
Import of manufactured goods	−0.754 (0.685)	0.151 (0.524)
US trade, % of GDP	0.127 (0.079)	0.173** (0.078)
Financial development, index	0.978 (1.409)	−0.530 (0.728)
Infrastructure access	1.883** (0.722)	2.672*** (0.544)
Governance index	0.047 (0.307)	0.080 (0.211)
Observations	264	247
R^2	0.562	0.521
Number of countries	20	19
Country fixed effects	Yes	Yes
Year fixed effects	Yes	Yes

*** $p<0.01$, ** $p<0.05$, * $p<0.1$, GDP = gross domestic product, PRC = People's Republic of China, R&D = research and development, US = United States.

Note: Robust standard errors in parentheses.

Source: Qureshi et al., forthcoming.

The results suggested that patent flows positively relate to investment in R&D in developing Asia, as well as to human capital accumulation. A 1.0% increase in R&D investment per capita increased patent flow by 0.2% in developing Asia. The coefficient was only slightly lower if the PRC was excluded, underscoring higher innovation not only in large market economies but overall, extending the findings of Ulku (2004).

Findings on secondary school enrollment as a significant driver of patent flows in the region highlight the key role education plays in innovation (Raghupathi and Raghupathi 2017) and the importance of human capital in upgrading a nation's innovative capacity (Stern, Porter, and Furman 2000, Ulku 2004).

Among trade-related variables, only the share of two-way trade with the US in GDP had a significant coefficient, and only when the PRC was excluded from the sample for developing Asia. The result possibly reflected spillover from the region's high volume of trade with the US, which is the main source of technological know-how for developing Asia.

The provision of infrastructure positively and significantly related to patent flows. This captured how infrastructure such as roads, electrical power, water supply, and ICT connectivity complement innovation. In contrast, financial development did not seem to be a significant determinant of innovation.

To sum up, the evidence from empirical analysis of country-level data suggests that R&D investment, human capital, and infrastructure all have positive and significant impact on innovation in developing Asia. The finding that a 1% increase in secondary education enrollment increases patent flows by 2% reinforces the notion that innovation is fundamentally a human endeavor. The next section takes a closer look at the role of education, human capital, and entrepreneurship in innovation in the region.

Fostering innovators and a culture of innovation

The empirical evidence in the preceding section points to human capital having a significant role in innovation. This is not surprising given that innovation is fundamentally and intrinsically a human enterprise. Indeed, the history of mankind is basically one of innovations, from the first fire and sharp-edged tools to the wheel, the compass, and the internal combustion engine, and on to space rockets and the internet. All these great inventions are testaments to human ingenuity. A prerequisite for an innovative society is therefore a large pool of creative innovators who are willing to ask new questions and seek alternative solutions. A sound education system that encourages curiosity, originality, and new ways of thinking helps create a pool of potential innovators. Another important source of innovation is high-quality entrepreneurship as epitomized by Steve Jobs of Apple and Jack Ma of Alibaba. As these examples illustrate, ICT has dramatically expanded opportunities for innovative entrepreneurship.

This section first provides empirical evidence of the relationship between human capital and innovation at the firm level in developing Asia. Next, it focuses on the role of education in nurturing future innovators and the critical challenges that education systems in the region face in fulfilling that role. Finally, because innovators need the right entrepreneurial ecosystem to convert their ideas into marketable products and services, the discussion turns to the basic framework and grounded assumptions of entrepreneurship and innovation.

The role of human capital in innovation: Evidence from firms

Human capital strengthens the capacity of a firm to absorb and develop new knowledge (Cohen and Levinthal 1990, Smith, Collins, and Clark 2005), which makes it essential to innovation, both at the frontier and catching up to it. In fact, even when they use technologies and products already available elsewhere, firms still need a workforce with the appropriate skills and knowledge. While policies such as R&D tax credits and direct public funding may boost innovation in the short run, it is more effective in the long run to increase the stock of human capital (Bloom, Van Reenen, and Williams 2019).

Previous studies found a robust positive association between human capital and innovation output, but their proxies for human capital were often restricted to formal schooling (Ayyagari, Demirgüç-Kunt, and Maksimovic 2011, Robson, Haugh, and Obeng 2009, Toner 2011). Increasing the stock of human capital through training sponsored by firms often engenders greater innovation (Dostie 2018). Employee schooling and the provision of training improve human capital within a firm and positively influence innovation output, as does slack time made available for such creative activities as ideation, experimentation, and prototype development (van Uden, Knoben, and Vermeulen 2017).

While firm-level surveys for several economies in developing Asia offer detailed information on innovative activity and human capital, cross-country analysis is made extremely challenging by differences in survey instruments, sampling methodology, and populations of reference. World Bank Enterprise Surveys, on the other hand, have somewhat less detailed indicators of innovation and human capital, but they cover a substantial number of Asian economies. These surveys are therefore useful to explore the relationship between a firm's propensity to innovate and its human capital, the latter proxied by employee educational attainment, employee training, and the industry-specific experience of the top manager, which is a neglected but important attribute when studying innovation. Another question to explore is whether offering training to employees has greater impact on firm-level innovation when a firm's operations are constrained by the inadequate skills of its workers. Box 2.3.1 discusses the empirical specification for this analysis.

Box 2.3.1 The role of human capital in innovation: An empirical approach

The following equation was used to estimate a linear probability model of the relationship between a firm's human capital and its innovation, controlling for broad firm characteristics (Model 1 in Table 2.3.1):

$$Innov_{ijc} = \alpha + \beta \cdot HC_{ijc} + \gamma \cdot F_{ijc} + \delta_j + \sigma_c + \epsilon_{ijc}$$

where $Innov_{ijc}$ is a binary indicator of whether firm i in industry j in country c introduced either a new product or a new process, as defined in the *Oslo Manual 2018*.

HC_{ijc} is a set of proxies for firm-level human capital: the share of employees that completed high school (a proxy for the stock of generic skills and basic knowledge available within the firm), the number of years of experience the top manager has accrued working in the industry, and formal training provided to employees, which includes classroom work, seminars, lectures, workshops, audio-visual presentations, and demonstrations with a structured and defined curriculum. Formal training does not include, however, employee orientation upon being hired or training to familiarize workers with equipment and machinery on the shop floor or the establishment's standard operating procedures.

F_{ijc} is a vector of other firm characteristics shown in the literature to affect the firm's propensity to innovate, such as firm size, age, foreign ownership, export orientation, and R&D; δ_j is industry fixed effects; and σ_c is country fixed effects, while ϵ_{ijc} captures unobserved firm, industry, and country characteristics.

Also estimated is a model that includes an interaction term capturing how employer-sponsored training can compensate for a paucity of skills (Model 2 in Table 2.3.1).

Source: Khatiwada and Arao, forthcoming(b).

Table 2.3.1 reports the results of the linear probability model in Box 2.3.1. Model 1 shows all three proxies for human capital positively and significantly associated with the predicted probability of firms to introduce a new product, but only employee training is positively and significantly associated with the probability of implementing a new process. This finding suggests that different aspects of human capital matter for product versus process innovation.

Table 2.3.1 Linear probability model estimates

Variable	New product		New process	
	Model 1	Model 2	Model 1	Model 2
Workforce with high school education, %	0.000479*** (0.00373)	0.000483*** (0.00362)	0.000326* (0.0990)	0.000321 (0.107)
Manager experience	0.0161*** (0.00292)	0.0158*** (0.00366)	0.00954 (0.129)	0.00937 (0.145)
Training	0.0771*** (0)	0.0650*** (1.36e-08)	0.0782*** (1.90e-08)	0.0748*** (5.18e-07)
Skill constraint		−0.0215 (0.274)		0.0269* (0.0937)
Interaction of training and skill constraint		0.0857*** (0.000547)		0.0122 (0.620)
Medium-sized, default: small	0.0439*** (4.57e-06)	0.0440*** (3.73e-06)	0.0748*** (0)	0.0741*** (0)
Large, 100+	0.0713*** (5.95e-07)	0.0713*** (8.20e-07)	0.117*** (0)	0.116*** (0)
Mature, default: young	0.0258** (0.0259)	0.0266** (0.0239)	0.0161 (0.212)	0.0164 (0.208)
Older	0.0333** (0.0133)	0.0332** (0.0141)	0.00772 (0.545)	0.00715 (0.577)
Foreign owned	0.00637 (0.711)	0.00741 (0.666)	−0.0157 (0.343)	−0.0155 (0.352)
Exporter	0.00643 (0.559)	0.00603 (0.586)	0.0270** (0.0109)	0.0258** (0.0145)
Research & development	0.362*** (0)	0.362*** (0)	0.376*** (0)	0.377*** (0)
Industry fixed effects	Yes	Yes	Yes	Yes
Country fixed effects	Yes	Yes	Yes	Yes
Observations	20,670	20,567	20,532	20,428

* = significant at 10%, ** = significant at 5%, *** = significant at 1%.

Notes: Robust p-values in parentheses. The results are based on enterprise surveys for Armenia, Afghanistan, Azerbaijan, Bangladesh, Bhutan, Cambodia, Georgia, India, Indonesia, Kazakhstan, the Kyrgyz Republic, the Lao People's Democratic Republic, Malaysia, Myanmar, Nepal, Pakistan, Papua New Guinea, the Philippines, Solomon Islands, Sri Lanka, Tajikistan, Thailand, Timor-Leste, Uzbekistan, and Viet Nam.

Source: Khatiwada and Arao, forthcoming(b).

The predicted probability of firms that provide training to employees reporting a new product was 7.7% and a new process 7.8%. This supports the argument that firm-level training can update or upgrade employees' knowledge and, more importantly, provide specific knowledge not available in general education. The predicted probabilities of reporting a new product were 0.048% for the share of the workforce with a high school education and 1.6% for the top manager's experience. The estimates were similar in magnitude for the implementation of a new process but not statistically significant.

The estimated coefficients for other firm characteristics were mostly in line with the literature: Medium-sized and large firms were more likely to report a new product or process than small firms, and firms that exported were more likely to report a new product or process than firms that sold exclusively on the domestic market. R&D expenditure was positively associated with innovative outcomes, the predicted probability of a firm that spent on R&D reporting a new product being 36% and a new process 38%.

Model 2 investigated whether employer-sponsored training was more strongly associated with innovative activity for firms reporting skill constraints. Once again, the results varied between product and process innovation. For product innovation, the positive and significant association between employer-sponsored training and reporting a new product was stronger for skill-constrained firms than for firms that did not face severe or very severe skill constraints. For process innovation, on the other hand, the interaction was smaller and statistically insignificant. In sum, model 2 suggests that employer-sponsored training may be a mechanism to compensate for the constraints resulting from an inadequately educated workforce.

The conclusion is that a firm's human capital—proxied by the percentage of the workforce with high school education, managerial experience, and employer-sponsored training—is positively and significantly associated with likelihood to engage in product innovation and, to a lesser extent, process innovation, suggesting that different aspects of human capital matter to different types of innovation. These findings are consistent with the literature, which shows that the quality of a firm's human capital is a key determinant of its capacity to absorb new technology and knowledge (Almeida and Fernandes 2008, Comin and Hobijn 2004, Lederman and Maloney 2003, Keller 2004). Additionally, the findings show that providing training to employees has more impact than other measures of human capital, especially for firms whose operations are constrained by inadequately skilled workers.

Education plays a vital role in fostering innovation

Human capital has many determinants: health and nutrition; education, training, and work experience; social and communication skills; habits and personality traits; and individual fame and brand image. It is evident that education plays a fundamental role in building human capital in the form of knowledge, skills, values, beliefs, and habits. Further, a sound education system can create a pool of potential innovators by fostering inquisitiveness and creativity.

Unfortunately, education often fails to deliver on its basic mission to create employable graduates, let alone future innovators. The world faces a learning crisis, in which hundreds of millions of children and young people in developing Asia today learn very little.

Focus first on basic skills

Figure 2.3.1 shows the estimated fraction of 10-year-olds in a range of Asian economies who are unable to read a simple sentence—a metric that the World Bank has termed "learning poverty." In a number of economies, this figure is greater than 50%, meaning that the majority of children do not have even basic literacy. Asia's learning crisis is most pronounced in South Asia, where millions of children are in school but learning at low levels (ASER Pakistan Secretariat 2019, ASER Centre 2018).

Figure 2.3.1 Learning poverty and GDP per capita in Asian economies

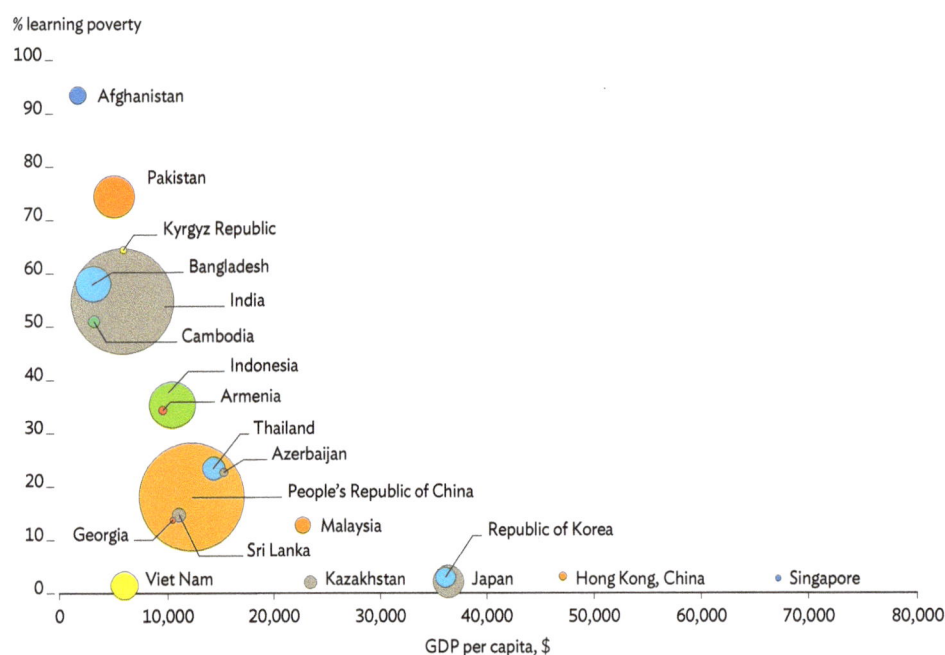

Note: Bubble size represents population size. Learning poverty is the percentage of children aged about 10 who are unable to read and comprehend a short text appropriate for their age. Data from World Bank (2019).

Source: Newman, Gentile, and dela Cruz, forthcoming.

The performance in other parts of Asia and the Pacific is mixed. Some economies perform better in achieving basic literacy in primary school but still underperform in secondary school, as shown in Figure 2.3.2. In a number of Asian economies, the majority of 15-year-olds do not meet even minimum expected proficiency in reading. However, there are also examples of Asian economies performing far better than expected based on their GDP per capita. Further, among the more developed economies of Southeast and East Asia, one can find some of the best education systems in the world.

Figure 2.3.2 Reading proficiency of 15-year-olds in Asian economies

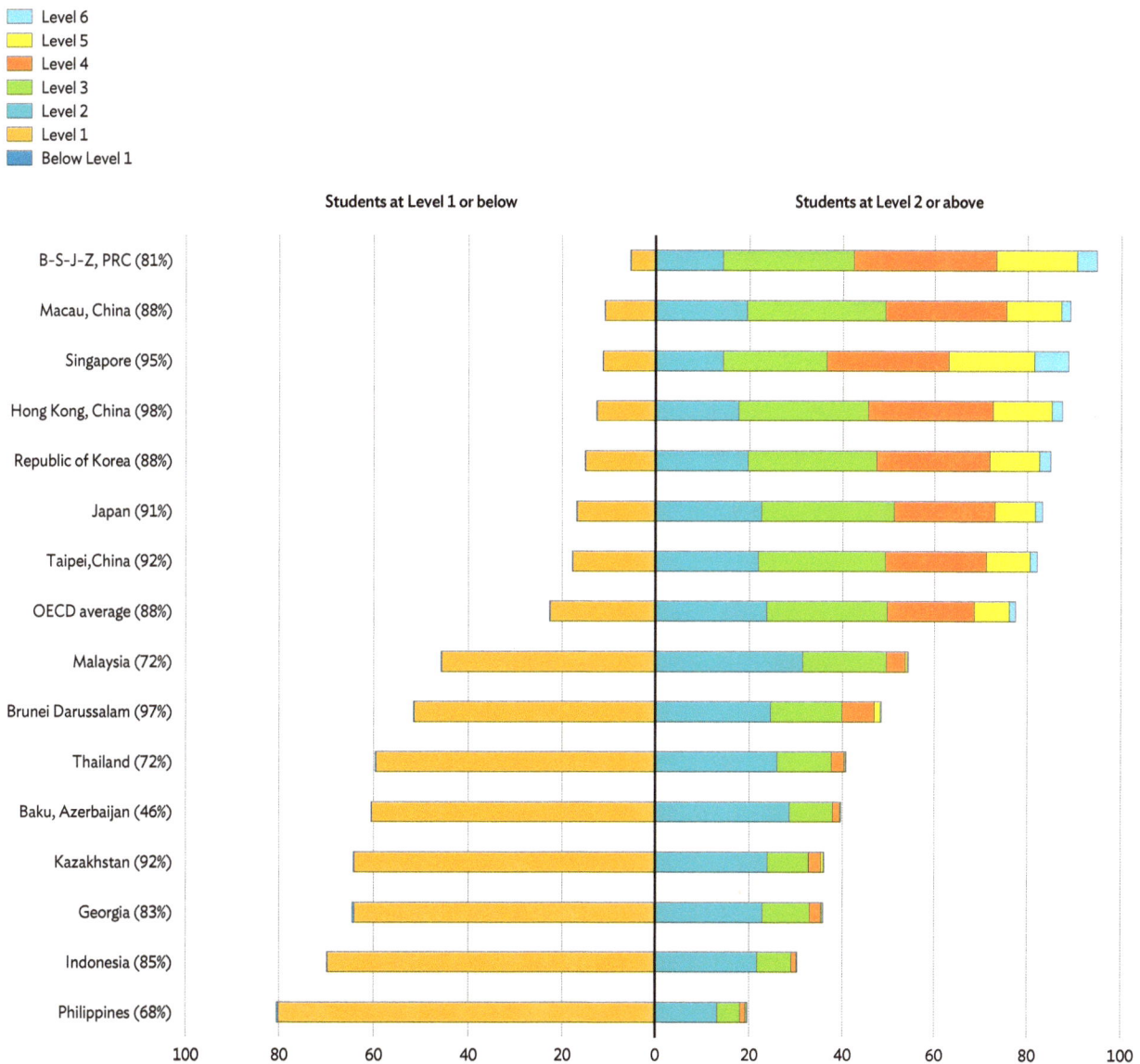

B-S-J-Z = Beijing, Shanghai, Jiangsu, and Zhejiang, OECD = Organisation for Economic Co-operation and Development, PRC = People's Republic of China.

Note: The figure in parentheses following the economy's name is the percentage of 15-year-olds covered by the sample. Students were classified as having reading skills from below level 1 to level 6. Students performing at level 1 can read and understand short, simple sentences. Students performing at level 6 can understand lengthy, complex texts and make complex inferences about the sources of information. The United Nations Sustainable Development Goals state that level 2 is the minimum proficiency that all students should have by the end of secondary school.

Source: Newman, Gentile, and dela Cruz, forthcoming.

For most economies, data are available only on basic skills, mainly literacy and numeracy. However, it can be assumed that, if education systems are not managing to develop even these basic skills, they are very unlikely to be developing higher-order skills such as problem solving and critical thinking.

Given the huge variation in learning outcomes across developing Asia, any economy wishing to drive innovation through its education system needs to assess the current state of this system. Economies achieving good outcomes have a range of options to foster innovation. Those where learning outcomes are low, on the other hand, need to acknowledge this weakness and focus on improving the quality of basic education. Without basic foundational skills including literacy and numeracy, it is almost impossible for students to go on to achieve higher learning.

To develop the education system, policy makers need to ensure that learning outcomes are measured and that the education system is sufficiently aligned with the goal of improved learning. Facing up to the learning crisis can be painful for governments and societies, but if it is not done, countries are left unable to embrace the innovation needed to drive development.

Shift teaching practices to develop innovation capabilities

Innovation requires a range of capabilities that can be grouped into two categories: "opening capabilities" and "closing capabilities."[5] Both kinds are needed in the general population and in leadership positions (Figure 2.3.3).

Figure 2.3.3 Opening and closing innovation capabilities

- Openness to questioning
- Failure tolerance
- Consultative management style

- Monitoring and enforcing goal attainment
- Results focus
- Performance management

Opening Innovation Capability

Closing Innovation Capability

- Creativity
- Problem solving
- Critical thinking

- Grit
- Perseverance
- Long-term orientation

Leadership

Population

Source: Newman, Gentile, and dela Cruz, forthcoming.

Opening capabilities are the set of skills and approaches required to enable the generation of new ideas. Ordinarily, they are a range of overlapping "soft skills" such as creativity, problem solving, evidence literacy, and critical thinking (Ueki and Guaita Martínez 2019, Saidi et al. 2019, Brazdauskas 2015). However, having innovative people with strong opening capabilities in an organization is not sufficient. Also needed is an enabling environment created by leaders who possess capabilities such as openness to questioning, failure tolerance, and a consultative management style (Barsh, Capozzi, and Davidson 2008, Burpitt and Bigoness 1997, Lewis, Ricard, and Klijn 2018, Fischer et al. 2018, Baer and Frese 2003). These leadership attributes are critical, as innovation often fails not for lack of innovative ideas but because leaders have not created an environment that enables innovation to flourish. Indeed, evidence exists that having people with many new ideas in an organization that does not enable innovation can actually hinder performance more than having no innovative people at all (Baer and Frese 2003).

Closing capabilities, on the other hand, are the set of skills and approaches needed to see an innovation through to completion. In a population, they include such attributes as grit, perseverance, and long-term orientation. They enable people to push forward the implementation of new ideas even in the face of challenges. In leadership, the attributes include the ability to monitor and enforce goal attainment, a strong focus on results, and performance management.

As innovations proceed through organizations, a gradual shift will see less time spent on opening processes and more time on closing processes. This requires careful balancing by leaders in particular, as the approaches that enable opening may conflict with those that facilitate closing (Bledow et al. 2009).

Some of the capabilities needed for innovation are influenced by culture, so different countries need to consider where their strengths and opportunities lie (Bledow et al. 2009). For example, failure intolerance is a particular issue in parts of Asia, where people tend to harbor more fear of failure than in other parts of the world (OECD 2019). Indeed, a number of countries in the region now explicitly nurture tolerance of failure. Recent results from Hubner et al. (forthcoming) highlights differences in the distribution of innovation capabilities across Asia and the Pacific. The study observed that teams in the PRC were particularly strong in closing capability but weaker in opening capability, while teams in India had the opposite distribution.

For decades, education experts have discussed how pedagogical approaches affect learning. One way to consider teaching approaches is to see them as a continuum running from teacher-centered approaches, which use traditional and didactic techniques to impart knowledge, to learner-centered approaches, which use more interactive approaches that help students direct their own learning (Weimer 2013, Brown 2003).

Learner-centered approaches—which include problem-based learning, group discussions, learning by doing, individual and group assignments, discussion, experimentation, competitions, debate, and games—have long been advocated as means to develop opening innovation capabilities. The theory is that enabling students to experiment, seek out information, and solve problems imparts skills that can be applied throughout their lives.

No globally comparable data exists on teaching practice. Studies have been carried out using ratings by observers, teachers, or students, but it is unclear how comparable these scores are across cultures. Evidence from cross-cultural comparisons has found that self-reported cultural values are not good indicators of cultural practices, as ratings are greatly affected by cultural norms (Taras, Steel, and Kirkman 2010), and the same problem may affect data on teaching practice (Aldridge et al. 2000, among others).

Table 2.3.2 presents a traffic light assessment of teaching practice in selected economies in Asia and the Pacific. Two indicators are chosen to assess the degree of learner-centeredness in teaching practice and are graded using qualitative descriptions from classroom observation studies: "group work and interactive learning" and "stimulation of higher-order thinking." These teaching practices are known to stimulate opening innovation capabilities in students (Scott 2015). Red indicates evidence that practice is generally not present. Amber indicates either evidence that practice is partly present or conflicting evidence from two or more studies. Green indicates evidence that practice is often or usually present. Gray indicates the absence of evidence on this practice.

The first indicator for learning outcomes in Table 2.3.2 is "early literacy," which is based on the World Bank Learning Poverty Indicator. Red indicates that more than 50% of 10-year-olds are unable to read a simple text, amber indicates a portion from 10% to 49%, and green indicates a portion less than 10%. The second learning outcome is the average Programme for International Student Assessment (PISA) 2018 reading, math, and science scores, with red indicating a score below 450, amber 450–500, and green above 500. It is expected that those with high learning outcomes will have strong closing innovation capabilities since there is a significant correlation between students' academic achievement and their possession of qualities like grit and perseverance (Kutlu, Kartal, and ŞimŞek 2017, Karlen et al. 2019, Christopoulou et al. 2018). High academic learning outcomes—and therefore strong closing innovation capabilities—can be developed through either learner-centered or teacher-centered approaches; however, by using learner-centered approaches, teachers can instill opening innovation capabilities as well.

Table 2.3.2 Descriptions of teaching practice in Asia and the Pacific

	Teaching practice		Learning outcomes	
	Group work and interactive learning	Stimulation of higher-order thinking	Early literacy	Average reading, math, and science score at age 15
Afghanistan	● (red)	● (red)	● (red)	● (gray)
Australia	● (green)	● (gray)	● (green)	● (amber)
Bangladesh	● (red)	● (red)	● (red)	● (gray)
Cambodia	● (red)	● (red)	● (red)	● (gray)
Hong Kong, China	● (red)	● (amber)	● (green)	● (green)
India	● (amber)	● (red)	● (red)	● (gray)
Indonesia	● (amber)	● (red)	● (amber)	● (red)
Japan	● (amber)	● (green)	● (green)	● (green)
Malaysia	● (amber)	● (red)	● (amber)	● (red)
People's Republic of China[a]	● (amber)	● (amber)	● (amber)	● (green)
Philippines	● (red)	● (red)	● (gray)	● (red)
Republic of Korea	● (red)	● (green)	● (green)	● (green)
Singapore	● (amber)	● (amber)	● (green)	● (green)
Viet Nam	● (amber)	● (amber)	● (green)	● (gray)

[a] The average reading, math, and science score at age 15 in the People's Republic of China is not representative of the country because only Beijing, Shanghai, Zhejiang, and Jiangsu participated in the Programme for International Student Assessment 2018.

Notes: The two indicators for teaching practice, "group work and interactive learning" and "stimulation of higher-order thinking," were graded in the study based on qualitative descriptions from published classroom observation studies. Red indicates evidence that the practice is generally not present. Amber indicates either evidence that the practice is partly present or conflicting evidence from two or more studies. Green indicates evidence that the practice is often or usually present. Gray indicates the absence of evidence on this practice. The two indicators of learning outcomes were chosen on the assumption that the achievement of academic outcomes is a proxy for closing innovation capabilities. "Early literacy" is based on the World Bank Learning Poverty Indicator, with red indicating a score greater than 50%, amber 10%–49%, and green less than 10%. Learning outcomes at age 15 are based on average Programme for International Student Assessment 2018 reading, math, and science scores, with red indicating a score below 450, amber 450–500, and green above 500.

Source: Newman, Gentile, and dela Cruz, forthcoming.

Table 2.3.2 shows that teaching practice varies significantly across the region. This is consistent with other studies that challenge the stereotype of Asian education as uniformly didactic and dependent on rote learning (Takayama 2017, You 2019). A number of Asian economies have teaching practices that are both poor quality and teacher-centered. Developing high-quality, learner-centered teaching strategies will help these economies to improve both opening and closing innovation capabilities. Other economies achieve high learning outcomes using relatively teacher-centered approaches. Policy makers in these economies may wish to promote the further evolution of teaching practice to optimize innovation capabilities.

Achieving change in pedagogical practice is notoriously difficult (Weimer 2013). Attempts by external actors to transplant learner-centered practices developed in one culture into an entirely different one have usually failed to achieve the intended outcomes (Schweisfurth 2013). Even where learner-centered rhetoric has been adopted by policy makers, this may translate into a relatively superficial impact on actual teaching practice (You 2019, Brinkmann 2019). However, policy makers across the region have scope to consider the types of capabilities their society needs and to design culturally embedded approaches to teaching and learning to develop them. There is nothing particularly Western about educational practices that can drive innovation. Cultural practices influence teaching practice across Asia and can contribute to developing innovative capabilities. For example, Confucius advocated that learners should take ownership of their learning and develop higher-order thinking skills, and this has had a strong influence on teaching in the PRC (Tan 2015). Similarly, India celebrates *jugaad*, or improvisation to create solutions when constraints are harsh or resources limited. This clearly encourages problem solving and experimentation (Prabhu and Jain 2015).

In recent decades, countries across Asia have exerted considerable effort to shift their educational practices toward strengthening innovative capability. Singapore initiated its Thinking Schools, Learning Nation reform in 1997 and its Teach Less and Learn More policy in 2006 (Takayama 2017). The PRC initiated its New Curriculum Reform in 2001 with the aim of promoting "pupils' creative and critical spirits and capabilities" (You 2019). Japan introduced initiatives designed to promote "zest for living" and "low pressure, room for growth" in 2002 (Takayama 2017). Philippine basic education policy states that "every graduate of basic education shall be an empowered individual who has learned ... to engage in autonomous, creative, and critical thinking" (Care and Luo 2016).

Policy makers need to be realistic and bear in mind that achieving change in pedagogical practice can be challenging. However, only by fostering new ways of teaching and by investing in new approaches in schools can Asian countries tackle the learning crisis and forge ahead to bolster innovative capability.

Broaden and diversify the skill mix

No single formula exists for blending school subjects to drive innovation. The ability to experiment and test ideas, which can be developed through effective science, technology, engineering, and math (STEM) teaching, is certainly important for innovation. Experts warn, however, against overemphasizing STEM subjects at the expense of those that can develop creativity, such as art and design, or critical thinking, such as social science and humanities. In fact, the literature suggests that a mix of different skills is key to driving innovation (Toner 2011).

Innovation in some sectors requires advanced technical skills and therefore requires graduates with qualifications as high as doctoral degrees (Marvel and Lumpkin 2007, Larson 2011, Toner 2011). It is almost impossible for someone to develop an innovative treatment for malaria, for example, without first honing advanced skills in microbiology and pharmacology. Similarly, innovations in car manufacturing are likely to come only from someone highly skilled in engineering. However, innovation in services or the public sector may depend less on technical skills than on general management and business skills (Marvel and Lumpkin 2007, Toner 2011). Policy makers need to assess which skills are needed and ensure the availability of mechanisms to link the tertiary education provided with the needs of industry.

Also important is to maintain diversity in skills, as innovation often results when different skill sets collide. One way to achieve this is for individuals to develop skills in more than one area. A doctor with skills in coding may be excellently prepared to identify novel approaches to digital health delivery, for example, as would an architect with knowledge of social development to identify and overcome physical barriers to inclusion. The advantages of developing more than one area of expertise are demonstrated by a study that found students pursuing dual majors are more innovative than those focused on a single major (Selznick and Mayhew 2018).

Some universities are now exploring how to guide students along more flexible learning journeys that allow them to develop skills across disciplines. In the PRC, for example, a number of prestigious universities are attempting to make undergraduate learning more diverse. Fudan University has changed the undergraduate curriculum to allow students to study a broad range of subjects in their first 2 years before having to choose a specialization in their third year. Similarly, Yuanpei College at Peking University requires students to take general education courses in one of four areas: humanities, social issues, science, and art (Godwin and Pickus 2017). Another approach to stimulate innovation is to supplement single major studies with courses specifically designed to build innovation skills (Wright et al. 2007, Thongpravati, Maritz, and Stoddart 2016).

Entrepreneurship and innovation in developing Asia

How entrepreneurship, innovation, and economic development interact is more complex than is often thought. Entrepreneurs are a mixed bag, as are the teams they form and the new businesses they create. Most entrepreneurs are not economically innovative, as few create new jobs in any significant number or have the means to be productive.

A telling discovery is that only a small minority of new firms in any cohort, dubbed "gazelles," are responsible for a disproportionate share of employment generation (Birch, Haggerty, and Parsons 1997).

This section looks closely at what determines the productivity potential of entrepreneurial ecosystems. The hypothesis is that institutional conditions can shape the productivity potential of new entrepreneurial firms through their impact on entrepreneurs' decisions to start a business and how to approach innovation in the pursuit of growth.

Not all firms are born equal

Data on entrepreneurial startups in a set of ADB developing member economies show that, although only 0.4% of new entrepreneurial businesses had grown enough to have 250+ employees within 42 months, these firms provided 44% of new jobs created by this group. In contrast, 54% of all new businesses employed no more than two people and created only 9% of new jobs. Obvious questions ask what drives this heterogeneity and whether it is possible to design policy measures that effectively help new entrepreneurial firms fulfill their productivity potential and thus better contribute to economic development. This does not imply that micro firms are unimportant. Although their job creation is limited, they nevertheless provide an important number of livelihoods, particularly in situations where individuals may have few alternatives.

New entrepreneurial firms are defined as companies launched and owner-managed by individuals or groups of individuals. Table 2.3.3 shows that new entrepreneurial businesses vary considerably in terms of their dominant activity; their patterns of innovative activity; how locationally specific their activities, resources, and markets are; and their resulting productivity potential and ability to contribute to economic development. One type of entrepreneurial business is worth highlighting: new digital ventures.

Table 2.3.3 New and entrepreneurial business categories

Type of business	Description of the business	Specialization and innovation drivers	Location specificity of activities	Location specificity of demand	Productivity potential
Local service businesses	Low-technology service providers such as personal services, cafes and restaurants, transport services, and construction and maintenance services	Reputation based on service quality or price, location specificity, business premises, personal relationships, and branding	Highly localized, with local sourcing of resources and supplies	Highly localized	Low
Low- to medium-technology small and medium-sized enterprises	Low- to medium-technology manufacturing businesses operating in supply chain niches or manufacturing specific products, such as parts and component suppliers, furniture manufacturers, and the like	Mainly through process innovation in the form of specialized manufacturing assets and coordinated investment when the innovation requires complementary assets; also through product innovation and branding	Mainly localized supply chain relationships	Localized for supply chain interactions, but regional, national, and even international for specific products	Low to medium
New high-technology ventures	High-technology businesses that commercialize technology-based products	Mainly product innovation by translating advances in basic and applied research and development into new and innovative products	Typically dependent on localized spillover of knowledge from research-intensive activities and local specialized resources, such as specialized human capital	Typically national and international, sometimes even global	High
Software businesses	Software development businesses that code useful functionalities in algorithmic form, such as accounting software and smartphone applications	Product innovation in the form of codification of useful functionalities in software packages	Increasingly tapping spillover of knowledge and ideas not local but distributed through digital platforms; reliance as well on regional specialized resources such as human capital and funding	National, international, and global, especially if software is offered through application software platforms such as Google Play	High
Digitally enhanced service businesses	Businesses that rely on digital technologies and infrastructure to deliver and coordinate digital and other services, such as personal transportation and delivery websites, accommodation service websites, bookkeeping services	Business model innovation in the form of digitally enhanced, organized, and coordinated services	Tapping into partly localized insights regarding what works in terms of digitally enhanced business model innovation derived from business model experiments; reliance as well on regional specialized resources such as human capital, funding, new venture accelerators	National, international, and global, depending on the type of service, typically needing to connect with localized resources such as cab drivers, physical accommodation providers, and the like	Medium to high, depending on their ability to establish platform leadership

Source: Autio, forthcoming.

These enterprises come in two major forms: (i) new ventures that create software products and applications and software-based services delivered through the internet (sometimes called software as a service) and (ii) new ventures that leverage the internet and the digital resources obtainable from it to innovate new ways of creating, delivering, and capturing customer value (new business models).

Figure 2.3.4 shows employment by both baby businesses and established businesses at the time of the interview. Baby businesses are entrepreneurial businesses owned and managed by individuals and teams that had not yet paid salaries or wages to an employee in their first 42 months of operations. Established entrepreneurial businesses have been operating for longer than 42 months. Micro businesses in the smallest category of 1–2 employees including owner-manager(s) evidently dominate both samples. Among baby businesses, 53.7% qualified as micro businesses. Among established businesses, 53.8% did. In contrast, entrepreneurial businesses with 250 or more employees represented only 0.4% of either baby businesses and established businesses. Contributions to employment were dramatically different, however. While micro businesses generated 8.8% of total employment if baby businesses, and 8.7% if established businesses, baby businesses with 250+ employees generated 44.1% of employment and established businesses of that size generated 43.1%.

The same skewed pattern can be observed in entrepreneurial businesses offering new products that are unfamiliar to customers (Figure 2.3.5). Among baby businesses, 16.4% indicated that their product or service was new and unfamiliar to all of their customers. Among established businesses, 14.4% did. Among baby businesses, 34.2% indicated their product or service was new and unfamiliar to only some of their customers. Among established businesses, 25.0% did. Nearly half of baby businesses, or 49.3%, said none of their customers found their product or service new or unfamiliar, as did 61.0% of established businesses.

The survey confirmed that most new businesses are not innovative. Note that the threshold for qualifying as a "product innovator" was quite low, as it did not require patenting or formal investment in R&D. As most new and entrepreneurial businesses failed to meet even relatively soft criteria for innovation, it is plain to see how growth impact from new firms tends to be highly skewed within any cohort.

Figure 2.3.4 A few firms providing a disproportionate share of employment

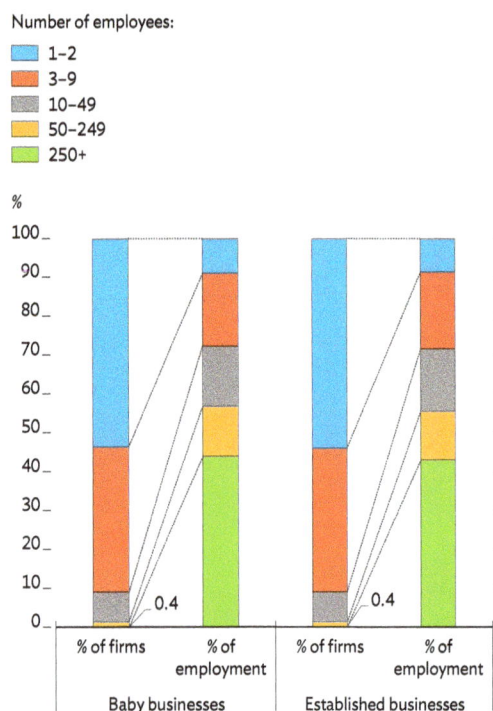

Note: Data cover 2006–2016 in Bangladesh; Georgia; Hong Kong, China; India; Indonesia; Kazakhstan; Malaysia; Pakistan; the People's Republic of China; the Philippines; the Republic of Korea; Singapore; Taipei,China; Thailand; Tonga; Vanuatu; and Viet Nam.
Source: Autio, forthcoming.

Figure 2.3.5 Less than one-sixth of businesses are product innovators

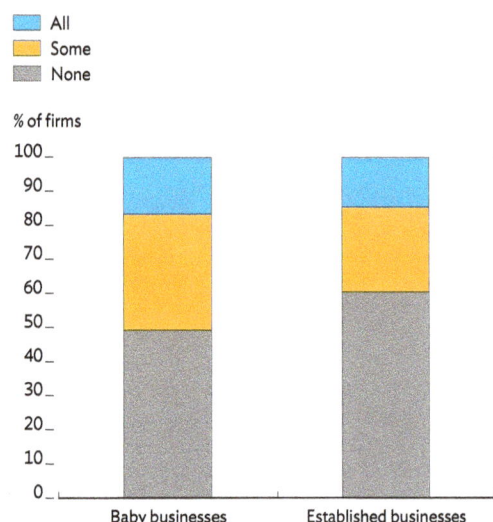

Note: Data cover 2006–2016 in Bangladesh; Georgia; Hong Kong, China; India; Indonesia; Kazakhstan; Malaysia; Pakistan; the People's Republic of China; the Philippines; the Republic of Korea; Singapore; Taipei,China; Thailand; Tonga; Vanuatu; and Viet Nam.
Source: Autio, forthcoming.

In a weak institutional environment, entrepreneurs choose informality

Whether or not an entrepreneurial firm has formally registered is a good proxy of its productivity potential because informal businesses are less likely to accumulate property and invest in innovation to grow their operation. A panel regression empirically assesses at the country level the impact of institutions, including entry regulations, on informal entrepreneurial activity—that is, the creation of new firms without entering them on business registers. Data from the Global Entrepreneurship Monitor and World Bank Enterprise Surveys are combined to construct country-level estimates of the population density of formal and informal entries.

Table 2.3.4 presents the results of three estimation models showing the impact on outcomes of interest from entry regulations, property rights protection, and the rule of law. Entry barriers include the number of registration procedures, the cost of registration, and the minimum paid-in capital needed to start a business in a particular country. Outcomes of interest are formal entry, defined as the population density of formal business registrations, and informal entry, defined as the population density of informal business entries.

The results in Table 2.3.4 support the notion that entrepreneurs choose informality if property right protection and the legal environment are weak. The number of registration procedures significantly influenced formal registrations but not correspondingly informal entries. Other dimensions of entry regulation had no significant effect, though one should note that the analysis focused on a relatively small sample of economies in developing Asia. The analysis nonetheless provides evidence suggesting that the rules of the game affect the allocation of entrepreneurial effort and, therefore, the productivity potential of new entrepreneurial businesses (Baumol 1996, Murphy, Schleifer, and Vishny 1991).

A large informal sector makes formal firms less productive

High density of informal entrepreneurial entries constitutes for formally registered entrepreneurs a negative externality because unfair competition undermines their willingness to innovate and grow their enterprises. This matters because fair market competition is a vital ingredient of innovation (ADB 2020). A cross-level regression that combines data from economies and firms explores the effect of the national population density of informal entrepreneurial entries and institutional determinants on the propensity of entrepreneurial firms to innovate, use new technologies, export, and expand employment. Data on product innovation, the use of new technology, and export activity is used to measure firm-level productivity potential, estimating the effects separately for baby businesses less than 42 months old and established businesses older than 42 months.

Table 2.3.4 Institutional influences on formal and informal entrepreneurship density rates

	(1)		(2)		(3)		(4)	
	Formal	Informal	Formal	Informal	Formal	Informal	Formal	Informal
Starting a business: number of procedures	−0.285** (0.102)	0.120 (0.251)					−0.279** (0.103)	0.284 (0.185)
Starting a business: registration cost (% per capita income)	0.002 (0.039)	−0.104 (0.114)					0.007 (0.041)	−0.137 (0.105)
Starting a business: paid-in minimum capital (% of income per capita)	0.016 (0.039)	−0.042 (0.112)					0.003 (0.043)	0.129 (0.115)
Property right protection			0.052 (0.076)	−0.345** (0.117)			0.067 (0.080)	−0.346** (0.115)
Rule of law					0.216 (0.183)	−0.401* (0.182)	0.242 (0.177)	−0.415** (0.159)
Population size	−0.058 (0.392)	−0.120 (0.186)	−0.241 (0.323)	−0.125 (0.124)	−0.378 (0.289)	0.006 (0.172)	−0.087 (0.355)	−0.021 (0.137)
Population growth (%)	−0.082 (0.060)	0.123 (0.127)	−0.154* (0.063)	0.230* (0.107)	−0.133* (0.062)	0.139 (0.115)	−0.086 (0.063)	0.190+ (0.101)
Development stage (second quintile of GDP per capita at PPP)	0.030 (0.137)	0.584+ (0.311)	0.039 (0.146)	0.906** (0.292)	−0.013 (0.152)	0.682* (0.294)	−0.019 (0.144)	0.923*** (0.277)
Development stage (third quintile of GDP per capita at PPP)	−0.090 (0.180)	−0.662+ (0.391)	0.104 (0.185)	−0.444 (0.354)	0.034 (0.187)	−0.333 (0.396)	−0.107 (0.188)	0.079 (0.390)
Development stage (fourth quintile of GDP per capita at PPP)	−0.281 (0.228)	−0.573 (0.465)	0.080 (0.210)	−0.224 (0.375)	0.038 (0.209)	−0.093 (0.436)	−0.275 (0.232)	0.589 (0.485)
Development stage (fifth quintile of GDP per capita at PPP)	−0.453 (0.327)	−0.831 (0.615)	0.232 (0.251)	−0.254 (0.462)	0.185 (0.250)	−0.226 (0.529)	−0.453 (0.330)	1.123 (0.689)
GDP growth (%)	−0.023 (0.026)	0.026 (0.084)	−0.023 (0.029)	0.070 (0.086)	−0.030 (0.030)	0.029 (0.082)	−0.036 (0.028)	0.067 (0.080)
Established firm rate (%)	0.022 (0.060)	0.416** (0.130)	0.017 (0.066)	0.365*** (0.109)	0.000 (0.066)	0.270* (0.134)	0.022 (0.062)	0.254* (0.117)
Constant	0.294 (0.390)	0.316 (0.312)	0.049 (0.347)	−0.009 (0.271)	0.095 (0.326)	0.008 (0.296)	0.345 (0.337)	−0.541+ (0.327)
Observations	58	58	58	58	58	58	58	58
Number of economies	11	11	11	11	11	11	11	11

* $p<0.05$, ** $p<0.01$, *** $p<0.001$, + $p<0.10$, GDP = gross domestic product, PPP = purchasing power parity.

Notes: Standard errors in parentheses. Data cover 2006–2016 in 11 ADB developing member economies: Bangladesh; Hong Kong, China; India; Indonesia; Kazakhstan; Malaysia; Pakistan; the Philippines; the Republic of Korea; Singapore; and Thailand.

Source: Autio, forthcoming.

The results in Table 2.3.5 show a negative association between informal entry density and new product development among both baby and established entrepreneurial businesses. Additionally, informal entry density suppresses new technology use among established businesses and export activity among baby businesses. The patterns are negative throughout, though not all associations are statistically significant.

For entry regulations, the number of procedures required to start a business had a positive link with new product innovation among established businesses, a negative link with their use of new technology (only borderline significant for baby businesses), and a negative link with export activity among baby businesses. The cost of registering a new business exhibited negative association with product innovation and export activity among established businesses. A minimum paid-in capital requirement meanwhile exhibited negative association with new product innovation and export activity for both baby and established businesses.

Table 2.3.5 Cross-level effects on entrepreneur innovation

	New product		New tech		Export	
	Baby business	Established business	Baby business	Established business	Baby business	Established business
Informal entrepreneurship (entry density per 1,000 adults aged 16–64 years)	−0.137** (0.045)	−0.158*** (0.035)	−0.015 (0.064)	−0.336*** (0.079)	−0.200* (0.084)	−0.000 (0.070)
Entry regulations						
Starting a business: number of procedures	0.162+ (0.098)	0.184* (0.079)	−0.219+ (0.129)	−0.461*** (0.105)	0.268* (0.116)	0.144 (0.088)
Starting a business: registration cost (% per capita income)	−0.045 (0.046)	−0.467*** (0.078)	0.059 (0.059)	0.072 (0.045)	−0.107 (0.068)	−0.410*** (0.118)
Starting a business: paid-in minimum capital (% per capita income)	−0.182*** (0.038)	−0.118** (0.041)	−0.036 (0.046)	0.036 (0.051)	−0.241*** (0.045)	−0.161*** (0.042)
Country institutions						
Property right protection	0.110+ (0.060)	0.339*** (0.052)	0.305*** (0.074)	0.645*** (0.091)	0.010 (0.101)	−0.074 (0.082)
Individual-level controls						
Gender (male = 1, female = 2)	0.028 (0.047)	0.049 (0.040)	0.149** (0.057)	0.050 (0.049)	−0.047 (0.067)	−0.150* (0.059)
Age	−0.065** (0.024)	−0.027 (0.021)	−0.143*** (0.028)	−0.155*** (0.025)	−0.016 (0.033)	−0.024 (0.030)
Income 1 (middle 33% tier)	−0.062 (0.059)	0.101* (0.051)	−0.020 (0.073)	−0.026 (0.061)	−0.012 (0.088)	0.017 (0.075)
Income 2 (upper 33% tier)	0.076 (0.063)	0.184*** (0.054)	−0.197** (0.076)	−0.024 (0.065)	0.377*** (0.087)	0.215** (0.076)
Education 1 (some secondary)	0.014 (0.093)	0.078 (0.068)	−0.131 (0.112)	−0.095 (0.081)	0.190 (0.148)	−0.012 (0.106)
Education 2 (secondary)	0.214* (0.085)	0.247*** (0.063)	0.111 (0.103)	0.144+ (0.076)	0.444** (0.138)	0.316** (0.100)
Education 3 (postsecondary)	0.386*** (0.090)	0.423*** (0.069)	−0.019 (0.105)	0.198* (0.084)	0.625*** (0.140)	0.421*** (0.104)
Education 4 (graduate experience)	0.632*** (0.139)	0.551*** (0.117)	0.373* (0.157)	0.188 (0.150)	0.784*** (0.193)	0.892*** (0.151)
Fear of failure (yes = 1)	0.147** (0.047)	−0.002 (0.040)	0.028 (0.057)	−0.047 (0.049)	0.039 (0.067)	−0.027 (0.057)

continued next page

Table 2.3.5 *Continued*

Country-level controls	New product		New tech		Export	
	Baby business	Established business	Baby business	Established business	Baby business	Established business
Population size	0.423*	1.309	1.415**	0.767	0.402	-1.303+
	(0.170)	(0.951)	(0.462)	(0.507)	(0.436)	(0.737)
Population growth (%)	0.115	0.218*	-0.102	0.238*	-0.011	0.358***
	(0.076)	(0.104)	(0.084)	(0.113)	(0.106)	(0.108)
Development stage (second quintile of GDP per capita at PPP)	-0.187	-1.888***	0.800***	0.451*	-0.367+	-3.394***
	(0.159)	(0.311)	(0.203)	(0.208)	(0.216)	(0.576)
Development stage (third quintile of GDP per capita at PPP)	0.191	-1.883***	1.633***	1.217***	-1.859***	-3.195***
	(0.185)	(0.321)	(0.310)	(0.212)	(0.318)	(0.614)
Development stage (fourth quintile of GDP per capita at PPP)	-0.098	-2.405***	1.196***	0.688**	-0.799*	-3.017***
	(0.222)	(0.334)	(0.337)	(0.223)	(0.397)	(0.643)
Development stage (fifth quintile of GDP per capita at PPP)	-0.291	-2.603***	1.867***	0.699*	-0.573	-2.701***
	(0.302)	(0.403)	(0.411)	(0.296)	(0.469)	(0.716)
GDP growth (%)	-0.084**	-0.222***	-0.042	-0.112***	-0.047	-0.045
	(0.032)	(0.027)	(0.035)	(0.033)	(0.041)	(0.034)
Constant	-0.685**	-0.184	-1.319*	-2.583***	-0.946+	0.103
	(0.237)	(0.579)	(0.531)	(0.619)	(0.503)	(0.717)
Observations	8,514	12,808	8,116	12,365	8,500	12,759
Number of groups	12	12	12	12	12	12
Observations per group: minimum	100	140	92	146	97	145
Observations per group: average	709.5	1067.3	676.3	1030.4	708.3	1063.3
Observations per group: maximum	2567	4689	2469	4618	2626	4711

* $p<0.05$, ** $p<0.01$, *** $p<0.001$, + $p<0.10$, GDP = gross domestic product, PPP = purchasing power parity.
Note: Standard errors in parentheses.
Source: Autio, forthcoming.

Finally, property right protection displayed positive association with both new product innovation and new technology use for both baby and established businesses. Among the control variables, higher educational attainment seemed to play a significant role in innovation, especially product innovation.

In sum, informal entry density appeared to have a generally negative relationship with innovative activity in new entrepreneurial firms. Onerous entry regulations broadly indicate negative links with innovativeness, though the number of required entry procedures deviated from this pattern. Property right protection showed positive association with new product innovation and new technology use.

The findings of the cross-level analysis broadly confirmed that an economy's institutional conditions regulate the productivity potential of new entrepreneurial firms, and that the economy's entry density of informal entrepreneurs constitutes a broad negative externality that dampens innovative activity.

This analysis provides rare direct evidence of cross-level effects of this density at the firm level.

While the broad associations confirm the importance of institutional conditions in shaping the productivity potential of new entrepreneurial ventures, the patterns revealed are not entirely consistent, pointing to a need for finer analysis with larger sample sizes and better firm-level controls.

Nonetheless, the key policy message is that broader institutional conditions matter and should be carefully addressed by governments seeking to enhance entrepreneurial dynamism and new firms' productivity potential. The next section examines in greater detail three specific elements of the institutional environment that innovators face: intellectual property rights, financial systems, and urban innovation clusters.

Conducive institutions and environment for innovators

This study has examined the role of human capital in spurring innovation in developing Asia, taking into account the intrinsically and fundamentally human nature of innovation. It analyzed the role of the education system and the entrepreneurial ecosystem in fostering an innovative culture that can encourage more Asian innovators. Notwithstanding the central role played by brilliant individuals in innovation, it takes teamwork, networking, and collaboration to transform innovative visions into reality. A well-known example is Steve Jobs working with Steve Wozniak and other friends to create Apple in a garage in a California suburb. More fundamentally, the most successful innovators do not innovate in a vacuum but rather within institutions and environments that foster innovation. Not even the greatest innovative concepts can get off the ground if innovators lack financing. Success may also be unlikely in the absence of adequate intellectual property rights (IPRs), as an environment lacking protection may deter innovators from investing time and effort in innovation. Yet another important dimension of the innovation environment is the availability of innovation networks, of which Silicon Valley is perhaps the most famous.

Intellectual property rights, innovation, and performance as an economy develops

IPRs take many forms, each appropriate at a different stage of economic development. The ROK is widely viewed as a benchmark for innovation among developing countries because it transformed itself from only one among many into a highly innovative high-income economy within just a few decades. The ROK experience can therefore be very informative about how IPRs evolve as an economy develops and moves up the innovation ladder. It can offer valuable lessons for countries in developing Asia that aspire to emulate ROK success in becoming a knowledge-based economy.

In such an economy, technological innovation and intellectual capital are important determinants of economic growth. IPRs are among the most powerful intangible assets that determine a firm's productive capacity. Lee (2013) referred to this capability to explain the ROK and Asian experience in catch-up development. This approach can be considered an extension of the view crediting technology, whereby the accumulated technological capability of firms sustained ROK economic growth for several decades (OECD 1992, Hobday 1995, Kim 1997).

Figure 2.4.1 Registration of intellectual property rights in the Republic of Korea, 1970–2010

- Patent
- Utility model
- Trademark
- Design

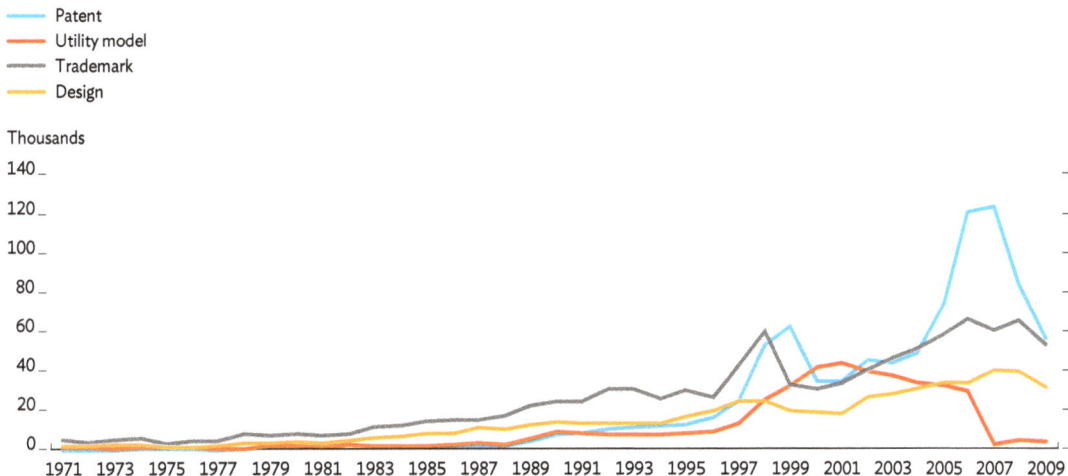

Note: Utility model registration rapidly diminished because that process changed in 2006 into an evaluation system. At the same time, patent registrations decreased because large firms such as Samsung and LG reduced their registration of patents with the Korean Intellectual Property Office. Since the mid-2000s, large firms in the Republic of Korea have applied for and registered patents with the United States Patent and Trademark Office instead, to better compete in the global market.

Source: Lee, Kang, and Park, forthcoming.

The data resoundingly confirm the conventional wisdom that the ROK engineered a spectacular transformation from a poor developing country into one of the world's most innovative economies. As latecomers and followers with limited technological capacity at the outset, ROK firms initially, before the 1980s, relied heavily on reverse engineering and imported equipment or machinery (Lee, Park, and Lim 2003). Then, after accumulating sufficient technological capability, ROK firms intensified their innovative activities, expanding the number of IPR registrations each year from 8,418 in 1971 to 145,927 in 2009 (Figure 2.4.1).

A recurring debate on the relationship between IPRs and innovation has been whether strong or weak protection better stimulates innovation (Maskus and Penubarti 1995, Smith 1999, Awokuse and Yin 2010). However, without innovation capability, nothing is produced even with strong IPRs (Lee 2019). Recent literature has correspondingly shifted focus from the effects of strong-versus-weak IPR protection on economic growth at different stages of development to, instead, the various roles of the diverse forms of protection, which include, in addition to regular invention patents, utility models, trademarks, and design patents (Kim et al. 2012). Conventional patent rights alone, for example, are not always effective in promoting innovation, particularly imitative innovation. Such issues need to be considered in developing Asia, which faces the challenge of managing its transition from imitation to innovation.

Existing empirical research on diverse IPR forms

Kim et al. (2012) showed that, in developing countries, simply strengthening patent rights does not promote innovation and growth, which is better promoted by minor IPR forms such as utility models, often called petty patents.[6] Lee (2019) and Kang, Jung, and Lee (2019) observed two different paths for technological development, one driven by patents, the other by trademarks. Which path to follow depends on the nature of business, some of which rely more on trademarks than patents. For instance, trademarks are more important when the innovation involves tacit knowledge that cannot be filed as patents, or when firms are more oriented toward domestic markets than world markets. The literature on trademarks regards them as expressions of the quality and variety of products (Block et al. 2015, Sandner and Block 2011) and as a measure of product innovation (Mendonça, Pereira, and Godinho 2004).

The shift from research into the strength of IPRs toward that which identifies the role of diverse forms of IPRs can be seen most clearly in Kim et al. (2012) and Kang, Jung, and Lee (2019), warranting a closer look at these two studies.

Kim et al. (2012) exploited data at the level of the country and firm to empirically research the effects of IPR protection on innovation and economic growth. It focused on the roles of two types of protection: patents and utility models. The results from both datasets are complementary. First, differences in economic growth and innovation can be explained in high-income countries by variations in patent rights but not by utility model rights. Second, the reverse is seen in middle- and low-income countries. That is, utility models help a developing country to build its technological capacity. Incremental, adaptive R&D generates innovations that qualify for such utility model protection and provide a foundation for becoming more sophisticated and eventually producing patentable innovations.

These results suggest that the correct goal for developing countries is not to ensure either strong or weak IPR protection, but rather to determine the appropriate kind of protection for their stage of development. However, this point is seemingly neglected in previous research and in current policy debates informed by it. Correspondingly, data on firms in the ROK show that, when ROK firms still lagged technologically from 1970 to 1986, incremental innovations had a positive impact on firm performance when controlling for other variables, but patents did not have a statistically significant effect. This finding strongly supports the view that utility models are a good strategy for growth in latecomers, particularly at the early stages.

In the period 1987–1995, when the ROK had already acquired greater technological and R&D capability, patents positively and significantly influenced sales growth, with utility model applications becoming insignificant. This exemplifies how a role reversal may occur after considerable technological competence is achieved, as firms rely less on minor innovations for their performance and increasingly on patentable innovations. Moreover, this suggests that utility model innovations can be important inputs toward generating future patentable innovations.

Kang, Jung, and Lee (2019) showed how dynamic changes in leading industries were reflected in applications for different types of IPR protection, with utility models and trademarks filed mostly in light manufacturing until the 1980s. Faced with challenges caused by macroeconomic factors such as rising wages and changing competitive landscapes with the rise of new rivals, ROK firms turned their attention to developing technological capability, from the mid-1980s especially in ICT. Corporate in-house R&D centers started to mushroom, and private and public R&D expenditure climbed steeply. As they globalized, ROK industries departed from the previous catch-up model based on imitative technologies and embarked on more advanced innovation.

This structural transformation was fully reflected in the transition from the early dominance of utility models and trademarks to the later dominance of patents. An interesting division between patent-dominated and trademark-dominated industries was observed. The former included electronics, ICT, machinery, and automobiles, and the latter pharmaceuticals and light manufacturing such as food, apparel, and leather. This pattern is even more visible in firm-level IPR statistics, in which trademark domination tends to reflect the nature of knowledge and the initially low or slow development of technological capability in areas such as pharmaceuticals, where firms have focused on the domestic market rather than exports.

The evolving role of design in innovation: New empirical evidence

The assertion that different IPR forms offer more appropriate protection at different development stages can best be illustrated by the growing importance of industrial design in ROK innovation. Perhaps because design is viewed as a less important dimension of innovation, in contrast to a new technology, design is the most neglected, least analyzed IPR form in economics.

Design (or industrial design) as defined by the World Intellectual Property Organization is the ornamental or aesthetic aspects of a product or service. Design is defined as "the shape, pattern, color, or any combination thereof in an article, which produces an aesthetic impression on the sense of sight." Design is an important way to add value to products and services and make them more competitive (Rothwell and Gardiner 1983). Designs make a product more attractive and appealing, adding commercial value and facilitating marketability. In addition, design is an important driver of innovation, acting as a bridge between technical and customer-oriented functions (Kline and Rosenberg 1986, Rothwell 1992, Walsh 1996). Appropriate design for a user-friendly feature helps satisfy customers.

Product differentiation is often achieved through better design. Moreover, technology gaps can be overcome by design. The relationship between the national economy and design can be discussed in relation to the stage of development of the national industrial strategy. Design is not important when the national economy is underdeveloped because growth relies on low wages enabling the mass production of low-cost goods. However, the importance of design increases as the economic structure advances. International competitiveness can be maintained only through product differentiation and quality improvement achieved through technological innovation and design development.

In the ROK, examples of the relationship between product competitiveness and industrial design can be seen in the electronics, rubber, and plastic industries. A case in point is Samsung Electronics.[7] This largest *chaebol*, or industrial conglomerate, in the ROK, founded in 1969, expanded its design center, Samsung Design, from a small group into, by 1981, a companywide R&D organization that declared in 1993 its renowned "new management initiative." During this period, good design was identified by the company's leaders as the critical element needed to excel in world markets.

The company declared 1996 "the year of design revolution" and the time to build a unique design identity. Samsung thereafter grew to become a global brand. Figure 2.4.2 shows the trend in the firm's design registrations and total sales since 1993. The emergence of Samsung Electronics as a highly innovative world-class tech giant—in fact, Apple's main rival in the global marketplace—coincided with its prioritizing, as a matter of corporate strategy, industrial design as a core ingredient of product differentiation (Box 2.4.1).

Figure 2.4.2 Design registration and sales growth of Samsung Electronics

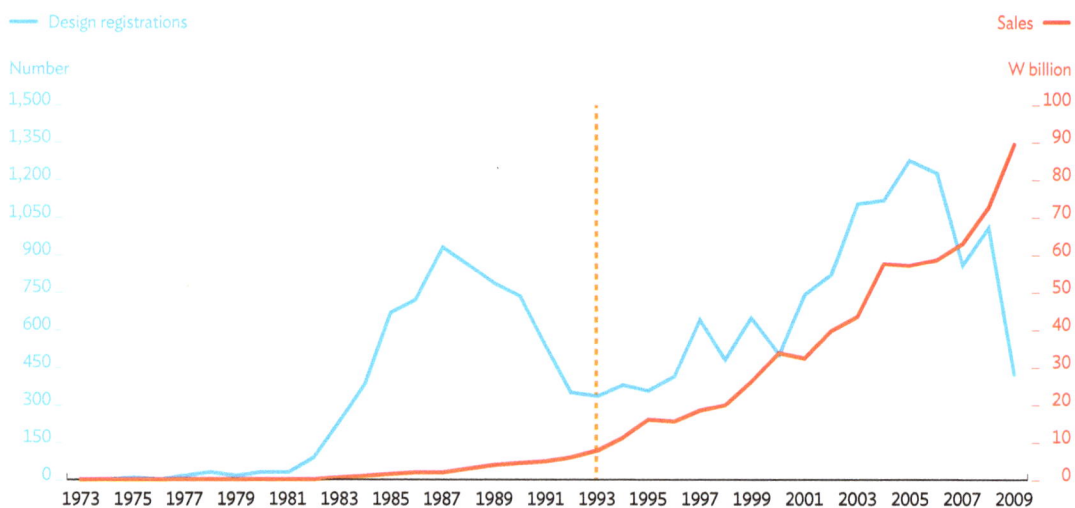

Source: Lee, Kang, and Park, forthcoming.

Box 2.4.1 The growing role of design and patents as economies mature

Lee, Kang, and Park (forthcoming) looked deeper into the role of design in innovation and firm performance in the Republic of Korea (ROK) at different stages of its development. For this purpose, the study built a rich firm-level panel database covering 7,094 externally audited firms in 22 manufacturing industries during 1971–2010. The database includes data for patents and design for all firms in the sample, as well as their financial variables.[a]

The sample period is divided into three subperiods that reflect important episodes in ROK economic history: 1971–1986, 1987–1998, and 1999–2010. Since the mid-1980s, the ROK has emphasized in-house R&D in the private sector, and considerable public–private joint R&D has been established to pursue projects (Lee 2013). In 1987, extensive revision of patent law included the introduction of substance patents. The Asian financial crisis of 1997–1998 precipitated major structural reform that had far-reaching effects on economic structure and innovative activity in the ROK.

To assess the effects of IPRs on each group and period, the study ran system generalized method of moments (GMM) regression with 1-year lagged variables, setting out the relationship between IPRs and firm performance, which was proxied by firms' sales growth (box table). A full set of year dummies was included to account for time-dependent overall effects in markets. Full sets of industry dummies were also included to capture industry-specific variations. The empirical specification is as follows:

$$Performance_{i,t} = \beta_0 + \beta_1 Performance_{i,t-1} +$$
$$\beta_2 Performance_{i,t-2} + \beta_3 Design\ intensity_{i,t-1}$$
$$+ \beta_4 Patent\ intensity_{i,t-1} + \beta_5 (Design$$
$$intensity_{i,t-1} * Patent\ intensity_{i,t-1})$$
$$+ \alpha_1 Advertisement\ Ratio_{i,t-1} +$$
$$\alpha_2 R\&D\ intensity_{i,t-1} + \alpha_3 Employees_{i,t-1} +$$
$$\alpha_4 Age_{i,t} + \varepsilon_{it}$$

Evidence from firm-level analysis confirmed that sales growth was significantly associated with high design intensity. However, a positive relationship emerges only after firms attain a certain capability—in the ROK since the 1990s but not during the 1970s and 1980s. It should be noted that, in the early stages of ROK development, utility models or petty patents substantially shaped the innovation landscape.

System GMM regression to test links between design and performance

Variables	Period 1: 1971–1986	Period 2: 1987–1998	Period 3: 1999–2010
Sales growth (t–1)	-0.173***	0.027*	0.016
	(-2.926)	(1.935)	(1.519)
Sales growth (t–2)	-0.030**	-0.003	-0.002
	(-2.036)	(-1.264)	(-0.813)
Design intensity (t–1)	-1.108	1.909	0.627***
	(-1.068)	(1.029)	(2.747)
Patent intensity (t–1)	7.823	0.407	0.992***
	(1.291)	(0.720)	(4.243)
Export sector dummy	0.049	0.015***	0.018***
	(1.266)	(2.886)	(2.977)
Employees (t–1)	-0.109	-0.291***	-0.160***
	(-0.661)	(-3.870)	(-3.020)
Firm age (t–1)	-1.026	-0.052	-0.414**
	(-0.813)	(-0.411)	(-2.495)
Advertisement ratio (t–1)	0.145	0.019***	0.065***
	(0.912)	(3.572)	(6.835)
R&D intensity (t–1)	0.013***	0.003***	0.003***
	(2.929)	(3.583)	(2.874)
Constant	7.055	2.839	0.131
	(0.654)	(0.951)	(0.029)
Observations	1,880	15,093	38,177
AR2	0.5805	0.2003	0.8227
Number of firms	634	2,653	5,892

* = p<0.10, ** = p<0.05, *** = p<0.01, AR2 = Arrelano-Bond Test for second-order serial correlation, GMM = generalized method of moments, R&D = research and development.

Note: t-statistics in paretheses.

Source: Lee, Kang, and Park, forthcoming.

In the full sample of firms, design and patent intensities positively contributed to firm performance only in the last period. In sum, the evidence from ROK firms points to a growing influence from design over time, in conjunction with a growing role for patents.

[a] The dataset is the same one used in Kang, Jung, and Lee (2019). The IPR variables for each firm are retrieved from the Korean Intellectual Property Rights Information Service (www.kipris.or.kr), and accounting variables are data from the Korea Information Service Value (www.kisvalue.com).

Policy implications

Several policy implications can be derived from existing studies and new firm-level analysis that focuses on the design–performance link. The evolution of ROK innovation from 1971 to 2010 suggests that different IPR forms are more appropriate at different development stages. During the country's early stage of development, firms' sales growth was more closely associated with petty patents or utility models (Kim et al. 2012). During the post-1987 catch-up phase, two innovation pathways emerged: one oriented toward trademarks and for firms tending to sell mostly domestically (Kang, Jung, and Lee 2019), and one oriented toward design and for firms tending mostly to export. Since the 2000s and the globalization and maturing of the ROK economy, regular patents and designs have assumed greater importance.

The key takeaway for developing Asia is that industrial designs, petty patents, and trademarks can, like regular patents, be effective forms of IPR protection, but at different stages or for different industries. Finally, better design is an important way for firms to differentiate their products and compete successfully in global markets. The rise of Samsung Electronics as a world-class tech giant underlines the high value added by design in the innovation process, especially at later stages of economic development.

Financial architecture and innovation

Access to finance is indispensable to innovation, which is inherently costly and fraught with risk and uncertainty. There is almost no way of knowing beforehand which particular innovations will turn out to be commercially successful. It is even more difficult to predict whether an innovator can turn his innovative vision into a viable reality. Yet even the greatest inventions need financing to succeed. While Apple is widely associated with Steve Jobs, for example, the iconic tech giant would never have emerged without the bold, high-risk investment of Mike Markkula, who provided critical seed money and managerial support during Apple's embryonic phase. A crucial component of viable innovation is, therefore, a sound and efficient financial system that can channel resources to aspiring innovators.

This study now takes a close look at the link between finance and innovation through cross-country empirical analysis (Box 2.4.2). It asks in particular whether financial intermediaries such as banks or capital markets are more conducive to innovation—and, if markets, what kind? Given widely varying stages of economic development in developing Asia, an additional question is whether a country's income affects the analytical comparison of intermediaries versus markets.

Box 2.4.2 Innovation under various types of financing

To determine the influence of financial architecture on innovation, a fixed-effect panel regression was performed on the following model:[a]

$$y_{i,j,t+1} = \beta_0 + \beta_1 Equity_{it} + \beta_2 Debt_{it} + \beta_3 Bank_{it} + \rho Controls_{it} + \delta_{i,j} + \mu_t + \delta_{i,j,t+1}$$

in which the subscripts *i*, *j*, and *t* refer to a country, industry, and year.[b] The dependent variable $y_{i,j,t+1}$ represents innovation measured in different ways: the *quantity* of innovation, measured by the number of patents, and the *quality* of innovation based on how innovative and exclusive patents were, measured by the number of citations and independent claims. $Equity_{it}$, $Debt_{it}$, and $Bank_{it}$ are proxies for the development of equity markets, private debt markets, and financial intermediaries such as ordinary savings banks and other financial institutions, divided by GDP.

Patent data are from the US Patent and Trademark Office, and annual financial market development and other economy-level information are from the World Development Indicators database and its Global Financial Development database. The sample included 47 developed and emerging economies. Each economy had at least one patent granted by the US Patent and Trademark Office by March 2019 and a mixed financial architecture, combining banks and markets, during the sample period 1997–2016.

The results showed that financial structures in an economy mattered disproportionately to innovation by industry. In particular, the findings indicated that market-based financial systems, as represented by both equity and debt markets, had a positive and significant effect on both R&D efficiency, as measured by the number of patents granted (box table) and on innovation quality and exclusiveness, based on the number of citations and claims. However, intermediary-based financial systems failed to encourage innovation and even rendered lower-quality patents during the period.

Financial architecture and innovation

	Relative number of patents			
	(1)	(2)	(3)	(4)
Equity	0.017*** (2.74)			0.030*** (5.20)
Debt		0.041*** (4.10)		0.047*** (3.36)
Bank			0.008 (0.40)	-0.020 (-0.81)
GDP growth	-0.007*** (-5.03)	-0.005*** (-3.12)	-0.005* (-1.74)	-0.010*** (-2.93)
Population growth	0.001 (0.35)	0.006* (1.87)	-0.001 (-0.41)	0.009*** (3.49)
Labor	-0.049*** (-4.19)	-0.064*** (-4.43)	-0.053*** (-4.98)	-0.056*** (-4.00)
Export	-0.009 (-0.57)	-0.021 (-1.35)	0.004 (0.23)	-0.050*** (-3.01)
R&D	0.126*** (4.78)	0.154*** (5.14)	0.128*** (4.71)	0.155*** (4.88)
Export to the US	0.082 (0.76)	0.071 (0.66)	0.078 (0.76)	0.077 (0.74)
Observations	28,841	20,445	28,761	20,445
adj. R^2	0.912	0.912	0.912	0.912
Country–industry FEs	Yes	Yes	Yes	Yes
Year fixed effects	Yes	Yes	Yes	Yes

* = $p<0.10$, ** = $p<0.05$, *** = $p<0.01$, adj. R^2 = adjusted R-squared, FE = fixed effect, GDP = gross domestic product, R&D = research and development, US = United States.

Note: Robust standard errors are clustered by country and industry and adjusted for heteroscedasticity.

Source: Huang and Tian, forthcoming.

[a] This analysis is based on Huang and Tian (forthcoming).

[b] A fixed-effect approach combined with lags was adopted primarily to address the possibility of reverse causality. Note that country–industry fixed effects denoted by $\delta_{i,j}$ absorb any time-invariant difference across countries and across different industries in a country, and the addition of time fixed effects denoted by μ_t mitigates the variation of common trends in the economy over time.

Although the regional financial system has historically been centered on banks, capital markets now play a large and growing role and have rapidly expanded in the past few decades. Further, regional economies show wide variation in financial development and maturity, ranging from global financial centers such as Singapore and Hong Kong, China to less developed countries with only rudimentary capital markets.

Empirical analysis in this section has focused on the effect of financial architecture on innovation quantity and quality. But, as much as finance can affect innovation, innovation can also affect finance. Indeed, financial technology, or the integration of new technology and financial services, is currently reshaping the global financial landscape. It has potential to become a powerful agent for financial inclusion, which can contribute to inclusive growth.

Financing modalities analyzed in this section are by no means complete or comprehensive. Precisely because innovation is inherently risky and uncertain, financing innovation has given rise to more specialized forms of financing modalities that are more capable of mobilizing and allocating seed money. Silicon Valley is replete with sophisticated mechanisms for channeling high-risk capital. Venture capital is perhaps the best-known example today, having been among the first to emerge. With the financial industry undergoing rapid change, other revolutionary mechanisms are sure to follow.

Cities as engines of innovation

Urban agglomeration plays an important role in fostering innovation (Feldman and Audretsch 1999, O'Huallachain 1999). As shown above, economies in developing Asia are becoming increasingly innovative. At the same time, they are experiencing rapid urbanization. Urban innovation clusters or hubs can be powerful promoters of innovation. Silicon Valley, the birthplace of the global tech industry, is perhaps the best-known example. Some well-known urban innovation clusters in developing Asia are Shenzhen, Zhangjiang, and Zhonguancun in the PRC; Bangalore and Hyderabad in India; and Pangyo Tech Valley in the ROK. But is there a systematic relationship between innovation and urbanization? Most existing evidence on the effect of urban agglomeration on innovation comes from developed economies. Systemic evidence is lacking as to whether urban agglomeration affects innovation, and if so, what the channel might be for it to occur in the developing world, including Asia.

A few generally accepted assumptions, however, provide insight on the issue. One is that innovation tends to be concentrated in a few cities that serve as innovation hubs.

Another is how firms in larger cities tend to be more innovative. Finally, the presence of top-tier universities often helps to explain host cities' disproportionate role in innovation. These findings are discussed in greater detail below.

Emergence of innovation hubs

It is widely recognized in the existing literature that innovation tends to be highly concentrated spatially. Within a given country, there are generally a few cities that are innovation hubs. These hubs host a large share of the country's innovative activities—one that is typically disproportionate to its share of the country's population. For instance, Nieto Galindo (2007) found that over 70% of Colombia's innovations were concentrated in three main cities that together were home to less than 40% of the country's population. In the US, Moretti (2019) showed that the top 10 innovative cities in computer science were home to 70% of inventors, in semiconductors 79%, and in biology and chemistry 59%.

Similar patterns were clearly observed in Asia. Each city's share of firms reporting process innovation, product innovation, and R&D expenditure was calculated and then compared with its share of national population (Table 2.4.1). A city with a share of firms engaged in innovation that was higher than its share of total population reflected concentration of innovation. In the PRC, 10 cities were found to host 64% of the country's firms involved in process innovation, 72% of firms in product innovation, and 64% of firms investing in R&D, while together accounting for only 55% of the national population. The contrast is even starker in India, where the top 10 cities host 70% of firms involved in process innovation, 76% in product innovation, and 73% undertaking R&D, while together accounting for only 43% of the country's population.

Table 2.4.1 Share of urban population and innovative firms in the 10 most innovative cities in selected countries

Feature concentrated, %	PRC	India	Indonesia	Kazakhstan	Malaysia
Urban population	55	43	72	67	70
Process innovation	64	70	99	94	99
Product innovation	72	76	93	83	80
R&D	64	73	100	91	92

PRC = People's Republic of China, R&D = research and development.

Note: The 10 most innovative cities in each country are the ones with the highest share of firms that undertake process innovation. Each cell is the sum of shares of these 10 cities.

Source: Chen, Hasan, and Jiang, forthcoming.

Figure 2.4.3 plots the cumulative share of firms against cumulative population share in India, Indonesia, Kazakhstan, Malaysia, and the PRC—the five countries in the sample with the most natural cities, or urban conglomerations delineated without regard for municipal boundaries. Each data point in the figure represents one natural city, and the cities are ranked by their share of firms involved in each of the three innovation activities. All the curves in the figure demonstrate a Lorenz-type convex feature, implying consistent spatial concentration of innovation across different countries and innovation activities. In general, curves for Malaysia and India are more convex than those for the PRC, suggesting a higher degree of innovation concentration in those two countries.

The figure also shows that many large cities have high shares of innovative firms, indicated by segments with relatively long projections on the horizontal axis and slopes greater than 45 degrees. However, some megacities are shown to have disproportionately low shares of innovative firms, indicated by segments with long projections on the horizontal axis and slopes of less than 45 degrees. Kuala Lumpur in Malaysia, Jakarta in Indonesia, and Almaty in Kazakhstan all have shares of national population larger than their shares of innovative firms.

Greater innovation in larger cities

Having established how innovation tends to concentrate in a few cities, how does city size affect firms' innovative activities? And to what extent may this relationship be causal? The answers to these questions emerge from an investigation into the impact of urban agglomeration on a firm's propensity to undertake product innovation, process innovation, and R&D (Box 2.4.3).

Top-tier universities as catalysts of urban innovation hubs

What drives the disproportionate role of cities in Asian innovation? Among a number of potential channels are economies of agglomeration, access to markets and finance, and the clustering of the different skills that engender innovation. In light of the previous finding that human capital affects innovation, another channel worth exploring is the role of top-tier universities, which tend to be highly concentrated spatially. According to ADB (2020), modern technology clusters are often located near universities and research institutes. Universities, especially the top campuses, are pioneers in exploring the uncharted and leaders in pushing the knowledge frontier. Countries often allocate abundant resources to their top-ranked universities to boost innovation capacity.

Figure 2.4.3 Cumulative shares of innovative firms versus urban population

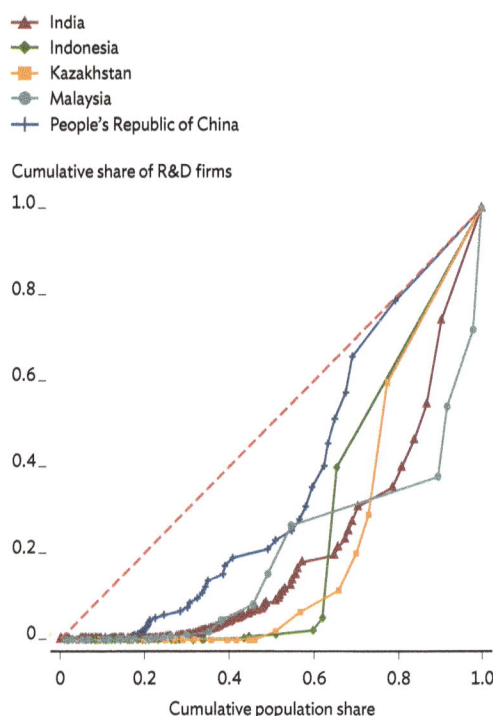

R&D = research and development.
Notes: Each data point represents a natural city, or an urban agglomeration delineated without regard for municipal boundaries. Natural cities are sorted by innovative firm share in ascending order. Population share is measured by the population in each natural city over the total population in all natural cities. The same method applies for innovative firm share.
Source: Chen, Hasan, and Jiang, forthcoming.

Box 2.4.3 How cities affect innovation

The econometric analysis is most appropriately undertaken by employing a probit model. However, endogeneity issues could arise in the baseline specification, biasing the estimated coefficients. One concern is that a city's size and a firm's innovation activities may be determined simultaneously (Moomaw 1981). This could happen if the innovative outputs of firms expand production scale, thereby attracting more employment to a city and reversing causality (Duranton 2007, 2014). Another explanation for simultaneity is missing local variables that correlate with both city size and innovation. For example, highly skilled workers at innovative firms could be attracted to large cities by amenities not adequately controlled in the regressions.

The box table shows that greater city size was still associated with a higher propensity for firm innovation even after addressing endogeneity.[a] The second-stage coefficients were significant at the 1% level, though the marginal effects became slightly different. For process innovation, if population size doubled, the predicted propensity for process innovation increased by 3.14 percentage points from an average propensity of 44.0%, or a 7.1% increase. For product innovation, the effect became smaller: an increase of 4.54 percentage points from a predicted average propensity of 32.6%, or a 13.9% increase. For firm R&D, the marginal effect was an increase of 1.84 percentage points from predicted propensity of 20.9%, or an 8.8% increase.

To summarize, after accounting for endogeneity, economically and statistically significant effects of city size were associated with its firms' innovation inputs and outputs. The average propensity for firms to engage in process innovation, product innovation, and R&D increased by 1.8–4.5 percentage points, or by 7%–14%, when city size doubled.

Instrumental variable estimates of elasticities of firm innovation–city population

Variables	(1) Process innovation	(2) Product innovation	(3) Firm R&D
First-stage estimates	log Population (2010)		
log Population (1950–1959)	.809*** (.0118)	.809*** (.0116)	.812*** (.0118)
Other controls	Yes	Yes	Yes
F statistic	5,713.3	5,707.6	5,714.8
Second-stage estimates			
log Population (2010)	.0796*** (.0295)	.126*** (.0302)	.0642** (.0306)
Marginal effect	.0314*** (.0116)	.0454*** (.011)	.0184** (.0087)
Predicted probability	.44*** (.0114)	.326*** (.0121)	.209*** (.011)
Sector/year/country FEs	Yes	Yes	Yes
Observations	17,838	18,903	17,673
Number of cities	285	287	283
F statistic	31.00	20.29	24.77

* = $p<0.1$, ** = $p<0.05$, *** = $p<0.01$, FE = fixed effect, log = logarithm, R&D = research and development.

Note: Robust standard errors clustered by country in parentheses.

Source: Chen, Hasan, and Jiang, forthcoming.

[a] The instrument used in the estimation was the average of a city's 1950–1959 population size. The instrument is quite strong, with first-stage F-statistics above 5. This further validates the first condition for the instrument.

Although patents, knowledge, and innovation produced by universities are often widely transmitted and adopted, evidence from developed countries shows that there exists a pronounced localized effect in the transfer of innovations from universities to firms. The presence of a university may enable localized knowledge spillover into firms' commercial innovations.

Of the top 500 universities in developing Asia, 248 are found in 99 cities in 9 countries (Table 2.4.2). The pattern that emerges is a high degree of spatial concentration of top universities. First, top universities are unevenly distributed across countries. Only 9 of the 25 countries in developing Asia have top universities, and 211 of them, or 85%, are located in only 5 countries: the PRC with 78, India with 64, Malaysia with 25, and Pakistan and Indonesia with 22 each.

Table 2.4.2 Distribution of top universities by country

Country	Number of universities	Number of cities with top universities	Number of cities in sample
Bangladesh	6	1	11
India	64	43	207
Indonesia	22	9	40
Malaysia	25	10	25
Pakistan	22	5	11
Philippines	6	2	11
PRC	78	17	74
Thailand	18	7	20
Viet Nam	7	5	17
Total	**248**	**99**	**416**

PRC = People's Republic of China.
Source: Chen, Hasan, and Jiang, forthcoming.

Second, universities are unevenly distributed across cities within a single country, more so in some countries than in others. Analysis found that 14 of the 25 top universities in Malaysia are located in Kuala Lumpur, and 12 of the 18 in Thailand are located in Bangkok, making them the second- and third-ranked cities with the most top universities in developing Asia (after Beijing, which hosts 20 of the 78 top universities in the PRC). By contrast, concentration is less intense in India, whose 64 top universities are distributed across 43 cities, the greatest concentration being 7 universities in Delhi.

High concentrations of both universities and firm innovation suggest correlation. To investigate whether firms located in cities with a large presence of top universities are more likely to innovate, a logit model was adopted with firm innovation activity as the dependent variable and a university dummy as the main explanatory variable. To account for the fact that cities with large populations and amenities tend to be ideal location choices for both innovative firms and universities, the model controlled for city characteristics including population, temperature, and other geographic factors. In addition, it controlled for fixed effects and firm characteristics that could affect innovation behavior.

Results showed that correlation between innovation and the presence of top universities was positive and significant. The odds that firms innovate in new production processes were 72% higher in cities with at least one top university than for firms in cities without any top universities (Table 2.4.3).

Table 2.4.3 Firm performance and top university presence

Variable	(1)	(2)	(3)	(4)	(5)	(6)	(7)	(8)
	Process innovation				Product innovation			
Top university	1.72***	1.6***	1.77***	2.11***	1.99***	1.96***	1.71***	1.32*
	(0.14)	(0.134)	(0.164)	(0.302)	(0.187)	(0.181)	(0.182)	(0.193)
Firm characteristics	No	Yes	Yes	Yes	No	Yes	Yes	Yes
City characteristics	No	No	No	Yes	No	No	No	Yes
Sector/year/country FEs	No	No	Yes	Yes	No	No	Yes	Yes
Observations	20,578	20,374	20,374	20,374	21,741	21,496	21,496	21,496
Number of cities	483	483	483	483	489	489	489	489
F statistic	44.08	45.64	29.54	27.54	54.55	24.54	20.15	17.80

* = $p<0.1$, ** = $p<0.05$, *** = $p<0.01$, FE = fixed effect.

Notes: Robust standard errors clustered by country are in parentheses. A logit model was used in all columns. Coefficients on top university are expressed as odds ratios. Process innovation is used as the dependent variable in columns (1) to (4), and product innovation in columns (5) to (8). Firm characteristics include firm age, size, a foreign direct investment dummy, a headquarters dummy, and the share of skilled workers. City characteristics include log of population in 2010, log of distance to port, average precipitation, maximum temperature, minimum temperature, and terrain ruggedness.

Source: Chen, Hasan, and Jiang, forthcoming.

After controlling for firm characteristics, sector, year, and country fixed effects, the odds were slightly higher still, at 77%. The positive effect of top universities on process innovation was even more pronounced after controlling for city characteristics, indicating that firms in cities with top university presence were twice as likely to undertake process innovation than were firms in cities without any top university. For product innovation, the correlation was smaller, with 30% greater likelihood of innovation, but remained significantly positive.

To conclude, both firm innovation and quality were highly concentrated spatially in particular cities. Firms in cities with top university presence were more likely to innovate new products and processes. Holding everything else constant, firms in cities with university presence were 111% more likely to undertake process innovation, and 32% more likely to undertake product innovation. Additional analysis indicated that greater top university presence is related to a higher likelihood of process innovation by local firms.

Toward a more innovative Asia

Innovation is an indispensable ingredient of economic growth and contributes greatly to improving the quality of life. Further, innovation brings a tireless parade of new technologies that improve on and replace old technologies. Currently, the Fourth Industrial Revolution, epitomized by revolutionary technologies such as artificial intelligence, autonomous vehicles, robotics, nanotechnology, and 3-D printing, is creating a palpable sense of excitement. For developing Asia, the current moment is especially opportune for examining the relationship between innovation and development. The region needs more and better innovation both to sustain growth by fostering productivity and to improve the quality of growth by making it more inclusive and sustainable.

It may seem that innovation and its impact on growth and development are relevant mostly to relatively advanced economies. Nothing could be further from the truth. Innovation is not limited to momentous new technologies that push the global technology frontier. Much of innovation is incremental and marginal, which may be less glamorous than self-driving cars but no less important for growth and the quality of life. Encouragingly, the evidence suggests that firms in less developed countries in the region are already doing plenty of such innovation. Further, ICT is opening up plenty of opportunities for innovative entrepreneurship in countries at all income levels. One prime example is Indonesia's Gojek, which started out as a motorbike taxi-hailing service but, in 2017 and again in 2019, joined the *Fortune* list of 50 Companies that Changed the World.

More generally, new technologies, most notably ICT, can enable less developed countries to leapfrog from obsolete to more advanced technologies by, for example, skipping over fixed-line phones by going straight to mobiles. This suggests that they can advance toward the global technology frontier in relatively short order. But leapfrogging remains a contentious issue, and it obscures the much bigger point: the need to get the basics right. As stated above, there is no shortcut to an innovative economy and society, no escaping the need to satisfy basic prerequisites for an innovative economy. For example, the exciting opportunities for innovation that ICT presents, especially for creative business models tailored to the local context, can never be realized without good ICT infrastructure, an enabling regulatory environment, and a workforce with solid numeracy and literacy, including digital literacy.

The first step on the journey to an innovative society must be to nurture a workforce that is capable of absorbing and utilizing more advanced technology from more advanced economies. This is what the NIEs did and what any aspiring economy must do. In addition to the NIE experience, growing innovative prowess in Viet Nam, where the education system produces superior learning outcomes as measured by Programme for International Student Assessment tests, attests to the central importance of human capital in innovation. A top priority in this regard is to build on basic education by creating a conducive entrepreneurial ecosystem that allows innovative entrepreneurs to flourish.

The education system must guarantee good basic learning outcomes. Despite stories about entrepreneurs dropping out of school to succeed beyond imagination, it is a pipe dream to think that individuals without basic literacy and numeracy can become innovators. The prerequisite of an education system that can produce a large pool of innovators is to get the basics right. Although some economies in developing Asia excel at delivering strong learning outcomes, others do not. In economies that fail, education must be reformed thoroughly with the objective of dramatically improving the quality of basic education. Strong basic education is one thing no country can leapfrog past because even the most creative thinkers need it.

A focus on learners nurtures innovators, as does an optimal skill mix. A growing body of robust evidence demonstrates that learner-centered approaches are superior to teacher-centered ones. Asian countries should therefore consider shifting their teaching practices to more student-centric approaches that encourage students to think for themselves. While the STEM quartet of science, technology, engineering, and math is certainly important for innovation, so are other subjects that develop creativity, such as art and design, or critical thinking, such as social science and humanities. In fact, individuals commanding a mix of disparate skills are key to driving innovation.

High-quality, innovative entrepreneurship needs favorable institutions. New entrepreneurial businesses constitute a potent force driving countries' productivity and innovation, particularly now in the digital age. This effect operates through business model innovation that challenges established industry incumbents. The evidence broadly indicates that strong property rights, impartial rule of law, and simplified entry regulations promote high-quality entrepreneurship. On the other hand, a high incidence of informal, unregistered businesses deters innovative businesses through potentially unfair competition. This suggests that fair competition and, more broadly, policies to promote competition can also promote innovative entrepreneurship (Box 2.5.1). National policy should focus on building high-quality institutions and a smooth regulatory regime to encourage more innovative formal entrepreneurship.

Box 2.5.1 Competition and innovation: evidence from the Republic of Korea

The quintessential example of a transition from an economic model based on investment to one based on innovation is the Republic of Korea (ROK). The ROK successfully leveraged an investment model until the Asian financial crisis of 1997–1998. From 1963 to 1997, GDP per capita in the ROK grew at an average rate of 7% per year. The pre-crisis model was structured around large conglomerates, called *chaebols*. The government supported *chaebols* through various means, providing preferential access to credit and bailout guarantees, and restricting domestic and foreign competition.

While this model delivered impressive results, the Asian financial crisis undermined the legitimacy of the model and opened the way for reform. Reform to favor competition had already been discussed, but without the catalyst of the crisis. The ROK undertook sweeping reform, restructuring inefficient *chaebols* and removing entry barriers for competitors and foreign investors. The antitrust agency strengthened enforcement, pushing the number of corrective orders up by threefold and financial penalties for anticompetitive behavior up by a factor of 25. Foreign direct investment quadrupled from the equivalent of 0.5% of GDP to 2.0%.

Pro-competitive reform opened the economy to competition. This revived economic growth, now driven by innovation rather than factor accumulation. In early 1990s, the ROK filed only an eighth as many patent applications with the US Patent and Trademark Office as did Germany. In 2012, it overtook a larger united Germany in terms of US patent applications and, in 2015, filed 30% more of them.

How did this transformation take place? Aghion, Guriev, and Jo (2019) undertook granular analysis of data from firms, using the censuses of ROK manufacturing firms in 1992 and 2003—before and after the 1998 reform—to analyze firm dynamics in industries formerly dominated by *chaebols*.

The results were consistent with the predictions of the Schumpeterian growth paradigm, which states that different types of institutions and policies promote growth at different stages of development. Before the crisis, total factor productivity (TFP) was stagnating or even falling, especially among *chaebols*. But after reform, rapid TFP growth resumed in both *chaebols* and independent firms (box figure). TFP growth was especially impressive in industries previously dominated by *chaebols* and thus most affected by reform. In those industries, firms outside of *chaebols* experienced notably rapid productivity growth. Further, the entry of these firms increased significantly in all industries after reform.

Data from firms on patenting activity confirm that reform promoted innovation, especially among independent firms. Before the crisis, *chaebol* firms had slightly faster growth in patent applications per year than their independent counterparts. However, after the crisis, the number of *chaebol* firm applications stopped growing, while patenting by independent firms accelerated.

All in all, the ROK experience suggests that fair competition and competition policy can facilitate a transition from growth led by investment to that led by innovation. This holds valuable lessons for the PRC and other middle-income Asian economies.

Logarithm of total factor productivity in *chaebol* and independent firms in industries with high, low, and zero *chaebol* share

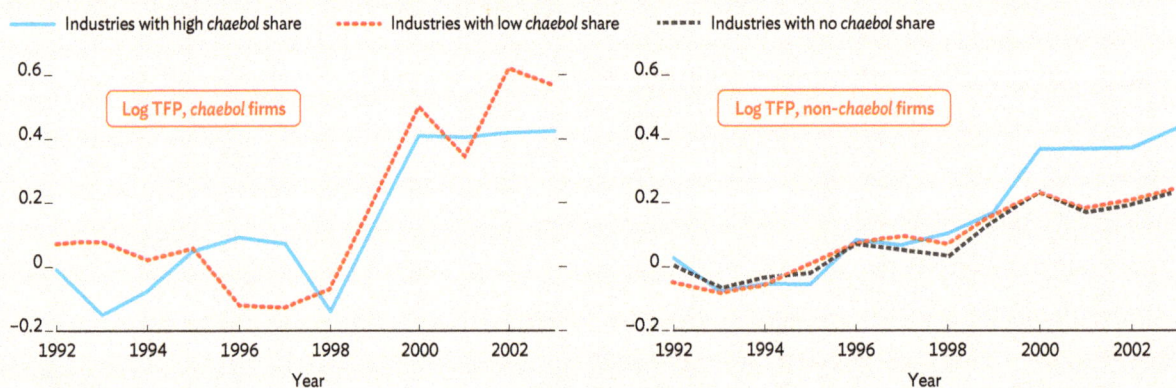

TFP = total factor productivity.

Notes: The figures are logarithms of average TFP in each industry after winsorizing the top and bottom 1% for the whole sample period in each industry category. Industries are classified by the average 1992–1997 *chaebol* share: high (above the 1992–1997 median of 20%), low (below median), and zero. Industry-level log TFPs are normalized by the 1992–1997 average = 0.

Source: Aghion, Guriev, and Jo 2019.

Digital entrepreneurs need better policies nationally and across the region. The focus regionally should be on nurturing and facilitating regional entrepreneurial ecosystems. Key principles include the following: (i) Adopt a bottom–up, facilitative approach, as opposed to a top–down, hierarchical approach. (ii) Seek close engagement with all stakeholders. (iii) Nurture close communities of entrepreneurs, accelerators, financiers, large businesses, mentors, public agencies, educational institutions, and regional agencies by serving as a secretariat. (iv) Sponsor open interaction and knowledge sharing among entrepreneurs regarding their business model experiments by promoting networking platforms. (v) Encourage active public–private interaction through systematic and institutionalized dialogue.

Although individual creativity and ingenuity are undeniably vital elements in the process, innovation occurs not in a vacuum but within institutions. Three key elements of an innovation architecture are intellectual property rights, an efficient financial system, and urban innovation hubs. Given the heterogeneity of Asian economies in terms of their innovation capacity and stage of development, the appropriate national innovation system will necessarily differ from country to country.

Different types of IPR serve better at different stages of development. There are four types of IPR: design, trademark, patents on core technologies, and utility or petite patents on incremental improvements. In the ROK, petite patents and trademarks initially provided the biggest impetus to firm growth, with design assuming a bigger role during the subsequent catch-up phase. As the ROK transformed itself into global innovation leader, patents became prominent. Therefore, not only patents but also design protection and trademarks can be effective forms of IPR. The ROK experience strengthens the case for a nuanced approach to IPR policy.

Equity and other capital markets are key to financing innovation. Analysis of industry-level patent data from 47 economies in 1997–2016 reveals that financial structures matter disproportionately to innovation. More precisely, both equity and debt markets have positive and significant effects on R&D efficiency, as measured by the number of patents granted, but capital markets also have a positive and significant effect on innovation quality. The effect is more pronounced and robust for equity markets. The obvious implication for Asian economies is to continue to develop their capital markets.

Evidence reconfirms the importance of cities as engines of innovation. Innovation tends to be concentrated in relatively few cities that serve as innovation hubs. Across Asia, the spatial concentration of innovation can be seen in product innovation, process innovation, and R&D. In addition, firms in larger cities tend to be more innovative.

Even after accounting for potential endogeneity, city size has a significant effect on innovative activity. Finally, the presence and number of top-tier universities in a city seems to have a positive impact on the propensity of the city's firms to pursue innovation. This finding underlines the importance of high-quality education in promoting innovation.

Institutions and policy must evolve with economic development. Each country has a unique national innovation system to cope with market failures and complement its successes according to its innovation capability. While such systems may have served innovation well in the past, they may stop doing so as a country's capability matures. The government should play a direct and leading role in the national innovation system at early stages of development but only an indirect and supportive role when the private sector assumes a bigger role. Yet, evidence is mixed on how effective activist innovation policy is. The subsidies of Innofund, a PRC government fund dedicated to supporting technology-based small and medium-sized enterprises, seem to have only a limited effect on innovative output (Li, Liu, and Gentile, forthcoming). This highlights that government intervention needs to be nuanced.

Beyond ensuring an enabling environment, governments can catalyze. Governments play a major direct role in innovation, accounting for a substantial share of R&D. The government share of economy-wide R&D from 1996 to 2017 was 24% in the ROK, 23% in the PRC, and 42% in Viet Nam. Government R&D tends to carry out basic research with large potential for spillover, while private sector research centers on commercial applications (Bernanke 2011). The internet is a classic example. Although much of the basic technology came from government laboratories, the countless innovations that it spawned and that made the internet what it is today came predominantly from the private sector. Plenty of scope exists for innovation within the public sector to improve the products and processes offered by governments. Public sector innovation labs such as those in Armenia and Sri Lanka can promote experimentation and openness to new approaches (Roth, Mohamed Asmi, and Husar, forthcoming).

Finally, there are no short cuts to the creation of an innovative society. The task is a long-term commitment requiring a lot of hard work. Similarly, education systems that aim to nurture innovation cannot leapfrog the stage of instilling strong basic skills, notably literacy and numeracy. However, Asia's past record and robust fundamentals suggest that it can and will dedicate the time and effort it takes to become a more innovative region.

Endnotes

1 First published in 1992, the *Oslo Manual* is the international reference guide for collecting and using data on innovation. The most recent edition, published in 2018, considers a broader range of innovation-related phenomena and the experience gained from recent rounds of innovation surveys in member countries of the Organisation for Economic Co-operation and Development (OECD) and partner economies and organizations.

2 An increase in one input while holding other inputs constant will initially increase output but then will generate lower returns per unit the more that one input is increased. In other words, increasing one factor of production while keeping the other factors constant is not productive past a certain point.

3 Most surveys that collect data on innovation, including World Bank Enterprise Surveys, are based on the *Oslo Manual*. The *Oslo Manual 2005* divides innovation into four main subtypes: (i) *Product innovation* is the introduction of a good or service that is new or significantly improved with respect to its characteristics or intended uses. (ii) *Process innovation* is the implementation of a new or significantly improved production or delivery method. (iii) *Marketing innovation* is the implementation of a new method of distribution involving significant changes in product design or packaging, placement, promotion, or pricing. (iv) *Organizational innovation* is the implementation of new firm business practices, workplace arrangements, or external relations.

4 Five countries in the Pacific—Fiji, Micronesia, Samoa, Tonga, and Vanuatu—are excluded from innovation variables for lack of data.

5 These terms follow Rosing et al. (2011). Other authors have used "creating" and "implementing" or "exploring" and "exploiting" to describe similar concepts (Bledow et al. 2009).

6 Whereas patents protect innovations that are highly inventive, utility models protect those that are less so. The latter offer second-tier protection for minor inventions that exhibit a practical or functional advantage over existing ones. Utility models are usually sought for small, marginal innovations that may not meet criteria for a patent (Bently and Sherman 2001, Beneito 2006).

7 http://www.design.samsung.com/global/contents/design-history/index.html.

Background papers

Autio, E., K. Fu, and J. Levie. Forthcoming. *Entrepreneurship as a Driver of Innovation in the Digital Age.* Asian Development Bank.

Chen, L., R. Hasan, and Y. Jiang. Forthcoming. *Urban Agglomeration and Firm Innovation: Evidence from Asia.* Asian Development Bank.

Huang, Z. and X. Tian. Forthcoming. *Does One Size Fit All? Financial Architecture and Innovation in the 21st Century.* Asian Development Bank.

Khatiwada, S. and R. M. Arao. Forthcoming(a). *Human Capital and Innovation at the Firm-Level.* Asian Development Bank.

——. Forthcoming(b). *Landscape of Innovation in Developing Asia: Firm-Level Perspective.* Asian Development Bank.

Lee, K., R. Kang, and D. Park. Forthcoming. *Diverse Forms of Intellectual Property Rights, Innovations, and Firm Performance at Different Stages of Development: Findings from the Firm-Level Study in the Republic of Korea, 1970s–2010s.* Asian Development Bank.

Li, J., C. Liu, and E. Gentile. Forthcoming. *The Effects of the Innofund Program on Technology-Based SMEs' Performance: Evidence from Zhongguancun National Innovation Demonstration Zone (ZNID).* Asian Development Bank.

Luan, F. S., Y. Chen, M. He, and D. Park. Forthcoming. *Is City Innovation Accumulative?* Asian Development Bank.

Newman, K., E. Gentile, and N. A. Dela Cruz. Forthcoming. *Education for Innovation: Sorting Fact from Fiction.* Asian Development Bank.

Park, T. and J. Kim. Forthcoming. *Innovation Policy in Asia.* Asian Development Bank.

Qureshi, I., D. Park, G. A. Crespi, and J. M. Benavente. Forthcoming. *Trends and Determinants of Innovation in Asia-Pacific and Latin America and the Caribbean.* Asian Development Bank.

All background papers are available at
https://www.adb.org/documents/asian-development-outlook-2020-background-papers

Background notes

Aghion, P., S. Guriev, and K. Jo. 2019. Chaebols and Firm Dynamics in the Republic of Korea. *CEPR Discussion Paper* 13825. Centre for Economic Policy Research.

Allen, E., P. Aji, and Y. Basnett. Forthcoming. *Catch up Innovation: A Stratified Approach to Support Technology Upgrading of Firms in Indonesia.* Asian Development Bank.

Autio, E. Forthcoming. *Large and Small Firm Roles in Innovation.* Asian Development Bank.

Cameron, C. Forthcoming. *Build Digital Societies*. Asian Development Bank.

Huang, B. Forthcoming. *Financing for Innovation*. Asian Development Bank.

Kim, J. and C. Castillejos-Petalcorin. Forthcoming. *Bottom of the Pyramid Innovation in Asia*. Asian Development Bank.

——. Forthcoming. *The Role of Government R&D in Fostering Innovation in Asia*. Asian Development Bank.

Kim, K. Forthcoming. *e-Mobility—A Promising Option for Reducing GHG in Transport Sector*. Asian Development Bank.

Nair, R. and J. E. Corpus. Forthcoming. *Incubating Future Innovators and Entrepreneurs*. Asian Development Bank.

Qureshi, I. Forthcoming. *Competition Policy and Innovation*. Asian Development Bank.

——. Forthcoming. *Frontier vs. Catch-up Innovation*. Asian Development Bank.

Rohrbeck, R., O. Kokshagina, and S. Roth. Forthcoming. *Vertical Innovation Industry Development to Enable Leapfrogging, Superior Competitiveness and Innovation*. Asian Development Bank.

Roth, S., Y. B. Mohamed Asmi, and A. Husar. Forthcoming. *Accelerating Innovation through Public Sector Innovation Labs and Vertical Industry Development Models*. Asian Development Bank.

Särkioja, T. Forthcoming. *Viet Nam's Digital Transformation is Driven by Policies Fostering Innovation and Start-ups*. Asian Development Bank.

Schweiger, H. and A. Stepanov. Forthcoming. *Innovation in Emerging Europe*. Asian Development Bank.

Tian, S. Forthcoming. *Innovation in the Financial Sector*. Asian Development Bank.

Yoon, S. Forthcoming. *e-Government and the Efficiency of Public Service*. Asian Development Bank.

Zhai, Y. and Y. Lee. Forthcoming. *Solving the Energy Trilemma through Innovation*. Asian Development Bank.

All background notes are available at https://www.adb.org/documents/asian-development-outlook-2020-background-papers

References

Acs, Z., L. Anselin, and A. Varga. 2002. Patents and Innovation Counts as Measures of Regional Production of New Knowledge. *Research Policy* 31(7).

ADB. 2014. *Innovative Asia: Advancing the Knowledge-Based Economy*. Asian Development Bank. https://www.adb.org/sites/default/files/publication/41752/innovative-asia-knowledge-based-economy.pdf.

——. 2017. *Asian Development Outlook (ADO) 2017: Transcending the Middle-Income Challenge.* Asian Development Bank. https://www.adb.org/sites/default/files/publication/237761/ado-2017.pdf.

——. 2018. *Inclusive Green Growth Index: A New Benchmark for Quality of Growth.* Asian Development Bank. https://www.adb.org/sites/default/files/publication/462801/inclusive-green-growth-index.pdf.

——. 2020. *Asia's Journey to Prosperity: Policy, Market, and Technology Over 50 Years.* Asian Development Bank. https://www.adb.org/sites/default/files/publication/549191/asias-journey-prosperity.pdf.

Aghion, P., N. Bloom, R. Blundell, R. Griffith, and P. Howitt. 2005. Competition and Innovation: An Inverted-U Relationship. *The Quarterly Journal of Economics* 120(2).

Aghion, P., W. Carlin, and M. E. Schaffer. 2002. Competition, Innovation and Growth in Transition: Exploring the Interactions between Policies. *William Davidson Institute Working Paper.* No. 501. DOI: https://ssrn.com/abstract=311407 or http://dx.doi.org/10.2139/ssrn.311407.

Aghion, P. and P. Howitt. 1992. A Model of Growth through Creative Destruction. *Econometrica* 60(2).

Aldridge, J. M., B. J. Fraser, P. C. Taylor, and C. C. Chen. 2000. *International Journal of Science Education* 22(1).

Almeida, R. and A. M. Fernandes. 2008. Openness and Technological Innovations in Developing Countries: Evidence from Firm-Level Surveys. *The Journal of Development Studies* 44(5).

Andersen, A. D., A. Marìn, and E. O. Simensen. 2018. Innovation in Natural Resource-Based Industries: A Pathway to Development? Introduction to Special Issue. *Innovation and Development* 8(1). DOI: 10.1080/2157930X.2018.1439293.

ASER Centre. 2018. *Annual Status of Education Report (Rural) 2018.* New Delhi, India. http://img.asercentre.org/docs/ASER%202018/Release%20Material/aserreport2018.pdf.

ASER Pakistan Secretariat. 2019. *Annual Status of Education Report (ASER) Pakistan 2018.* http://aserpakistan.org/document/aser/2018/reports/national/ASER_National_2018.pdf.

Awokuse, T. O. and H. Yin. 2010. Intellectual Property Rights Protection and the Surge in FDI in China. *Journal of Comparative Economics* 38(2).

Ayyagari, M., A. Demirgüç-Kunt, and V. Maksimovic. 2011. Firm Innovation in Emerging Markets: The Role of Finance, Governance, and Competition. *Journal of Financial and Quantitative Analysis* 46(6).

Baer, M. and M. Frese. 2003. Innovation is not Enough: Climates for Initiative and Psychological Safety, Process Innovations, and Firm Performance. *Journal of Organizational Behavior: The International Journal of Industrial, Occupational and Organizational Psychology and Behavior* 24(1).

Barro, R. J. 1990. Government Spending in a Simple Model of Endogeneous Growth. *Journal of Political Economy* 98(5, Part 2).

Barsh, J., M. M. Capozzi, and J. Davidson. 2008. Leadership and Innovation. *McKinsey Quarterly* 1.

Baumol, W. J. 1996. Entrepreneurship: Productive, Unproductive, and Destructive. *Journal of Business Venturing* 11(1).

Beneito, P. 2006. The Innovative Performance of In-house and Contracted R&D in terms of Patents and Utility Models. *Research Policy* 35(4).

Bently, L. and B. Sherman. 2001. *Intellectual Property Law.* Oxford University Press, England.

Bernanke, B. S. 2011. Promoting Research and Development: The Goverment's Role. *Issues in Science and Technology* 27(4).

Birch, D., A. Haggerty, and W. Parsons. 1997. *Who's Creating Jobs?* Cognetics.

Bledow, R., M. Frese, N. Anderson, M. Erez, and J. Farr. 2009. A Dialectic Perspective on Innovation: Conflicting Demands, Multiple Pathways, and Ambidexterity. *Industrial and Organizational Psychology* 2(3).

Block, J. H., C. O. Fisch, A. Hahn, and P. G. Sandner. 2015. Why Do SMEs File Trademarks? Insights from Firms in Innovative Industries. *Research Policy* 44(10).

Bloom, N., J. Van Reenen, and H. Williams. 2019. A Toolkit of Policies to Promote Innovation. *Journal of Economic Perspectives* 33(3).

Borensztein, E., J. De Gregorio, and J. W. Lee. 1998. How Does Foreign Direct Investment Affect Economic Growth? *Journal of International Economics* 45(1).

Brazdauskas, M. 2015. Promoting Student Innovation-Driven Thinking and Creative Problem Solving for Sustainability and Corporate Social Responsibility. *Innovation* 1.

Brinkmann, S. 2019. Teachers' Beliefs and Educational Reform in India: From "Learner-Centred" to "Learning-Centred" Education. *Comparative Education* 55(1).

Brown, K. L. 2003. From Teacher-Centered to Learner-Centered Curriculum: Improving Learning in Diverse Classrooms. *Education* 124.

Burpitt, W. J. and W. J. Bigoness. 1997. Leadership and Innovation among Teams: The Impact of Empowerment. *Small Group Research* 28(3).

Calestous, J. and Y. C. Lee. 2005. UN Millennium Project 2005. *Innovation: Applying Knowledge in Development.* Task Force on Science, Technology, and Innovation.

Care, E. and R. Luo. 2016. *Assessment of Transversal Competencies: Policy and Practice in the Asia-Pacific Region*. UNESCO Office Bangkok and Regional Bureau for Education in Asia and the Pacific.

Chataway, J., R. Hanlin, and R. Kaplinsky. 2014. Inclusive Innovation: An Architecture for Policy Development. *Innovation and Development* 4(1).

Christopoulou, M., A. Lakioti, C. Pezirkianidis, E. Karakasidou, and A. Stalikas. 2018. The Role of Grit in Education: A Systematic Review. *Psychology* 9(15).

Cirera, X. and W. F. Maloney. 2017. *The Innovation Paradox: Developing-Country Capabilities and the Unrealized Promise of Technological Catch-up*. World Bank.

Cirera, X. and S. Muzi. 2016. *Measuring Firm-Level Innovation Using Short Questionnaires: Evidence from an Experiment*. World Bank.

Cohen, W. M. and D. A. Levinthal. 1990. Absorptive Capacity: A New Perspective on Learning and Innovation. *Administrative Science Quarterly* 35.

Comin, D. and B. Hobijn. 2004. Cross-Country Technology Adoption: Making the Theories Face the Facts. *Journal of Monetary Economics* 51(1).

Dostie, B. 2018. The Impact of Training on Innovation. *ILR Review* 71(1).

Duranton, G. 2007. Urban Evolutions: The Fast, the Slow, and the Still. *American Economic Review* 97(1).

———. 2014. *Growing through Cities in Developing Countries*. World Bank.

Fagerberg, J., M. Srholec, and B. Verspagen. 2010. Innovation and Economic Development. In B. H. Hall and N. Rosenberg, eds. *Handbook of the Economics of Innovation* (2). North-Holland.

Feldman, M. P. and D. B. Audretsch. 1999. Innovation in Cities: Science-Based Diversity, Specialization and Localized Competition. *European Economic Review* 43(2).

Fischer, S., M. Frese, J. C. Mertins, and J. V. Hardt-Gawron. 2018. The Role of Error Management Culture for Firm and Individual Innovativeness. *Applied Psychology* 67(3).

Godwin, K. and N. Pickus. 2017. Liberal Arts and Sciences Innovation in China: Six Recommendations to Shape the Future. *Center for International Higher Education Perspectives* (8).

Griliches, Z. 1980. Returns to Research and Development Expenditures in the Private Sector. In J. W. Kendrick and B. Vaccara, eds. *New Developments in Productivity Measurements. NBER. Studies in Income and Wealth* 44. University of Chicago Press.

Grossman, G. M. and E. Helpman. 1991. Trade, Knowledge Spillovers, and Growth. *European Economic Review* 35(2-3).

———. 1994. Endogenous Innovation in the Theory of Growth. *Journal of Economic Perspectives* 8(1).

Hall, B. H. and J. Lerner. 2010. Chapter 14—The Financing of R&D and Innovation. In B. H. Hall and N. Rosenberg, eds. *Handbook of the Economics of Innovation.*

Hall, B. H., F. Lotti, and J. Mairesse. 2009. Innovation and Productivity in SMEs: Empirical Evidence for Italy. *Small Business Economics* 33(1).

Harrison, R., J. Jaumandreu, J. Mairesse, and B. Peters. 2008. Does Innovation Stimulate Employment? A Firm-Level Analysis Using Comparable Micro-Data from Four European Countries. *International Journal of Industrial Organization* 35.

Hobday, M. 1995. East Asian Latecomer Firms: Learning the Technology of Electronics. *World Development* 23(7).

Hubner, S., N. Tripathi, M. Frese, Z. Song, X. L. Kong, and T. Kaschner. Forthcoming. *Innovation in China, India, and Singapore: How Culture Affects Team Exploration, Exploitation, and Innovation Performance.* Publisher.

Kang, R., T. Jung, and K. Lee. 2019. Intellectual Property Rights and Korean Economic Development: The Roles of Patents, Utility Models and Trademarks. *Area Development and Policy.* DOI: 10.1080/23792949.2019.1585889.

Karlen, Y., F. Suter, C. Hirt, and K. M. Merki. 2019. The Role of Implicit Theories in Students' Grit, Achievement Goals, Intrinsic and Extrinsic Motivation, and Achievement in the Context of a Long-Term Challenging Task. *Learning and Individual Differences* 74(101757).

Katz, M. L. and C. Shapiro. 1987. R and D Rivalry with Licensing or Imitation. *The American Economic Review* 77(3).

Keller, W. 2004. International Technology Diffusion. *Journal of Economic Literature* 42(3).

Kerr, W. R., R. Nanda, and M. Rhodes-Kropf. 2014. Entrepreneurship as Experimentation. *Journal of Economic Perspectives* 28(3).

Kim, L. 1997. *Imitation to Innovation: The Dynamics of Korea's Technological Learning.* Harvard Business Press.

Kim, Y. K., K. Lee, W. G. Park, and K. Choo. 2012. Appropriate Intellectual Property Protection and Economic Growth in Countries at Different Levels of Development. *Research Policy* 41(2).

Kline, S. J. and N. Rosenberg. 1986. An Overview of Innovation. In R. Lindau and N. Rosenberg, eds. *The Positive Sum Strategy, Harnessing Technology for Economic Growth.* National Academy Press.

Kutlu, Ö., S. K. Kartal, and N. T. Şimşek. 2017. Identifying the Relationships between Perseverance, Openness to Problem Solving, and Academic Success in PISA 2012 Turkey. *Eğitim Bilimleri Araştırmaları Dergisi* 7(1).

Larson, E. 2011. International PhDs Will Drive Innovation into the Future. *Research Technology Management* 54(3).

Lederman, D. and W. Maloney. 2003. R&D and Development. *Policy Research Working Paper Series.* No. 3024. World Bank.

Lee, K. 2013. How Can Korea Be a Role Model for Catch-up Development? A 'Capability-Based' View. In A. K. Fosu, ed. *Achieving Development Success: Strategies and Lessons from the Developing World.* Oxford University Press.

——. 2019. *The Art of Economic Catch-up: Barriers, Detours and Leapfrogging in Innovation Systems.* Cambridge University Press.

Lee, K., D. Park, and C. Lim. 2003. Industrial Property Rights and Technological Development in the Republic of Korea. *WIPO Policy Monograph.* April.

Lewis, J. M., L. M. Ricard, and E. H. Klijn. 2018. How Innovation Drivers, Networking and Leadership Shape Public Sector Innovation Capacity. *International Review of Administrative Sciences* 84(2).

Lucas, R. E., Jr. 1988. On the Mechanics of Economic Development. *Journal of Monetary Economics* 22(1).

Mairesse, J., P. Mohnen, and E. Kremp. 2005. The Importance of R&D and Innovation for Productivity: A Reexamination in Light of the 2000 French Innovation Survey. *Annales d'Economie et de Statistique* 79(80).

Mansfield, E. 1980. Basic Research and Productivity Increase in Manufacturing. *American Economic Review* 70(5).

Marvel, M. R. and G. T. Lumpkin. 2007. Technology Entrepreneurs' Human Capital and Its Effects on Innovation Radicalness. *Entrepreneurship Theory and Practice* 31(6).

Maskus, K. E. and M. Penubarti. 1995. How Trade-Related Are Intellectual Property Rights? *Journal of International Economics* 39(3-4).

Mendonça, S., T. S. Pereira, and M. M. Godinho. 2004. Trademarks as an Indicator of Innovation and Industrial Change. *Research Policy* 33(9).

Moomaw, R. L. 1981. Productivity and City Size: A Critique of the Evidence. *The Quarterly Journal of Economics* 96(4).

Morck, R. and B. Y. Yeung. 2001. The Economic Determinants of Innovation. *University of Alberta School of Business Research Paper* No. 2013-645. https://ssrn.com/abstract=2277064.

Moretti, E. 2019. The Effect of High-Tech Clusters on the Productivity of Top Innovators. *NBER Working Paper* No. 26270. National Bureau of Economic Research.

Murphy, K. M., A. Schleifer, and R. W. Vishny. 1991. The Allocation of Talent: Implications for Growth. *The Quarterly Journal of Economics* 106(2).

Nieto Galindo, V. M. 2007. La Aglomeración Como Una Causa de la Innovación en Colombia. *Planeación & Desarrollo* 38(1).

OECD. 1992. *Technology and the Economy: The Key Relationships.* Organisation for Economic Co-operation and Development.

———. 2019. *PISA 2018 Results (Volume III): What School Life Means for Students' Lives.* Organisation for Economic Co-operation and Development. https://www.oecd-ilibrary.org/docserver/2f9d3124-en.pdf?expires=1584960998&id=id&accname=guest&checksum=DAB8CEF8E85A6254AA4E7E62599CC6C6.

O'Huallachain, B. 1999. Patent Places: Size Matters. *Journal of Regional Science* 39(4).

Prabhu, J. and S. Jain. 2015. Innovation and Entrepreneurship in India: Understanding Jugaad. *Asia Pacific Journal of Management* 32(4).

Raffo, J. D., S. L'huillery, and L. Miotti. 2008. Northern and Southern Innovativity: A Comparison across European and Latin American Countries. *European Journal of Development Research* 20(2).

Raghupathi, V. and W. Raghupathi. 2017. Innovation at Country-Level: Association between Economic Development and Patents. *Journal of Innovation and Entrepreneurship* 6(1).

Robson, P. J., H. M. Haugh, and B. A. Obeng. 2009. Entrepreneurship and Innovation in Ghana: Enterprising Africa. *Small Business Economics* 32(3).

Romer, P. M. 1986. Increasing Returns and Long-Run Growth. *Journal of Political Economy* 94(5).

———. 1990. Endogenous Technological Change. *Journal of Political Economy* 98(5, Part 2).

———. 2010. What Parts of Globalization Matter for Catch-up Growth? *American Economic Review* 100(2).

Rosing, K., M. Frese, and A. Bausch. 2011. Explaining the Heterogeneity of the Leadership–Innovation Relationship: Ambidextrous Leadership. *The Leadership Quarterly* 22(5).

Rothwell, R. 1992. Developments towards the Fifth Generation Model of Innovation. *Technology Analysis & Strategic Management* 4(1).

Rothwell, R. and P. Gardiner. 1983. The Role of Design in Product and Process Change. *Design Studies* 4(3).

Saidi, T., D. van der Westhuizen, N. Conrad, T. Mutsvangwa, and T. S. Douglas. 2019. Learning by Solving as a Pedagogical Approach to Inclusive Health Innovation. *Development Southern Africa.*

Sandner, P. G. and J. Block. 2011. The Market Value of R&D, Patents, and Trademarks. *Research Policy* 40(7).

Sawada, Y., A. Matsuda, and H. Kimura. 2012. On the Role of Technical Cooperation in International Technology Transfers. *Journal of International Development* 24(3).

Schweisfurth, M. 2013. *Learner-Centred Education in International Perspective: Whose Pedagogy for Whose Development?* Routledge.

Scott, C. L. 2015. The Futures of Learning 3: What kind of pedagogies for the 21st century? *UNESCO Education Research and Foresight Working Papers.*

Selznick, B. S. and M. J. Mayhew. 2018. Measuring Undergraduates' Innovation Capacities. *Research in Higher Education* 59(6).

Seyfang, G. and A. Smith. 2007. Grassroots Innovations for Sustainable Development: Towards a New Research and Policy Agenda. *Environmental Politics* 16(4). DOI: 10.1080/09644010701419121.

Smith, K. G., C. J. Collins, and K. D. Clark. 2005. Existing Knowledge, Knowledge Creation Capability, and the Rate of New Product Introduction in High-Technology Firms. *Academy of Management Journal* 48.

Smith, P. J. 1999. Are Weak Patent Rights a Barrier to US Exports? *Journal of International Economics* 48(1).

Solow, R. M. 1956. A Contribution to the Theory of Economic Growth. *The Quarterly Journal of Economics* 70(1).

Stern, S., M. Porter, and J. Furman. 2000. The Determinants of National Innovative Capacity. *NBER Working Paper.* No. 7876. September. The National Bureau of Economic Research.

Takayama, K. 2017. Imagining East Asian Education Otherwise: Neither Caricature, nor Scandalization. *Asia Pacific Journal of Education* 37(2).

Tan, C. 2015. Beyond Rote-Memorisation: Confucius' Concept of Thinking. *Educational Philosophy and Theory* 47(5).

Taras, V., P. Steel, and B. L. Kirkman. 2010. Negative Practice-Value Correlations in the GLOBE Data: Unexpected Findings, Questionnaire Limitations and Research Directions. *Journal of International Business Studies* 41(8).

Thongpravati, O., A. Maritz, and P. Stoddart. 2016. Fostering Entrepreneurship and Innovation through a Biomedical Technology PhD Program in Australia. *International Journal of Engineering Education* 32(3).

Toner, P. 2011. Workforce Skills and Innovation: An Overview of Major Themes in the Literature. *OECD Education Working Papers.* No. 55. DOI: https://doi.org/10.1787/5kgk6hpnhxzq-en.

Ueki, Y. and J. M. Guaita Martínez. 2019. The Impact of Engineers' Skills and Problem-Solving Abilities on Process Innovation. *Economic Research-Ekonomska Istraživanja.*

Ulku, H. 2004. R&D, Innovation, and Economic Growth: An Empirical Analysis. *IMF Working Paper.* No. 04/185. International Monetary Fund.

van Uden, A., J. Knoben, and P. Vermeulen. 2017. Human Capital and Innovation in Sub-Saharan Countries: A Firm-Level Study. *Innovation* 19(2).

Walsh, V. 1996. Design, Innovation and the Boundaries of the Firm. *Research Policy* 25(4).

Weimer, M. 2013. *Learner-Centered Teaching: Five Key Changes to Practice (2nd Ed.).* Jossey-Bass.

Wooldridge, A. 2010. First Break All the Rules: The Charms of Frugal Innovation. *The Economist.* 17 April.

World Bank. 2019. Ending Learning Poverty: What Will It Take? https://openknowledge.worldbank.org/bitstream/ handle/10986/32553/142659.pdf?sequence=6&isAllowed=y.

Wright, M., K. M. Hmieleski, D. S. Siegel, and M. D. Ensley. 2007. The Role of Human Capital in Technological Entrepreneurship. *Entrepreneurship Theory and Practice* 31(6).

You, Y. 2019. The Seeming "Round Trip" of Learner-Centred Education: A "Best Practice" Derived from China's New Curriculum Reform? *Comparative Education* 55(1).

3

ECONOMIC TRENDS
AND PROSPECTS
IN DEVELOPING ASIA

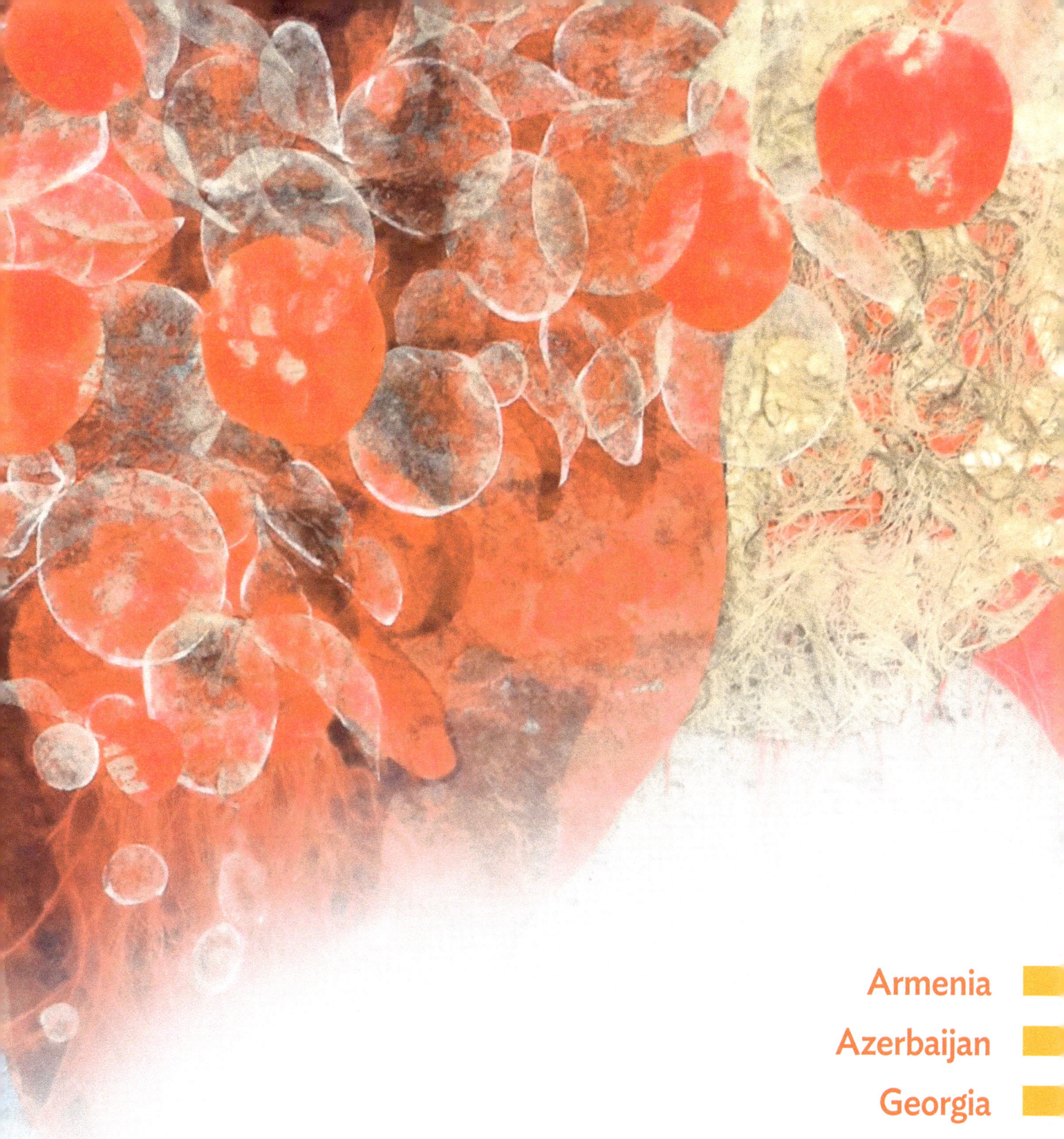

CENTRAL ASIA

Armenia

Azerbaijan

Georgia

Kazakhstan

Kyrgyz Republic

Tajikistan

Turkmenistan

Uzbekistan

Armenia

Growth accelerated in 2019 on stronger domestic demand. Lower import costs kept inflation subdued, and fiscal and current account deficits narrowed. Growth is projected to ease in 2020 under the adverse effects of the COVID-19 outbreak but recover in 2021. Inflation and the current account deficit are expected to rise slightly in 2020 before moderating in 2021. Boosting public investment is essential for inclusive and sustainable growth.

Economic performance

Growth accelerated from 5.2% in 2018 to 7.6% in 2019 on strong gains in services, industry, and private consumption.

On the supply side, growth accelerated in industry and services but not in agriculture. Growth in industry including construction almost doubled from 4.4% in 2018 to 8.6% as mining and quarrying recovered from a slump in 2018 and expanded by 21.3%. Manufacturing rose by 12.0% on continued gains in processed foods, beverages, tobacco, textiles, and nonferrous metal products. Construction grew by 4.2%, reflecting higher fixed investment, both public and private. Growth in services edged up from 9.4% in 2018 to 10.1% with gains in all subsectors but led by double-digit growth in finance, insurance, health care, recreation, accommodation, and food services. Adverse weather caused agriculture to contract in 2019 for a fourth consecutive year, by 4.0% (Figure 3.1.1).

On the demand side, private consumption underpinned the expansion while net exports dragged on growth, as did investment including changes in inventories. Private consumption grew by 12.7%, supported by recovering consumer confidence, higher consumer lending, and wage increases for selected categories of public employees. Public consumption was flat, in line with the government's conservative fiscal stance. Investment declined by 5.2% in 2019 as a 34.3% plunge in inventories offset a 4.7% rise in gross fixed capital formation. Exports grew at a faster rate than imports.

Easing global food prices, lower import costs, and a stable exchange rate trimmed average annual inflation from 2.5% in 2018 to 1.4% (Figure 3.1.2). Price rises for food slowed from 2.5% in 2018 to 2.1%, for other goods from 4.5% to 1.5%, and for services from 1.2% to 0.5%. The 12-month inflation rate from December to December eased from 1.8% in 2018 to 0.7% in 2019, well below the 2.5%–5.5% target band set by the Central Bank of Armenia.

Figure 3.1.1 Supply-side contributions to growth

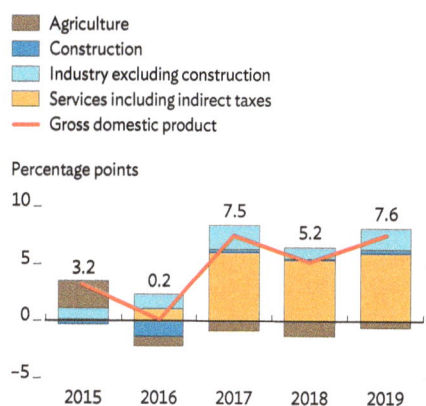

Source: Central Bank of Armenia. http://www.cba.am (accessed 25 February 2020).

Figure 3.1.2 Inflation

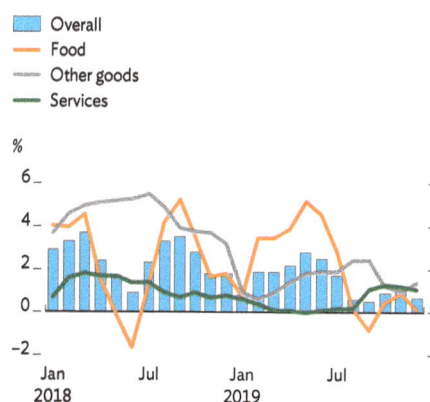

Source: Statistical Committee of Armenia. http://www.armstat.am (accessed 25 February 2020).

This chapter was written by Grigor Gyurjyan of the Armenia Resident Mission, ADB, Yerevan.

With inflation low, monetary policy remained accommodative to support domestic demand. The central bank relaxed its policy rate by 25 basis points in January 2019 to 5.75% and again in September 2019 to 5.50%. Broad money growth accelerated from 7.4% in 2018 to 11.2% last year as a rise in net domestic assets outpaced a drop in net foreign assets (Figure 3.1.3). Net domestic assets benefitted from an 18.5% rise in credit driven by higher mortgage and consumer lending. The decline in net foreign assets came as those held by commercial banks fell by 35.2%, more than offsetting a 39.4% rise in net foreign assets held by the central bank. A relatively stable exchange rate and attractive terms for deposits and loans in local currency helped reduce the share of foreign currency loans from 56.0% at the end of 2018 to 50.9% a year later, and that of foreign currency deposits from 60.4% to 57.6%.

Fiscal consolidation continued in 2019. The budget deficit narrowed from 1.8% of GDP in 2018 to 1.0%, well below the 2.5% target. Higher economic growth, improved tax administration, and increased nontax revenue lifted revenue by 16.2% to equal 23.8% of GDP. Expenditure grew at a lower rate of 12.2% to the equivalent of 24.8% of GDP, reflecting efforts to rationalize current spending and capital outlays that underperformed expectations. Capital expenditure was about 15% below target but nevertheless grew by 23.3% to equal 2.8% of GDP (Figure 3.1.4).

The ratio of public debt to GDP declined for a second consecutive year, from 55.8% at the end of 2018 to 53.6% a year later, as GDP growth outpaced a rise in debt (Figure 3.1.5). External public debt grew by 4.5% to $5.8 billion, equal to 44.2% of GDP, while domestic public debt rose by 10.9% to $1.5 billion. In September 2019, Armenia successfully issued its third round of eurobonds, which totaled $500 million and had a 10-year maturity with annual interest at 4.2%. This allowed the redemption of $403 million from its first eurobond issue, in 2015.

A smaller trade deficit in goods, relatively stable net trade in services, and a moderate rise in remittances helped narrow the current account deficit from the equivalent of 9.4% of GDP in 2018 to an estimated 8.0% in 2019 (Figure 3.1.6). The merchandise trade deficit narrowed from 14.4% of GDP in 2018 to 14.0% in 2019 as exports grew by an estimated 9.7%, reflecting gains in agriculture, processed foods, other manufactures, and minerals. Import growth moderated to 8.5% as lower imports of investment goods partly offset much higher vehicle imports. The service deficit narrowed, reflecting gains in finance and travel-related services.

Gross international reserves rose by 25.7% to an all-time high of $2.84 billion at the end of 2019, or cover for 4.9 months of imports, on the combined effects of the improved trade position, eurobond issuance, central bank purchases of foreign exchange, and public borrowing.

Figure 3.1.3 Contributions to broad money growth

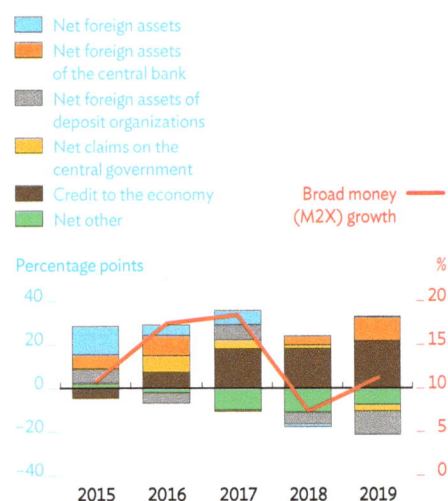

- Net foreign assets
- Net foreign assets of the central bank
- Net foreign assets of deposit organizations
- Net claims on the central government
- Credit to the economy
- Net other
- Broad money (M2X) growth

Source: Central Bank of Armenia. http://www.cba.am (accessed 25 February 2020).

Figure 3.1.4 Fiscal indicators

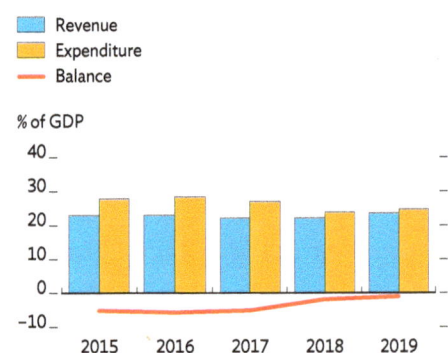

- Revenue
- Expenditure
- Balance

Sources: Ministry of Finance. http://www.minfin.am; Statistical Committee of Armenia. http://www.armstat.am (accessed 25 February 2020).

Figure 3.1.5 Public debt

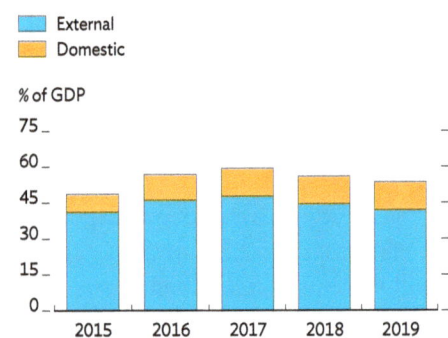

- External
- Domestic

Sources: Ministry of Finance. http://www.minfin.am; Statistical Committee of Armenia. http://www.armstat.am (accessed 25 February 2020).

The Armenian dram appreciated in nominal effective terms against a basket of major currencies by 17.2% in the 12-month period ending in December 2019, though real effective appreciation was by only 0.5% because of lower inflation (Figure 3.1.7).

Economic prospects

Reflecting the impact of COVID-19 on the economy, growth is projected to slow to 2.2% in 2020 with less rapid expansion in consumption, then edge up to 4.5% in 2021 as reforms initiated in 2019 and 2020 take hold and improve infrastructure, human capital, finance, and public administration (Figure 3.1.8). Planned increases in capital spending over the medium term are seen as supporting growth.

On the supply side, industry and services are expected to be the main drivers of growth. Industry including construction is projected to grow by 1.4% in 2020 and 4.0% in 2021, supported by further expansion in manufacturing and in particular food processing, while expansion in mining and quarrying should moderate following the strong recovery in 2019. Agriculture is projected to rebound by 1.8% in 2020 and accelerate to 2.6% in 2021, assuming favorable weather and continued government efforts to promote productivity and modernization through subsidized loans and the introduction of crop insurance. Construction is projected to expand by 3.3% in 2020 and 4.8% in 2021 on further construction by households and higher public investment. Growth in services is expected to moderate to 2.6% in 2020 before edging up to 5.6% in 2021, supported mainly by finance and information technology.

On the demand side, consumption and investment will lead growth. Expansion in private consumption is expected at 3.9% in 2020 and 5.9% in 2021, supported by minimum wage and pension increases in January 2020, higher bank credit, a moderate rise in remittances, further improvements in consumer sentiment, and the introduction in January 2020 of lower personal income tax at a flat rate of 23%, falling to 22% in 2021. With higher spending for social services, public consumption is expected to rebound in 2020 and accelerate slightly in 2021. Investment is also forecast to recover and grow by 2.1% in 2020 and 2021, benefitting from higher infrastructure spending, a cut in the profit tax rate from 20% to 18%, and simpler taxation of small firms.

Monetary policy is expected to remain broadly accommodative. Inflation is projected to accelerate slightly to 2.8% in 2020 on a continued rise in aggregate demand and expansionary fiscal policy, and assuming only a small effect on prices from increasing import tariffs on selected goods in the transition to the common external tariff under the Eurasian Economic Union, as well as normal weather.

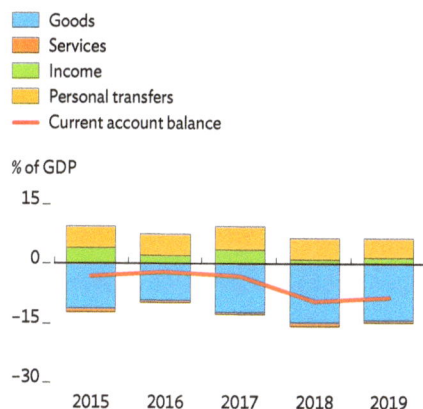

Figure 3.1.6 Current account components

Goods
Services
Income
Personal transfers
Current account balance

Source: Central Bank of Armenia. http://www.cba.am (accessed 25 February 2020).

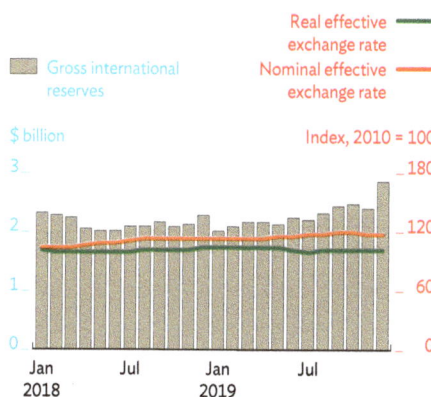

Figure 3.1.7 Reserves and effective exchange rates

Gross international reserves
Real effective exchange rate
Nominal effective exchange rate

Sources: Central Bank of Armenia. http://www.cba.am; International Monetary Fund. International Financial Statistics online database (accessed 20 January 2020).

Table 3.1.1 Selected economic indicators (%)

	2018	2019	2020	2021
GDP growth	5.2	7.6	2.2	4.5
Inflation	2.5	1.4	2.8	2.2
Current acct. bal. (share of GDP)	−9.4	−8.0	−8.6	−8.2

Sources: Central Bank of Armenia. http://www.cba.am (accessed 25 February 2020); ADB estimates.

Inflation is seen slowing to 2.2% in 2021. The 12-month inflation rate December to December is expected to remain within the central bank target band of 2.5%–5.5% at least to the end of 2021.

Higher growth, a smaller budget deficit, and a lower ratio of debt to GDP in 2019 allowed the budget to become mildly expansionary in 2020, before likely returning to a more neutral stance in 2021. The 2020 budget projects a fiscal deficit equal to 2.3% of GDP, with revenue rising to 23.9% of GDP and expenditure to 26.2%. Tax revenue is projected to rise by 9.5% to reach 22.6% of GDP as further improvements in tax administration, simplified tax procedures, and a wider tax base offset the effects of cutting corporate profit and personal tax rates and raising the threshold for taxing small and medium-sized enterprises. Public debt will likely decline to equal 50%–53% of GDP.

The current account deficit is forecast to widen to the equivalent of 8.6% of GDP in 2020 and narrow to 8.2% in 2021 (Figure 3.1.9). The merchandise trade deficit is seen widening to 14.6% of GDP in 2020 before narrowing to 14.2% in 2021, reflecting only a modest rise in domestic demand, the waning effects of higher vehicle reexports, higher import tariffs, and a possible rise in the price of imported natural gas, offset partly by higher agricultural and mining exports. Merchandise exports are projected rising by 2.5% in 2020 and 7.5% in 2021, with imports rising by 7.5% and then 6.5%. Services are likely to remain broadly unchanged, though with rising receipts from finance and from information and technology services. Remittance inflow may be affected by slower growth prospects in the Russian Federation as oil prices decline. Public and publicly guaranteed external debt is projected to decrease slightly to the equivalent of 48.5% of GDP at the end of 2020 and 46.8% a year later.

Armenia's major trade partners are likely to be adversely affected by recent developments in the global economy, including the spread of COVID-19 and the sharp decline of global oil prices, both of which pose risks to Armenia's economic outlook.

Policy challenge—boosting capital expenditure for inclusive and sustainable growth

Armenia's upgraded fiscal framework in 2017 helped rebuild fiscal space while allowing higher capital spending during the past 3 years, which raised capital outlays from the equivalent of 2.5% of GDP in 2018 to 2.8% in 2019 and a projected 4.5% in 2020. However, capital spending fell short of its target in 2018 and 2019 and, as a percentage of GDP, remains below the

Figure 3.1.8 GDP growth

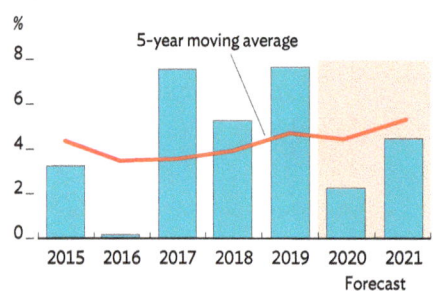

Sources: Statistical Committee of Armenia. http://www.armstat.am (accessed 25 February 2020); ADB estimates.

Figure 3.1.9 Current account balance

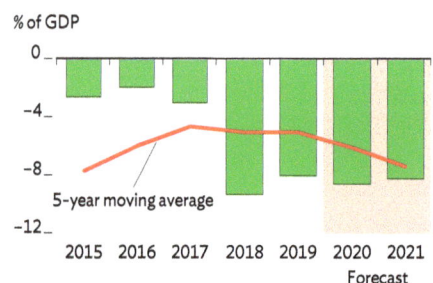

Sources: Central Bank of Armenia. http://www.cba.am; Statistical Committee of Armenia. http://www.armstat.am (both accessed 25 February 2019); ADB estimates.

average for upper-middle-income countries. Moreover, with capital outlays at less than 5.0% of GDP since 2012, the public capital stock, or the value of government-owned assets, is estimated to have fallen by two-thirds from the equivalent of 160% of GDP in 2000 to 62% in 2017. While expenditure under-execution can reduce public debt and deficits in the short run, in the long run the under-execution of capital spending imposes a limit on a country's production capacity and growth potential. Thus, boosting capital expenditure through a sound process of public investment management is important.

In a 2019 assessment of public investment management, the International Monetary Fund concluded that, while Armenia performs well in its adherence to fiscal rules, its budget comprehensiveness, and the availability of funding, it lags in project appraisal, budgeting for investment, project selection, and performance across the project cycle. Boosting capacity to plan, prioritize, and implement well-targeted capital spending is thus critical. The assessment proposed a two-stage gateway for project planning. The first gateway reviews project proposals before they are submitted to the cabinet, and the second gateway requires further review and full appraisal of cleared flagship projects.

Planning is important to ensure that each project's objectives align with national strategic priorities. To this end, the government has started preparing its Armenia Transformation Strategy 2050 to provide an overarching national strategy for five areas—infrastructure, human capital, finance and the economy, public administration, and justice—and 16 sectors, with closely aligned medium-term budgeting.

Allocating public investment to the most productive projects is a key concern. To streamline and maximize efficiency in appraising and selecting projects, the government established in 2019 a public investment unit in the Ministry of Economy. Guidelines are to be introduced in 2020 for appraising planned projects through cost–benefit analysis and in terms of cost-effectiveness.

Another problem is substantial bunching of expenditure at the end of the year, especially for foreign-financed projects, which is a contributing cause of underspending. Addressing this problem requires continued capacity development in project executing and implementing agencies to better satisfy the procedures and policies required by development partners regarding procurement, contract management, and financial reporting.

All of these reforms should be considered parts of a broader effort to improve public financial management. Strong implementation of reform is thus important, as envisaged by the Public Financial Management Reform Strategy for 2019–2023, approved in November 2019.

Azerbaijan

Fiscal stimulus and higher gas production lifted growth in 2019 as food prices boosted inflation. Lower oil prices narrowed the current account surplus. A further decline under COVID-19 will slash growth in 2020 despite higher public spending, with growth recovering in 2021. Inflation is forecast to slow before it accelerates in 2021 as growth picks up. The current account surplus will narrow in 2020 with lower oil prices and then widen in 2021 as oil prices recover. The government needs to allocate spending more efficiently.

Economic performance

Growth accelerated from 1.4% in 2018 to 2.2% in 2019 with 3.5% expansion in the three-fifths of the economy outside of the large petroleum industry (Figure 3.2.1). Petroleum expanded by 0.4% as the Shah Deniz II field spurred a 27.7% rise in gas production, which offset a 3.3% decline in oil output attributable to maintenance at the Central Azeri oil field in April and the West Chirag field in October.

On the supply side, industry reversed an average decline of 2.9% in 2015–2018 with 0.7% growth as all subsectors grew except construction, which contracted by 6.1% because of lower public investment and the completion of major petroleum projects. Growth in agriculture rose from 4.6% in 2018 to 7.3%, led by an 11.7% rise in crops, mainly cereals and cotton, supported by continued exemptions from taxes and duties on production inputs. Services, supplying 37% of GDP, grew by 3.7% on gains in trade, communications, and tourism, with the number of tourists rising by 11.3%.

On the demand side, consumption and net exports expanded. Private consumption benefited from rising incomes as salaries and pensions increased, as well as increased consumer lending, while public wage increases boosted public consumption. Gross fixed capital formation declined by 2.3% as public investment in the petroleum industry fell.

Average annual inflation increased from 2.3% in 2018 to 2.6% as prices rose by 3.8% for food, 1.2% for other goods, and 2.0% for services (Figure 3.2.2). To limit food price inflation, the authorities continued to organize public produce markets to let farmers sell directly to the public. The State Oil Fund of Azerbaijan (SOFAZ), the sovereign wealth fund and main source of hard currency, sold $6.6 billion in foreign exchange to the domestic market in 2019, 2.1% more than in 2018. A stable

Figure 3.2.1 GDP growth by sector

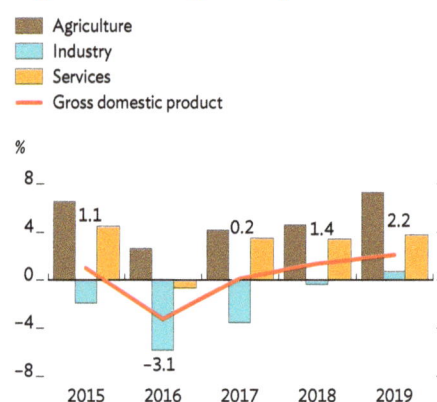

- Agriculture
- Industry
- Services
- Gross domestic product

Source: State Statistical Committee of the Republic of Azerbaijan.

Figure 3.2.2 Monthly inflation

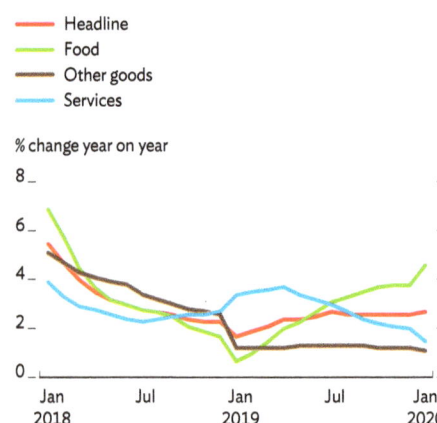

- Headline
- Food
- Other goods
- Services

Sources: State Statistical Committee of the Republic of Azerbaijan; Haver Analytics.

This chapter was written Nail Valiyev of the Azerbaijan Resident Mission, ADB, Baku.

exchange rate, pegged at 1.7 Azeri manats per $1 since 2017, has helped keep inflation moderate, though the manat appreciated slightly on average in 2019 in real effective terms (Figure 3.2.3).

As inflation remained within its target band of 2%–6%, the central bank reduced the policy rate from 9.75% to 7.50% in eight steps during 2019. Despite some decrease, dollarization in the bank sector remains high, with nearly 34.6% of loans and 61.0% of deposits in foreign currency. Dollarization and a shallow domestic capital market continue to constrain monetary policy. Credit growth accelerated from 10.7% in 2018 to 17.5%, with loans to households rising by 31.2% to reach 45.6% of all lending. Broad money growth accelerated from 5.7% in the whole of 2018 to 11.1% in the 11 months from January to November 2019 (Figure 3.2.4). The government's efforts to resolve nonperforming loans by paying down some overdue household loans helped cut the share of nonperforming loans from 12.1% in 2019 to 8.2%. Nevertheless, the bank sector remains weak, and the country's largest bank, the state-owned International Bank of Azerbaijan, does not yet appear ready for privatization despite extensive restructuring.

Fiscal policy remained somewhat expansionary during 2019. The budget deficit narrowed slightly from 0.4% of GDP in 2018 to 0.3%, but the deficit excluding transfers from SOFAZ remained large at 14.2% of GDP (Figure 3.2.5). Central government outlays grew from 28.5% of GDP in 2018 to 29.9% as the government raised public sector wages and the national minimum salary and compensated household borrowers to offset the impact of past devaluations. Improved tax administration helped raise revenue from 28.1% of GDP in 2018 to 29.6%. The government also moved to strengthen fiscal sustainability and reduce dependence on oil revenue by implementing a new fiscal rule requiring the non-oil primary deficit to decline as a percentage of GDP from 31.1% in 2019 to 28.1% in 2022.

The current account surplus is estimated to have narrowed from 12.9% of GDP in 2018 to 7.3%. The trade surplus shrank from $9.6 billion to $5.8 billion, while imported construction and transport services expanded the service deficit. Merchandize exports, of which hydrocarbons are nearly 90%, reversed a 31.2% rise in 2018 to decline by 4.2% as oil export earnings fell, though non-oil exports increased marginally. Higher aggregate demand boosted merchandise imports by 24.8%. Net foreign direct investment in the first 9 months of 2019 plunged by 70% to $304 million, with most investment in petroleum. The official foreign exchange reserves of the central bank rose by 12.5% to a record high of $6.3 billion. Strategic reserves including SOFAZ assets totaled an estimated $49 billion at the end of 2019, with external public debt estimated at $9.1 billion (Figure 3.2.6). The government aims to reduce the ratio of external debt to GDP to 11% by 2025 in line with a debt management strategy approved in 2018.

Figure 3.2.3 Inflation and exchange rate

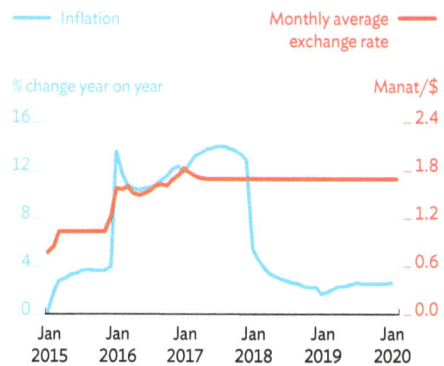

Sources: Central Bank of the Republic of Azerbaijan; State Statistical Committee of the Republic of Azerbaijan; Haver Analytics.

Figure 3.2.4 Contributions to money supply growth

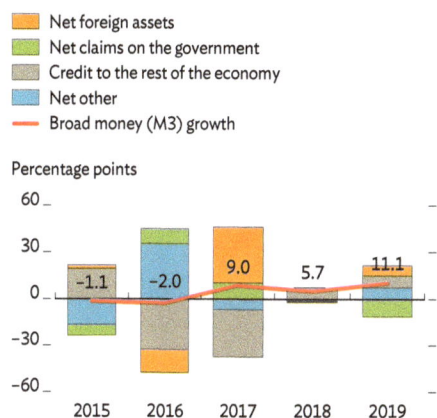

Note: Data for 2019 are to November 2019.
Source: Central Bank of the Republic of Azerbaijan.

Figure 3.2.5 Fiscal indicators

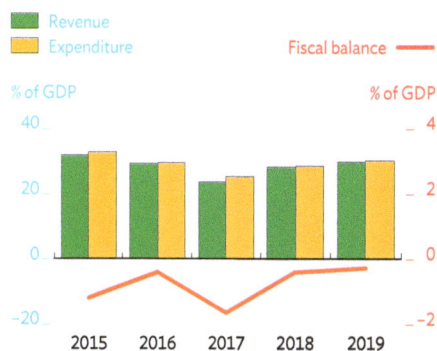

Source: Ministry of Finance of the Republic of Azerbaijan.

Economic prospects

As diversification remains elusive, Azerbaijan's growth prospects will continue to hinge on petroleum prices for the foreseeable future. A decline in oil prices under COVID-19, will slash growth to 0.5% in 2020. A recovery in prices and higher oil and gas production are projected to raise growth to 1.5% in 2021 (Figure 3.2.7). Expansion in industry, projected at 0.5% in 2020 and 2.0% in 2021, will come from stronger hydrocarbon performance, in particular higher output at the Shah Deniz II gas field with the completion in 2020 of the Trans Adriatic Pipeline to carry gas from Turkey to Italy. Growth in agriculture is expected to slow to 4.5% in 2020 and 4.0% in 2021, though continued subsidies for imports of fertilizer and seed should promote higher cash crop production. Services are expected to show little growth in 2020 as the COVID-19 outbreak hits tourism and retail trade, but they will expand by 1.0% in 2021 as the economy improves.

On the demand side, higher civil service income will fuel public consumption, and a 34% increase in minimum salaries should boost private consumption. Investment is expected to slow in 2020 as low oil income cuts public investment before stabilizing in 2021 as private investment picks up. Strong gas output will strengthen net exports, supporting growth.

Fiscal policy is expected to become more expansionary in 2020 with the budget deficit rising to at least 3.4% of GDP—or 17.2% when excluding transfers from SOFAZ— as higher social spending and continued strong public investment boost total expenditure by 10.2%. The government has budgeted AZN1.0 billion to mitigate the impact of COVID-19 on macroeconomic stability, the labor market, and entrepreneurship. It will approve criteria to support the private sector. The budget originally projected revenue, including transfers from SOFAZ, equal to 29.4% of GDP in 2020, based on an assumed oil price of $55 per barrel. Actual revenue could be lower if March 2020 oil prices persist for the rest of the year. With changes in the tax code expanding tax collections, transfers from SOFAZ were earlier projected to cover 47% of revenue in 2020 and 45% in 2021. The government projected SOFAZ to receive $12.4 billion in revenue from export earnings in 2020, of which 91% would be transferred to the budget.

Inflation is projected to decelerate slightly to 2.5% in 2020 with economic activity sluggish and increase to 3.5% in 2021 on the lagged impact of higher social spending to expand private consumption (Figure 3.2.8). These forecasts assume modest growth in food prices and a stable exchange rate. However, the sharp rise in social expenditure is expected to pose additional inflationary pressures, as will nationwide salary increases following the rise in minimum salaries. A prolonged decline in petroleum prices may trigger exchange rate adjustments and a surge in inflation, as occurred in 2016.

Figure 3.2.6 State oil fund assets and central bank reserves

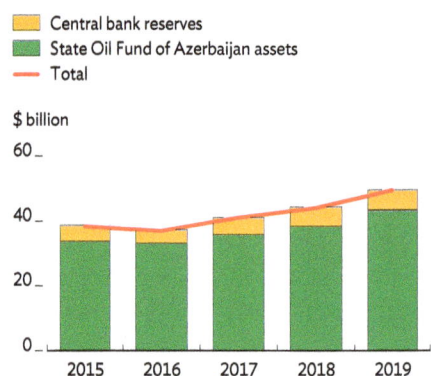

Sources: Central Bank of the Republic of Azerbaijan; State Oil Fund of Azerbaijan. http://www.oilfund.az (both accessed 2 March 2020).

Figure 3.2.7 GDP growth

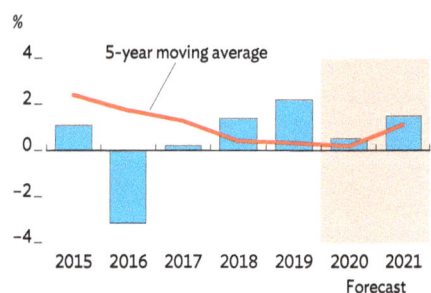

Sources: Central Bank of the Republic of Azerbaijan; ADB estimates.

Table 3.2.1 Selected economic indicators (%)

	2018	2019	2020	2021
GDP growth	1.4	2.2	0.5	1.5
Inflation	2.3	2.6	2.5	3.5
Current acct. bal. (share of GDP)	12.9	7.3	4.4	6.3

Sources: Central Bank of the Republic of Azerbaijan; ADB estimates.

Nevertheless, as current and forecast inflation remain within the target band of 2%–6% (4±2%), the central bank reduced the policy rate again in January 2020, to 7.25%. Further relaxation of monetary policy is possible if the exchange rate remains stable, though regulated interest rates would likely contribute to faster credit growth. The central bank will continue its auctions of deposits and notes to stabilize the monetary base, contain currency in circulation, and avoid creating downward pressure on the manat, thus delaying any move toward a floating exchange rate regime. The government will maintain tight control over administered prices to keep core inflation in check.

The current account surplus is forecast to narrow to 4.4% of GDP in 2020 and widen to 6.3% in 2021 (Figure 3.2.9). Merchandise imports are projected to contract by 37.8% in 2020 as COVID-19 cuts total trade, in particular the 10% of imports that come from the People's Republic of China, and recover by 23.5% in 2021 as domestic demand recovers and the situation stabilizes. Import costs may rise if more expensive imports replace cheaper goods from the People's Republic of China. Merchandise exports are projected to decline by 32.7% in 2020, as lower oil prices cut hydrocarbon export earnings, before rising by 24.4% in 2021 with higher gas export volumes and oil price recovery. Despite less income from tourism, the deficit in services is expected to narrow with the completion of major construction services in the oil industry. Public and publicly guaranteed debt will remain limited in line with the government's debt management strategy. The budget law allows $600 million in external borrowing in 2020. With strategic international reserves including SOFAZ assets projected to remain near $50 billion, Azerbaijan's external debt should remain sustainable over the medium term.

Policy challenge—creating a medium-term expenditure framework for more efficient use of government revenue

Since 2008, central budget expenditure has grown steadily to reach AZN24.4 billion, equal to 29.9% of GDP in 2019, thanks to substantial revenue from petroleum exports. SOFAZ was established to promote the efficient use of this income and ensure its availability for multiple generations. It transfers money annually to the budget to support budget expenditure, in particular public investment. From 2012 to 2019, transfers from SOFAZ provided on average nearly half of central budget revenue (Figure 3.2.10). However, transfers are determined year by year, not as part of a longer-term plan.

Because budgets are currently developed on an annual cycle, fiscal policy typically lacks a long-term, strategic focus.

Figure 3.2.8 Inflation

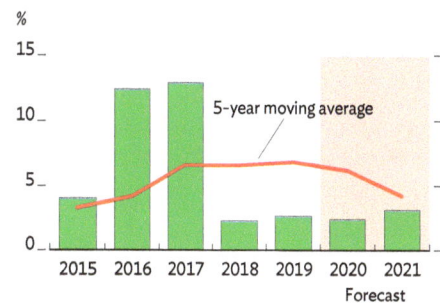

Sources: Central Bank of the Republic of Azerbaijan; ADB estimates.

Figure 3.2.9 Current account balance

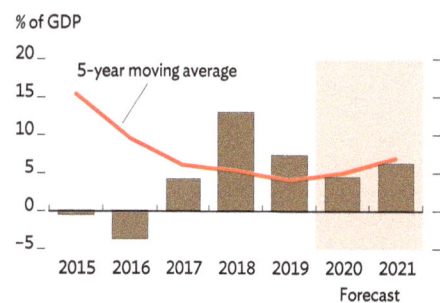

Sources: Central Bank of the Republic of Azerbaijan; ADB estimates.

This has contributed to the ad-hoc nature of investment projects that are often poorly designed and implemented. To address this problem, the government adopted in 2018 fiscal rules governing the use of oil revenues and creating a medium-term expenditure framework (MTEF). To implement this framework, the government has agreed to develop strategic plans for each sector, including detailed costing; established an MTEF center at the Ministry of Finance; and identified three areas—agriculture, education, and the environment—to pilot the framework starting with the 2021 budget. Implementing the MTEF is a challenge for the government, and its success will require strong efforts from spending ministries.

The government needs to develop a medium-term strategy linked to its main development objectives, with clear performance indicators and a sound monitoring and evaluation framework. In addition, strong capacity for macroeconomic forecasting is needed to ensure sound fiscal forecasting and accurate identification of available fiscal resources.

The MTEF process is expected to bridge gaps between the government's national strategic vision, its strategic plans for different sectors, and annual budget allocations, with a focus on applying public expenditure to attain set objectives. Once the government's strategic priorities are set, the MTEF will guide budgetary allocations toward attaining them over the medium term. Successful implementation of the MTEF depends on ministries' ability to translate government objectives into sectoral goals and prepare detailed programs and procurement plans to specify realistic annual costs within the framework.

The MTEF requires a strong monitoring and reporting mechanism. Modern information and communication technology should replace the outdated budget recording and reporting system currently used. The MTEF should bring strong accountability, thereby improving fiscal transparency and public understanding of budget policy.

Capacity and institutional weaknesses are major hurdles to implementing the MTEF. Spending agencies currently lack the capacity to formulate sector strategies or medium-term action plans. It is thus important that the implementation of the MTEF be properly phased. MTEF implementation will be more successful if done incrementally, progressively refining existing systems rather than suddenly replacing them with an unfamiliar new process.

Figure 3.2.10 State Oil Fund of Azerbaijan budget transfers

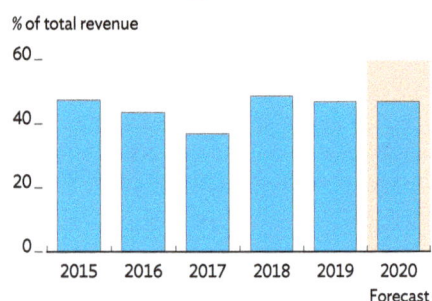

% of total revenue

Source: Ministry of Finance of the Republic of Azerbaijan.

Georgia

Infrastructure spending and continued export gains boosted growth in 2019. Inflation accelerated with currency depreciation. Growth is projected at zero in 2020 under continued monetary tightening and COVID-19 before recovering in 2021 on stronger demand and foreign investment. Monetary tightening will slow inflation in both years. Having narrowed in 2019, the current account deficit will narrow further to 2021 as imports continue to decline. Promoting technological innovation would spur business development.

Economic performance

Growth is estimated to have accelerated from 4.8% in 2018 to 5.1% in 2019, reflecting record spending on public investment and a sharp rise in exports. On the supply side, service growth accelerated from 5.6% in 2018 to 6.8% in 2019 on strong 15.2% expansion in information and communication technology; 14.1% in arts, entertainment, and recreation; and 9.1% in tourist-related accommodation and food services. Industry expanded by 2.7%, with gains in electricity and gas utilities by 5.5% and construction by 4.1%. Agriculture decreased by 1.0% on low investment in the sector (Figure 3.3.1).

On the demand side, preliminary data show growth in public investment more than doubling from 9.2% in 2018 to a record 25.1%. Expansion in net exports accelerated from 11.0% in 2018 to 14.5% as growth slowed in consumption from 5.1% to 2.4% and in private investment from 6.5% to 4.7%.

Average inflation nearly doubled from 2.6% in 2018 to 4.9% with currency depreciation and prices rising sharply toward year-end (Figure 3.3.2). Food prices jumped by 8.2%, and excise tax increases boosted prices for alcoholic beverages and tobacco by 16.3%. Core inflation—excluding food and nonalcoholic beverages, tobacco, energy, and regulated utility tariffs—was 2.0%.

A sharp rise in capital spending to the equivalent of an estimated 7.0% of GDP widened the fiscal deficit from 0.7% of GDP in 2018 to 2.1% (Figure 3.3.3). This occurred despite high collections of value-added tax and improved tax administration that raised tax revenue by 8.7% to equal 22.8% of GDP and total revenue by 9.2% to equal 25.8% of GDP.

Figure 3.3.1 GDP growth by sector

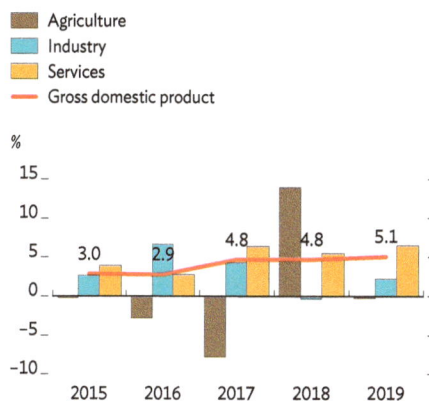

Source: National Statistics Office of Georgia.
http://www.geostat.ge.

Figure 3.3.2 Monthly inflation

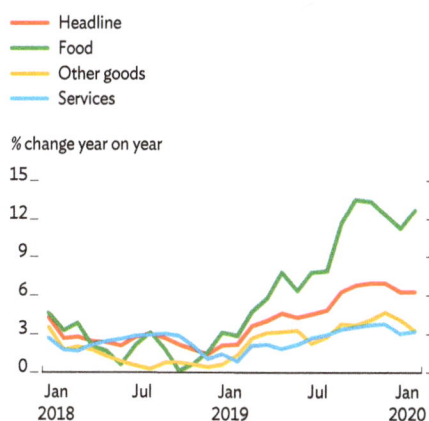

Source: National Statistics Office of Georgia.
http://www.geostat.ge.

This chapter was written by George Luarsabishvili of the Georgia Resident Mission, ADB, Tbilisi.

Outlays for wages expanded by only 5.9%, helping limit growth in noninterest expenditure to 10.0%. Public debt climbed from the equivalent of 44.9% of GDP in 2018 to 47.9% in part because of currency depreciation. Private debt excluding intercompany lending rose by nearly 4 percentage points to equal 58.0% of GDP (Figure 3.3.4).

To cope with rising inflationary pressures and currency depreciation as the US dollar strengthened and foreign exchange inflow fell short of expectations, the National Bank of Georgia, the central bank, raised its policy rate by 250 basis points to 9.0% in four steps in the period from September to mid-December 2019 and maintained the rate in the first quarter of 2020, while cutting reserve requirements on deposits denominated in foreign currency by 5 percentage points to 25% in October 2019. The Georgian lari depreciated in 2019 by 8.9% against the US dollar, 6.2% against the euro, 4.9% in nominal effective terms, and 5.3% in real effective terms. The currency lost further ground in the first quarter of 2020 with the global rise of the US dollar and a risk premium that the market sees in response to COVID-19 (Figure 3.3.5). In response, the central bank sold $193 million in foreign exchange from August 2019 to March 2020.

Banks remained well capitalized, with improved asset quality and higher liquidity but less profitability. Bank capital as a percentage of assets was 19.5%, the percentage of nonperforming loans 1.9%, and the liquid asset ratio 19.6%— all improvements in 2019. However, dollarization in the banking system remained high, with deposits unchanged from a year earlier at 61.1% and loans down from 56.1% to 54.6%. Average interest rates were 11.8% for loans and 5.7% for deposits.

The current account deficit narrowed from the equivalent of 6.8% of GDP in 2018 to an historic low of 4.5% in 2019, though growth in merchandise exports slowed from 22.4% in 2018 to an estimated 13.5%. Merchandise import growth plunged from 15.1% in 2018 to only 0.8% despite record high public spending on infrastructure, as the lari depreciated and oil prices fell. Growth in remittances slowed from 13.9% in 2018 to 9.7%. Tourism revenues increased by 1.4% even as the Russian Federation banned direct flights to Georgia. Foreign direct investment—concentrated mainly in finance, manufacturing, tourism, and construction, increased by 0.2% despite profit repatriation and a gradual winding down of energy projects. Foreign reserves rose by $72 million to $3.3 billion at the end of 2019, while external debt reached the equivalent of 95.2% of GDP and the public portion of it 37.2%. Standard & Poor's and Fitch raised Georgia's credit rating at the end of 2019 from BB– to BB.

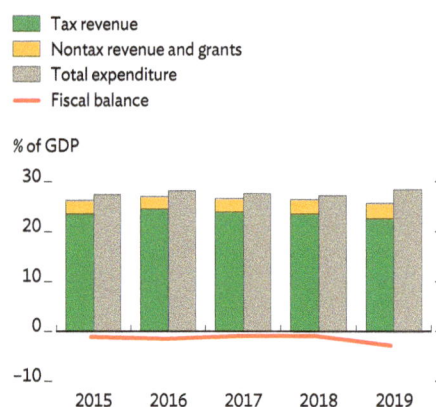

Figure 3.3.3 Fiscal indicators

Source: International Monetary Fund. www.imf.org; Ministry of Finance of Georgia. www.mof.ge.

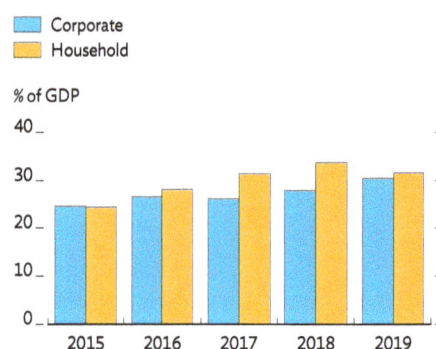

Figure 3.3.4 Corporate and household debt

Source: National Bank of Georgia. http://www.nbg.gov.ge.

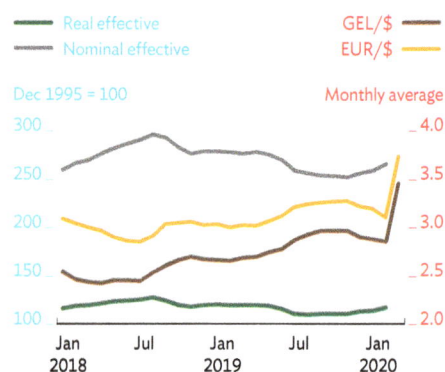

Figure 3.3.5 Exchange rates

Source: National Bank of Georgia. http://www.nbg.gov.ge.

Economic prospects

Growth is projected to decline to zero in 2020 as monetary tightening and the impact of COVID-19 constrain consumption and limit expansion in tourism and trade, before recovering to 4.5% in 2021 with higher domestic demand fueled by increased bank credit to households, increased foreign direct investment, and a rebound in workers' remittances (Figure 3.3.6). Gains in retail trade and higher government education spending are projected to boost services by 1.1% in 2020 and 6.3% in 2021, with the latter reflecting an expected recovery in tourism. Growth in industry is projected to contract to 3.1% in 2020 with a slowdown in construction and manufacturing before recovering to 2.1% in 2021 with higher mining output. Agriculture is forecast to decline marginally by 0.7% in 2020 and expand by 0.4% in 2021 as investment in the sector strengthens.

The introduction of administered prices for food, which represents 31.3% of the consumer price index, should help slow inflation to 4.5% in 2020 and 3.0% in 2021, the central bank target (Figure 3.3.7). Fiscal policy is projected to be expansionary, as the budget deficit is projected to widen somewhat to 2.5% in both 2020 and 2021 with social spending forecast at 9.0% of GDP. This reflects phased increases in the basic pension and a gradual rise in education outlays to 6.0% of GDP, despite savings from better targeting of social insurance benefits and improved procurement practices. A revised fiscal framework should help minimize fiscal risk by including injections to state-owned enterprises and liabilities to public–private partnerships under an overall debt ceiling equal to 60.0% of GDP. However, public debt is expected to increase to 48.5% in 2020 and 49.5% in 2021 in part from the need to continue financing infrastructure projects (Figure 3.3.8).

Georgia's external prospects will depend heavily on developments in its trade partners. The current account deficit is projected to narrow further, to 4.4% of GDP in 2020 and 4.2% in 2021, with a continued decline in imports as much lower oil prices help trim the trade deficit by 2.5% in 2020 and 0.5% in 2021 (Figure 3.3.9). Exports are projected to grow by 3.6% in 2020 and 11.9% in 2021, with modest domestic expansion and higher foreign direct investment raising imports by 1.1% in 2020 and 7.0% in 2021. Gross international reserves are expected to reach $3.5 billion in 2020 and $3.6 billion at the end of 2021. External debt is expected to equal 96.0% of GDP at the end of 2020 and 96.5% at the end of 2021 (Figure 3.3.10).

Risks to economic growth include lower than expected domestic demand and growth in trade partners, slower growth in tourism revenues, and tighter liquidity in global financial markets, in part reflecting the impact of COVID-19.

Figure 3.3.6 GDP growth

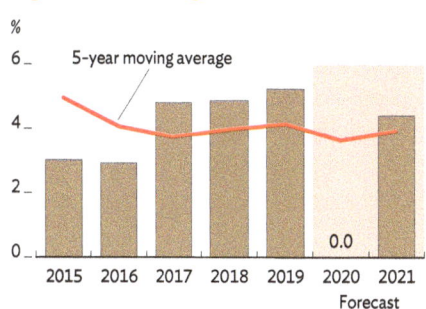

Sources: National Statistics Office of Georgia; ADB estimates.

Figure 3.3.7 Inflation

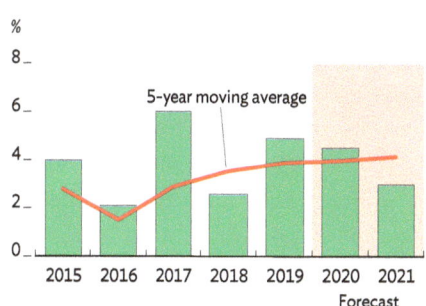

Source: National Bank of Georgia. http://www.nbg.gov.ge.

Table 3.3.1 Selected economic indicators (%)

	2018	2019	2020	2021
GDP growth	4.8	5.1	0.0	4.5
Inflation	2.6	4.9	4.5	3.0
Current acct. bal. (share of GDP)	-6.8	-4.5	-4.4	-4.2

Source: ADB estimates.

Policy challenge—promoting technological innovation for business development

Georgia has made tangible progress in creating innovative digital services for business development. However, it is constrained by limited mobile broadband coverage and internet connectivity, especially in rural areas. Georgia has improved its adoption of information and communication technology (ICT), the third pillar of the enabling environment component cited in the World Economic Forum's Global Competitiveness Index 2019, where Georgia ranks 55 of 141 economies. However, Georgia has made little progress in improving the technological sophistication of firms, ranking only 91 in innovation capability and 93 in entrepreneurial culture. The report highlighted slow progress toward improving university–industry collaboration in research and development and digital skills in the workforce, with research and development expenditure equal to only 0.3% of GDP, well below the 1.8% average for upper-middle-income countries.

To promote start-ups, the government has inaugurated two new agencies. The Georgian Innovation and Technology Agency supports competitiveness in small and medium-sized enterprises and promotes innovative start-ups. It also supports innovation laboratories, business incubators, and new technology firms. The Georgian Entrepreneurship Development Agency facilitates private sector development through a variety of financial and other facilities to support start-ups during their incubation, especially those oriented toward exports. While these efforts have helped firms advance through better use of ICT, Georgia's Global Competitiveness Index rank remains low at 108 for growth in innovative companies and 120 for cluster development.

Advances in science and labor market analysis can help enable firms to innovate. Georgia is taking steps to integrate ICT into school curricula. ICT is a mandatory subject and part of computer-based instruction and learning. In addition, ICT modules are used to train teachers. The government has created an information system to collect and analyze labor market data to identify mismatches between the labor skills required and educational programs. Despite these efforts, the local workforce needs further training, especially in ICT.

The government receives international support for technological innovation, including help in formulating a development strategy for broadband infrastructure and narrowing the digital divide between urban and rural areas. Supporting dedicated and open-access digital platforms for a variety of commercial, government, and research activities would help firms integrate ICT more effectively, thereby raising their productivity. Greater openness to trade and further competition among firms would also help.

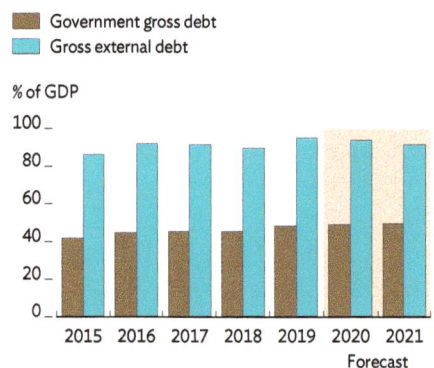

Figure 3.3.8 Government gross debt and gross external debt

Sources: Ministry of Finance of Georgia. www.mof.ge; International Monetary Fund. www.imf.org.

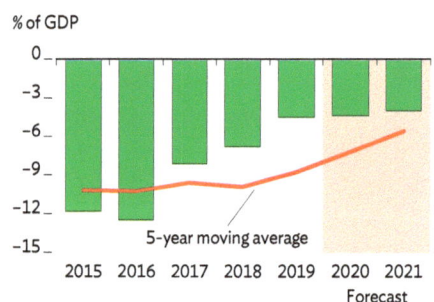

Figure 3.3.9 Current account balance

Sources: National Bank of Georgia; ADB estimates.

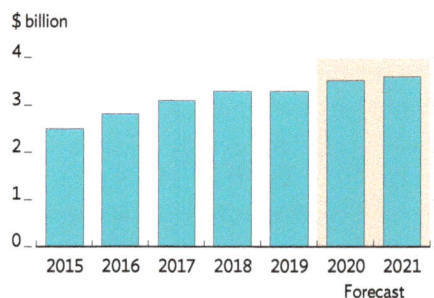

Figure 3.3.10 Gross international reserves

Sources: National Bank of Georgia. www.nbg.gov.ge; International Monetary Fund. www.imf.org; ADB estimates.

To make electronic commerce more trustworthy and viable, the government must improve its legal and regulatory framework for electronic commerce while creating more efficient mechanisms for setting taxes and tariffs. Promoting technology-oriented start-ups in business process outsourcing, information services, and computer services could help advance innovation and the use of more modern technology, thereby making firms more dynamic. Doing so would require further investments in research and development, as well as reducing the cost of doing business by extending computer systems that link business and government. Cutting operating costs for service users and other cost-cutting investments could allow firms to become more efficient and technologically sophisticated. Meanwhile, firms could do more to boost their own innovative capacity by, for example, offering ICT training to workers. Promoting cluster development, where Georgia ranks poorly by international standards, could support innovative links among firms.

The government should continue educational reform, including measures to reform vocational education and expand education in science and technology, to enhance productivity by increasing the supply of workers with relevant skills. Improving education and familiarity with digital technologies, particularly in rural areas, would make growth more broadly based and inclusive.

Kazakhstan

Expansionary fiscal policy lifted consumption, investment, and growth in 2019. Price controls and tight monetary policy trimmed inflation. Growth is projected to plummet in 2020 because of COVID-19 and lower oil export earnings before rebounding in 2021 from a low base with stronger oil production and expansionary fiscal policy. Administrative and monetary measures should contain inflation, but a smaller trade surplus will widen the current account deficit. Social assistance needs to be more sustainable.

Economic performance

Growth rose from 4.1% in 2018 to 4.5% in 2019, led by gains in services, consumption, and investment (Figure 3.4.1). On the supply side, growth in industry slowed from 4.4% in 2018 to 3.8% as lower commodity prices and planned maintenance on major oil fields limited mining growth. Expanded state housing programs and continued infrastructure spending tripled growth in construction from 4.6% in 2018 to 12.9%. Growth in agriculture slowed from 3.8% to 0.9% as a drought-induced 1.7% decline in crop production nearly offset 4.0% expansion in livestock. Services improved slightly from 3.9% growth in 2018 to 4.4%, led by gains of 7.6% in trade, 5.2% in communications, and 5.1% in transport.

On the demand side, data for which are available for only the first 9 months of 2019, growth in consumption jumped from 1.6% in the comparable period of 2018 to 6.7%. Public consumption reversed a 13.9% drop to rise by 10.2%, reflecting higher wages for civil servants and increased social spending, while a minimum wage increase and expanded credit boosted growth in private consumption from 5.1% to 6.0%. Investment growth accelerated from 2.8% to 8.9%, driven by a 12.9% increase in gross fixed capital formation mainly for mining, infrastructure, and housing. Net exports fell by 16.3%, with real imports rising by 10.8% and real exports by 2.5%.

Inflation in 2019 slowed from 6.0% in 2018 to 5.3%, reflecting tight monetary policy and government measures to constrain prices directly (Figure 3.4.2). Food inflation accelerated from 5.1% in 2018 to 8.2%, despite government actions, but slowed for other goods from 7.8% to 5.7%. Inflation slowed more steeply for services, from 5.3% to 1.2%, as a government review prompted a 3.1% drop in utility charges and self-sufficiency in oil and tight control of the domestic petroleum market cut gasoline prices by 5.6%.

Figure 3.4.1 Supply-side contributions to growth

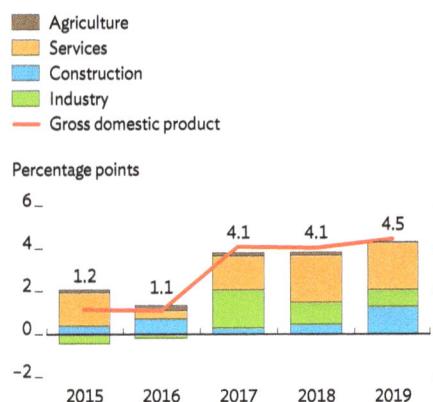

Agriculture
Services
Construction
Industry
Gross domestic product

Percentage points

Source: Republic of Kazakhstan. Ministry of National Economy. Statistics Committee.

Figure 3.4.2 Monthly inflation

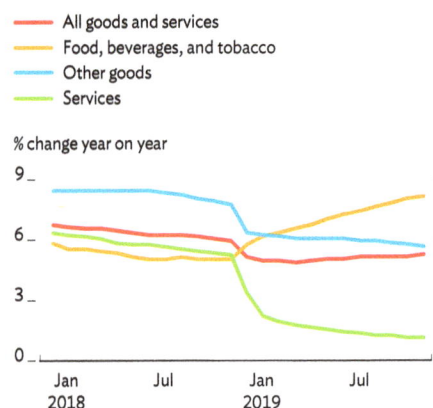

All goods and services
Food, beverages, and tobacco
Other goods
Services

% change year on year

Source: Republic of Kazakhstan. Ministry of National Economy. Statistics Committee.

This chapter was written by Genadiy Rau of the Kazakhstan Resident Mission, ADB, Nur-Sultan.

Fiscal policy was expansionary in 2019, with expenditure increases to accommodate expanding social programs. The state budget deficit expanded from the equivalent of 1.3% of GDP in 2018 to 1.9% as the deficit aside from the large petroleum industry widened from 7.3% to 8.0% (Figure 3.4.3). Improved tax administration raised revenue from 17.5% of GDP in 2018 to 18.6%, while expenditure climbed from 18.8% of GDP to 20.5% as a quadrupling of social assistance recipients helped raise social spending by 26.0%. Transfers to the budget from the National Fund of the Republic of Kazakhstan exceeded receipts by 6.3%, a reversal from 2018 when receipts exceeded transfers. With higher growth, government and government-guaranteed debt declined from the equivalent of 26.0% of GDP at the end of 2018 to 25.2% a year later.

Monetary policy pursues an inflation target of 4%–6% in 2019–2021, revised down to 3%–5% in 2022 and beyond. After cutting the policy rate in April 2019, the National Bank of Kazakhstan, the central bank, raised it in September by 25 basis points to 9.25% while increasing sales to banks of its own securities by 34.6% during the year to reduce liquidity and counter inflationary pressures. Broad money (M3) growth slowed from 7.0% in 2018 to 2.4% as deposits grew by 5.5% and credit to the economy by 5.9% (Figure 3.4.4). While consumer credit exceeded the 16.8% increase in 2018 to rise by 24.4%, credit to firms dropped, deepening a 5.0% decline in 2018 with a further 7.5% decline last year. The quality of loans deteriorated, with the nonperforming loan ratio edging up from 7.4% of banks' portfolios at the end of 2018 to 8.1% a year later, while nonperforming loans to small and medium-sized enterprises rose from 9.3% to 14.6%. Foreign currency deposits declined from 46.8% of the total at the end of 2018 to 42.3%, while foreign currency loans decreased from 22.9% of all loans to 16.6% (Figure 3.4.5).

Preliminary estimates show the current account deficit widening from the equivalent of 0.2% of GDP in 2018 to 3.1% as the merchandise trade surplus decreased by 23.4% to equal 10.9% of GDP. Declining global oil prices and stagnant production volume contributed to reducing merchandise exports by 4.0%, while rising demand for consumer and capital goods boosted imports by 10.6%. Primary income was stagnant, with net foreign investors' earnings at $20.2 billion. Net foreign direct investment rose by 15.9% to $5.6 billion, mainly for mining and infrastructure projects, while net outflow of portfolio investment rebounded to $4.7 billion.

Portfolio capital outflow and repayment of eurobonds reduced gross international reserves by 6.4% to $29 billion at the end of 2019, or cover for 7.1 months of imports. The central bank continued rebalancing its international reserves portfolio, raising the share of gold to an all-time high of 65.2%. Assets in the sovereign wealth fund increased by 6.8% to $61.9 billion, reflecting robust portfolio earnings (Figure 3.4.6).

Figure 3.4.3 Fiscal indicators

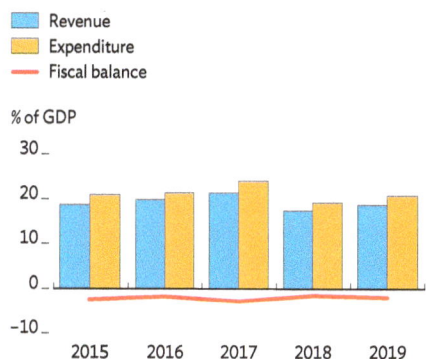

Sources: Ministry of Finance; Ministry of National Economy.

Figure 3.4.4 Growth in broad money

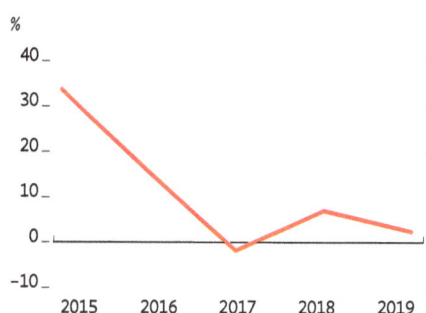

Source: National Bank of the Republic of Kazakhstan.

Figure 3.4.5 Dollarization in the banking system

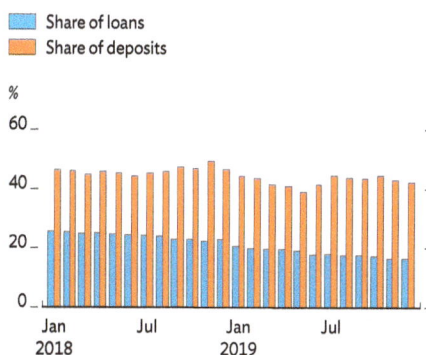

Source: National Bank of the Republic of Kazakhstan.

External debt, 62.4% of which is private intercompany debt, eased slightly to an estimated 88% of GDP as state-owned enterprises repaid debt (Figure 3.4.7). In September, the government issued two tranches of eurobonds totaling €1.15 billion, with 7-year bonds yielding 0.6% annually and 15-year bonds 1.5%, the lowest rates ever granted to an emerging market rated BBB. The central bank reported no monthly net interventions in the foreign exchange market over the year. In early 2020, it started publishing monthly amounts of conversions and transfers from the sovereign wealth fund to the state budget.

Economic prospects

Doubly hit by the plunge in oil prices and other economic implications of COVID-19, growth is forecast to drop to 1.8% in 2020 as oil and gas production recedes with prices in decline, despite the introduction of stimulus packages aiming to boost infrastructure investment and maintain social expenditure. Substantial downside risks to the outlook stem from a protracted COVID-19 crisis and a continued plummeting of global oil prices, which could hit Kazakhstan's economy more than anticipated in the absence of measures by the Organization of the Petroleum Exporting Countries and other leading producers to stabilize prices. In 2021, growth is expected to rebound to 3.6%, supported by rising hydrocarbon and manufacturing output and higher investment (Figure 3.4.8).

On the supply side, industry is forecast to expand by 1.2% in 2020, with continued government support for manufacturing, and by 4.5% in 2021 with the waning impact of external shocks. Mining will shrink in 2020 as global demand for commodities plunges but recover the following year. In agriculture, growth is forecast to accelerate to 2.9% in 2020 and 3.2% in 2021 on a rebound of crop production and further livestock expansion. Services are projected to grow by only 1.5% in 2020 as a state of emergency declared to contain COVID-19 adversely affects transport, trade, and the hospitality industry, then recover to 3.3% growth in 2021. Construction is forecast to expand by 6.1% in 2020 and 4.9% in 2021 as it receives support from the government's countercyclical stimulus package, which will expand and accelerate irrigation programs and other infrastructure investment, and from ongoing housing policy and infrastructure modernization programs.

On the demand side, growth in consumption is projected to moderate to 2.0% in 2020 with slower expansion in credit to households and despite further increases in government social spending, recovering to 3.2% in 2021. Expansion in investment is forecast to slow to 3.6% in 2020 because of external shocks before recovering to 4.1% in 2021, with gross fixed capital formation benefiting from government-led infrastructure

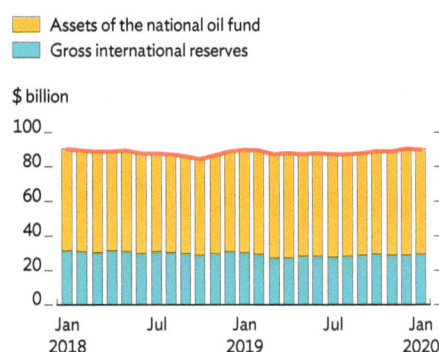

Figure 3.4.6 Foreign currency reserves and oil fund assets

Source: National Bank of the Republic of Kazakhstan.

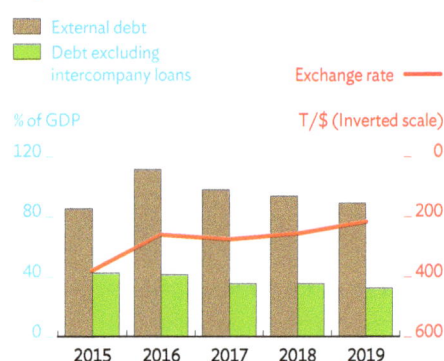

Figure 3.4.7 External debt

Sources: National Bank of Kazakhstan; ADB estimates.

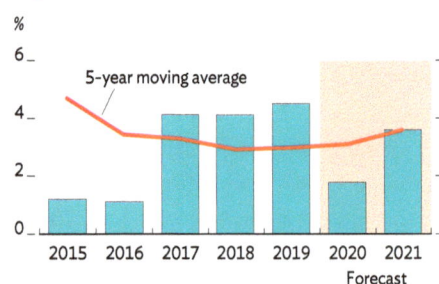

Figure 3.4.8 GDP growth

Source: Asian Development Outlook database.

programs, as well as foreign direct investment in commodities. The deficit in net exports is projected to expand in 2020 but narrow in 2021 as exports of goods and services outgrow imports.

Inflation is projected to accelerate to 6.0% in 2020 and edge down to 5.7% in 2021, partly as an effect of administrative and monetary measures (Figure 3.4.9). In March 2020, the central bank raised the policy rate by 275 basis points to 12.00% to stabilize the national currency, which depreciated dramatically in the aftermath of the sharp decline in global oil prices and because of COVID-19. The government pledged to use regional food stockpiles to maintain price stability. Such measures should help trim food price inflation to 6.2% in 2020 and 4.7% in 2021, as should greater domestic crop production and government limitations on markups for staple foods. Currency depreciation will likely raise inflation for other goods to 6.4% in 2020 and 6.5% in 2021, while prices for services should rise by 5.4% in 2020 and 6.1% in 2021. The central bank is expected to continue issuing its own securities to remove excess liquidity and possibly raise the policy rate further to contain inflation. Meanwhile, external shocks have the potential to further depreciate the tenge against the US dollar, with the central bank intervening to smooth exchange market fluctuations.

Fiscal policy over the next 2 years is expected to remain expansionary, with countercyclical measures in response to COVID-19 and continued support to social protection. The state budget is projected to record a deficit equal to 3.5% of GDP in 2020 as tax receipts decline, diminishing though to 2.1% of GDP in 2021 (Figure 3.4.10). The non-oil deficit will expand to the equivalent of 8.7% of GDP in 2020 and subside to 8.2% in 2021. Revenue is projected slipping to 17.1% of GDP in 2020 following tax breaks and with the economic impact of COVID-19 and then recovering to 18.4% in 2021. Expenditure is forecast at 20.6% of GDP in 2020, declining slightly to 20.5% in 2021 despite rising social outlays and continued programs for industrialization, infrastructure, and housing. Notwithstanding the government's plans to reduce sovereign wealth fund transfers to the budget, the rapidly deteriorating economic situation will cause a shortfall in tax collection, thus increasing reliance on such transfers. Government and government-guaranteed debt are projected to rise to 26.4% of GDP in 2020 and 27.8% in 2021, reflecting the higher fiscal deficit and currency depreciation.

Monetary policy over the next 2 years will focus on limiting the rise in inflation while supporting the government's efforts to mitigate the effects of COVID-19 on the economy. With more expansionary fiscal policy, broad money growth will increase to 10.0% in 2020 before slowing to 4.9% in 2021 as the central bank strives to drain excess liquidity. Since January 2020, the central bank has prohibited financial institutions from offering consumer loans to the unemployed and has introduced means testing for other borrowers, which should cool consumer credit growth.

Table 3.4.1 Selected economic indicators (%)

	2018	2019	2020	2021
GDP growth	4.1	4.5	1.8	3.6
Inflation	6.0	5.3	6.0	5.7
Current acct. bal. (share of GDP)	-0.2	-3.1	-5.3	-2.4

Sources: Republic of Kazakhstan, Ministry of National Economy, Statistics Committee; ADB estimates.

Figure 3.4.9 Inflation

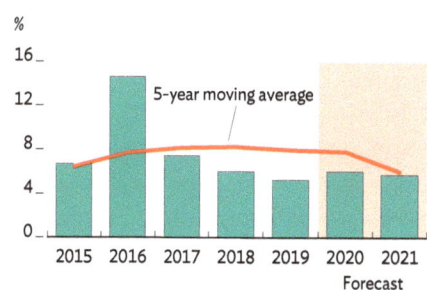

Source: *Asian Development Outlook* database.

Figure 3.4.10 Fiscal balance

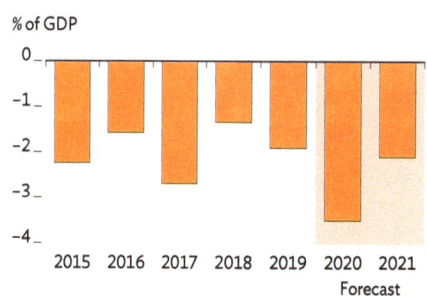

Source: *Asian Development Outlook* database.

The current account deficit is forecast to widen to the equivalent of 5.3% of GDP in 2020 as the trade surplus drops sharply and then narrow again to 2.4% in 2021 as exports recover (Figure 3.4.11). After an initial drop in 2020, merchandise exports are projected to bounce back by 42.2% in 2021, reflecting gains in agriculture and minerals. Imports, projected to decline moderately in 2020, will also rebound in 2021, expanding by 11.5% as the government raises social assistance payments and incomes continue to grow. Cost-cutting on international events, new COVID-19 travel restrictions, and a weak currency will reduce demand for imported services, narrowing the deficit in services in both 2020 and 2021.

International reserves, after declining in 2020, are projected to increase gradually to $23.5 billion at the end of 2021. Assets in the sovereign wealth fund are forecast to follow a similar trend and decline from the currently estimated $60 billion with guaranteed budget transfers exceeding commodity export revenue in 2020, and then recover to about $55 billion at the end of 2021. External debt, which is primarily intercompany debt, should increase to equal 97% of GDP at the end of 2020 with currency depreciation, and then moderate to 95% a year later as foreign subsidiaries and state-owned enterprises continue repaying their external debt.

Policy challenge—building a sustainable welfare system

As the plunge in oil prices and the challenges created by COVID-19 put the economy of Kazakhstan under unprecedented stress, the sustainability of its welfare system remains a critical concern in light of the role it plays as a stabilizer during crises.

For the welfare system to provide sufficient funding during difficult times, it must accumulate resources during the good times. Rapid economic growth since 2000 has allowed such accumulation while dramatically reducing poverty in Kazakhstan. The share of the population living below the national poverty line fell from 44.5% in 2002 to 2.6% in 2016. The World Bank estimates that 4 million–5 million people were pulled out of poverty from 2006 to 2015, while the middle class, defined as those living on more than $10 per person per day using 2005 purchasing power parity, grew from 8.5% of the population in 2006 to 25.0% in 2015.

Substantial currency devaluation since 2015 cut real incomes by 4.3% over the subsequent 3 years. Peaking at 14.6% in 2016, inflation eroded savings and drove the population living below the poverty line up to 4.3% in 2018. In response, the government broadened its social assistance program in 2019, easing eligibility requirements and raising payments. The number of social assistance recipients nearly quadrupled

Figure 3.4.11 Current account balance

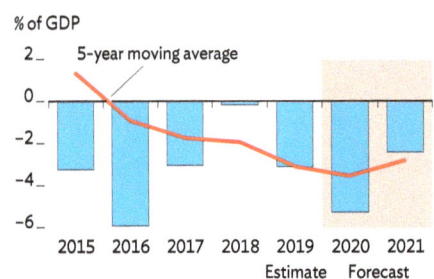

% of GDP

Source: *Asian Development Outlook* database.

in 2018 to 2.2 million people, while the average payment more than doubled (Figure 3.4.12). In the same year, social assistance outlays jumped by 26.0%, exceeding a quarter of the state budget or 5.1% of GDP, while transfers from the sovereign wealth fund and other state budget revenue each rose by 18.0%.

The government's assistance program helped moderate the impact of external shocks on the vulnerable population. However, the current financing model is not sustainable over the long run. Lower oil prices and stagnant production caused sovereign wealth fund receipts to fall by 11.0% in 2019, and they are likely to deteriorate further in the near future. Wealth fund assets, estimated at $60 billion, provide the fiscal space needed to meet growing social obligations for some time. Eventually, however, sustaining the welfare system will require the authorities to ensure some combination of higher revenue, increased borrowing, and/or lower expenditure from tighter eligibility requirements or smaller benefits.

The government is working to improve program targeting and streamline administration. In September 2019, careful verification removed more than 72,000 people from social assistance. In 2020, eligibility became conditional on able-bodied family members seeking employment, complemented by the state-run Enbek employment program. Further, the government is opening support centers across the country to provide advice and assistance to large and low-income families.

On the revenue side, the government is gradually implementing the twice-postponed Universal Declaration of Income and Property (UDIP) to facilitate compliance and reduce tax evasion. Civil servants will begin submitting declarations in 2021, and the goal is to require declarations from all taxpayers by 2025. While most of the work needed for the new system has been completed, implementing the UDIP is a complex task, with success depending on many factors, most notably proper data protection to prevent its misuse. The UDIP rollout is expected to help the government shrink the shadow economy to 15%–17% of GDP from current estimates of somewhat less than 30%, according to the Statistics Committee of Kazakhstan. Also, the UDIP may improve the targeting of social assistance by providing additional information on household income.

To complement these measures, the government may decide to replace the current flat income tax with a progressive tax, increasing rates for high-earning households. This system would leave more money with low-wage earners, who are likely to spend it on basic necessities, possibly increasing government tax receipts overall.

Improving revenue collection and the administration of the social assistance program should make social assistance more sustainable. It is preferable to increasing public debt or relying on additional transfers to the budget from the sovereign wealth fund.

Figure 3.4.12 Social assistance

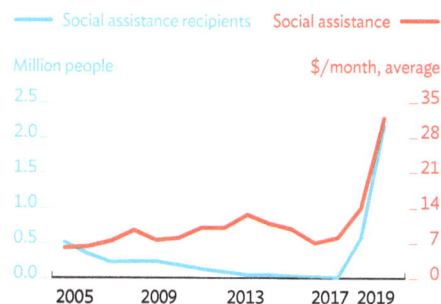

Source: Republic of Kazakhstan. Ministry of National Economy. Statistics Committee.

Kyrgyz Republic

Growth accelerated in 2019, driven by mining and manufacturing. Inflation decelerated as substantial food imports held prices down, and high gold exports narrowed the current account deficit. Growth is projected to decelerate in 2020 in tandem with a slowdown in the country's main trade partners amid the global COVID-19 outbreak, but recover in 2021 as gold exports rise. For a third consecutive year, the government is promoting development in lagging regions.

Economic performance

GDP growth in the first 3 quarters of 2019 was strong, rising above 6.0%, but it slowed during the fourth quarter (Q4) and finally averaged 4.5% in the full year (Figure 3.5.1). Growth outside the large gold-mining industry reached 3.8%.

On the supply side, growth in industry accelerated from 5.9% in 2018 to 8.1%. Although gold production slowed in Q4 as yields declined, steady growth in gold production in the first 3 quarters of 2019 allowed mining growth overall to reverse 2.1% contraction in 2018 with 18.4% growth in 2019. Growth in manufacturing rose from 5.1% in 2018 to 8.3% on increased production of metals, mineral products, coal, apparel, and food products. Expansion in construction rose from 7.8% in 2018 to 10.6% with robust investment in mining, energy, transport infrastructure, and trade facilities. Growth in agriculture was little changed at 2.6%. Expansion in services was also about the same in both years, at 2.9%. Transport growth jumped from 1.2% in 2018 to 3.3%, but retail and wholesale trade growth slid from 5.7% in 2018 to 4.9% in 2019.

On the demand side, public expenditure is estimated to have risen as spending increased on energy and transport infrastructure projects. Meanwhile, private consumption is estimated to have grown as wage increases in public schools and hospitals in Q4 of 2019 more than offset a 13.5% fall in remittances (Figure 3.5.2).

Inflation slowed from an average annual rate of 1.5% in 2018 to 1.1%, with prices held down by 0.3% Kyrgyz som appreciation versus the US dollar and substantial food imports (Figure 3.5.3). Food prices fell in the first half but were pushed up by seasonal factors in Q4. Meanwhile, prices for other goods increased by 0.6%, and for services by 0.1%.

Figure 3.5.1 GDP growth by sector

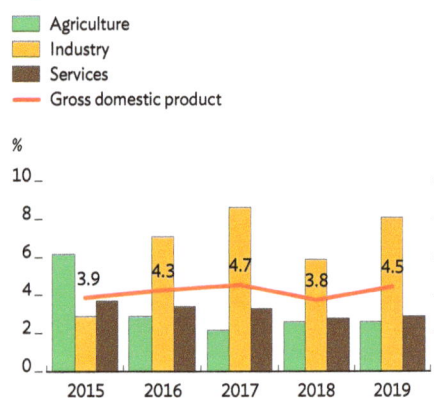

Source: National Statistics Committee of the Kyrgyz Republic. http://www.stat.kg (accessed 5 March 2020).

Figure 3.5.2 Remittances

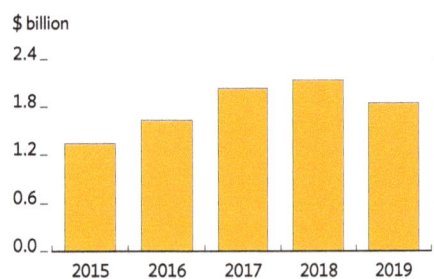

Source: National Bank of the Kyrgyz Republic. http://www.nbkr.kg (accessed 5 March 2020).

This chapter was written by Gulkayr Tentieva of the Kyrgyz Republic Resident Mission, ADB, Bishkek.

In December, inflation rose to 3.1% year on year, indicating that inflation was picking up (Figure 3.5.4).

The end-year fiscal deficit narrowed from 1.1% of GDP in 2018 to 0.1% in 2019. Expenditure rose from 27.7% of GDP to 28.4%, but revenue rose faster, from 26.6% of GDP to 28.3%. The smaller deficit and higher nominal GDP cut external government debt from 48.0% of GDP at the end of 2018 to 44.8% at the end of Q3 of 2019. Domestic government debt remained less than 6.0% of GDP.

During 2019, the National Bank of the Kyrgyz Republic, the central bank, loosened monetary policy and restricted its currency interventions to smoothing excess som volatility. With inflation low, the policy interest rate was cut from 4.75% at the end of 2018 to 4.25%, supporting economic expansion with strong domestic credit growth for a third year in a row. The average deposit interest rate increased from January to December 2019 by 0.07 percentage points to 4.2%, while the average lending rate fell by 0.2 percentage points to 14.8%. Deposits rose by 13.4% and credit by 14.5%, while growth in broad money accelerated from 5.5% in 2018 to 8.8%. Nonperforming loans worsened from 7.5% of all loans at the end of 2018 to 8.4% a year later. Dollarization remains extensive but is declining, with the share of foreign currency loans falling from 38.0% in 2018 to 35.7%, and deposits from 44.5% to 40.7%.

The current account deficit is estimated to have narrowed from the equivalent of 12.3% of GDP in 2018 to 10%. Exports rose by 7.5%, driven by gold exports up by 25.4%, vegetables 44%, meat products 43%, and cement 32%. Imports fell by 6.3%, reflecting imports of apparel and shoes down by 28%, sugar 26%, and chemical products 23%. Year-end international reserves rose from $2.1 billion in 2018 to a record high of $2.3 billion, or cover for 4.1 months of imports. External debt, including government-guaranteed and private debt, is estimated to have fallen from the equivalent of 85.6% of GDP at the end of 2018 to 82.6% at the end of Q3 of 2019 (Figure 3.5.5).

Economic prospects

Growth is forecast at 4.0% in 2020 (Figure 3.5.6). Although gold exports could benefit from global financial volatility, import disruption under COVID-19 affecting raw materials, equipment, and food from the People's Republic of China and other countries will hold back manufacturing, construction, and other import-dependent industries. If the outbreak worsens and border closures are prolonged, growth could slow even further. It should then pick up to 4.5% in 2021, assuming recovery in the region.

Figure 3.5.3 Exchange rate

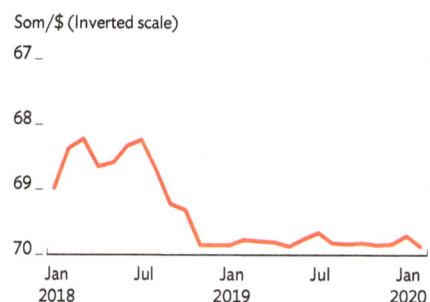

Som/$ (Inverted scale)

Source: National Bank of the Kyrgyz Republic. http://www.nbkr.kg (accessed 5 March 2020).

Figure 3.5.4 Monthly inflation

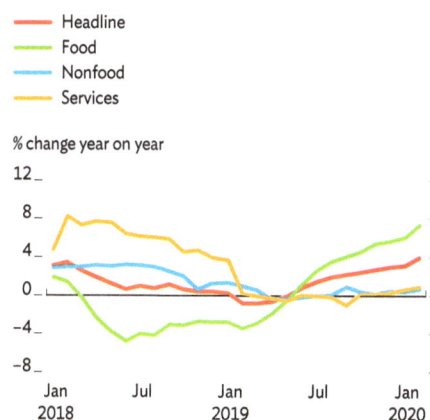

— Headline
— Food
— Nonfood
— Services

% change year on year

Sources: Bulletin of the National Bank of the Kyrgyz Republic. http://www.nbkr.kg (accessed 5 March 2020).

Figure 3.5.5 External debt

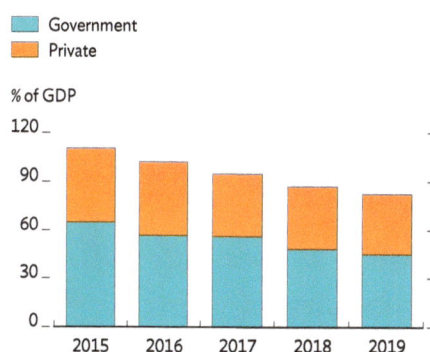

■ Government
■ Private

% of GDP

Note: Government debt refers to both government and government-guaranteed debt. Data for 2019 are to the end of the third quarter.

Sources: The Ministry of Finance; National Statistics Committee. http://www.stat.kg; National Bank of the Kyrgyz Republic. http://www.nbkr.kg (both accessed 5 March 2020).

On the supply side, gold production is expected to stay healthy. On the demand side, however, spending may shrink, especially private consumption, if remittances fall following an economic slowdown in Kazakhstan and the Russian Federation.

Average inflation will rise to 3.5% in 2020 on higher prices for food and other products, with border closures and possible depreciation of the Kyrgyz som against the US dollar. The central bank is expected to remain focused on maintaining price stability and a flexible exchange rate, and continue to intervene only to smooth excessive som volatility. Inflation in 2021 is expected to fall to 3.0% as conditions stabilize (Figure 3.5.7).

The fiscal deficit is projected to widen to the equivalent of 2.0%–3.0% of GDP in 2020 and 2021, with higher current spending on measures to contain COVID-2019. Nevertheless, the government is expected to continue to restrain unprioritized expenditure while improving tax policy and administration. Over the longer term, fiscal consolidation will remain a major concern. Efforts will focus on reforming public wages, cutting subsidies, improving the targeting of social benefits, broadening the tax base, and strengthening tax and customs administration. The aim is to keep public external debt below the equivalent of 50% of GDP in the medium term.

The current account deficit is expected to widen to the equivalent of 12.0% of GDP in 2020 as exports other than gold fall, but then ease back to 10.0% in 2021 (Figure 3.5.8). Healthy gold exports are projected to push export growth above 7.0% in both years, while other exports will be held back by Kyrgyz products' poor compliance with Eurasian Economic Union sanitary and phytosanitary standards. Meanwhile, imports could fall by about 5%–7% in 2020 as border closures delay infrastructure projects. Remittances will likely slow by 5%–10% in 2020, reflecting possible depreciation of the ruble and a growing trend among Kyrgyz migrant workers to obtain citizenship or long-term residency in the Russian Federation.

While debt sustainability has improved, the International Monetary Fund sees the Kyrgyz Republic at moderate risk of debt distress. Barring shocks, if public external debt is held below 50% of GDP, total external debt could be kept below 85% of GDP over the medium term.

Policy challenge—promoting development in lagging regions

Promoting development and reducing poverty in lagging regions have been government priorities since 2018. Currently, Bishkek and the adjoining Chui Region produce more than half of GDP with 30% of the population, while the southern regions of Osh, Jalal-Abad, and Batken produce less

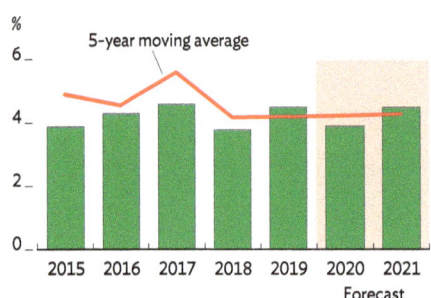

Figure 3.5.6 GDP growth

Sources: National Statistics Committee of the Kyrgyz Republic. http://www.stat.kg (accessed 5 March 2020); ADB estimates.

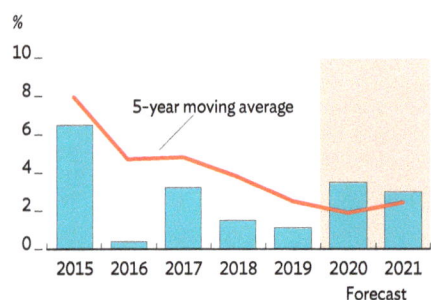

Figure 3.5.7 Inflation

Sources: National Bank of the Kyrgyz Republic; ADB estimates.

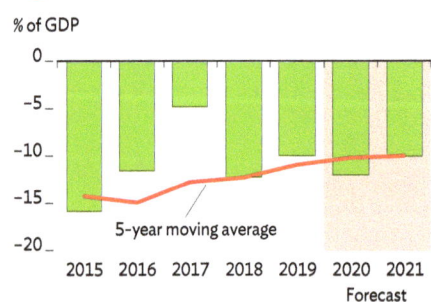

Figure 3.5.8 Current account balance

Sources: National Bank of the Kyrgyz Republic. http://www.nbkr.kg (accessed 5 March 2020); ADB estimates.

than a quarter of GDP with close to half of the population. Policies to narrow the gap need to foster private sector development and economic growth in lagging regions.

Poverty and inequality remain significant despite some improvement, with the national poverty rate improving from 30.6% in 2014 to 22.4% in 2018 and the Gini coefficient from 0.314 in 2008 to 0.273 in 2017. However, the Kyrgyz Republic ranked only 122 of 189 in the United Nations' *Human Development Report 2019*. Further, poverty is unevenly distributed at 20.1% in urban areas, and 23.7% in rural areas. About 68% of the poor are found in rural areas, with Osh, Jalal-Abad, and Batken accounting for 60%.

Limited access to jobs is a common factor in lagging regions, especially in remote ones. Lagging regions' share in overall employment plunged from 53.1% in 2000 to 29.3% in 2018. To cope, residents have moved to informal jobs elsewhere in the country or emigrated to take low-skilled jobs. More than 663,000 migrant workers are now estimated to be in the Russian Federation and another 150,000 in Kazakhstan. Workers' remittances, which equaled 12.7% of GDP in 2005, averaged 30% in 2011–2016 and have stabilized at about 22%. Excluding remittances, poverty rates remain high, especially in the southern regions.

Although increased investment could promote growth in lagging regions, both foreign and domestic investment currently remain weak. Foreign direct investment is low, equal to 9.0% of GDP in 2010–2018 and concentrated in mining. Meanwhile, policy support for small and medium-sized enterprises such as preferential tax, financing, and regulatory treatment remains limited, inhibiting their growth and competitiveness and hindering their adoption of new technologies and shift toward export orientation. To enable more participation in global and regional value chains, the Kyrgyz Republic should improve its ranking of 80 out of 190 in the World Bank's *Doing Business 2019*.

The government's Regional Policy of the Kyrgyz Republic, 2018–2022 is an integrated development program for targeted regions over the medium to long term. The objective is to develop economically competitive clusters of small and medium-sized enterprises that use local raw materials available in their region. The program is expected to narrow the gap between the more prosperous regions of Bishkek, Chui, and Issyk-Kul and other economically deprived regions: Batken, Jalal-Abad, Naryn, Osh, and Talas. It has identified 20 regional development centers or growth points, 5 or 6 of which are to be developed initially.

Special attention will be paid to developing agriculture by creating new irrigation projects and better maintaining existing ones. Regional and strategic roads are being developed to facilitate trade. With an improved investment climate and

Table 3.5.1 Selected economic indicators (%)

	2018	2019	2020	2021
GDP growth	3.8	4.5	4.0	4.5
Inflation	1.5	1.1	3.5	3.0
Current acct. bal. (share of GDP)	–12.3	–10.0	–12.0	–10.0

Sources: National Statistics Committee of the Kyrgyz Republic; Bulletin of the National Bank of the Kyrgyz Republic; ADB estimates.

better infrastructure, agro-industrial clusters have potential to be growth drivers. Other areas with potential are tourism, livestock breeding, construction, petrochemicals, and pharmaceuticals.

The government is implementing measures to improve the tax regime and strengthen capacity in local governments for public administration. The Russian–Kyrgyz Development Fund and the Guarantee Fund have developed mechanisms to support business in the regions. Decentralization will be pursued. The government will directly undertake infrastructure development and encourage private enterprise, notably in manufacturing, through public–private partnership. Human resource development in the identified growth centers will receive priority. It is expected that regional development will create jobs, thus slowing migration. Further development of free trade zones and industrial parks can complement the development of economic corridors toward promoting balanced regional growth.

Finally, a digital transformation program aims to promote the use of information and communication technology to connect government, businesses, and citizens. A high-tech park to promote the development of a domestic tech industry and attract foreign investment has been operational for more than 5 years.

Accelerating development in lagging regions and improving the lives of their residents would (i) foster higher economic growth by diversifying the manufacturing and export base and promoting new growth drivers and centers to create jobs; (ii) make economic growth more inclusive, improve the quality of basic services such as water supply and sanitation, and enhance the employability of the population through skill development; (iii) improve the business environment for attracting investment into the regions and developing private sector activity and public–private partnership; (iv) and catalyze solutions that enable the country to better leverage cross-border regional cooperation by utilizing potential for export and trade facilitation, agriculture value chains, and single markets in industry and services with other countries under the Eurasian Economic Union.

Tajikistan

Acceleration across sectors and a rebound in remittances boosted growth in 2019. Higher domestic demand lifted inflation, but the current account deficit narrowed slightly. Lower public investment, along with weak remittances and foreign direct investment under COVID-19, are projected to slow growth in 2020 and 2021, with inflation remaining in single digits. The current account deficit will be little changed as rising electricity exports offset low remittances. Reforming tax policy is important to spur investment.

Economic performance

Growth rose marginally from 7.3% in 2018 to 7.5% in 2019 with continued heavy public investment, higher remittances, and ongoing state-led industrialization that boosted manufacturing, despite weak private investment and unresolved problems in banking.

On the supply side, growth in industry expanded from 11.8% in 2018 to 13.6% on gains of 12.6% in mining, 16.2% in manufacturing, and 5.3% in electricity generation. Aluminum production reversed a 6.8% plunge in 2018 to grow by 5.2%, while gold production rose by 26.2% to a new record (Figure 3.6.1). Expansion in agriculture accelerated from 4.0% in 2018 to 7.1% on moderate gains in fruit and vegetable production and a strong recovery in cotton after a drought-induced fall in output in 2018. Growth in services, the largest sector (Figure 3.6.2), increased from 2.1% to 2.9% as a 6.3% rise in remittances helped expand retail trade by 9.6%. Construction reversed a 7.8% rise in 2018 to fall by 6.3%, reflecting weak demand for housing.

On the demand side, increased consumer demand boosted growth, though fixed capital investment reversed from a 7.8% rise in 2018 to a 6.3% decline with less growth in public investment. Net exports fell by 4.8% as continued but slower growth in infrastructure spending boosted imports, particularly for capital goods. Exports rose on higher electricity generation and cement production but remained lower than imports.

Inflation accelerated from 5.4% in 2018 to 8.0% as prices rose by 10.9% for food, 4.2% for other goods, and 5.5% for services (Figure 3.6.3). Contributing to higher inflation were seasonal supply shocks from adverse weather and higher prices for imported food, as well as rising household income, faster credit growth, and a 15.0% increase in electricity tariffs in September 2019.

Figure 3.6.1 GDP growth by sector

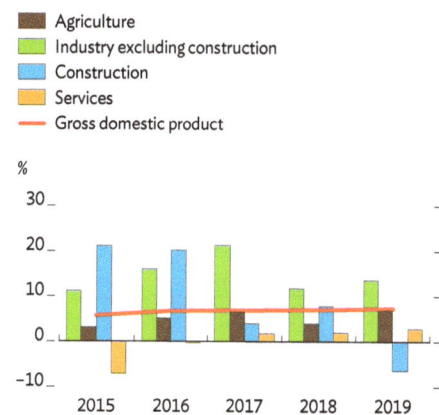

- Agriculture
- Industry excluding construction
- Construction
- Services
- Gross domestic product

Source: Tajikistan State Statistical Agency.

Figure 3.6.2 GDP production structure

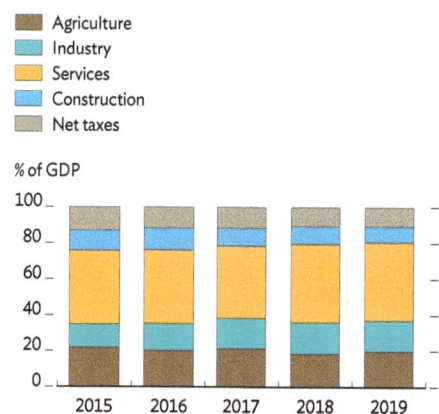

- Agriculture
- Industry
- Services
- Construction
- Net taxes

Source: Tajikistan State Statistical Agency.

This chapter was written by Muhammadi Boboev of the Tajikistan Resident Mission, ADB, Dushanbe.

Fiscal policy remained expansionary as continued spending for the Rogun hydropower project and disappointing revenue performance widened the government's budget deficit from the equivalent of 2.8% of GDP in 2018 to 3.8% (Figure 3.6.4). Shortfalls in corporate profit and value-added tax collections cut revenue from 29.1% of GDP in 2018 to 26.7%, though higher imports and better tax administration boosted excise and custom duty receipts. Expenditure declined from 31.9% of GDP in 2018 to 30.4% as outlays to complete and launch the second unit of Rogun in September proved smaller than anticipated. Robust GDP growth, external debt repayment, and limited new borrowing reduced public and publicly guaranteed external debt from 38.9% of GDP at the end of 2018 to 36.8% a year later, with total public debt declining from 47.9% of GDP in 2018 to 45.2% (Figure 3.6.5).

The National Bank of Tajikistan, the central bank, struggled to contain monetary expansion despite setting an inflation target of 5%–9% and expanding sales of Treasury bills and central bank securities to restrain liquidity. Growth in broad money tripled from 5.1% in 2018 to 16.9%, while expansion in private credit almost doubled from 6.5% to 12.0% (Figure 3.6.6). Reserve money growth also jumped, from 7.0% in 2018 to 20.1%. The central bank raised the refinancing rate from 14.00% to 14.75% in February 2019 before cutting it to 13.25% in June and 12.25% in December—then raised it again to 12.75% in February 2020 to cool the economy. Efforts to combat dollarization and tighten foreign exchange controls trimmed the share of foreign currency deposits from 53.2% at the end of 2018 to 46.9% a year later, and loans in foreign currency from 57.1% to 48.7%.

Improved bank supervision helped cut nonperforming loans from 31.1% of total credit in 2018 to 26.1%, as did greater loan volume enabled by higher remittances. The return on bank assets improved marginally from 1.9% in 2018 to 2.1%, and the return on bank equity from 7.0% to 7.7% (Figure 3.6.7). Two large banks remained troubled, however, and their resolution plans remain to be approved. In December 2019 the central bank launched the National Processing Center for Remittances, which requires transfer operators in the subregion and further afield to register and deposit remittances there.

The current account deficit narrowed from the equivalent of 5.0% of GDP in 2018 to an estimated 4.5% last year. The trade deficit widened marginally from $2.1 billion to $2.2 billion as export growth slowed from 10.4% in 2018 to 9.3%, but a slowdown in capital inputs for the Rogun hydropower project slashed growth in imports from 13.5% in 2018 to 6.3%. With some economic growth during 2019 in the Russian Federation, remittances edged up from $2.6 billion in 2018 to $2.7 billion, equal to 33.4% of GDP. Gross international reserves remained at $1.4 billion at the end of September 2019, cover for 5.4 months of imports, thanks to purchases of domestically produced gold and proceeds from a $500 million eurobond issue (Figure 3.6.8).

Figure 3.6.3 Sources of inflation

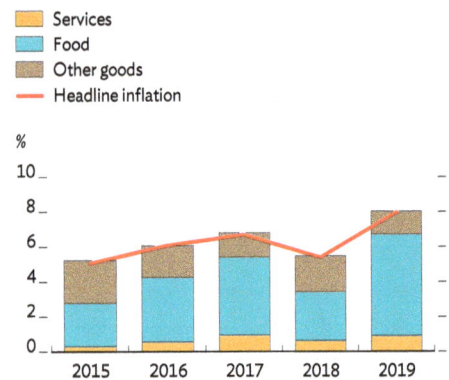

Source: Tajikistan State Statistical Agency.

Figure 3.6.4 Fiscal indicators

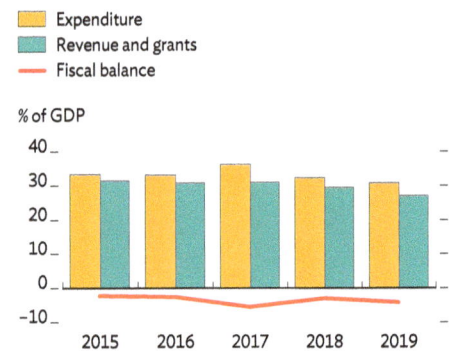

Sources: Ministry of Finance; Tajikistan State Statistical Agency.

Figure 3.6.5 Public debt

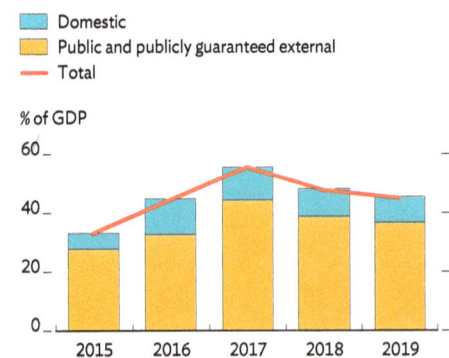

Sources: Ministry of Finance; Tajikistan State Statistical Agency.

Economic prospects

With the global outbreak of COVID-19, growth is forecast to slow to 5.5% in 2020 and 5.0% in 2021. Fiscal consolidation will reduce public investment, a weak business climate will discourage private investment, and low remittances from sluggish growth in the Russian Federation will limit domestic consumption. A pickup in private credit along with increased production and exports will support growth, as will additional electricity generation and improving economic relations with neighboring countries (Figure 3.6.9). Downside risks stem from weakness at two large banks and several state-owned enterprises, along with the possibility of greater declines in remittances, foreign direct investment, and tourism receipts as a result of COVID-19.

On the supply side, expansion in industry will likely slow as COVID-19 reduces foreign direct investment, despite continuing efforts to boost electricity generation, mining, and manufacturing. Reduced activity at Rogun and expected delays in constructing of Tajikistan's segment of a gas pipeline from Turkmenistan to the People's Republic of China should slow construction. Agriculture is expected to rise modestly with additional area under cultivation. Growth in services will slow in 2020 with low remittances but recover somewhat in 2021 as remittances expand.

On the demand side, public investment will remain the main growth driver, despite a further slowdown, as a weak business climate limits private investment. Private consumption will fall with low remittances. Net exports are forecast to improve as the implementation of Rogun and construction of a new transmission line reconnecting Tajikistan's electricity system to the Central Asia Power Grid boost electricity exports and support the domestic production of import substitutes.

Inflation is projected to remain under 10% in 2020 with moderating demand, despite the expectation of greater exchange rate flexibility, external currency pressures from ruble depreciation, potential supply shocks, and possibly faster monetary expansion during an election year, along with increases in public salaries expected in September 2020 and higher electricity tariffs expected in November. With slower growth in demand, inflation will moderate to 8.0% in 2021, within the central bank's 2020 target of 4%–8% (Figure 3.6.10). Inflation could be higher if currency depreciation accelerates or budgetary needs for domestic financing, including election year spending, exceed current plans, boosting money growth.

The budget deficit is projected to widen to 4.3% of GDP in both 2020 and 2021, with continued but moderating outlays for the Rogun project, election year spending in 2020, and the 30th anniversary of Tajikistan's independence in 2021.

Table 3.6.1 Selected economic indicators (%)

	2018	2019	2020	2021
GDP growth	7.3	7.5	5.5	5.0
Inflation	5.4	8.0	9.0	8.0
Current acct. bal. (share of GDP)	–5.0	–4.5	–4.5	–4.2

Sources: Tajikistan State Statistical Agency; ADB estimates.

Figure 3.6.6 Monetary indicators

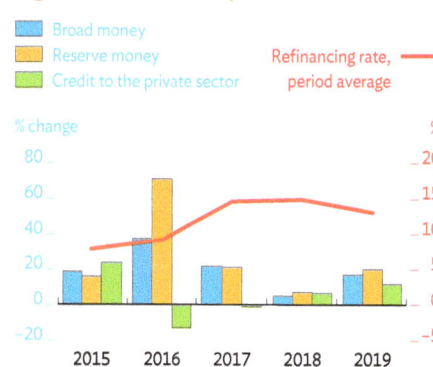

Source: National Bank of Tajikistan.

Figure 3.6.7 Indicators of banking system soundness

Q = quarter.
Source: National Bank of Tajikistan.

Tax revenue is projected to fall by 10% in 2020 as customs duties decline with lower imports attributable to disruption in trade, a decline in investment projects, and weaker domestic demand reflecting the unfavorable external environment. Total revenue is forecast at 25.1% of GDP in 2020 and 25.6% in 2021. Expenditure is forecast equal to 29.4% of GDP in 2020 and 29.9% in 2021 but could be higher with additional recapitalization of troubled banks, any clearing of arrears at state-owned enterprises, or faster currency depreciation, which would raise the cost of imports to supply investments. Although foreign assistance now comes entirely through grants because of Tajikistan's high risk of debt distress, the authorities anticipate covering any financing gaps for infrastructure through external borrowing, raising total external debt—all of it public—to $3.5 billion, or 39.0% of GDP, by the end of 2021. The prospect of continued large fiscal deficits from heavy investment spending risks making an already heavy debt burden unsustainable while weakening the external position through higher imports.

Monetary policy will likely aim to contain inflation and limit depreciation by tightening liquidity but may be constrained by demand for budget financing. The central bank could raise the refinancing rate if needed to limit inflation. Resources for lending to private firms may increase with the gradual recovery of the banking system.

The current account deficit is forecast to remain equal to 4.5% of GDP in 2020 and narrow slightly because of slower growth to 4.2% in 2021, with continued heavy capital-intensive imports (Figure 3.6.11). Exports are projected to grow by 10% annually in both 2020 and 2021 with higher electricity generation, including substantial exports of electricity to Afghanistan and Uzbekistan. With weak growth in the Russian Federation and the adverse effects of COVID-19 there and in other countries, remittances are projected to fall by 10% in 2020 and recover by 5% in 2021. Imports are expected to moderate in 2020 and expand by 5% in 2021 with rising disposable income and despite continued efforts to replace imports of food and manufactures with local alternatives. Reserves may fall below the current level despite purchases of domestically produced gold to offset sales of foreign exchange aimed at stabilizing the exchange rate.

Policy challenge—reforming tax policy

Heavy infrastructure spending has created pressure to mobilize more revenue. Tax revenue averaged the equivalent of 22.2% of GDP during 2015–2019 and provided nearly 70% of total revenue, above the average for low-income developing countries. Much of the burden falls on companies, for which the effective tax rate including required pension and insurance contributions

Figure 3.6.8 Gross international reserves

Q = quarter.
Source: National Bank of Tajikistan.

Figure 3.6.9 GDP growth

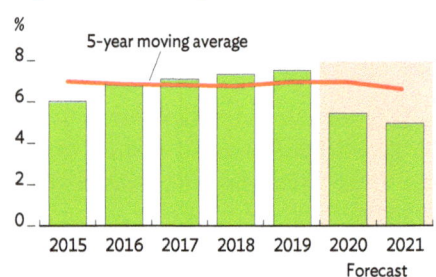

Sources: Tajikistan State Statistical Agency; ADB estimates.

Figure 3.6.10 Inflation

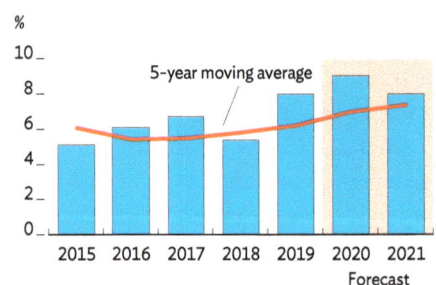

Sources: National Bank of Tajikistan; ADB estimates.

Figure 3.6.11 Current account balance

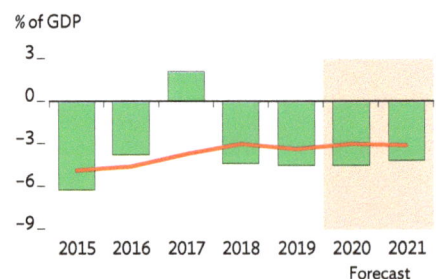

Source: ADB estimates.

averages 67% for a typical firm. This is more than double the norm for transitional economies in Europe and Central Asia, according to the World Bank's *Doing Business 2020* website. The unfavorable tax regime makes tax compliance costly and time consuming, prompting firms to relocate to neighboring countries. To improve the investment climate, Tajikistan must reconsider how to make its tax policy more business friendly while finding other ways to increase revenue.

Current tax policy has unrealistic revenue collection targets using reported GDP growth, which mainly reflects heavy public spending and overstates likely income growth at private firms. At the same time, tax laws provide generous tax exemptions estimated to exceed 5% of GDP, but they have failed to promote innovation and investment even as they distort markets and excessively burden small and medium-sized enterprises. Retroactive tax inspections and reviews invite corruption by some tax officers and have induced some investors to leave the country or close or sell their businesses. At the same time, the tax base has shrunk under inconsistent tax legislation, poor comprehension of tax provisions, and substantial tax avoidance and evasion, creating a large informal economy while undermining business prospects.

The government has begun a comprehensive process to introduce a new tax code in 2021. Goals include reducing the number of taxes, lowering corporate tax rates, and providing preferential rates for small businesses while widening the tax base and simplifying business operations. Electronic filing of tax returns and online payment of tax liabilities have already been introduced to simplify taxpaying and reduce corruption. However, more could be done to advance reform: reviewing tax exemptions to further broaden the tax base, moving from tax inspections toward risk-based assessment, and shifting more of the tax burden from income and profit to consumption. In particular, tax incentives should be limited to activities with clear and monitorable impacts on investment, innovation, regional development, and/or employment generation. In addition, administrative and compliance burdens should be reduced.

Meanwhile, the government must assess how proposed reform will affect revenue mobilization. Reform that lightens administrative burdens but reduces revenue will intensify fiscal pressures and make it harder to finance existing expenditure commitments. Unless the government wants to trim spending, reform will require new revenue measures, such as higher taxes on consumption and household income, to offset lower corporate taxes and boost revenue from sources other than income.

Turkmenistan

Faster expansion in hydrocarbon production modestly spurred growth in 2019. Inflation remained in double digits, and the current account fell into a marginal deficit. Growth is projected to moderate this year and next, with a corresponding decline in inflation. Robust imports to supply government investment projects are projected to widen the current account deficit in 2020 and 2021. Risk persists, given the likely global economic slowdown caused by the COVID-19 pandemic and a fall in commodity prices. Extensive reform is needed to diversify exports and mitigate vulnerability to commodity price shocks.

Economic performance

The government reported GDP growth rising slightly from 6.2% in 2018 to 6.3% in 2019, driven by expansion in both the large hydrocarbon industry and the rest of the economy (Figure 3.7.1). The International Monetary Fund (IMF) estimated that higher oil and gas output boosted growth in hydrocarbons from 5.4% in 2018 to 6.6%. Government support for import substitution kept expansion in the rest of the economy stable at 6.3%.

According to preliminary ADB estimates, higher gas output boosted growth in industry from 6.0% in 2018 to 6.9%. Expansion in services remained at 7.0% but with gains in retail trade, catering, and transport. Growth in agriculture is estimated to have accelerated from 3.5% in 2018 to 4.0% as cotton and wheat harvests met government targets.

On the demand side, higher gas exports supported growth, as did public investment though less so than in previous years. The IMF estimated that spending cuts required by fiscal adjustment trimmed gross investment from 28.2% of GDP in 2018 to 24.4% (Figure 3.7.2). Growth in private consumption remained sluggish as rising prices constrained real household incomes.

No official estimate has been released for inflation in 2019, but the IMF projected in its October 2019 World Economic Outlook that average annual inflation would rise slightly from 13.2% in 2018 to 13.4%, driven mainly by credit growth and increases in utility tariffs and other administered prices (Figure 3.7.3). Shortages of foreign exchange widened the gap between the official exchange rate and the parallel market rate, pushing up prices for imported goods. To contain inflation, the government maintained price controls on selected locally produced foods and services in state-run shops.

***

This chapter was written by Jennet Hojanazarova of the Turkmenistan Resident Mission, ADB, Ashgabat.

Figure 3.7.1 GDP growth

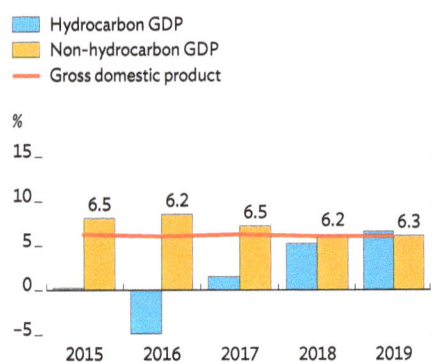

- Hydrocarbon GDP
- Non-hydrocarbon GDP
- Gross domestic product

Sources: International Monetary Fund. 2019. *Regional Economic Outlook: Middle East and Central Asia.* October; ADB estimates.

Figure 3.7.2 Gross investment including foreign direct investment

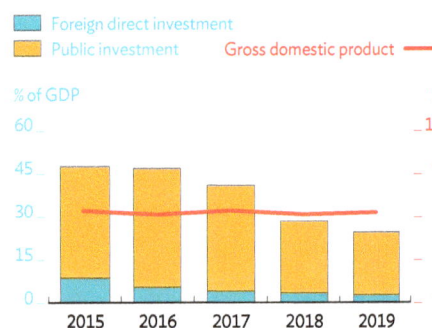

- Foreign direct investment
- Public investment
- Gross domestic product

FDI = foreign direct investment, GDP = gross domestic product.
Sources: International Monetary Fund. 2019. Press release following a staff visit; ADB estimates.

For its part in containing inflation, the Central Bank of Turkmenistan maintained strict control of cash in circulation while promoting noncash payments. It also kept the exchange rate fixed, limiting access to foreign exchange. Credit growth remained sizable, with credit rising to equal 63% of GDP. Lending mainly entailed subsidized credit to state-owned enterprises in priority sectors, with some credit provided to private firms involved in import substitution.

The state budget deficit is estimated to be unchanged at the equivalent of 0.1% of GDP in 2019, held down by cuts to capital spending and consumer subsidy programs, while the nonhydrocarbon fiscal deficit reportedly narrowed from 6.2% of GDP in 2018 to 5.2% (Figure 3.7.4). Revenue was estimated to have slipped from the equivalent of 13.5% of GDP in 2018 to 12.9%, and expenditure from 13.7% in 2018 to 13.2%. The central bank financed most of the budget deficit. Extrabudgetary spending remained considerable. Public sector debt was estimated to have risen from 29.1% of GDP at the end of 2018 to 30.7% a year later.

The current account is estimated to have recorded a small deficit equal to 0.6% of GDP, reversing a 5.7% surplus in 2018 as export growth slowed from 49.6% in 2018 to 8.0% while imports reversed a 47.8% drop in 2018 to expand by 1.6%. Hydrocarbon export revenue rose on increased gas purchases by the People's Republic of China as per intergovernmental contracts stipulating a gradual rise in gas shipments, as well as on the resumption of some exports to the Russian Federation. Foreign direct investment inflows, mainly for gas, oil, and chemical processing, were estimated to equal 3.0% of GDP. External borrowing for large infrastructure projects remained significant, helping to push external debt from 25.4% of GDP at the end of 2018 to 27.1% a year later (Figure 3.7.5).

Economic prospects

Growth is projected to moderate to 6.0% in 2020 and 5.8% in 2021 as expansion slows in hydrocarbon output and exports (Figure 3.7.6). On the supply side, industry is projected to expand by 6%–7%, reflecting gains in agricultural processing, light industry and food products, construction materials, and chemicals—all areas that have been targeted for import substitution. With the government having announced support for farmers, agriculture is forecast to expand by 4% in both years, while growth in services is projected to slow to 5%–6% as growth in domestic demand moderates.

With some slowing in domestic demand, inflation is likely to decelerate, though continued foreign exchange shortages will likely mean further price increases for imported goods. The authorities are expected to continue their efforts to limit inflation with administrative price controls while promoting import substitution and maintaining a fixed exchange rate.

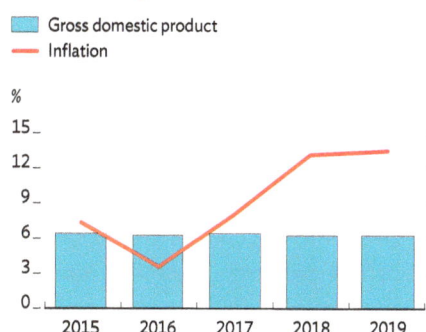

Figure 3.7.3 Gross domestic product growth and inflation

Sources: International Monetary Fund. 2019. *Regional Economic Outlook: Middle East and Central Asia.* October; ADB estimates.

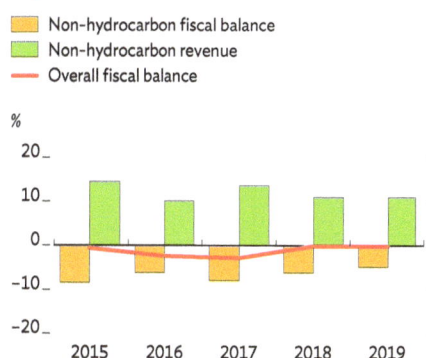

Figure 3.7.4 Government fiscal balances

Note: Fiscal data refer to the general government. Non-hydrocarbon fiscal balance and revenue are percentages of non-oil gross domestic product, and the overall fiscal balance is a percentage of total gross domestic product.
Sources: International Monetary Fund. 2019. *Regional Economic Outlook: Middle East and Central Asia.* October; ADB estimates.

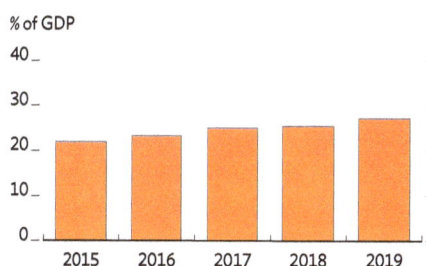

Figure 3.7.5 External debt

Sources: International Monetary Fund. 2019. *Regional Economic Outlook: Middle East and Central Asia.* October; ADB estimates.

Banks will likely continue direct lending to state-owned enterprises in priority sectors in the near term but have longer-term plans to shift from directed lending to loan pricing based on risk.

The state budget is projected to record small deficits of less than 1% of GDP in 2020 and 2021. The government aims to continue support for social services and announced that 70% of expenditure would go to such outlays, while also announcing a 10% rise in wages, pensions, and stipends. Domestic treasury securities are projected to provide budget financing equal to 3% of GDP, allowing some domestic debt to be refinanced.

Contracts for gas shipments are forecast to lift export revenue by 7%–8% in both 2020 and 2021. With large projects requiring imports of equipment and services, the current account deficit is projected to widen to equal 3%–5% of GDP in 2020 and 2021 (Figure 3.7.7). External debt could rise to equal 30% of GDP by 2020 or 2021.

Recent adverse developments in the global economy, including the spread of COVID-19, and grim prospects for global hydrocarbon prices, could pose downside risks to Turkmenistan's economic outlook.

Policy challenge—diversifying exports

Turkmenistan's exports are the most concentrated in Central Asia (Figure 3.7.8). Hydrocarbons accounted for 90.1% of all exports in 2018, with natural gas providing 55.2%, oil 22.6%, and oil products 12.3%. Most exports go to a single market, previously the Russian Federation but now the People's Republic of China. Such export concentration leaves the country vulnerable to commodity price shocks observed since mid-2014.

Economic diversification has been a key element of Turkmenistan's national program of socioeconomic development for 2011–2030. The President's program for 2019–2025, adopted in February 2019, reemphasizes the need to diversify the economy through import substitution, export promotion, and structural transformation, while raising the number and quality of jobs in manufacturing and services with higher value added.

Several measures have been introduced over the past decade to promote diversification both within and beyond the hydrocarbon economy. To move up the value chain, the government prioritized foreign direct investment for natural gas processing and the production of liquid fuels, polyethylene, polypropylene, ammonia, and urea toward developing chemical and fertilizer industries with higher value added. Beyond the hydrocarbon economy, large public investments aim to improve domestic and regional connectivity through new and improved roads, railways, airports, and telecommunications, thereby promoting growth. Targeted government support to

Table 3.7.1 Selected economic indicators (%)

	2018	2019	2020	2021
GDP growth	6.2	6.3	6.0	5.8
Inflation	13.2	13.4	13.0	8.0
Current acct. bal. (share of GDP)	5.7	-0.6	-3.0	-4.7

Sources: International Monetary Fund. 2019. *Regional Economic Outlook: Middle East and Central Asia.* October; ADB estimates.

Figure 3.7.6 GDP growth

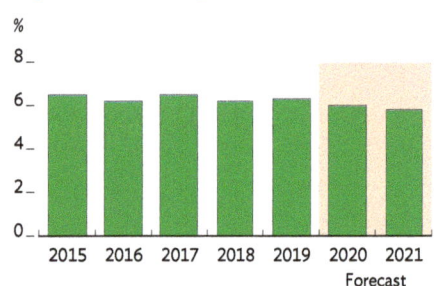

Source: *Asian Development Outlook* database.

Figure 3.7.7 Current account balance

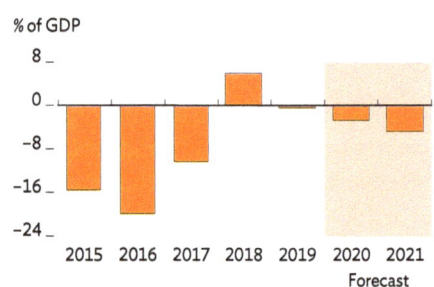

Sources: International Monetary Fund. 2019. *Regional Economic Outlook: Middle East and Central Asia.* October; ADB estimates.

export-oriented small and medium-sized enterprises has, along with steps to lower impediments to local private businesses, increased the production of import substitutes for building materials and in light industry, mainly textiles, clothing, and such food products as meat, dairy goods, flour, and flavorings. These developments have raised the share of manufacturing and processing in industry (Figure 3.7.9). Local production now meets a large share of domestic demand, reducing the need to import.

Meanwhile, Turkmenistan has significant potential to expand its export-oriented manufacturing and services. Greater participation in global trade would, however, require making the economy more open. For that to succeed, domestic firms would need to upgrade and diversify their output with new and more sophisticated products. This would mean jobs with higher productivity and therefore able to provide higher incomes.

Shifting the focus in Turkmenistan from import substitution to export promotion would require deeper institutional and structural reform to overcome current obstacles to doing business internationally, make the country more open to trade, and conform with international standards. This should include, among other measures, pursuing more efficient investment projects, creating a conducive business and investment climate, fostering private sector activity, improving access to finance in a more effective financial system, and upgrading the skills of the workforce.

Making investment projects more efficient is paramount, as high investment in the past, nearly equal to half of GDP, has generated only limited improvements in productivity and competitiveness except in hydrocarbons. Careful assessment of possible export activities outside of the hydrocarbon economy is needed to gauge their potential to be competitive and viable over the long term. This would depend on demand in international markets and the impact of new activities on domestic employment and income. Reviewing and prioritizing current investment projects based on such assessments is important to guide the selection of the most efficient investments for export-oriented production.

Attracting foreign direct investment in the non-hydrocarbon economy could help bring capital, skills, and managerial know-how while providing greater access to foreign markets. The major prerequisite for this is creating a business-friendly environment.

Reforming the investment and business climate could facilitate greater foreign investment inflow and invigorate the private sector. The European Bank for Reconstruction and Development contends in its Transition Report 2019–2020 that Turkmenistan needs to improve in many institutional dimensions, notably governance, transparency, competitiveness, private sector development, and financial intermediation.

Figure 3.7.8 Export concentration index, 2018

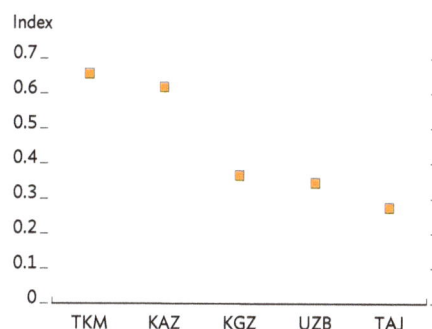

KAZ = Kazakhstan, KGZ = Kyrgyz Republic, TAJ = Tajikistan, TKM = Turkmenistan, UZB = Uzbekistan.
Source: United Nations Development Program. *Human Development Report 2019: Human Development Indices and Indicators.*

Figure 3.7.9 Change in the composition of industrial production

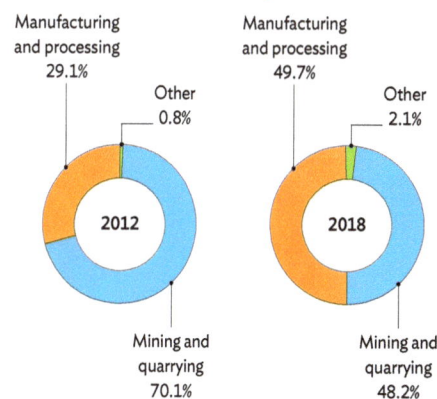

Manufacturing and processing 29.1%
Other 0.8%
2012
Mining and quarrying 70.1%

Manufacturing and processing 49.7%
Other 2.1%
2018
Mining and quarrying 48.2%

Source: *Statistical Yearbook of Turkmenistan 2019.*

Loosening the state monopoly in banking, deepening financial intermediation, and improving exchange rate management would enhance reform and remove current disincentives for efficient investment and business.

Developing human capital and a more skilled workforce is essential to boost labor productivity and competitiveness. This requires improving the quality of education at all levels, especially tertiary education, which has the most impact on innovation and graduating to higher value added. According to the United Nations Development Program's *Human Development Report 2019*, Turkmenistan needs to boost its tertiary education programs, as only 8% of its rapidly expanding young population is enrolled in tertiary education. Expanding tertiary education, strengthening research and development capacity for innovation would help enhance workforce productivity.

Turkmenistan would also benefit from greater data dissemination, closer ties with development partners, and more participation in international surveys and assessments such as the *Doing Business* report of the World Bank, *Global Competitiveness Report* of the World Economic Forum, and *Public Investment Management Assessment* framework of the IMF, which would help identify existing bottlenecks and suggest steps to overcome them.

Uzbekistan

An improved business climate spurred investment, boosting growth. Inflation moderated, and higher exports narrowed the current account deficit. Growth is anticipated to slow in 2020 with lower demand and prices for natural gas and copper, as well as the effects of COVID-19, then recover in 2021 as industry and agriculture pick up. Monetary tightening will trim inflation further in 2020 and 2021, and slower import growth will narrow the current account deficit. Inflation must be contained even as structural reform continues.

Economic performance

The government reported that growth accelerated marginally from 5.4% in 2018 to 5.6% in 2019.

On the supply side, expansion in agriculture rose from 0.3% in 2018 to 2.5% as abundant water supply and price incentives for cotton and wheat raised crop harvests by 3.7% and livestock production by 1.7%. Growth in construction accelerated from 14.3% in 2018 to 19.0%, driven by housing, infrastructure development, and modernizing industrial facilities. Expansion in industry declined from 10.8% in 2018 to 6.6% as a slowdown in hydrocarbon production trimmed output from mining and quarrying by 1.0%, reversing 26.5% expansion in 2018, though growth in manufacturing rose from 7.9% to 9.4%. Growth in services also moderated, from 5.5% in 2018 to 5.1%, reflecting smaller gains in trade, accommodation, catering, transportation, storage, and information and communication (Figure 3.8.1).

On the demand side, investment was the main growth driver, with gross fixed capital formation jumping from 29.9% expansion in 2018 to 33.9% on higher investment in manufacturing, mining and quarrying, energy, and housing. An improved investment climate boosted foreign loans and foreign direct investment (FDI) into modernizing machinery and equipment, upgrading inventories, and construction. Growth in private consumption slipped from 5.9% in 2018 to an estimated 5.7%, but public consumption accelerated from 4.8% to an estimated 5.5%. Wages and income were higher for civil servants and workers generally, augmented by increased remittances and lending to households. Net exports improved by 4.2% as growth in exports outpaced imports.

Figure 3.8.1 GDP growth by sector

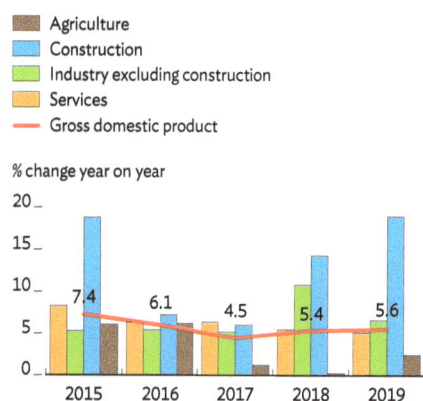

- Agriculture
- Construction
- Industry excluding construction
- Services
- Gross domestic product

% change year on year

Sources: State Statistics Committee; ADB estimates.

This chapter was written by Begzod M. Djalilov of the Uzbekistan Resident Mission, ADB, Tashkent.

Inflation slowed from 17.5% in 2018 to 14.6% as tight monetary policy and delayed adjustments to utility prices cut inflation by more than a quarter in the first 7 months of 2019 (Figure 3.8.2). Inflation reaccelerated during the rest of the year on price increases averaging 21.6% for regulated items such as bread and electricity in the second half and with 5.5% depreciation of the Uzbek sum against the US dollar in August 2019, after the exchange rate was floated (Figure 3.8.3).

The consolidated budget reversed a surplus in 2018 equal to 0.5% of GDP with a 1.5% deficit. The overall fiscal balance, comprising the consolidated budget balance and expenditure on state programs financed by external borrowing and covered by the state budget, also showed a deficit, up from 2.5% of GDP a year earlier to 3.9%. Higher spending on social and infrastructure development, coupled with a 39.0% increase in salary expenditure, boosted total outlays by 37.0%. Revenue rose by 27.0%, benefiting from a broader base for value-added tax (VAT), the adoption of a 12% personal income tax, the cancellation of customs exemptions on imports beginning in October 2019, and higher reporting of taxable wages brought about by stronger tax enforcement. External borrowing financed an estimated 57.1% of the deficit and domestic sources the rest.

Despite declining inflation, the central bank kept the policy rate at 16.0% as credit growth accelerated from 51.4% to 54.8%. Loans in foreign currency outgrew domestic currency loans because interest rates on US dollar loans averaged only 7.0% versus 24.4% for those denominated in Uzbek sum. Policy-guided lending at an average interest rate of 7.6% boosted credit expansion, kept state-owned banks' share in total assets at 86.0%, and weakened the impact of monetary policy.

Growth in broad money accelerated slightly from 13.2% to 13.8% (Figure 3.8.4). Broad money in Uzbek sum grew by 14.4%, down from 21.7% a year earlier, while net foreign assets rose by 12.7%, reversing 1.7% decline in 2018.

In the first half of 2019, excess demand for foreign exchange helped depreciate the sum by 2.8% despite occasional central bank intervention. With rapid credit growth fueling import demand, the central bank floated the currency on 20 August, following 8.7% depreciation against the US dollar from January. Cumulative depreciation reached 14.0% during the year. To avoid a run on deposits, the central bank advised commercial banks to adjust interest rates on deposits, which in August 2019 averaged 18.0% for local currency and 5.0% for US dollar deposits, and to be flexible about changing credit terms so that borrowers could repay loans at the new exchange rate. As part of structural reform, the government abolished from 1 October exemptions from customs payments, which encouraged importers to boost inventories of intermediate and capital goods beforehand.

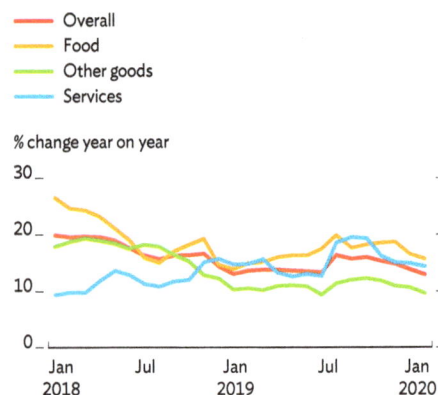

Figure 3.8.2 Monthly inflation

— Overall
— Food
— Other goods
— Services

% change year on year

Source: State Statistics Committee.

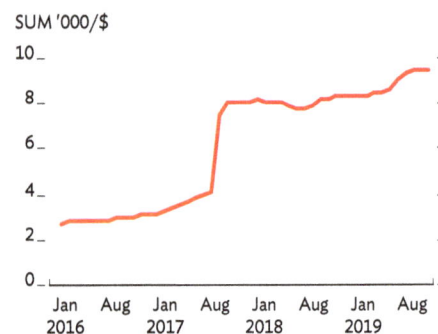

Figure 3.8.3 Exchange rate

SUM '000/$

Sources: The Central Bank of the Republic of Uzbekistan; ADB estimates.

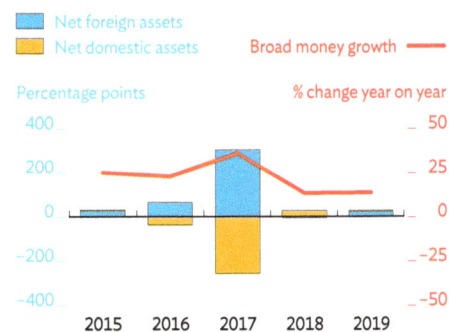

Figure 3.8.4 Contributions to money supply growth

Net foreign assets
Net domestic assets
Broad money growth —

Percentage points   % change year on year

Source: The Central Bank of the Republic of Uzbekistan.

The current account deficit narrowed from 7.1% of GDP in 2018 to 4.2% as the trade deficit shrank from $9.3 billion to $8.9 billion (Figure 3.8.5). Exports of goods and services expanded by 25.3%, a significant rise, albeit less than the 39.1% rise in 2018. Import growth slowed sharply from 42.3% in 2018 to 13.6%, with the lesser increase coming from imports of capital and intermediate goods for industry and construction. Cross-border transfers, mainly worker remittances, rose from $5.1 billion a year earlier to $5.8 billion, or 10.0% of 2019 GDP. FDI rose from the equivalent of 6.2% of GDP in 2018 to 7.3%, driven by investment in petrochemicals, cement, and textiles. External public debt climbed from 19.8% of GDP in 2018 to 26.2%. Foreign reserves rose from $27.1 billion at the end of 2018 to $29.2 billion a year later, providing cover for 13 months of imports (Figure 3.8.6).

Economic prospects

Growth is likely to slow to 4.7% in 2020 with the adverse impact of COVID-19 and lower demand and prices for natural gas and copper, despite support from the government's stabilization measures. It is expected to reaccelerate to 5.8% in 2021 on higher investment and further gains in agriculture and industry from structural reform (Figure 3.8.7). Risks to stability remain from persistent inflation.

On the supply side, price liberalization for wheat and cotton and structural reform to production are expected to expand crop production, boosting agriculture by 2.5% in 2020 and 3.0% in 2021. Growth in industry is forecast to slow to 5.0% in 2020 as mining and quarrying output is curtailed by COVID-19 and lower external demand and prices for natural gas and copper. With government plans to improve production infrastructure and enterprise export potential, industry is projected to grow by 7.0% in 2021, reflecting higher domestic and foreign demand and further trade liberalization. Construction is expected to expand by 17.0% in 2020 and 15.0% in 2021 on housing reform and urban infrastructure development. Higher wages and pensions and ongoing reform in transport and finance should sustain growth in trade, transport, and banking. Thus, services are expected to increase by 4.0% in 2020 and 5.5% in 2021, despite possible fallout affecting tourism in the aftermath of the global COVID-19 outbreak.

On the demand side, investment will remain the key growth driver as government programs to develop urban infrastructure and upgrade manufacturing facilities should maintain high rates of fixed capital formation in 2020 and 2021. Periodic increases in wages coupled with slowing inflation will likely support private consumption in 2020–2021 despite the adverse effect on remittances of currency depreciation in the Russian Federation. Net exports will remain negative.

Figure 3.8.5 Current account components

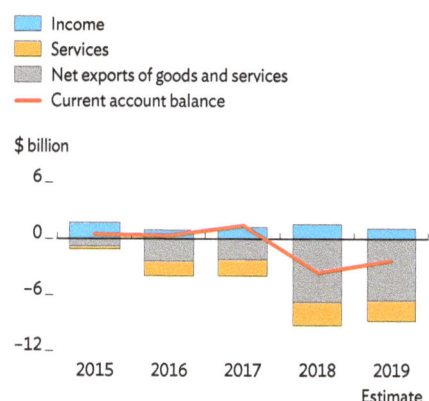

Sources: International Monetary Fund; ADB estimates.

Figure 3.8.6 Gross international reserves

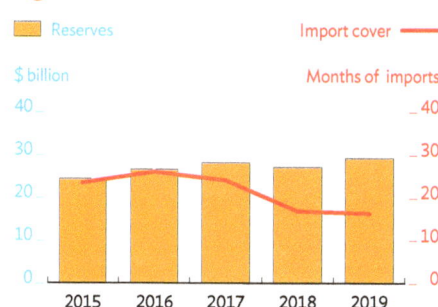

Sources: International Monetary Fund; ADB estimates.

Figure 3.8.7 GDP growth

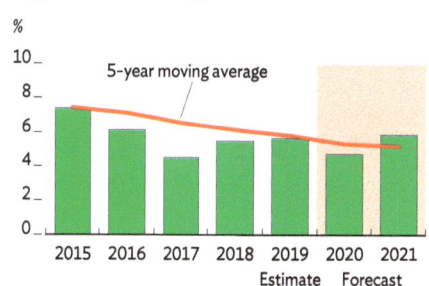

Source: *Asian Development Outlook* database.

Table 3.8.1 Selected economic indicators (%)

	2018	2019	2020	2021
GDP growth	5.4	5.6	4.7	5.8
Inflation	17.5	14.6	13.0	10.0
Current acct. bal. (share of GDP)	-7.1	-4.2	-4.0	-3.5

Sources: State Statistics Committee; ADB estimates.

Inflation is anticipated slowing to 13.0% in 2020 and 10.0% in 2021 (Figure 3.8.8). This reflects a gradual central bank shift toward inflation targeting and an expected halving of credit growth to 25.0% in 2020 and 20.0% in 2021 through fiscal tightening coupled with joint efforts by fiscal and monetary authorities to reform policy-guided lending. However, planned price hikes for electricity and natural gas and further deregulation of prices in agriculture will maintain inflationary pressures.

Broad money is anticipated to grow by 12.0% in 2020 and 11.0% in 2021 (Figure 3.8.9). In 2020, the central bank and the Ministry of Finance will jointly start reforming preferential lending, and by the end of 2021 all interest rates on loans will be at or above the central bank policy rate. To mitigate the adverse impact of slower credit growth on firms, banks are advised to relend credit accrued during the credit boom in 2018–2019 to efficient investment projects. In anticipation of price hikes for electricity and natural gas and their impact on inflation, the central bank kept the policy rate at 16.0% after its meeting on 5 March 2020 despite an expected slowing of inflation. However, the policy rate could decline if inflationary pressures and expectations diminish.

The consolidated fiscal deficit is projected equal to 0.5% of GDP in 2020, moving to a small surplus of 0.1% of GDP in 2021, while the overall fiscal deficit is expected to shrink to 2.7% of GDP in 2020 and 2.1% in 2021, financed by domestic and external borrowing (Figure 3.8.10). A cut in the VAT rate to 15.0% is projected to reduce consolidated budget revenue from 27.9% of GDP in 2019 to 24.3% in 2020 before it edges back to 24.6% in 2021. Expenditure is projected at 24.8% of GDP in 2020 and 24.5% in 2021, with outlays favoring education, health care, social protection, public services, and capital spending for agriculture, irrigation, and tourism infrastructure. The response to COVID-19 may require higher public expenditure, with implications for the country's fiscal position.

The current account deficit is forecast to narrow further, to 4.0% in 2020 and 3.5% in 2021, as the expected halving of credit expansion slows growth in imports of capital goods (Figure 3.8.11). Exports of natural gas and copper are expected to decline in 2020, offset by higher gold exports. In 2021, exports should expand with structural reform in agriculture, improved infrastructure for services and industry, and higher external demand for natural gas.

To contain rapid growth in external debt, the Ministry of Finance has limited external borrowing under public guarantees to $4.0 billion in 2020, and disbursements under external loans to $1.5 billion. Public external debt is nevertheless expected to reach the equivalent of 29.5% of GDP at the end of 2020 and 32.0% in 2021 (Figure 3.8.12).

Figure 3.8.8 Inflation

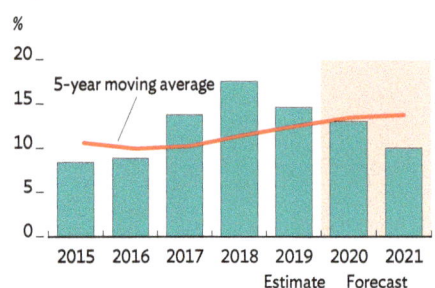

Source: *Asian Development Outlook* database.

Figure 3.8.9 Broad money and credit growth

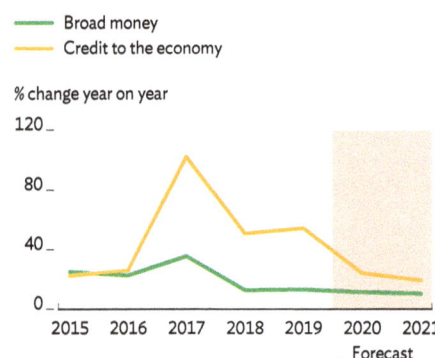

Sources: The Central Bank of the Republic of Uzbekistan; ADB estimates.

Figure 3.8.10 Fiscal components

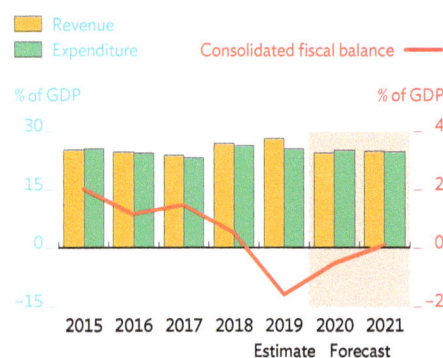

Sources: International Monetary Fund; ADB estimates.

Following issues in 2019 of $1.0 billion in sovereign eurobonds and a corporate eurobond debut by the state-owned Uzbek Industrial and Construction Bank, several commercial banks and state-owned enterprises are expected to issue eurobonds in 2020 and 2021.

Policy challenge—containing inflation during reform

Uzbekistan introduced comprehensive reform in 2017 to facilitate the transformation of a state-led economy into a market economy by eliminating distortions in key areas, notably agriculture, energy, and finance. The government eliminated a regime of multiple exchange rates, liberalized capital movement, streamlined procedures to facilitate trade with neighbors, and began deregulating prices for electricity, natural gas, bread, and cotton. Reform was partly to blame for inflation surging from 8.8% in 2016 to 17.5% in 2018 before slowing to 14.6% in 2019. The government faces the challenge of containing double-digit inflation to mitigate the adverse impact of structural reform on the population, 11.4% of whom live below the national poverty line. It must do so despite expected further adjustments to regulated prices and increases in import tariffs on such basic foodstuffs such as sugar, wheat, and edible oil. The dangers of high inflation include discouraging investors and undermining people's willingness to save in the banking system.

To contain inflation, the central bank has instituted an inflation-targeting regime to attain single-digit inflation in 2021 and 5% inflation in 2023. It adopts a base rate and interest rate corridor and open market operations. In addition, the central bank board has doubled to eight the number of annual meetings on the policy rate. Commercial banks will play a role as market makers in foreign exchange, and the central bank will further improve its market intervention methods using derivatives such as swaps, options, and futures. In 2020, the central bank and the Ministry of Finance began to unsegment the credit market by reforming preferential lending, with all lending to be based on market rates by the end of 2021. The central bank further aims to strengthen its macroeconomic analysis and forecasting and scrutinize firms' and individuals' inflationary expectations, while continually communicating monetary policy to the public.

Growth in state budget spending is projected to slow to 11.0% in 2020, and the cut in the VAT rate from 20% to 15% in 2019 is expected to have a lagged impact slowing inflation. In addition, the Ministry of Finance plans to reduce external borrowing and keep total external debt below 45% of GDP over the medium term. The government will further pursue a policy

Figure 3.8.11 Current account balance

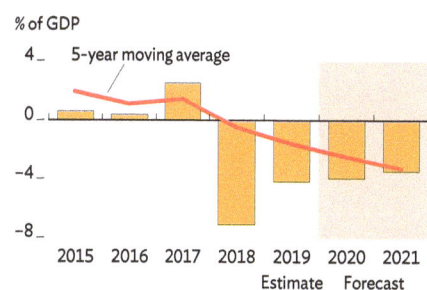

Sources: International Monetary Fund; ADB estimates.

Figure 3.8.12 Public external debt

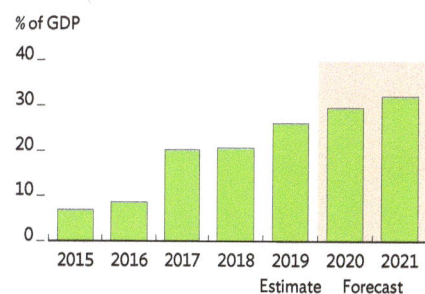

Sources: International Monetary Fund; ADB estimates.

of developing infrastructure to expand agricultural production and storage capacity, and to improve logistics for agriculture and food, which should ease seasonal shortages and price swings for vegetables, meat, and cereals.

It is critical to strengthen the transmission of monetary policy by further consolidating the credit market. Fiscal and monetary authorities should avoid market-distorting loans with preferential rates to households and firms. While price adjustments for electricity and other utilities to eliminate past distortions are inevitable in structural reform, the authorities should smooth these adjustments with targeted offsets to mitigate their impacts on the poor and improved service quality to boost productivity and limit rises in production costs. This requires accelerating reform in utilities such as state-owned electricity suppliers.

Curbing inflation also requires measures to address a lack of competition in transportation, education, and health care. The government should move to facilitate competition by promoting private sector involvement in these industries and by strengthening the institutional and regulatory capacity of the State Antimonopoly Committee. Finally, slowing inflation requires tackling administrative barriers that escalate costs for imports of consumption and intermediary goods, in particular food and construction materials. In this regard, the government should streamline customs clearance procedures by accelerating the adoption of risk management and customs administration that uses information and communication technology.

EAST ASIA

Hong Kong, China
Mongolia
People's Republic of China
Republic of Korea
Taipei,China

Hong Kong, China

Anemic domestic and external demand caused GDP to contract in 2019. Inflation edged up, and the current account surplus widened. Weakness will likely continue this year as domestic challenges and various external threats persist, but recovery is likely in 2021. Inflation will trend down in 2020 but up in 2021, and the current account surplus should stabilize in 2020, then narrow in 2021. Worsening inequality can be addressed through inclusive growth, strengthened labor productivity, and better jobs.

Economic performance

After growing by 2.9% in 2018, GDP shrank by 1.2% in 2019, marking the economy's first contraction since the global financial crisis of 2008–2009 (Figure 3.9.1). Growth moderation deepened as civil unrest took a huge toll on investment sentiment, private consumption, and tourism-dependent businesses, especially in the second half of the year. This dealt a severe blow to the economy already undermined by a global economic slowdown and trade conflict between the US and the People's Republic of China (PRC).

Domestic demand weakened significantly in 2019. Falling by 1.1% in real terms in 2019, private consumption recorded its first decline in 16 years and subtracted 0.8 percentage points from growth. The volume of retail sales fell by 12.3%, and the value of restaurant receipts by 5.9% (Figure 3.9.2). Fixed investment recorded its biggest drop in 2 decades, at 12.3%, subtracting 2.6 percentage points from growth. Machinery and equipment acquisition and intellectual property licensing plunged by 20.0%, while expenditure on buildings and construction fell by 6.1%. Meanwhile, new public services and higher allocations for existing ones pushed government consumption expenditure up by 5.1%, contributing 0.5 percentage points to growth.

Exports reversed 3.5% growth in 2018 to fall by 4.7% in real terms in 2019 amid a global economic slowdown and further slackening of manufacturing and trade worldwide. Exports to the US worsened sharply to a double-digit decline in 2019 as US demand for imports from the PRC moderated. Dragged down by faltering economic performance in major European economies, exports to the European Union also declined significantly, by 5.6%. Service exports slumped by 10.4%,

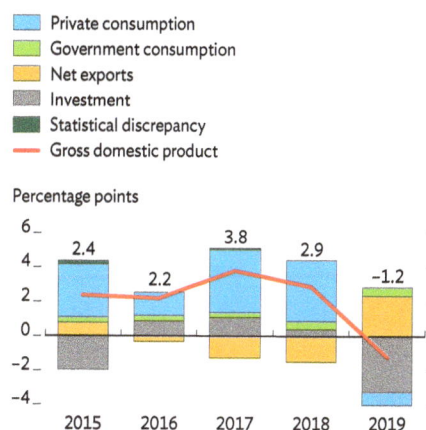

Figure 3.9.1 Demand-side contributions to growth

- Private consumption
- Government consumption
- Net exports
- Investment
- Statistical discrepancy
- Gross domestic product

Percentage points

Source: Census and Statistics Department, https://www.censtatd.gov.hk/home/ (accessed 22 March 2020).

Figure 3.9.2 Retail sales

- Volume
- Growth

Index, Oct 2014 to Sep 2015 = 100

Source: Census and Statistics Department, https://www.censtatd.gov.hk/home/ (accessed 22 March 2020).

This chapter was written by Matteo Lanzafame of the Economic Research and Regional Cooperation Department, ADB, Manila, and Michael Timbang, consultant, Economic Research and Regional Cooperation Department, ADB, Manila.

the biggest annual decline on record, undercut by a fall in tourist arrivals, which plunged by 14.2% last year amid local tensions in the second half and slashed receipts from travel services by 21.0% (Figure 3.9.3). Exports of financial, business, and other services also fell as cross-border financial and commercial activities weakened. Meanwhile, imports of goods and services were severely hit by weakening domestic demand and plummeted more sharply than exports, by 6.8% (Figure 3.9.4). The upshot was net exports adding 2.3 percentage points to growth.

On the supply side, most sectors saw significant declines in the first 3 quarters of 2019 as they suffered under the prevailing malaise. The exceptions were agriculture, fishing, mining, and quarrying, which narrowed their combined contraction from 2.9% in the first 3 quarters of 2018 to 0.2%; information and communications, which expanded by 5.4%; and real estate, professional, and business services, which grew by 1.4%. Import and export, wholesale, and retail trade services were severely hit by the unrest, reversing 5.3% growth to plummet by 5.3%. Accommodation and food services were also badly buffeted in the first 3 quarters of last year, plummeting from 7.0% growth in the same period in 2018 to contraction by 4.0%. Growth in the entire service sector fell from 3.5% in the first 3 quarters of 2018 to 0.4% in real terms. Manufacturing output growth also slowed, from 1.3% to 0.7%, in response to a weak external environment. Construction registered the biggest decline, reversing 5.4% growth in the first 3 quarters of 2018 to fall by 5.8%.

Headline consumer price inflation accelerated from an average of 2.4% in 2018 to 2.9% in 2019 as pressures on food prices continued to build, led by the disrupted supply of fresh pork owing mainly to an outbreak of African swine fever in the PRC (Figure 3.9.5). Netting out the effects of all government one-off relief measures, the underlying inflation rate rose from an average of 2.6% in 2018 to 3.0% in 2019. Average residential property prices rose by 1.5%, while residential rents retreated by 5.2% in December from their recent peak in August.

The current account surplus widened to equal 6.4% of GDP in the first 3 quarters of 2019, almost doubling a 3.3% surplus in the same period of 2018. This reflected a narrower trade deficit and a slight increase in net inflow of primary income, partly offset by a lower service surplus. The overall balance of payments turned around a deficit equal to 0.8% of GDP in the first 3 quarters of 2018 to record a 0.1% surplus in the same period of 2019. Gross official reserves rose to $441.4 billion at the end of 2019, or cover for 9.4 months of imports. Net external financial assets amounted to 3.9 times GDP at the end of the third quarter of last year, providing the economy with a strong cushion against sudden external shocks.

Figure 3.9.3 Tourism indicators

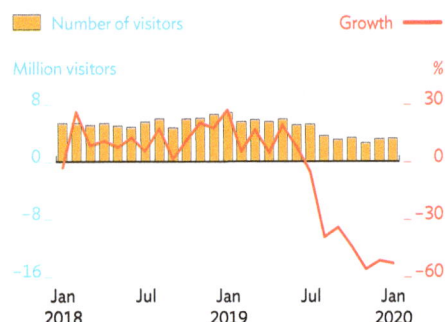

Source: CEIC Data Company (accessed 22 March 2020).

Figure 3.9.4 External trade

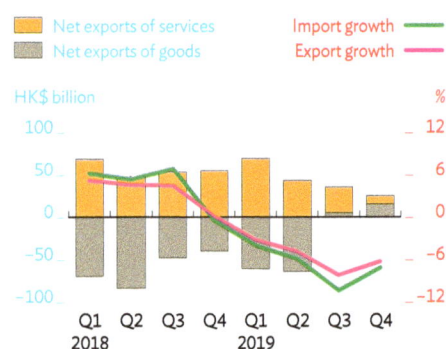

Source: Census and Statistics Department, https://www.censtatd.gov.hk/home/ (accessed 22 March 2020).

Figure 3.9.5 Monthly inflation

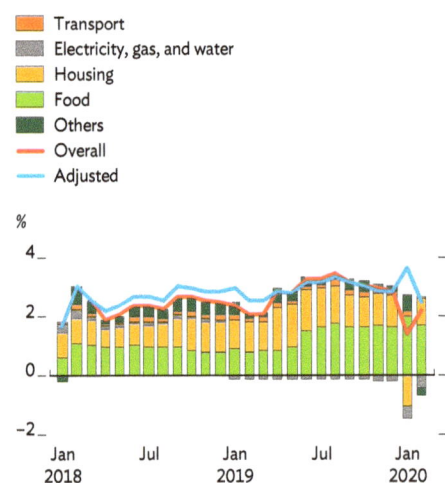

Note: Adjusted inflation refers to the rate once the effects of temporary subsidies by the government are removed.
Source: CEIC Data Company (accessed 22 March 2020).

The government revised its budget estimate for fiscal year 2019 (FY2019, ended 31 March 2020) from a surplus equal to 0.6% of GDP to a deficit of 1.3%, mainly because revenue was 9.4% lower than expected and expenditure 0.6% higher than budgeted to finance the establishment of an anti-epidemic fund (Figure 3.9.6). Revenue from profit tax, salaries tax, and stamp duties declined significantly under subdued economic conditions, enhanced tax concessions, and deferred tax assessment cycles.

Monetary conditions remained broadly accommodative in 2019. Following a US interest rate cut in October, the Hong Kong Monetary Authority reduced its base rate by 25 basis points to 2.0% to support the local dollar peg against the US dollar. Domestic credit grew by 7.1% in December, and the broad money (M2) supply rose by 2.8% (Figure 3.9.7). Reflecting ongoing unrest and softening global growth, the local stock market exhibited considerable volatility last year. The Hang Seng Index fell by 12.1% from May to September 2019, but, spurred by the phase one trade deal between the US and PRC, rebounded in December to rise 9.1% higher than in December 2018 (Figure 3.9.8).

Economic prospects

GDP is projected to contract further by 3.3% in 2020 as the economy faces significant downward pressure from faltering domestic and external demand (Figure 3.9.9). The adverse impact of persistent unrest will continue to dampen consumer spending and investor sentiment. The COVID-19 outbreak will weigh on already weak private consumption and inbound tourism, evidenced by sharp contraction in retail sales and services receipts. The composite purchasing managers' index remained contractionary at 46.8 in January and plunged further to 33.1 in February as the COVID-19 threat snowballed, signaling the sharpest deterioration of private sector conditions in more than 2 decades (Figure 3.9.10). Moreover, business surveys in the first quarter of 2020 remained pessimistic and suggested broad and continued deterioration in investor sentiment.

The labor market has started to weaken, with the unemployment rate rising from 2.8% in June to 3.3% in December. Given soft global trade, weighed down by growth moderation in the PRC and several other key partners, exports are unlikely to rise this year. In mid-January 2020, business sentiment in the service sector remained pessimistic, but services will continue to be the main driver of growth, supported by trade-related and professional activities. Assuming that unrest subsides and the impact of COVID-19 is contained, gradual recovery is forecast for all sectors later this year and next year, with growth forecast at 3.5% in 2021, buttressed by expansionary fiscal measures and recovery in demand, both domestic and external.

Figure 3.9.6 Fiscal indicators

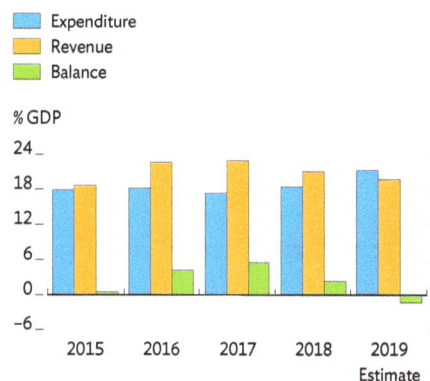

Note: Years are fiscal years ending 31 March of the next year.
Sources: The Government of the Hong Kong Special Administrative Region of the PRC. The 2020–2021 Budget, and other years. http://www.budget.gov.hk; CEIC Data Company; *Asian Development Outlook* database.

Figure 3.9.7 Domestic credit and money supply growth

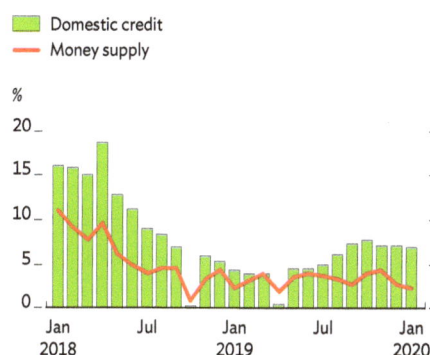

Source: CEIC Data Company, Hong Kong Monetary Authority, https://www.hkma.gov.hk/ (accessed 22 March 2020).

Table 3.9.1 Selected economic indicators (%)

	2018	2019	2020	2021
GDP growth	2.9	–1.2	–3.3	3.5
Inflation	2.4	2.9	2.0	2.5
Current acct. bal. (share of GDP)	3.7	6.4	7.0	5.0

Sources: Census and Statistics Department, https://www.censtatd.gov.hk/home/ (accessed 22 March 2020); ADB estimates.

Headline consumer price inflation is forecast to average 2.0% in 2020 and 2.5 in 2021 (Figure 3.9.11). The inflation rate may stay somewhat elevated in the coming months as pork supply disruption continues, but overall price pressures are expected to be moderate in tandem with subdued economic performance and the near absence of external price pressures. Domestic cost pressures, on the other hand, will depend on developments in local economic conditions and real estate, especially private residential rent.

The FY2020 budget deficit is forecast to widen to the equivalent of 4.8% of GDP as cash payouts and other one-off relief measures are introduced. Meanwhile, operating expenditure, which increased by 22.2% in FY2019, is estimated to grow further by 16.9% as the government labors to stimulate the economy. Recurrent expenditure on education, social welfare, and health care is expected to absorb some 60% of government recurrent expenditure. Fiscal reserves, which equaled 22 months of government expenditure at the beginning of FY2020, will drop to 16 months of expenditure by the end of March 2021. In the medium term, fiscal reserves are forecast to approximate 26.5% of GDP, equal to 15 months of government expenditure.

Sharp growth moderation in the PRC beyond earlier forecasts will substantially slash external demand, and the remaining uncertainty spawned by the US–PRC trade conflict will dent export growth. Imports are likely to be restrained as well by weak domestic demand. The trade deficit will likely narrow, as will the surplus in the services account with tourist arrivals falling further under the current domestic situation and recent developments pertaining to the COVID-19 outbreak. On the upside, the US–PRC phase one trade deal may improve global economic sentiment in the short run, providing lift to external trade for Hong Kong, China. On balance, the current account surplus is forecast to equal 7.0% of GDP this year and, as exports and service receipts recover in 2021, narrow to 5.0% (Figure 3.9.12).

The two main downside risks to the outlook are deepening public dissatisfaction and the sharp global economic downturn caused by COVID-19. If local tensions in the city persist, confidence in the economy from foreign investors and local residents alike will dampen further, adding downward pressure to private consumption and investment, worsening labor market pressures, and lowering output. Meanwhile, the economy's geographic proximity and close economic ties with the PRC heighten the potential economic impact posed by the COVID-19 health crisis, weighing severely on private consumption, inbound tourism, investment, and perhaps even forcing business closures. In a worse-case scenario—in which the outbreak is protracted and widespread, precautionary behavior and policies are extended, and the PRC sees a large

Figure 3.9.8 Hang Seng Index

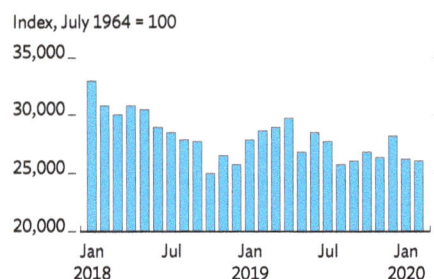

Index, July 1964 = 100

Source: CEIC Data Company (accessed 22 March 2020).

Figure 3.9.9 GDP growth

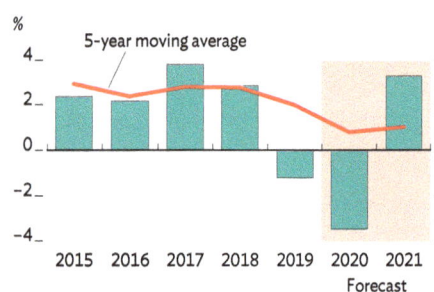

Source: Asian Development Outlook database.

Figure 3.9.10 Purchasing managers' index

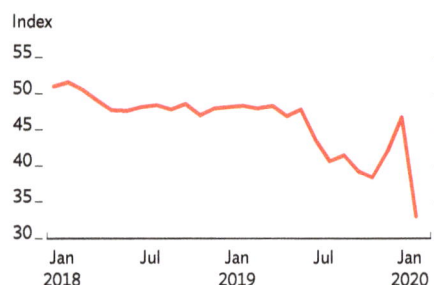

Source: CEIC Data Company (accessed 22 March 2020).

decline in consumption and investment—growth could be lower by an estimated 0.9 percentage points. Mounting trade barriers could, along with deepening geopolitical tensions between the US and Iran, further disrupt global supply chains and hit global economic confidence and international investment, adversely affecting growth in Hong Kong, China.

Policy challenge—fostering shared prosperity and inclusive growth

Hong Kong, China has enjoyed remarkable growth over the past 4 decades, but the same period saw income disparities widen, and the city now suffers significant inequality. High income inequality and relative poverty can have severe repercussions on the political and social environment, and growing evidence supports the view that they damage economic performance as well. The challenge for policy makers in Hong Kong, China is to adopt appropriate measures to address these issues.

According to World Bank data, gross national income per capita in Hong Kong, China increased nearly ninefold from the early 1980s to 2018, reaching $50,300 ($67,810 when adjusted for purchasing power parity) and ranking it the fourteenth highest in the world (tenth in PPP terms). Meanwhile, data from the Standardized World Income Inequality Database indicate that the net Gini index, a widely used index of inequality based on disposable income after taxes and social transfers, worsened steadily from 0.37 in the early 1960s to 0.41 in 2016, which is even further removed from the average of 0.31 for wealthy countries worldwide and less equal than in other advanced economies in Asia (Figure 3.9.13). Moreover, a large share of the population appears not to be sharing fully in the benefits of prosperity. Median household income excluding foreign domestic workers grew moderately by 59.3% over the past decade. According to the *Hong Kong Poverty Situation Report 2018*, 613,000 households had incomes below the official poverty line in 2018, based on monthly household income before any government intervention, the cutoff set at 50% of the median household income adjusted by household size. This yielded a poverty rate of 20.4%, the highest since 2010. Taking into account recurrent government cash handouts, the poverty rate falls to 14.9% for all households but only 8.0% for working households. This suggests that generating more employment for the poor is the most effective policy against income disparity.

In the short term, additional redistributive measures can help, but a sustainable solution to the multifaceted problems associated with income inequality can come only from the creation of more stable employment in the formal sector. Such employment helps build solid foundations for social development and promotes civic engagement and a healthier

Figure 3.9.11 Inflation

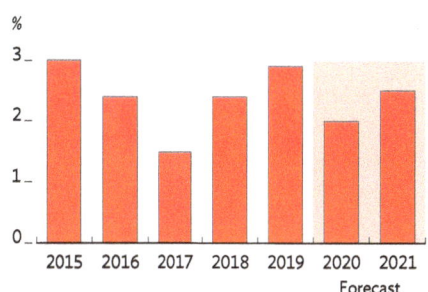

Source: *Asian Development Outlook* database.

Figure 3.9.12 Current account balance

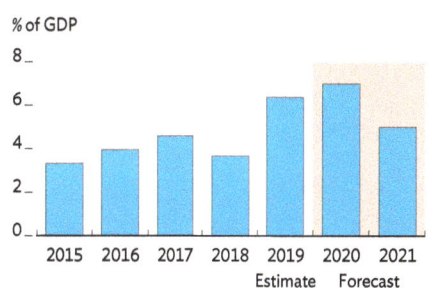

Source: *Asian Development Outlook* database.

Figure 3.9.13 Net Gini

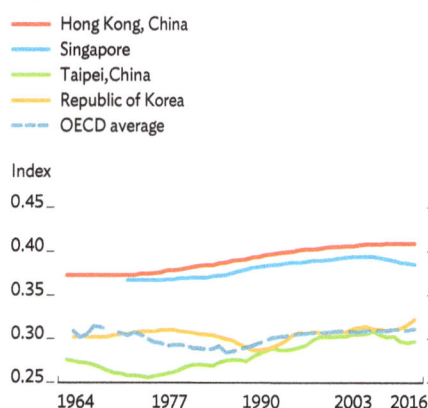

OECD = Organisation for Economic Co-operation and Development.
Source: The Standardized World Income Inequality Database (accessed 22 March 2020).

economic and political environment. These objectives cannot be attained by income redistribution alone. Policy in the medium- to long-term should thus promote inclusive growth through the generation of good jobs—those that pay wages able to support a comfortable living standard and include essential labor protection, such as safe working conditions, regulations against arbitrary dismissal, and collective bargaining rights. Increasing the rate at which good jobs are created is key to a long-term strategy to reduce inequality and achieve inclusive growth.

Boosting the number of good jobs requires improvements in labor productivity, a necessary prerequisite for higher real wages, and the provision of more stable employment and better working conditions. In this respect, the local policy toolkit already includes several useful measures. Subsidies encourage and enable small and medium-sized enterprises to innovate toward greater use of labor-complementing technologies, as opposed to labor-substituting technologies. Tax incentives reward research and development. And major public co-work spaces and incubators foster a startup-friendly environment in which the number of startups expanded from 2,625 in 2018 to 3,184 in 2019.

Labor market policies and training programs should focus on upgrading skills in the current and future labor force. Set up by the government in 2002, the Continuing Education Fund provides subsidies to adults who study to improve their work skills. Statutory bodies, including the Employees Retraining Board and the Vocational Training Council, play integral roles in the provision of market-oriented training and retraining services. The one-off Love Upgrading Special Scheme, launched in October 2019, provides skills-enhancing assistance free of charge to underemployed or recently unemployed workers with courses across 23 industries and generic skills. Eligible graduates receive follow-up placement services for 3–6 months. The Researcher Programme for holders of bachelor and master's degrees, and the Postdoctoral Hub for PhDs, aim to encourage these highly educated beneficiaries to pursue careers in innovation and technology. These initiatives provide funding to Cyberport, the Hong Kong Science Park, and a number of start-ups and technology companies to employ local university graduates and researchers in research and development projects. Both programs have received additional funding in the budget for FY2020.

The challenge for policy makers in Hong Kong, China is to meld these initiatives into a comprehensive and effective strategy to generate good jobs for an increasing number of workers, by bolstering measures that work, revising or discarding the ones that do not, and continuing to innovate the policy toolkit to adjust to a fast-changing global economic and technological environment. The prospects for gradually more inclusive growth in Hong Kong, China in the future depend in large part on the success of this strategy.

Mongolia

Growth slowed in 2019 as mining slumped and export expansion moderated. Inflation edged up, and the current account deficit narrowed. Growth is expected to fall sharply in 2020 because of COVID-19 but rebound in 2021 as the outbreak subsides. In 2020, the current account deficit will widen as inflation moderates, then 2021 will reverse both trends. Mongolia faces the challenge of strengthening policy credibility to ensure financial stability in these uncertain and turbulent times.

Economic performance

The economic expansion that began in 2017 reached its peak in late 2018. Lower contributions from mining, transportation, and manufacturing dragged growth down to 5.1% in 2019 from 7.2% in 2018. The contribution of mining to growth declined by 1.8 percentage points as output was lower for gold, copper, zinc, and fluorspar. This spilled over into other sectors, pushing down the contribution of services to 2.7 points and of other industry to 1.2 points, for a combined drop of 0.6 points from 2018. Agriculture grew by 8.1% as both crops and livestock output rose, contributing 1.2 points (Figure 3.10.1).

On the demand side, investment contributed 6.9 percentage points to growth, an increase of 0.6 points from 2018 as government capital expenditure increased by 75.3%—and despite stabilized net foreign direct investment. Fueled by rising nominal incomes and recourse to credit from nonbank financial institutions, private consumption contributed 6.8 percentage points to growth, while government consumption added another 1.8 points. Net exports continued to be a major drag on growth, subtracting 10.4 points (Figure 3.10.2).

Average inflation increased by 0.5 percentage points to 7.3% in 2019. Food price inflation rose by 3.6 points as supplies of meat and vegetables declined. Utility and transportation costs rose, and the pass-through of currency depreciation pushed up import prices (Figure 3.10.3). The Mongolian togrog depreciated against the US dollar by 3.4% on average, though the Bank of Mongolia, the central bank, doubled its sales of US dollars over those in 2018 (Figure 3.10.4).

The budget recorded an overall surplus equal to 1.4% of GDP and a primary surplus equal to 3.7%—both in surplus for a second year in a row—as revenue grew by 18.6% on rising receipts from corporate income tax, value-added tax, and social insurance. Budgetary expenditure and net lending

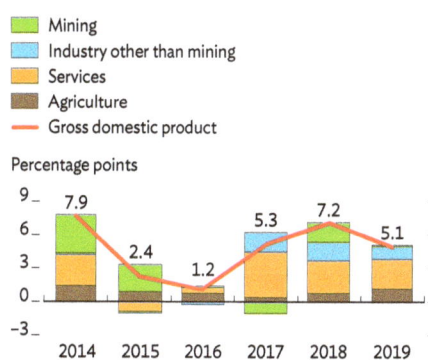

Figure 3.10.1 Supply-side contributions to growth

- Mining
- Industry other than mining
- Services
- Agriculture
- Gross domestic product

Percentage points

7.9   2.4   1.2   5.3   7.2   5.1

2014 2015 2016 2017 2018 2019

Sources: National Statistics Office of Mongolia. 2020 Statistical Information Services. http://1212.mn; ADB estimates.

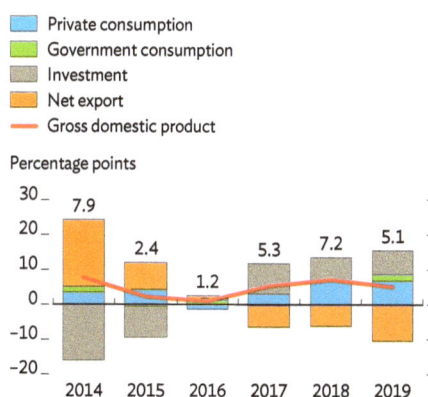

Figure 3.10.2 Demand-side contributions to growth

- Private consumption
- Government consumption
- Investment
- Net export
- Gross domestic product

Percentage points

7.9   2.4   1.2   5.3   7.2   5.1

2014 2015 2016 2017 2018 2019

Note: Trends in contributions of net exports to growth are based on National Statistics Office data, which do not reflect the latest Bank of Mongolia revision of balance of payments data.

Sources: National Statistics Office of Mongolia. 2020 Statistical Information Services. http://1212.mn; ADB estimates.

This chapter was written by Declan Magee and Bold Sandagdorj of the Mongolia Resident Mission, ADB, Ulaanbaatar.

increased by 23.9%, the largest expansion in 3 years, though budgetary interest payments declined by 17.8%. The structural balance fell from a surplus equal to a scant 0.04% of GDP in 2018 to a deficit of 1.7%, which was less than the deficit approved by the parliament (Figure 3.10.5). Public debt including central bank external liabilities fell by 5.4 percentage points to equal 79.1% of GDP.

The central bank maintained positive real interest rates throughout the year, imposed consumer loan restrictions on banks, increased risk weights on loans denominated in US dollars, required conservation buffers for tier-1 capital from systemically important banks, and increased the US dollar reserve requirement ratio by 3 percentage points to 15%. Broad money growth slowed from 22.8% in 2018 to 7.0% last year on sharply lower credit growth, down from 25.8% in 2018 to 4.9%. Nonperforming and overdue loans rose to 14.3% of the total (Figure 3.10.6).

Based on the central bank balance of payments data, the current account deficit shrank by 17.8% to equal 13.1% of GDP and was fully financed by net inflow of foreign direct investment (Figure 3.10.7). The merchandise trade surplus rose by 69.1% as export growth at 9.1% outpaced import growth at 2.2%. The deficit in the service account fell by 17.1% as transportation, tourism, and other service receipts increased. Despite continued trade tensions between the US and the People's Republic of China (PRC) dampening commodity market expectations, PRC demand for coking coal and iron ore soared, and these two commodities accounted for 86.0% of Mongolia's export growth. By contrast, copper exports decreased by 10.7%, mainly from lower prices. Foreign exchange reserves grew to $4.4 billion or cover for 5.8 months of imports.

Economic prospects

GDP growth is forecast to decelerate sharply to 2.1% in 2020 despite a higher contribution from agriculture thanks to favorable weather (Figure 3.10.8). The slowdown became apparent in the second half of 2019, when fourth quarter growth dipped to 2.2%, making it the slowest quarter since the third quarter of 2016. Reduced demand for raw materials and lower commodity prices caused by a slowdown in the PRC, and now the COVID-19 outbreak, will reduce exports of coal, copper, iron ore, zinc, and crude oil, pushing growth down further. The outbreak, having brought a sudden temporary stop to coal exports to the PRC and caused a significant drop in passenger transport, will reduce value added in mining and dampen expansion in other areas. Growth will recover to 4.6% in 2021 as growth rebounds in the PRC and trade tensions and COVID-19 concerns ease, allowing recovery in coking coal exports, and as ore quality and output improve at the Oyu Tolgoi mineral deposit.

Figure 3.10.3 Inflation

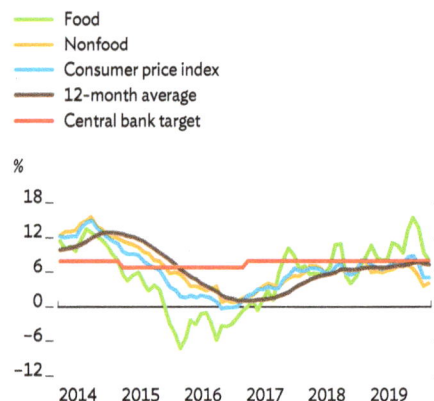

Sources: National Statistics Office of Mongolia. 2020 Statistical Information Services. http://1212.mn; Parliament resolution on monetary policy guidelines for 2013–2018; ADB estimates.

Figure 3.10.4 Exchange rate and central bank bills

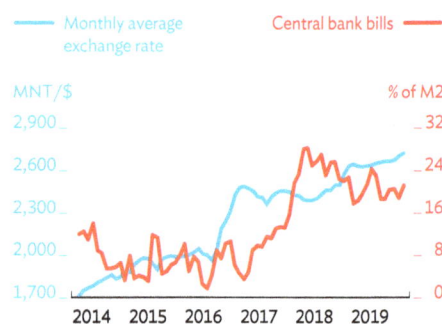

Source: Bank of Mongolia. 2020 Monthly statistical bulletin and bank sector consolidated balance sheet.

Table 3.10.1 Selected economic indicators (%)

	2018	2019	2020	2021
GDP growth	7.2	5.1	2.1	4.6
Inflation	6.8	7.3	6.6	7.9
Current acct. bal. (share of GDP)	-16.8	-13.1	-13.9	-7.8

Sources: National Statistics Office of Mongolia. 2020 Statistical Information Services. http://1212.mn; ADB estimates.

The COVID-19 outbreak likely means that record expenditure planned under the 2020 budget will not be realized, so contributions from government consumption and investment to growth are expected to decline. Private consumption will be lower in 2020 because of COVID-19 and the lagged effect of consumer credit restrictions imposed in 2019. Net exports will continue to drag on growth as exports fall.

Inflation will moderate to 6.6% in 2020 as the economy slows (Figure 3.10.9). However, it is forecast to reaccelerate in 2021 and approach the central bank target as demand and economic activity recover, the effect of COVID-19 on growth fades, and the delayed impact of togrog depreciation is realized.

The current account deficit is projected to widen in 2020, mainly on an expected decline in the merchandise trade surplus as exports fall, the terms of trade deteriorate (Figure 3.10.10), the economic slowdown continues in the PRC, and negative spillover materializes from COVID-19. The deficit will narrow somewhat in 2021 as these effects wane.

Several downside risks loom on the horizon. Deeper and more prolonged consequences from COVID-19 may cause even lower growth in 2020 than projected, raise unemployment, and impose major pressures on the balance of payments and the fiscal position, making investors less willing to take on Mongolia's debt and engendering a liquidity problem for the banking system. In addition, household indebtedness could worsen the risk exposure of nonbank financial institutions, which are subject to less stringent regulation. Asset quality in the banking system could be jeopardized, causing a credit crunch with adverse effects on economic activity.

Policy challenge—strengthening fiscal policy and improving exchange market interventions

As Mongolia moves beyond current program support from the International Monetary Fund and into a new political cycle, it needs to convince investors that policy will be guided by the objectives of financial stability and growth. Mongolia has a weak track record in macroeconomic policy continuity and predictability, especially immediately before and after elections. In the past four parliamentary cycles, budget expenditure has expanded by 29.2% on average in an election year and then contracted by 1.7% the following year.

Further, after the successful conclusion of an earlier 18-month International Monetary Fund program in 2010, budget spending soared by 62.2% in 2011 and by 20.4% in 2012—doubling the amount in absolute terms. This partly reversed previous policy reform, including by failing to establish fiscal and reserve buffers, and worsened economic vulnerability

Figure 3.10.5 Government budget

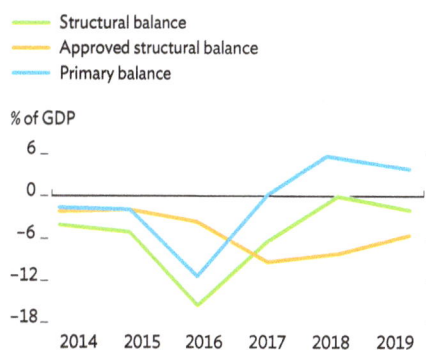

- Structural balance
- Approved structural balance
- Primary balance

Note: Structural balance is the difference between expenditure and underlying revenue.

Sources: National Statistics Office of Mongolia. 2020 Statistical Information Services. http://1212.mn; Parliament Resolution of the Government Budget, 2014–2019. http://legalinfo.mn.

Figure 3.10.6 Money and credit growth

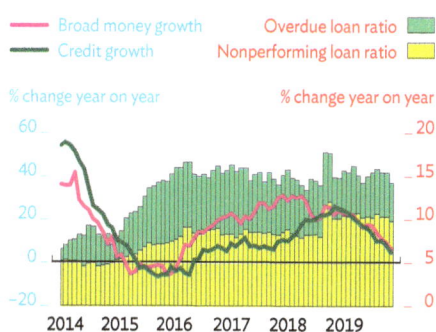

- Broad money growth
- Credit growth
- Overdue loan ratio
- Nonperforming loan ratio

Source: Bank of Mongolia. 2020. Banking sector consolidated balance sheet. http://mongolbank.mn.

Figure 3.10.7 Balance of payments

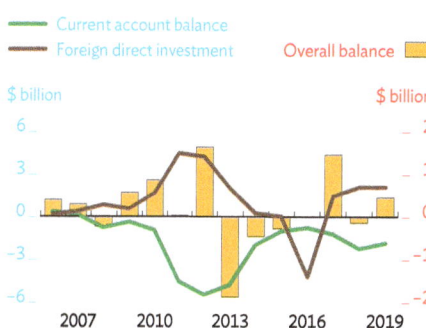

- Current account balance
- Foreign direct investment
- Overall balance

Source: Bank of Mongolia. 2020. Banking sector consolidated balance sheet. http://mongolbank.mn.

in 2012 by elevating inflation to 14.0% and widening the current account deficit to the equivalent of 43.8% of GDP. These policy disruptions have been hugely damaging, causing debt-servicing costs to spiral by a factor of 7.8 from 2012 to 2016.

Mongolia now has an opportunity to buck this trend by demonstrating that the latest macroeconomic improvement is not just a flash in the pan but part of a new macroeconomic policy framework that will be strictly followed to tackle outstanding macroeconomic challenges. Robust positive swings in primary and structural balances in recent years should be maintained through strict adherence to the Fiscal Stability Law. Fiscal policy should be consistent with broad macroeconomic objectives and responsible public debt management, continuously building buffers through rising primary surpluses. Budget planning, forecasting, and approval should be more realistic, and fiscal policy should be countercyclical. Policies on reprioritizing spending and implementing stimulus packages should be designed with these issues in mind, to avoid possible fiscal cliffs, better manage cycles of boom and bust, and create fiscal space to boost human development and growth.

Further, the government should absorb excessive togrog liquidity by issuing medium-term government securities to finance public investment. This would ease pressure on the exchange rate, which has built up from market expectations and excess togrog deployed only in short-term central bank bills. Also useful would be to issue securities with various maturities to recreate the togrog benchmark yield curve abandoned in 2017 and thereby facilitate the pricing of private securities. Foreign exchange reserves should be accumulated opportunistically—that is, carried out through occasional central bank interventions in the foreign exchange market to smooth large fluctuations in the exchange rate or effect monetary policy. Exporters should be able to sell their foreign exchange holdings freely on the market and not solely to the central bank.

Further, the government should tackle supply shock inflation, which tends to persist in Mongolia and be highly disruptive, by building strategic reserves of consumer staples. These policies should be buttressed by ensuring financial sector stability and its smooth functioning, which requires effective control to stop excessive risk-taking by financial institutions and measures to facilitate interbank and securities transactions. These controls are necessary to raise confidence in the economy and encourage capital inflow to finance a potentially large gap in the external accounts. With $4.8 billion in government debt maturing from 2020 and 2024, equal to 34.9% of GDP, it is essential to manage public external debt proactively before external financing conditions worsen.

Figure 3.10.8 GDP growth

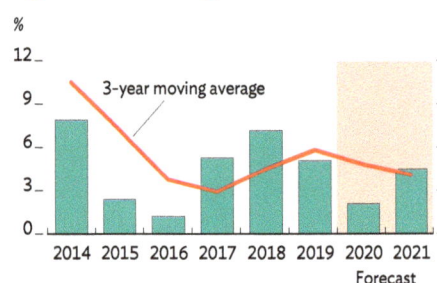

Source: *Asian Development Outlook* database.

Figure 3.10.9 Inflation

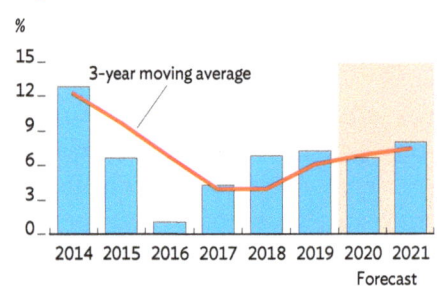

Source: *Asian Development Outlook* database.

Figure 3.10.10 Terms of trade

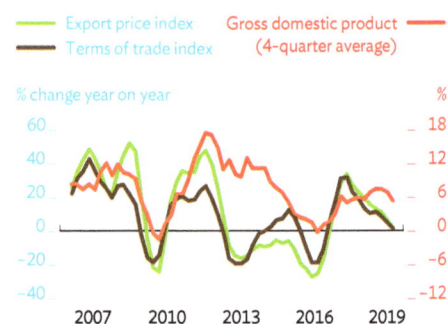

Sources: National Statistics Office of Mongolia. 2020 Statistical Information Services. http://1212.mn; Bank of Mongolia. 2020 Statistical Database; ADB estimates.

People's Republic of China

Weak domestic demand and external headwinds slowed growth in 2019. The extent of a COVID-19 shock to both supply and demand will depend on how the outbreak spreads and is handled, and on how economic policy makers respond. GDP growth is forecast to decelerate sharply in 2020 before bouncing back in 2021. Inflation is projected to surge, led by high pork prices, before retreating substantially in 2021. The current account surplus will widen in 2020 before narrowing in 2021.

Economic performance

Reflecting weaker domestic demand and challenging external conditions, economic growth in the People's Republic of China (PRC) slowed from 6.7% in 2018 to 6.1% in 2019 (Figure 3.11.1). Growth was supported by fiscal and monetary policy and stayed within the government target of 6.0%–6.5%.

On the demand side, consumption remained the main driver of growth, though its contribution declined from 4.4 percentage points in 2018 to 3.5 points (Figure 3.11.2). Consumption decelerated as both household disposable income and consumption expenditure softened, reflecting a rapid increase in food prices, which drove down consumers' purchasing power in real terms. Real growth in household income moderated to 5.8%, and in consumption expenditure to 5.5%, each down by 0.7 percentage points from 2018. Similarly, real growth in retail sales of consumer goods decelerated from 6.9% in 2018 to 6.0% in 2019, owing mostly to a decline in car sales, which were down by 0.8% from 2018, and moderating growth in property-related purchases such as household appliances, furniture, and decoration materials. Rural households' real income and consumption expenditure increased faster than those of urban residents, reflecting government efforts to revitalize rural areas and the expansion of online shopping (Figure 3.11.3).

The contribution of investment to growth fell from 2.8 percentage points in 2018 to 1.9 points in 2019 because of sharp deceleration in manufacturing investment as domestic demand softened, profits declined, overcapacity in some upstream industries continued to be cut, and external demand deteriorated (Figure 3.11.4). A reduction in value-added tax (VAT) seems not to have incentivized companies to increase investment in 2019 as they saw growth in sales revenue moderate and profits decline (Figure 3.11.5).

Figure 3.11.1 Economic growth

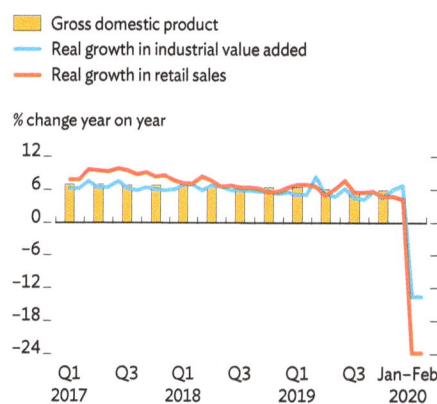

- Gross domestic product
- Real growth in industrial value added
- Real growth in retail sales

% change year on year

Q = quarter.
Sources: National Bureau of Statistics; ADB estimates.

Figure 3.11.2 Demand-side contributions to growth

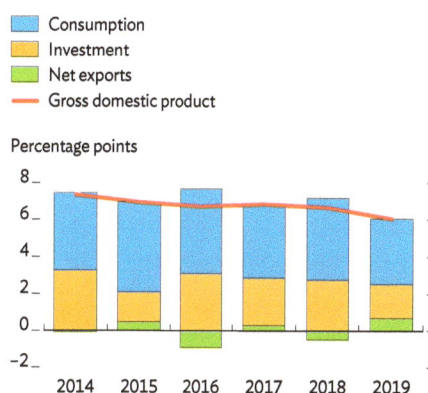

- Consumption
- Investment
- Net exports
- Gross domestic product

Percentage points

Source: National Bureau of Statistics.

This chapter was written by Dominik Peschel, Jian Zhuang, and Wen Qi of the People's Republic of China Resident Mission, ADB, Beijing.

Growth in manufacturing investment plummeted from 9.5% in 2018 to 3.1% in 2019, with investment in chemical fibers, textiles, and electrical machinery hard hit, though investment in high-tech manufacturing such as medical, electrical, and communication equipment kept growing at double-digit rates.

Supported by increased special bond issuance by local governments, growth in infrastructure investment accelerated slightly in the first 3 quarters of 2019. However, as local governments issued virtually no new special bonds in October–December 2019, growth in infrastructure investment declined by about 3 percentage points in the fourth quarter (Q4) of 2019, dragging infrastructure investment growth down to only 3.8% in the whole year. Meanwhile, growth in real estate investment, comprising land purchases and new construction, accelerated marginally from 9.5% in 2018 to 9.9% in 2019.

Net exports reversed their 0.5 percentage point drag on growth in 2018 to contribute 0.7 points in 2019 as merchandise imports declined. This mostly reflected lower imports of investment goods such as machinery and electrical equipment as domestic demand softened and uncertainty pertaining to trade clouded the outlook for exports, while exports grew only marginally.

On the supply side, services remained the main driver of growth, contributing 3.6 percentage points despite moderating from 8.0% growth in 2018 to 6.9% last year (Figure 3.11.6). Transport, financial services, leasing and commercial services, and information technology services grew quickly. Growth in real estate services moderated, however, as growth in housing sales slowed, and retail sales similarly felt the moderation in consumption expenditure. Robust service sector growth helped stabilize the surveyed unemployment rate in cities in a range of 5.0%–5.3% during the year.

The contribution to growth from industry including construction and mining slipped marginally by 0.1 percentage points to 2.2 points as real growth in the sector likewise moderated by 0.1 percentage points to 5.7% in 2019. Strong increases in high tech, mining, and raw materials partly offset deceleration in export-oriented manufacturing. A sharp decline in investment in agriculture, and rising costs for pork production owing to African swine fever, decelerated agriculture growth by 0.4 percentage points to 3.1% in 2019. As a result, the sector's contribution to GDP growth declined marginally to 0.2 points in 2019.

Consumer price inflation averaged 2.9% in 2019, rising from 2.1% in 2018 as food and other prices diverged (Figure 3.11.7). Food prices soared—driven by sharply higher pork prices as a result of African swine fever—to average 9.3%, while nonfood inflation declined slightly to average 1.4%. Although the share of pork in household consumption has fallen gradually in recent years as living standards improved, pork alone still accounted

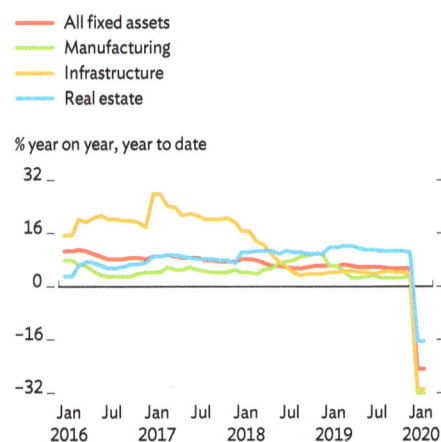

Figure 3.11.3 Growth in urban and rural income and consumption expenditure per capita

Q = quarter.
Source: National Bureau of Statistics.

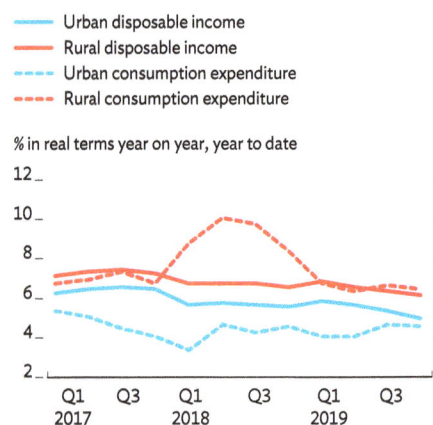

Figure 3.11.4 Growth in fixed asset investment

Source: National Bureau of Statistics.

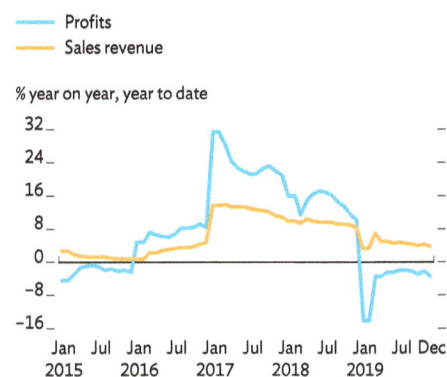

Figure 3.11.5 Growth in industrial enterprise profits and sales revenue

Source: National Bureau of Statistics.

for an estimated 2.3% of the consumer price basket in 2019, and for nearly two-thirds of meat production and consumption. Producer price inflation turned negative in July 2019 to average –0.3% for the year. Prices for newly constructed homes in the top 70 cities were on average 9.7% higher in 2019 than a year earlier, with price increases more pronounced in second- and third-tier cities (Figure 3.11.8).

Monetary policy remained largely accommodative in 2019. Support for banks and the real economy included several rounds of cuts in the reserve requirement ratio for various types of banks (Figure 3.11.9). In addition, a new pricing mechanism was established in August 2019 to reduce financing costs for the real economy and improve the transmission of monetary policy. Under the new mechanism (described in *ADO 2019 Update*), banks were required to price most new loans according to the applicable loan prime rate, which is chiefly linked to the medium-term lending facility rate set by the central bank plus a premium. Under the new mechanism, the 1-year loan prime rate gradually declined from 4.25% on 20 August 2019 to 4.05% on 20 February 2020 (Figure 3.11.10).

Bank loans remained the driver of credit growth to the real economy in 2019. Total social financing—a broad credit aggregate, the scope of which has been revised frequently and now includes all types of government bonds—was up by 10.7% at the end of 2019 from a year earlier with the integration of government bonds. Bank loans outstanding increased by 12.3% and government bonds by 14.3%, while shadow bank finance outstanding declined by 7.4%. Net special bond issues from local governments picked up rapidly, as did net corporate bond issues, but new equity financing was negligible. Broad money (M2) was 8.7% higher at the end of 2019 than a year earlier (Figure 3.11.11).

Deficit spending kept fiscal policy expansionary in 2019. General government fiscal expenditure grew by 8.1%, more than double 3.8% growth in revenue. Increased spending was most pronounced in education, health care, employment, and social security, while weaker revenue stemmed from slower growth, a cut in VAT effective on 1 April 2019, and earlier reform to personal income taxes that became effective in two phases, in October 2018 and January 2019. As a result, the consolidated budget deficit of the central and local governments reached the equivalent of 4.9% of GDP in 2019 (Figure 3.11.12).

To support the real economy, the government cut taxes and fees for corporations. In March 2019, it announced CNY2 trillion in cuts to taxes and fees for enterprises. This included a 3 percentage point cut for the highest VAT bracket, which includes manufacturing, and a 1 point cut for a lower bracket that includes transportation and construction, as well as a 3–4 point cut in employers' social security contributions.

Figure 3.11.6 Supply-side contributions to growth

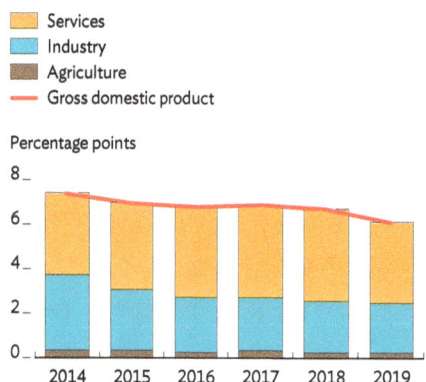

Source: National Bureau of Statistics.

Figure 3.11.7 Monthly consumer price inflation

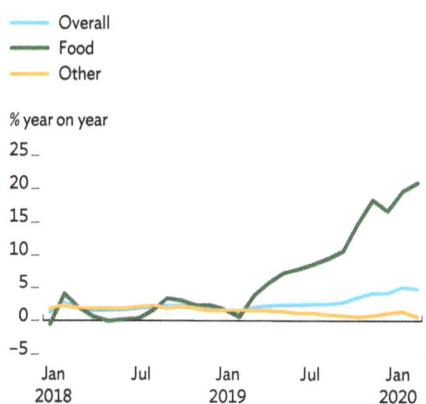

Source: National Bureau of Statistics.

Figure 3.11.8 Price increase for newly constructed homes

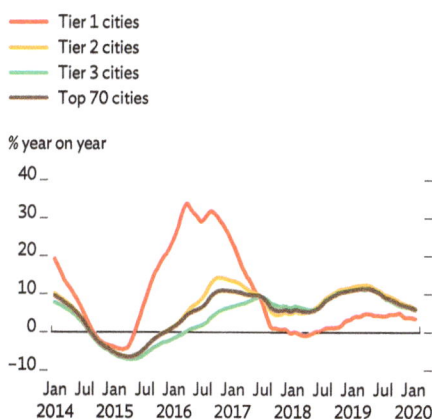

Note: Tier 1 cities are Beijing, Guangzhou, Shanghai, and Shenzhen; tier 2 has 31 provincial capitals and larger municipalities; and tier 3 has 35 other cities.
Sources: National Bureau of Statistics; ADB estimates.

The government also increased special bond issuance to finance infrastructure investment. The full 2019 annual quota of CNY2.15 trillion for new local government special bond issues, equal to 2.2% of GDP, was nearly reached by the end of September. In the remainder of 2019, local governments remained within that quota, despite being allowed to continue issuing new special bonds worth up to CNY1 trillion by using part of the 2020 quota (Figure 3.11.13).

The current account surplus recovered from 0.4% of GDP in 2018 to 1.3% in 2019 (Figure 3.11.14). While growth in merchandise trade decelerated in 2019 as the trade conflict between the US and the PRC persisted, the deficit in the service balance narrowed by 10.6%, reflecting lower outbound tourism. Following the imposition of additional US tariffs on $351 billion worth of imports from the PRC, export growth weakened with a sharp decline in merchandise exports to that market (Figure 3.11.15). A decline in merchandise imports reflected moderating growth in domestic demand, lower demand for investment goods as the escalating trade conflict soured the outlook for exports, and a decline in imports for processing and assembly for reexport. In sum, despite merchandise exports increasing by only 0.5% in 2019, the surplus in the merchandise trade balance expanded to equal 3.3% of GDP as imports declined by 2.7%.

A phase one agreement reached with the US in mid-December 2019 brought a stop to new tariffs and reduced rates in some bilateral tariffs imposed earlier. The trade conflict had an adverse impact on foreign direct investment (FDI). Net FDI narrowed by half from the equivalent of 0.8% of GDP in 2018 to 0.4% in 2019 as investor confidence waivered. In 2019, FDI inflow declined by 23.0%, outflow by only 1.1%.

The renminbi came under downward pressure while official reserves stayed broadly stable. The renminbi depreciated by 1.7% in nominal terms per US dollar, from CNY6.86 at the end of 2018 to CNY6.98 by the end of 2019 (Figure 3.11.16). Depreciation was driven primarily by heightened uncertainty and a deteriorating outlook for the domestic economy. An increase in unregistered capital outflow, proxied by errors and omissions in the balance of payments, mirrored depreciation pressure on the renminbi, with unregistered outflow nearly doubling to the equivalent of 1.6% of GDP in the first 3 quarters of 2019 from 0.9% in the same period of 2018. Official reserves increased by $54.9 billion in 2019 and stood at $3.22 trillion by year-end.

Figure 3.11.9 Reserve requirement ratios for financial institutions

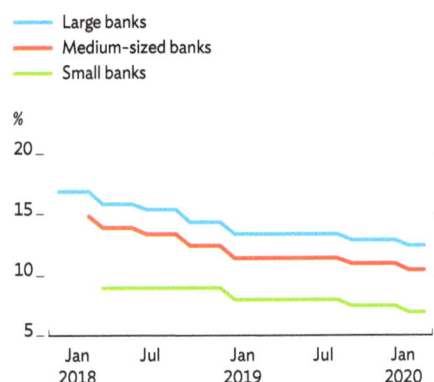

Source: People's Bank of China.

Figure 3.11.10 Bank lending and policy rates

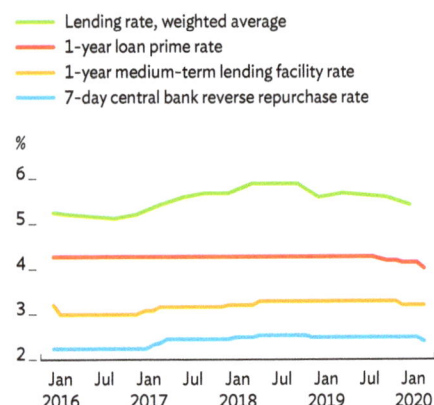

Sources: People's Bank of China; National Interbank Funding Center.

Figure 3.11.11 Growth in broad money, credit outstanding, and government bonds outstanding

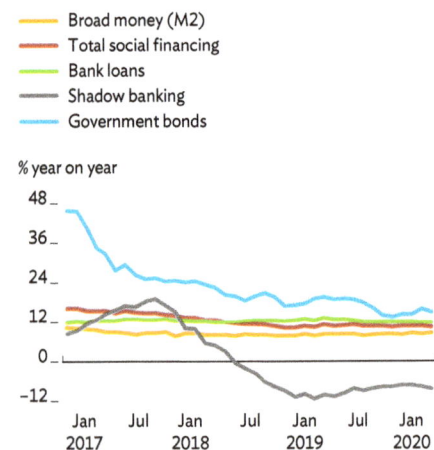

Note: Shadow banking comprises entrust loans, trust loans, and banks' acceptance bills.
Sources: People's Bank of China; ADB estimates.

Economic prospects

COVID-19 exploded in January and February 2020, disrupting business in the PRC and upending earlier economic forecasts (Figure 3.11.17). The outbreak became a demand shock as people stayed home. It became a supply shock as companies suffered shortages of labor, with migrants unable to return to work from the Lunar New Year holiday, and of materials as supply chains faltered. Though the government took several measures to alleviate the impact on the economy (Box 3.11.1), economic indicators for January–February 2020 signal sharp GDP contraction in Q1 of 2020 (Figure 3.11.1). With substantial fiscal and monetary policy support, economic growth should recover in the remainder of 2020. Notwithstanding some local finetuning, restrictions on the housing market are unlikely to be relaxed substantially. Restrictions on shadow banking and pollution controls will be sustained. GDP growth is now expected to average 2.3% in 2020 and then bounce back to 7.3% in 2021 (Figure 3.11.18).

On the demand side, consumption is expected to remain a driver of growth despite COVID-19. Consumer staples are expected to hold up fairly well, but discretionary consumer spending will likely take a hit as growth in household income decelerates in 2020, higher prices for daily necessities weigh on purchasing power, and housing market moderation drags on property-related spending. Government spending, especially on health care, is expected to increase further to support the economy this year and then grow moderately in 2021.

Infrastructure investment is expected to pick up from Q2, reflecting an increase in new local government special bond issues in early 2020 (Figure 3.11.13). Government support for high technology and continued industrial upgrading should help stabilize investment in manufacturing. At the same time, COVID-19 has deepened uncertainty about manufacturing investment, the investment category that plummeted furthest in January–February 2020 (Figure 3.11.4). Growth in real estate investment will likely moderate in the whole of 2020 as weak construction in Q1 is unlikely to be fully caught up in the remainder of the year. As imports of goods and services are expected to decline faster than exports, the contribution of net exports to growth is projected to stay positive in 2020 but to drag on growth in 2021 as imports outpace exports. The current account surplus is expected to increase in 2020 before narrowing in 2021.

On the supply side, services will be hit hard by sharp deceleration in domestic consumption. Value added in financial services should grow solidly on increased bank profits from expanded lending, but COVID-19 will hammer other services, especially wholesale and retail trade, accommodation, transportation, and entertainment. This trend is expected to reverse as COVID-19 comes under control and these subsectors

Figure 3.11.12 General government fiscal revenue and expenditure

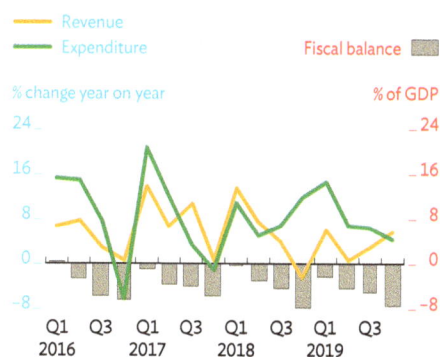

GDP = gross domestic product, Q = quarter.
Sources: Ministry of Finance; ADB estimates.

Figure 3.11.13 Local government special bond issues

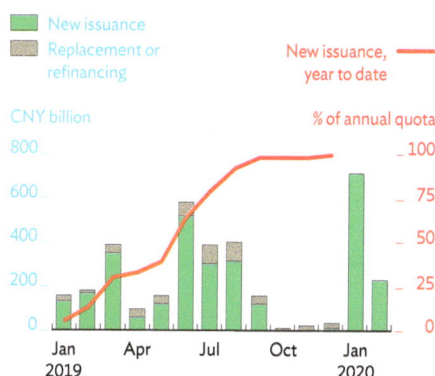

Note: The annual quota for new local government special bond issues in 2020 has yet to be approved.
Sources: Ministry of Finance; ADB estimates.

Figure 3.11.14 Balance of payments

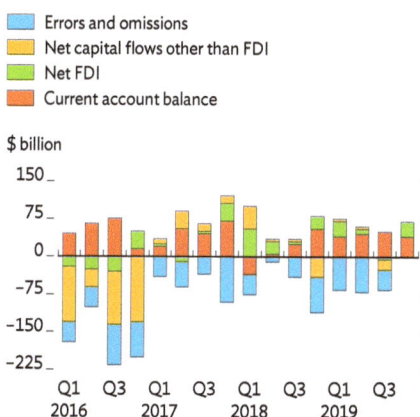

FDI = foreign direct investment, Q = quarter.
Note: Data only on the current account and FDI are available for Q4 of 2019.
Sources: State Administration of Foreign Exchange; ADB estimates.

Box 3.11.1 Measures to counter the economic impact of COVID-19

As the COVID-19 outbreak spread in late January 2020, the authorities aimed to contain it by extending the Lunar New Year vacation, for which people traditionally return to their hometowns. This meant that production could restart only gradually as workers belatedly trickled back to work. Tourism suffered as group tours were cancelled, as did restaurants and other entertainment venues as people avoided crowds. In addition to epidemic prevention-and-control measures, the central and local governments acted to protect the economy, notably with the following:

(i)   On 5 February, the State Council announced targeted tax cuts for some industries—including medical suppliers, public transportation, logistics, and home services—and waived the registration fee for drugs and medical equipment needed to contain the virus.

(ii) On 11 February, the State Council increased the front-loaded local government bond quota by CNY848 billion, bringing the preapproved quota to CNY1,848 billion: CNY1,290 billion for special bonds and CNY558 billion for general bonds.

(iii) On 19 February, the State Council suspended employers' social insurance contributions to cover pensions, unemployment, and vocational injury and deferred the collection of housing provident funds. This excepted all companies in Hubei and small and medium-sized enterprises (SMEs) across the PRC from February to June and, for larger companies outside of Hubei, waived half of the payments from February to April. In addition, employers' contributions to basic medical insurance were halved from February for up to 5 months.

(iv) On 25 February, the State Council exempted smaller taxpayers in Hubei from value-added tax and cut it from 3% to 1% for those outside Hubei, effective from 1 March to 31 May, as well as approved various measures to support the job market.

(v)   On 3 March, the State Council decided that local governments can retain a bigger proportion of fiscal revenue collected for a certain period of time and will receive faster allotment of transfer payments. Also, further tax and fee cuts will be made to logistics-related services.

(vi) On 5 March, the State Council provided guidance on medical insurance reform that, among other things, mandated special medical insurance payment policies to ensure that, during major epidemics, medical institutions treat patients before charging fees.

(vii) On 12 March, the Ministry of Commerce said it would improve export tax rebate policies, increase foreign trade loans, expand coverage of short-term export credit insurance, and push for lower insurance premiums.

(viii) On 13 March, the National Development and Reform Commission announced new measures to boost consumption, including encouraging local governments that have restricted car purchases to increase the number of license plates available as appropriate.

(ix) On 17 March, the National Development and Reform Commission said that the central government would increase the quota for local government special bond issues and accelerate the development of infrastructure, citing 5G networks and data centers.

Monetary policy measures taken included the following:

(i)   On 3 February, the central bank cut 7-day and 14-day reverse repo rates by 10 basis points, lowering them to 2.40% and 2.55%, respectively. It also injected sizable liquidity into the banking system.

(ii) On 5 February, the State Council called on banks to offer preferential loans at fiscally subsidized interest rates below 1.6% to enterprises that produce, transport, or sell medical supplies and other essentials.

(iii) On 9 February, the central bank announced a special relending program to support industries involved in epidemic prevention and control with interest rates not higher than 100 basis points below the 1-year loan prime rate. A quota of CNY300 billion became available on 10 February for relending to selected banks across 10 provinces and municipalities.

(iv) On 17 February, the central bank cut the medium-term lending facility rate by 10 basis points. The loan prime rate benchmark for pricing bank loans fell by the same magnitude to 4.05% on 20 February.

(v)   On 25 February, the State Council encouraged banks to defer loan payments and increase lending at concessional rates to micro and small enterprises. State-owned banks were urged to increase lending to them by 30% in the first half of 2020. The relending quota through which banks can refinance their lending to micro businesses and SMEs from the central bank will be increased by CNY500 billion. Policy banks will add a special credit quota of CNY350 billion for lending to such firms at preferential rates.

(vi) On 1 March, the central bank and the banking regulator said in a joint statement that all enterprises in Hubei with principal or interest due from 25 January to 30 June can apply for a delay to the end of Q2, as can qualified micro businesses and SMEs nationwide.

(vii) On 13 March, the central bank announced a targeted cut in the reserve requirement ratio by 50–100 basis points for banks that have met inclusive financing targets and an additional cut of 100 basis points for qualified joint-stock banks.

bounce back. Growth in real estate services will likely moderate further in tandem with a less dynamic housing market. Manufacturing—earlier poised to profit from the phase one trade deal with the US—is now expected to suffer lower domestic demand and declining exports. However, government support will help high-tech manufacturing and innovative industries continue to grow in both 2020 and 2021. Despite lost dynamism in the housing market, construction will profit from increased infrastructure investment, but mining is expected to be hit by weaker demand, both domestic and external. Growth in agriculture, still suffering from African swine fever, should gradually stabilize and recover in 2021.

The outlook for the labor market remains clouded by COVID-19, which puts tremendous pressure on companies, especially small and medium-sized enterprises (SMEs) with little or no financial reserves. While larger companies and state-owned enterprises are unlikely to lay off workers, this benefit to labor in the short term will likely dent firms' profitability and further increase corporate debt (Figure 3.11.19).

Despite slowing domestic growth and lower global oil prices, consumer price inflation is expected to surge in 2020 to 3.6% on higher food prices (Figure 3.11.20). Then, with pork prices having normalized, consumer prices are forecast higher in 2021 by only 1.9%. Some producer prices may rise temporarily because COVID-19 has disrupted some supply chains, but slower growth and lower commodity prices should depress producer prices on average in 2020, before they increase moderately in 2021.

Monetary policy is expected to become more accommodative, with the central bank likely reducing the medium-term lending facility rate to further bring down the loan prime rate. In addition, further targeted cuts to the reserve requirement ratio will provide additional liquidity to banks, and the central bank will likely keep liquidity ample in the interbank market. Targeted measures include a special relending program for certain industries and SMEs (Box 3.11.1). The central bank may also cut the 1-year benchmark deposit rate to bolster banks' interest margins, which came under pressure from recent reductions in the loan prime rate.

Shadow banking is unlikely to be unleashed, as this would negate some of the progress made in reducing its outstanding amount (Figure 3.11.11). With further room to cut policy interest rates, but a difficult environment for corporate bond issues and initial public offerings, financing will increasingly come from financial institutions. Banks are encouraged to continue lending to keep companies going and thereby prevent a sharp rise in unemployment, and not worry too much about nonperforming loans. Despite temporary regulatory forbearance, this will likely mean, at the least, more special-

Figure 3.11.15 Growth in PRC exports, by region or country, and imports

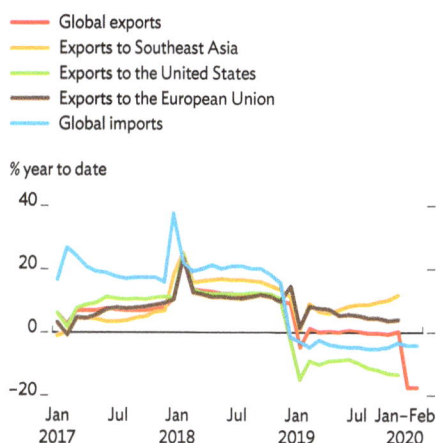

PRC = People's Republic of China.
Note: No breakdown by region or country is available for the first 2 months of 2020.
Sources: General Administration of Customs; ADB estimates.

Figure 3.11.16 Renminbi exchange rates

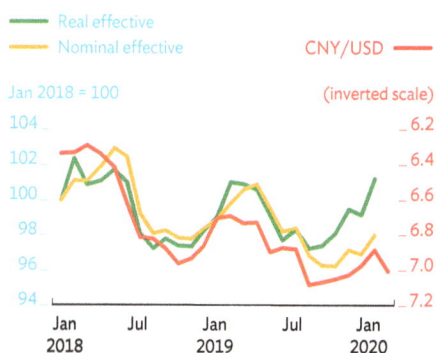

Sources: Bank for International Settlements; People's Bank of China; ADB estimates.

Table 3.11.1 Selected economic indicators (%)

	2018	2019	2020	2021
GDP growth	6.7	6.1	2.3	7.3
Inflation	2.1	2.9	3.6	1.9
Current acct. bal. (share of GDP)	0.4	1.3	1.6	1.2

Sources: National Bureau of Statistics; ADB estimates.

mention loans, rated a notch above nonperforming (Figure 3.11.21). A concern is banks accumulating credit risk and how to deal with it once the economy has recovered.

Poor access to finance will continue to challenge private firms despite government measures in February 2020 to increase lending to SMEs (Box 3.11.1). With many corporate bonds coming due from March 2020, private firms seeking longer-term financing in the bond market are in a difficult position. Meanwhile, state-owned enterprises will aim to roll over their short-term debt. Sales revenue growth and profits in industry already declined notably in 2019 (Figure 3.11.5). Many companies may struggle to survive another year of declining revenue growth and profits in 2020 caused by production shortfalls or reduced demand for services induced by COVID-19. Private SMEs are particularly vulnerable, as they enjoy less access to bank loans than do state-owned and other larger companies with better collateral and lower default rates.

Fiscal policy will likely become more supportive, including a further increase in new local government special bond issues, which were already higher in early 2020 (Figure 3.11.13). With the government aiming to shore up growth through infrastructure investment, the local government special bond quota will very likely be fixed significantly above last year's CNY2.15 trillion. As government spending is expected to accelerate while tax revenue suffers from recent temporary tax cuts and slower economic growth, the consolidated budget deficit looks set to expand markedly. Despite recent efforts by the central government to temporarily support local government finances (Box 3.11.1), lower tax revenue will burden the finances of local governments as they are not allowed to levy taxes or incur debt without central government approval, limiting their means to stimulate the local economy. In 2021, the consolidated budget deficit is expected to retreat as growth in tax revenue recovers and the increase in public expenditure moderates.

The current account is forecast to record surpluses equal to 1.6% of GDP in 2020 and 1.2% in 2021. Merchandise exports and imports are both expected to contract substantially in 2020 before picking up in 2021. The service deficit is expected to shrink notably in 2020 in line with sharply lower outbound tourism before widening again in 2021. In terms of capital flows, FDI inflow is projected to moderate because COVID-19 has roiled uncertainty stemming from the trade conflict with the US, and FDI outflow will also be lower owing to tight capital controls and weaker domestic growth, limiting the funds available for acquisitions overseas. Despite recently increased global uncertainty and volatility, some portfolio inflow is expected to continue as long-term foreign investors acquire PRC bonds and stocks to diversify their portfolios, profiting from the spread between PRC and US bond yields

Figure 3.11.17 COVID-19 cases in the People's Republic of China

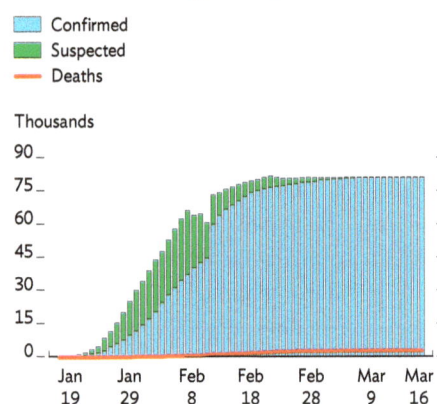

Source: National Health Commission.

Figure 3.11.18 GDP growth

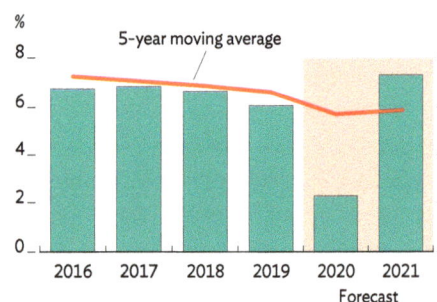

Source: *Asian Development Outlook* database.

Figure 3.11.19 Debt structure

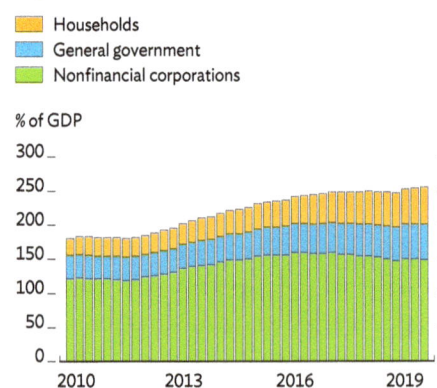

Source: Bank for International Settlements.

(Figure 3.11.22). While unregistered capital outflow is expected to remain sizeable, it should be manageable under strict capital controls.

The forecast is subject to large risks, both domestic and external. The main downside risks come from COVID-19: a new round of domestic infections or the virus spreading globally could further damage both investor sentiment and consumer spending. Another domestic downside risk is to credit sustainability, if COVID-19 keeps the economy from normalizing soon. Either a substantial number of companies, especially SMEs, would face bankruptcy, or bank lending loosened to stabilize growth in the short run would burden banks with heightened credit risks. This could cause nonperforming loans to spike, undermining financial stability and leaving banks in need of recapitalization. Externally, the trade conflict with the US could revive in the absence of a durable deal, generating an additional obstacle to economic recovery.

Policy challenge—further integrating into global capital markets

By increasingly opening its bond and equity markets to foreign investors in recent years, the PRC has enabled sizable portfolio inflow further spurred by its inclusion and increased weighting in global indexes. In 2019, the PRC saw financial assets held by foreign investors expand by $213.0 billion, including increases of $75.0 billion in bond holdings and $133.5 billion in equity holdings (Box 3.11.2). This flow could reverse.

With the current account surplus narrowing in the medium term and net FDI inflow moderating, volatility in portfolio flows could pose a challenge. Whereas the current account surplus once guaranteed foreign exchange inflow, as did rather stable FDI flows most of the time, portfolio flows can reverse quickly on changeable market sentiment. Even as the current account surplus declined and net FDI inflow moderated, unregistered capital outflow—proxied by errors and omissions in the balance of payments—has remained sizeable despite strict capital controls (Figure 3.11.23). From 2018 to Q3 of 2019, net FDI inflow and the current account surplus combined could not fully cover unregistered capital outflow. Against this backdrop, managing capital outflow could be a challenge if investors suddenly withdrew from the market, especially if foreign participation in the bond market reversed abruptly. That said, reserve assets stood at an ample $3.22 trillion at the end of 2019, and foreign bond and equity holdings equaled only 19.4% of these reserves at the end of 2019.

Foreign equity and bond investment will increasingly drive capital flows into the PRC and potentially out of it.

Figure 3.11.20 Inflation

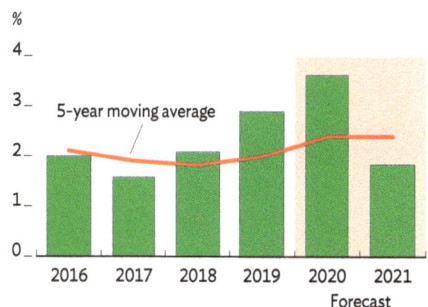

Source: *Asian Development Outlook* database.

Figure 3.11.21 Problematic bank loans by category

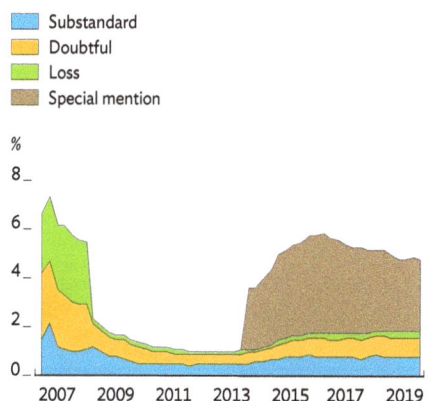

Note: Data on special-mention loans, a category one notch above substandard, started in 2014.
Source: China Banking and Insurance Regulatory Commission.

Figure 3.11.22 Difference in government bond yields

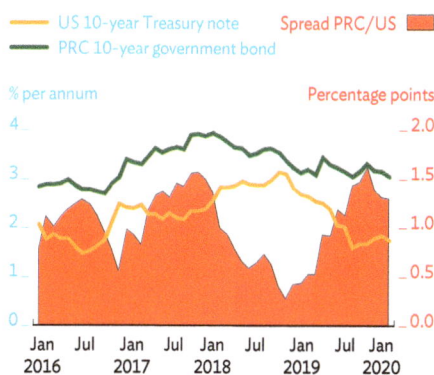

PRC = People's Republic of China, US = United States.
Sources: PRC National Interbank Funding Centre; US Federal Reserve Board; ADB estimates.

Box 3.11.2 Steps in the opening of bond and equity markets in the People's Republic of China

At the end of 2019, foreign investors' holdings stood at $919.2 billion, of which $301.3 billion was in equities and $324.4 billion in bonds (box figure). Capital market reform and opening to foreign investors made bonds and equities the two main financial assets held by foreigners since 2018, after inflow into PRC bond and equity markets had picked up. This reflected improved access for foreigners to the capital market as Shenzhen–Hong Kong Stock Connect was launched in December 2016, followed by Bond Connect in July 2017.

Financial assets in the People's Republic of China held by overseas entities

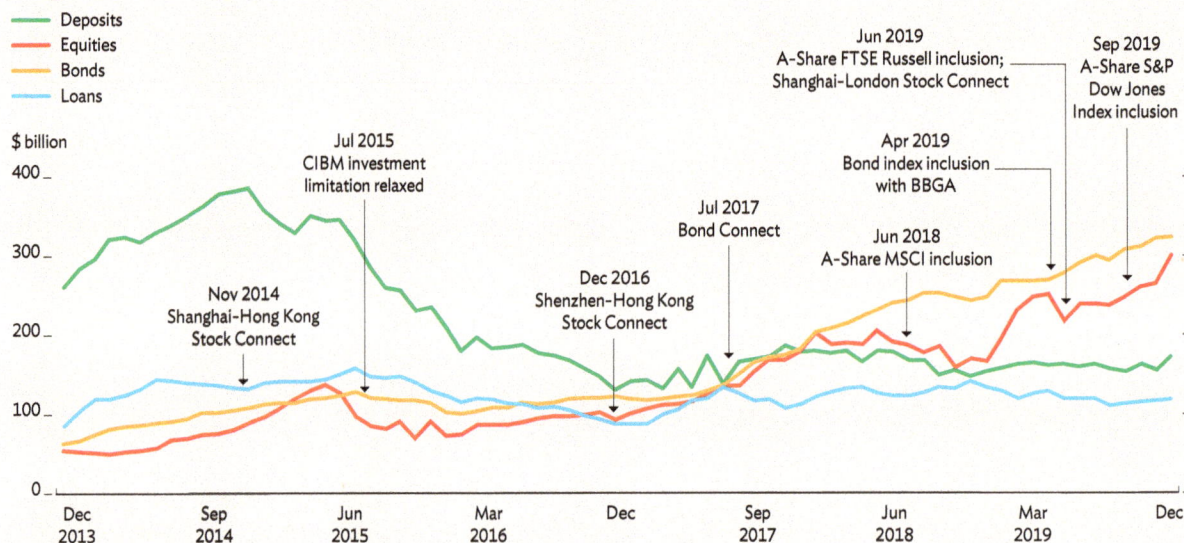

BBGA = Bloomberg-Barclays Global Aggregate Index, CIBM = China Interbank Bond Market, FTSE = Financial Times Stock Exchange, MSCI = Morgan Stanley Capital International, PRC = People's Republic of China, S&P = Standard & Poor's.
Sources: People's Bank of China; ADB compilation.

The recent COVID-19 outbreak may excite capital flow volatility temporarily, but in the long run net inflow to the PRC is likely to continue for two main reasons. First, the PRC capital market is large while foreign participation remains low, indicating further catch-up potential. In 2018, the PRC accounted for 8.5% of global equity market capitalization, according to the latest data from the World Federation of Exchanges, and 12.6% of the global bond market outstanding, according to data from the Bank for International Settlements. However, at the end of 2019, foreign ownership of PRC equities was only 4.4%, and of bonds only 3.3%. Secondly, PRC inclusion and stepwise increases in weighting in global bond and equity indexes is expected to continue, bringing further capital inflow. Most of it is currently directed toward relatively liquid and safe central government bonds, which accounted for 59.7% of foreign bond holdings in the PRC at the end of 2019. Policy bank bonds accounted for 22.8%, and negotiable certificates of deposit 9.9% (Figure 3.11.24).

Figure 3.11.23 Balance of payments: breakdown of capital flows

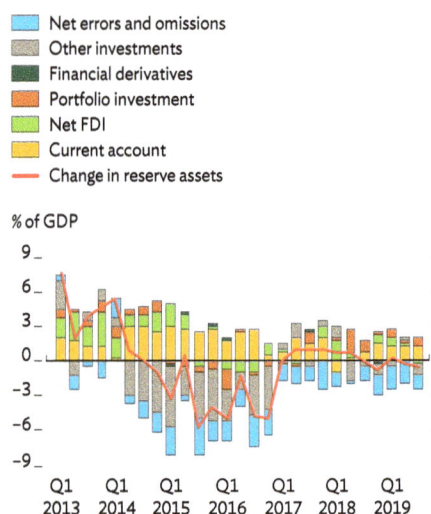

FDI = foreign direct investment, GDP = gross domestic product, Q = quarter.
Sources: State Administration of Foreign Exchange; ADB estimates.

The way to effectively manage capital flow volatility and potential reversal is to strengthen financial system stability and deepen the domestic bond market. As PRC integration into the global financial market remains limited, portfolio inflow is currently only marginally affected by the global financial cycle. Thus, domestic financial regulation and supervision should be strengthened and the macroprudential policy framework enhanced to better reflect the expanding role of portfolio flows.

Deep and liquid capital markets—in which financial derivatives, especially Treasury bond futures, are available to foreign investors for managing risk—are key to attracting long-term international investors. Meanwhile, broadening foreign investors' market participation beyond treasuries, which still attract the bulk of their investment, requires more depth, liquidity, and transparency in other market segments. In addition, further clarifying and unifying currently fragmented tax and regulatory frameworks for foreign investors would mean fewer uncertainties and easier market access.

Figure 3.11.24 Structure and market share of foreign investors' bond holding in the PRC

Sources: China Central Depository & Clearing Co., Ltd, Shanghai Clearing House; ADB estimates.

Republic of Korea

GDP growth in 2019 decelerated to its slowest in a decade, weighted down by moderating export growth and contraction in private investment. Weak global demand and COVID-19 are expected to hit growth hard this year. Consumption will weaken, and exports and private investment will fall as support is delayed, but accommodative fiscal and monetary policies should cushion some COVID-19 effects. Factory data need to be better used to strengthen manufacturing.

Economic performance

GDP slowed from 2.7% in 2018 to 2.0% in 2019, its slowest in a decade, as the economy faced domestic and external headwinds (Figure 3.12.1). On the demand side, investment deepened 1.8% contraction in 2018 with further contraction by 2.5% as gains from a fiscal stimulus package were offset by sharper reduction in private investment, and despite government investment expanding to a 10-year high of 11.1%. Private investment contraction by 6.0% reflected continued weakening in global trade. Private consumption, the main engine of growth, also slowed, from 2.8% in 2018 to 1.9%, as declining wages and deteriorating consumer confidence constrained household spending. Meanwhile, government consumption growth rose from 5.6% in 2018 to 6.5% on higher government subsidies and transfers.

Growth in exports of goods and services moderated from 3.5% in 2018 to 1.7% this year as the economy grappled with two trade conflicts, one between the US and the People's Republic of China (PRC) and the other between Japan and the Republic of Korea (ROK) (Figure 3.12.2). A downturn in global electronics trade further crimped exporters. Growth in shipments of semiconductor and information technology products, metals, and heavy industry products languished in negative territory for most of the year. Meanwhile, imports continued to contract as lower world crude oil prices cut the fuel import bill, and as subdued domestic consumption and private investment reduced demand for capital and transport goods.

By sector, growth in services slowed from 3.2% in 2018 to 2.7%. Growth in wholesale and retail trade, information and communications, transport and storage, and finance and

Figure 3.12.1 Demand-side contributions to growth

- Government consumption
- Private consumption
- Gross fixed capital formation
- Exports of goods and services
- Imports of goods and services
- Change in inventories
- Statistical discrepancy
- Gross domestic product

Percentage points

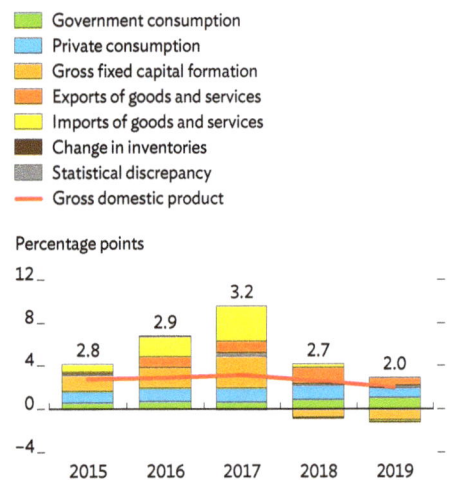

Source: Haver Analytics (accessed 5 March 2020).

Figure 3.12.2 Supply-side contributions to growth

- Agriculture
- Services
- Industry
- Taxes less subsidies
- Gross domestic product

Percentage points

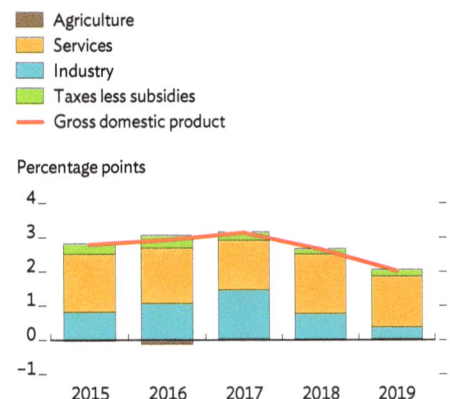

Source: Haver Analytics (accessed 5 March 2020).

This chapter was written by Shiela Camingue-Romance and Donghyun Park of the Economic Research and Regional Cooperation Department, ADB, Manila.

insurance, which together comprise two-fifth of services, all slid from their recorded expansions in 2018, while real estate and business services both recorded modest increases.

Industry growth slowed from 2.1% in 2018 to just 0.9% last year as coal production was curtailed in line with the government's commitment to reduce reliance on this fuel, continuing policies to cap property prices, and softening global and domestic demand. Mining contracted by 1.4%, and construction by 3.0%, while growth in manufacturing fell by more than half from 3.4% in 2018 to 1.4%. Manufacturing was hit by shrinking global trade and by structural and cyclical factors but nonetheless stayed in positive territory on growth higher than expected in its top two sectors: growth in computer, electronic, and optical products unexpectedly picking up in the second half of the year on higher demand for electronic devices, and transport equipment also expanding on higher shipbuilding orders and increased demand for automobiles in major trade partners. Agricultural output improved on 1.5% growth in 2018 with expansion by 2.4% on better weather and increased livestock production.

As growth decelerated, inflation fell from 1.5% in 2018 to 0.4% last year (Figure 3.12.3). This is far below the central bank target of 2.0% and the lowest annual inflation in 6 decades. Core inflation, which excludes food and energy, also fell, from 1.2% a year earlier to 0.7%.

The current account surplus slipped from the equivalent of 4.5% of GDP in 2018 to 3.7% in 2019 (Figure 3.12.4). Growth in merchandise exports decelerated from 10.3% in 2018 to 7.9% on lower external demand and subdued prices for semiconductors and petrochemicals. Growth in merchandise imports contracted by 6.0% on account of lackluster demand for consumer goods and intermediate inputs for production. Net foreign direct investment contracted by 4.1% last year. This, combined with a sharp decline in net portfolio investment, narrowed the surplus in the overall balance of payments to $1.5 billion, less than a tenth of the $17.5 billion recorded in 2018. This small surplus raised official foreign exchange reserves by a modest 1.3% to $408.8 billion at the end of 2019.

Fiscal and monetary policies remained supportive of growth in 2019. The government introduced two supplementary budgets that raised government expenditure on continuing programs to create jobs, spur innovation, and improve household incomes. As a result, expenditure in the first 11 months of the year increased by 12.5%, greatly exceeding the government target for annual rises at 7.3% until 2022. Meanwhile, growth in government revenue in the first 11 months of 2019 braked from 8.8% a year earlier to a scant 0.2%, largely reflecting lower corporate profits. As a result, the fiscal deficit excluding social security funds in the consolidated balance came to W45.6 trillion,

Figure 3.12.3 Monthly inflation

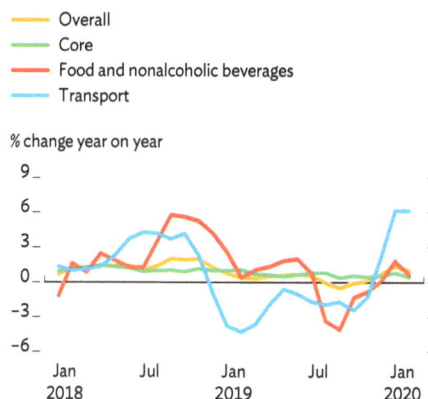

- Overall
- Core
- Food and nonalcoholic beverages
- Transport

Source: Haver Analytics (accessed 5 March 2020).

Figure 3.12.4 Current account components

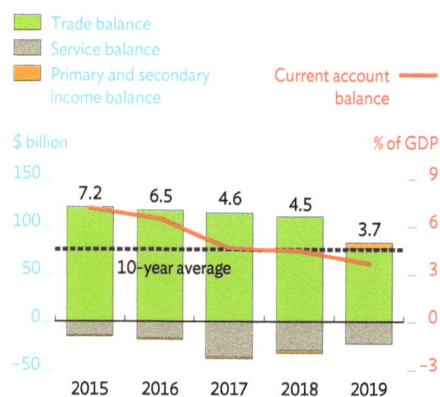

- Trade balance
- Service balance
- Primary and secondary income balance
- Current account balance

Sources: Bank of Korea, Economics Statistics System, available: http://ecos.bok.or.kr/EIndex_en.jsp; Haver Analytics (both accessed 5 February 2020).

the largest since 2011 and higher than the full year target of W42.3 trillion. With the economy weakening and inflation low, monetary policy was accommodative as the central bank cut its policy interest rate twice last year, first by 25 basis points in July and then by another 25 basis points in October, lowering the rate to 1.25%.

Economic prospects

As growth in major trade partners deteriorates, COVID-19 spreads around the world, and access to export markets tightens, growth is expected to slow markedly to 1.3% this year, picking up to 2.3% in 2021 (Figure 3.12.5). With weaker growth anticipated in the PRC and major advanced economies, exports are less likely to grow this year. Supply chain disruption from the outbreak is expected to affect private investment as well, as firms cut or delay facility upgrades. Meanwhile, consumption will moderate, but the slowdown will be tempered by continued government support, including accommodative fiscal and monetary policy. Such support and a projected recovery in global growth in 2021 should lift growth in the ROK to 2.3% next year.

Exports of goods and services are set to fall again this year. Exports to the US and rest of the world picked up in the first 2 months of the year, but exports to the PRC, the largest trade partner of the ROK, contracted. Meanwhile, a projected rebound in electronics and potential gains from the US–PRC phase one agreement are likely to be delayed. Imports are similarly expected to slow as demand for consumer and capital goods falls, but they should recover toward the end of the year as business activity and consumer spending recover.

Private investment is expected to weaken in tandem with exports. The business confidence index fell from 77 in February 2020 to 69 in March, signaling lower fixed investment in the months ahead as firms foresee weakening in corporate sales and incomes (Figure 3.12.6). New product launches and the establishment of new data centers to support plans by big companies to export 5G content and connectivity have spurred investment in information technology since the end of 2019. However, with factory closures in the PRC in response to COVID-19 and sluggish global trade, business expansion is likely to pause.

Growth in private consumption is expected to soften in 2020. After reaching a 19-month high in January 2020, consumer confidence fell below 100 in February, indicating lower household spending in the near term. Confidence should improve later in the year as the outbreak is brought under control. A proactive approach to monitoring and tracing the outbreak in the ROK should lessen fears of massive infection.

Figure 3.12.5 GDP growth

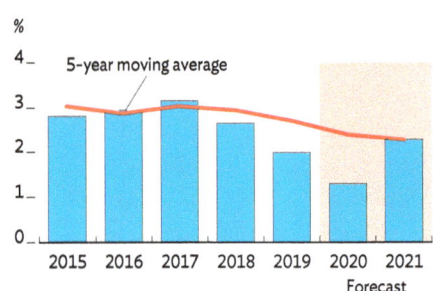

Source: *Asian Development Outlook* database.

Figure 3.12.6 Private investment indicators

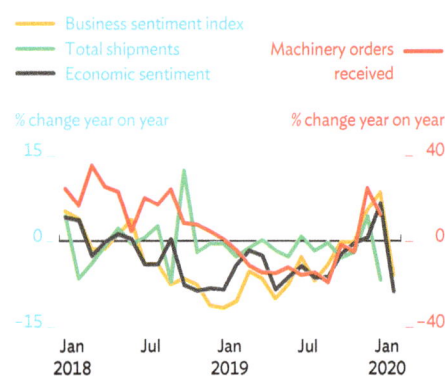

Source: Haver Analytics (accessed 5 March 2020).

Table 3.12.1 Selected economic indicators (%)

	2018	2019	2020	2021
GDP growth	2.7	2.0	1.3	2.3
Inflation	1.5	0.4	0.9	1.3
Current acct. bal. (share of GDP)	4.5	3.7	2.8	3.5

Sources: Haver Analytics (accessed 5 March 2020); ADB estimates.

Despite supply constraints imposed by COVID-19, declining fuel prices and price cutting on manufactures to stimulate demand will keep price increases to a minimum. Inflation is therefore forecast at only 0.9% this year (Figure 3.12.7). Prices are projected to pick up gradually to 1.3% in 2021, once the virus is contained and growth revives price pressures.

Merchandise exports are expected to moderate during most of this year, improving only toward the end as demand for electronics and other exports from major markets slowly picks up. The Nikkei purchasing managers' index slipped from an 8-month high of 50.1 in December 2019 to below 50 in January and February 2020 on lower export orders, indicating lower production. A pickup in export growth to 4.5% in February, largely on higher shipments of memory chips and car components to the US, is unlikely to impart momentum in light of a contraction now expected in major advanced economies.

Merchandise imports are likely to follow the same trend, picking up toward year-end as domestic activity rebounds. The service account will likely record a larger deficit as tourism receipts decline with lower tourist arrivals, while income accounts will shrink as the outbreak hampers corporate incomes and profits. As a result, the current account surplus will fall to the equivalent of 2.8% of GDP this year, rising again to 3.5% in 2021 (Figure 3.12.8).

Monetary policy should remain accommodative to support growth. In March, the central bank slashed its benchmark interest rate by 50 basis points and introduced measures to aid small companies and boost liquidity. Depending on how the macroeconomic situation unfolds in the near term, the central bank may adjust policy further to sustain growth and keep inflation low. Fiscal policy too will remain expansionary with continued efforts to revitalize the economy through government spending and measures to contain COVID-19. On 17 March 2020, the government passed a W11.7 trillion supplemental budget for disease prevention and treatment and financial assistance to affected families and business. On 19 March, it launched a W50 trillion package to ease financial burdens on smaller businesses and boost their liquidity—doubling it to W100 trillion on 24 March to include conglomerates and big companies. Excluding the additional budget and emergency package, a consolidated fiscal deficit equal to 3.5% of GDP is planned under the 2020 budget.

The key downside risk to the outlook would be a wider and more protracted COVID-19 pandemic, which threatens to damage economies through multiple channels. Given strong trade relations between the PRC and the ROK and the role of the latter in global manufacturing supply chains, extended factory closures and lockdowns in major trade partners could exact a heavy toll on domestic production.

Figure 3.12.7 Annual inflation

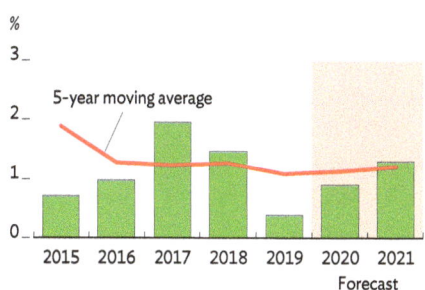

Source: *Asian Development Outlook* database.

Figure 3.12.8 Current account balance

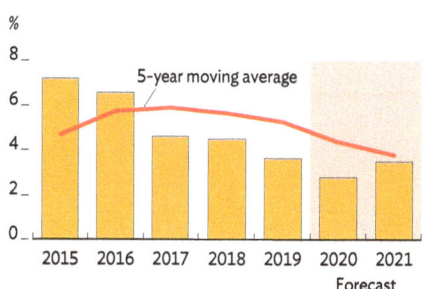

Source: *Asian Development Outlook* database.

Policy challenge—smarter manufacturing

To boost manufacturing, some countries have actively pursued polices to make production more efficient and flexible by digitalizing data. Factory smartization, as some choose to call it, denotes the digitalization and networking of all processes, products, and resources. According to this definition, workers, machines, and parts share all information relevant to production and have the capacity to utilize the information in the production process. For example, Nobilia, a German kitchen equipment maker, applies information and communication technology to automatically order, process, and assemble parts. Factories then digitalize all relevant information and use it in decision making. Smart production is widely credited with turning Nobilia, which has just two factories, into Europe's biggest kitchen equipment manufacturer.

In the ROK, government support for factory smartization began in 2014. In the next 5 years, the government spent W414 billion on subsidies for smart factories. In 2019, the government allocated W1 trillion in its budget for smart factories, making it a top structural policies. The government has proposed a target of 30,000 smart factories by 2022.

According to a 2019 study by the Korean Development Institute (KDI) based on a survey of 1,000 ROK manufacturing firms, such concerted policy support still leaves significant scope for making factories smarter. The survey indicated that the factory smartization rate was 31% in 2015, rising to only 37% in 2017 (Figure 3.12.9). This indicates that most factories still engage in little system integration or data sharing and utilization.

Of course, the ultimate purpose of smarter factories is to make firms more productive. The KDI study confirmed that it did improve factory performance. In particular, it significantly and positively affected daily output, which is the most comprehensive performance indicator.

A number of policy directions exist as options for further fostering smart factories in the ROK. First, government could strive to acquire a longer-term and more sustainable policy perspective on smart factories. Rushing into smartization without adequate preparation can be costly and wasteful. Second, smart factories require smart policy support. In practice, this means systematically linking and analyzing the information gleaned from past policy experience. Third, retraining systems must be reconfigured to meet firms' specific emerging needs. Such reconfiguration would facilitate the reallocation of workers away from skill categories that will shrink as factories become smarter. Finally, smart factory policy should make good use of public–private partnership in place of top–down government-led initiatives. More specifically, network-based management platforms can link various stakeholders and foster their collaboration, and thus spearhead the upgrading of ROK manufacturing through digitalization.

Figure 3.12.9 Smartization of factories

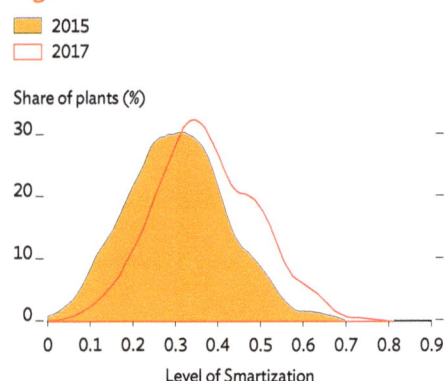

Source: Adapted from Kim, M., S. Chung, and C. Lee. 2019. Smart Factory: Economic Impact and Policy Implications. *Research Monograph 2019-01*, Korea Development Institute (in Korean).

Taipei,China

Domestic demand kept growth stable in 2019. Inflation moderated despite rising food prices, and the current account surplus narrowed. Growth is expected to moderate in 2020 as COVID-19 takes its toll but revive in 2021 on higher exports and public outlays. Inflation should trend down this year, as oil and other commodity prices moderate, but rise slightly in 2021 as demand strengthens. The current account surplus will likely fall in 2020 but expand next year as export growth accelerates. Improving labor productivity is essential for maintaining growth as the population ages.

Economic performance

GDP growth stabilized in 2019 at 2.7%, the same rate as in the previous year. Domestic demand remained the main driver of growth. Gross capital formation expanded by 5.4% and contributed 1.2 percentage points to GDP growth as companies re-shored operations back to Taipei,China, mainly from the People's Republic of China (PRC). Private consumption increased by 2.1% and added 1.1 percentage points, while government consumption grew by only 0.1%, making its contribution to GDP growth negligible. As export growth almost doubled to 1.2% in real terms while import growth slowed by nearly half to 0.8%, net exports reversed contraction in the previous year to expand by 3.0% and add 0.4 points to growth (Figure 3.13.1).

On the supply side, growth in services declined marginally to 2.7% in 2019, mainly with slower expansion in wholesale and retail trade. Industry growth decelerated from 3.2% to 0.6% as manufacturing moderated in line with a downturn in semiconductors, while excessive rainfall caused agriculture to contract, reducing to nil its contribution to growth. Services added 1.6 percentage points, and industry 0.2 points, but sectoral contributions do not add up to GDP growth, leaving a statistical discrepancy in the official data. The unemployment rate was unchanged at 3.7%.

Inflation remained subdued in 2019, falling to 0.6%, less than half of the 2018 rate. While food price inflation almost doubled to 1.9% as heavy rains disrupted the supply of vegetables and fruit, nonfood prices dropped considerably as oil prices fell and the communication industry began to experience more competition (Figure 3.13.2).

Figure 3.13.1 Demand-side contributions to growth

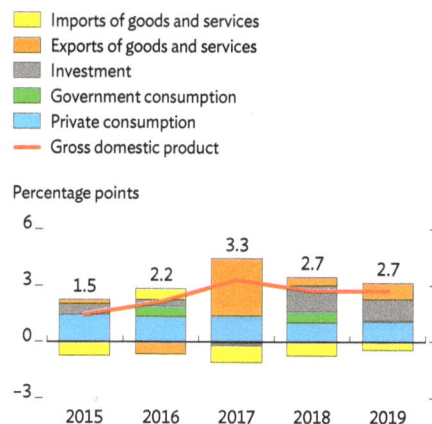

- Imports of goods and services
- Exports of goods and services
- Investment
- Government consumption
- Private consumption
- Gross domestic product

Percentage points

Source: Haver Analytics (accessed 2 March 2020).

Figure 3.13.2 Inflation

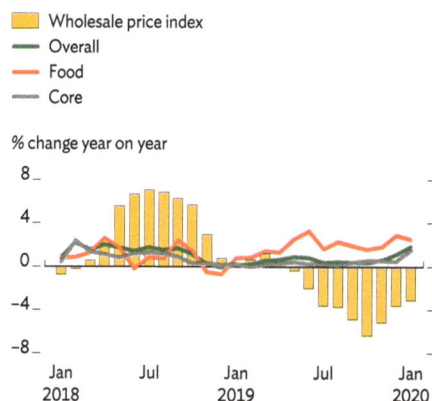

- Wholesale price index
- Overall
- Food
- Core

% change year on year

Source: CEIC Data Company (accessed 2 March 2020).

This chapter was written by Irfan Qureshi and Nedelyn Magtibay-Ramos of the Economic Research and Regional Cooperation Department, ADB, Manila.

Core inflation, which excludes food and energy, eased from 1.0% in 2018 to 0.3%, and wholesale prices plummeted by 2.3% with declining prices for fertilizers, fibers, petroleum, and coal products.

Merchandise exports contracted in 2019 even as they doubled to the US, the second largest market for Taipei,China after the PRC, raising their share of total exports from 11.8% in 2018 to 14.0%. Exports of electrical machinery and apparatuses, which account for more than a third of merchandise exports, grew faster than in the previous year. The trade surplus narrowed as imports declined less than exports and the service account registered a deficit despite faster growth than in 2018 in investment income and net tourism receipts (Figure 3.13.3). The current account surplus thus narrowed from the equivalent of 11.6% of GDP in 2018 to 10.5%. Gross foreign exchange reserves grew by 3.5% in 2019. The local dollar depreciated by 2.5% against the US dollar (Figure 3.13.4). However, it appreciated by 0.4% in nominal effective terms (against a trade-weighted basket of currencies) and by 3.3% in real effective terms (taking inflation into account).

Both fiscal and monetary policy were accommodative in 2019. Budgetary revenue contracted by 1.2% while expenditure expanded by 5.0%, reversing a central government budget surplus equal to 0.1% of GDP in 2018 with a provisional deficit of 0.6%. In March 2020, the central bank reduced the discount rate, for the first time in almost 4 years, to 1.125%, its lowest ever. The decision seeks to facilitate business continuity and avoid adverse implications of massive cross-border capital flows for financial stability. Outstanding credit to the private sector increased by 5.7%, and net foreign assets in banks grew by 5.5%. Broad money expansion accelerated from 2.7% in 2018 to 4.5% but remained within the central bank target range.

Economic prospects

Economic growth is forecast to slow to 1.8% in 2020 as growth in private consumption and investment moderate in response to COVID-19 and a slower increase in government outlays. It will rise to 2.5% in 2021 on solid expansion in exports and public investment, albeit at a lower rate than in 2019 because of a high base. Private investment will continue to be driven by re-shoring from the PRC. Public investment in infrastructure is expected to rise, though less than in previous years, again because of base effects. Consumption spending, especially on services, is expected to be depressed by COVID-19, but this may be partly offset by a rise in the minimum wage at the start of the year and steady employment.

On the supply side, services will continue to make the largest contribution to growth this year and next. Services are followed by industry, which is shown recovering gradually by

Figure 3.13.3　Tourist arrivals

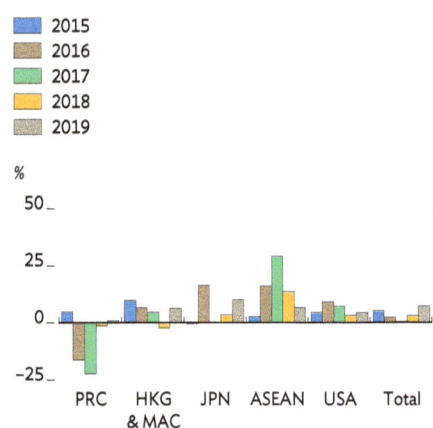

ASEAN = Association of Southeast Asian Nations, HKG = Hong Kong, China, JPN = Japan, MAC = Macau, China, PRC = People's Republic of China, USA = United States.
Source: Haver Analytics (accessed 2 March 2020).

Figure 3.13.4　Exchange rates

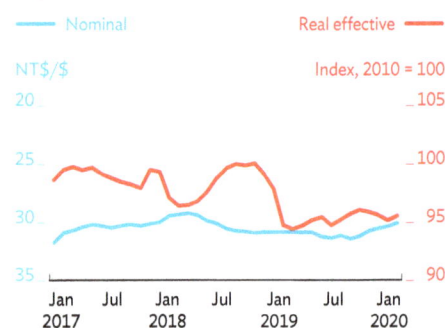

Source: Haver Analytics (accessed 2 March 2020).

Table 3.13.1　Selected economic indicators (%)

	2018	2019	2020	2021
GDP growth	2.7	2.7	1.8	2.5
Inflation	1.3	0.6	0.4	0.8
Current acct. bal. (share of GDP)	11.6	10.5	10.0	12.0

Sources: Haver Analytics (accessed 11 March 2020); ADB estimates.

the latest readings of the seasonally adjusted manufacturing purchasing managers' index. The index improved from 51.3 in January 2020 to 52.7 in February.

Inflation will remain subdued at 0.4% in 2020 and 0.8% in 2021 with softening oil and other commodity prices and— continuing a trend that began in 2019—as communications companies cut prices to boost market share before 5G mobile phones are rolled out. These developments should limit the inflationary impact of continued accommodative monetary policy.

On the external front, export growth is forecast to trend upward as it benefits from trade redirection to sidestep the US–PRC trade conflict. Imports of machinery, industrial parts such as ICT components, and transport equipment are also expected to rise strongly on robust public investment and demand from export-oriented industries. The trade surplus is nevertheless projected to rise, pushing the current account surplus to the equivalent of 10.0% of GDP in 2020 and 12.0% in 2021.

The budget deficit is projected to shrink to 0.6% of GDP this year as revenue outgrows expenditure on a projected rise in income tax revenue as the economy expands and 5G broadband licenses are auctioned. Outstanding central government debt will fall below 30% of GDP at the end of 2020 as budget financing requirements decline. Because debt is entirely domestic, there is no exchange rate risk.

Risks to the outlook tilt to the downside. One main risk is deepening uncertainty over the US–PRC trade conflict or a collapse of their phase one deal, further slowing global growth, especially in the PRC. Another is a prolonged COVID-19 outbreak, to which tourism, retail, and food and beverage services are especially vulnerable.

Policy challenge—raising labor productivity as the population ages

Taipei,China is aging rapidly, as shown by the so-called support ratio of working age population to total population. The decline is faster than in Hong Kong, China; the Republic of Korea (ROK); the PRC; Singapore; and several advanced economies (Figure 3.13.5). The median age is rising sharply, from 19.31 in 1970, then the lowest in the world, to 55.8 in 2050, one of the highest (Figure 3.13.6). These trends mainly reflect high life expectancy at more than 80 years and low fertility at only 0.9 per 1,000 women (Figure 3.13.7). Fertility is expected to start recovering in 2020 but will remain below the birth rate of 2.1 required to sustain a population.

An aging population strains fiscal resources by requiring more public services to ensure suitable housing, economic

Figure 3.13.5 Working age population

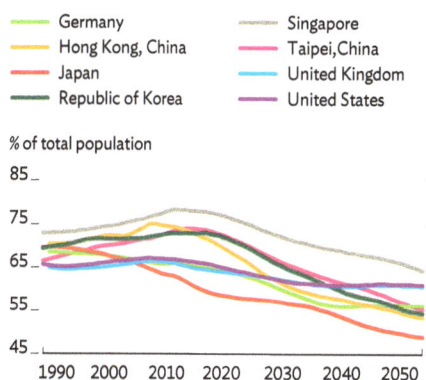

Source: ADB calculations using data from Haver Analytics (accessed 6 February 2020).

Figure 3.13.6 Median age

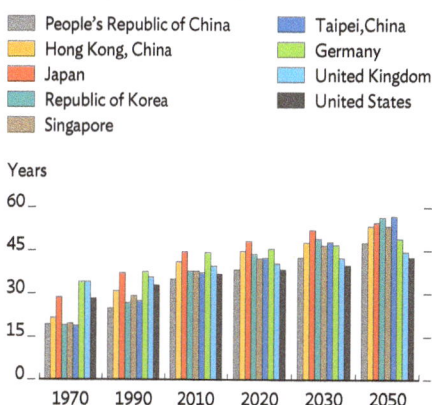

Source: ADB calculations using data from Haver Analytics (accessed 6 February 2020) and the UN World Population Prospects 2019.

Figure 3.13.7 Life expectancy and fertility rate

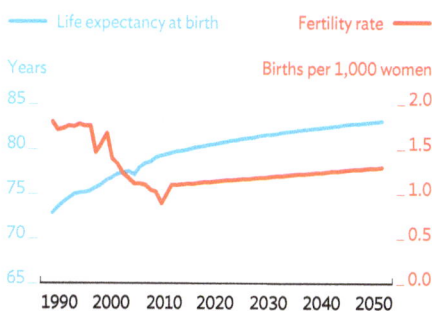

Source: ADB calculations using data from Haver Analytics (accessed 6 February 2020).

security, health care, and long-term care. This crimps the resources available for investment into either human or physical capital and thereby stagnates potential output. Raising productivity is essential to counter a worsening demographic outlook.

The government should devise incentives to encourage companies to take advantage of existing innovation in areas such as robotics and artificial intelligence to automate aggressively and raise productivity. While Taipei,China has more robots installed per manufacturing worker than most advanced economies, it lags the leaders: in descending order, the ROK, Singapore, Germany, and Japan (Figure 3.13.8). Taipei,China enjoys the fiscal space, meanwhile, to offer tax incentives to spur robot adoption across industries (Figure 3.13.9). Public expenditure on research and development should be increased to develop and enhance mechanical devices and robots able to take the heavy lifting out of the hands of older factory workers and increase their productivity.

It should also strengthen measures that make labor markets more flexible and efficient: allowing easier hiring and firing of employees, increasing participation, and encouraging the training of women and older workers. The government has already acted to provide cheaper childcare to boost fertility and raise female workforce participation, as well as increased subsidies to employers that hire older workers, introduced a pension reform bill that will encourage workers to remain in the workforce, limited age discrimination in hiring, and set up an employment database for older workers. These steps can be complemented by promoting flexible work arrangements to facilitate part-time employment and working from home.

To address talent shortages, visa regulations for skilled workers have become less restrictive, but more can be done to attract highly skilled foreign workers by adjusting residency requirements, health insurance, taxes, and compensation. More broadly, to encourage innovative start-ups and other new firms, Taipei,China should improve on its rating for ease of doing business, which the World Bank index puts below those of other high-income economies (Figure 3.13.10). In particular, access to credit should be enhanced by allowing moveable assets to serve as collateral.

Figure 3.13.8 Installed industrial robots in manufacturing, 2017

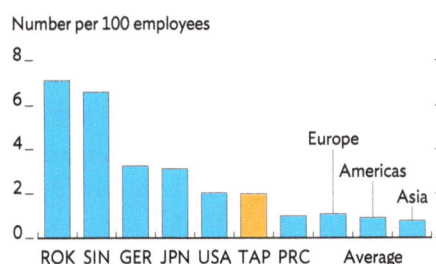

GER = Germany, JPN = Japan, PRC = People's Republic of China, ROK = Republic of Korea, SIN = Singapore, TAP = Taipei,China, USA = United States.
Source: International Federation of Robotics, https://ifr.org/.

Figure 3.13.9 Manufacturing robot stock in Taipei,China by industry, 2015

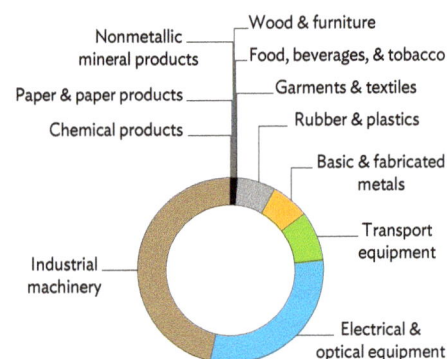

Source: International Federation of Robotics.

Figure 3.13.10 Ease of doing business score, 2020

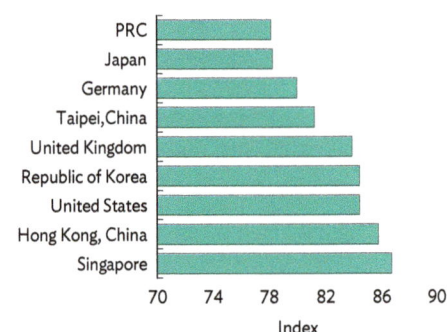

PRC = People's Republic of China.
Source: World Bank. Doing Business 2020. https://www.doingbusiness.org/en/data/doing-business-score (accessed 4 February 2020).

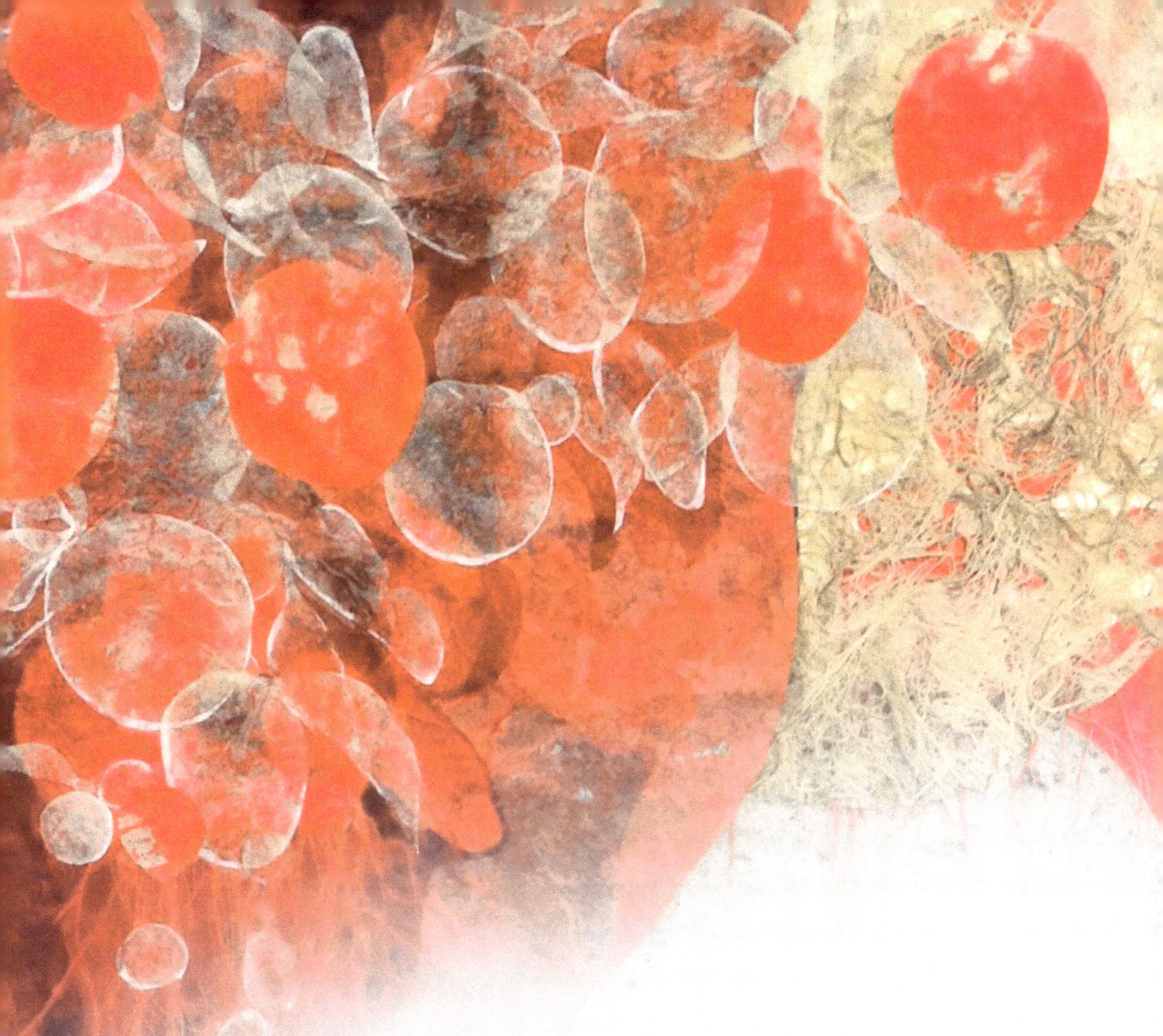

SOUTH ASIA

Afghanistan
Bangladesh
Bhutan
India
Maldives
Nepal
Pakistan
Sri Lanka

Afghanistan

Growth improved marginally in 2019 as robust agriculture compensated for slowing industry. Inflation accelerated, and the current account surplus narrowed. Growth is forecast unchanged this year despite COVID-19 but picking up in 2021 on improving business and consumer confidence. Inflation is expected to accelerate in 2021, and the current account surplus to narrow further as grant assistance falls in the next 2 years. To reduce grant dependence and become more self-reliant, the government needs to raise more domestic revenue.

Economic performance

GDP improved on 2.7% growth in 2018 to grow by 3.0% in 2019 (Figure 3.14.1). Precipitation above average enabled recovery in agriculture, which provides 19% of GDP, from 0.9% decline in 2018. Uncertainty surrounding delayed presidential elections caused industry to decelerate in 2019 from strong 7.6% growth in 2018, and growth in services remained sluggish.

Business confidence was further eroded by continued violence that took a high toll on Afghan civilians, causing private investment to decline. Private consumption improved thanks to rising agricultural incomes. Public expenditure on development projects marginally decreased, further softening domestic demand.

Inflation increased from 0.6% in 2018 to average 2.3% in 2019 as the local currency, the afghani, depreciated and food prices reversed their steep fall in 2018 to rise by 3.8% last year (Figure 3.14.2). Nonfood inflation fell from 2.3% in 2018 to 0.9% as demand slackened. The afghani depreciated against the US dollar by 7.5% on average in 2019 as US dollars were smuggled out of the country in response to political uncertainty prior to presidential elections, with the steepest depreciation recorded in June 2019 (Figure 3.14.3).

Broad money growth rose from 2.6% in 2018 to 5.7% in 2019, as the issuance of new banknotes increased currency in circulation by 7.1% in the first 3 quarters of the year (Figure 3.14.4). To mitigate excessive fluctuation in the afghani exchange rate and reduce liquidity in the market, Da Afghanistan Bank, the central bank, auctioned $1,781 million in the first 3 quarters of 2019, or 6% more than in the same period of the previous year. Credit to the private sector contracted by 2.1% in the first 3 quarters of 2019 as credit demand waned along with business confidence.

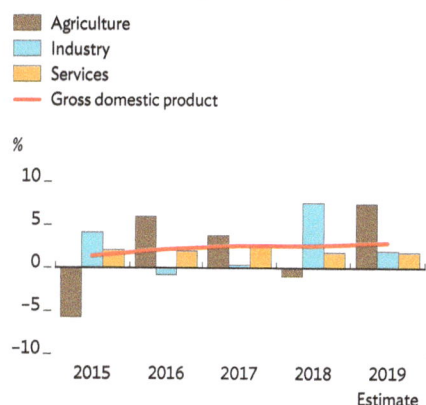

Figure 3.14.1 GDP growth by sector

Sources: World Development Indicator, World Bank; International Monetary Fund; ADB estimates.

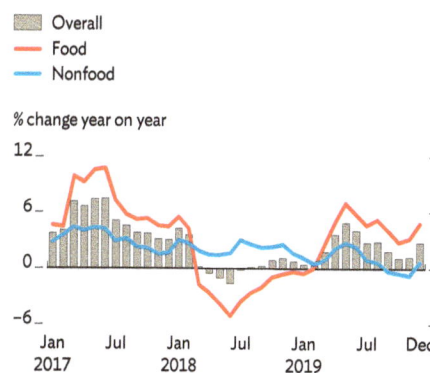

Figure 3.14.2 Inflation

Source: Central Statistical Office (accessed 3 March 2020).

This chapter was written by Abdul Hares Halimi of the Afghanistan Resident Mission, ADB, Kabul.

Nonperforming loans rose to 13.1% of all bank loans at the end of September 2019, reflecting weak economic conditions but also improved bank compliance with classification and provisioning regulations (Figure 3.14.5). Dollarization increased, with the share of foreign-denominated loans rising from the equivalent of 54% of GDP in 2018 to 60%.

Despite a slowdown in revenue collection during the election months from June to September 2019, domestic revenue increased from the equivalent of 13.3% of GDP in 2018 to a record high of 13.8%, contributing more than half of total revenue including grants. Strong revenue growth was supported by improved tax administration, higher customs revenue following afghani depreciation, and a surge in nontax revenues, notably a one-off transfer of central bank profits to the Treasury. Public expenditure equaled an estimated 58.0% of GDP in 2019, however, substantially widening the fiscal deficit excluding grants from 4.5% of GDP in 2018 to 5.4%. Including grants, the budget surplus shrank from 1.5% of GDP in 2018 to 0.1%. Public debt declined slightly from 7.6% of GDP in 2018 to 7.0%.

Including grants, the current account surplus is estimated to have narrowed from the equivalent of 9.6% of GDP in 2018 to 2.0%; excluding grants, the current account deficit widened from 27.5% of GDP in 2018 to 32.2% (Figure 3.14.6). The trade deficit widened slightly from 29.0% of GDP in 2018 to 30.6%. In the first 11 months of 2019, exports declined by 10.4% despite afghani depreciation, following a 25.0% decline in 2018, while strong agricultural output decelerated import growth to only 0.2% in the same period. Gross international reserves rose slightly to $8.5 billion, covering more than 12 months of imports (Figure 3.14.7).

Economic prospects

Growth is expected to remain unchanged at 3.0% in 2020, with continuing political uncertainty and now COVID-19 likely to dampen any prospects for further economic growth. Despite the announcement of presidential election results, the political situation remains unsettled, and proposed intra-Afghan peace talks are not yet scheduled. A significant COVID-19 outbreak in Afghanistan has become more likely with high numbers of Afghans recently returning from Iran, which is suffering its own major outbreak. GDP growth is nevertheless projected to rise to 4.0% in 2021, supported by improved prospects for long-term political stability and security, as well as a successor to the Extended Credit Facility program of the International Monetary Fund that reached completion in December 2019—and despite a gradual decline in international grants. These developments promise to raise consumer confidence and, triggering the repatriation of capital held overseas, boost investment. Initial steps taken to shift public spending from security to development should contribute to economic growth.

Figure 3.14.3 Nominal exchange rate

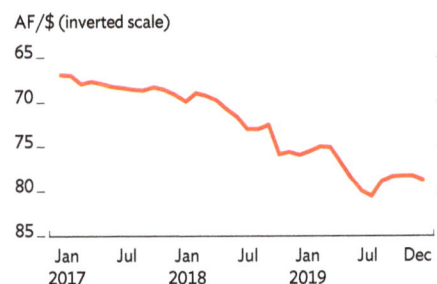

AF/$ (inverted scale)

Source: CEIC Data Company (accessed 2 March 2020).

Figure 3.14.4 Monetary indicators

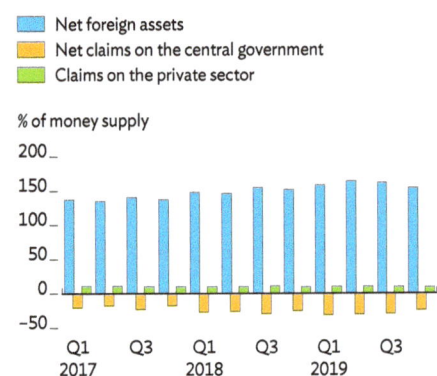

- Net foreign assets
- Net claims on the central government
- Claims on the private sector

% of money supply

Source: International Monetary Fund. International Financial Statistics (accessed 2 March 2020).

Figure 3.14.5 Nonperforming loans

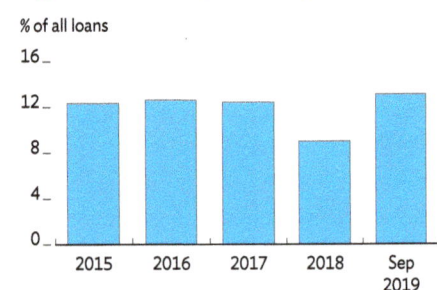

% of all loans

Source: Da Afghanistan Bank (accessed 27 February 2020).

The expected decline in foreign financial assistance and continued capital flight through smuggling will cause further afghani depreciation, despite likely central bank intervention to contain pressure on the currency. While pass-through from depreciation adds to inflationary pressure, higher inflation is unlikely, given sluggish consumption growth, which will contain the rise in aggregate demand. On balance, inflation should remain unchanged at 2.3% in 2020, then increase to 3.5% in 2021 as economic activity improves and domestic demand strengthens.

The fiscal deficit is expected to increase slightly in both 2020 and 2021 as revenue declines. Grants as a percentage of GDP are forecast to be little changed from 2019. Domestic revenue will remain at the 2019 amount as nontax revenue mobilization weakens—and despite total revenue rising to 27.7% of GDP in 2021, as expected, after the implementation of value-added tax (VAT). Expenditure will likely rise somewhat but remain close to the 2019 percentage of GDP, with priority given to financing expenditure in response to COVID-19.

The current account surplus will likely narrow in 2020 and 2021. International grants are expected to fall gradually despite expected commitments at an international conference later this year and strengthened partnership to support objectives under the Afghanistan National Peace and Development Framework. Exports are expected to trend upward with stronger agriculture exports, enhanced efforts by the government to facilitate trade, and the development of new trade corridors. However, export growth will be insufficient to offset import growth and lower grants. International reserves are projected to remain comfortable over the next 2 years at cover for nearly 12 months of imports.

The outlook is subject to significant risks. On the upside, a successful political settlement and sustainable peace would open a new window of opportunity for Afghanistan and unleash significant growth, raising business confidence and paving the way for prosperity and socioeconomic development. On the downside, uncertainty and lower domestic demand could ensue from a prolonged period of political transition after the September presidential elections, delays in commencing intra-Afghan talks, and a steeper reduction in foreign aid than is currently expected. These risks could be compounded by rising tensions in the Middle East or a worsening COVID-19 outbreak in Afghanistan or Iran, which is a major trade partner and source of remittances.

Policy challenge—accelerating domestic revenue growth

Afghanistan's ratio of revenue to GDP reached a historic high of 13.8% in 2019 but remained below the ratio in most neighboring countries and the average in low-income economies.

Table 3.14.1 Selected economic indicators (%)

	2018	2019	2020	2021
GDP growth	2.7	3.0	3.0	4.0
Inflation	0.6	2.3	2.3	3.5
Current acct. bal. (share of GDP)	9.6	2.0	1.0	0.5

Source: ADB estimates.

Figure 3.14.6 Current account balance

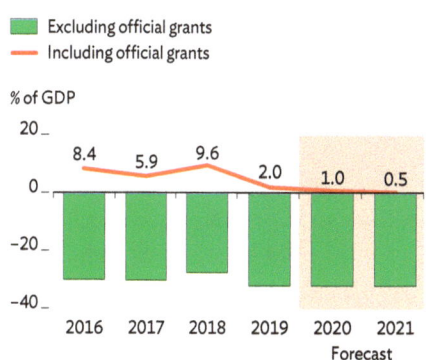

■ Excluding official grants
— Including official grants

% of GDP

Note: Years are fiscal years ending on 21 December of the same calendar year.
Sources: International Monetary Fund Article IV, December 2019; ADB estimates.

Figure 3.14.7 International reserves

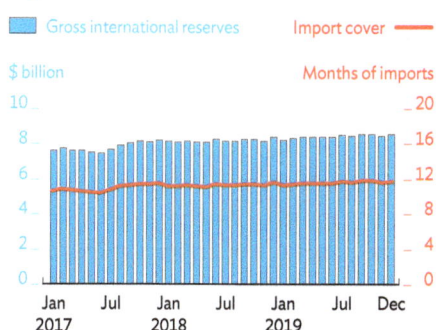

■ Gross international reserves   Import cover —

$ billion   Months of imports

Sources: CEIC Data Company; International Financial Statistics, IMF; Da Afghanistan Bank (accessed 18 March 2020).

Revenue covered 51% of government expenditure, the rest financed by development partners. Indeed, as a fragile country in armed conflict, Afghanistan has limited revenue sources and weak government institutions but daunting security and development needs, leaving public finances heavily dependent on foreign assistance. This dependence is not sustainable, though, so the country needs to become more self-sufficient in financing public expenditure. Accelerating domestic revenue mobilization is one of the most pressing policy challenges facing Afghanistan.

Over the past 2 decades, Afghanistan has made notable progress in building a revenue system able to help generate rising government revenue. Since 2016, the government has successfully followed a strategy of boosting prospects for self-reliance through domestic revenue mobilization that, together with foreign grant assistance, helped achieve a balanced budget and keep public debt low. Tax administration reform over the last 2 years has made revenue collection more efficient, and customs revenue benefitted from afghani depreciation in 2019.

While past revenue collection benefitted from an expanding tax base and improved efficiency, it has also increasingly relied on risky indirect and one-off measures that create uncertainty. The World Bank estimates that 2019 nontax revenue drove revenue growth by contributing 1.3 percentage points to GDP, while tax revenue deducted 0.15 percentage points from GDP. Going forward, realizing self-reliance and reducing grant dependence will depend on how successfully the government builds a sound domestic revenue base by further broadening the tax base and reducing reliance on nontax revenues. Key to revenue mobilization policy in the near future is the planned adoption of VAT by early 2021. According to the International Monetary Fund, the successful administration of VAT could gradually raise revenue by up to the equivalent of 1.8% of GDP, but it will be a challenge without resolving currently daunting political and business uncertainty.

The government should pursue structural reform as outlined in the Afghanistan National Peace and Development Framework to ensure sustained progress towards self-reliance. Strenuous efforts are needed to improve governance and public financial management. Policies should continue to work toward strengthening revenue collection, improving customs and tax administration and compliance, introducing carefully designed and appropriate new taxes, and improving the tax policy mix. In the short term, policy actions can focus on introducing digital technology into revenue collection, reinforcing controls and tax audits, strengthening antifraud measures, and sanctioning noncompliance. Over the medium term, additional excises and property taxes should be introduced, a fiscal regime for natural resource taxation developed, and enforcement and compliance strengthened.

Bangladesh

GDP grew by 8.2% in fiscal 2019 on robust growth in both industry and services. Inflation slowed following a good crop harvest, and the current account deficit narrowed as the trade deficit shrank and remittances expanded further. Growth is expected to remain strong in fiscal 2020 and 2021. Inflation is expected to stay in check, and the current account deficit will narrow further. Achieving higher growth requires reform to better mobilize domestic resources.

Economic performance

Growth increased to 8.2% in FY2019 (ended 30 June 2019) from 7.9% in the previous year on robust growth in industry and services (Figure 3.15.1). Growth in industry rose from 12.1% in FY2018 to 12.7% in FY2019, reflecting brisk growth in manufacturing output to supply markedly higher export demand, notably to the US and some previously unpenetrated markets. Growth in services increased from 6.4% to 6.8% mainly on improvements in wholesale and retail trade, transport, education, and health and social services. Agriculture growth moderated from 4.2% to 3.9%.

On the demand side, growth in FY2019 was buoyed by robust growth in exports. Private investment expanded, though at a slower pace than a year earlier, while public investment remained steady. Total investment increased from the equivalent of 31.2% of GDP in FY2018 to 31.6% as private investment increased from 23.3% of GDP to 23.5% and public investment remained unchanged at 8.0%.

Inflation moderated from 5.8% in the previous year to average 5.5% in FY2019 with lower domestic rice prices following a good harvest and lower food prices on the international market (Figure 3.15.2). While food inflation eased, nonfood inflation moved a bit higher owing to upward adjustments in natural gas prices and currency depreciation.

Growth in broad money accelerated from 9.2% in FY2018 to 9.9% but remained well below the FY2019 monetary program target of 12.0% (Figure 3.15.3). Growth in private credit moderated from 16.9% in FY2018 to 11.3%, well below its

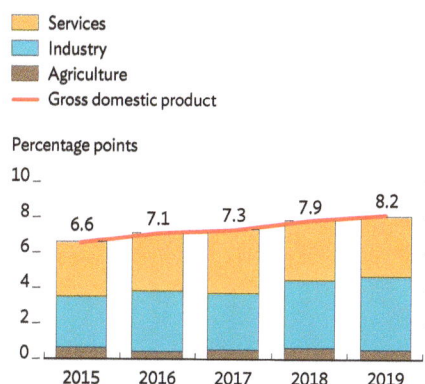

Figure 3.15.1 Supply-side contributions to growth

- Services
- Industry
- Agriculture
- Gross domestic product

Percentage points

6.6 (2015), 7.1 (2016), 7.3 (2017), 7.9 (2018), 8.2 (2019)

Note: Years are fiscal years ending on 30 June of that year.
Sources: Bangladesh Bureau of Statistics. http://www.bbs.gov.bd; ADB estimates.

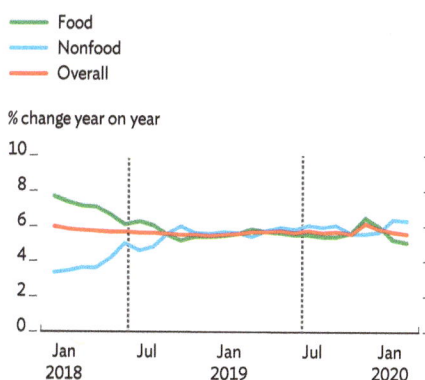

Figure 3.15.2 Monthly inflation

- Food
- Nonfood
- Overall

% change year on year

Note: Dotted lines denote ends of fiscal years.
Source: Bangladesh Bank. 2020. Monthly Economic Trends. February. https://www.bb.org.bd.

This chapter was written by Jyotsana Varma, Soon Chan Hong, and Barun K. Dey of the Bangladesh Resident Mission, ADB, Dhaka. The projections presented here were made before the COVID-19 global pandemic struck and its impact has not been incorporated. It is estimated that spillover from global pandemic could cost Bangladesh 0.2%–0.4% of GDP. If a significant outbreak occurs in Bangladesh, the impact could be more significant. The outlook will be updated as more information becomes available.

16.5% program target. Net credit to the public sector, however, increased strongly to 19.8%, substantially exceeding the 10.9% program target. It reflects both an overshot budget deficit and measures to reduce reliance on sales of national savings certificates by increasing budget financing from banks at lower market rates.

Bangladesh Bank, the central bank, kept its policy rates unchanged in FY2019 as inflation remained stable. With increased demand for foreign exchange to pay for imports and for bank financing of the budget, market liquidity tightened, pushing the call money rate to 4.6% in June 2019 from 3.4% a year earlier, while the yield on 91-day Treasury bills rose from 3.7% to 6.8%. The weighted average rate on new lending remained broadly steady in FY2019, however, declining by 20 basis points to 9.7% in June, while the average deposit rate was unchanged at 5.5% (Figure 3.15.4).

Budget revenue rose slightly from the equivalent of 9.6% of GDP in FY2018 to 9.9%. With national elections occurring, government spending increased significantly from 14.3% of GDP to 15.4%, reflecting a rise in current spending from 7.9% to 8.6% and annual development spending from 5.3% to 5.8%. Slower growth in revenue collection and accelerated spending pushed the overall deficit up from 4.7% of GDP to 5.5%, crossing the budget ceiling of 5.0% for the first time in more than a decade (Figure 3.15.5). This deviation reflected temporary circumstances and not a departure from policy that has kept the government medium- and long-term debt ratio low, amounting to just 29.1% of GDP in FY2019.

Exports reached $39.9 billion in FY2019, reflecting growth acceleration from 6.7% a year earlier to 10.1%. Growth in garment exports, accounting for over 84% of the total, rose from 8.8% to 11.5% on strong demand from the US and newly penetrated markets such as Australia, India, Japan, the People's Republic of China, and the Republic of Korea. Exports other than garments rose by 5.8%. Imports—following explosive 25.2% expansion in FY2018—grew in FY2019 by only 1.8% to reach $55.4 billion. Imports of petroleum products, garment intermediates, and construction materials grew substantially to support industry growth. However, imports of capital goods increased slightly as investment slowed, and a good crop harvest sharply reduced food import requirements. Consequently, the trade deficit narrowed substantially from $18.2 billion to $15.5 billion. Remittances markedly increased by 9.6% to $16.4 billion, benefitting by measures to encourage transfer through official channels.

Substantial improvement in the trade deficit and strong remittances narrowed the current account deficit in FY2019 by about half to $5.3 billion, equal to 1.7% of GDP. After adjusting for errors and omissions, the surplus in the combined capital and financial account fell from $8.7 billion to $5.3 billion,

Figure 3.15.3 Growth of monetary indicators

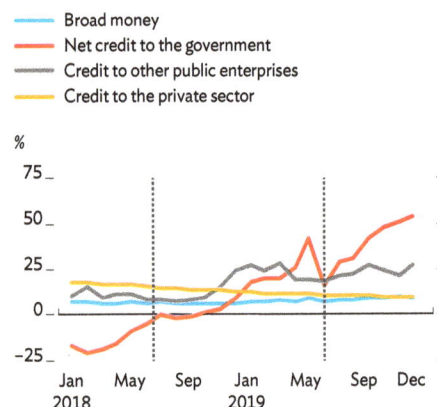

Note: Dotted lines denote ends of fiscal years.
Source: Bangladesh Bank. 2019. *Major Economic Indicators: Monthly Update.* January. https://www.bb.org.bd.

Figure 3.15.4 Interest rates

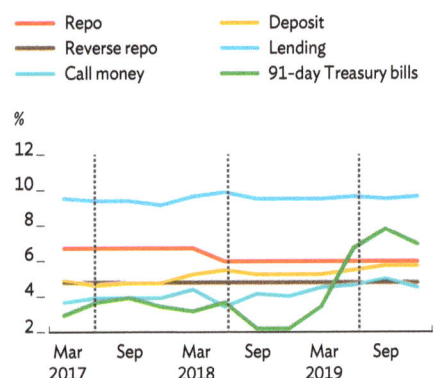

Note: Dotted lines denote ends of fiscal years.
Source: Bangladesh Bank. 2020. *Major Economic Indicators: Monthly Update.* January. https://www.bb.org.bd.

Figure 3.15.5 Fiscal indicators

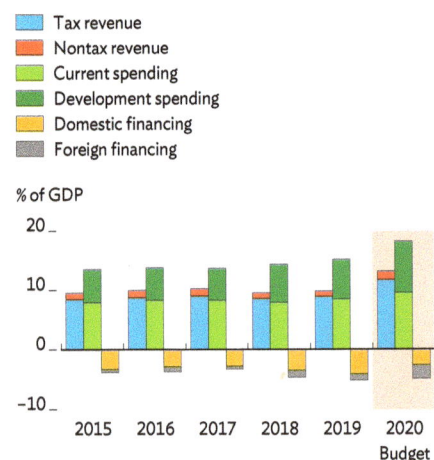

Note: Years are fiscal years ending on 30 June of that year.
Source: *Asian Development Outlook* database.

mainly owing to larger repayments of trade credit and less use of commercial bank credit and short-term loans. Nonetheless, the overall balance reversed a $857 million deficit in FY2018 with a small surplus of $12 million. Central bank gross foreign exchange reserves including valuation adjustments decreased marginally from $32.9 billion to $32.7 billion, or cover for 6.0 months of imports (Figure 3.15.6).

The Bangladesh taka depreciated against the US dollar by 0.9% in FY2019 as the central bank intervened, selling $2.3 billion to commercial banks to tamp down excessive market volatility (Figure 3.15.7). Reflecting inflation differentials, the taka appreciated by 5.0% in real effective terms, eroding competitiveness.

Economic prospects

Forecasts for FY2020 and FY2021 rest on several assumptions: political calm will continue, helping to maintain consumer and investment confidence; exports and imports will be depressed in FY2020 by a global economic slowdown but will improve in FY2021; central bank monetary policy will be expansionary enough to support economic growth yet maintain price stability; and the weather will be normal. The impact of COVID-19 has not been included.

GDP growth is expected to moderate but remain strong at 7.8% in FY2020 as domestic demand is supported by continued healthy growth in workers' remittances (Figure 3.15.8). Private investment is expected to remain subdued. Economic activity is forecast to accelerate in the second half of the year with expanded government development spending, higher imports of liquefied natural gas and construction materials, favorable trends in power production, and the authorities pursuing policies to boost exports.

On the supply side, industry growth is expected to moderate to 11.5% as growth in manufacturing output slows in tandem with expected zero growth in exports. Likewise, service growth is expected to ease to 6.5%, following the trend in industry and reflecting an only moderate uptake of credit in a period of prevailing uncertainty. However, growth in agriculture is expected to pick up to 4.0% thanks to continued government policy support, notably to reduce fertilizer prices and finance mechanization to counter labor shortages at harvest time.

In FY2021, GDP growth is expected to edge up to 8.0% as a foreseen improvement in global growth permits expansion in both exports and imports to pick up. Aided by continued strong remittances, private consumption will continue to drive growth. Private investment will revive on a stronger outlook supported by regulatory improvements to conditions for doing business and an initiative to have banks maintain their lending

Figure 3.15.6 Foreign exchange reserves

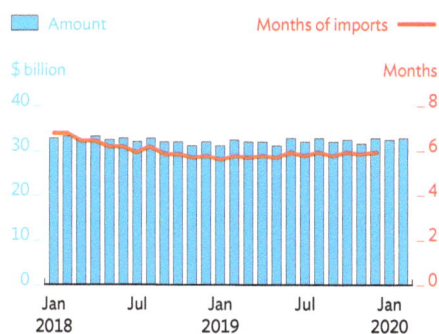

Note: Source: Bangladesh Bank. http://www.bb.org.bd.

Figure 3.15.7 Exchange rates

Note: Dotted lines denote ends of fiscal years.
Source: Bangladesh Bank. 2020. Monthly Economic Trends. January. http://www.bb.org.bd.

Figure 3.15.8 GDP growth by sector

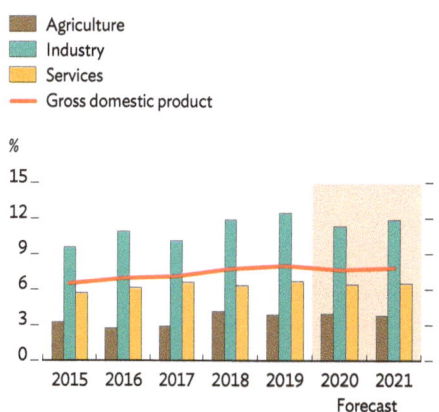

Note: Years are fiscal years ending on 30 June of that year.
Sources: Bangladesh Bureau of Statistics. http://www.bbs.gov.bd; ADB estimates.

rates in single digits. A planned rise in public investment in large projects should buttress expansion in domestic demand. Industry growth is projected to rise to 12.0% on earnings from larger apparel exports and expected government policy support to strengthen industry. Service growth is forecast to move higher to 6.6% following the trend in industry. Agriculture growth will moderate slightly to 3.8%, however, reflecting the high base anticipated in FY2020.

Inflation is expected to slightly edge up to average 5.6% in FY2020 on higher global and regional food prices, especially for fish, vegetables, fruit, and spices (Figure 3.15.9). Nonfood prices are also expected to rise on account of a hike in natural gas prices on 1 July 2019 and upward adjustment to administered prices for electricity by 5.3% retail and 8.4% wholesale, effective 1 March 2020. Inflation is expected to ease to average 5.5% in FY2021 on better supply conditions.

Broad money grew by 12.0% year on year in December 2019, somewhat above the monetary program target of 11.3% for the first half of FY2020. Bank borrowing by the government was strong, reflecting FY2020 budget policy to markedly reduce the use of national savings certificates from the equivalent of 3.0% of GDP in FY2018 to 1.0%. Private sector credit continued to grow slowly with subdued import demand. Net foreign assets showed a small gain. Interbank call money rates and interest on government Treasury bills and bonds of various maturities remained broadly stable at higher rates established in FY2019 as bank liquidity remained tight.

Exports fell by 4.8% in the first 8 months of FY2020, reversing 13.0% expansion in the same period a year earlier. This reflected garment exports plunging in the period from 14.2% growth to 5.5% decline (Figure 3.15.10). This abrupt change in fortune came in large part from a cyclical downturn in global apparel trade but was compounded by a lack of product diversification to keep up with changes in consumer demand, as well as lower prices offered by buyers and currency depreciation in competitor countries. Given high demand for low-cost fast-fashion products, government policy designed to revive sales—reducing source tax on export proceeds for all sectors from 1.00% to 0.25%, slashing interest rates on loans under the Export Development Fund, and providing a 1.0% special cash incentive for apparel and textile exports—are expected to boost exports in second half such that overall exports in FY2020 match the previous year. With expected global growth recovery in FY2021, exports are expected to pick up to 10.0% as pent-up consumer demand is released.

Import payments declined by 4.4% in the first 7 months of FY2020, reversing 7.4% growth in the same period a year earlier and mostly reflecting lower demand for garment intermediates and capital imports and a sharp decline in rice imports. With the expected pickup in garment exports, import

Table 3.15.1 Selected economic indicators (%)

	2018	2019	2020	2021
GDP growth	7.9	8.2	7.8	8.0
Inflation	5.8	5.5	5.6	5.5
Current acct. bal. (share of GDP)	-3.5	-1.7	-0.8	-0.3

Sources: Bangladesh Bureau of Statistics. http://www.bbs.gov.bd; ADB estimates.

Figure 3.15.9 Annual inflation

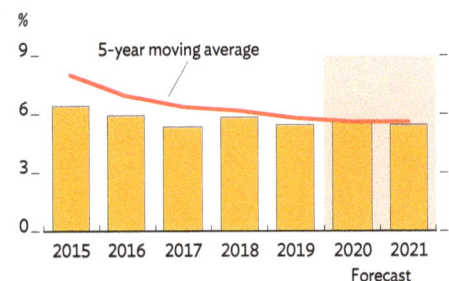

Note: Years are fiscal years ending on 30 June of that year.
Sources: Bangladesh Bank. 2020. Monthly Economic Trends. January. http://www.bb.org.bd; ADB estimates.

Figure 3.15.10 Export growth

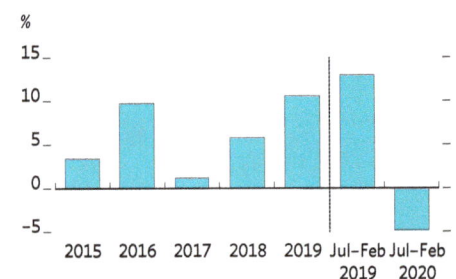

Note: Years are fiscal years ending on 30 June of that year.
Source: Export Promotion Bureau, Bangladesh. Export performance, various issues.

growth is expected to improve in the second half. Imports are thus forecast to decline by only 0.5% in the whole of FY2020. Import growth is projected to pick up to 7.0% in FY2021 as the government expedites the completion of several large infrastructure projects. Imports of construction materials, capital machinery, and export-related items are expected to increase sharply.

This outlook makes the trade deficit likely to moderate as a share of GDP in both years. Notably, overseas worker remittances increased handsomely in the first 8 months of FY2020, doubling growth from 10% a year earlier to 20% (Figure 3.15.11). Government efforts are taking hold to promote money transfers through formal channels, including a 2% cash incentive, and to curb the role of unauthorized intermediaries. Remittances are therefore expected to grow by 16% in FY2020. Growth will then moderate to 9% in FY2021 as the number of outgoing workers declines and uncertainty limits scope for increased employment and higher wages.

The current account deficit is expected to narrow to the equivalent of 0.8% of GDP in FY2020 on these projected developments in trade and remittances, as well as other factors (Figure 3.15.12). With growth in exports picking up faster than imports and continued healthy remittances, the FY2021 current account deficit is projected lower, at only 0.3% of GDP.

To avoid excessive volatility in the foreign exchange market, the central bank tackled market demand by selling $489 million in FY2020 to 4 March 2020. The taka depreciated by 1.1% against the US dollar in the year to the end of January 2020 but appreciated by 2.5% in real effective terms.

The FY2020 budget, announced in June 2019, targets a ratio of revenue to GDP at 13.1%. Public spending is targeted at 18.1% of GDP, with current spending at 9.6% and development spending at 8.5%. Revenue collection by the National Board of Revenue, however, grew by only 7.5% in the first 7 months of FY2020, suggesting revenue may fall short of its target. Weak revenue collection reflects the marked decline in export and import activity and complications encountered in the transition to a new value-added tax (VAT) regime. As in the past, any revenue shortfall is expected to be compensated by adjustment in spending to meet the targeted deficit of 5.0% of GDP.

Policy challenge—boosting public resource mobilization to sustain high growth

Prudent macroeconomic management has allowed Bangladesh to achieve impressive economic and social development. Robust growth has increased per capita income and reduced poverty. Notwithstanding impressive economic and social gains, mobilizing domestic resources in the public sector poses

Figure 3.15.11 Remittance growth

Note: Years are fiscal years ending on 30 June of that year.
Source: Bangladesh Bank. http://www.bb.org.bd.

Figure 3.15.12 Current account balance

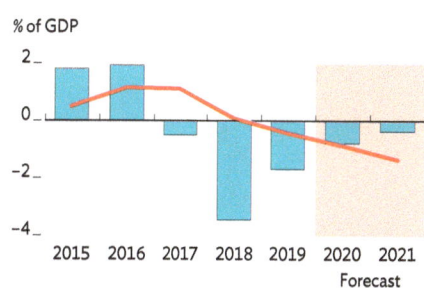

Note: Years are fiscal years ending on 30 June of that year.
Sources: Bangladesh Bank. *Annual Report 2017–2018*.
https://www.bb.org.bd; ADB estimates.

a major challenge. Shortfalls in revenue are regular annual occurrences, as is the resulting need to cut back spending plans. The ratio of revenue to GDP in Bangladesh is, at 9.9%, the lowest in South Asia and much lower than the average in developing countries worldwide (Figure 3.15.13). It undercuts the country's potential to sustain high economic growth and reduce poverty. Revenues thus need to be raised significantly from both taxes and other sources to support much-needed public expenditure on infrastructure and social development.

Tax revenue provides about 90% of total revenue, its major components being VAT, income tax, customs duties, and supplementary duties. Other revenue is from profits and dividends remitted by public institutions and administrative fees and charges (Table 3.15.2).

To improve the tax structure and strengthen revenue mobilization, the authorities have adopted a number of measures in the past. Two such reforms were a sales tax at the import stage and the introduction of VAT in 1991 with a single rate to replace excise duties on domestic manufactures and services. In addition to VAT, supplementary duties were introduced on luxuries and certain other goods, to discourage consumption on various grounds. Though VAT and supplementary duties expanded the revenue base, the system was not comprehensive in scope and contained some distortions. Reform to the customs tariff in the early 1990s reduced the number of rates and lowered duties, moderating protection for local producers. Income tax reform rationalized personal and corporate tax rates, and the introduction of universal self-assessment procedures brought more taxpayers within the tax net. Parliament enacted the Value Added Tax and Supplementary Duty Act in 2012, but its rollout was delayed, coming into effect only in July 2019 with VAT implemented using several rates. The government is working on other reform to incorporate transfer pricing into the Income Tax Ordinance, 1984 and alternative dispute resolution into income tax, VAT, and custom acts; draft a new direct tax code and customs act; and improve tax administration by automating and digitalizing operations.

Despite several attempted reforms, anticipated progress has been elusive as many of them were ad hoc. While the new VAT law addressed some deficiencies and distortions in the previous law, it retained multiple VAT rates, keeping administration inefficient. Income tax remains complex, depressing income tax collection below its potential. Only 2.2 million Bangladeshis pay income tax despite scope to increase the number to some 10 million by simplifying collection and refunds. Income tax law is outdated, and its administration is not automated despite an acute shortage of trained tax administrators.

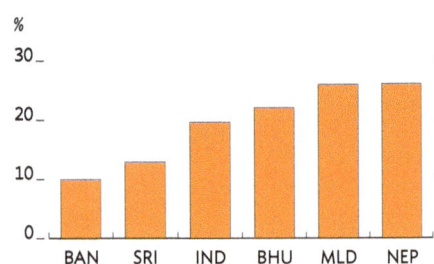

Figure 3.15.13 Ratio of revenue to GDP in South Asian countries, 2019

BAN = Bangladesh, BHU = Bhutan, GDP = gross domestic product, IND = India, MLD = Maldives, NEP = Nepal, SRI = Sri Lanka.

Source: International Monetary Fund. World Economic Outlook database (accessed 28 January 2020).

Table 3.15.2 Structure of Bangladesh revenue, % of gross domestic product

Revenue source	FY2015	FY2016	FY2017	FY2018	FY2019
Tax revenue	8.5	8.8	9.0	8.6	8.9
Income tax	2.7	2.6	2.7	2.6	2.7
Customs duty	1.0	1.0	1.1	0.9	1.0
Value-added tax	3.0	3.1	3.2	3.0	3.3
Supplementary duty	1.4	1.5	1.6	1.6	1.5
Other taxes	0.4	0.5	0.5	0.5	0.4
Nontax revenue	1.1	1.2	1.2	1.0	1.0
Total revenue	9.6	10.0	10.2	9.6	9.9

Note: Years are fiscal years ending on 30 June of that year.

Sources: Ministry of Finance, Annual Budget FY2017–FY2020; ADB estimates.

Further, the tax system contains many concessions, exemptions, and incentives that make it unwieldy. Several categories of workers, such as the self-employed and service providers, are not included in the tax net.

The challenge is thus to raise the ratio of tax to GDP closer to the developing country average. Comprehensive tax reform would help by expanding the tax base and making resource mobilization more efficient.

To expand the tax base, the authorities can consider (i) lowering tax rates and the tax-free income threshold; (ii) simplifying tax system procedures and structure by limiting the number of rates, thereby fostering compliance and making tax administration less challenging; (iii) curbing tax exemption policy to remove costly tax holidays and other incentives that have been ineffective at attracting new investment; (iv) tapping new sources of VAT and income tax such as e-commerce and online services and platforms; and (v) enforcing tax laws and regulations more strictly to curb leakage.

To make resource mobilization more efficient, the authorities can consider (i) establishing modern information technology systems and automation in key compliance areas such as registration, filing, and the management of payment obligations, which would strengthen institutional capacity; (ii) improving management and governance by ensuring the recruitment of competent tax and customs officials; (iii) adopting a risk-based audit linked to taxpayers' inherent risks, to encourage compliance and improve internal control of tax administration; and (iv) improving human resources with proper training programs on tax administration and compliance.

Bhutan

Higher consumption expenditure in fiscal 2019 lifted growth from its 2018 slump. However, growth remains sluggish because of prevailing weakness in investment and hydropower. Inflation fell, and the current account deficit widened. The outlook is uncertain as the pandemic may be protracted and spill over beyond tourism. Growth will be driven by fiscal expansion to offset the impact of the pandemic, and inflation is expected to remain benign. Policies need to be implemented to reduce regional inequalities.

Economic performance

Provisional estimates show growth accelerating to 4.4% in fiscal year 2019 (FY2019, ended 30 June 2019) from 3.8% a year earlier (Figure 3.16.1). The pickup was underpinned by consumption expenditure, reflecting recent rebalancing away from growth driven by fixed investment. Growth remained sluggish for a second year as a substantial decline in construction tracked a large drop in government investment and as hydropower production, a major industry driver, suffered a marked fall.

On the supply side, industry contracted again, by 0.9%. Construction in particular fell further by 5.4% with the completion of the Mangdechhu hydropower project and with government capital expenditure much lower than average. This downdraft was compounded by a decline in hydropower production for a second straight year, by over 5%, with lower water flows. Growth in services, at 10.4%, once again picked up the slack, supported by broad expansion in wholesale and retail trade, transportation and storage, and hotels and restaurants. Offsetting near stagnation in international tourist arrivals, a 25.0% increase in tourists from the region was a key driver of services. Agriculture, a traditional laggard, grew by 3.8% under targeted policy interventions.

On the demand side, investment contracted for a second year, by 2.6%. This reflected a marked drop in budgetary capital expenditure as the country transitioned to a new government and the Twelfth Five-Year Plan, 2019–2023 with spending to mop up spillover projects but no new ones initiated. Once again, domestic demand was held aloft by consumption growth, which accelerated from 8.6% in FY2018 to 10.3% (Figure 3.16.2). Private consumption improved on 10.1% growth a year earlier with 11.8% expansion in FY2019, fueled by growth in private credit accelerating to 20.0%. Government current expenditure

This chapter was written by Kanokpan Lao-Araya, Tshering Lhamo, and Nyingtob Norbu of the Bhutan Resident Mission, ADB, Thimphu.

Figure 3.16.1 Supply-side contributions to growth

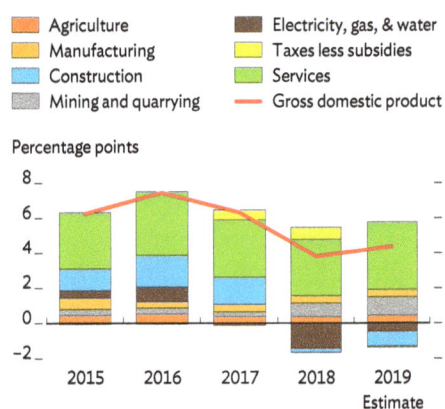

- Agriculture
- Manufacturing
- Construction
- Mining and quarrying
- Electricity, gas, & water
- Taxes less subsidies
- Services
- Gross domestic product

Percentage points

Note: Years are fiscal years ending 30 June of that year.
Sources: National Statistics Bureau. National Accounts Statistics, 2019. http://www.nsb.gov.bt; ADB estimates.

Figure 3.16.2 Demand-side contributions to growth

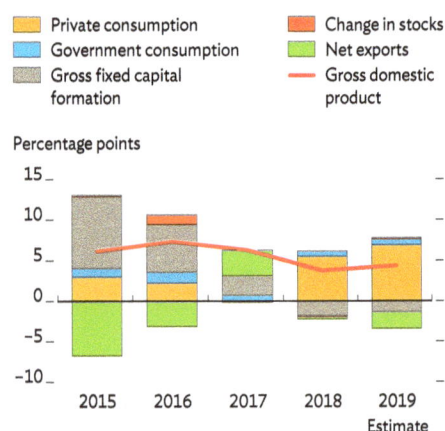

- Private consumption
- Government consumption
- Gross fixed capital formation
- Change in stocks
- Net exports
- Gross domestic product

Percentage points

Note: Years are fiscal years ending 30 June of that year.
Sources: National Statistics Bureau. National Accounts Statistics, 2019. http://www.nsb.gov.bt; ADB estimates.

rose from 3.7% to 5.0%. Private investment declined again, reflecting completion at Mangdechhu and a slowdown at other hydropower construction sites, but not as steeply as in FY2018. Net exports deteriorated by 9.0% with a 12.7% fall in exports.

Inflation reached its lowest average in a decade at 2.8% in FY2019 (Figure 3.16.3). This decline reflected lower food prices as domestic supply improved and import prices declined. Nonfood inflation rose moderately from an average of 1.8% in FY2018% to 2.4%. Imported inflation, primarily from India and accounting for 52% of all inflation, was low for dual reasons. In addition to lower prices for agricultural imports, the Indian goods and services tax lowered prices for other imported goods from India. That said, price transmission from India can be observed weakening in recent years as non-tradables assume greater significance in driving nonfood inflation; notable last year were domestic services, particularly hotels and restaurants, and housing, in anticipation of a civil service salary raise.

Government spending fell from the equivalent of 32.2% of GDP in FY2018 to 27.4% in FY2019, reflecting transition to a new plan period (Figure 3.16.4). The overall budget deficit rose from 0.3% of GDP in FY2018 to 2.2% as a decline in expenditure was outweighed by a revenue decline by 7.4 percentage points to 24.5% of GDP, mainly reflecting a very large reduction in external grants with the winding up of the Eleventh Five-Year Plan, 2014–2018. Tax revenue also declined, from 16.6% of GDP to 15.2%, largely reflecting reduced receipts from state-owned enterprises. Bucking the cyclical capital spending downswing, current expenditure increased by 6.0%.

The primary mandate of monetary policy, to maintain price stability, continues to be underpinned by a parity peg with the Indian rupee. Broad money (M2) grew at a slower rate of 5.6% in FY2019, tracking lackluster growth, but still found impetus in an increase in net foreign assets and private credit (Figure 3.16.5). Private sector credit remains concentrated in building and construction, and in tourism and services, with each group growing by over 25%. Continued rapid expansion in credit in recent years has enabled a sharp worsening of nonperforming loans, from 11.5% of all private loans outstanding in FY2018 to 16.5% in FY2019. Reflecting credit developments, the risk-weighted capital adequacy ratio fell from 16.2% in FY2018 to 12.6%, only marginally meeting the prudential requirement of 12.5%. Despite the steep deterioration, Bhutan's macro-prudential requirements are generally more stringent than international norms, so its macro-financial situation is far from needing corrective action. Having appreciated by 2.1% in FY2018, the Bhutan ngultrum closely followed the Indian currency as it depreciated by 7.8% against the US dollar in FY2019.

The current account deficit widened further from the equivalent of 19.1% of GDP in FY2018 to 22.6% (Figure 3.16.6).

Figure 3.16.3 Inflation

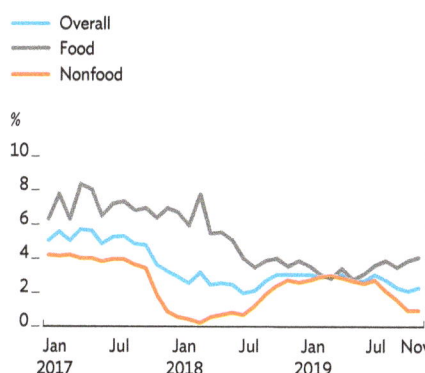

Source: National Statistics Bureau. Monthly Consumer Price Index Bulletin. December 2019. http://www.nsb.gov.bt.

Figure 3.16.4 Fiscal indicators

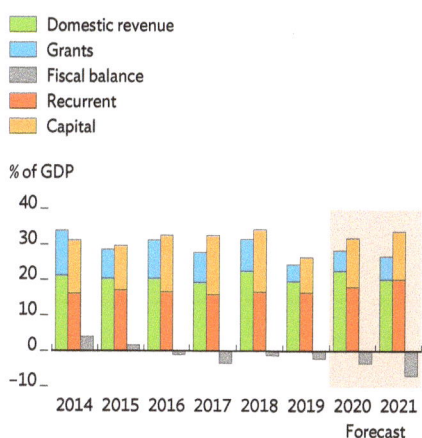

Note: Years are fiscal years ending 30 June of that year.
Source: National Budget, Financial Year 2019/20, Ministry of Finance. http://www.mof.gov.bt.

Figure 3.16.5 Monetary indicators

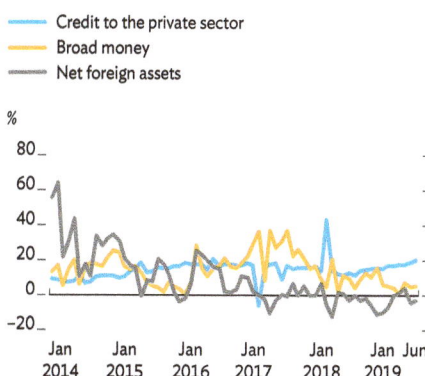

Source: Royal Monetary Authority. Monthly Statistical Bulletin February 2020. http://www.rma.org.bt.

About 40% of this deterioration was caused by a widening net service deficit, and the remainder reflected higher interest and transfer payments and lower export receipts and grants. A 6.6% fall in imports helped to contain the damage. Though wider, the current account deficit was covered by a slightly larger sum of capital and financial account inflows plus a very large positive errors and omissions.

Gross international reserves were, at $1.1 billion in June 2019, essentially unchanged from a year earlier and adequate to cover 10.3 months of merchandise and service payments (Figure 3.16.7). Public external debt rose from $2.6 billion to $2.7 billion, reaching the equivalent of 109.7% of GDP (Figure 3.16.8). Of this, 73.6% is rupee denominated, largely concentrated in hydropower debt. The remaining 26.4% in convertible currencies is mostly on concessional terms from multilateral development banks. Though the debt ratio is high, the International Monetary Fund considers Bhutan's risk of debt distress only moderate because hydropower debt is essentially self-liquidating through electricity sale agreements.

Economic prospects

Growth is forecast to pick up to 5.2% in FY2020 on increased hydropower capacity, assumed normal water flow, and an anticipated sharp increase in government expenditure to offset the dampening effect of COVID-19. A further uptick to 5.8% is expected in FY2021 as ripples from the pandemic dissipate and government spending remains elevated.

Industry is forecast to expand by 5.4% in FY2020, fueled by strong growth in hydropower and construction revived by the large pickup in government capital expenditure. Favored by priority credit and other government initiatives, agriculture is expected to grow by 3.9%. Growth in services is projected to slow to 5.6%, a steep deterioration caused by the impact of COVID-19 on tourism, revenue from which is projected to decline by 30%. It is evident that the aggregate impacts of the pandemic will be more severe than what the estimates capture. In addition to other second-round impacts caused by social distancing, demand in the informal sector will probably slow.

Consumption expenditure is expected to be a consistent growth driver, expanding by 6.4% in FY2020 and 8.4% FY2021 mostly on a strong increase in government consumption as moderating expansion in private credit slows growth in private consumption. Fixed investment is projected to expand by 2.0% in FY2020 and 2.6% in FY2021, underpinned by accelerated implementation at two major hydropower projects and the development of four special economic zones.

Fiscal policy is thus planned as expansionary. It is the main driver of growth in the outlook, with expenditure forecast to increase by 31.5% in FY2020—featuring a 50.7% spike in capital expenditure—and then grow by 16.1% in FY2021.

Figure 3.16.6 Components of the current account

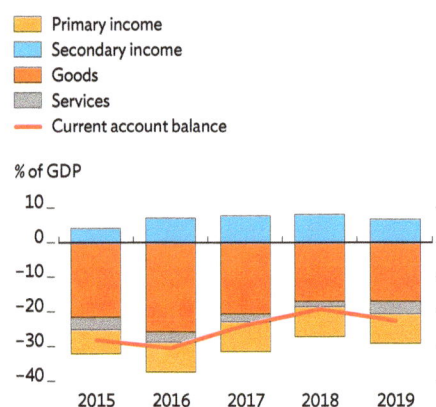

Note: Years are fiscal years ending 30 June of that year.
Source: Royal Monetary Authority. Monthly Statistical Bulletin February 2020. http://www.rma.org.bt.

Table 3.16.1 Selected economic indicators (%)

	2018	2019	2020	2021
GDP growth	3.8	4.4	5.2	5.8
Inflation	3.7	2.8	3.8	4.0
Current acct. bal. (share of GDP)	–19.1	–22.6	–19.1	–18.4

Sources: National Statistics Bureau. National Accounts Statistics, 2019. http://www.nsb.gov.bt; ADB estimates.

Figure 3.16.7 External reserves

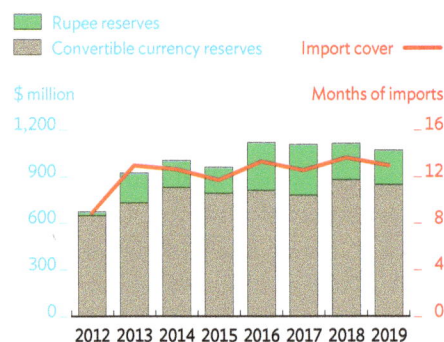

Note: Years are fiscal years ending 30 June of that year.
Source: Royal Monetary Authority. Monthly Statistical Bulletin February 2020. http://www.rma.org.bt.

Revenue including grants is projected to increase by 26.9% in FY2020 but only 3.9% of FY2021. The surge in resources in FY2020 reflects a large increase in nontax revenue from high dividend receipts and transfers from state-owned corporations, in large part reflecting revenue generated by the Mangdechhu Power Plant. Current grants and transfers are expected to grow strongly to support new projects as a new plan period opens. From a higher base, expansion in revenue and grants will slow in FY2021. Accordingly, the budget deficit is projected to widen to the equivalent of 3.5% of GDP in FY2020 and 6.2% in FY2021, largely financed by domestic and external concessional borrowing.

Monetary policy is expected to remain accommodative to support private sector growth and stimulus measures. Despite scant global pressure on prices, inflation is projected to accelerate to 3.8% in FY2020 and 4.0% in FY2021 as domestic demand increases.

Current account deficits are forecast to improve slightly but remain high at the equivalent of 19.1% of GDP in FY2020 and 18.4% in FY2021, continuing to require substantial external financing. Exports of ferrous metals are expected to improve and supplement increased electricity exports. Imports are also expected to expand, by 5.8% in FY2020 and 2.9% in FY2021, largely to supply hydropower project construction.

Downside risks to the growth forecasts include a significantly lower contribution from services if COVID-19 impacts are protracted. If the pandemic constricts supplies for manufacturing and construction, this would render the government's stimulus plan to bolster demand less effective and possibly spur inflation. Another risks would be continuing low water flow or other technical problems hindering the full operation of hydropower plants.

Policy challenge—enhancing agricultural productivity to address regional inequality

Equity is a pillar of Bhutan's pursuit of gross national happiness. Yet, free access to social services notwithstanding, inequality persists as large sections of the population continue to depend heavily on agriculture, and a large productivity gap persists between agriculture, and other sectors of production, accentuating disparity between urban and rural areas and within regions (Figure 3.16.9).

Monthly urban average expenditure is Nu45,508, but rural average expenditure is only Nu26,937. At the district level, Thimphu and Paro exhibit higher average urban expenditure, a wider range, and higher top incomes than do agrarian districts such as Dagana. Like agricultural employment, poverty is significantly higher in rural Bhutan (Table 3.16.2).

Figure 3.16.8 External debt indicators

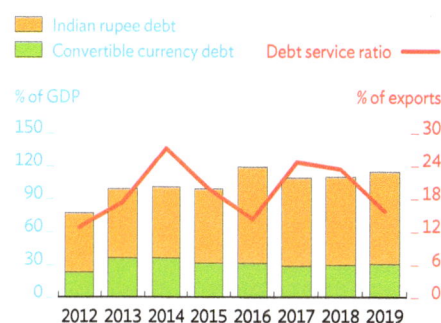

Note: Years are fiscal years ending 30 June of that year.
Source: Royal Monetary Authority. Monthly Statistical Bulletin February 2020. http://www.rma.org.bt.

Figure 3.16.9 Asymmetry in productivity and employment, 2017

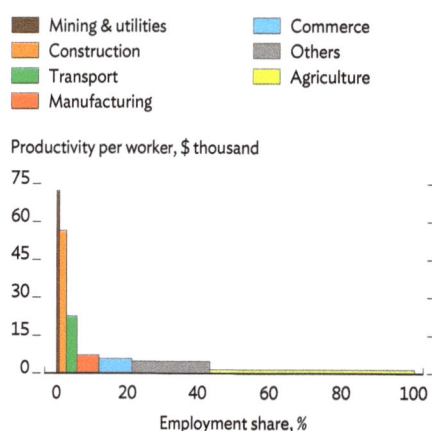

Note: Years are fiscal years ending on 30 June of that year.
Sources: ADB estimates using data from UN National Main Accounts Aggregate 2019 and ILOSTAT 2019.

Thus, tackling inequality must target the rural population, where 76% are stuck in agriculture.

A Theil index decomposition suggests that, both within-region and between-region drivers of inequality are significant, the latter explaining about 35% of disparity (Table 3.16.3). However, the rural Gini coefficient is higher than the urban one, which runs counter to the assumption that disparity in urban areas is higher, given wider distributional possibilities. Perhaps this is because households on the urban periphery, who do not depend on agriculture, are classified as rural. The disparity between the two is evident. An alternative reason could be shortcomings in the measure itself. Existing inequality measures are based on consumption, not income. Consumption measures underestimate inequality as people consume only a portion of their income, with the poor consuming a significantly larger portion. Further, debt-financed consumption artificially inflates the income of households that take out loans, most of them in urban Bhutan. Including debt-financed consumption misleads surveyors on the income of these households, causing them to underestimate inequality, though it could be that consumption expenditure is a more accurate reflection of incomes in rural than in urban areas because rural access to credit is lower. In any case, informed policy making requires a more accurate picture of inequality, which can be obtained by combining data on income taxes and from surveys of living standards.

Inclusive growth has been impeded primarily by the challenges of generating adequately modern employment and of lifting agricultural productivity. Interventions must therefore be geared toward modernizing agriculture. A high priority should be to promote agricultural value chains that would enable farmers to integrate better with markets and other sectors. To realize this, a concerted drive toward commercially oriented infrastructure and enabling policies is critical, as is enhancing mechanization and fostering deeper penetration of technologies. With an inherent limit to farm mechanization in mountainous Bhutan, interventions should focus on mechanizing activities higher up the value chain and beyond the farm, stimulating off-farm employment. As fragmented landholdings deter large-scale investments in mechanization, exploring modalities for spreading the costs over larger units could offer commercially viable alternatives. Additionally, more affordable technologies to monitor small farms, particularly against wildlife, are also worth exploring.

Public investments thus far have focused primarily on rural connectivity and input subsidies. It may be timely to begin investing in cold-storage facilities, enhancing and standardizing products, and promoting enabling supply contract. Recent efforts to boost agricultural productivity and rural incomes are prioritized lending and targeted measures to enhance commercialization, including support through financial inclusion and rural credit.

Table 3.16.2 Key indicators by region

	Rural	Urban	Bhutan
Poverty rate	11.9	0.8	8.2
Gini	0.35	0.32	0.38
Monthly expenditure (Nu)	26,937	45,508	33,542
Agri. employment (% of population)	76.0	4.3	51.0

Sources: Bhutan Living Standards Survey, 2017; Poverty Analysis Report, 2017; Labour Force Survey, 2017.

Table 3.16.3 Decomposing drivers of inequality, 2017

Within	Between	Overlap	Aggregate
0.168	0.126	0.071	0.366

Source: Based on data from Bhutan Living Standards Survey, 2017.

India

Growth slowed last year as a credit shortage lowered domestic demand. Inflation spiked on surging vegetable prices, but the current account deficit shrank as demand slowed. GDP growth will decline further this year owing to COVID-19 but rebound next year on government initiatives and better credit. Inflation will decelerate as demand weakens, then reaccelerate as it revives. The current account deficit will narrow as global growth and oil prices falter, then widen as the economy strengthens.

Economic performance

Economic growth slowed to 5.0% in fiscal year 2019 (FY2019, ended 31 March 2020), according to advance official estimates. This was below the average of 7.0% in the past decade and the slowest since the global financial crisis, when growth was 3.1% in FY2008. Within FY2019, growth hit a 27-quarter low of 4.7% in the third quarter. With the COVID-19 outbreak starting in late January and subsequently affecting India, the advance estimate of GDP growth in FY2019 is likely to be downgraded.

Agriculture growth improved from 2.4% in FY2018 to a robust 3.7% in FY2019 on higher grain output supported by rainfall above normal in the second half, adding 0.5 percentage points to growth (Figure 3.17.1). Industry growth slowed to 1.8%, its lowest rate since economic liberalization in FY1991, as manufacturing and construction weakened. With automobile sales down significantly, manufacturing grew by only 0.9%, its slowest in more than 20 years. After contracting in FY2018, mining recovered to grow by 2.8%. In sum, the contribution of industry to growth fell by more than half to 0.5 percentage points. With public administration and other services expanding by 8.8%, service growth at 7.0% contributed 3.5 percentage points. Government measures to address financial sector stress helped growth in financial services, real estate, and other professional services accelerate from 6.8% in FY2018 to a robust 7.3%.

On the demand side, a decline in investment severely dragged down growth (Figure 3.17.2). After growing by an annual average of 7.2% over the past decade, gross fixed capital formation contracted by 0.6% in FY2019, its worst showing since FY2002. With consumer confidence sagging to its lowest in a decade (Figure 3.17.3), growth in private

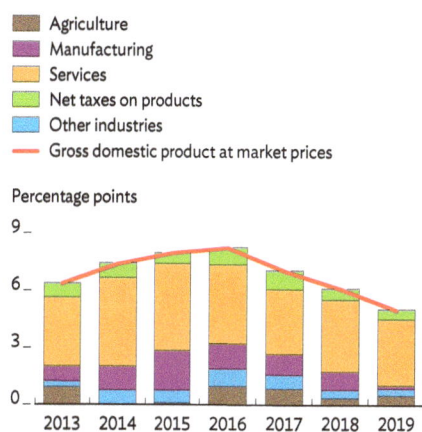

Figure 3.17.1 Supply-side contributions to growth

Legend:
- Agriculture
- Manufacturing
- Services
- Net taxes on products
- Other industries
- Gross domestic product at market prices

Percentage points

Notes: Other industries include mining and quarrying; construction; and electricity, gas, and other utilities. Years are fiscal years ending on 31 March of the next year.

Sources: Ministry of Statistics and Programme Implementation. http://www.mospi.nic.in; CEIC Data Company (accessed 3 March 2020).

This chapter was written by Lei Lei Song of the South Asia Department, ADB, New Delhi, and Shalini Mittal, consultant, India Resident Mission, ADB, New Delhi.

consumption slowed from 7.2% in FY2018 to 5.3%, adding only 3.0 percentage points to GDP growth in FY2019, the least since FY2009. Government consumption rose by 9.8%, contributing 1.0 percentage point to GDP growth, as the government acted to support growth from the second quarter of FY2019. As domestic demand slowed, imports of goods and services fell, allowing net exports to improve and contribute 0.9 percentage points to growth despite falling exports.

The growth slowdown in the past 3 years from a recent high of 8.3% in FY2016 reflects both cyclical and structural factors. The economy had enjoyed fast growth at an annual average of 7.5% from FY2013 to FY2016, driven largely by consumption, both private and government. Credit from banks and in particular nonbanking financial companies (NBFCs, including housing finance companies) supported this expansion. Banks, particularly public sector banks constrained by high nonperforming loans (NPLs) from earlier periods, were not as aggressive as before (Figure 3.17.4). NBFCs stepped up lending to consumers and businesses, expanding their share of nonfood credit (which excludes public sector loans for procuring crops from farmers) from 19.0% to 22.1% in FY2013–FY2016, with annual expansion averaging 16.3% in the period (Figure 3.17.5).

The growth trajectory was influenced by the demonetization of large banknotes starting at the end of 2016 and the launch of a goods and services tax in mid-2017. Fueled by surging nonfood credit from NBFCs at 30.9%, growth in final domestic demand (private and public consumption plus gross capital formation) remained strong at 10.3% in FY2017. Yet, the cash crunch induced by demonetization adversely affected domestic supply. As imports exploded and net exports subtracted 2.8 percentage points, GDP growth declined to 7.0% in FY2017.

Structural weakness underlay the cyclical downturn. As the economy slowed, the asset quality of NBFCs deteriorated, with NPLs rising from 2.4% of credit outstanding in FY2013 to 6.1% in FY2018. This induced banks and institutional investors to cut their exposure to NBFCs, drying up their finance. A large NBFC defaulted on its bond obligations in September 2018, sparking an NBFC crisis (see *Policy Challenge* below). With banks and NBFCs stressed, a credit crunch ensued as the flow of financial resources to businesses collapsed from the equivalent of 11.7% of GDP in FY2018 to 4.0% in the first half of FY2019 (Figure 3.17.6). The credit crunch directly induced a continued slowdown in FY2018 and FY2019.

Other structural constraints were subdued job and wage growth and continued rural stress, which affected consumption; inadequate infrastructure; progress of reform in key markets such as labor and land; and low tax revenue constricting fiscal space.

Figure 3.17.2 Demand-side contributions to growth

- Private consumption
- Government consumption
- Gross fixed capital formation
- Net exports
- Other investments
- Statistical discrepancy
- Gross domestic product at market prices

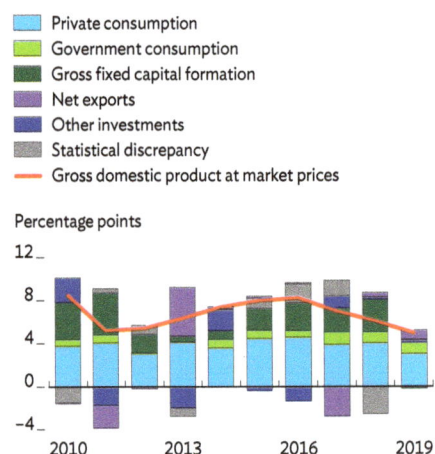

Percentage points

Notes: Other investments include valuables and changes in stocks. Years are fiscal years ending on 31 March of the next year.
Sources: Ministry of Statistics and Programme Implementation. http://www.mospi.nic.in; CEIC Data Company (accessed 3 March 2020).

Figure 3.17.3 Consumer confidence

- Current situation
- Future expectations

Index

Source: Reserve Bank of India (accessed 11 March 2020).

Figure 3.17.4 Nonperforming loans held by banks

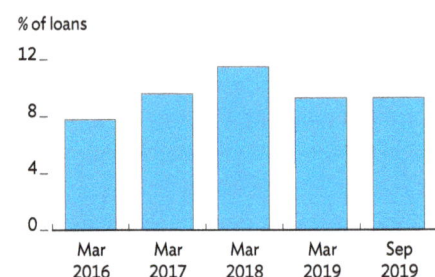

% of loans

Source: Reserve Bank of India. http://www.rbi.org.in (accessed 6 March 2020).

Consumer price inflation, benign in the first half of FY2019, spiked above the target zone of 2%–6% in December 2019 for the first time since the adaption of inflation targeting. The spike was caused by a surge in prices for vegetables, particularly onions as the harvest was hit by a late monsoon. Inflation remained elevated in early 2020 and averaged 4.7% in FY2019. Inflation excluding food and fuel rose slightly to 4.2% in FY2019, with housing, health care, and education contributing more than half to the increase (Figure 3.17.7).

Monetary policy was accommodative as the Reserve Bank of India, the central bank, cut its policy rate by a total of 135 basis points from February to October 2019. It refrained from further cuts before March 2020, citing elevated inflation. Lending rates had come down by only 69 basis points since the monetary easing cycle started, however, indicating weak monetary transmission (Figure 3.17.8). With inflation above the target zone, the central bank pursued unconventional monetary policy to improve both the cost and the availability of credit. It introduced long-term repurchase operations with 1-year and 3-year tenors at the policy rate and removed the quantitative restriction on liquidity provisions. It also exempted banks temporarily from the cash reserve requirement for loans to micro, small, and medium-sized enterprises (MSMEs), as well as to finance car and home purchases; allowed the declaration of NPLs for commercial real estate to be delayed by 1 year; and extended restructuring for stressed MSME loans. As a result, bond yields fell immediately, and lending rates also started to fall.

With weak economic growth and falling tax collection, the central government invoked an escape clause in the Fiscal Responsibility and Budget Management Act, which allows deviation from fiscal targets during structural reform. The fiscal deficit in FY2019 was revised up by 0.5 percentage points to 3.8% (Figure 3.17.9). Fiscal stimulus equal to 0.5% of GDP was provided by lowering corporate tax rates.

Central government revenue grew less than budgeted to 9.4% of GDP in FY2019, largely from shortfalls in tax revenue. Budgeted to expand by 18.2% a year earlier, gross tax revenue grew by only 3.8% as noncompliance and inefficient implementation slowed growth in revenue from the goods and services tax. Further, the central government missed its disinvestment target with its failure to sell Air India, but nontax revenue still increased to equal 1.7% of GDP after the central bank transferred a dividend of $21.5 billion.

The government had little room to use fiscal policy to boost economic activity in FY2019. Central government expenditure grew less than budgeted, to equal 13.2% of GDP. Recurrent expenditure was reduced to 11.5% of GDP largely through cuts to food subsidies, but capital expenditure rose to equal 1.7% of GDP as the government pushed ahead with infrastructure projects.

Figure 3.17.5 Nonfood credit growth

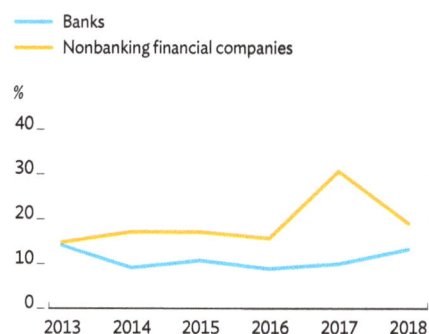

Notes: Nonbanking financial companies include systemically important firms, some of which take deposits and some not, as well as housing finance companies. Years are fiscal years ending on 31 March of the next year.
Sources: Reserve Bank of India; National Housing Bank (accessed 9 March 2020).

Figure 3.17.6 Flows of financial resources to businesses

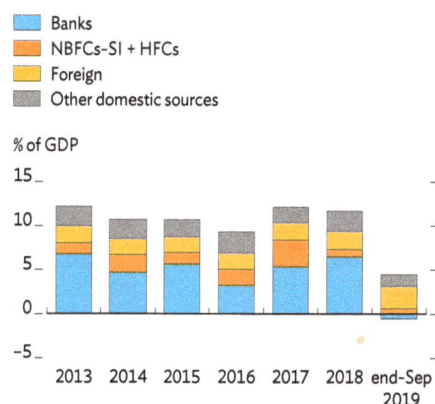

HFC = housing finance company, NBFC-SI = systemically important nonbanking financial company that does not take deposits.
Note: Years are fiscal years ending on 31 March of the next year.
Source: Reserve Bank of India (accessed 6 March 2020).

Figure 3.17.7 Inflation

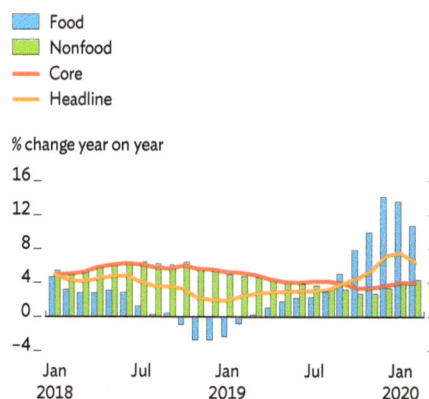

Sources: CEIC Data Company (accessed 15 March 2020); ADB estimates.

Slowing domestic demand and falling oil prices suppressed imports of goods and services, which fell in FY2019 by 3.2% (Figure 3.17.10). This narrowed the trade deficit despite exports of goods and services growing by a meager 0.9% because of the global economic slowdown during the year. Rising trade tensions between the US and the People's Republic of China (PRC) did not benefit Indian exports. Their weak performance in a competitive manufacturing market was reflected by declining exports of textiles excluding readymade garments, agriculture and allied products, leather, engineering goods, and other manufactures.

After growing at a robust pace over the past 2 years, the surplus in service exports rose modestly by 1.7% in FY2019 as net receipts from financial, transport, travel, and other businesses increased despite generally weak global demand. Remittances, on the other hand, grew by double digits. On balance, the current account deficit shrank from the equivalent of 2.1% of GDP in FY2018 to 0.9% in FY2019.

Net foreign direct investment (FDI) inflow remained healthy at $54.1 billion in FY2019, an increase of $10.7 billion supported by the opening of contract manufacturing, single-brand retailing, and insurance intermediaries for FDI, among other liberalizations. Net foreign portfolio flow remained positive as investors became newly allowed to subscribe to listed debt securities issued by real estate investment trusts, then turned negative in March 2020 under COVID-19. Equity inflow similarly grew only modestly from the beginning of the fiscal year in April 2019 to February 2020, as the Bombay Stock Exchange Sensex Index rose by 9.8% over the same 11 months of FY2018, before a substantial fall in March 2020 (Figure 3.17.11).

The Indian rupee depreciated against the US dollar by 7.8% in FY2019, more than half of the decline occurring in March (Figure 3.17.12). In real effective terms based on consumer prices, however, it appreciated by 3.8% in FY2019 with the recent spike in domestic inflation. The impact of appreciation on trade competitiveness may be muted as this transitory quickening of inflation dissipates. India's international reserves increased by $58.4 billion in FY2019 to $471.3 billion, or cover for 9.3 months of imports (Figure 3.17.13).

Economic prospects

The COVID-19 pandemic jeopardizes global growth and India's recovery. GDP growth in India is forecast to slow further to 4.0% in FY2020 before rebounding sharply to 6.2% in FY2021, assuming that the pandemic dissipates in the second half of 2020.

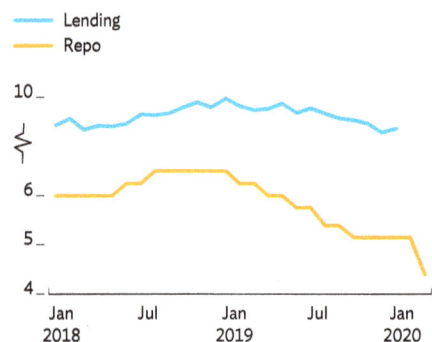

Figure 3.17.8 Interest rates

Source: Reserve Bank of India (accessed 27 March 2020).

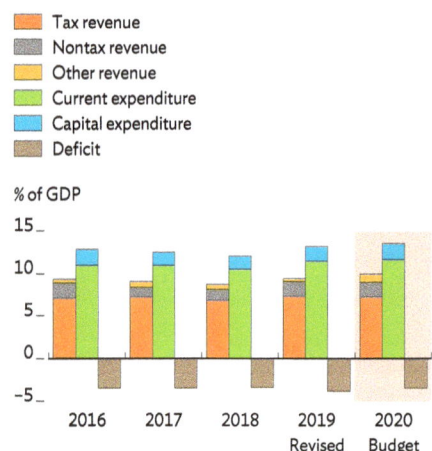

Figure 3.17.9 Federal budget indicators

Note: Years are fiscal years ending on 31 March of the next year.
Source: Ministry of Finance Union Budget 2018–2020. http://indiabudget.nic.in.

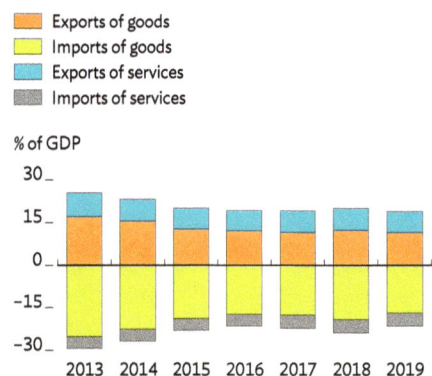

Figure 3.17.10 Trade indicators

Note: Years are fiscal years ending on 31 March of the next year.
Sources: CEIC Data Company (accessed 11 March 2020); ADB estimates.

The spread of the virus within India, while still limited at the end of March, is widening. Indian central and state governments have moved to contain the outbreak by closing borders and initiating a national lockdown from 25 March for 21 days. Consumption and investment are expected to be severely affected in the first quarter of FY2020, though demand will recover strongly when the pandemic is eventually contained in India and globally. India's low participation in global supply chains may help limit impact. The lowest oil prices in more than 15 years will, if sustained, benefit India as a large oil importer and partly offset the adverse impact of COVID-19.

Economic growth showed signs of improvement before the pandemic struck. New investment projects announced in the third quarter of FY2019 were the highest in 7 quarters, with more projects completed (Figure 3.17.14). The composite Nikkei purchasing managers' index for February 2020 remained above 50, predicting expansion (Figure 3.17.15). In agriculture, the area reported sown with winter crops is higher than in FY2018, indicating a higher harvest to come. Industrial production grew in January 2020. In February, steel production rose year on year for the first time in 6 months, and motor vehicle retail sales rose after 11 months of decline.

In FY2020, the national lockdown and travel restrictions will constrain economic activity. Financial market sell-offs and volatility may dampen consumer sentiment and investor confidence, aggravating the impact. Financial conditions may stay strained as financial markets roil. Private consumption may suffer as it did during the global financial crisis of 2008–2009 or even more. Gross fixed capital formation is likely to contract further as risk perception heightens and uncertainty deepens under the pandemic.

To counter the impact of COVID-19, the central government has allocated $2 billion to strengthen the health system and introduced a $22.5 billion relief package, equal to 0.8% of GDP, including direct cash transfers and increased free distribution of food and gas to the poor and vulnerable, insurance for health workers, welfare support for construction workers, and support for small businesses. The central government had increased capital expenditure to the equivalent of 1.8% of GDP in the FY2020 budget announced before the pandemic. To support an ambitious plan to invest $1.4 trillion in designated National Infrastructure Pipeline projects in the next 5 years, the central government has allocated $3 billion as equity support to infrastructure finance companies to leverage more long-term lending from the market. Central government expenditure was budgeted to grow by 13.9% in FY2020.

The central bank on 27 March cut its policy rate by 75 basis points to 4.4%, the lowest ever, and rolled out a range of measures to preserve financial stability and mitigate the

Figure 3.17.11 Stock prices

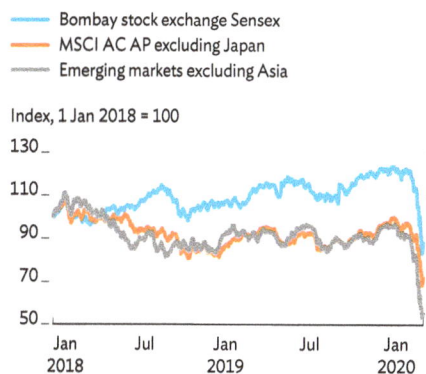

Index, 1 Jan 2018 = 100

Source: Bloomberg (accessed 21 March 2020).

Figure 3.17.12 Exchange rate

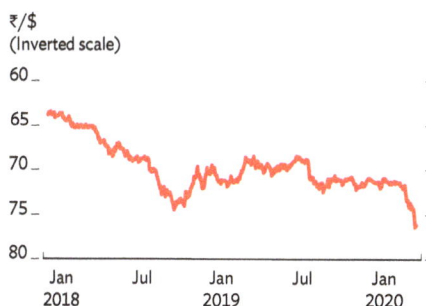

₹/$
(Inverted scale)

Source: Bloomberg (accessed 20 March 2020).

Figure 3.17.13 Gross international reserves

SDR = special drawing right.
Note: Years are fiscal years ending on 31 March of the next year.
Source: CEIC Data Company (accessed 9 March 2020).

economic impact of COVID-19. Targeted long-term repo operations, an increase in the amount banks may borrow from an emergency window of the central bank, and a cut in the cash reserve ratios for banks will ensure ample liquidity. All lending institutions will allow a 3-month moratorium on term loans and defer interest payments on working capital. In March 2020, when Indian financial markets joined a global sell-off in response to the COVID-19 pandemic, the central bank undertook open market operations and US dollar–rupee swaps to ensure adequate rupee and dollar liquidity. With inflation expected to ease into the target zone soon, the central bank is likely to cut policy rates further to counter financial volatility and support growth. The central bank has committed to using all instruments, conventional and unconventional, to fight the pandemic.

Assuming a normal monsoon in FY2020, agriculture is likely to remain strong and support rural incomes. Government measures will alleviate rural distress and help revive rural consumption. The FY2020 budget increased allocations to agriculture and the rural sector by 28.1% to equal 0.8% of GDP. A 16-point action plan in the budget includes hikes to minimum support prices that aim to ensure a minimum 50% profit margin to farmers, an ambitious target of $210 billion in credit to agriculture from public and private financial institutions, and an increased allocation to a central government program of conditional cash transfers to small landholders. A record high winter crop in the second half of FY2019 will increase farmers' incomes.

Domestic demand will rebound strongly once the pandemic passes and full economic activity resumes. As consumer sentiment and investor confidence are restored, growth in consumption and investment are expected to return to rates similar to before FY2019, or perhaps higher.

Government initiatives introduced in late 2019 and in the FY2020 budget will aid recovery and sustain growth in the coming years. The recent budget introduced a simplified personal income tax option that reduces tax rates for those earning less than $20,000 per year but forgoes exemptions and deductions. This will increase household disposable income, thereby boost private consumption, and potentially expand the tax base. A taxpayers' charter enumerating their rights aims to engender more trust in government.

Private investment, both domestic and foreign, will be encouraged by corporate tax cuts introduced in September 2019, which eased the average effective corporate tax rate including all surcharges from 30% to 25% and, for new manufacturing companies, to 17%. Investor sentiment should improve as well with the removal of the dividend distribution tax, the extension of concessional corporate tax rates to new power companies, and tax relief introduced for start-ups. An investment clearance

Table 3.17.1 Selected economic indicators (%)

	2018	2019	2020	2021
GDP growth	6.1	5.0	4.0	6.2
Inflation	3.4	4.7	3.0	3.8
Current acct. bal. (share of GDP)	–2.1	–0.9	–0.3	–1.2

Note: Years are fiscal years ending on 31 March of the next year.
Sources: Ministry of Statistics and Programme Implementation. http://www.mospi.nic.in; ADB estimates.

Figure 3.17.14 Investment projects

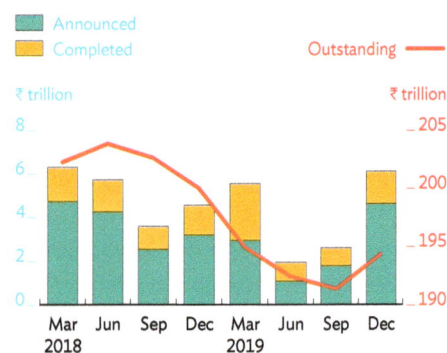

Source: Centre for Monitoring Indian Economy Pvt. Ltd. (accessed 5 March 2020).

Figure 3.17.15 Purchasing managers' indexes

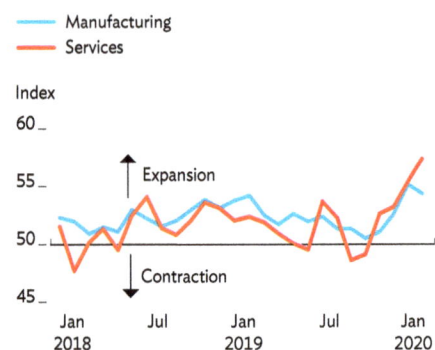

Note: Nikkei, Markit. Years are fiscal years ending on 31 March of the next year.
Source: Bloomberg (accessed 11 March 2020).

cell is being set up to provide end-to-end facilitation and support for investment, including pre-investment advice, and improve the ease of doing business. Foreign sovereign wealth funds are incentivized to invest in infrastructure.

Reform is under way to alleviate financial sector stress, a major factor behind the recent slowdown. Reform recapitalized and merged state-owned banks and reduced their tax burdens, and it will sell the balance of the government stake in Industrial Development Bank of India to private and institutional investors, as well as broaden deposit insurance coverage. Credit to MSMEs is promoted by measures that increase turnover limits for audits of accounts, provide subordinate debt, and extend a restructuring window.

Inflation is expected to fall significantly in FY2020 as oil prices and domestic demand weaken. Food inflation will come down as supply improves and the transitory effects of the recent spike in onion prices dissipates. Prices for some manufactures are likely to rise with supply disruption and rupee depreciation. Headline inflation is forecast to average 3.0% in FY2020 and rise to 3.8% in FY2021 as domestic demand strengthens.

Before the pandemic struck, the central government had committed in its FY2020 budget to a moderate path of fiscal consolidation, lowering the fiscal deficit to the equivalent of 3.5% of GDP in FY2020, 3.3% in FY2021, and 3.1% in FY2022. Central government tax revenue is likely to fall short of targeted growth at 12.0% in FY2020 as GDP growth falters. Ambitious disinvestment targets may be difficult to achieve under current circumstances. The fiscal deficit is unlikely to shrink as budgeted. However, this crisis requires expansionary fiscal policy to mitigate its effects and facilitate recovery.

After growing by 0.5% in FY2019, exports of goods and services are expected to contract in FY2020 with lower oil prices and global demand. Imports of goods and services are likely to contract more than last year as falling oil prices reduce the net oil import bill and domestic demand remains sluggish. The surplus in services will decline, but the overall trade deficit is likely to shrink. Remittances will be hit by weak earnings abroad under depressed global growth and falling oil prices. On balance, the current account deficit is expected to narrow to the equivalent of 0.3% of GDP in FY2020 (Figure 3.17.16).

In FY2021, exports of goods and services are expected to recover as the global economy rebounds. Exports are expected to grow at a pace similar to the 11.5% average in FY2016–FY2018. Imports of goods and services, supported by rising domestic demand and oil prices, are likely to outgrow exports. As the trade deficit widens, the current account deficit is forecast to rise to equal 1.2% of GDP in FY2021.

Figure 3.17.16 Current account indicators

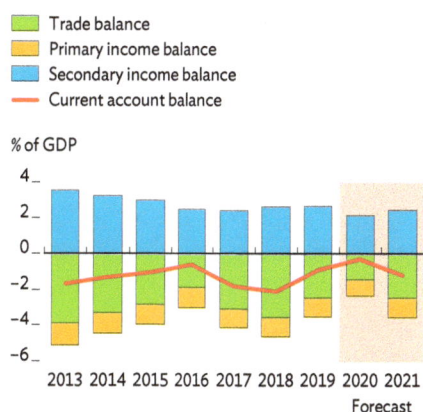

- Trade balance
- Primary income balance
- Secondary income balance
- Current account balance

% of GDP

2013 2014 2015 2016 2017 2018 2019 2020 2021

Forecast

Note: Years are fiscal years ending on 31 March of the next year.
Sources: CEIC Data Company (accessed 9 March 2020); ADB estimates.

The pandemic will slow global FDI flows in FY2020, but FDI flow into India is expected to rebound in FY2021 as global conditions improve and India remains an attractive investment destination. Portfolio inflow is expected to drop significantly in FY2020 after market slumps tighten global financial conditions but should rebound in FY2021 as Indian financial markets continue to offer healthy returns (Figure 3.17.17). Reform will help. From FY2020, certain categories of government securities will be fully open to nonresident investors, and the limit on foreign portfolio investment in corporate bonds will be raised. Foreign exchange reserves may fall in FY2020 but are expected to increase in FY2021.

Risks to the outlook are firmly on the downside. A prolonged COVID-19 pandemic would push the global economy into deep recession and further slow Indian growth. Were the virus to spread widely within India, economic activity would be severely constrained. Failure to implement reform to address structural weakness would further hamper recovery after the pandemic.

Policy challenge—strengthening nonbank financing to support growth

Nonbanking financial companies (NBFCs) have become increasingly important to financing the Indian economy, particularly after 2013, as bank credit growth slowed in response to NPLs rapidly increasing to an 11.2% share of all loans outstanding in FY2017. Recently, NBFCs have become fragile, and the collapse of a large one triggered the credit crunch that slowed growth in FY2019. Ensuring NBFC health has become essential.

Complementing regular commercial banks, NBFCs provide credit to a wide variety of niche segments, ranging from infrastructure to consumer durables. Some take deposits (NBFCs-D) and some not (NBFCs-ND). No new license has been issued to an NBFC-D since 1997. NBFCs-ND rely on markets and banks to raise money and are divided into those that are systemically important (NBFCs-SI), with assets greater than ₹5 billion, and smaller ones. At the end of September 2019, there were 82 NBFCs-D, 274 NBFCs-SI, and 9,187 others. Data on smaller NBFCs-ND are not readily available and therefore not discussed here. About 100 housing finance companies (HFCs) extend housing finance to individuals, cooperative societies, and corporations and lease commercial and residential premises. They are also included as NBFCs after their regulation shifted from the National Housing Bank to the central bank in August 2019.

Figure 3.17.17 Portfolio capital flows

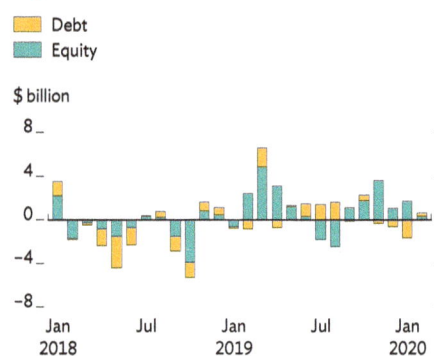

Source: Security and Exchange Board of India.
https://www.fpi.nsdl.co.in/web/Reports/Archive.aspx.
(accessed 11 March 2020).

NBFCs constitute the third largest segment in the Indian financial sector, after commercial banks and insurance companies. At the end of FY2018, NBFCs had assets of ₹44.4 trillion, equal to 23.4% of GDP, with NBFCs-SI accounting for 60.0%, NBFCs-D 9.5%, and HFCs 30.5%. The government owns the two largest NBFCs-SI and 39.8% of this group's assets, as well as 10.3% of NBFCs-D but only 5.4% of HFC assets. At the end of September 2019, NBFCs had raised funds mainly from debentures at 37.3% of the total, bank borrowing at 25.4%, and commercial papers at about 5.0% (Figure 3.17.18).

Nonfood credit extended by NBFCs has registered average annual growth at 20.0% since FY2013, financing mainly industry, housing, services, and automobile purchases (Figure 3.17.19). As this doubled growth in bank nonfood credit, the share of NBFCs in outstanding of nonfood credit increased from 19.0% in FY2013 to 26.1% in FY2018 (Figure 3.17.20).

However, the asset quality of NBFCs has deteriorated as they expanded. The NPLs of NBFCs excepting HFCs increased from 2.6% of all loans at the end of FY2013 to 6.1% just 5 years later. In September 2018, one of largest NBFCs, Infrastructure Leasing and Finance Company (IL&FS), defaulted on its bond obligations. IL&FS had borrowed heavily from banks and the corporate bond market, attracting investors like mutual funds, pension funds, and corporations, and was rated highly by domestic rating agencies.

The IL&FS default triggered panic in the financial market. Liquidity soon dried up in the entire NBFC segment as banks and mutual funds cut their exposure to NBFCs. This dramatically cut the flow of resources from NBFCs to businesses, by 69.2% in FY2018 and a further 66.3% in the first half of FY2019. As bank credit flows fell as well, total financial flows to businesses plunged by 60.3% year on year in the first half of FY2019, creating the credit crunch.

In the wake of the IL&FS crisis, the central government has moved to cushion its impact. It launched a ₹1 trillion partial credit guarantee program to protect NBFC lending that satisfied program criteria, and it contributed ₹100 billion to a ₹250 billion alternative investment fund to provide last-mile funding to stalled housing developments.

As the regulator, the central bank acted to ensure the flow of bank lending to NBFCs: reducing risk weights on lending to NBFCs to make them similar to weights for other companies, increasing limits on bank exposure to single-borrower NBFCs from 10% to 20% of the bank's tier-1 capital, and allowing banks to lend to registered NBFCs (other than micro-finance institutions) for onlending to micro and small enterprises, to the housing sector, and, as term loans only, to agriculture.

These measures have prevented further NBFC-SI failures and perhaps a financial crisis. Since then, banks have increased lending to NBFCs and improved their liquidity.

Figure 3.17.18 Borrowing by nonbanking financial companies

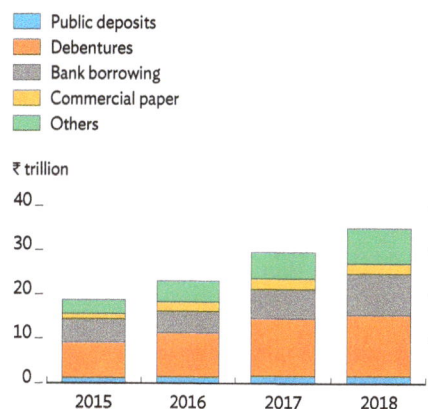

Notes: Nonbanking financial companies include systemically important firms, some of which take deposits and some not, as well as housing finance companies. Years are fiscal years ending on 31 March of the next year.
Source: Reserve Bank of India (accessed 9 March 2020).

Figure 3.17.19 Nonbanking financial companies lending, by sector

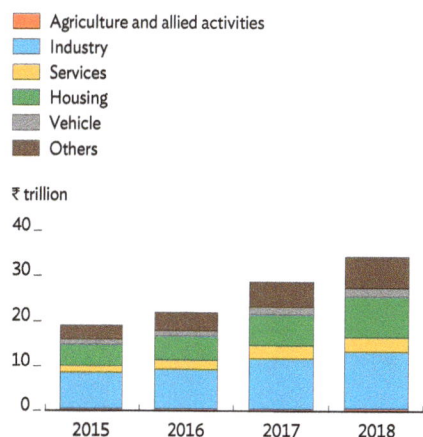

Notes: Nonbanking financial companies include systemically important firms, some of which take deposits and some not, as well as housing finance companies. Years are fiscal years ending on 31 March of the next year.
Sources: Reserve Bank of India; National Housing Board.

Yet, bank lending may be skewed in favor of large and highly rated NBFCs. Smaller, less-established, and lower-rated NBFCs continued to struggle for funds. Bond market liquidity for NBFCs and HFCs remained tight.

NBFCs carry risks inherent to their business nature. They rely on wholesale funding and face liquidity risks when markets seize up. Their focus on particular market segments concentrates risk. With less stringent regulation and supervision, NBFCs tend to be excessively leveraged, and their lending is likely procyclical. Further, unlike banks, NBFCs cannot borrow from the central bank when in difficulty, and deposit insurance schemes do not apply.

Reform is needed to address the structural issues in NBFCs. They need to diversify funding sources by accessing broader pools of capital, especially those with long-maturity liabilities such as pension funds and insurance companies. Debt pooling to securitize NBFC assets would help but would require better disclosure and market transparency. Credible and reliable ratings are crucial for attracting large pools of investments in NBFCs. Further regulatory intervention is necessary to improve governance in rating agencies and strengthen their capacity.

Regulatory and supervisory oversight of NBFCs-SI in particular must be enhanced, given their strong links with the economy. A proper mechanism is needed to control risk and ensure soundness, which could include regular and detailed audits and inspection by the regulator, new limits on liquidity and asset liability mismatch, and regular reviews of asset quality.

Making NBFC supervision more stringent and comparable to bank supervision will be a challenge for the central bank. While there are some 90 scheduled commercial banks, NBFCs-SI number close to 300. Supervising such a large number of entities to the same standard of coverage and detail will require the central bank to significantly expand its capacity.

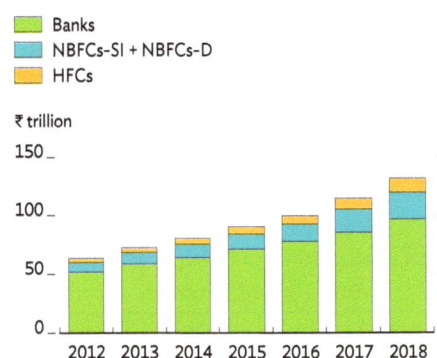

Figure 3.17.20 Nonfood credit, by institution type

NBFC-D = nonbanking financial company that takes deposits, NBFC-SI = systemically important nonbanking financial company that does not take deposits, HFC = housing finance company.

Note: Years are fiscal years ending on 31 March of the next year.

Sources: Reserve Bank of India and National Housing Board.

Maldives

Growth slowed in 2019 with a steep fall in construction and moderation in tourism income despite higher visitor arrivals. Policy support kept inflation minimal. Lower imports narrowed the current account deficit, which remained large and is forecast higher in 2020 and 2021. The outlook is for a growth collapse in 2020 as tourism plummets under the COVID-19 pandemic but then a revival in 2021. Decentralizing governance across the county's widely scattered islands would benefit from gradual implementation.

Economic performance

Economic growth moderated from 6.9% in 2018 to an estimated 5.7% in 2019 as construction significantly weakened, growth in tourism income slowed, and other sectors including fisheries contracted (Figure 3.18.1).

Construction growth braked sharply from 12.5% in 2018 to only 1.7% in 2019 as large projects were completed, substantial delays slowed the implementation of the government's investment program, and expansion in privately led projects eased. Public Sector Investment Program spending in 2019 fell by 26% from a year earlier, and growth in bank loans to private developers for construction and real estate slowed from 22.1% in 2018 to 9.3%. Tracking this falloff in spending, growth in imports of construction goods reversed a marked 35.6% increase in 2018 to decline by 11.7%.

Growth in tourist arrivals increased from 6.8% in 2018 to 14.7%, to reach a record of 1.7 million visitors in 2019. Arrivals benefited from political stability, increased flight connections, the opening of new resorts, and extensive marketing campaigns. European tourists grew by 14.8%, accounting for almost half of the increase and maintaining the highest regional market share at 49.0%. Asian arrivals substantially recovered from a 1.0% decline in 2018 to expand by 13.8% in 2019. The recovery was largely an 83.5% expansion in Indian visitors, accounting for 34.6% of growth in arrivals. Tourist arrivals from the People's Republic of China (PRC) reversed a 7.6% drop in 2018 to grow by a marginal 0.3%. Although declining in recent years, visitors from the PRC were 16.7% of arrivals in 2019, while the Indian share rose from 6.1% to 9.7%.

Despite higher growth in tourist arrivals and a 12.8% increase in hotel bed-nights—an occupancy measure used as a proxy for tourism earnings—preliminary estimates show growth in travel

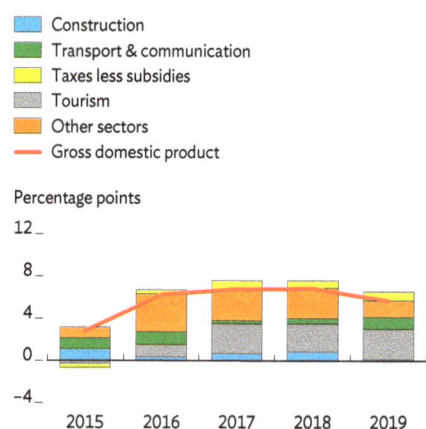

Figure 3.18.1 Supply-side contributions to growth

- Construction
- Transport & communication
- Taxes less subsidies
- Tourism
- Other sectors
- Gross domestic product

Percentage points

Source: Maldives Monetary Authority. 2020. Monthly Statistics. February. http://www.mma.gov.mv.

This chapter was written by Masato Nakane of the South Asia Department, ADB, Manila, and Abdula Ali and Macrina Mallari, consultants, South Asia Department, ADB, Manila.

receipts slowing sharply from 10.4% in 2018 to 4.3% in 2019, indicating weaker tourist spending. Apart from preliminary data, the failure of income growth to match increased arrivals may reflect more tourists staying at the country's new mid-priced hotels and fewer at luxury resorts (Figure 3.18.2).

Fish exports in 2019 fell by 14.3% in volume terms and by 13.6% in earnings as both demand and prices fell. Financial services, transportation, and communications performed well in 2019.

Average inflation remained subdued at 0.2% in 2019, owing mainly to the government's administrative price controls on the staples rice, flour, and sugar, as well as lower global prices for oil and food products (Figure 3.18.3). With inflationary pressure low, the Maldives Monetary Authority has maintained the accommodative policy in force since it lowered the indicative monetary policy rate in 2015.

Fiscal policy was expansionary. With a supplementary budget approved during the year, the budget deficit increased from the equivalent of 5.2% of GDP in 2018 to 5.7%. Recurrent expenditure increased by 14.0%, mainly reflecting the first full year of a new pay structure for civil servants introduced in 2018, as well as additional employees recruited for newly established government agencies. This increase pushed growth in total expenditure, despite weak capital expenditure, up by 9.6%, raising expenditure as a percentage of GDP from 32.3% in 2018 to 33.1%. A large increase in grants raised total revenue slightly to 27.4% of GDP even as weaker economic growth during the year held growth in domestic revenue to only 2.8%. As a percentage of GDP, domestic revenue slipped from 26.1% in 2018 to 25.0% in 2019 (Figure 3.18.4).

Government external debt including Rf11.8 billion in state loan guarantees increased to Rf33.8 billion in 2019, equal to 38.5% of GDP, mainly with the disbursement of guaranteed loans to state-owned enterprises. Government domestic debt including Rf966 million in debt guarantees rose to reach Rf33.2 billion or 37.8% of GDP, up from 35.8% in 2018. At the end of 2019, total public debt including state guarantees was estimated to have increased by 12.0% to Rf67.02 billion, or 76.3% of GDP (Figure 3.18.5). This development underscores an International Monetary Fund assessment that Maldives continues to face a high risk of public external debt distress.

The current account deficit narrowed from the equivalent of 26.1% of GDP in 2018 to an estimated 21.5% as provisional estimates indicate that the merchandise trade deficit reversed 27.1% deterioration a year earlier with 5.5% improvement. Imports fell by 4.0% on lower demand for construction goods, machinery, and electrical equipment as investment slackened, while exports rose by 7.4% as fuel reexports more than offset the drop in fish exports. The current account deficit was financed by net financial account inflow, mainly foreign direct

Figure 3.18.2 Tourism indicators

Source: Maldives Monetary Authority. 2020. Monthly Statistics. February. http://www.mma.gov.mv.

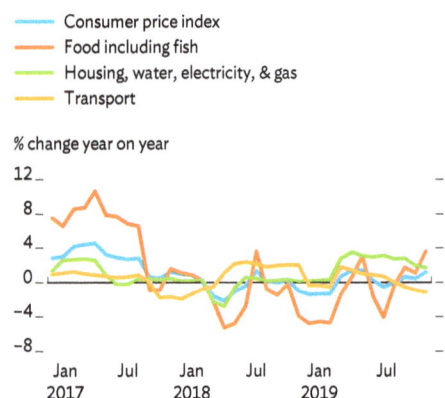

Figure 3.18.3 Inflation

Source: Maldives Monetary Authority. 2020. Monthly Statistics. February. http://www.mma.gov.mv.

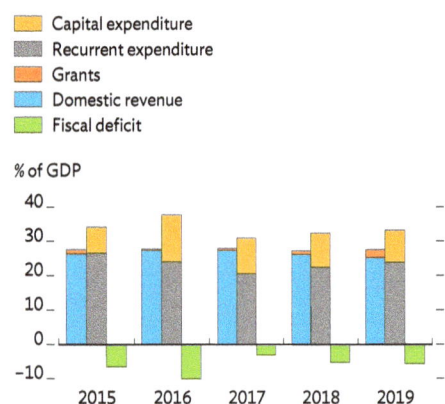

Figure 3.18.4 Fiscal indicators

Source: Maldives Monetary Authority. 2020. Monthly Statistics. February. http://www.mma.gov.mv.

investment and other investment liabilities predominantly incurred by state-owned enterprises with government guarantees (Figure 3.18.6).

Gross international reserves climbed by about 6% to $753 million in 2019 while usable reserves—gross international reserves less the foreign currency deposits of commercial banks—amounted to $315.9 million. They provided cover for only 1.3 months of imports (Figure 3.18.7).

Economic prospects

Economic growth is expected to plunge in 2020 as tourism gets hammered by COVID-19, then bounce back strongly in 2021 with expected recovery in tourism. Preliminary numbers for February 2020 indicate a 14% decline in tourist arrivals from February 2019, including a 95% drop in visitors from the PRC. Notably, the government has suspended direct flights from the PRC, some European countries, and several other countries and all cruise ship arrivals and has restricted entry of all persons, regardless of nationality, who have embarked or transited through the countries with travel bans. Consequently, earnings will fall substantially, as the PRC is the largest single source market for Maldives, and Europe collectively supplies about half of visitors.

Initial estimates show a wide range of possible impacts on the economy from reduced tourism depending on the severity and duration of contagion in Maldives' main tourist markets. In terms of lost income, the impact could be in the range of $329 million–$657 million, which would contract GDP by 6.2%–12.3%. Though the impact may well be near the upper end of estimates in 2020, tourism can be expected to make a strong comeback in 2021 as pent-up demand is released— assuming that efforts to test for and contain the virus succeed.

Slowing in construction and real estate will likewise continue in 2020 as financing becomes a problem with decreased tourism earnings, which on average provide more than 50% of government revenues. If the decline in tourist arrivals lasts, the government anticipates a shortfall in revenue of between $135.9 million and $446.6 million. The supply of construction materials is likely to be affected by COVID-19 halting some infrastructure projects, notably for housing. Private-led investment in housing and tourism is also expected to be adversely affected.

Construction, however, is poised to recover in 2021, especially with a number of large and high-priority projects slated to commence, including three bridges connecting Greater Malé with an international port in Gulhifalhu.

Prospects for fisheries might be hurt as well by COVID-19, particularly affecting exports of chilled and frozen fish. Exports of chilled yellowfin tuna to Europe have declined, and exports to Asian markets are likely to follow similar trends in the coming months.

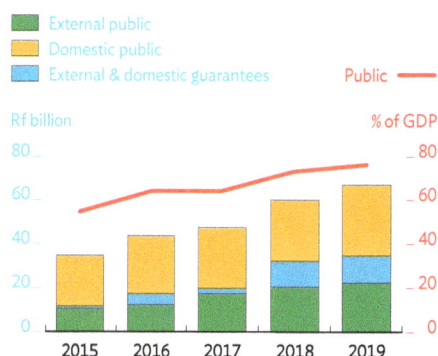

Figure 3.18.5 Public debt including guarantees

Sources: Maldives Monetary Authority. 2020. Monthly Statistics. February; 2019 Budget. http://www.mma.gov.mv.

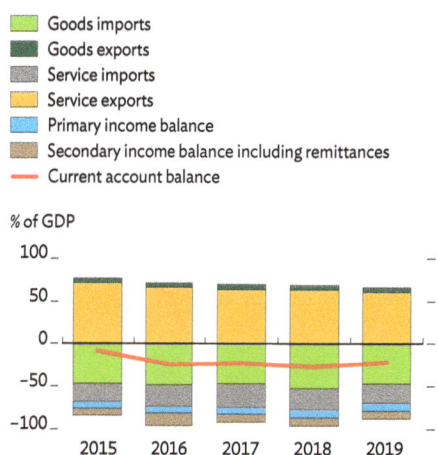

Figure 3.18.6 Balance of payments

Source: Maldives Monetary Authority. 2020. Monthly Statistics. February. http://www.mma.gov.mv.

Table 3.18.1 Selected economic indicators (%)

	2018	2019	2020	2021
GDP growth	6.9	5.7	–3.0	7.5
Inflation	–0.1	0.2	1.0	1.2
Current acct. bal. (share of GDP)	–26.1	–21.5	–23.0	–22.0

Sources: Maldives Monetary Authority. 2020. Monthly Statistics. February. http://www.mma.gov.mv; ADB estimates.

On balance, GDP growth is expected to contract by 3.0% in 2020, given the bleak outlook for tourism and other industries in the shadow of COVID-19, before it rebounds to 7.5% in 2021 with the anticipated rebound in tourism and robust construction growth.

The main downside risk to the outlook is a continuing spread of COVID-19 that keeps global tourism prostrate. Consequences would be suppressed tourism earnings for a second year and renewed concerns about fiscal and public debt sustainability, given the country's very high debt ratio and persistently thin stock of usable foreign exchange reserves.

Downward pressure on inflation will continue under the government's prevailing policies to lower electricity prices and harmonize staple food prices across the country, and with more subdued prices anticipated for oil on the world market. However, late shipments of imported products disrupted by COVID-19—especially products from the PRC, which account for more than 16% of all imports—may create supply shortages and push local prices up for a time. On balance, though, inflation is forecast to average 1.0% in 2020, marginally increasing to 1.2% in 2021.

The current account deficit is projected to worsen to the equivalent of 23.0% of GDP in 2020 as tourism income dwindles. The anticipated tourism recovery in 2021, though, will help narrow the current account deficit that year to 22.0% of GDP.

Policy challenge—implementing decentralized governance

The 2008 Constitution and the Decentralization Act, 2010 provide a legal framework for decentralization in Maldives. The Constitution formally established the role of local councils in governance, and the Decentralization Act paved the way for the first elections of island, atoll, and city councils in 2011. The act mandated councils to ensure democratic and accountable governance, deliver social services, and foster economic growth while protecting the local environment. It also created the Women's Development Committee as an integral part of local governance, advancing gender inclusion.

However, the implementation of the act and of decentralization have been slow, mainly because local councils' institutional capacity has been weak and amendments to the act returned certain devolved powers to the central government.

In 2018, a new government brought decentralization back again to the fore as a priority of the Maldives Strategic Action Plan, 2019–2023. In December 2019, the newly elected President ratified eight amendments to the Decentralization Act that granted more fiscal autonomy to local councils by allotting at least 5.0% of national revenue, or more than 4.0% of the budget, to local councils as block grants, empowering them to collect fees for municipal services and to borrow and manage

Figure 3.18.7 Gross international reserves

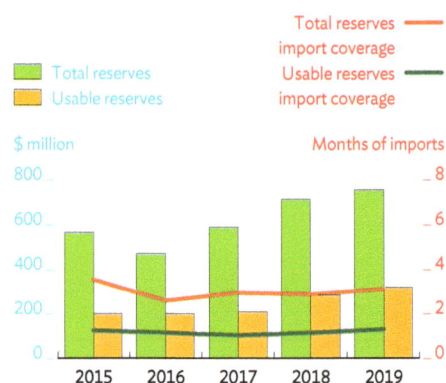

Source: Maldives Monetary Authority. 2020. Monthly Statistics. February. http://www.mma.gov.mv.

Box 3.18.1 Grant distribution under the eight amendments to the Decentralization Act

Starting in 2020, budget allocations will provide block grants from the central government for local governance, with 76% apportioned to island councils, 8% to atoll councils, and 16% to city councils. Distribution to the 200 councils will depend mainly on population and land area weighted as in the box table.

An equalization grant, also following the weights in the table, will be distributed to councils before the full grant transaction to ensure that all councils have sufficient funding to implement their programs.

With this change, an estimated Rf1.6 billion will be allocated to local councils as block grants in 2020. This change is expected to increase island council budgets by 165.8%, atoll council budgets by 38.5%, and city council budgets by 463.2% over 2019 budget allocations.

The 200 councils will be elected in 2020, comprising 4 city councils, 18 atoll councils, and 178 island councils.

Grant distribution

	Weights, %		
Variable	Island council	Atoll council	City council
Block grant	76	8	16
Population	75	60	65
Land area	10	5	15
Distance from capital of the administrative atoll	5	25	0
Distance from Malé	5	5	15
Council performance	5	5	5
Equalization grant	10	50	10

debt, provided it aligned with national fiscal policy (Box 3.18.1 and Figure 3.18.8). They transfer municipal functions to local councils that can more efficiently and effectively deliver services locally and give councils authority to manage human resources in council administration. Finally, they further increase women's participation in decision making by allocating a minimum quota of 33% of council seats to women.

Notwithstanding its good intent, a recent amendment to the act will not address all challenges to successful and efficient decentralization and may even pose additional hurdles in the absence of an enabling environment and necessary institutional support during implementation. The country's current fiscal and debt circumstances leave little fiscal space to fully allocate the envisaged resources to local councils. Worryingly, the power to borrow may further deepen national debt.

As experience in other countries has demonstrated, decentralization is not a simple or linear process. Sri Lanka's devolution entailed high administrative costs arising from complexity, duplication, conflict, and fragmentation. Decentralization in the Philippines was constrained by a lack of human, technical, and financial capacity in local governments.

Maldives would be well advised to adopt a gradual approach to decentralization, rather than devolving substantial functions all at once. The central government should start by devolving a small selection of services and functions to local governments while providing proper training to strengthen local council capacity. Then devolution can build on established success. As noted by a World Bank study, successful cases of decentralization in developing countries followed an incremental process in which policies and programs were carefully designed, organized, and carried out to build local institutional capacity.

Figure 3.18.8 Local council budget

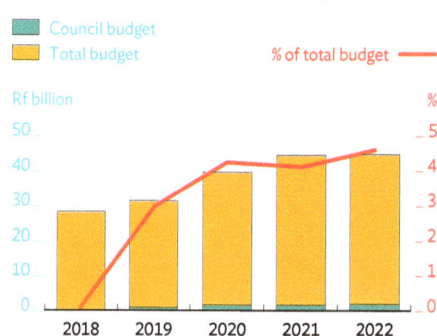

Source: Ministry of Finance. 2020. *Budget in Statistics 2020.*

Nepal

Growth accelerated in fiscal 2019 on a bumper harvest, buoyant tourism and remittances, and accelerated private investment. Inflation was moderate, and the large current account deficit narrowed. The outlook is for moderating growth under COVID-19, weaker tourism, and less buoyant remittances and agriculture. The current account deficit will narrow as stabilizing investment reduces imports. The authorities should strengthen the small export sector by facilitating the creation of well-considered special economic zones.

Economic performance

GDP growth accelerated to an estimated 7.1% in fiscal year 2019 (FY2019, ended 16 July 2019) from 6.7% a year earlier. Strong recovery in agriculture accounted for the bulk of the advance, but support came as well from stepped-up tourist arrivals and remittances and an uptick in private investment (Figure 3.19.1). Services, contributing slightly over half of GDP, saw growth rise to 7.3% on higher remittances, which supported retail trade, and on buoyant tourist arrivals, which favored hotels, restaurants, and other tourism services. Industry, providing 15.2% of GDP, saw growth broadly unchanged at 8.1%, sustained by strengthening in other sectors and a stable political environment.

On the demand side, accelerated consumption expenditure facilitated by remittance growth dominated spending in FY2019. Private investment, mostly in energy and services, grew by 27.0% to equal almost a third of GDP. Public investment increased by only 5.5%, however, following a 54.2% surge in FY2018, owing to construction delays affecting national pride projects.

Inflation edged up from 4.2% in FY2018 to 4.6% in FY2019 (Figure 3.19.2). Food inflation rose from 2.7% in FY2018 to average 3.1% as floods and landslides in early July created food price pressures, as did delayed food supply from India caused by strict tests for pesticide residues conducted at customs points along the border. Price pressures markedly escalated in the final months of the year as food inflation accelerated in India and further intensified in the first half of FY2020. Strong demand pushed inflation for other goods and services higher, from an average of 5.3% in FY2018 to 5.9%.

The fiscal deficit, having risen to the equivalent of 6.7% of GDP in FY2018, moderated to 5.1% in FY2019 as capital expenditure underperformed expectations (Figure 3.19.3).

This chapter was written by Manbar Singh Khadka and Neelina Nakarmi of the Nepal Resident Mission, ADB, Kathmandu.

Figure 3.19.1 Supply-side contributions to growth

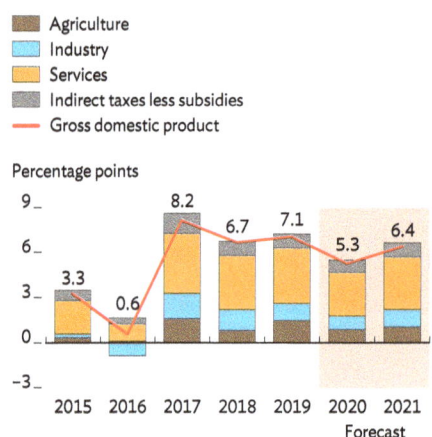

- Agriculture
- Industry
- Services
- Indirect taxes less subsidies
- Gross domestic product

Percentage points

Note: Years are fiscal years ending in mid-July of that year.
Sources: Central Bureau of Statistics. 2018. National Accounts of Nepal 2017/18. http://cbs.gov.np/; ADB estimates.

Figure 3.19.2 Monthly inflation

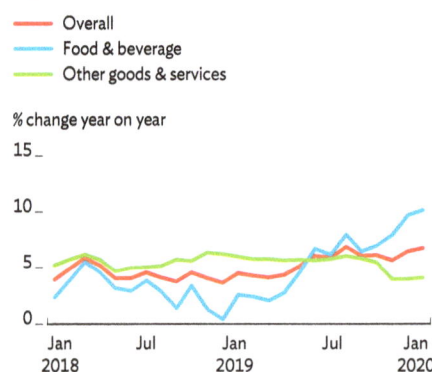

- Overall
- Food & beverage
- Other goods & services

% change year on year

Source: Nepal Rastra Bank. 2020. Recent Macroeconomic Situation. http://www.nrb.org.np.

A capital expenditure decline by 10.8% reflected long-standing challenges to project readiness, procurement processes, and project management. Revenue increased by 4.2% mainly on higher customs earnings from import growth and improvements in tax administration, notably advances in custom valuation procedures, the adoption of risk-based custom clearance, and the implementation of an e-payment system.

Growth in broad money (M2) supply moderated from 19.4% in FY2018 to 15.8% in FY2019, slowed by dwindling net foreign assets and only a modest rise in net domestic assets (Figure 3.19.4). Credit to the private sector decelerated from 22.3% growth in FY2018 to 19.1% a year later, suppressed by higher lending rates and intermittent liquidity crunches. A contributing cause of these liquidity crunches was increased domestic borrowing since FY2018 to enable fiscal transfers to newly created subnational governments. Nepal Rastra Bank, the central bank, sought to address liquidity shortages by lowering the cash reserve ratio for banks and financial institutions.

Export earnings exceeded expectations with a surge in exports of palm oil and jute. But with a low export base and rising imports of oil and other products, Nepal's large trade deficit was little changed from a year earlier, at the equivalent of 37.1% of GDP. Workers' remittances increased healthily by 7.8% as the Nepalese rupee depreciated against the US dollar and the authorities cracked down on informal means of remitting. Net invisible earnings increased slightly to equal 29.4% of GDP, narrowing the current account deficit slightly to 7.7% of GDP (Figure 3.19.5). The deficit was financed primarily by external borrowing but required a drawdown of foreign exchange reserves, shrinking them by 5.8% to $9.5 billion at the end of FY2019 but leaving import cover strong at 7.8 months (Figure 3.19.6).

Economic prospects

GDP growth is expected to moderate from 7.1% in FY2019 to 5.3% in FY2020 for several reasons, notably COVID-19. Growth prospects will be undermined by a nationwide lockdown imposed from 24 March to 7 April and its effects mainly on industry and services, as well as a potential fall in remittances. Lower agricultural output—in particular of rice, which supplies nearly 7% of GDP—will further dampen growth prospects. A late monsoon, flooding in some areas in early July, and pest infestation in others are the main causes. The global outbreak of COVID-19 has dampened services, constricting growth prospects.

Industrial output will slacken in response to reduced domestic demand further worsened by the COVID-19 pandemic. Both supply and demand of industrial output, except essential goods and services, substantially dropped during the lockdown.

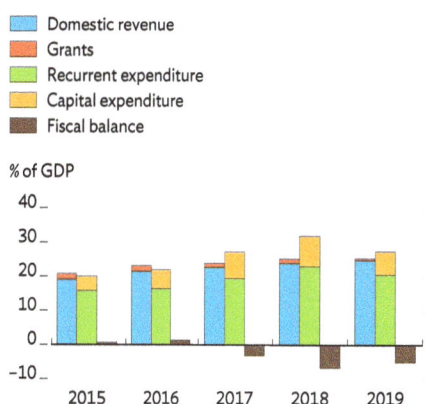

Figure 3.19.3 Fiscal indicators

Note: Years are fiscal years ending in mid-July of that year.
Source: Ministry of Finance. Budget Speech 2020.

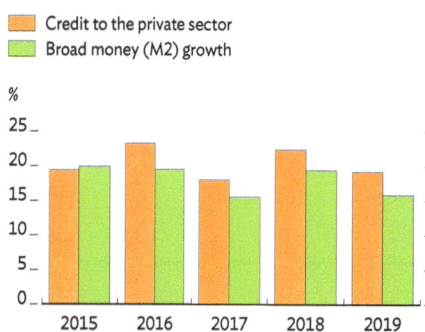

Figure 3.19.4 Monetary indicators

Note: Years are fiscal years ending in mid-July of that year.
Source: Nepal Rastra Bank. 2019. Recent Macroeconomic Situation. http://www.nrb.org.np.

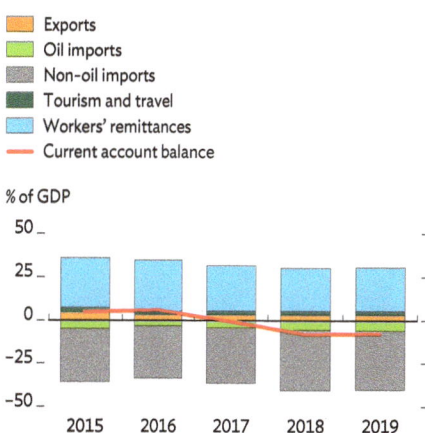

Figure 3.19.5 Current account indicators

Note: Years are fiscal years ending in mid-July of that year.
Source: Nepal Rastra Bank. 2019. Recent Macroeconomic Situation. http://www.nrb.org.np.

Major industries like cement, iron, steel, and bricks are operating below their full potential. Weaker demand is partly a matter of earthquake reconstruction winding down after 2 fiscal years of acceleration. Further, slack budget execution in the first 6 months of FY2020 has curbed demand, most notably for construction materials. Capital expenditure grew by 13.2% in FY2020 to mid-January, down from 14.7% a year earlier, while the execution of the annual capital budget fell to 15.2% from 17.2% (Figure 3.19.7). Limited disbursement of large allocations for national pride projects has deepened the slowdown.

Service growth will wane in FY2020 with a slowdown in tourist arrivals. The global outbreak of COVID-19 has markedly reduced tourist arrivals. January 2020 arrivals from all markets were 2.0% lower than a year earlier (Figure 3.19.8).

Private consumption growth will decelerate on diminishing remittance growth that fell to a mere 1.3% in the first half of FY2020 after rising by 17.6% in the year-earlier period (Figure 3.19.9). Remittance income will be lower in the fourth quarter of this fiscal year because of COVID-19, which will cause domestic spending, particularly on travel and recreation, to plunge this fiscal year. The extent of weakening will depend on the persistence of the pandemic. The decline could be greater if there is a wide and prolonged outbreak of the COVID-19. Budget execution on large infrastructure projects was sluggish in the first 6 months of FY2020, limiting growth in fixed investment. The midyear review of the FY2020 budget envisages a deficit equal to 6.5% of GDP, but it will likely be lower as capital expenditure is expected to continue to underperform allocation. Moreover, COVID-19 has affected the implementation of ongoing projects. The lockdown has worsened uncertainty with regard to project implementation.

The trade deficit reversed marked 19.2% expansion in the first half of FY2019 to narrow by 5.5% in the first half of FY2020. About two-thirds of the improvement reflected reduced imports, especially of vehicles and construction materials, and the balance a strong increase in exports, in particular a surge in palm oil shipments to India. The improved trade balance in the period combined with remittance growth, however tepid, shrank the current account deficit from $1.3 billion to $0.7 billion. Reflecting developments to date, the full-year current account deficit is forecast to narrow from the equivalent of 7.7% of GDP in FY2019 to 5.0%, mainly reflecting slowing import growth.

Inflation will accelerate from 4.6% in FY2019 to average 6.0% this year. Headline inflation averaged 6.4% in the first 6 months of FY2020, significantly higher than 4.2% a year earlier. Food inflation increased by 10.2% in the first half of FY2020 with big increases in prices for vegetables, spices, and alcoholic beverages. Food prices escalated owing to the late

Table 3.19.1 Selected economic indicators (%)

	2018	2019	2020	2021
GDP growth	6.7	7.1	5.3	6.4
Inflation	4.2	4.6	6.0	5.5
Current acct. bal. (share of GDP)	–8.2	–7.7	–5.0	–5.6

Sources: Central Bureau of Statistics. 2018. *National Accounts of Nepal 2017/18*; ADB estimates.

Figure 3.19.6 Gross international reserves

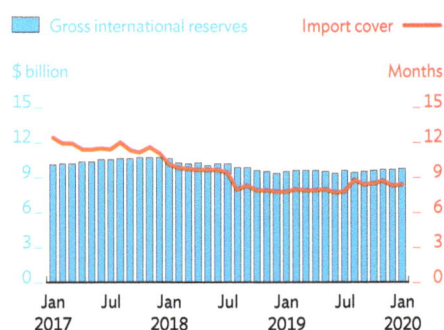

Source: Nepal Rastra Bank. 2020. Recent Macroeconomic Situation. http://www.nrb.org.np.

Figure 3.19.7 Midyear capital expenditure

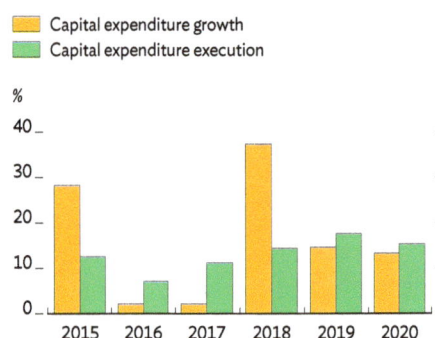

Note: Years are fiscal years ending in mid-July of that year.
Sources: Ministry of Finance. Budget speech various years; Financial Comptroller General Office.

monsoon, which depressed agricultural yields, and a ban on onion exports imposed by India, a major supplier.

The temporary closure of international borders over COVID-19 concerns has also nudged up food prices. Prices for other goods such as clothing and footwear, furnishings and household equipment, health-care and education services soared in the first half of FY2020. Rising inflationary pressure in neighboring India has a direct bearing on inflation in Nepal, as nearly two-thirds of its international trade is with India.

GDP growth at 6.4% is envisaged for FY2021, assuming a quick end to the COVID-19 pandemic, a rapid recovery from it, a normal monsoon, and success in ongoing efforts to improve the business climate. Two very large infrastructure projects— the 456-megawatt Upper Tamakoshi Hydroelectric Project and Gautam Buddha International Airport—will underpin investment, with both expected to begin operations by FY2021. Further growth stimulation is expected from higher spending by subnational governments.

Inflation is forecast to moderate to an average of 5.5% in FY2021, assuming a better harvest, subdued oil prices, and more moderate inflation in India. The current account deficit is expected to widen from the equivalent of 5.0% of GDP in FY2020 to 5.6% as imports of capital goods surge. However, the deficit will be largely contained by low oil prices, a gradual reduction in the quantity of fuel imports as hydroelectricity increasingly replaces internal combustion generators, and higher hydroelectricity exports to India.

Possible downside risks to the outlook are natural hazards like erratic monsoons and floods, which would depress farm output and damage infrastructure. Subnational spending may underperform for lack of capacity to utilize grants and execute projects in provincial and local governments. Exogenous shocks such as COVID-19 may weaken global demand more than expected and slash out-migration for employment, undermining the outlook for narrowing the current account deficit.

Policy challenge—operationalizing special economic zones

Special economic zones (SEZs) are delineated areas in a country that have distinct economic regulations and incentives that are more liberal or business friendly than those generally prevailing in the economy. SEZs are established to promote more rapid economic growth, in particularly by attracting foreign direct investment. Notably, about 70% of foreign greenfield investment in developing economies has been made in SEZs in recent years.

Well-functioning SEZs could play a key role in expanding exports, which currently finance only 8% of imports, thereby

Figure 3.19.8 Tourist arrivals

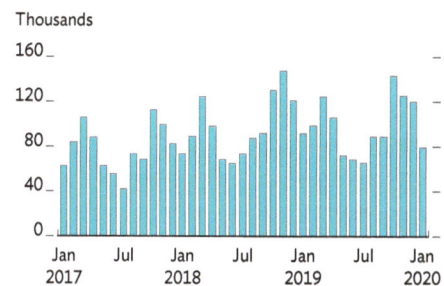

Source: Department of Immigration.

Figure 3.19.9 Migrant workers and remittances

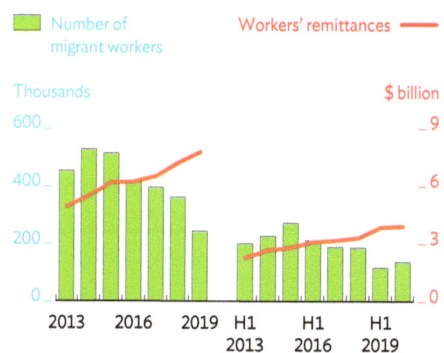

Note: Years are fiscal years ending in mid-July of that year.
Sources: Department of Foreign Employment; Nepal Rastra Bank.

reducing a large trade deficit and its risks to Nepal's external position as rapid growth in remittances fades. Export growth is hindered by the country's poor business climate, reflected in *Doing Business 2020* ranking Nepal at 94 out of 190 economies because of its lengthy processes for initiating a business, registering property, and paying taxes. Such hurdles have constrained foreign investment and deterred diversification, largely confining exports to primary products with little value added.

A well-considered SEZ can offer qualifying investors necessary infrastructure and associated services; an incentivized tax regime with varying exemptions from income tax, excise duty, and value-added tax; and quick one-stop services for investment approvals, customs clearances, immigration concerns, foreign workers' employment, banking, income repatriation, and other business requirements.

The government created in 2004 what is now called the Special Economic Zone Authority. The SEZ Act was promulgated in 2016, and SEZ regulations in 2017 (Box 3.19.1). The legislation was intended to give the Special Economic Zone Authority the means to induce greater investment by providing a favorable business environment and tax incentives. The authority currently operates the Bhairahawa SEZ near the border with India.

When the Bhairahawa SEZ was initiated in 2014, nearly two dozen firms applied to establish business operations in it. However, several later withdrew, and just three have begun production. The apparently unsuccessful takeoff of this initial SEZ is traceable to a dearth of services, notably a lack of one-stop services such as a customs desk, inadequate provision of dedicated electricity and water supplies, and muddled tax incentives. Various amenities such as banks, insurance companies, and a medical center are not yet established.

For industries within an SEZ to flourish and boost the economy, provisions envisaged under the SEZ Act must be effectively implemented. Apart from one-stop services that most importantly address administrative hurdles, the provision of serviced land, water and electricity supplies, and connectivity to major highways and border points is crucial to attracting investment in an SEZ. The experience at Bhairahawa indicates that higher priority needs to be placed on properly developing SEZs and ensuring that adequate capacity and resources are available to the SEZ Authority to execute its mandate effectively.

Strong coordination among stakeholders will be crucial for SEZs to succeed under Nepal's new federal system. Although SEZs are a central government responsibility, it would seem that provincial and local governments need to be consulted and brought on board for greater consensus and quick implementation. Effective mechanisms therefore need to be devised to generate this cooperation.

Box 3.19.1 Selected features of Special Economic Zone Act, 2016

Tax concessions:
  i. Industries within SEZs situated in high mountain and other government-designated mountain districts receive 100% exemption from income tax for the first 10 years of operations, reduced to 50% in following years.
  ii. Dividend tax is 100% exempted for the first 5 years, reduced to 50% for another 3 years.
  iii. Foreign investors are entitled to a 50% tax concession on income generated from service fees or royalties on the transfer and/or management of foreign technology in industries established within SEZs.

Export requirements:
  i. Industries in SEZs can sell their production in the domestic market during their first year but will not receive tax benefits on the goods and services sold domestically.
  ii. Industries are to export at least 60% of their goods or services from their second year of operation.

Establishment and operation of SEZs:
  i. With government approval, a private company may establish and manage an SEZ, including the development of necessary infrastructure.
  ii. SEZs can be created as public–private partnerships.

VAT exemption:
VAT will be zero-rated on exports of goods and services produced in SEZs and on raw materials sold to industries within SEZs. Exemptions will not be given if the export requirement is not met.

Income repatriation:
Foreign investors can repatriate the dividends generated from their investments and sell their interest in a SEZ business.

SEZ = special economic zone.
Source: SEZ Act, 2016 and the First Amendment to it.

Pakistan

Decisive policy helped narrow the current account deficit last year, but growth moderated and sharp currency depreciation caused inflation to accelerate. Growth is expected to be further constrained this year by ongoing stabilization efforts, slower growth in agriculture, and the impact of the COVID-19 outbreak, before recovering next year. The current account and fiscal deficits will narrow further, but inflation is expected to leap briefly into double digits. Expanding social protection is crucial for ensuring inclusive growth.

Economic performance

GDP growth dropped from 5.5% in fiscal year 2018 (FY2018, ended 30 June 2018) to 3.3% in FY2019, the lowest rate in 8 years. The slowdown reflected macroeconomic imbalances and faltering investment. Policy measures geared toward fiscal consolidation and monetary tightening were implemented as prior actions agreed with the International Monetary Fund (IMF) under an Extended Fund Facility arrangement approved in July 2019. Slower growth spanned all sectors. Growth in livestock, which contributes almost two-thirds of agricultural output, accelerated slightly to 4.0% in FY2019, but agricultural production as a whole expanded by only 0.8%, owing to high input costs and water shortages. The sector's contribution to GDP growth dropped from 0.7 percentage points in FY2018 to only 0.2 points in FY2019.

Growth in industry fell markedly from 4.9% in FY2018 to 1.4% in FY2019, sharply lowering its contribution to growth to 2.8 percentage points. Large-scale manufacturing output fell by 2.1% in FY2019, the first decline in a decade, because demand weakened and construction slumped as public development spending plummeted. Electricity production, by contrast, surged by 40.5% as new generation projects were completed and came online. The slowdown in agriculture and manufacturing, exacerbated by weaker demand and higher costs, caused growth in service output to slow from 6.2% in FY2018 to 4.7% in FY2019, lowering the sector's contribution to GDP growth from 3.8 percentage points in FY2018 to 2.8 points (Figure 3.20.1).

On the demand side, private consumption, which accounts for 81.8% of GDP, grew more slowly in FY2019 as subdued output growth translated to lower incomes. The contribution of total consumption to GDP growth thus fell from 6.1 percentage points in FY2018 to 4.1 points in FY2019.

Figure 3.20.1 Supply-side contributions to growth

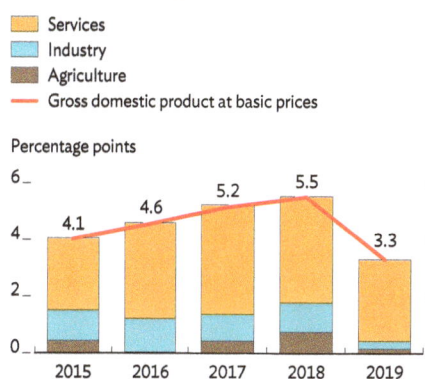

Note: Years are fiscal years ending on 30 June of that year.
Source: Ministry of Finance. Pakistan Economic Survey 2018–19. http://www.finance.gov.pk.

This chapter was written by Khadija Ali and Kiyoshi Taniguchi of the Pakistan Resident Mission, ADB, Islamabad, and Cara Tinio of the Pacific Department, ADB, Manila.

Investment contracted, shaving 0.9 points from growth, as uncertainty caused by a delay in the government's decision to seek support from the IMF lowered private investment, and public investment began to taper as infrastructure projects were completed. The contribution of net exports, which subtracted 2.3 percentage points from growth in FY2018, recovered to a 0.1 point contribution in FY2019 (Figure 3.20.2).

Inflation accelerated from 4.7% in FY2018 to 6.8% in FY2019 on poor harvests, tariff increases, and Pakistan rupee depreciation against the US dollar by 24.0% following the adoption of a more flexible exchange rate. Food price inflation rose to 4.6%, while inflation for other goods accelerated to 9.2% as tariffs on energy products were raised to manage mounting fiscal pressures. Inflation was estimated using rebased prices from FY2016 (Figure 3.20.3).

To counter inflation, the State Bank of Pakistan, the central bank, raised its policy interest rate by a cumulative 575 basis points to 12.25% at the end of FY2019 (Figure 3.20.4). Private sector credit remained stable during the fiscal year at the equivalent of 17.3% of GDP, while government borrowing from commercial banks continued to decline and be replaced mainly by external borrowing (Figure 3.20.5). Growth in broad money increased from 9.7% in FY2018 to 11.3% in FY2019.

The consolidated federal and provincial budget deficit rose sharply from the equivalent of 6.5% of GDP in FY2018 to 8.9% in FY2019, mainly as revenue collection faltered. Revenue subsided from 15.1% of GDP in FY2018 to 12.7% in FY2019 as tax receipts, which provide over 90% of revenue, declined to the equivalent of 11.6% of GDP because of economic deceleration, tax concessions on personal income, and the suspension of sales and withholding taxes on petroleum products and mobile phone loads. Nontax revenues were halved to 1.1% of GDP in FY2019 as central bank profits fell. Public spending remained stable at the equivalent of 21.6% of GDP in FY2019 despite a rise in current expenditures to 18.4% of GDP as tighter monetary policy pushed up interest payments. Federal and provincial development spending was curtailed to offset this increase (Figure 3.20.6).

Gross public debt climbed to equal 84.8% of GDP in FY2019, still well above the 60.0% threshold mandated under the Fiscal Responsibility and Debt Limitation Act. Less than half of the increase was traceable to the high fiscal deficit. Borrowing increased during the fiscal year mainly in response to the steep currency depreciation, bilateral and multilateral inflows to finance the deficit in the balance of payments, and planned borrowing from the central bank above budgetary requirements to provide some fiscal space for FY2020.

Pakistan's current account deficit narrowed from 6.3% of GDP in FY2018 to 4.9% in FY2019 as remittances rose by 9.7%, and the trade balance improved (Figure 3.20.7).

Figure 3.20.2 Demand-side contributions to growth

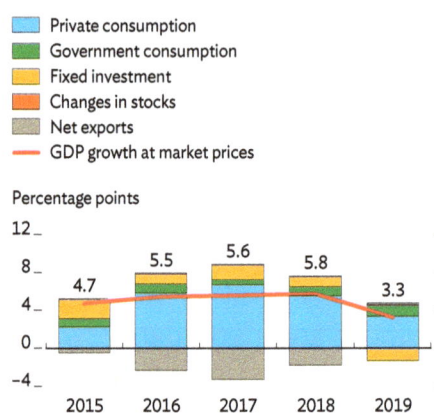

Note: Years are fiscal years ending on 30 June of that year.
Source: Ministry of Finance. Pakistan Economic Survey 2018–19. http://www.finance.gov.pk.

Figure 3.20.3 Inflation

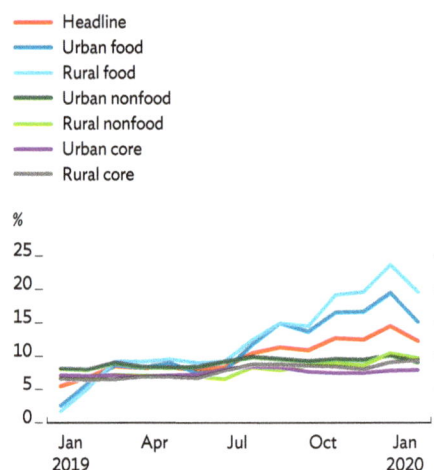

Notes: Core inflation excludes food and energy. The base year is FY2016.
Source: State Bank of Pakistan. Economic Data. http://www.sbp.org.pk (accessed 13 March 2020).

Figure 3.20.4 Interest rates

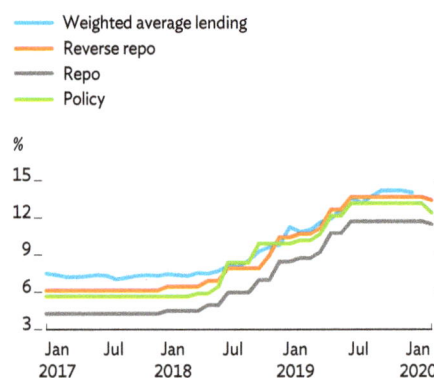

Sources: State Bank of Pakistan. Economic Data. http://www.sbp.org.pk (accessed 13 March 2020); Monetary Policy Information Compendium Mar 2020.

Merchandise imports declined by 6.8% as local currency depreciation and the imposition of regulatory duties depressed demand, but also because of lower international oil prices. Despite currency depreciation, merchandise exports also declined by 2.1% as softening international prices forced down the prices fetched by key textile products (Figure 3.20.8).

The investment needs of some energy projects under the China–Pakistan Economic Corridor eased as they neared completion, which lowered financial inflow in FY2019. Foreign direct investment (FDI) plunged by 52.0% to $1.7 billion. Portfolio investment recorded net outflow of $1.4 billion as the government retired a $1.0 billion eurobond, and private investors exited the equity market in anticipation of substantial currency depreciation and monetary tightening. Gross foreign exchange reserves fell by $2.5 billion to reach $7.3 billion at the end of FY2019, enough to cover a scant 1.5 months of imports (Figure 3.20.9). With FDI subdued in FY2019, Pakistan managed to finance its current account deficit and meet debt repayment obligations only with the help of higher official inflows from multilateral and bilateral partners, including one-off payments from the People's Republic of China, Saudi Arabia, and the United Arab Emirates.

Economic prospects

GDP growth is forecast to decelerate to 2.6% in FY2020 as ongoing stabilization efforts further curtail economic activity. Agriculture is expected to see slow growth as the worst locust infestation in over 2 decades damages harvests of cotton, wheat, and other major crops. The government has declared a national emergency to combat the infestation. Modest growth is expected in some export-oriented industries such as textiles and leather. However, large-scale manufacturing, which provides over half of industrial production, will likely contract, as it did in the first half of FY2020 when currency depreciation ran up production costs for some industries and forced them to raise their prices. The ongoing COVID-19 outbreak will pose a downside risk to growth prospects as it further dampens consumer demand and as private businesses are temporarily shut down in efforts to control the pandemic.

Growth is expected to accelerate to 3.2% in FY2021, driven by a rebound in investment as macroeconomic imbalances are corrected, currency depreciation is contained, and the locust infestation subsides. Investment may also receive a boost from the implementation of critical structural reform to improve energy production and distribution and the business climate overall, as well as Moody's recent upgrade of Pakistan's credit rating outlook from *negative* to *stable*—all of which should enhance investor confidence.

Figure 3.20.5 Government budget indicators

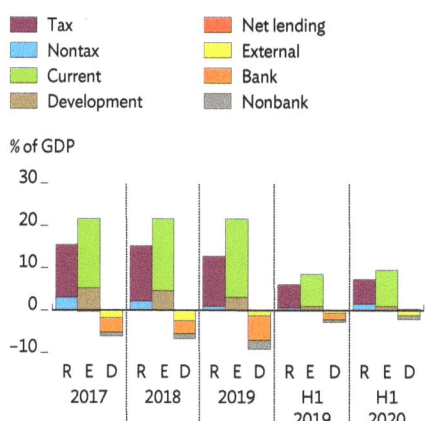

Legend: Tax, Nontax, Current, Development, Net lending, External, Bank, Nonbank

% of GDP

D = deficit financing, E = expenditure, H = half, R = revenue.
Note: Years are fiscal years ending on 30 June of that year.
Source: Ministry of Finance. *Pakistan Summary of Consolidated Federal & Provincial Budgetary Operations, Jul–Dec 2020.*

Figure 3.20.6 Government domestic and external debt

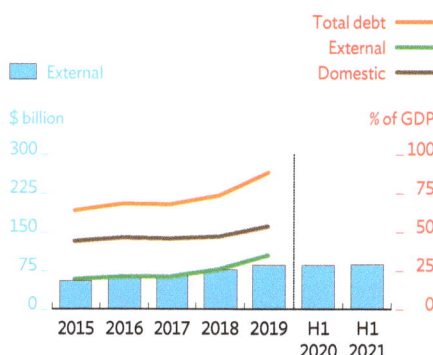

Total debt, External, Domestic, External

$ billion   % of GDP

H1 = first half.
Note: Years are fiscal years ending on 30 June of that year. External debt includes government and other external liabilities and public corporations.
Source: State Bank of Pakistan. *Economic Data.* http://www.sbp.org.pk (accessed 13 March 2020).

Figure 3.20.7 Remittances

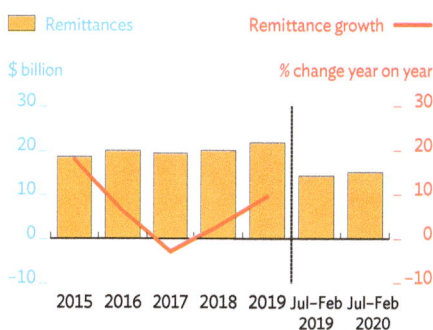

Remittances, Remittance growth

$ billion   % change year on year

Note: Years are fiscal years ending on 30 June of that year.
Source: State Bank of Pakistan. *Economic Data.* http://www.sbp.org.pk (accessed 13 March 2020).

Inflation is projected to accelerate to 11.5% in FY2020, reflecting a sharp rise in food prices in the first part of the fiscal year and a 9.8% drop in the value of the local currency against the US dollar in the first 7 months of FY2020. A new price series that tracks price movements in rural as well as urban markets showed rural food inflation averaging 16.3% in the first 7 months of FY2020, while urban food inflation stood at 14.5%. However, high food inflation is expected to be mostly transitory, likely to dissipate as food supplies improve in the second half of the fiscal year. Further, a drop in international oil prices forecast in the second half of FY2020 should translate to lower production and transport costs for goods and services, which could be passed on to consumers.

After raising the policy rate to 13.25% at the beginning of FY2020, the central bank reduced it in 2 steps to 11.00% in March 2020 following the decline in global oil prices and sluggish demand under COVID-19. Growth in private sector credit has slowed considerably. Inflation is forecast to decelerate to 8.3% in FY2021 with the central bank expected to take further policy action to both manage inflation and boost economic activity.

The fiscal deficit is expected to narrow to 8.0% of GDP in FY2020 as the government continues to prioritize consolidation. In the first half of FY2020, the deficit fell as revenue collection rebounded from the equivalent of 6.1% of GDP a year earlier to 7.3%. A fall in import duties caused by import contraction was compensated by the reinstatement of levies on petroleum products and telecommunication services, the elimination of exemptions for export-oriented industries, and higher profit transfers from the central bank and the Pakistan Telecommunication Authority. On the expenditure side, spending increased from 8.7% of GDP in the first half of FY2019 to 9.6% on higher interest payments and public development programs to protect public investments and support business activity, particularly activity connected with construction. Further, health care and other social expenditure is expected to be significantly higher as the government addresses COVID-19. The decline in the oil price may adversely affect government revenues through reduced petroleum tax receipts.

To finance the fiscal deficit, the government restructured its short-term borrowing from the central bank into long-term securities in a bid to increase the average maturity of domestic debt and reduce its interest rate. Improving the primary budget balance as planned will reduce public debt ratios, moving the economy closer to debt sustainability as GDP growth recovers somewhat in FY2021 and further in subsequent years.

The current account deficit is expected to continue narrowing to the equivalent of 2.8% of GDP in FY2020 with a reduction in the trade deficit resulting from currency

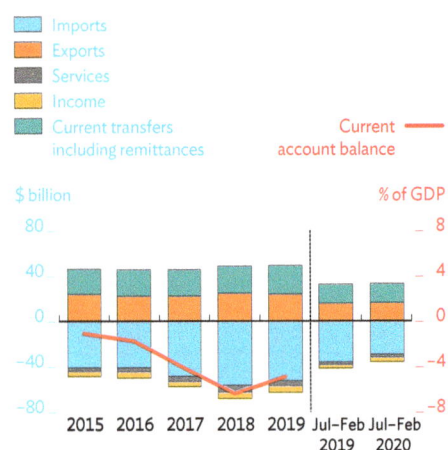

Figure 3.20.8 Current account components

Note: Years are fiscal years ending on 30 June of that year.
Source: State Bank of Pakistan. *Economic Data.*
http://www.sbp.org.pk (accessed 13 March 2020).

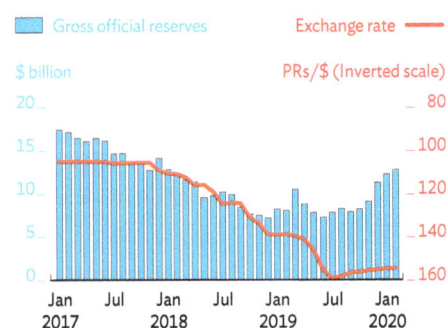

Figure 3.20.9 Gross official reserves and exchange rate

Source: State Bank of Pakistan. *Economic Data.*
http://www.sbp.org.pk (accessed 6 March 2020).

depreciation, the imposition of regulatory duties to contain import demand, and continued recovery in workers' remittances following declines in FY2016–FY2018. In the first half of FY2020, the current account deficit narrowed sharply from 5.8% of GDP a year earlier to 1.5%. Modest growth in the key exports textiles, rice, and leather was supported by loans under a central bank export finance scheme and a long-term financing facility for exporters. This was complemented by a notable reduction in imports restrained by higher import duties. Weaker demand under COVID-19 could adversely affect exports, but, on balance, exports should strengthen thanks to policy stability, improvement in the ease of doing business, and lagged effects from currency depreciation. Thanks primarily to the lower oil price, the current account deficit is projected to narrow further to equal 2.4% of GDP in FY2021.

FDI inflow soared by 62.5% year on year in the first half of FY2020. Short-term capital has also poured in rapidly to buy government securities denominated in Pakistan rupees that offer attractive returns. Supported by these flows, international reserves are expected to improve to 2.2 months of import coverage at the end of FY2020.

Policy challenge—expanding social protection for inclusive growth

The ongoing COVID-19 pandemic underscores the importance of strengthening social protection in Pakistan, especially as spending on social development has not kept up with the growing need. The *Human Development Report 2019* ranked Pakistan at 152 among 189 economies. Health outcomes remain poor, featuring one of the highest maternal mortality ratios in the region and the third-highest child stunting rate in the world. An estimated 23 million children are out of school. While the portion of the population living below the national poverty line declined significantly from 64.0% in 2001 to 24.3% in 2016, the share of rural residents in poverty is consistently more than double that of urban residents. Gender inequality continues to be pervasive, with women facing poor economic opportunity and restricted mostly to informal work. Limited employment opportunities and high out-of-pocket health care expenditure routinely lock people in poverty and all too often inflict economic shocks that drag them down into it.

A main factor behind poverty and continued gender inequality is insufficient investment in human capital, especially for women, which is further exacerbated by rapid population growth. Over 63% of the population is under the age of 30, and gaps in education and technical and vocational skills mean that significant efforts are needed to absorb the sizable incoming labor force effectively. Against a backdrop of slow growth,

Table 3.20.1 Selected economic indicators (%)

	2018	2019	2020	2021
GDP growth	5.5	3.3	2.6	3.2
Inflation	4.7	6.8	11.5	8.3
Current acct. bal. (share of GDP)	-6.3	-4.9	-2.8	-2.4

Sources: Ministry of Finance. Pakistan Economic Survey 2018–19. http://www.finance.gov.pk; ADB estimates.

fiscal consolidation, and monetary tightening, a comprehensive social protection strategy is crucial to promote inclusive growth and protect the most vulnerable.

In 2019, the government launched Ehsaas, a comprehensive program for social protection and poverty alleviation that, among other things, extends the social safety net program called the Benazir Income Support Program (BISP). Since its inception in 2008, BISP has disbursed $3.6 billion through unconditional cash transfers to over 5.6 million beneficiary families, reaching about 17% of the population. Exclusively targeting poor female beneficiaries, the program provides a financial cushion to enable increased household consumption, improve nutrition, and promote women's economic and political empowerment. Its conditional cash transfer component, Waseela-e-Taleem, provides financial support as well to the children of BISP beneficiaries who are enrolled and receiving a primary education.

The government has demonstrated a steady commitment to social protection, including under the IMF Extended Fund Facility arrangement, which calls for expanding social spending to help protect the most vulnerable. The allocated budget for BISP has risen from PRs102 billion in FY2016 to PRs180 billion in FY2020 and has attracted additional support from international partners. Government pro-poor spending, including on social protection, was estimated to equal 9.2% of GDP in FY2018, but spending on education was only 2.4%, and health expenditure fell short of 1.0%. While budget allocations for social protection and pro-poor programs are growing, a continuing concern is the scale of need highlighted above. Higher spending on social protection, including the Ehsaas program, will be crucial in response to COVID-19 and the serious implications it may have on poor and vulnerable segments of the population.

The implementation of social protection programs should focus on the quality of delivery, factoring a large informal labor market, high rates of transient and vulnerable poverty, and the need to target beneficiaries appropriately. Technological innovations—such as a comprehensive, regularly updated national socioeconomic registry, biometric identification systems to improve targeting, and digital payment mechanisms to facilitate transfers—will help overcome implementation challenges as social protection under Ehsaas is scaled up. Independent evaluation will be key to assessing Ehsaas program effectiveness over time and help policy makers formulate appropriate and timely action plans to improve beneficiary targeting and coordinate federal and provincial efforts.

The government will need to remain committed to ensuring the sustainability of Ehsaas even as it strives to manage the consequences of COVID-19, stabilize Pakistan's macroeconomic situation, and implement the structural reform essential to laying a foundation for inclusive growth.

Table 3.20.2 Ehsaas policy

The objective is to reduce inequality, invest in people, and lift lagging districts.

Pillar I Addressing elite capture and making the government system work for equality

- Institutional reform
- Institutional strengthening
- Improved performance
- Increased transparency and accountability

Pillar II Safety nets

- National socioeconomic registry
- Kifalat
- Tahafuz
- Housing for the poor
- Protection against catastrophic health expenditure
- Welfare programs for the disabled
- Welfare of the elderly poor
- Labor welfare
- Welfare of workers abroad

Pillar III Human capital development

- Malnutrition
- Pro-poor education initiatives
- Health

Pillar IV Jobs and livelihoods

- Innovation challenge, prize funding, and venture capital
- Information technology
- Technical and vocational education and training
- Manpower exports
- Poor farmers
- Poor women

Source: Government of Pakistan.

Sri Lanka

The economy faced two major adverse shocks in less than 12 months—terror attacks in April 2019 and the global spread of COVID-19 from January 2020. Despite earlier signs of revival, the domestic outbreak of COVID-19 in March will markedly curtail economic activity, dimming growth in 2020 while adding to downside risks. However, a broad range of quickly adopted government policy actions should sustain households, businesses, and the economy at large. Greater participation in global value chains could lift and broaden manufacturing.

Economic performance

GDP growth slowed from 3.2% in 2018 to an estimated 2.6% in 2019 (Figure 3.21.1). Following the resolution of a political impasse in the fourth quarter of 2018, growth rebounded in the first quarter of 2019 but slowed in the following quarters after coordinated terror attacks on Easter Sunday disrupted economic activity. Other contributing factors were subdued growth in agriculture in the second half of the year and uncertainty over the outcome of presidential elections in November. Tourist arrivals declined year on year each month from April to December 2019, adding up to an 18.0% decline in the whole year (Figure 3.21.2). Government promotional campaigns and deep discounting sped recovery in arrivals faster than earlier expected. Just as the tourist arrivals were returning to normal, the global spread of COVID-19 has once again buffeted arrivals, driving them down by a cumulative 12.2% in the first 2 months of 2020.

Agriculture saw growth fall from 4.0% in 2018 to 1.7% in 2019 largely because of excessive rain in the latter part of the year. Industry expanded by 2.6% in 2019 as construction recovered to grow by 3.7% after contracting in 2018, but manufacturing growth slowed to 1.5% as consumer demand weakened. Services grew at a lower rate of 2.9%, with growth sluggish in wholesale and retail trade and transportation, and accommodation and food and beverage services contracting by 4.2% as tourist arrivals plummeted after the Easter Sunday terror attacks. Financial services showed robust growth at 7.8% in 2019 but slowed from 11.8% in 2018 as nonperforming loans proliferated, credit growth weakened, and taxes and capital requirements rose.

Figure 3.21.1 GDP growth by sector

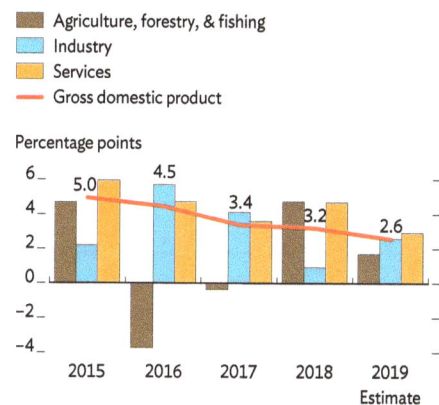

Sources: Department of Census and Statistics of Sri Lanka. http://www.statistics.gov.lk/ (accessed 15 March 2020); ADB estimates.

Figure 3.21.2 Tourism indicators

Source: Sri Lanka Tourist Development Authority. https://www.sltda.gov.lk/index.html (accessed 15 March 2020).

This chapter was written by Eshini Ekanayake and Hasitha Nimali Wickremasinghe of the Sri Lanka Resident Mission, ADB, Colombo.

On the demand side, net exports made the largest contribution to GDP growth, reflecting a significant fall in imports (Figure 3.21.3). Having contracted in 2017 and 2018, consumption expenditure returned to marginal growth at 2.1% as government consumption recovered. Gross fixed capital investment contracted again by 3.0%, even as construction revived moderately.

Inflation as measured by the Colombo consumer price index averaged 4.3% in 2019 (Figure 3.21.4). While food prices were lower than a year earlier for much of 2019, higher administered prices for fuel and transport, and pass-through from currency depreciation in 2018, pushed nonfood inflation higher to an average of 5.9%. This eased in the latter half of 2019 as fuel and cooking gas prices declined. Though food inflation averaged only 0.8%—partly owing to a base effect but also thanks to better supplies of key crops—supply shortages in the latter part of the year caused an uptick that carried into 2020. Core inflation rose from an average of 3.5% in 2018 to 5.5% but moderated to 4.8% at the end of 2019 as nonfood inflation eased. Inflation measured by the national consumer price index averaged 3.5%, slightly less than the Colombo index.

With economic activity subdued, growth in private sector credit weak, and inflation moderate because of high real interest rates, the Central Bank of Sri Lanka eased monetary policy in 2019 (Figure 3.21.5). From the end of 2018 to the end of January 2020, it cut the statutory reserve ratio by 100 basis points to 5.0% and the standing deposit facility rate and standing lending facility rate by 150 basis points each to 6.5% and 7.5%, respectively. Bank lending rates were unresponsive in the first half of the year, prompting the central bank to impose a cap on deposit rates. This was later replaced by a cap on lending rates as the lower cost of funds had not been passed on to borrowers. Most market interest rates finally fell in the second half of 2019, and the weighted average prime lending rate was 194 basis points lower at the end of 2019 than a year earlier (Figure 3.21.6).

The budget deficit for 2019 equaled 6.5% of GDP, up from 5.3% in 2018, and the primary balance was a 0.7% deficit after surpluses in 2017 and 2018 (Figure 3.21.7). The revenue ratio fell from 13.4% of GDP in 2018 to 12.2% as indirect tax collection in particular suffered from weak excise and VAT collection because of a large decline in imports and subdued economic activity after the terror attacks. Direct tax revenue, however, improved significantly from 2.1% of GDP in 2018 to 2.7% in 2019. In November, the new government announced tax relief measures, lowering the VAT rate from 15% to 8%, abolishing the economic service charge of 0.5% and the nation-building tax of 2%, and retracting some direct taxes introduced by the Inland Revenue Act. These declines were partly offset

Figure 3.21.3 GDP growth by demand components

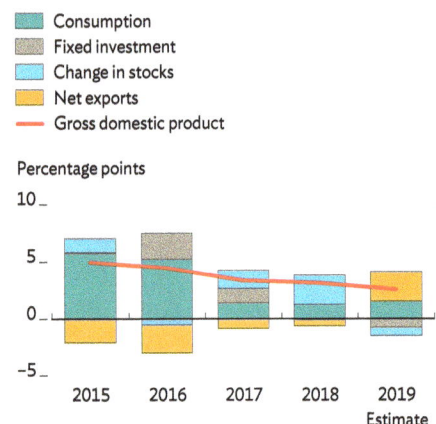

Sources: Department of Census and Statistics of Sri Lanka. http://www.statistics.gov.lk/ (accessed 15 March 2020); ADB estimates.

Figure 3.21.4 Inflation

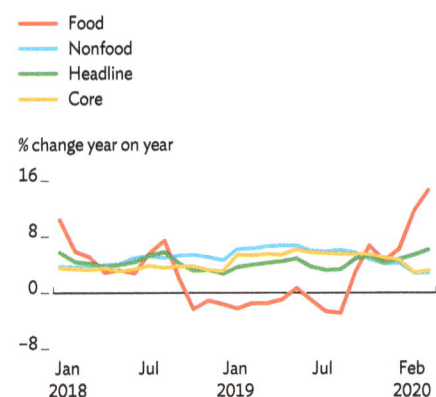

Source: Department of Census and Statistics of Sri Lanka. http://www.statistics.gov.lk/ (accessed 15 March 2020).

Figure 3.21.5 Policy rates

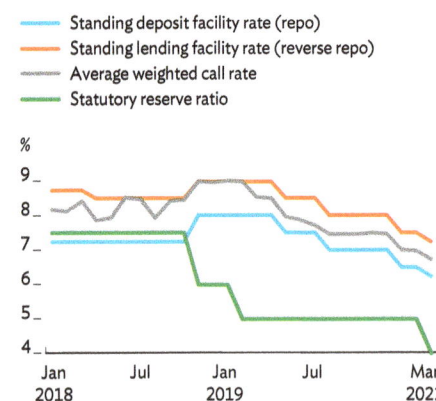

Source: Central Bank of Sri Lanka. https://www.cbsl.gov.lk/en (accessed 20 March 2020).

by increases in a number of excise taxes and levies on imports. The expenditure ratio increased marginally from 18.6% of GDP in 2018 to 18.7% on higher recurrent expenditure for salaries and pensions, while public investment fell further from 4.3% of GDP in 2018 to 4.1% in 2019. In sum, the ratio of central government debt to GDP increased from 82.9% at the end of 2018 to 83.7% a year later (Figure 3.21.8).

The current account deficit narrowed from 3.2% of GDP in 2018 to 2.1% as imports contracted by 10.3%, slicing the trade deficit by 22.7% (Figure 3.21.9). The drop in imports reflected weak domestic demand, substantial currency depreciation in 2018, and measures introduced in 2018 to curtail nonessential imports, though they were withdrawn in March 2019 (Figure 3.21.10). Weak imports helped offset an 18% decline in tourism receipts after the terror attacks. Worker remittances fell by 4.2% in 2019, reflecting a structural decline as the composition of migrants changed in recent years. Exports grew by only 0.4% as a strong 5.2% increase in garment exports more than compensated for declines in petroleum products and agricultural exports, the latter accounting for a fifth of the total.

The Sri Lanka rupee depreciated against the US dollar by an average of 10%, from SLRs162.5 in 2018 to SLRs178.8 in 2019, but by year-end rates it appreciated by a marginal 0.6%, from SLRs182.8 to SLRs181.6 (Figure 3.21.11). Subdued imports and the proceeds from $4.4 billion in sovereign bond issues in March and June lifted reserves to $7.5 billion at the end of 2019 despite sizeable debt repayment (Figure 3.21.12).

Economic prospects

Sri Lanka's prospects for recovery from 2 years of declining growth held promise at the open of 2020. Indeed, a key forward-looking indicator, the service purchasing managers' index, reached a 24-month high of 60.2 in December 2019 (Figure 3.21.13). However, it fell sharply to 50.2 in February 2020 as it became increasingly evident that COVID-19 would lower global growth and disrupt supply chains, tourism, and transport. With the March outbreak of COVID-19 in Sri Lanka, the *ADO 2020* growth projection of 2.2% has taken on significant downside risks—emanating from the severity and the duration of domestic infection as well as apparently intensifying economic impact from the pandemic—which could lower growth by another 1.0–1.5 percentage points. GDP growth is expected to recover to 3.5% in 2021. If the pandemic is contained by mid-2020, recovery could begin in the latter part of 2020 and into 2021, driven by the release of pent-up demand.

The disruption caused by COVID-19 and the necessary containment measures to limit the spread of the disease will stunt economic activity and lower consumer and business

Figure 3.21.6 Commercial bank rates, and private sector credit growth

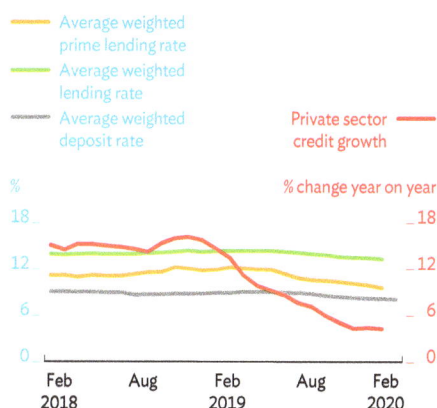

Source: Central Bank of Sri Lanka. https://www.cbsl.gov.lk/en (accessed 15 March 2020).

Figure 3.21.7 Central government finance

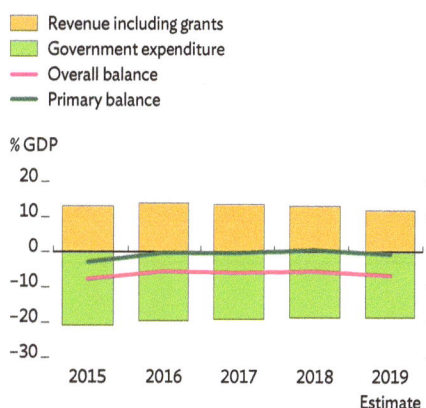

Note: Figures exclude revenue and expenditure transfers to provincial councils.

Sources: Central Bank Annual report various years; Ministry of Finance, Economy and Policy Development estimate.

Figure 3.21.8 Government debt

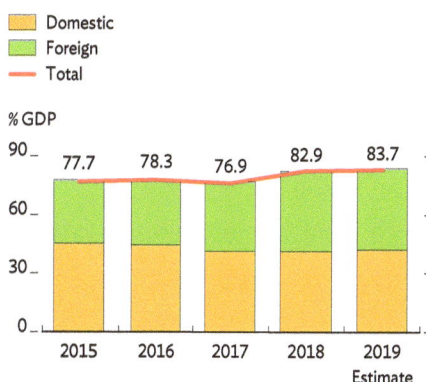

Sources: Central Bank Annual report various years; Ministry of Finance, Economy and Policy Development estimate.

confidence, limiting household income and consumption and private sector business sales and investment through most of 2020. Moreover, remittances will moderate as the global economy slows and oil prices fall because about half of remittances originate in the Middle East.

After a sustained period of stressed cash flow for firms, private investment will likely be weaker than expected. Public investment is also uncertain because a full budget for 2020 will be passed only after parliamentary elections. With limited fiscal space, pressure to meet higher health-care expenditure and income support measures is likely to constrain investment spending.

The government has acted to contain the spread of COVID-19 and provided economic support to individuals and business adversely affected by containment measures. On 16 March, at an emergency meeting, the central bank cut the statutory reserve ratio by 100 basis points and cut both the standing lending facility rate and the standing deposit facility rate by 25 basis points, adding to the 50 basis points reduction in policy rates made in January. Financial support measures include granting a 6-month moratorium on debt servicing for firms in the tourist and apparel industries and for all small and medium-sized enterprises, calling for new working capital loans at 4% interest, postponing repayment on small personal loans for 3 months, providing SLRs10,000 in interest-free loans and weekly food assistance for beneficiaries of the poverty-alleviation program Samurdhi, extending the deadline for tax payments and utility bills, and other interventions to support specific groups that are at financial risk.

Inflation is expected to trend higher to average 5.0% in 2020 and fall marginally lower to 4.8% in 2021. Higher food prices owing to a low base, tighter supply conditions, and supply-chain disruptions will drive inflation. The pass-through of lower indirect taxes announced in November 2019, weak demand, and much lower global fuel prices will provide some offset to price pressures in 2020.

Although Sri Lanka has good public health infrastructure, greater support required for public health services and financial support for households and businesses add significant new spending pressures in 2020. The budget deficit will be higher than the 7.9% of GDP estimated by the International Monetary Fund in February 2020, before the spread of COVID-19 into Sri Lanka. That estimate reflected a fall in tax revenue from tax cuts, hikes to some excise rates and levies, and increases in expenditure to cover arrears accrued in 2019. With higher required spending and tighter global liquidity, more deficit financing from the domestic market is expected.

Larger fiscal deficits will push the central government domestic and external debt ratios even higher. Sri Lanka's external debt repayment obligations are already substantial,

Figure 3.21.9 Current account components

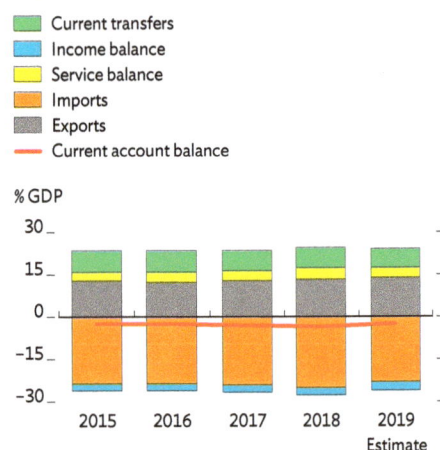

Sources: Central Bank of Sri Lanka. https://www.cbsl.gov.lk/en (accessed 20 March 2020); ADB estimate.

Figure 3.21.10 Trade indicators

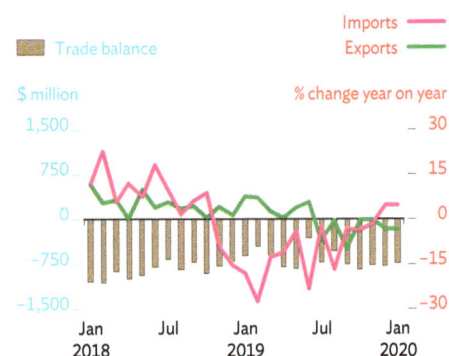

Source: Central Bank of Sri Lanka. https://www.cbsl.gov.lk/en (accessed 20 March 2020).

Figure 3.21.11 Exchange rates

Source: Central Bank of Sri Lanka. https://www.cbsl.gov.lk/en (accessed 20 March 2020).

estimated at $17.0 billion from 2020 to 2023, with the next eurobond maturity of $1 billion scheduled for September 2020. Moreover, the country's refinancing risk and borrowing cost will likely increase with the downgrading of its outlook to *negative* by two rating agencies and with investor retreat to safe havens in times of crisis.

The current account deficit is expected to widen to 2.8% of GDP in 2020 and then fall to 2.6% in 2021 on forecasted improvement in exports, tourist earnings, and remittances. Export revenues will weaken in 2020 on reduced sales—especially to Europe and the US, key markets for garments and rubber products—as well as to Iran, which buys 10% of tea exports. Service exports, including tourist and information technology earnings, will also weaken in 2020, as will remittances on a reduction in migrant worker departures. However, the negative impact of these developments will be partly offset by lower imports as global oil prices and energy demand ebb, subdued domestic demand, and restrictions imposed for 3 months in March by the central bank on imports of vehicles and nonessential consumer items.

Prospects for a more substantial pickup in growth have been diminished by the global spread of COVID-19 and its outbreak in Sri Lanka, which underlines preexisting downside risks for the economy. Clearly a recovery in tourism is delayed, and restrictions on normal economic activity will entail financial pressures on many firms and individuals, as experienced in countries with extended lockdowns.

Policy challenge—boosting participation in global value chains

Manufacturing has become increasingly fragmented across borders with improvements in global connectivity and widening opportunities to benefit from wage differentials across countries. Stages of production now take place across several countries in what are known as global value chains (GVCs), which expanded significantly from the 1990s to 2007 but slowed following the global financial crisis of 2008–2009. Fragmented, cross-border production remains significant, and participation in GVCs encourages technology transfer, creates better jobs, and provides access to wider markets.

As standard trade statistics do not adequately track how much value each economy in a GVC adds to a product, new methodologies have been developed to measure contributions. These new frameworks are used to divide gross exports into foreign and domestic value added and "pure double-counted" terms, which refers to value added to a good that cross a border between two countries more than once in a GVC.

Figure 3.21.12 Gross official reserves

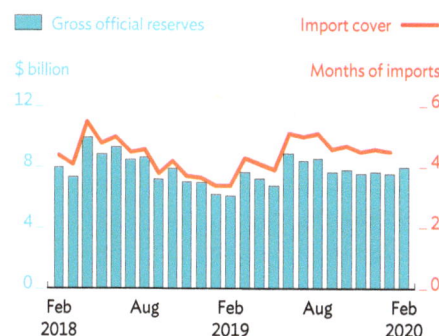

Source: Central Bank of Sri Lanka. https://www.cbsl.gov .lk/en (accessed 20 March 2020).

Figure 3.21.13 Purchasing managers' index

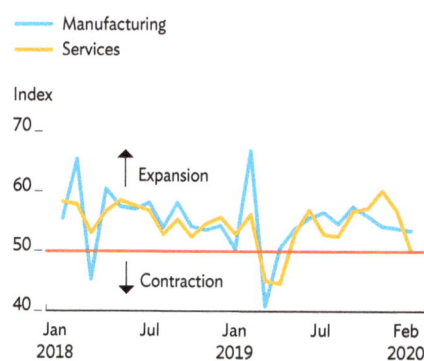

Source: Central Bank of Sri Lanka. https://www.cbsl.gov .lk/en (accessed 20 March 2020).

Table 3.21.1 Selected economic indicators (%)

	2018	2019	2020	2021
GDP growth	3.2	2.6	2.2	3.5
Inflation	4.3	4.3	5.0	4.8
Current acct. bal. (share of GDP)	-3.2	-2.1	-2.8	-2.6

Note: Inflation as measured by the Colombo consumer price index.

Sources: Department of Census and Statistics of Sri Lanka. http://www.statistics.gov.lk/; ADB estimates.

These approaches are used to derive appropriate measures of participation, such as backward linkages (foreign inputs into a country's exports), forward linkages (intermediate inputs that go into a receiving country's exports), and upstreamness. These measures offer a more realistic view of an economy participating in GVCs.

Sri Lanka's backward linkages are higher than its forward linkages, indicating that its industries tend to rely more on foreign intermediates than they supply to foreign producers. Its forward and backward GVC participation trails that of Malaysia, Thailand, and Viet Nam but is on par with South Asian neighbors such as Bangladesh, India, and Nepal (Figure 3.21.14).

Upstreamness, or the distance of a product from the final good, is indicated with ascending numbers, with 1 denoting zero distance from the final good. In 2018, Sri Lanka's upstreamness indexes were from 1.5 to 1.9 for its largest exporting industries, agriculture and clothing, which indicate that most of the products in these categories were close to final production (Figure 3.21.15).

Another GVC indicator commonly used is vertical specialization, which measures a country's total foreign value added (imported inputs in its exports) and the pure double-counted terms. This data show that Sri Lanka's participation in GVCs was limited in 2017, with vertical specialization less than 20% of its exports in all major export categories, well below the rate in Malaysia, at 44% in some industries, and in Viet Nam, at 58%.

Research by the Organisation for Economic Co-operation and Development identifies factors that determine a country's participation in GVCs as trade policy, which includes tariff structures and trade facilitation measures, and nonpolicy factors such as country size, proximity to GVC hubs, and income. Sri Lanka is ranked 96 of 190 countries in trading across borders in *Doing Business 2020*, indicating that it needs to improve logistical support and the efficiency of border agencies to facilitate greater GVC participation. While Sri Lanka is distant from the GVC hubs of Europe and North America, it can exploit proximity to GVC hubs in Asia by strengthening links and participating in regional trade agreements, which would improve its access to this market.

Recent positive measures by Sri Lanka include building a web-based portal to streamline and fast-track investment approvals and setting up a one-stop trade information portal. A customs single window based on the Automated System for Customs Data World enables the electronic submission and processing of customs declarations and cargo manifests. Sri Lanka's participation in the Trade Facilitation Agreement of the World Trade Organization provides opportunities for guidance in systematically improving its trade facilitation.

Figure 3.21.14 Backward participation across economies

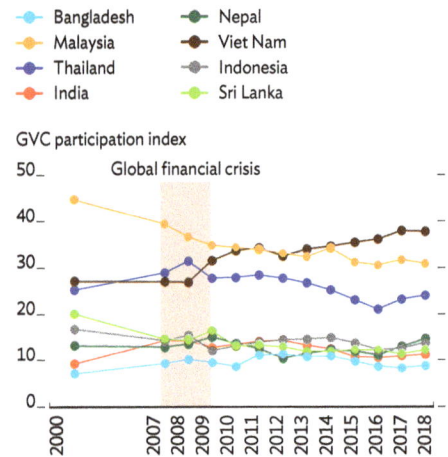

GVC = global value chain.
Source: ADB estimates using data from the Multi-Region Input–Output Table Database.

Figure 3.21.15 Upstreamness by sector

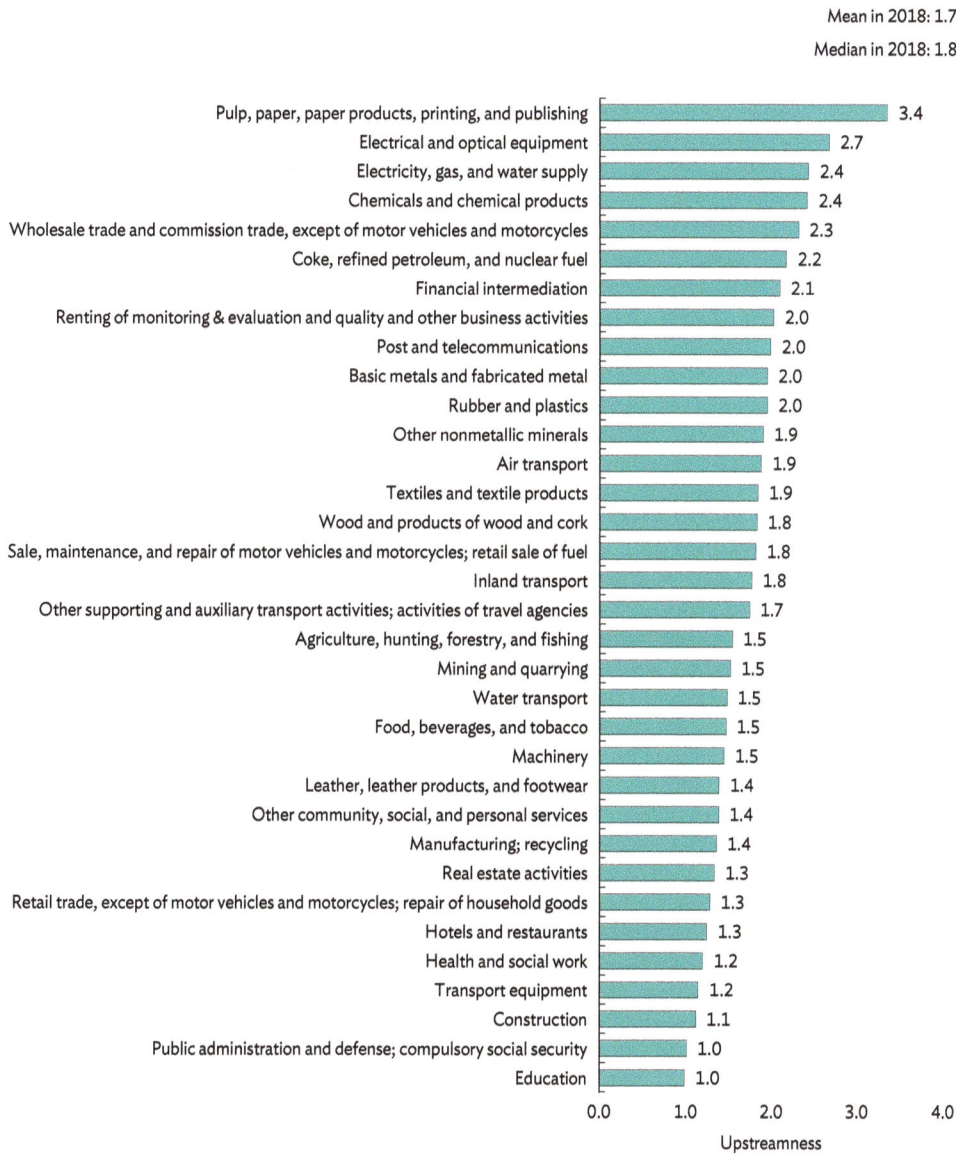

Mean in 2018: 1.7

Median in 2018: 1.8

Sector	Upstreamness
Pulp, paper, paper products, printing, and publishing	3.4
Electrical and optical equipment	2.7
Electricity, gas, and water supply	2.4
Chemicals and chemical products	2.4
Wholesale trade and commission trade, except of motor vehicles and motorcycles	2.3
Coke, refined petroleum, and nuclear fuel	2.2
Financial intermediation	2.1
Renting of monitoring & evaluation and quality and other business activities	2.0
Post and telecommunications	2.0
Basic metals and fabricated metal	2.0
Rubber and plastics	2.0
Other nonmetallic minerals	1.9
Air transport	1.9
Textiles and textile products	1.9
Wood and products of wood and cork	1.8
Sale, maintenance, and repair of motor vehicles and motorcycles; retail sale of fuel	1.8
Inland transport	1.8
Other supporting and auxiliary transport activities; activities of travel agencies	1.7
Agriculture, hunting, forestry, and fishing	1.5
Mining and quarrying	1.5
Water transport	1.5
Food, beverages, and tobacco	1.5
Machinery	1.5
Leather, leather products, and footwear	1.4
Other community, social, and personal services	1.4
Manufacturing; recycling	1.4
Real estate activities	1.3
Retail trade, except of motor vehicles and motorcycles; repair of household goods	1.3
Hotels and restaurants	1.3
Health and social work	1.2
Transport equipment	1.2
Construction	1.1
Public administration and defense; compulsory social security	1.0
Education	1.0

Upstreamness

Source: ADB estimates using data from the Multi-Region Input–Output Table Database.

SOUTHEAST ASIA

Brunei Darussalam

Cambodia

Indonesia

Lao People's Democratic Republic

Malaysia

Myanmar

Philippines

Singapore

Thailand

Timor-Leste

Viet Nam

Brunei Darussalam

Continued recovery is forecast on increased activity in oil and gas and in other areas, and as completed projects come online and other large investment projects begin. Exports of goods and services picked up in 2019, and growth in private consumption surged. Despite higher imports, the current account is expected to stay well in the black. With growth recovering, the government should turn its attention to tackling youth unemployment, which has worsened in recent years.

Economic performance

The economy posted 3.9% GDP growth in 2019 on a strong performance by industry as it reversed contraction in 2018 (Figure 3.22.1). The oil and gas industry, having contracted by 1.1% in 2018, expanded by 4.7% in 2019. Hydrocarbon production appeared to continue its recovery in the fourth quarter of 2019 and, together with new downstream production of petroleum and chemical products, further boosted economic activity. In the whole of 2019, oil production rose by 8.8% and natural gas production by 2.2% (Figure 3.22.2). By contrast, construction slowed following the completion of some big infrastructure projects. The service sector improved upon 0.8% growth in 2018, with substantial contributions from finance, wholesale and retail trade, and health services.

On the demand side, growth in private consumption surged from 2.2% in 2018 to a 6-year high of 5.9% in 2019 thanks to improved labor market conditions and lower inflation. For example, domestic sales of automobiles, a key consumer durable in Brunei Darussalam, rose by 6%. Similarly, increased global demand for oil and gas and reduced import growth with the slowdown in infrastructure spending lifted net external demand (Figure 3.22.3). However, after double-digit growth in 2018, fixed investment contracted by 4.4% owing to reductions in both construction and investment by the oil industry. Growth in public consumption remain muted, meanwhile, constrained by government efforts to consolidate its finances.

Even as growth picked up, inflation returned to habitual negative territory as the consumer price index fell by 0.4% in 2019. The decrease was largely attributed to lower prices for transport, housing, utilities, and food. The current account surplus is estimated to have widened from the equivalent of 7.9% of GDP in 2018 to 9.0% in 2019 with a rebound in

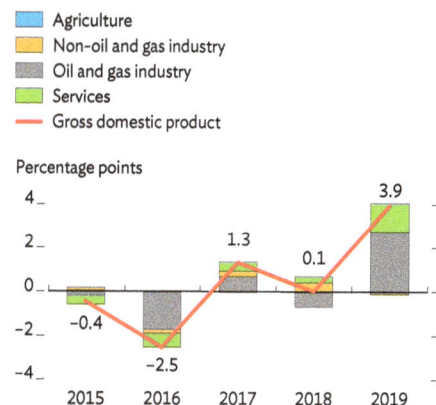

Figure 3.22.1 Supply-side contributions to growth

- Agriculture
- Non-oil and gas industry
- Oil and gas industry
- Services
- Gross domestic product

Percentage points

Source: CEIC Data Company (accessed 17 March 2020).

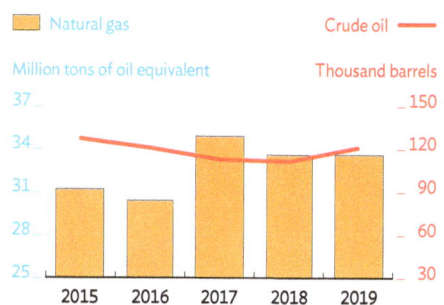

Figure 3.22.2 Average daily oil and gas production

- Natural gas
- Crude oil

Million tons of oil equivalent / Thousand barrels

Source: Brunei Darussalam Ministry of Energy.

This chapter was written by Pilipinas Quising of the Economic Research and Regional Cooperation Department, ADB, Manila, and Thiam Hee Ng of the Southeast Asia Department, ADB, Manila.

exports following the completion of a program to repair and restore aging oil and gas facilities and the start of downstream production. Consequently, international reserves increased slightly to $4.3 billion, providing cover for 10 months of imports.

Income from hydrocarbons through taxes, dividends, and royalties provided the government with revenue to fund relatively large public sector projects as well as invest in infrastructure. Provisional estimates to the third quarter of fiscal year 2019 (FY2019, ending 31 March 2020) show revenue reaching B$3.31 billion, more than three-fourths of the targeted B$4.36 billion. Conversely, expenditure may end up below budget as the government continues to rein in spending.

Economic prospects

The economy is expected to sustain its recent recovery. On the demand side, the recent uptick in private consumption should continue in the near term. With the completion of large refinery projects in 2019, investment may take a breather, but exports of oil and petroleum products should increase. In November 2019, the country started exporting petroleum and gas products, mainly automotive diesel, their value rising by $205 million that month to $357 million in December (Figure 3.22.4).

The Hengyi refinery was expected to run at full capacity starting in the second half of 2020, and Brunei Fertilizer Industries' ammonia and urea production plant was scheduled to start operation in the second quarter of 2021, though volatile oil prices and the spread of COVID-19 have slightly dimmed the outlook. GDP is still forecast to continue to grow above trend, albeit at a slower pace of 2.0% this year before picking up to 3.0% next year (Figure 3.22.5).

Gradual diversification of the production base away from oil and gas is starting to show additional green shoots. Several aquaculture projects are in the works, notably Golden Corporation Sdn Bhd in marine shrimp culture, capture fisheries, and seafood processing, and Hiseaton Fisheries Sdn Bhd producing pompano fish and Barramundi Asia (B) Sdn Bhd producing barramundi fish. The opening to the public of the 30-kilometer Temburong Bridge this year, linking the capital Bandar Seri Begawan with the lush rainforests of Temburong, is expected to boost tourism in Temburong District once the COVID-19 pandemic has passed. Complementing the bridge is the construction of Temburong's first luxury eco-resort, which is slated for completion by the end of 2020.

In finance, the monetary authority has established regulatory requirements for the operation of a peer-to-peer financing platform to facilitate the growth and development of capital markets. It also established a national credit scoring system known as the Bureau Credit Score to help banks and finance companies objectively assess the creditworthiness of potential clients.

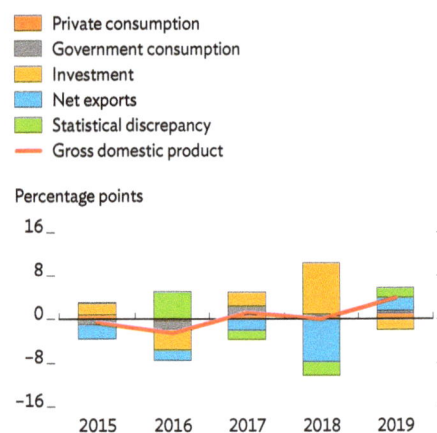

Figure 3.22.3 Demand-side contributions to growth

Source: CEIC Data Company (accessed 17 March 2020).

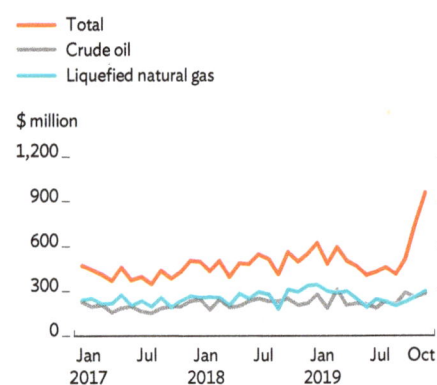

Figure 3.22.4 Exports of mineral fuels

Source: CEIC Data Company (accessed 20 March 2020).

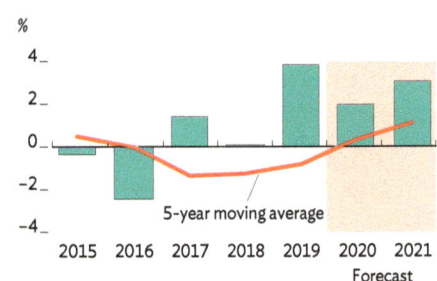

Figure 3.22.5 GDP growth

Sources: CEIC Data Company (accessed 17 March 2020); ADB estimates.

Inflationary pressure is expected to remain muted in the next 2 years, with little imported inflation because of low global commodity prices, and with government subsidies for many products. Liquefied natural gas and crude oil prices are expected to fall in 2020 owing to weak global demand, which will weigh heavily on exports earnings. In 2021, anticipated recovery in liquefied natural gas and crude oil prices should, along with exports from a newly built fertilizer plant, support export growth. Although imports of petroleum feedstock and for infrastructure investments are expected to increase, the value of exports will continue to exceed imports, keeping the current account in surplus.

Policy challenge—tackling youth unemployment

A latest labor force survey in Brunei Darussalam shows that the unemployment rate hit 8.7% in 2018. Although this was down somewhat from 9.3% in 2017, it was still the highest unemployment rate in Southeast Asia. What is more, the unemployment rate among youths aged 15–24 increased from 28.8% in 2017 to 29.9% in 2018. By educational attainment, 40% of the unemployed have tertiary and technical and vocational education and technical training (TVET) (Figure 3.22.6).

High unemployment among TVET graduates and those with tertiary education indicates a mismatch between the skills and qualifications possessed by the local labor force and the skills and qualifications demanded in the labor market. The share of employment across sectors and occupations and between locals and nonlocals speaks of a need to identify and develop, in close consultation with the private sector, skills that are relevant to the demands of industry, both public and private. The country's education system would be well advised to take a fresh look at the knowledge and skills it imparts.

Recognizing this, the government recently initiated several programs to tackle the problem. To develop better vocational training and education, reskilling, and the professionalization of manual jobs, it established several initiatives such as the i-Ready Apprenticeship Program and strengthened collaboration and engagement with industry through the Manpower Industry Steering Committee. These efforts are intended to ensure alignment between industry needs, in terms of numbers and qualifications, and manpower supply, and to address the current mismatch between general education and TVET training and the requirements of industry. The programs will help youths develop their skills and prepare for future employment. Further initiatives aim to develop aspiring entrepreneurs, such as those under Darussalam Enterprise and the Ministry of Finance and Economy, as well as the Entrepreneurship Innovation Centre under the Ministry of Education.

Table 3.22.1 Selected economic indicators (%)

	2018	2019	2020	2021
GDP growth	0.1	3.9	2.0	3.0
Inflation	1.0	-0.4	-0.2	0.1
Current acct. bal. (share of GDP)	7.9	9.0	5.5	9.5

Sources: CEIC Data Company (accessed 17 March 2020); ADB estimates.

Figure 3.22.6 Unemployment by educational attainment and gender

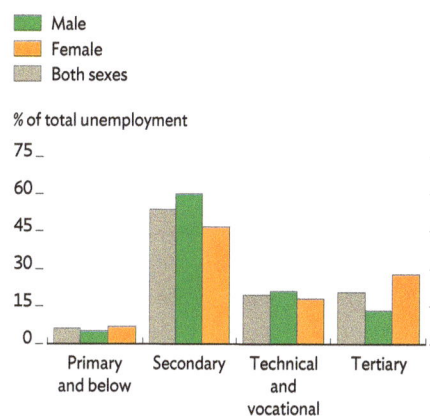

Source: Department of Economic Planning and Statistics. Labour Force Survey 2018. http://www.deps.gov.bn.

Cambodia

Despite slowing a little in 2019, growth remained strong as garment manufacturing, construction, and tourism continued to expand. The current account deficit widened significantly. Growth is expected to slow sharply in 2020 as export growth eases following partial suspension by the European Union of trade preferences for Cambodia and as the external environment worsens under COVID-19. Issuing government bonds in local currency would promote the development of local capital markets and domestic investment.

Economic performance

Growth slowed slightly in 2019 as the economy expanded by an estimated 7.1% (Figure 3.23.1). Robust construction and rising exports of garments, footwear, and travel goods were the main contributors to growth. Agriculture contracted by an estimated 0.5% as low rainfall affected fisheries and crops. Industry including construction expanded by an estimated 11.3% and contributed 4.0 percentage points to real GDP growth. The service sector contribution of 2.4 percentage points to growth in 2019 was lower than in previous years. Strong growth in visitor arrivals from the People's Republic of China (PRC) pushed all arrivals up by 10.0% in the first 3 quarters, but arrivals declined in the fourth quarter, following Cambodia's decision to ban online gambling. In the end, growth in visitor arrivals decelerated substantially from 10.7% in 2018 to 6.6% in 2019 (Figure 3.23.2).

Inflation was subdued in most of 2019 but rose to 3.1% year on year at the end of December on price increases for food. Across the full year, low increases for food and continued easing of fuel prices saw average annual inflation decline from 2.5% in 2018 to 1.9% in 2019.

The general government budget, which combines central and local government budgets, projected a deficit equal to 2.3% of GDP in 2019, but high revenue and low expenditure instead created a surplus at 5.3% of GDP (Figure 3.23.3). Strong tax collection boosted government revenue to an estimated 25.1% of GDP, with expenditure initially estimated at 19.8% of GDP. The estimated outcome for 2019 will be revised as new data become available.

Cambodia remains a highly dollarized economy, with the riel accounting for only about 20% of currency in circulation.

Figure 3.23.1 Supply-side contributions to growth

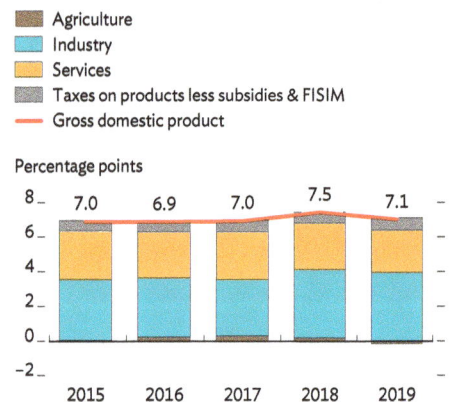

FISIM = financial intermediation services indirectly measured.
Sources: National Institute of Statistics; ADB estimates.

Figure 3.23.2 Tourist arrivals

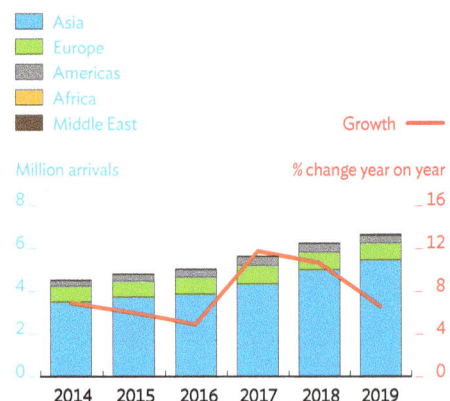

Sources: Ministry of Tourism; ADB estimates.

This chapter was written by Poullang Doung of the Cambodia Resident Mission, ADB, Phnom Penh.

The National Bank of Cambodia, the central bank, has taken measures to promote the use of the riel, notably requiring banks to denominate at least 10% of their loan portfolios in the local currency. The central bank has sought partners to help promote the use of the riel for transactions. Growth in the money supply (M2) slowed from 24.0% in 2018 to 18.0% last year, largely maintained by foreign currency deposits, which accounted for 83% of the liquidity. Growth in credit to the private sector accelerated from 23.2% in 2018 to 26.3%. This rapid growth in lending raised private sector credit outstanding from the equivalent of 82.8% of GDP in 2018 to 94.7%.

Cambodia's current account deficit widened from 12.2% of GDP in 2018 to an estimated 17.6% as import growth outpaced exports (Figure 3.23.4). The dollar value of merchandise exports is estimated to have grown by 13.5% as merchandise imports rose by an estimated 19.5% on significant increases in imports of construction materials, fuel, and vehicles. Buoyant foreign direct investment inflow—recorded at $3.7 billion, a 15.4% increase from the previous year—continued to finance the current account deficit. This permitted international reserves to accumulate to $18.8 billion in 2019, or cover for 8.8 months of imports.

Economic prospects

Growth is expected to slow dramatically to 2.3% in 2020 as a direct result of the COVID-19 outbreak, low growth in the PRC and contraction in major advanced economies, and reduced access to export markets, before rebounding to 5.7% in 2021 (Figure 3.23.5). COVID-19 will hit services hard by reducing foreign visitor arrivals and is expected to affect construction and manufacturing through supply chain disruption and reduced demand. The service sector is projected to contract by 1.7% in 2020 as tourism falls and growth in real estate slows. Industry growth is forecast to slow to 6.5% in 2020 with deceleration in garment production for export and in construction in line with arrested growth in major advanced economies and a sharp slowdown in the PRC, and in particular with the curtailment of European Union trade preferences starting in August 2020. Agriculture growth is expected to be low at 0.5% or so in 2020, reflecting a forecast for extended hot weather this year and the authorities' instruction to cultivate only one rice crop during the dry season.

Inflation is expected to remain low, averaging 2.1% in 2020 in line with foreseen decelerating growth and lower international fuel prices. Inflation is projected to remain subdued in 2021 as international fuel prices likely stay low (Figure 3.23.6).

The general government budget for 2020 has a deficit equal to 2.8% of GDP. Revenue in 2020 is budgeted at 23.5% of GDP,

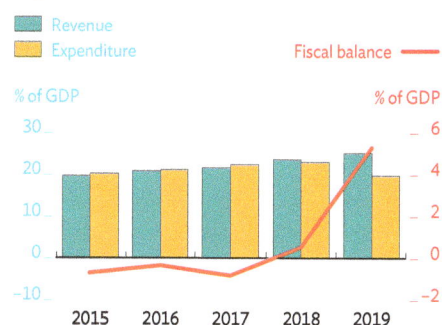

Figure 3.23.3 Fiscal indicators

Source: Ministry of Economy and Finance.

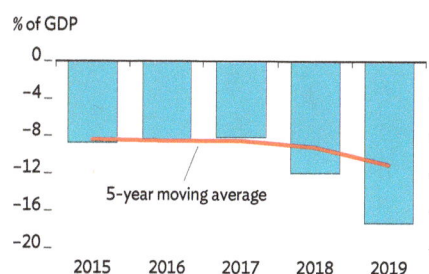

Figure 3.23.4 Current account balance

Source: *Asian Development Outlook* database.

Table 3.23.1 Selected economic indicators (%)

	2018	2019	2020	2021
GDP growth	7.5	7.1	2.3	5.7
Inflation	2.5	1.9	2.1	1.8
Current acct. bal. (share of GDP)	-12.2	-17.6	-19.0	-16.9

Sources: National Institute of Statistics; ADB estimates.

up from a 2019 budget target of 20.0% of GDP. However, the impact of COVID-19 on trade and services is likely to depress revenue below target. Expenditure is budgeted to rise from 22.4% of GDP in 2019 to 26.3%. This reflects government plans for significant stimulus to offset the short-term impacts of COVID-19 and lost trade preferences. Public external debt relative to GDP is anticipated to hover at about 29% in 2020, keeping Cambodia at low risk of sovereign debt distress.

As the economy faces the COVID-19 threat, the central bank is taking several measures to increase liquidity in the local market and support businesses as they struggle under the effects of COVID-19. It is also promoting local currency use with incentives for riel-denominated loans. The central bank plans to continue to support the development of equity and bond markets, including a forthcoming initial public offering for one of Cambodia's largest banks. Over time, developing financial markets and increased use of the local currency will give the central bank more channels through which to transmit monetary policy.

The current account deficit is forecast to equal 19.0% of GDP in 2020, narrowing to 16.9% in 2021. The wider current account deficit in 2020 will reflect slower growth in exports and disrupted tourism. Gross international reserves are expected to increase to more than $20.6 billion in 2020, providing cover for 9 months of imports. Reserves could come under pressure, though, if the COVID-19 outbreak causes foreign direct investment to fall sharply.

Growth prospects are subject to significant downside risks, including export demand falling faster than expected under curtailed trade preferences, disruption linked to COVID-19, and advanced economies falling into recession. Increased bank lending connected to real estate continues to pose risks to financial and macroeconomic stability, particularly under a slowdown linked to COVID-19. The outbreak and temporary border closures in Southeast Asia could apply additional pressure on consumer prices.

Policy challenge—developing a local bond market

Cambodia has achieved high economic growth over the past 2 decades to become one of the fastest-growing economies in the subregion. The authorities are committed to developing financial services to support growth and ensure macroeconomic stability.

Local issues of government bonds could help diversify the nonbank financial sector and deepen local capital markets. Government bond issues would help to establish a risk-free benchmark for pricing locally issued corporate bonds.

Figure 3.23.5 GDP growth

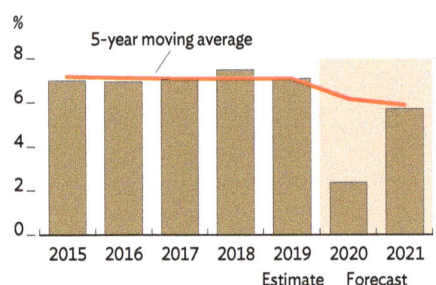

Source: Asian Development Outlook database.

Figure 3.23.6 Inflation

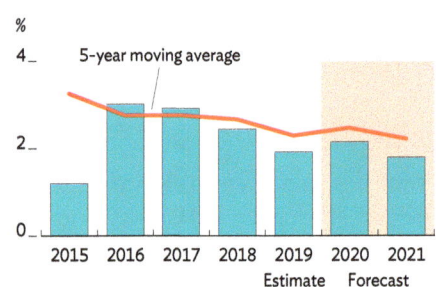

Source: Asian Development Outlook database.

The development of a corporate bond market would help to reduce companies' reliance on bank credit while offering new channels for long-term financial intermediation. This would support private sector development, diversify the nonbank financial sector, and channel domestic savings into investment, thus reducing reliance on foreign capital flows. Also important would be to cultivate long-term institutional investors in government bonds in addition to banks, such as insurance companies and pension funds, to deepen the market.

Efforts to develop a local currency bond market face a particular challenge in Cambodia, however, from its pervasive dollarization. The promotion of local currency bonds would be consistent with the broader goal of expanding the use of the riel.

Government authorities are working on a draft amendment to the Law on Government Securities that would provide a clear legal framework and pave the way for issuing government bonds. The development of an overarching legal framework could be complemented by the development of a roadmap for bond market development over the medium term. This roadmap could be guided by analysis of the experiences of peer countries in the subregion. Based on these experiences, the roadmap would include steps such as establishing a coordination body and trade and settlement systems to facilitate the development of primary and secondary markets.

Indonesia

Growth slowed last year as stronger domestic consumption only partly offset a worsening external environment and weakening domestic investment. Inflation fell, and the current account deficit narrowed. Disruption from COVID-19 and recent developments in commodity and financial markets will have severe implications for both the world and Indonesia in 2020. Over the medium and long term, Indonesia needs to improve its productivity and resilience, not least through greater technology adoption.

Economic performance

GDP growth slowed from 5.2% in 2018 to 5.0% in 2019 (Figure 3.24.1). Stronger domestic consumption partly offset a worsening external environment and weakening domestic investment.

On the demand side, domestic consumption remained strong, supported by robust household spending and election-related expenditure (Figure 3.24.2). Household consumption was bolstered by spending on health care and education services as visits to heath facilities increased and the use of EdTech services grew rapidly. The labor market remained robust, adding 2.5 million jobs in the 12 months to August 2019, though unemployment stayed at 5.3%. With revenue receipts undershooting targets, the government reined in consumption, particularly in the second half of the year.

Growth in fixed investment slid from 6.6% in 2018 to 4.4% (Figure 3.24.3). Investment in buildings and plantation agriculture remained strong, while investment in equipment and vehicles declined sharply. Plantation agriculture investment is set to continue, to meet the target of producing 50 million tons of palm oil by 2024, which would entail investing $2.3 billion over the next 5 years.

Exports contracted by 0.9% in 2019, a broad decline partly buffered by sustained demand for coal and palm oil. With natural resources accounting for a large share of Indonesia's exports, growth in mining and quarrying also performed poorly. Imports shrank by 7.7%, partly as several import-dependent high-tech manufacturing areas slowed production.

On the supply side, growth in agriculture and industry both slowed (Figure 3.24.4). Growth in agriculture fell from 3.9% in 2018 to 3.6% in 2019 as a mild drought damaged food crops.

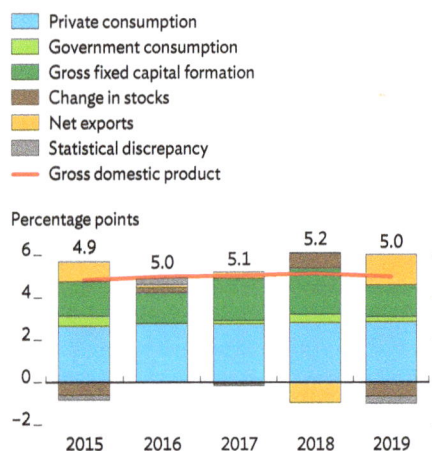

Figure 3.24.1 Demand-side contributions to growth

- Private consumption
- Government consumption
- Gross fixed capital formation
- Change in stocks
- Net exports
- Statistical discrepancy
- Gross domestic product

Percentage points

Source: CEIC Data Company (accessed 13 March 2020).

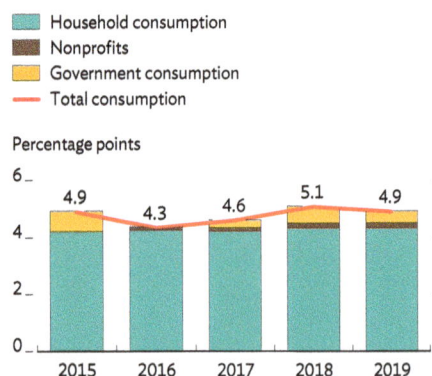

Figure 3.24.2 Contributions to consumption growth

- Household consumption
- Nonprofits
- Government consumption
- Total consumption

Percentage points

Source: CEIC Data Company (accessed 13 March 2020).

This chapter was written by Emma Allen and Priasto Aji of the Indonesia Resident Mission, ADB, Jakarta.

The downturn in food crops was partly offset by stronger growth in plantations, livestock, and fisheries. Manufacturing growth declined from 4.3% in 2018 to 3.8%, with losses from capital-intensive industries partly offset by gains in labor-intensive ones. Growth in construction held relatively steady, slowing only from 6.1% a year earlier to 5.8% in 2019.

Growth in services was strong and broad based, rising from 5.8% in 2018 to 6.4%. It was stoked by strengthening domestic consumption and election spending by political parties. Modern services such as information and communications did especially well from surges in mobile phone ownership and internet usage (Figure 3.24.5).

With administered prices unchanged and core inflation stable, headline inflation continued to moderate. It averaged 2.8% in 2019, at the lower end of the 2.5%–4.5% target set by Bank Indonesia, the central bank (Figure 3.24.6). Prices for transport and communications were contained, as were those for housing. However, El Niño weather disturbances caused food prices to fluctuate. Exchange rate stability has been supported by regular central bank auctions of derivatives called domestic non-deliverable forwards since late 2018. In 2019, the Indonesian rupiah appreciated against the US dollar by 0.6% on average, or by 4.2% at year-end, recovering some ground lost in 2018.

The current account deficit narrowed from $30.6 billion in 2018, equal to 2.9% of GDP, to $30.4 billion in 2019, or 2.7% (Figure 3.24.7). Trade deficits persisted in services and primary income, but a small surplus of $3.5 billion was recorded in goods as imports contracted faster than exports. Oil imports fell partly because of import controls that include a requirement that diesel engines burn blends with at least 20% locally produced biofuel. Subdued domestic investment clipped imports of capital goods.

The balance of payments turned a $7.1 billion deficit in 2018 into a $4.7 billion surplus in 2019 (Figure 3.24.8). Net inflow of portfolio investment rose from $9.3 billion in 2018 to $21.5 billion as global financial market conditions improved following interest rate cuts by the US Federal Reserve. Inflow of foreign direct investment also increased, to $24.4 billion, channeled into utilities, transport, telecommunications, and e-commerce. In 2019, the Jakarta Composite Index gradually recovered by 1.7% in line with other markets in Southeast Asia. These financial inflows more than offset a deficit in the current account. Foreign reserves stood at $129.2 billion at the end of 2019, sufficient to cover 7.3 months of imports and government external debt servicing.

With inflation benign and the balance of payments in surplus, the central bank supported growth with four rate cuts totaling 100 basis points from July to October 2019 (Figure 3.24.9), reducing the policy rate to 5.0%.

Figure 3.24.3 Contributions to fixed investment growth

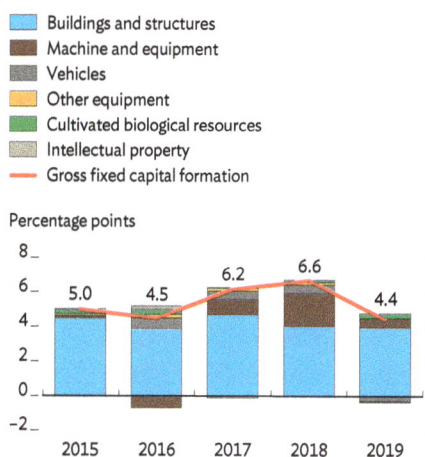

Source: CEIC Data Company (accessed 13 March 2020).

Figure 3.24.4 Supply-side contributions to growth

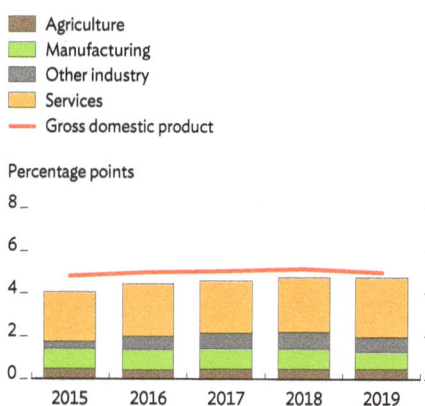

Source: CEIC Data Company (accessed 13 March 2020).

Figure 3.24.5 Internet and mobile phone usage

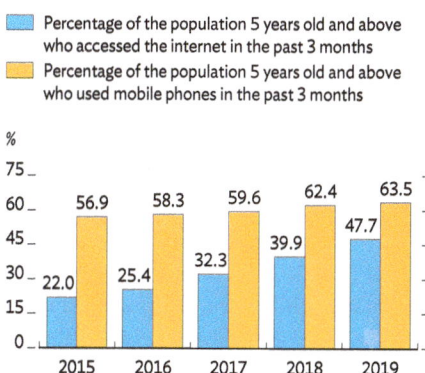

Source: CEIC Data Company (accessed 13 March 2020).

However, credit growth remained muted, even decelerating to 6.1% year on year in December 2019 as loans to the public sector, including state-owned enterprises, tailed off.

The 2019 budget set a fiscal deficit equal to 1.8% of GDP, but year-end estimates indicate that it reached 2.2% of GDP as growth and revenue both fell short of expectations, with revenue reaching only 90.4% of the budget target. The ratio of GDP to revenue declined from 14.7% in 2014 to 12.4% in 2019 as tax revenue fell from 10.8% of GDP to 9.8% in the period, and as oil and gas revenue also declined. Expenditure reached 93.9% of the 2019 budget target, or 14.5% of GDP, with spending on subsidies and capital investment declining while social transfers increased. Gross budget financing in 2019 equaled 5.9% of GDP, higher than the target of 5.4%, and was met with additional issues of government securities. Central government debt reached Rp4,778 trillion in December 2019, equal to 29.8% of GDP.

Economic prospects

Disruption from COVID-19 and developments in commodity and financial markets will have severe implications for Indonesia in 2020. As events unfold, Indonesia's key trade partners already expect severe impacts on their economies. Domestic demand is likely to weaken as business and consumer sentiment falls. GDP growth is accordingly forecast at 2.5% this year. As the global economy recovers in 2021 and investment reform gains traction, growth is forecast at 5.0%.

Earnings from exports of goods and services are expected to contract for a second year in 2020. As the COVID-19 outbreak halts production in economies that import Indonesian commodities, earnings from petroleum, palm oil, and coal are likely to suffer this year. Travel bans and flight cancellations will hit tourism receipts. To counter flagging export growth, the government is accelerating licensing and customs processing by removing regulations that impose unnecessary burdens on businesses. The central bank has lowered rupiah reserve requirements by 50 basis points for banks financing trade. As the outbreak wanes and the global economy recovers, export growth should recover in 2021.

As with exports, fixed investment is expected to remain subdued in the near term. Leading indicators such as credit growth and imports of machinery and equipment continued to moderate in early 2020 (Figure 3.24.10). As the People's Republic of China is the dominant supplier of capital goods for investment in Indonesia, infrastructure projects that require imports may be put on hold until the second half of 2020, and new project approvals may also be delayed. These losses may be partly offset by temporary measures to help businesses cope with impacts from the outbreak, including reductions

Figure 3.24.6 Inflation

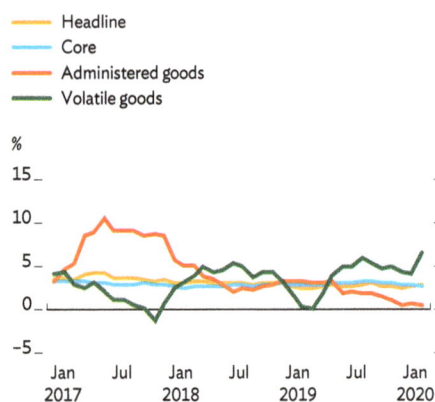

Note: Inflation rates based on 2012 prices.
Source: CEIC Data Company (accessed 13 March 2020).

Figure 3.24.7 Current account balance

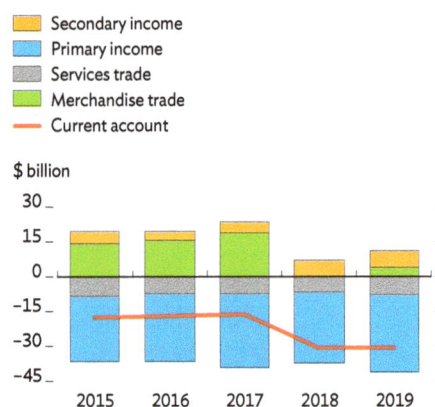

Source: CEIC Data Company (accessed 13 March 2020).

Figure 3.24.8 Balance of payments

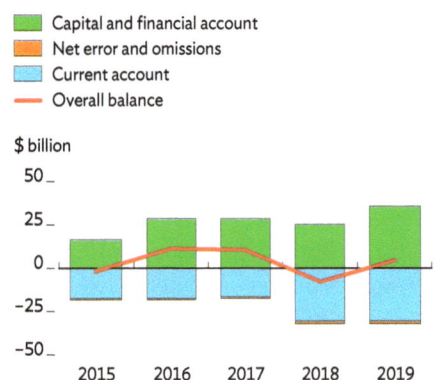

Source: CEIC Data Company (accessed 13 March 2020).

to corporate income tax and deferred import tax payments for manufacturing. Fresh reform should gain traction in 2021 with the introduction in early 2020 of two omnibus bills in parliament on job creation and taxation. The legislation tackles many longstanding issues concerning business licensing, labor, land procurement, and tax systems. Investment in urban real estate and construction should also gain momentum in 2021.

Signs already show domestic consumer confidence beginning to decline (Figure 3.24.11). The impact of the COVID-19 outbreak on consumer sentiment and spending is likely to be especially strong in urban areas. Unless the government successfully contains the outbreak, household spending on health care could jump, productivity fall, and discretionary spending shrink. As these impacts spread, jobs and worker incomes will be affected. One in four jobs is in wholesale or retail trade or in accommodation and food services, many of them informal. Occupations in these areas, as well as in construction, agriculture, manufacturing, and transport, are less amenable to working from home and thus highly exposed to business downturns.

To counter job and income losses, the government is stepping up efforts to ensure the timely disbursement of social transfers and exempting manufacturing workers with incomes below $14,000 per year from income tax for 6 months. Workers' incomes are also supported by temporarily allowing businesses affected by COVID-19 to use funds from death and accidence insurance to prevent layoffs. Anticipating employment losses—and in a bid to boost skills to create a tech-savvy workforce—the government is accelerating the rollout of its new flagship program Kartu Pra Kerja, which provides youths with training subsidies and job incentives.

With better weather and recent investment in palm oil plantations, growth in agriculture should hold up this year and next. However, manufacturing and construction face headwinds in 2020 from an unfavorable external environment. Growth in services will moderate as consumers hold off on spending. Exceptions may be information and communications as the digital economy facilitates remote work and education services as online learning rapidly expands.

Inflation will likely remain within the revised central bank target range of 2%–4% both this year and next, forecast at 3.0% in 2020 and declining to 2.8% in 2021 as global and domestic conditions improve. The government is expected to maintain administered prices for energy in the near term, while lower commodity prices may further ease inflationary pressures. But tight food supplies and sudden currency depreciation could push up volatile prices for imported goods. While such increases may be temporary, they could further depress household spending, which will already be under pressure from the economic slowdown.

Figure 3.24.9 Policy rate and credit growth

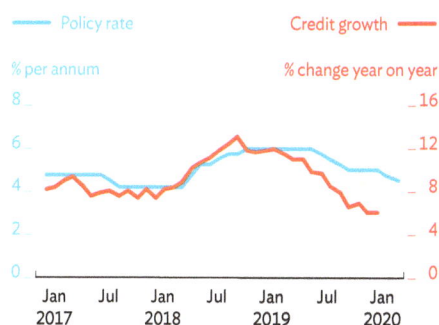

Note: Credit refers to commercial and rural banks outstanding loans.
Source: CEIC Data Company (accessed 13 March 2020).

Figure 3.24.10 Raw materials and capital goods imports

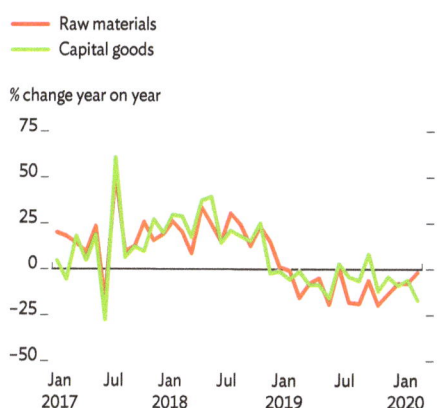

Source: CEIC Data Company (accessed 20 March 2020).

Figure 3.24.11 Consumer confidence and exchange rate

Source: CEIC Data Company (accessed 20 March 2020).

The current account deficit is forecast to equal 2.9% of GDP in 2020 and 2021. While the recent drop in oil prices could prompt gains in the near term, improvement may be eroded as prices for gas, coal, palm oil, and rubber soften. With domestic demand expected to wane in 2020, imports of goods and services are forecast to fall faster than exports, creating a small trade surplus. As exports recover and fixed investment gains traction under policy reform in 2021, increased imports of capital goods will keep the current account deficit unchanged from 2020. Export earnings from tourism are expected to decline sharply in 2020 before gradually recovering in 2021. The deficit in the primary income account is expected to persist as foreign investors repatriate dividends. By relying on investment inflow to finance the current account deficit, Indonesia remains vulnerable to global risk sentiment, particularly as two-thirds of equity and one-third of sovereign bonds are foreign held.

To counter the economic slowdown, the central bank lowered its 7-day reverse repurchase agreement policy rate in February and March by a total of 50 basis points to 4.50%. The rupiah came under pressure in March, prompting renewed central bank efforts to support exchange rate stability, minimize speculation, and smooth investment outflow by strengthened interventions in the bond, spot, and domestic non-deliverable forward markets. Interventions in the first quarter of 2020 helped preserve liquidity in the local currency money market. To alleviate foreign exchange pressures and boost banks' foreign exchange liquidity, the central bank halved reserve requirements for commercial banks from 8% to 4%.

Fiscal policy supports growth. The government has unveiled stimulus packages that offer incentives and subsidies for workers and businesses. In addition, it will maintain sizable expenditure on infrastructure at 16.5% of total expenditure, equal to 2.4% of GDP. Lower tax collection and a drop in taxes on oil production are likely to leave a revenue shortfall. This shortfall and heightened spending on stimulus measures are likely to push the fiscal deficit above the target of 1.8% of GDP in the 2020 budget.

Risks to the growth outlook are on the downside. External risks would include an extended COVID-19 outbreak, further declines in commodity prices, worsened finance market volatility, and capital outflows from Indonesia. The combination of these developments may induce a global recession. Domestic risks concern how quickly and effectively the spread and economic impacts of the COVID-19 outbreak are contained, as well as constraints on fiscal policy associated with sliding revenues and reliance on capital market financing. Limitations in the health care system could, along with difficult enforcement of social distancing measures, prolong impacts. If business and consumer sentiment remains subdued,

Table 3.24.1 Selected economic indicators (%)

	2018	2019	2020	2021
GDP growth	5.2	5.0	2.5	5.0
Inflation	3.2	2.8	3.0	2.8
Current acct. bal. (share of GDP)	−2.9	−2.7	−2.9	−2.9

Sources: CEIC Data Company (accessed 13 March 2020); ADB estimates.

potential second-round impacts could include bankruptcies and layoffs, with the poor and vulnerable greatly exposed because of social protection gaps. Timely action is therefore required, making any delay in stimulus program rollout particularly critical.

Policy challenge—a tech-savvy and innovative workforce

Growth in Indonesia has averaged 5% since 2015, yet much higher growth is needed for the country to achieve its ambition to join the world's five largest economies by 2045. The main factor constraining potential growth has been stagnant productivity partly attributed to limited technological sophistication in Indonesian industries. A study by ADB and the Ministry of Finance, *Innovate Indonesia*, indicates that, if Indonesia optimized its adoption of new technologies to enable industry to use resources more efficiently, it could increase GDP per capita to $14,747 by 2045, putting its economy in the high-income group.

To exploit the benefits of new technologies, companies and workers need to have the know-how to absorb and adopt them. However, the study notes, Indonesia currently lacks such workers. This concern is shared across the automotive, electronics, food and beverage, textiles and clothing, and footwear industries. Using LinkedIn data, a recent survey by the Mandiri Institute found that many firms struggle to find workers with the right competencies in software and information technology services, inducing them to move to other countries. The share of the population in the 25–34 age group with a tertiary education is still relatively low at 16.1%, below that of other countries in the Group of 20 (Figure 3.24.12).

Potential nevertheless exists for rapid technological adoption. Indonesia is projected to be among the world's largest producers of science, technology, engineering, and mathematics graduates because of rapid expansion in its population and tertiary education system (Figure 3.24.13). If this growing pool of local skills is well used, national capacity for development and innovation will jump.

The government is addressing skills gaps. Enrollment in technical and vocational education is being expanded, and a training subsidy for unemployed youths has been introduced. Fiscal incentives now encourage workforce training, as well as research and development.

However, the challenge of growing a tech-savvy workforce goes beyond expanding access to education. Indonesia needs to nurture knowledge and awareness of new technologies through an improved education and skills ecosystem that

Figure 3.24.12 Share of population aged 25–34 years with tertiary education, 2017

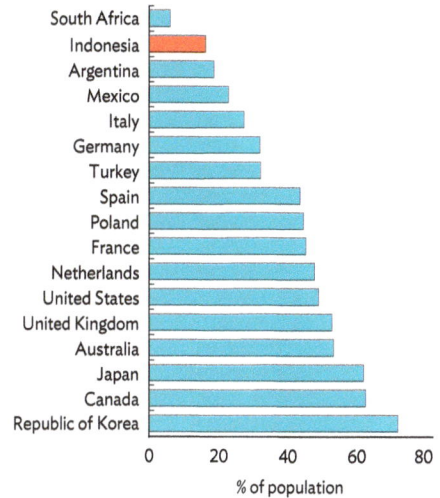

% of population

Source: OECD. 2019. OECD Data.

Figure 3.24.13 Projected share of graduates with STEM degrees across OECD and G20 countries in 2030

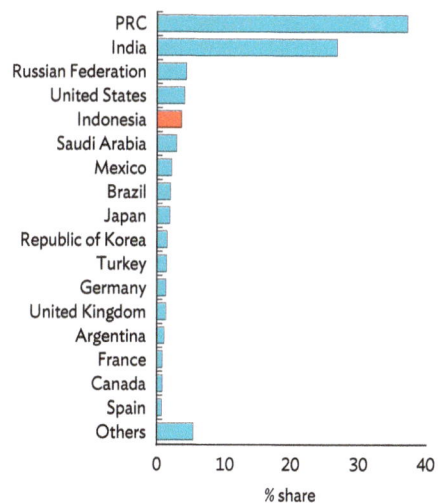

% share

OECD = Organisation for Economic Co-operation and Development, PRC = People's Republic of China, STEM = science, technology, engineering, and math.
Source: OECD. 2015. Education Indicators in Focus No. 31.

invests in skills for the future. To this end, firms should be encouraged to offer workforce training to enable workers' greater use of new technologies, while education and training providers should have greater autonomy to respond to industry-specific skill needs. Funding could be allocated to training programs that aim to develop digital literacy within firms, in particular small and medium-sized enterprises. In addition, hands-on technical assistance may be provided by intermediate technology centers, offering access to experts and to research and development facilities. These benefits could be provided through applied research centers that meld public and private innovation.

Other areas for policy action include upgrading capacity in existing higher education institutions to provide digital skills in demand, including through internships built into the curricula of university programs and by strengthening technology entrepreneurship programs.

Lao People's Democratic Republic

Flooding and drought in 2019 slashed growth in agriculture and hydroelectric generation. Growth could decelerate this year as services suffer under COVID-19 but should bounce back next year as services recover and electricity production capacity increases. Inflation rose sharply in the second half of last year, and the current account remained a concern. Following serious natural disasters in 2 successive years, fiscal reform is needed to better finance disaster preparedness, response, and recovery, especially as disasters worsen under climate change.

Economic performance

GDP growth fell from 6.2% in 2018 to 5.0% in 2019, a slowdown reflected in modest credit growth at 7.4% (Figure 3.25.1). Disasters slowed growth in both agriculture and hydroelectric production. The impact of flood, drought, and African swine fever on agriculture, which provides 15.5% of GDP, was mitigated, however, by increased cash crop production. Agriculture still reversed 1.3% growth in 2018 to contract by 0.2% last year.

Industry growth declined from over 7.0% in 2018 to just 4.1%. Drought caused electricity generation, the backbone of industry, to reverse growth at 10.6% in 2018 with 3.0% contraction in 2019. In contrast, robust construction growth at 16.8%—reflecting megaprojects for a railway, an expressway, and 16 special and specific economic zones—helped sustain growth in industry. Growth in services edged up from 7.0% in 2018 to 7.2%, sustained by strong expansion in tourist arrivals, notably from, in descending order, Thailand, the People's Republic of China, and Viet Nam. Growth in tourist arrivals overall accelerated sharply from 8.5% in 2018 to 14.4% (Figure 3.25.2).

Higher food prices and a weaker local currency raised average inflation from 2.0% in 2018 to 3.3% last year (Figure 3.25.3). A surge in rice, meat, and pork prices since the third quarter pushed food price inflation to 10.2% in December 2019, elevating overall inflation in December 2019 to 6.3% from 1.4% a year earlier.

Export growth softened from 18.7% in 2018 to 4.5% in 2019. Electricity exports fell but were offset by higher exports of commercial agricultural produce, garments, gold, and agro-processing products (Figure 3.25.4). Import growth plunged from 6.0% in 2018 to 0.5% as Lao kip depreciation made imports

Figure 3.25.1 Supply-side contributions to growth

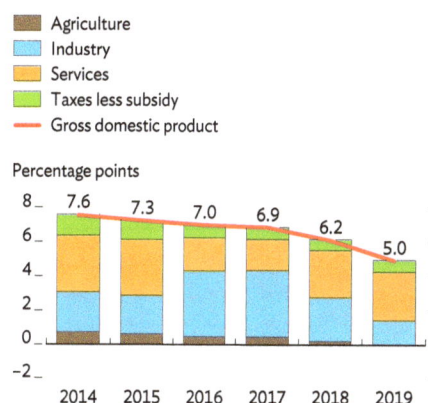

- Agriculture
- Industry
- Services
- Taxes less subsidy
- Gross domestic product

Percentage points

Sources: Lao Statistics Bureau; ADB estimates.

Figure 3.25.2 Tourist arrivals

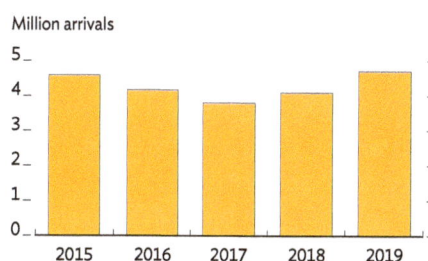

Million arrivals

Sources: Lao PDR Ministry of Information, Culture and Tourism; Haver Analytics (accessed 3 March 2020).

This chapter was written by written by Rattanatay Luanglatbandith and Soulinthone Leuangkhamsing of the Lao PDR Resident Mission, ADB, Vientiane.

more expensive and as economic growth faltered. The deficit in the income account rose slightly because of higher interest payments and repatriated profits. The current account deficit narrowed from the equivalent of 13.0% of GDP in 2018 to 9.5%. Gross international reserves edged up from $873.2 million at the end of 2018 to $997.3 million a year later, providing cover for only 1.5 months of imports. External debt declined from 92.8% at the end of 2018 to 92.2% at the end of 2019.

The fiscal deficit expanded partly because of higher spending to cope with contrary weather. As public expenditure fell slightly from the equivalent of 21.0% of GDP in 2018 to 20.7% last year, so did revenue collection, from 16.3% of GDP to 15.7%. The resulting fiscal deficit increased from 4.7% of GDP to 5.0%.

The central bank manages the exchange rate to stabilize inflation. By the end of 2019, monetary authorities had gradually allowed kip depreciation against the US dollar in the regulated commercial bank rate. In the parallel market, the kip depreciated by 5.8% against the dollar, reflecting a lack of confidence on the local currency.

Economic prospects

An ongoing regional growth slowdown and the COVID-19 outbreak will hinder economic growth as tourist arrivals, investment, trade, and services suffer downturns. COVID-19 may severely trim service growth from 7.2% in 2019 to just 1.3% in 2020. This will be offset in part by increases in electricity generation by at least 9,000 gigawatt-hours (GWh) per year—7,400 GWh from the Xayaburi Hydropower Project and 1,600 GWh from the Nam Ngiep 1 Hydropower Project—equal to 26.0% of current total capacity. Other offsetting factors will be a continuing public construction boom and agricultural recovery from drought in 2019. Growth is forecast at 3.5% in 2020 (Figure 3.25.5). As services recover from COVID-19 in 2021, growth should rise to 6.0%.

Agriculture is expected to grow by 2.5% this year and 2.7% in 2021, contingent on good weather and recovery in livestock and fishery output. Industry growth is forecast to recover to 5.7% in 2020 as electricity production and exports increase and then, with railway construction speeding up in 2021, to rise to 6.8%. Provided that COVID-19 is contained this year and its impact on tourism, transport, wholesale and retail trade, and related services begins to wind down, services growth should recover to about 6.4% in 2021.

Inflation is projected to accelerate to 4.0% in 2020 and 4.5% in 2021, reflecting higher prices for food, clothing, and transportation. Kip depreciation against the US dollar and the Thai baht will stoke higher prices for imports.

The current account deficit is forecast to narrow to 9.4% of GDP in 2020 and 8.1% in 2021 on robust growth in electricity

Figure 3.25.3 Monthly inflation

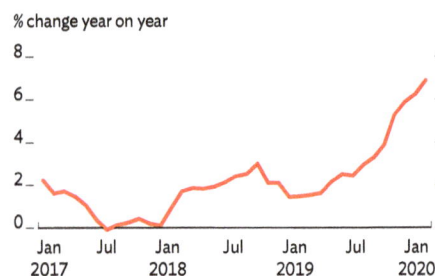

% change year on year

Sources: Lao Statistics Bureau; Haver Analytics (accessed 6 March 2020).

Figure 3.25.4 Electricity exports

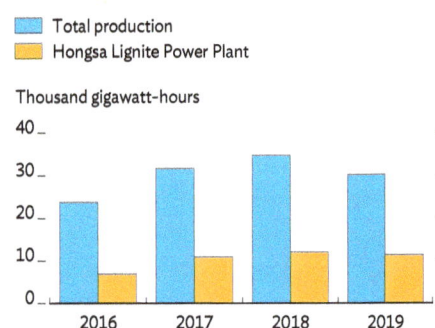

Total production
Hongsa Lignite Power Plant

Thousand gigawatt-hours

Source: Lao PDR Ministry of Energy and Mines.

Table 3.25.1 Selected economic indicators (%)

	2018	2019	2020	2021
GDP growth	6.2	5.0	3.5	6.0
Inflation	2.0	3.3	4.0	4.5
Current acct. bal. (share of GDP)	−13.0	−9.5	−9.4	−8.1

Sources: Lao Statistics Bureau; ADB estimates.

Figure 3.25.5 GDP growth

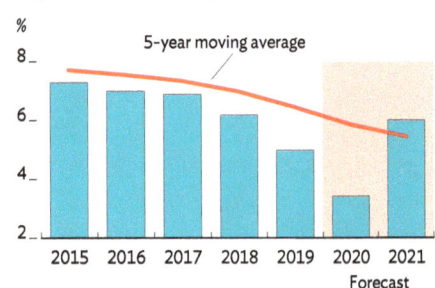

%

5-year moving average

Forecast

Source: Asian Development Outlook database.

exports at 6.0% and then 7.0% (Figure 3.25.6). Imports are expected to expand by 1.0% and then by 4.0% to supply equipment for hydropower and railway projects.

The projected slowdown in growth will add to continuing pressure on the budget arising from weak tax collection, large infrastructure spending needs, and adjustments to wages and benefits. Revenue and grants are projected to equal 14.8% of GDP in 2020 and 15.5% in 2021, and expenditure to equal 20.7% and then 21.0%. The budget deficit is thus expected to edge up to 5.9% of GDP in 2020, easing to 5.5% in 2021 (Figure 3.25.7).

Domestic risks to the growth outlook include adverse weather and the slow pace of public finance management reform. External risks include a regional slowdown caused by trade tensions between the US and the People's Republic of China and uncertain global financial conditions. Risks from COVID-19 are viewed as both domestic and external.

Policy challenge—building resilience and fiscal buffers

Disaster resilience in the Lao PDR is inadequate, and consequent damage is frequent and substantial. Agriculture, which employs more than 70% of the population, is particularly vulnerable. Floods in 2018 are estimated to have cost $371 million, and flooding and drought in 2019 at least $380 million, affecting transport, agriculture, economic growth and stability, social welfare, government finances, and the current account.

The social impact of disasters includes worsened personal vulnerability while living in temporary shelters, temporary loss of livelihood, forced migration, increased indebtedness, long-term unemployment, and malnutrition especially for children and young adults, the poor, women, and other disadvantaged groups.

To create fiscal space to cope with disasters, fiscal policy should aim to expand the revenue base, reduce the large fiscal deficit, and ensure the proper management of public finances and public debt. To augment government funds for disaster preparedness, response, and recovery, the government should explore the use of insurance, such as through the Southeast Asia Disaster Risk Insurance Facility.

Ultimately, the best way to deal with disasters is to build resilience. Climate resilience should be a feature of new infrastructure design and development. Risk-informed development planning, budgeting, and financing to strengthen resilience should be considered for high-risk economic and geographic areas. Disaster response should be better coordinated by national and local agencies, local communities, and development partners. The national development plan should incorporate disaster risk reduction, response, and recovery as crosscutting and multisectoral features.

Figure 3.25.6 Current account balance

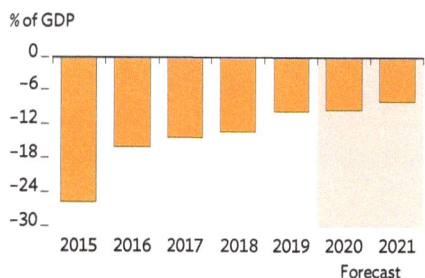

% of GDP

Source: *Asian Development Outlook* database.

Figure 3.25.7 Fiscal indicators

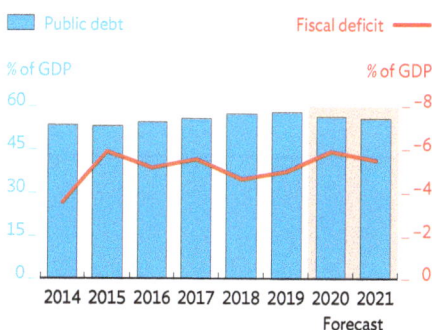

Sources: *Asian Development Outlook* database; International Monetary Fund estimates.

Malaysia

Weaker external demand and domestic investment dragged down growth in 2019. Inflation remained muted, and the current account surplus widened as imports fell more sharply than exports. Difficult global economic conditions and the spread of COVID-19 are expected to hit growth hard this year. Inflation will pick up slightly as it returns to trend, and the current account surplus will continue. Preparing the workforce for the future requires more reform of general education and technical and vocational education and training.

Economic performance

GDP growth dropped to 4.3% in 2019, its slowest in a decade (Figure 3.26.1). Growth in private consumption, the largest component of aggregate demand, remained strong but slipped a bit from 8.0% in 2018 to 7.6% in 2019. While employment growth, wage increases, and relatively stable consumer prices underpinned buoyancy in private consumption, other factors that supported consumer spending were government measures to counter the high cost of living, notably special pension payments and a doubling of grants and transfers. Robust consumer spending partly offset sluggish growth in exports and domestic investment. Weaker global growth, trade tensions between the US and the People's Republic of China, and lower commodity prices dragged down export earnings. Lackluster investment continued in 2019, partly as a result of a government program to rationalize expenditure. While private investment expanded by 1.5% in 2019, government investment plunged by nearly 11.0%.

By sector, growth in services decelerated from 6.8% in 2018 to a still robust 6.1%, with consumer services especially strong. Growth in industry decelerated from 3.1% in 2018 to 2.1% last year. Manufacturing growth decelerated from 5.0% in 2018 to 3.8% in 2019 as export demand weakened, particularly for electronics. Shutdowns of maturing oil fields, some but not all of them planned, caused mining and quarrying output to continue to decline but at a slower pace than in 2018. Construction mirrored the sluggish investment performance on the demand side, growing marginally only in the final quarter of the year on improvement in housing starts and civil engineering works on large transportation projects. Growth in agriculture markedly improved from 0.1% in 2018 to 1.8% in 2019 (Figure 3.26.2).

This chapter was written by Thiam Hee Ng and Maria Theresa Bugayong of the Southeast Asia Department, ADB, Manila.

Figure 3.26.1 Demand-side contributions to growth

- Private consumption
- Government consumption
- Public gross fixed capital formation
- Private gross fixed capital formation
- Change in stocks
- Imports
- Exports
- Gross domestic product

Percentage points

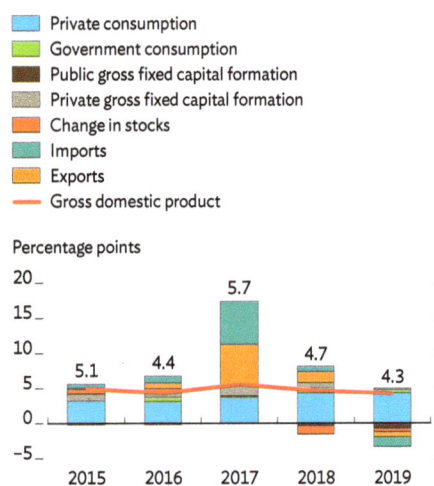

Sources: Haver Analytics; Bank Negara Malaysia. 2020. *Monthly Statistical Bulletin.* February. http://www.bnm.gov .my (accessed 28 February 2020).

Figure 3.26.2 Supply-side contributions to growth

- Agriculture
- Industry
- Services
- Import duties
- Gross domestic product

Percentage points

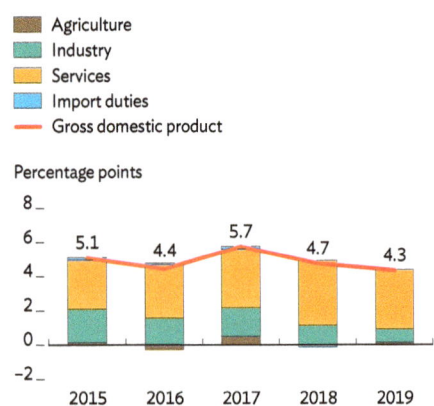

Sources: Haver Analytics; Bank Negara Malaysia. 2020. *Monthly Statistical Bulletin.* February. http://www.bnm.gov .my (accessed 28 February 2020).

Inflation remained muted even with strong consumption and some monetary policy easing with a central bank policy rate cut from 3.25% to 3.00% in May 2019. This suggests a lack of wage pressure and lower domestic oil prices but also higher subsidies for several commodities. A deflationary trend in 2018 stretched to the first quarter of 2019, but inflation slowly started rising in March to reach an average of 0.7% for the full year (Figure 3.26.3). Price increases were largest for food, housing, water, electricity, furnishings, and education. Transport prices declined, however, as domestic retail fuel price ceilings were maintained. Bank Negara Malaysia, the central bank, reduced its policy rate in January and again in March 2020 to 2.50%, mainly to prevent a further slowdown in the economy.

The financial sector remains stable with banks well capitalized. The share of nonperforming loans in bank portfolios remained low. Credit growth slowed partly as a deliberate measure to manage risk arising from high household indebtedness and also real estate speculation. With inflation under control and broad money growth decelerating from 9.1% at the end of 2018 to 3.5% a year later, the statutory reserve requirement was lowered from 3.5% to 3.0% on 16 November 2019 to further support domestic liquidity.

Government revenue improved significantly in 2019, climbing from RM236.5 billion in 2018 to RM261.8 billion and rising as a percentage of GDP from 16.3% to 17.3%. The improvement came primarily from Petronas nontax dividends amounting to RM54 billion in 2019, more than twice the amount remitted to the government in 2018. Expenditure increased by 8.3% to RM314.6 billion, equal to 20.8% of GDP. Operating expenditure—including salaries, interest payments, grants, transfers, and subsidies—increased by 10.4%. By contrast, development expenditure contracted, falling by 0.4% with revisions and timeline adjustments in the implementation of major infrastructure projects such as Light Rapid Transit 3, Mass Rapid Transit 2, and the East Coast Rail Link. The ratio of the fiscal deficit to GDP declined from 3.7% in 2018 to 3.4%. With the government strengthening its efforts to simplify and facilitate business procedures, Malaysia now ranks 12th among 190 economies in the World Bank survey *Doing Business 2020*.

Export earnings in US dollar terms declined by 4.3% in 2019 as commodity prices were generally depressed and external demand weak. Exports of electronics, comprising 46% of the total, declined by nearly 5.0%, while the combined export value of crude oil products and liquefied natural gas declined by 35.5% because of economic weakness in the US and the People's Republic of China, both of them key markets for Malaysia's exports. The dollar value of imports declined by 5.5% in 2019. As imports declined faster than exports, the

Figure 3.26.3 Monthly inflation

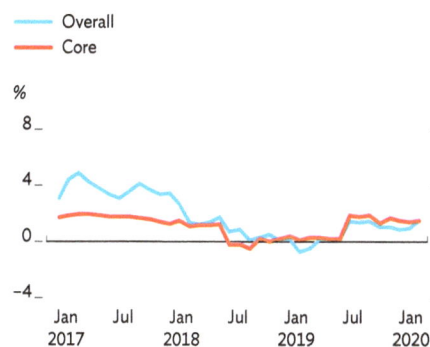

Sources: Haver Analytics; Bank Negara Malaysia. 2020. *Monthly Highlights and Statistics.* March. http://www.bnm.gov.my (accessed 9 March 2020).

Figure 3.26.4 Current account balance components

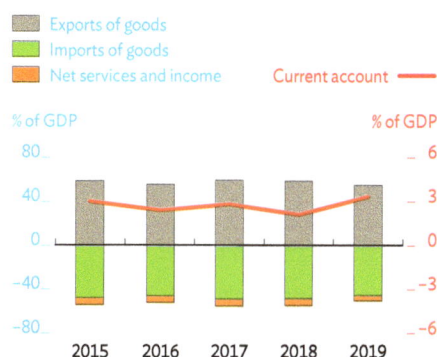

Sources: Haver Analytics; Bank Negara Malaysia. 2020. *Monthly Highlights and Statistics.* March. http://www.bnm.gov.my (accessed 9 March 2019).

current account surplus expanded by more than 1 percentage point of GDP, from 2.1% in 2018 to 3.3% (Figure 3.26.4). International reserves including gold were estimated at the end of December 2019 at $102.4 billion, sufficient to cover 7.4 months of imports. Trade tensions and an unstable growth outlook continued to put pressure on the Malaysian ringgit. External debt at the end of December 2019 stood at $231.2 billion.

Economic prospects

With global economic conditions worsening and COVID-19 spreading, Malaysia's economic performance is expected to be adversely affected. However, even as external demand falls sharply, domestic demand will continue to grow, albeit with private consumption expected to slow after strong growth last year and with public investment expected to remain sluggish.

The new administration that took office in March 2020 has announced it will continue implementing large infrastructure projects announced in the 2020 budget. Private investment, on the other hand, is expected to continue to be sluggish in response to disruption and uncertainty under the COVID-19 outbreak (Figure 3.26.5). On the positive side, two policy rate cuts in January and March this year totaling 50 basis points, and a reduction in the reserve requirement by another 100 basis points to 2.0%, could boost investment. With COVID-19 disrupting supply chains and travel, exports of goods and services are expected to continue to contract. GDP growth is thus expected to drop to 0.5% in 2020 before recovering to 5.5% in 2021 (Figure 3.26.6).

Growth in private consumption is expected to weaken in 2020 as the outbreak of COVID-19 discourages people from going out. Consumption growth is expected to be supported by continued income growth, a higher minimum wage, and a low unemployment rate. Effective on 1 February 2020, the minimum wage for workers in 16 city councils and 40 municipal councils was raised by about 9%.

With the number of COVID-19 infections in Malaysia picking up in March and the imposition of a restricted movement order nationwide, consumption spending is expected to take a hit, especially in restaurants and hotels. A stimulus package announced on 27 February 2020 could help mitigate some of the impact of COVID-19 on consumption by offering incentives for domestic tourism and a temporary optional reduction in employee contributions to the Employees Provident Fund. The new administration also introduced additional measures such as financial assistance to workers forced to take unpaid leave, discounts on electricity bills, bringing forward living cost assistance payments, and implementing RM2 billion worth of small projects.

Table 3.26.1 Selected economic indicators (%)

	2018	2019	2020	2021
GDP growth	4.7	4.3	0.5	5.5
Inflation	1.0	0.7	1.0	1.3
Current acct. bal. (share of GDP)	2.1	3.3	2.3	2.9

Source: ADB estimates.

Figure 3.26.5 Consumer and business confidence indexes

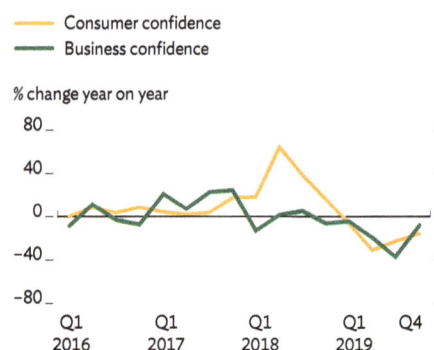

Q = quarter.
Note: Above 100 indicates improvement in business conditions and rising consumer confidence.
Source: Haver Analytics (accessed 9 March 2020).

Figure 3.26.6 GDP growth

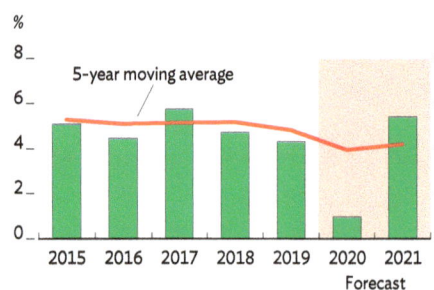

Source: Asian Development Outlook database.

After having failed to gain traction last year, investment is expected to remain lackluster this year and next with the bleaker global economic environment. The previous administration announced the resumption of several large infrastructure projects such as the East Coast Railway Link and two mass transit projects, which the new administration has announced it will continue to implement.

Inflation will remain muted given the drop in growth and limited demand pressure. Moreover, a big drop in global oil prices is expected to help keep inflation well under control, at 1.0% in 2020 and 1.3% in 2021 (Figure 3.26.7).

Multiple factors will continue to weigh in on Malaysia's export growth in 2020: a much weaker external environment, supply chain disruption, and lower agriculture and mining output (Figure 3.26.8). However, recovery in exports is seen in 2021 as the impact of COVID-19 fades. Meanwhile, import growth is expected to remain weak as investment growth continues to lag and demand for imports of intermediate goods remains depressed. The net result will likely be a narrower current account surplus equal to 2.3% of GDP in 2020, widening to 2.9% in 2021.

In response to the worsening global environment, the government will have to strike the right balance in its fiscal stance between supporting economic growth and maintaining fiscal sustainability. Public consumption is expected to maintain its trend growth. A stimulus package in February totaling RM20.0 billion included RM3.5 billion in additional federal government spending, RM3.5 billion in loan funds, and RM13.0 billion in optional cuts to Employees Provident Fund contributions. An additional RM3.9 billion in support was announced by the new administration in March 2020. Both of these stimulus packages are expected to counter the effects of COVID-19 on consumption and support affected businesses.

Risks to the outlook tilt to the downside as the global economic environment could suffer further and a prolonged COVID-19 crisis could place further downward pressure on Malaysia's growth prospects. A key domestic risk to the forecast would be any delay in implementing large infrastructure projects.

Figure 3.26.7 Inflation

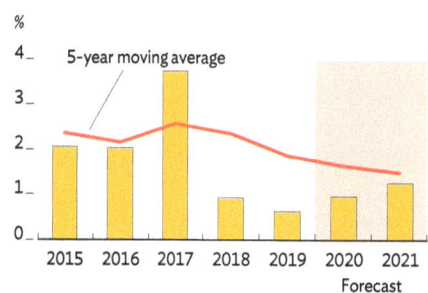

Source: *Asian Development Outlook* database.

Figure 3.26.8 Export and import growth

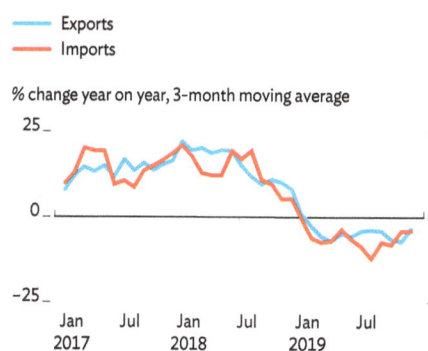

Source: Haver Analytics (accessed 10 March 2020).

Policy challenge—preparing the workforce for the future

The government unveiled its Shared Prosperity Vision 2030 last year with the aim of providing a decent living standard to all Malaysians by 2030. To achieve this vision, it has identified education, including technical and vocational education and training (TVET), as a key enabler. This will require considerable investment in the workforce to ensure that it is sufficiently educated and skilled to meet the vision of a prosperous society.

Over the years, Malaysia has made significant strides in education. By 2019, it had achieved near universal primary schooling and had improved access to secondary schooling. The number of universities in Malaysia has expanded considerably, and now 21 public universities and 38 private universities churn out about 51,000 graduates annually.

Despite these impressive achievements in the number of graduates from institutions of higher education, there are concerns that a large share of them are ill-prepared for the job market. One key challenge is reflected in the growing number of university graduates who are unable to find work (Figure 3.26.9). According to a study conducted in 2018 by the Ministry of Education, nearly 60% of graduates remain unemployed for at least a year after graduation. This partly reflects the view of employers that university graduates do not have the necessary technical and soft skills for the job. At the same time, there is considerable heterogeneity in the quality of graduates, encouraging some graduates to have unrealistically high expectations for their salary on the basis of their degree.

While there is no shortage of jobs overall, there is a problem of skills mismatch. Most graduates prefer white collar jobs, and many are unwilling to take up blue collar jobs. Further, TVET is not a popular education choice for many students, with only 13% of upper secondary students choosing to pursue it.

With employers preferring job candidates with a combination of hard skills such as analytical thinking and problem solving and the soft skills of communication and team work, it is important for educational curricula to strike a good balance between the two skills sets. Existing graduates can be encouraged to acquire soft skills through work experience or assignment at companies. The 2020 budget introduced the Graduates@Work program, through which the government will offer a wage incentive of RM500 per month for 2 years to graduates who obtain a job after being unemployed for more than 12 months. Employers will receive a hiring incentive of up to RM300 per month for each new hire for 2 years. This looks like a promising public program to help graduates upgrade their soft skills on the job.

Reforming TVET could help make the program more attractive to students. Currently there are over 1,000 TVET institutes, a number that can be rationalized to strengthen their quality. These TVET institutes should work closely with industry to identify skills gaps and train workers in the skills they need to fill these vacancies.

Figure 3.26.9 Unemployment rate

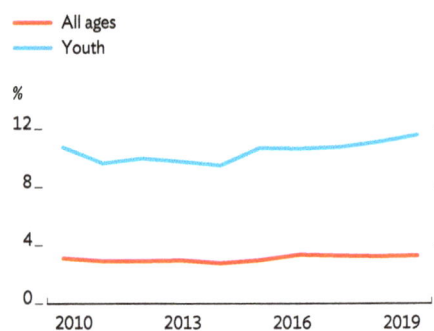

Note: Youth unemployment refers to the share of the labor force aged 15–24 without work but available for and seeking employment.

Source: The World Bank database, https://data.worldbank.org/indicator (accessed 10 March 2020).

Myanmar

Growth picked up last year, the current account deficit narrowed, and inflation accelerated. As COVID-19 poses an external risk in fiscal 2020, growth is projected to slow before picking up again in fiscal 2021. Inflation is forecast to ease slightly over the next 2 years. The current account deficit will widen as exports and service receipts weaken, while the fiscal deficit will remain manageable. Empowering the rural economy and reducing poverty depend on creating jobs and building climate change resilience.

Economic performance

GDP growth picked up to 6.8% in fiscal year 2019 (FY2019, ended 30 September 2019) from 6.4% in the previous year (Figure 3.27.1). Growth accelerated in two sectors. Agriculture growth recovered from a scant 0.1% in FY2018 to 1.6% in FY2019, reflecting improved weather and export demand for some agricultural products, notably beans, pulses, and fishery and livestock products. Industry grew by 8.4% in FY2019 as garment manufacturing and construction expanded. Services, on the other hand, saw growth moderate from 8.7% in FY2018 to 8.3% in FY2019 as growth in tourism slowed.

The pickup in GDP growth was accompanied by sharply higher inflation, surging from 5.9% in FY2018 to 8.6% as prices for food and imported fuel rose. Although agricultural production expanded, higher external and internal demand pushed up prices for some major food items despite exchange rate stability in 2019.

As net service receipts and export of goods increased while imports stalled with lower demand for investment goods, the current account deficit narrowed from the equivalent of 3.7% of GDP in FY2018 to 3.5% in FY2019. Export growth decelerated to 10.0%, reflecting a fall in primary exports such as gas, rice, and minerals in response to weaker regional and global demand. However, acceleration in garment exports moderated the slowdown in exports overall (Figure 3.27.2). Meanwhile, import growth was stable at just above 7% in both FY2018 and FY2019.

Foreign direct investment (FDI) commitments expanded from $3.3 billion recorded from October 2017 to September 2018 to $4.2 billion in FY2019 (Figure 3.27.3).

Figure 3.27.1 GDP growth

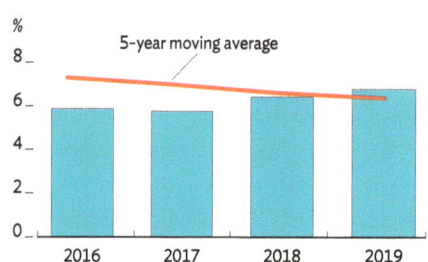

Note: Years are presented as fiscal years ending 30 September of that year.
Sources: Central Statistical Organization; Central Bank of Myanmar.

Figure 3.27.2 Garment exports

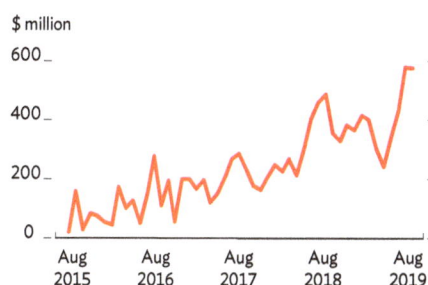

Source: Ministry of Planning, Finance and Industry.

This chapter was written by Yumiko Tamura and Eve Cherry Lynn of the Myanmar Resident Mission, ADB, Nay Pyi Taw.

Manufacturing, transport, and telecommunications remained the key FDI recipients in FY2019, with manufacturing garnering 32% of FDI approvals, and transport and telecommunications 37%.

The government has tried to keep the fiscal deficit within 4.0%–4.5% of GDP to maintain macroeconomic stability and debt sustainability. Yet the FY2019 budget estimated a higher deficit equal to 5.0% of GDP to accommodate an intended increase in capital expenditure.

To improve stability and compliance with finance rules and regulations, the government has undertaken several reforms: support to state-owned banks to improve their corporate governance, a gradual opening of the bank and insurance industries to foreign institutional investors, and partial relaxation of the interest rate cap on unsecured lending. Meanwhile, broad money supply growth slowed in the year to June from 18.6% in 2018 to 12.0% in 2019.

Economic prospects

GDP growth will likely slow significantly to 4.2% in FY2020 under the COVID-19 pandemic but, if the virus is confined quickly, recover to 6.8% in FY2021 (Figure 3.27.4). Lower growth in FY2020 reflects how severely the COVID-19 pandemic will hit global, regional, and local economies.

Thereafter, however, a pickup in industry and a gradual rebound in investment and exports should support an expected recovery of GDP growth to 6.8% in FY2021. Growth in agriculture will decelerate to 1.3% in FY2020, reflecting the potential negative impact of COVID-19 on exports of some primary products.

With weaker demand and possible supply-side constraints, including reduced availability of intermediate goods from countries affected by COVID-19, the purchasing managers' index fell to 49.8 in February 2020. This prompts a forecast that growth in industry will decelerate to 5.6% in FY2020.

Further growth in construction is expected, supported by continued reform to the legal and regulatory framework, the implementation of various infrastructure projects, and efforts to counter a housing shortage. Moreover, the extension of the European Union's generalized scheme of preferences for developing trade partners will enable expansion in export-oriented industries such as garments, particularly in FY2021. The outlook for industry thus remains positive, with growth expected to pick up to 8.7% in FY2021. A lower growth rate of 4.5% is expected for services in FY2020 as the COVID-19 pandemic could have a dramatic impact on tourism at its peak during the dry season, which continues to May.

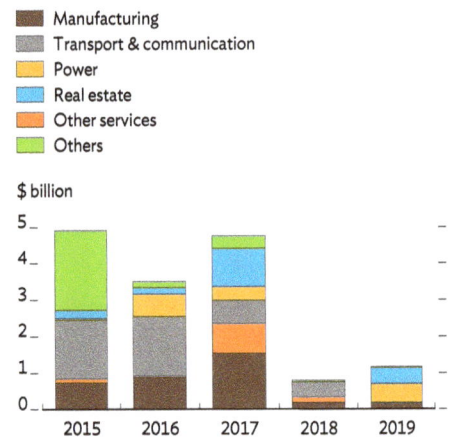

Figure 3.27.3 Foreign direct investment approvals by sector

Manufacturing
Transport & communication
Power
Real estate
Other services
Others

$ billion

Note: Years are presented as fiscal years ending 30 September of that year.
Source: Directorate of Investment and Companies Administration.

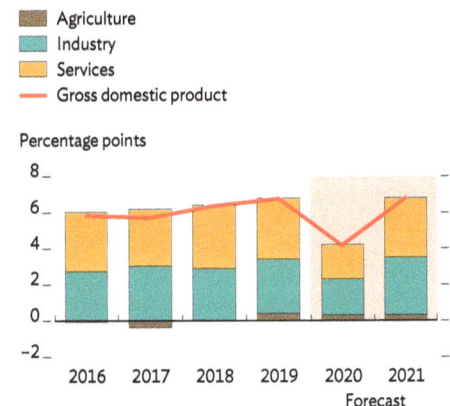

Figure 3.27.4 Supply-side contribution to growth

Agriculture
Industry
Services
Gross domestic product

Percentage points

Note: Years are presented as fiscal years ending 30 September of that year.
Sources: Central Statistical Organization; Central Bank of Myanmar; ADB estimates.

Inflation is expected to ease only slightly to 7.5% in FY2020 and FY2021, reflecting continuing rises both for food and other goods. Despite a likely stabilization of fuel prices, rising costs for imported raw materials are seen to keep inflationary pressures strong in the near term.

FDI inflows are expected to regain momentum in FY2020, supported by the opening of the finance industry to FDI, gradual reform to the tax and legal systems, improved electricity supply and other infrastructure, and a more conducive business and investment climate. As of January 2020, FDI commitments had increased from $1.3 billion a year earlier to $2.1 billion.

Despite growth in garment exports and net service receipts, the current account deficit is forecast to widen this year and next with the anticipated deceleration in exports and tourism service receipts resulting from the COVID-19 pandemic, as well as possibly higher intermediate imports. The current account deficit will thus expand to equal 4.5% of GDP in FY2020 and FY2021 (Figure 3.27.5).

The fiscal deficit is expected to widen to 5.2% in FY2020, mainly to accommodate a proposed increase in spending on public services such as education, health care, and social protection, as well as continued building to fill infrastructure deficits (Figure 3.27.6). The Central Bank of Myanmar has announced an interest rate cut by 100 basis points effective 1 April 2020 to stimulate growth and safeguard the economy from a possible fallout caused by the COVID-19 pandemic. Moreover, toward remedying the economic repercussions of COVID-19, the government introduced a comprehensive economic stimulus package that exempts and defers taxes, and establishes a COVID-19 fund to offer low-interest loans to the industries worst affected.

Growth prospects are subject to significant downside risks, including postponed FDI and lower export demand if advanced economies fall into a recession because of the COVID-19 pandemic. There also remains some uncertainty about the direction of government economic policy during the political transition starting with a general election in late 2020.

Policy challenge—empowering the rural economy

Following the implementation of comprehensive strategies to address poverty, Myanmar made significant progress in recent years. The national poverty rate shrank by almost half in little more than half a dozen years, from 42.2% in 2010 to 24.8% in 2017 (Figure 3.27.7). Aside from poverty reduction, improvements have been achieved in gender equality, electricity consumption (a proxy for economic activity), and

Table 3.27.1 Selected economic indicators (%)

	2018	2019	2020	2021
GDP growth	6.4	6.8	4.2	6.8
Inflation	5.9	8.6	7.5	7.5
Current acct. bal. (share of GDP)	−3.7	−3.5	−4.5	−4.5

Note: Years are presented as fiscal years ending 30 September of that year.

Sources: Central Statistical Organization; Central Bank of Myanmar ADB estimates.

Figure 3.27.5 Current account balance

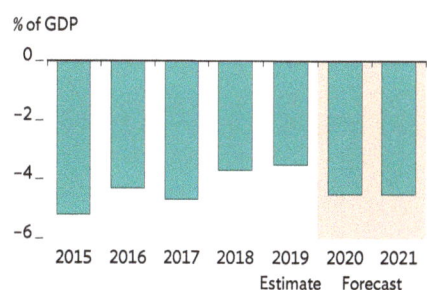

Note: From 2015 to 2017, years are fiscal years ending 31 March of the next year, and from 2018 the fiscal year is from 1 October of the previous year to 30 September of the current year.

Sources: Central Bank of Myanmar; ADB estimates.

Figure 3.27.6 Fiscal balance

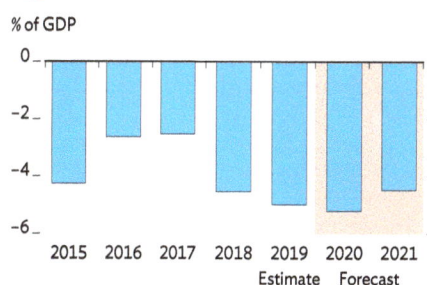

Note: From 2015 to 2017, years are fiscal years ending 31 March of the next year, and from 2018 the fiscal year is from 1 October of the previous year to 30 September of the current year.

Sources: Central Bank of Myanmar; ADB estimates.

living standards. However, this notable progress has been shadowed by a persistently higher poverty rate in rural areas. Poverty festers at more than twice the national rate in rural areas, where 70% of the population lives.

In recent years, the government has launched many projects to improve rural livelihoods, strength residents' skills, and upgrade transport and communications. The government continues to support financial inclusion in rural areas by encouraging commercial banks to expand into the countryside by opening branches, installing ATMs, and setting up mobile banking, as well as by providing microfinance to poor households. Further, the Myanmar Sustainable Development Plan, 2018–2030 underscores the need to empower local communities toward poverty reduction.

It is important to create a dynamic rural economy off the farm, strengthen human capital, enhance access to credit, build farm-to-market transport networks, upgrade agro-processing industries, and promote ecotourism to enhance off-farm job opportunities. Tourism could significantly contribute to rural development but would require an effective industry-management strategy, a solid legal framework, and further improvement in rural infrastructure.

At the same time, the government should accelerate its implementation of a comprehensive action plan for reducing disaster risk to ensure that disasters do not push more vulnerable rural residents into poverty. Facilitating the provision of jobs and enhancing disaster resilience are the two most immediate strategies to pursue to further reduce poverty and address inequality in rural areas. As government revenue is limited, public sector management should be improved to optimize funding as much as possible.

Figure 3.27.7 Poverty rate

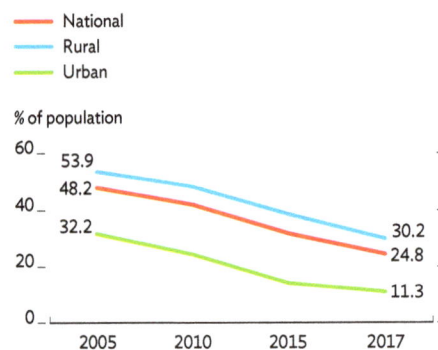

Source: Ministry of Planning, Finance and Industry.

Philippines

Growth moderated in 2019 as investment slowed, but it remained strong. The economy will slow sharply in 2020 under the impact of COVID-19 before rebounding in 2021. Expansionary fiscal and monetary policies will support growth recovery once the pandemic dissipates. Inflation will remain moderate, and the current account deficit relatively small. Greater focus on building climate change resilience is vital in light of the country's extreme vulnerability to natural hazards.

Economic performance

Economic growth went through an easing phase in 2019, dropping below its 6.3% long-term trend to 5.9%. The primary reason for moderation in growth was a slump in public spending on infrastructure in the first half of 2019 caused by congressional delay in passing the 2019 national budget. With public spending catching up in the second half of the year, economic growth rebounded with a strong fourth-quarter performance of 6.4% year on year.

On the demand side, private consumption sustained high growth at 5.8% and contributed most to GDP growth (Figure 3.28.1). This was achieved through strong employment generation, which created 1.3 million new jobs and pushed the unemployment rate down from 5.3% in 2018 to 5.1% in 2019—a historic low. Remittances from overseas workers expanded by 3.9%, also supporting robust consumption growth. With the catch-up in budgetary spending in the second half of the year, government consumption rose by 10.5% in 2019.

Investment plunged from 13.2% growth in 2018 to 0.6% contraction in 2019, primarily reflecting a 2.4% drop in public construction but also lower investment in transport equipment by 14.0% and in machinery by 4.1%. Partly offsetting these declines was a 13.8% increase in private construction. Weak external demand slashed real growth in exports of goods and services from 13.4% in 2018 to 3.2%. Import growth slowed even more, from 16.0% to 2.1%, reflecting lower demand for investment goods and components for export-oriented manufacturing—and allowing net exports to modestly contribute to growth.

On the supply side, service growth accelerated from 6.8% in 2018 to 7.1%, contributing 70% of economic growth in 2019 (Figure 3.28.2). Retail trade, tourism, business process

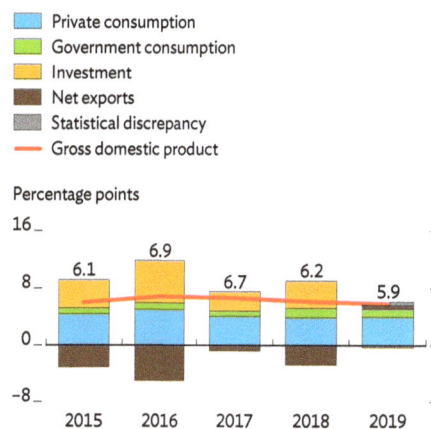

Figure 3.28.1 Demand-side contributions to growth

- Private consumption
- Government consumption
- Investment
- Net exports
- Statistical discrepancy
- Gross domestic product

Percentage points

Sources: *Asian Development Outlook* database; CEIC Data Company (accessed 12 March 2020).

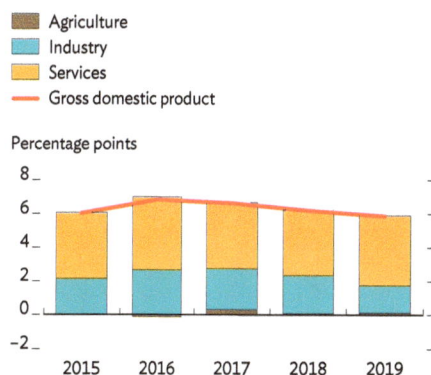

Figure 3.28.2 Supply-side contributions to growth

- Agriculture
- Industry
- Services
- Gross domestic product

Percentage points

Sources: *Asian Development Outlook* database; CEIC Data Company (accessed 12 March 2020).

This chapter was written by Teresa Mendoza of the Philippines Country Office, ADB, Manila.

outsourcing, finance, and real estate services were among the major contributors. Industry growth eased from 6.7% in 2018 to 4.9% but still generated nearly 30% of increased GDP in 2019. Manufacturing growth slipped to 3.8% on soft external demand, but food and beverages, chemicals, metal products, and electrical machinery posted strong gains supported by domestic demand. Brisk private construction partly countered a decline in public construction in the first half (Figure 3.28.3). Agriculture growth was again modest but improved from 0.9% in 2018 to 1.5% in 2019 despite being affected by weather disturbances, including drought caused by El Niño in the first half of the year.

Inflation declined throughout 2019, the average dropping by half from 5.2% in 2018 to 2.5%. Core inflation also slowed, from 4.2% to 3.2%, helping to ease inflation expectations (Figure 3.28.4). Rice prices declined on improved supply since the lifting of quantitative restrictions on rice imports in February of last year. In line with falling inflation expectations, Bangko Sentral ng Pilipinas, the central bank, began to loosen its monetary policy, reducing the overnight reverse repurchase rate by a cumulative 75 basis points in 2019. Additionally, the central bank lowered the reserve requirement ratio for most banks by 100 basis points from December 2019, bringing the cumulative ratio reduction to 400 basis points in 2019. Consequently, growth in domestic liquidity (M3) picked up to 11.9% year on year in January 2020 from 7.9% in January 2019.

Fiscal policy was automatically contractionary in the first half of 2019 because of the delay in passing the national budget (Figure 3.28.5). With strong catch-up in public spending in the second half, however, fiscal policy became expansionary (Figure 3.28.6). For the whole year, the fiscal budget deficit rose from the equivalent of 3.2% of GDP in 2018 to 3.5% in 2019. Budget expenditure excluding interest rose by 12.3% in 2019, peaking at 31.3% in the fourth quarter. Growth in budget revenue was higher by 10.1%, primarily through higher tax collection. Tax revenue as a share of GDP rose to 15.2%, the highest ratio achieved in over 2 decades. Reflecting this budget outcome, the ratio of government debt to GDP continued its downward trend to reach 41.5% in 2019. In February 2020, Fitch Ratings adjusted its outlook on its BBB investment grade credit rating for the Philippines from *stable* to *positive*.

The current account deficit narrowed to equal 0.1% of GDP in 2019 from 2.7% in 2018, mirroring the drop in domestic investment (Figure 3.28.7). Merchandise exports rose by 2.7% while imports declined by 3.0%, narrowing the merchandise trade deficit from 15.4% of GDP in 2018 to 12.9% last year. Higher remittances and earnings from exports of services substantially offset the merchandise trade deficit. Net inflow of foreign direct investment amounted to $7.6 billion, a 23.1% decline from 2018. Portfolio investment posted net inflow,

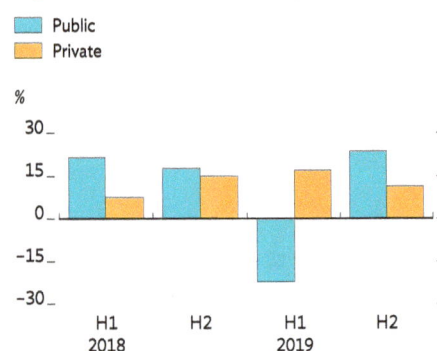

Figure 3.28.3 Construction growth

H = half.
Sources: *Asian Development Outlook* database; CEIC Data Company (accessed 12 March 2020).

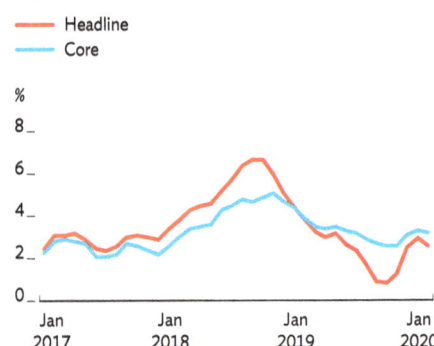

Figure 3.28.4 Inflation

Source: CEIC Data Company (accessed 12 March 2020).

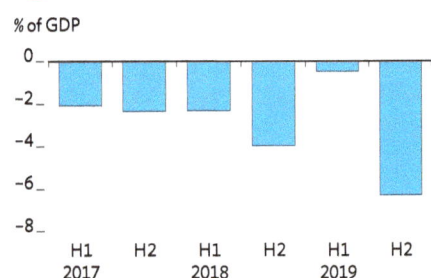

Figure 3.28.5 Fiscal balance

H = half.
Sources: *Asian Development Outlook* database; CEIC Data Company (accessed 12 March 2020).

reversing the previous year's net outflow. In sum, a $7.8 billion surplus in the overall balance of payments in 2019 reversed a deficit in 2018.

Foreign exchange reserves stood at $87.6 billion in February 2020, providing cover for more than 7 months of imports of goods and services and income payments. The Philippines' external debt position remains strong, with debt equal to only 23.3% of GDP in 2019, most of it with medium- to long-term maturity.

Economic prospects

Economic growth is projected to fall to 2.0% in 2020 before a strong recovery to 6.5% in 2021, assuming the COVID-19 outbreak is contained by June of this year.

The government has taken decisive action by instituting social distancing to stop the spread of COVID-19. However necessary, these enhanced community quarantine measures will weigh heavily on domestic demand. Following a sharp rise in reported cases of COVID-19 and incidences of local transmission, the government enforced community quarantine in Metro Manila on 15 March. It shortly expanded community quarantine to the entire island of Luzon, home to over half of the population and the generator of over 70% of GDP. Mass transit systems were suspended as home quarantine was imposed on households, public gatherings prohibited, schools suspended, and most retail establishments closed, with such exceptions as supermarkets, hospitals, and pharmacies. Quarantine has been enforced as well in some towns, cities, and provinces outside of Luzon. The schedule for lifting the quarantine is initially mid-April, but this will be reviewed in light of changes observed in the spread of the virus.

The negative effect on domestic demand is compounded by the impact of the outbreak in other countries on tourism, trade, and remittances. The first-round effect was a slump in tourism and aviation. Preliminary data show 9.8% growth in tourist arrivals year on year in January plunging to 41.4% contraction in February after travel restrictions were imposed. The People's Republic of China and the Republic of Korea, early hotspots of COVID-19, are key markets that together supplied 45% of international visitors to the Philippines in 2019 (Figure 3.28.8). Second-round effects that emerged as global supply chains were disrupted have affected manufacturing and merchandise exports.

Remittances from overseas Filipino workers, equal to 9% of GDP, will also slow. Large flows of remittances come from the US, Europe, and the Middle East, which collectively supply 70% of all remittances. Financial markets have been affected as well, with the stock market index dropping by 31% from the start of the year to late March.

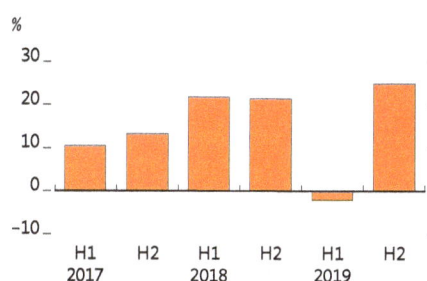

Figure 3.28.6 Government expenditure growth

H = half.
Note: Government expenditure excludes interest payments.
Sources: *Asian Development Outlook* database; CEIC Data Company (accessed 12 March 2020).

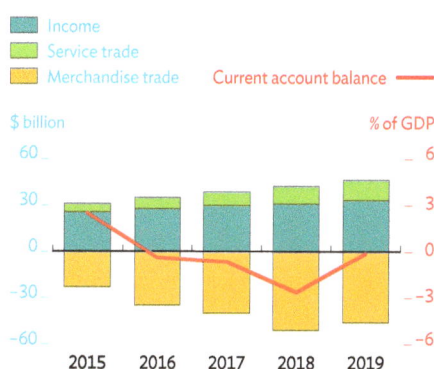

Figure 3.28.7 Current account components

Source: CEIC Data Company (accessed 20 March 2020).

Table 3.28.1 Selected economic indicators (%)

	2018	2019	2020	2021
GDP growth	6.2	5.9	2.0	6.5
Inflation	5.2	2.5	2.2	2.4
Current acct. bal. (share of GDP)	-2.7	-0.1	-0.3	-1.4

Sources: *Asian Development Outlook* database; CEIC Data Company (accessed 12 March 2020); ADB estimates.

The Philippine peso has depreciated by 0.9%, a relatively moderate decline compared with currency depreciation in other regional economies.

Expansionary monetary and fiscal policies remain supportive. The central bank cut policy interest rates by a total of 75 basis points in February and March, bringing the overnight reverse repurchase rate to 3.25% (Figure 3.28.9). It also announced a reduction by 200 basis points in the reserve requirement ratio for most banks from 30 March 2020. Under the 2020 budget, programmed expenditure is higher by 12%, with increased allocations for infrastructure and social services. Fiscal support has been announced, the first relief package featuring programs to contain COVID-19 and support affected businesses and vulnerable workers. Further relief and fiscal stimulus packages are expected. In the end, the planned budget deficit equal to 3.2% of GDP is likely to be significantly exceeded.

In 2021, a V-shape recovery is expected with growth reaching 6.5%, provided that the effects of the virus outbreak dissipate by June 2020.

Public investment and a rebound in private consumption will be the main drivers of the economic recovery. Public construction growth is expected to be strong with key public infrastructure projects under way. The government announced a revised infrastructure program in November 2019 that identified 100 projects under its Build Build Build infrastructure program, many of which are to be completed or substantially so by 2022. The revised program includes several infrastructure projects implemented by public–private partnerships.

Private consumption should recover strongly. Private investment is also expected to pick up in line with higher public spending on infrastructure and as lower interest rates stimulate investment. Acceleration in public spending on construction will drive investment in equipment and machinery, while private construction is sustained by demand for office and retail space and housing.

Also ready to help lift private investment are ongoing government reforms to ease the administrative and regulatory burden on businesses, championed through the recently established Anti-Red Tape Agency. Several bills currently under deliberation in Congress will, when approved, be catalysts for private investment. They include packages under the Comprehensive Tax Reform Program and initiatives to ease restrictions on foreign participation in some investment areas through amendments to the Public Services Act, Retail Trade Liberalization Act, and Foreign Investments Act. These reforms are part of the government's strategy to secure an A credit rating by 2022, to further lower the cost of borrowing in international and domestic credit markets.

Figure 3.28.8 International visitors, 2019

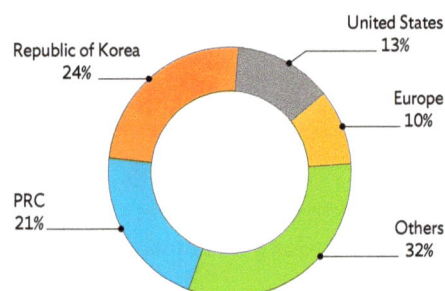

United States
13%

Republic of Korea
24%

Europe
10%

PRC
21%

Others
32%

PRC = People's Republic of China.
Note: Visitor arrivals exclude overseas Filipinos.
Source: CEIC Data Company (accessed 12 March 2020).

Figure 3.28.9 Policy interest rate

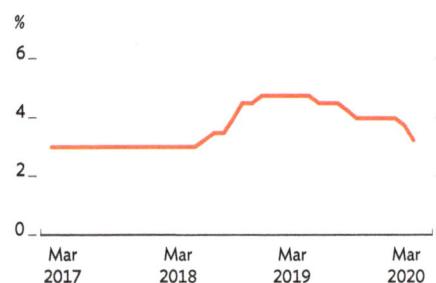

%

6

4

2

0

Mar
2017

Mar
2018

Mar
2019

Mar
2020

Note: Overnight reverse repurchase rate.
Source: CEIC Data Company (accessed 20 March 2020).

Inflation at 2.8% in the first 2 months of 2020 is projected to average 2.2% in the whole year and 2.4% in 2021. Lower global oil prices will be countered by price pressures caused by African swine fever. With inflation expected to remain within the central bank target range of 2.0%–4.0%, there is room for further monetary policy expansion.

The current account deficit is projected to remain modest this year. Exports of goods and services, particularly tourism, will slow under the COVID-19 pandemic, though imports will also be muted by sluggish domestic demand. The PRC, Japan, and the US are among the country's main trading partners. (Figure 3.28.10). Softer global oil prices should also cushion the deficit. The current account deficit will widen next year as imports strengthen to supply more robust public investment. On balance, the current account deficit is forecast to equal 0.3% of GDP in 2020 and 1.4% in 2021.

Risks tilt to the downside. The main downside risk to GDP growth in 2020 comes from COVID-19 and is therefore highly unpredictable. The impact on the economy will be larger than currently assumed if the global outbreak is prolonged beyond the first half, or if there is sustained local transmission in the Philippines. Also, a less-desirable U-shape recovery is possible if disrupted supply chains are not restored quickly, workers are not rehired immediately, or businesses are slow to restart operations. The government has space, however, for further fiscal and monetary expansion to mitigate the worst effects of the virus outbreak and to quicken economic recovery. Ensuring adequate resources to health care will help to prepare for the outbreak.

Policy challenge—building resilience under climate change

The global climate crisis is among the biggest challenges facing humanity in the 21st century. Rising temperatures and sea levels—and frequent extreme weather events such as heat waves, droughts, and coastal flooding—have already caused costly environmental damage in many countries in Asia and the Pacific in recent years. It has also contributed to frequent localized viral and bacterial epidemics within communities. Notably high profile in Australia, prolonged drought and high summer temperatures combined to spread catastrophic bushfires in 2019 and 2020.

The Philippines is a negligible contributor to global greenhouse gas (GHG) emissions, its emissions per capita far lower than global or Asian averages (Figure 3.28.11). However, the country does have a large stake in mitigating climate change, as it is among the world's most vulnerable, situated in a highly cyclone-prone region and experiencing

Figure 3.28.10 Main trade partners, 2019

Share of merchandise imports
Share of merchandise exports

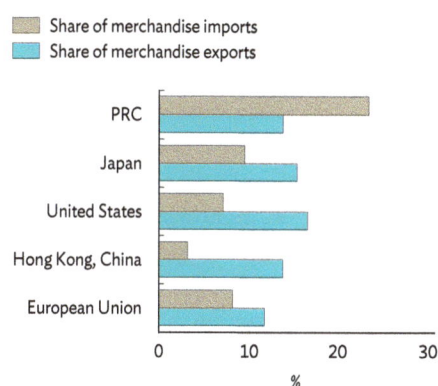

PRC = People's Republic of China.
Source: CEIC Data Company (accessed 12 March 2020).

Figure 3.28.11 Territorial carbon dioxide emissions

2000
2018

Tons per capita

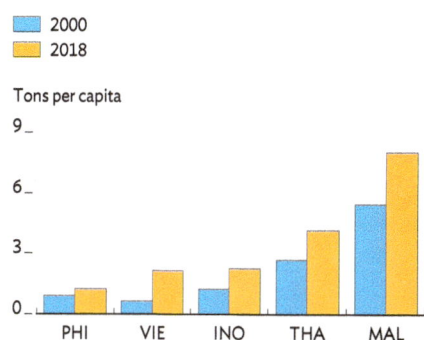

INO = Indonesia, MAL = Malaysia, PHI = Philippines, THA = Thailand, VIE = Viet Nam.
Source: Enerdata. https://www.enerdata.net/ (accessed 20 March 2020).

19–22 such storms most years. The 2019 Global Climate Risk Index ranked the Philippines fifth most affected by extreme weather events in 1998–2017. As an archipelago, the Philippines has extensive areas susceptible to rising sea levels, with most of its municipalities, home to nearly 60% of the population, located on the coast. Moreover, a significant share of the population depends on agriculture for its livelihood, and this is the sector likely to be worst affected by climate change.

The Philippines is active in global efforts to mitigate climate change. In 2015, the government announced an ambitious contribution to the Paris Agreement of a 70% reduction by 2030 in GHG emissions relative to business as usual, conditional on adequate international support. It ratified the Paris Agreement 2 years later and declared that it will update its GHG emission reduction contribution. In addition, the government has implemented an array of policies and programs to promote energy efficiency, renewable energy, and sustainable public transport systems. The Department of Tourism is rolling out its sustainable tourism development program for local governments, with investments in sewerage treatment plants, drainage, and solid waste management.

The climate challenge for the Philippines over the next 30 years is to avoid potentially large increases in GHG emissions while growing rapidly and to invest strategically in climate resilience. A good next step would be to strengthen its commitment to reducing GHG emissions. Some countries, such as New Zealand, have enacted or are considering legislation to lock in net zero GHG emissions by 2040 or 2050. The Philippines could do the same, as this would further encourage investment in climate change mitigation and resilience. The government and private sector could also consider new approaches to investments in energy, infrastructure, and agriculture.

The country can promote renewable energy sources further to drive economic growth. Significant GHG mitigation can come from making electricity generation less carbon intensive. Power generation contributes half of Philippine GHG emissions with its dependence on fossil fuels (Figure 3.28.12). The use of coal has expanded dramatically in recent years, more than doubling from 12% of the primary energy mix in 2000 to 27% in 2018. Setting aside transportation and concentrating on power generation, the share of renewables declined from 43% in 2000 to 23% in 2018, while the coal-fired share rose to 52%. Shifting the energy mix back to more renewables will require reform to incentivize large investments in renewable power generation. A carbon tax on polluting industries could be studied.

The emergence of affordable low-carbon technologies such as solar and wind power offer opportunities to scale up investments. Promoting renewable energy would facilitate

Figure 3.28.12 Greenhouse gas emissions by sector

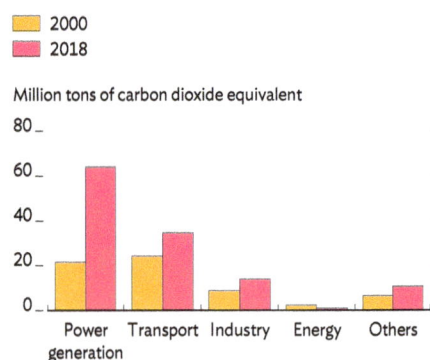

Million tons of carbon dioxide equivalent

Notes: Energy includes losses from oil refining.
Others include commerce, residences, and agriculture.
Source: Department of Energy.

technology transfer to the Philippines. Developing local expertise in renewables has potential to create a new growth industry that pioneers the export of renewable energy technology, creating new manufacturing industries and jobs.

Infrastructure programs, particularly when part of recovery and reconstruction following disasters, should be climate friendly and resilient. The government's Build Build Build program emphasizes mass urban transportation systems to help reduce GHG emissions. Such investments include expanding metro and light rail systems, a subway in Metro Manila, and an inter-region rail system such as from New Clark City in Central Luzon to Calamba, Laguna, in South Luzon, which could transport 700,000 passengers daily by 2030. These mass urban transit systems would help shrink the Philippine carbon footprint.

Agriculture offers opportunities for the government to invest in climate resilience, as it is the sector most vulnerable to changes in rainfall and weather patterns, rising sea levels, and more frequent outbreaks of crop pests. Institutional reform will be needed in water supply. A good first step would be for Congress to pass a bill to consolidate under one department the 30-plus agencies currently concerned with water. Investment will be needed to secure water resources and improve efficiency in irrigation and other water use. Institutional reform will be necessary to better enable agricultural extension services to transfer appropriate technologies to farmers, as well as to attract private sector participation in strengthening livestock and crop health systems to prevent, detect, and respond to pests and diseases. An array of emerging climate-smart technologies and practices are available for adoption such as solar- or wind-powered water pumps, drip irrigation, innovative greenhouse technologies, and more efficient field machinery.

Singapore

Growth last year slowed to a 10-year low in this wide open economy. As the global economy is likely to continue to slow with the spread of COVID-19, growth is forecast to be subdued this year, with a slight pickup in 2021. Inflation is expected to remain subdued and the current account surplus ample. Embracing financial technology is key to continued growth in this highly developed hub of Southeast Asia.

Economic performance

GDP growth decelerated to 0.7% in 2019, its lowest since 2009, as export-oriented industries like manufacturing and trade were affected by a downswing in the global electronics cycle, weaker global demand, and trade tensions between the US and the People's Republic of China (PRC). Having expanded by 8.1% in 2018, exports of goods and services contracted by 1.6% last year. Domestic demand remained robust, however, partly offsetting the export slowdown.

All major components of domestic demand—private consumption, government consumption, and investment—held up well. While growth in private consumption moderated from a 4.2% rise in 2018 to 3.7% last year, government consumption growth was only a trifle slower, edging down from 2.9% in 2018 to 2.8%. Consumption expanded by 3.5% on steady growth in private expenditure driven by higher spending on health care, clothing, food, education, and recreation. Meanwhile, domestic fixed investment continued to decline, but with the pace of contraction slowing from 3.4% in 2018 to 0.2% (Figure 3.29.1).

By sector, manufacturing shrank by 1.4%, dragged down mainly by weaker electronics exports. Among services, wholesale and retail trade declined by 2.9%, but all others posted positive growth. Finance and insurance, business services, and the "other services" category were the main drivers of service sector growth. Construction turned around contraction by 3.5% a year earlier to grow by 2.8%, with public and private construction both expanding (Figure 3.29.2).

Average consumer price inflation rose marginally from 0.4% in 2018 to 0.6%. An increase in administered prices for road transportation more than offset the slight decline in housing and utility prices. Transportation costs increased on

Figure 3.29.1 Demand-side contributions to growth

- Private consumption
- Government consumption
- Gross capital formation
- Net exports
- Statistical discrepancy
- Gross domestic product

Percentage points

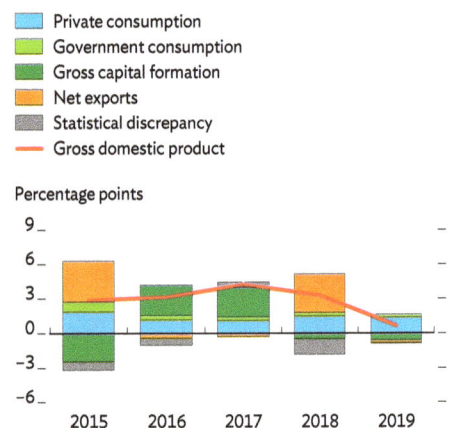

Source: Ministry of Trade and Industry. Economic Survey Singapore 2019 (accessed as of 17 February 2020).

Figure 3.29.2 Contributions to growth, by industry

- 2019
- 2018

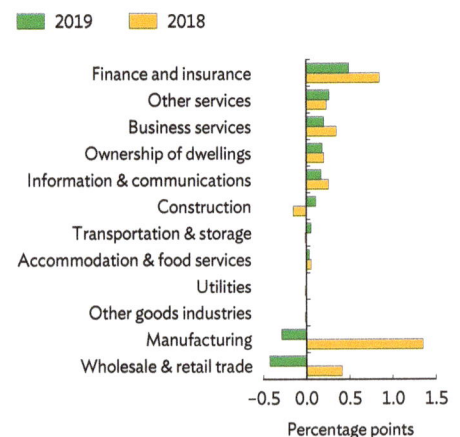

Finance and insurance
Other services
Business services
Ownership of dwellings
Information & communications
Construction
Transportation & storage
Accommodation & food services
Utilities
Other goods industries
Manufacturing
Wholesale & retail trade

Percentage points

Source: Ministry of Trade and Industry. Economic Survey Singapore 2019 (accessed as of 17 February 2020).

This chapter was written by Shu Tian and Mai Lin Villaruel of the Economic Research and Regional Cooperation Department, ADB, Manila.

higher fares for public transport and on higher gasoline prices coupled with a rise in prices for car certificates of entitlement and higher repair and maintenance costs. Core inflation, which excludes accommodation and private road transport, rose by 1.0% on increased costs for education, food, health care, and recreation and culture (Figure 3.29.3).

The trade surplus expanded to equal 26.3% of GDP in 2019, though both exports and imports of goods weakened in US dollar terms. Merchandise exports declined with the continued global slump in electronics, while merchandise imports contracted as those of both oil and other merchandise shrank. Service exports have recorded robust growth in recent years and now exceed merchandise exports. Net service exports amounted to 1.5% of GDP in 2019 as receipts in financial and insurance services and business services exceeded travel and transport payments. The current account surplus thus remained nearly unchanged at the equivalent of 17.0% of GDP, but the overall balance of payments fell to a deficit equal to 2.3% of GDP as financial accounts ran a greater deficit owing to higher net outflow of portfolio investment (Figure 3.29.4).

In April 2019, the Monetary Authority of Singapore maintained its policy of encouraging the modest and gradual appreciation of the Singapore dollar in nominal effective terms, but in October it slowed the rate of appreciation slightly. The Singapore dollar appreciated in nominal terms against US dollar in the second half of the year (Figure 3.29.5). The Singapore interbank offered rate had been rising since 2018 but fell by 0.22 basis points from its peak in July 2019 to the end of December 2019, which spurred higher credit growth in the second half of the year (Figure 3.29.6).

The fiscal deficit in fiscal year 2019 (FY2019, ended 31 March 2020) was S$5.1 billion, equal to 1.0% of GDP. Revenue in FY2019 grew by 1.3%, driven by growth in personal and corporate income tax, withholding tax, and an impressive increase in statutory boards contributions. A rise in government expenditure reflected higher outlays on health care, the environment, and economic development. Including net investment returns on Singapore's reserves and special transfers, however, the overall budget recorded a much lower deficit in FY2019 of S$1.7 billion, equal to 0.3% of GDP.

Economic prospects

In the fourth quarter of 2019, the economy showed signs of recovery as GDP grew by 1.0%, supported by higher growth in construction and services. Exports other than oil expanded in December by 2.4% year on year, after 9 months of decline, and Singapore had attracted S$6.3 billion in fixed asset investment in the fourth quarter of 2019, the highest recorded

Figure 3.29.3 Inflation

Source: CEIC Data Company (accessed as of 17 February 2020).

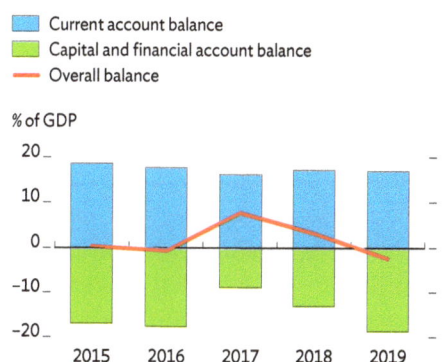

Figure 3.29.4 Balance of payments

Source: Ministry of Trade and Industry. Economic Survey Singapore 2019 (accessed as of 17 February 2020).

Figure 3.29.5 Exchange rates

Source: CEIC Data Company (accessed as of 17 February 2020).

in a decade. The manufacturing purchasing managers' index started to edge up to reach 50.1 in December 2019 and 50.3 in January 2020, when the electronics index reached 50.1, signaling broad-based economic expansion (Figure 3.29.7).

However, with COVID-19 spreading to more economies, Singapore's growth prospects have dimmed. Manufacturing and construction will be adversely affected by supply chain disruption and weaker exports. The outlook for the service sector is similarly bleaker than it was. Tourism-related services will suffer in the near term as tourist numbers are likely to decline sharply, especially from the PRC, which has provided about 20.0% of the tourist arrivals in Singapore in recent years. In response, the government has announced fiscal support for services likely to be affected by COVID-19 in the form of corporate income tax rebates, rental waivers, and expedited access to working capital loans.

Domestic demand will also be affected, though the damage is likely to be cushioned by public investment and government spending. The Ministry of Health has been granted an additional budget of S$800 million to contain COVID-19, and the government has introduced a stabilization and support package worth S$4.0 billion, aiming to aid businesses and boost consumer spending. As more economies become affected by COVID-19, these fiscal stimulus efforts may be partly offset by a greater weakening of external demand from major trade partners and supply chain disruption. Growth is thus forecast at 0.2% in 2020 and 2.0% in 2021.

Inflation is expected to remain tame both this year and next. Though rising prices for food and some services will continue to apply modest upward pressure on consumer prices, oil prices will drag on inflation in 2020. Low inflation allows monetary policy to ease further to cushion the effects from the COVID-19 outbreak.

As the PRC is a top trade partner of Singapore, external trade will be adversely affected by supply chain disruptions brought about by factory closures and weaker import demand. Trade is further weighed down as more trade partners are affected by COVID-19. On balance, the current account surplus is expected to continue at 17% of GDP this year and next.

In light of COVID-19, fiscal policy will likely continue to be expansionary in FY2020, with the overall deficit expected to reach S$10.9 billion, equal to 2.1% of GDP. The government passed its 2020 budget with a S$5.6 billion special economic package, including the above-mentioned S$800 million for the Ministry of Health, to mitigate the economic consequences of COVID-19 in the short run and to bolster growth. As the government has accumulated fiscal surpluses over the years, it enjoys enough fiscal space for an expansionary fiscal policy.

Table 3.29.1 Selected economic indicators (%)

	2018	2019	2020	2021
GDP growth	3.4	0.7	0.2	2.0
Inflation	0.4	0.6	0.7	1.3
Current acct. bal. (share of GDP)	17.2	17.0	17.0	17.0

Sources: Ministry of Trade and Industry. Economic Survey Singapore 2019; ADB estimates.

Figure 3.29.6 Financial indicators

Source: CEIC Data Company (accessed as of 17 February 2020).

Figure 3.29.7 Purchasing managers' indexes

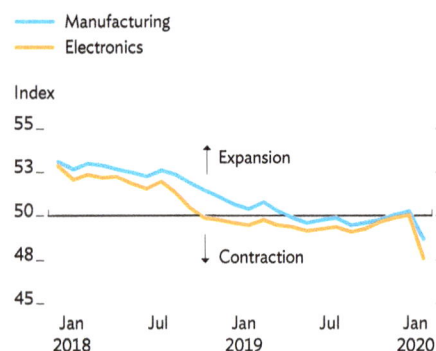

Source: CEIC Data Company (accessed as of 9 March 2020).

Risks to the outlook include uncertainty over the scope, duration, and impact of the pandemic; continuing trade tensions between the US and the PRC; and uncertain oil prices in light of geopolitical tensions in the Middle East and decisions by the Organization of the Petroleum Exporting Countries.

Policy challenge—embracing financial technology

Singapore has witnessed a rapid increase of financial technology (fintech), or digital innovation in financial service provision. Investment and adoption have soared in the past few years, and the city now hosts nearly 40% of the fintech businesses in Southeast Asia. Despite trade tensions, fintech investment in Singapore continued to expand to nearly S$1 billion during the first 3 quarters of 2019, a 69% increase over the same period in 2018 (Figure 3.29.8). Singapore owes its status as a leading global fintech hub partly to good infrastructure, a convenient location, a favorable intellectual property regime, and a fintech-friendly policy and regulatory environment. The country now hosts more than 1,000 fintech companies and more than 40 innovation labs.

Singapore's fintech development still faces some challenges. While it offers novel financial solutions for businesses, the rapid growth of fintech companies calls for more expertise and capacity in terms of compliance and risk-management practices. And, while markets in Southeast Asia present good business opportunities, differences in legal systems and regulatory frameworks across the region may limit the application and expansion of fintech solutions. Finally, while Singapore has a large pool of financial experts, demand is still high for experts with skills in big data analysis, business design, social media, and other emerging areas.

Fintech companies may collaborate with traditional financial institutions to enhance their capacity in compliance and risk management, with traditional financial institutions benefiting from exposure to new business models and higher efficiency. They can partner as well with law firms, commercial businesses, and fintech companies in other Southeast Asian markets to lower cultural barriers and better understand national regulations. In addition, collaboration by Southeast Asian central banks can engender a friendly regional regulatory environment for regional fintech companies aiming to tap the regional market. To increase the supply of fintech professionals, schemes to retrain workers and specially designed education programs for university students promise to close the supply gap over the long run.

Figure 3.29.8 Financial technology investment in Singapore

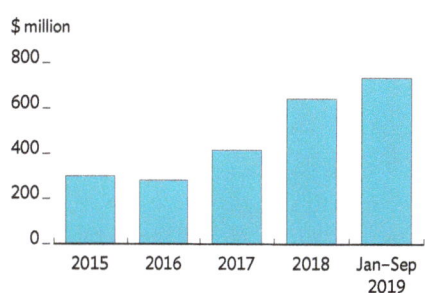

Source: Accenture Research analysis on CB Insights, Pitchbook, and Tracxn databases.

Thailand

Restrained largely by slowing exports, Thailand posted paltry growth at 2.4% last year. GDP growth is likely to slow further this year to 4.8% contraction but could pick up to 2.5% in 2021. Risks to the growth forecast remain tilted to the downside as COVID-19 could be especially damaging to an economy heavily dependent on international trade and tourism. Small and medium-sized enterprises could benefit from help in adapting their business models to digital technology.

Economic performance

GDP growth plummeted from 4.2% in 2018 to 2.4% in 2019 as merchandise exports continued to contract (Figure 3.30.1). Exports of goods and services reversed growth in 2018 at more than 3.0% to contract by 2.6% in 2019, largely reflecting a slowdown in global trade tied to trade conflict between the US and the People's Republic of China (PRC). Almost all major categories of merchandise exports contracted.

Manufacturing export declines hit electronic components and devices, automobiles, petroleum-related products, and agricultural products, in particular rice and rubber. Rice exports were made less competitive by the local currency strengthening against the US dollar. Meanwhile, exports of rubber declined following the implementation of the Agreed Export Tonnage Scheme of the International Tripartite Rubber Council, under which producers pledged to cut rubber exports for 4 months beginning in April 2019.

Combined exports to the European Union, the US, and Japan expanded by just 1.9%, with a 6.6% decline to the European Union. Meanwhile, exports to other markets declined by 4.6%, dragged down by softer demand from Southeast Asia. Exports of services bounced back in the second half of 2019 thanks to the return of PRC tourists, who stayed away after a fatal ferry accident in Phuket in July 2018; visa fee exemptions for tourists from India, the PRC, and Taipei,China; and increased flight frequencies between Thailand and the Russian Federation. Tourist arrivals in Thailand reached 39.8 million in 2019, or 4.2% higher than in the previous year (Figure 3.30.2). Meanwhile, government consumption remained lackluster, and growth in private investment slowed somewhat, from 4.1% in 2018 to 2.8%.

Figure 3.30.1 Demand-side contributions to growth

- Private consumption
- Government consumption
- Total investment
- Net exports
- Statistical discrepancy
- Gross domestic product

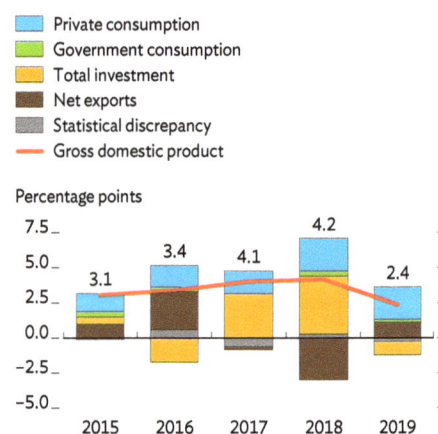

Percentage points

Source: Office of the National Economic and Social Development Council. http://www.nesdc.go.th (accessed 11 March 2020).

Figure 3.30.2 Tourism indicators

- Number of tourists
- Growth in the number of tourists

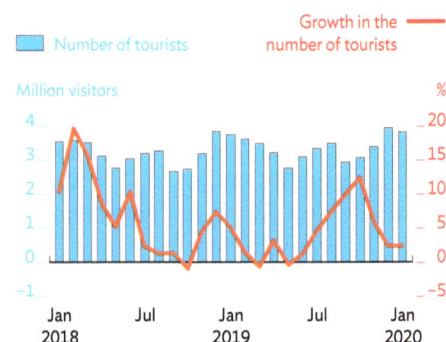

Million visitors

Sources: Bank of Thailand. http://www.bot.or.th; CEIC Data Company (both accessed 11 March 2020).

This chapter was written by Chitchanok Annonjarn of the Thailand Resident Mission, ADB, Bangkok.

Weak external demand kept investment and private consumption soft, with expansion in the latter declining from 4.6% in 2018 to 4.5% last year. Meanwhile, government consumption also remained subdued. Domestic demand woes were made worse by a continued slowdown in private investment growth from 4.1% in 2018 to 2.8% last year.

Weak external demand and domestic consumption lowered capacity utilization in manufacturing, inducing businesses to delay investment and crimping imports of capital goods. To boost sluggish domestic activity, the government introduced economic stimulus measures such as soft loans for farmers, more livelihood transfers to low-income earners, cash handouts and tax breaks to boost domestic tourist spending, and soft loans to small and medium-sized enterprises, but the impact seemed limited. Public spending recorded moderate growth, but its support for economic growth faltered in the last quarter of 2019 owing to delays affecting investment projects of state-owned enterprises, and the late enactment of the Annual Budget Expenditure Act for fiscal year 2020 (FY2020, ending 30 September 2020) caused by a delay in forming a new government. In FY2019, the fiscal balance recorded a small deficit equal to 2.6% of GDP (Figure 3.30.3).

As merchandise exports contracted, merchandise imports followed suit, reversing 13.7% expansion in 2018 to decline by 5.4% in 2019. Import contraction affected mostly imports of raw materials and intermediate goods, in line with broader economic softening.

Growth slowed across sectors in 2019 (Figure 3.30.4). Agricultural output fell especially for rice and sugarcane, but smaller harvests pushed up crop prices. In sum, agricultural growth sank from 5.5% expansion in 2018 to essentially zero. Industry output stagnated, and services, led by sluggish tourism, slowed from 4.8% expansion in 2018 to 4.0% in 2019.

As growth slowed, so did inflation, which edged down from 1.1% in 2018 to just 0.7% last year (Figure 3.30.5). Lower international oil prices played their part. Core inflation, which excludes volatile food and fuel prices, was even lower at 0.5%. In December 2019, the cabinet approved a new headline inflation target of 1%–3% for 2020, with which the Bank of Thailand, the central bank, shaved 1 percentage point off the top of a target range that had been in place since 2015. The central bank cited structural factors for driving down prices, including an aging population and technological advancements such as the growth in e-commerce, which reduce costs.

The current account balance posted a larger surplus of $37.3 billion thanks to expanded surpluses in both merchandise and services. The capital and financial account recorded a deficit of $12.6 billion, mostly reflecting a rise in outward investment. The surplus in the overall balance of payments thus rose from $7.3 billion in 2018 to $13.6 billion.

Figure 3.30.3 Fiscal balance

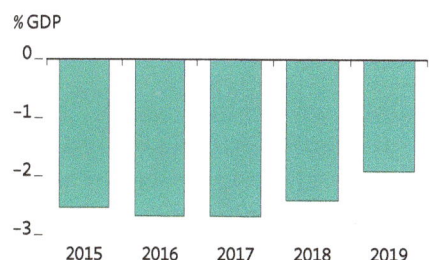

Note: Years are fiscal years ending on 30 September of that year.
Source: Bank of Thailand, http://www.bot.or.th (accessed 11 March 2020).

Figure 3.30.4 Supply-side contributions to growth

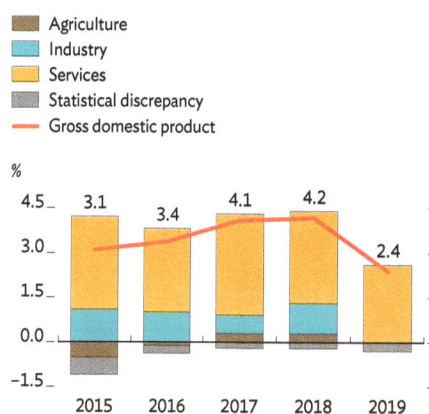

Source: Office of the National Economic and Social Development Council. http://www.nesdc.go.th (accessed 11 March 2020).

Figure 3.30.5 Inflation and policy interest rate

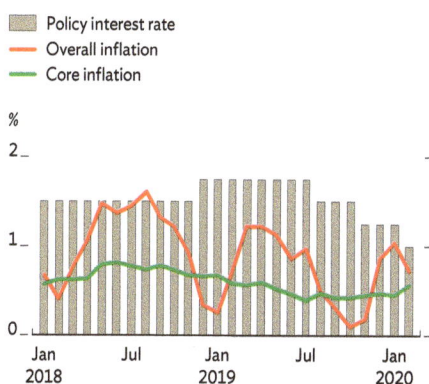

Sources: Bank of Thailand. http://www.bot.or.th; CEIC Data Company (both accessed 11 March 2020).

International reserves stood at $224.3 billion at the end of 2019, sufficient to cover 13 months of imports or 3.7 times short-term external debt. With a comfortable balance of payments and international reserves, the Thai baht appreciated by 4.1% against the US dollar in 2019 (Figure 3.30.6).

The central bank cut its policy rate, the 1-day repurchase rate, by 0.25% twice, in August and November 2019, to 1.25% to support growth during the slowdown and induce inflation toward the target. Fiscal policy remained supportive of growth, with an actual budget deficit rising from the equivalent of 2.8% of GDP FY2018 to 3.1%. Public debt remained sustainable at 41.2% of GDP, only 2.7% of it held overseas.

Economic prospects

Thailand's economy is expected to remain sluggish in the near term. GDP is projected to contract by 4.8% in 2020 and then recover to 2.5% in 2021 (Figure 3.30.7). Contraction and low growth will be accompanied by benign inflation. Public debt is likely to remain sustainable despite more government borrowing for large infrastructure projects. The current account is expected to maintain a large surplus in 2020 with slow economic activity and then narrow marginally in 2021 with increased imports to supply investment projects.

Exports of goods and services are projected to continue their declining trend this year, mainly because of the COVID-19 outbreak, before turning around in 2021. Phase one of the trade deal between US and PRC, signed earlier this year, could help Thai exports, but it remains to be seen whether or not the terms of the trade deal will actually be implemented. Meanwhile, the impact of COVID-19 on merchandise exports is likely to become clearer in the second quarter of 2020. Some exports such as electronics, automobiles, and chemical products are likely to suffer hits from supply chain disruption in the PRC. Meanwhile, other exports—notably metal products, machinery, and equipment—could gain from trade diversion, though probably not enough to offset the impact from supply chain disruption. Exports of services are also expected to deteriorate in 2020 with a significant decline in foreign tourists but rebound in 2021 as they return. Growth in private consumption is expected to slow in 2020 as growth in household income weakens. In addition, COVID-19 and drought in 2020 will dampen private consumption before improvement in 2021 with gradual economic recovery.

Private investment growth is projected to be negative this year as external demand continues to decline and business sentiment plunges mainly because of concern over COVID-19. Traction should return next year as some public–private partnership and public investment projects that were postponed in 2019 and 2020 finally begin implementation.

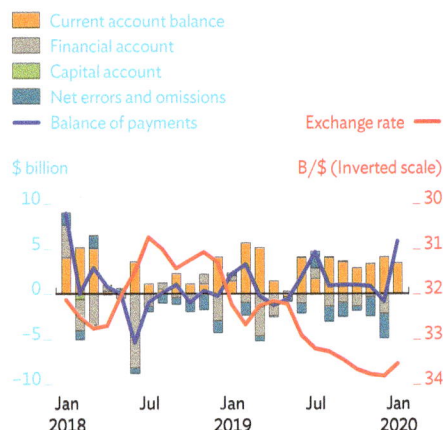

Figure 3.30.6 Balance of payments and exchange rate

Sources: Bank of Thailand. http://www.bot.or.th; CEIC Data Company (both accessed 11 March 2020).

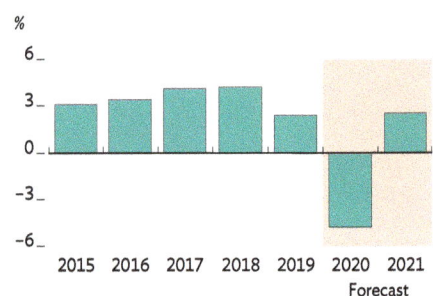

Figure 3.30.7 GDP growth

Source: *Asian Development Outlook* database.

Table 3.30.1 Selected economic indicators (%)

	2018	2019	2020	2021
GDP growth	4.2	2.4	−4.8	2.5
Inflation	1.1	0.7	−0.9	0.4
Current acct. bal. (share of GDP)	5.6	6.7	7.1	6.7

Sources: Office of the National Economic and Social Development Council. http://www.nesdc.go.th; Bank of Thailand. http://www.bot.or.th; CEIC Data Company (all accessed 11 March 2020); ADB estimates.

Thailand is expected to continue to benefit from government incentives to lure more foreign investors. In 2019, the value of investment applications to the Board of Investment rose by 69.0%. Actual foreign investment should be more evident in 2021. Merchandise imports are likely to improve with higher investment.

Growth is projected to moderate across sectors. Growth in agriculture is expected to be meager, with drought across nearly half of Thailand forecast to get worse in 2020. The water level in the Mekong River is at its lowest since 1992, affecting agricultural output and farm incomes. Manufacturing growth is likely to soften this year and gradually improve next year in line with economic recovery. The service sector is forecasted to record negative growth in 2020 as inbound tourism takes a substantially hit from the COVID-19 outbreak. Some tourism-related businesses temporarily close and lay off employees, which threatens off-farm income. However, tourism is expected to get back on track in 2021. Low growth and oil prices should be accompanied by tame inflation, which is projected at –0.9% in 2020 and slightly higher at 0.4% in 2021, in line with the economic outlook (Figure 3.30.8).

The current account surplus is expected to remain large in 2020 and 2021. It is projected to widen in 2020 as imports collapse in the slowdown. In 2021, import growth is expected to outpace that of exports, supported mainly by the rollout of infrastructure projects that will narrow the trade surplus. Net service exports should post only a small surplus in 2020, given the impact of COVID-19 on tourism. The current account surplus is projected to equal 7.1% of GDP in 2020 and 6.7% in 2021. The financial account could be balanced as Thai investors venture abroad more and foreign investment in Thailand rises. The surplus in the overall balance of payments should remain comfortable, as should international reserves (Figure 3.30.9).

Fiscal and monetary policies are expected to remain accommodative this year and next. The government anticipates a FY2020 budget deficit of B469 billion, up by 4.3% from FY2019. However, budget expenditure is lagging because of prolonged negotiations to establish a coalition government. This has delayed the start of new investment projects, weighing on an already faltering economy. Any boost from the planned increase in expenditure is heavily weighted toward the latter half of FY2020.

Meanwhile, the central bank is expected to continue to pursue an accommodative monetary policy to support economic growth. In February and March 2020, it cut its policy rate by further 0.50 percentage points in total to 0.75%, in response to COVID-19, delays in budget implementation, and severe drought. As the policy interest rate is already low, the central bank may consider using other measures jointly with monetary policy.

Figure 3.30.8 Inflation

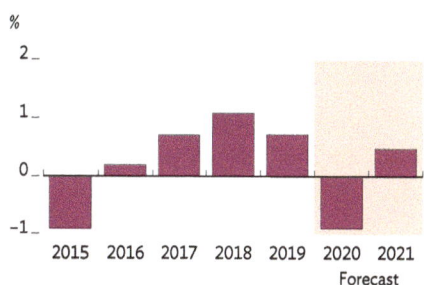

Source: *Asian Development Outlook* database.

Figure 3.30.9 Current account balance

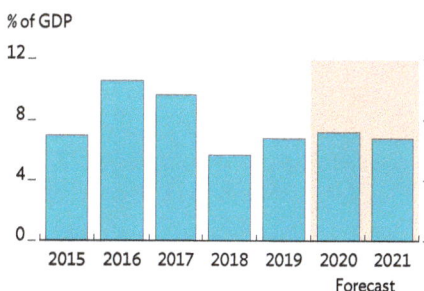

Source: *Asian Development Outlook* database.

Risks to the outlook tilt to the downside. The major external risks are deeper contraction in global economic growth and any reheating of the trade conflict between the US and the PRC. The impact of COVID-19 will depend on how quickly it can be brought under control. Knock-on impacts from a likely slowdown in inbound tourism could dent domestic confidence in the economy for many months. Purely domestic risks to growth could arise from delays in implementing the FY2020 budget or infrastructure investment projects, or from prolonged drought.

Policy challenge—strengthening smaller firms through digital transformation

Several global challenges and domestic structural issues have weighed on the Thai economy in recent years, keeping actual economic growth below potential. In response, the government has actively promoted Thailand 4.0, a new economic model to embrace digital transformation. The private sector similarly realizes the potential benefits of digital transformation, but some businesses, especially small and medium-sized enterprises (SMEs), struggle to transition their businesses into the digital phase.

SMEs are the backbone of economic growth in Thailand as they account for more than 90% of enterprises in the country, employ some three-quarters of the national workforce, and in 2018 supplied 43.0% of GDP growth (Figure 3.30.10). However, prolonged economic uncertainty in the past few years has kept SMEs from investing to improve their efficiency and productivity, adding to structural woes that undermine competitiveness.

Several forms of government support, notably soft loans, loan guarantees, and tax exemptions, could give a helping hand to struggling SMEs and keep them from going out of business. However, SMEs need more than money to recover. They need to transform themselves into smart SMEs, applying high technology and more innovation to production and upgrading their capability to trade using online channels.

A study conducted by Cisco Systems—the information technology, networking, and cybersecurity giant—and Thailand's Office of Small and Medium Enterprise Promotion enumerated the hurdles to digital transformation that SMEs face: lack of customer data, digital skills or talent, or a digital mindset. Policies should therefore provide more assistance toward improving SME access to technology, supporting links with larger firms to enable technological upgrades, and improving education to equip students with knowledge and skills to thrive in the digital economy. Once SMEs can upgrade their capability and become more advanced on a large scale, economic transformation and enhanced national competitiveness can follow (Figure 3.30.11).

Figure 3.30.10 SME expenditures

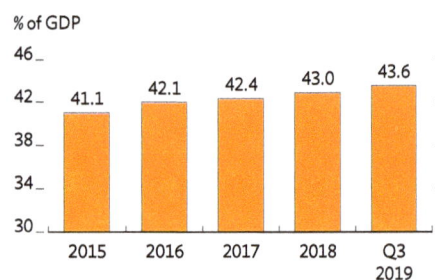

Q = quarter, SME = small or medium-sized economy.
Source: Office of SME Promotion.

Figure 3.30.11 Digital transformation challenges for SMEs in Thailand

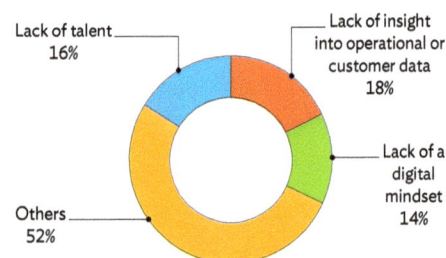

SME = small or medium-sized enterprise.
Source: IDC-Cisco SMB Digital Maturity Index 2019.

Timor-Leste

Fiscal stimulus brought the economy back to growth in 2019, reversing 2 years of economic contraction. Inflation eased on lower food prices, and the current account improved from deficit to surplus, if only briefly. The economy is expected to contract in 2020 under political uncertainty but should pick up in 2021. Improving air connectivity and reducing travel costs with the rest of the world would be important enablers of economic diversification.

Economic performance

GDP excluding the large offshore oil and gas industry (hereafter GDP) grew by 3.4% in 2019 (Figure 3.31.1). This return to growth was driven by modest fiscal stimulus. Public spending increased by 4.3% in 2019 as a 13.2% increase in recurrent expenditure more than offset an 8.4% decline in capital and development expenditure (Figure 3.31.2). Public spending was more evenly distributed throughout the year in 2019 than in some recent years as the work of government was uninterrupted by elections or the formation of a new government, as earlier feared.

While domestic revenue collection fell slightly, this was offset by high proceeds from petroleum taxes and Petroleum Fund investments, together generating a surplus equal to 8.0% of GDP. Government consumption rebounded strongly in 2019, reversing 1.0% contraction in the previous year to expand by 11.5%. Growth in private consumption slowed, however, from 2.6% in 2018 to 1.9% last year. Similarly, investment contracted despite ongoing work on major projects such as Tibar Bay port.

By sector, growth acceleration in 2019 was led largely by services, which account for two-thirds of the economy and are closely linked with government consumption. After contracting by 2.6% in 2018, the service sector posted robust 5.4% growth in 2019. Construction, by contrast, contracted by an estimated 4.0% in 2019 as public investment declined, and agricultural production also shrank slightly with somewhat unfavorable weather.

Even as GDP growth reversed a 2-year declining trend with fairly robust growth, inflation eased from 2.3% in 2018 to 0.9% in 2019, pulled down mostly by lower prices for imported food (Figure 3.31.3).

Figure 3.31.1 Supply-side contributions to growth

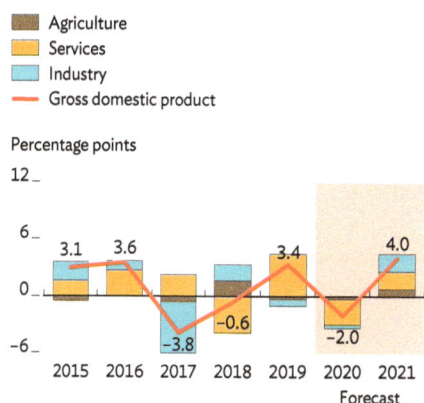

- Agriculture
- Services
- Industry
- Gross domestic product

Percentage points

Sources: Statistics Timor-Leste; ADB estimates.

Figure 3.31.2 Public expenditure components

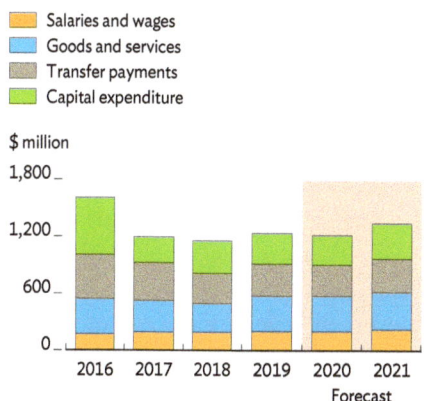

- Salaries and wages
- Goods and services
- Transfer payments
- Capital expenditure

$ million

Sources: Timor-Leste Budget Transparency Portal; ADB estimates.

This chapter was written by David Freedman of the Cambodia Resident Mission, ADB, Phnom Penh.

A large increase in petroleum income and a slight narrowing of the trade deficit moved a current account deficit equal to 12.2% of GDP in 2018 into a surplus of 8.1%. Earnings from coffee exports rose by 30.8% as export prices increased. With investment contracting and reduced imports of capital goods, the trade deficit narrowed slightly.

Turning to the offshore petroleum industry, a large increase in petroleum income lifted the fiscal balance from a deficit equal to 6.0% of GDP in 2018 into a surplus of 8.0% in 2019. Meanwhile, though, money supply went the other way, reversing 3.1% growth in 2018 with 13.1% contraction last year.

Economic prospects

The economy is expected to contract by 2.0% in 2020 as political uncertainty weighs on government activity, and as measures to mitigate the COVID-19 pandemic suppress demand. GDP growth is expected to accelerate to 4.0% in 2021 on moderate fiscal stimulus and reviving private investment.

The formulation of the 2020 budget was delayed by disagreement within the three-party coalition that forms the government. An initial proposal for $1.95 billion in appropriations in 2020 was submitted to the National Parliament but then withdrawn. The budget proposal was revised down and resubmitted but not approved. In the absence of an approved budget, the government will make monthly appropriations equal to one-twelfth of the previous year's budget.

A range of measures including restrictions on international travel have been introduced to control the spread of COVID-19. These measures and the ongoing budget impasse will slow the implementation of government programs and reduce demand during the first half of this year, thus slowing growth. Government activity may pick up in the second half of 2020, but the outlook is highly uncertain. More substantial stimulus is expected in 2021 as the government moves forward with the implementation of its investment program.

A long dry season and spotty rainfall in the second half of 2019, and an infestation of fall armyworms, are expected to reduce the production of food and cash crops. Inflation is thus projected to accelerate moderately to 1.3% in 2020 and 1.8% in 2021 as food prices rise locally and internationally.

Volatility in global bond and equity markets may affect the performance of the investment portfolio of the Petroleum Fund (Figure 3.31.4). Projected lower oil prices will also hit fiscal and current account balances and may dampen investor interest in developing new petroleum fields. The current account is therefore expected to fall back into large deficits in the near term.

Figure 3.31.3 Inflation

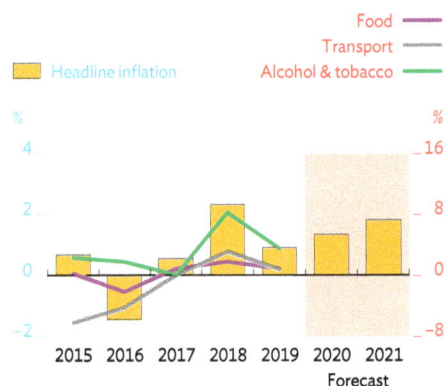

Sources: Statistics Timor-Leste; ADB estimates.

Table 3.31.1 Selected economic indicators (%)

	2018	2019	2020	2021
GDP growth	-0.6	3.4	-2.0	4.0
Inflation	2.3	0.9	1.3	1.8
Current acct. bal. (share of GDP)	-12.2	8.1	-10.5	-30.4

Sources: Statistics Timor-Leste; Timor-Leste Central Bank; ADB estimates.

Figure 3.31.4 Petroleum Fund balance at year-end

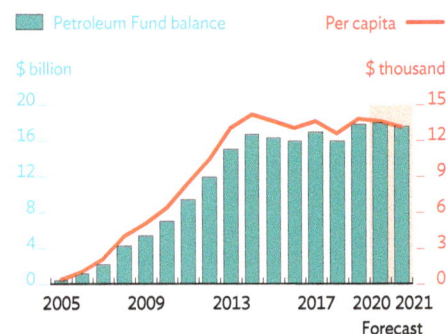

Sources: Timor-Leste national budget documents, various years; ADB estimates.

Policy challenge—improving air connectivity

Although the COVID-19 pandemic has prompted temporary restrictions on international air travel, improving air connectivity for Timor-Leste and reining in unusually high costs of air travel to neighboring countries will be crucial for achieving the country's medium-term objective of economic diversification.

Timor-Leste has scheduled flight services from Dili to Australia, Indonesia, and Singapore. Demand for air services has grown slowly, and the only route with sufficient demand to support daily flights by more than one airline is from Dili to Denpasar, on the Indonesian island of Bali (Figure 3.31.5). In October 2018, competition on the Dili–Denpasar route ceased after Citilink acquired operational control of rival Sriwijaya Air. Ticket prices rose immediately, and in January 2020 the cost per kilometer of flights between Dili and Denpasar was 2.7 times higher than for flights from Denpasar to Kupang in West Timor (Figure 3.31.6).

The government is committed to improving air connectivity. It has completed a major upgrade of the airport in Oe-Cusse Ambeno to support the development of that region's special economic zone. On the south coast, it has upgraded the airport at Suai to support oil and gas developments nearby. The government also plans to upgrade the international airport at Dili by extending the runway, improving safety, and developing a new terminal. These investments could help to attract new flight services by addressing important constraints such as flight loading restrictions but will not remove the need to consider changes to aviation policy.

As reducing flight costs is an immediate priority, the government should assess whether any immediate regulatory changes could reduce costs without compromising air safety or security. Encouraging competition on key routes such as Dili–Denpasar is likely to be central to reducing costs. The government should therefore consider embedding procompetitive principles in its framework for licensing airline operators. With some observers proposing the establishment of a national airline, the potential benefits and risks of this policy should be weighed against alternative approaches such as the airline-underwriting model that has been used by some small island states.

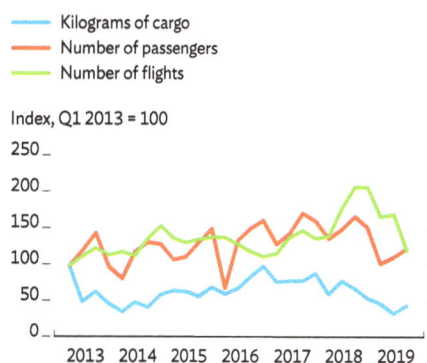

Figure 3.31.5 Growth in air traffic

- Kilograms of cargo
- Number of passengers
- Number of flights

Index, Q1 2013 = 100

Source: Statistics Timor-Leste.

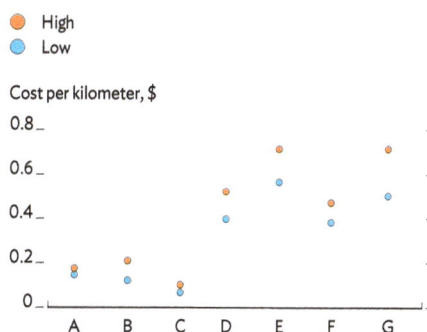

Figure 3.31.6 Flight costs

- High
- Low

Cost per kilometer, $

A = Bali to Kupang, B = Bali to other Indonesian cities, C = Bali to other international destinations in Southeast Asia, D = Dili to Bali, E = Dili to Darwin, F = Dili to Singapore, G = Dili to Kupang.

Source: ADB estimates using data from Google Flights as of 13 January 2020.

Viet Nam

Expansion in 2019 was robust underpinned by strong domestic demand, manufacturing, and foreign direct investment but is forecast to decelerate significantly in 2020 under COVID-19. Inflation eased to a 3-year low in 2019 but it is projected to rise moderately in 2020 and 2021. The current account surplus expanded in 2019 but will contract sharply this year. Despite economic deceleration and the downward risks from COVID-19, growth in Viet Nam will remain one of the highest in the region.

Economic performance

Growth recorded another stellar year, slipping only marginally off a record high of 7.1% in 2018 to 7.0% in 2019 (Figure 3.32.1). On the supply side, solid growth in industry at 8.9%, a rate sustained from 2018, and in services improving from 7.0% in 2018 to 7.3%, mostly offset a slowdown in agriculture. Manufacturing expanded by 11.3%, mining rebounded from 3.1% contraction in 2018 to grow by 1.3%, and construction sustained growth above 9%. Expansion in services was driven by tourism, banking and finance, wholesale services, and transportation (Figure 3.32.2). Prolonged drought and African swine fever slowed growth in agriculture by nearly half, from 3.8% in 2018 to 2.0%.

On the demand side, strong growth was led by a 7.4% rise in private consumption as higher incomes continued to expand the middle class and inflation remained fairly stable. Public consumption, meanwhile, slipped from 6.3% growth in 2018 to 5.8% as fiscal consolidation continued.

Investment growth remained robust despite slowing from 8.2% in 2018 to 7.9%. Viet Nam attracted $38 billion in foreign investment, up by 7.2% over the previous year. Equity investment was $15.5 billion, 56% higher than in 2018. Inflows from the People's Republic of China (PRC) and Hong Kong, China doubled in 2019. Disbursed foreign direct investment was, at $20.4 billion, 6.7% higher than in 2018 (Figure 3.32.3). These robust inflows of foreign capital drove private investment as slow disbursement held back public investment.

Exports expanded to $263 billion, partly reflecting diversion from the PRC to end run US tariffs. This powered the merchandise trade surplus to a 9-year high of some $10 billion.

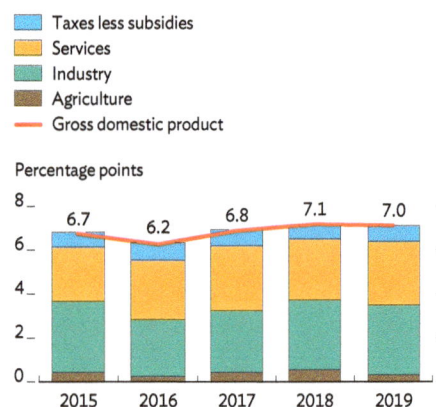

Figure 3.32.1 Supply-side contributions to growth

Taxes less subsidies
Services
Industry
Agriculture
Gross domestic product

Percentage points

Source: General Statistics Office of Viet Nam.

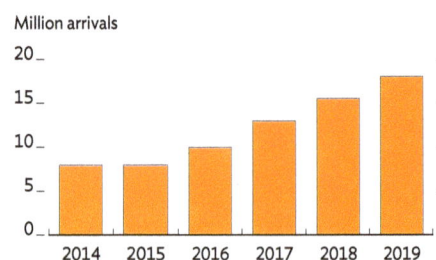

Figure 3.32.2 Tourist arrivals

Million arrivals

Source: General Statistics Office of Viet Nam.

This chapter was written by Cuong Minh Nguyen, Chu Hong Minh, Nguyen Luu Thuc Phuong, and Tomi Sarkioja of the Viet Nam Resident Mission, ADB, Ha Noi.

Foreign-invested firms accounted for 70% of exports. The PRC continued to be the largest source of imports, with a 33% share, followed by the Republic of Korea (ROK) with 19% and Southeast Asia with 13%.

Inflation averaged at 2.8% in 2019, its lowest in 3 years, held down by softening global fuel prices despite increases in administered prices for electricity, health care, and education, as well as food prices pushed higher by drought and African swine fever (Figure 3.32.4). Strong economic fundamentals including robust foreign capital inflow supported the Viet Nam dong, the strength of which also tamed inflation.

The State Bank of Viet Nam, the central bank, pursued prudent monetary policy in 2019. Low and stable inflation allowed it to cut policy rates. In September 2019, it cut the discount and refinancing rates by 0.25% to support growth. This first cut since July 2017 boosted market sentiment but not market liquidity, and credit growth remained under control at less than 14% (Figure 3.32.5). In November 2019, the central bank lowered interest rate caps on dong deposits of less than 6 months and on short-term dong lending to prioritized sectors.

The current account surplus expanded from the equivalent of 2.4% of GDP in 2018 to an estimated 5.0%, supported by a large trade surplus and stable remittances estimated at $9.3 billion. Merchandise exports rose by 8%, led by a 10% increase for mobile phones, electronics, and components, which comprise 33% of exports. Merchandise imports grew by 7% to supply higher production of computers, electronics, and parts— and reflecting a 21% increase in oil imports.

The financial account surplus was estimated to equal 7.3% of GDP, boosted by large net inflows of both foreign direct investment and portfolio capital. With the current and financial accounts both in surplus, the overall balance of payments amounted to a surplus estimated at 8.9% of GDP.

The stronger balance of payments enabled the central bank to build up international reserves, raising import coverage from 2.7 months at the end of 2018 to 3.6 months a year later. The dong exchange rate against the US dollar remained stable in 2019, but the dong appreciated by 2% against the PRC renminbi (Figure 3.32.6).

Fiscal consolidation continued in 2019 (Figure 3.32.7). The budget deficit narrowed from the equivalent of 3.7% of GDP in 2018 to an estimated 3.5%. Revenue growth rose from 5.0% in 2018 to 7.3%, notably from increased domestic excise tax collection. Meanwhile, public expenditure growth was slashed from 15.3% in 2018 to 6.7%. Continued tightening of government loan guarantees and robust economic growth further reduced the ratio of public and publicly guaranteed debt from a peak equal to 63.7% of GDP in 2016 to an estimated 54.8% in 2019.

The resolution of nonperforming loans progressed but only slowly, their official percentage of all outstanding bank credit

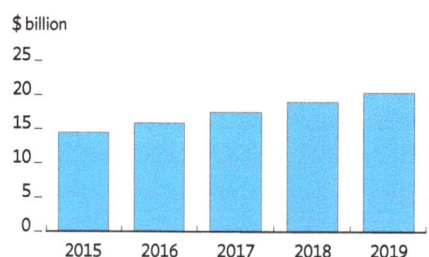

Figure 3.32.3 Disbursement of foreign direct investment

$ billion

Source: General Statistics Office of Viet Nam.

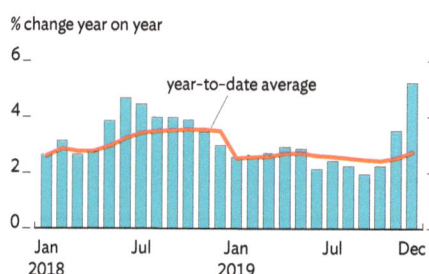

Figure 3.32.4 Inflation

% change year on year

Source: General Statistics Office of Viet Nam.

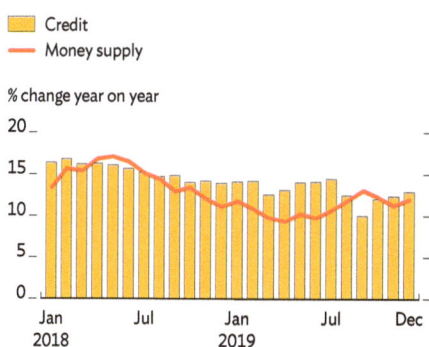

Figure 3.32.5 Credit and money supply growth

Credit
Money supply

% change year on year

Sources: State Bank of Viet Nam; General Statistics Office of Viet Nam; ADB estimate.

falling to 1.9% by the end of 2019. However, all nonperforming loans—those on bank balance sheets and those warehoused with the Viet Nam Asset Management Company—and other high-risk loans held by banks were 4.9% of all outstanding bank loans at the end of December 2019. Meeting Basel II capital adequacy requirements remained a challenge, with half of local banks not yet in compliance by the end of 2019, prompting an extension of the 2020 deadline to 2023.

Economic prospects

The spread of COVID-19 and the resulting abrupt global slowdown will slash growth to 4.8% in 2020 (Figure 3.32.8). Risks tilt to the downside as COVID-19 could cause an even sharper slowdown.

The outbreak spiraled into a new stage in March when it came to affect all of Viet Nam's principal trade and investment partners: the European Union, the PRC, the ROK, Japan, and the US. In Viet Nam itself, the number of COVID-19 infections has continued to climb. The impact on Viet Nam could therefore be severe, creating shocks to both supply and demand in almost every area of the economy. Growth decelerated to 3.8% in the first quarter of 2020 from 6.8% in the corresponding period in 2019.

On the demand side, travel restrictions held down growth in domestic consumption in the first quarter of 2020. Growth in retail sales dropped to 4.7% in the first quarter of the year from 12.0% in the same period last year. Inflow and disbursement of foreign direct investment have already slowed. In January and February 2020, foreign investment registration shrank by 23.6% against a year earlier, while disbursement dropped by 5.0%. With the sharp contraction in global trade, export growth is therefore forecast to ease to 5.3% in 2020, and import growth to 4.7%, before exports recover to 7.8% growth in 2021 and imports to 6.8%.

On the supply side, export-oriented manufacturing managed to weather headwinds in January–February with sufficient inventories of inputs, which prolonged supply chain disruption has since exhausted. As manufacturing occupies a substantial share of industry, sector expansion thus fell to 6.2% in February 2020 from 9.2% a year earlier. The manufacturing purchasing managers' index, a leading indicator, fell from 50.6 in January 2020 across the threshold at 50 into contractionary territory to 49.0 in February—the first such drop in over 4 years (Figure 3.32.9). Output fell at the fastest pace in over 6.5 years, while new orders shrank for the first time since November 2015, partly a result of lower export sales and orders from economies affected by COVID-19. Manufacturing has been further disrupted by travel restrictions that prevented the return after the Lunar New Year in late January of skilled workers from the

Figure 3.32.6 Exchange rate

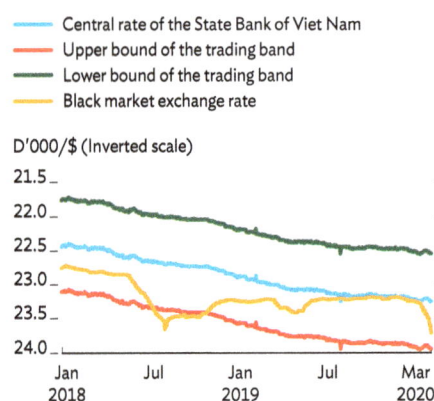

Sources: State Bank of Viet Nam; ADB observations.

Figure 3.32.7 Fiscal balance

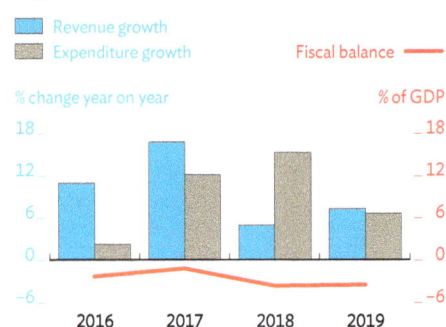

Note: Fiscal balance excludes off-budget spending and onlending.
Source: Ministry of Finance.

Figure 3.32.8 GDP growth

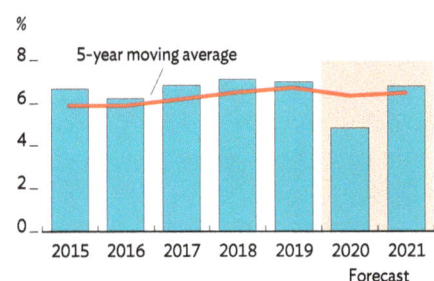

Source: Asian Development Outlook database.

PRC and the ROK, as well as by 14-day compulsory quarantine for those exposed to infected people. Industry slowed to 5.1% in the first quarter of the year from 8.6% in the same period last year. An enterprise survey conducted in March by the National Advisory Council for Administrative Reform found 74% of surveyed firms expecting to shut down operations temporarily if the outbreak is not controlled by June 2020.

The current account balance is expected to fall into deficit equal to 0.2% of GDP this year, recovering to 1.0% surplus in 2021. The financial account will also be hit by the outbreak. As of 24 March 2020, the stock market index had plummeted by 31.4% since the end of 2019.

The COVID-19 outbreak also harmed agriculture as the closing in January of almost all land border crossings between the PRC and Viet Nam froze agricultural exports. As the outbreak persists, demand for agricultural exports from Viet Nam will continue to fall. Separately, agricultural production is suffering severe salinity intrusion in the Mekong Delta. Growth in agriculture dropped sharply to 0.08% in the first quarter of the year from 2.7% in the same period last year. Agricultural growth is therefore seen to slow to 1.0% in 2020.

Services have so far been the sector hardest hit by the outbreak. Considering its 42% share of GDP, a slowdown in services will significantly dent growth. The largest impact is through lower tourism and associated services, which account for 40% of sector revenue. In January–February 2020, tourist arrivals grew by only 4.8%, the lowest rate in these months in the past 5 years. In February, tourist arrivals fell by 37.7% from a month earlier and by 21.8% year on year. Arrivals from the PRC, typically 30% of all foreign tourists, have ceased. As COVID-19 spreads globally, the government has stopped issuing visas and imposed temporary travel bans on tourist arrivals from all countries, sharply curtailing tourism. The International Air Transport Association estimates that the current extensive spread of the pandemic will cost Viet Nam 23% of its arriving passengers. Growth in services was halved to 3.2% in the first quarter of 2020 from 6.5% in the corresponding period in 2019.

Inflation in March dropped by 0.7% month on month, from a 0.2% decrease a year earlier. However, average inflation in the first quarter of 2020 rose to 5.6%, the highest rate in the same period since 2016, largely on higher health care and pork prices, the latter triggering higher prices for substitute meats. In the full year of 2020, inflation is expected to average at 3.3%, rising further to 3.5% in 2021 (Figure 3.32.10). If the pandemic worsens more than currently forecast, and particularly if prices stay elevated for pork, inflationary pressures could intensify.

Stagnant business has substantially weakened credit demand. At the end of February 2020, credit growth was

Figure 3.32.9 Purchasing managers' index

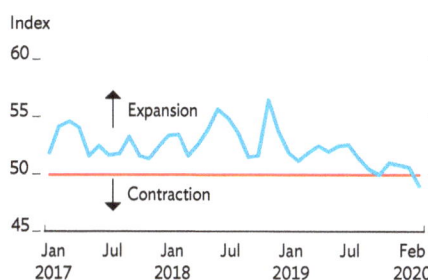

Source: Bloomberg (accessed 21 March 2020).

Figure 3.32.10 Inflation

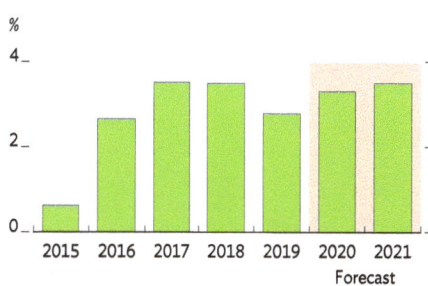

Source: *Asian Development Outlook* database.

estimated to have grown by 0.1% since the end of 2019, the lowest rate in the same period in the past 6 years. To support affected businesses, the government unveiled on 4 March 2020 a $10.8 billion relief package of debt restructuring and lowered and waived interest rates and fees. Subsequently, the central bank cut policy rates by 0.5%–1.0%, lowered interest rate caps on dong deposits of less than 6 months and on short-term dong lending to prioritized sectors, and instituted other measures.

The 3.4% fiscal deficit target for 2020 may now be hard to achieve, given reduced tax collection from incomes and export earnings, substantial increases in spending on health care and employment funds, and a recently launched fiscal package worth $1.3 billion that reduces taxes and fees for affected firms and defers tax payment. The fiscal deficit is therefore expected to widen to the equivalent of 4.2% of GDP in 2020 before improving to 3.5% in 2021.

Despite the potentially large impact of COVID-19, Viet Nam's economic fundamentals remain resilient. If the outbreak is contained within the first half of 2020, growth should rebound to 6.8% in 2021 and remain strong over the medium and long term.

Drivers of economic growth—a growing middle-income class and a dynamic private sector, notably household businesses and domestically held enterprises—remain robust. The middle class in Viet Nam is one of the fastest growing in Southeast Asia. According to Boston Consulting Group, the middle class has doubled in size since 2014 to 33 million, or a third of the population.

The business environment similarly continues to improve. The disbursement of public investment has increased significantly, growing by nearly 18% in January–February 2020 over the same period in 2019. Disbursement will continue to improve in 2020 as this is a priority fiscal measure in response to COVID-19.

The large number of bilateral and multilateral trade agreements in which Viet Nam participates promise the improved market access essential for an economic rebound after COVID-19. Containment of COVID-19 in the PRC and that market's likely return to normal will help revive global value chains and facilitate economic recovery in Viet Nam.

Policy challenge—high-tech industries and knowledge-intensive jobs

Viet Nam has rapidly integrated into the global economy and moved up the chain of value addition from agriculture to light manufacturing and on to electronics. Its total trade is now valued at twice its GDP, having swiftly emerged as a significant value chain hub in Southeast Asia for the manufacturing of

Table 3.32.1 Selected economic indicators (%)

	2018	2019	2020	2021
GDP growth	7.1	7.0	4.8	6.8
Inflation	3.5	2.8	3.3	3.5
Current acct. bal. (share of GDP)	2.4	5.0	-0.2	1.0

Sources: General Statistics Office of Viet Nam; ADB estimates.

information and communication technology (ICT) hardware and electronics. In 2019, ICT and electronics exports were estimated at $91.0 billion, accounting for 34.4% of all goods exported.

Viet Nam had 38,861 ICT companies in 2018 and currently boasts 2,000–3,000 tech start-ups. Investment by large multinational companies and other foreign investors explains much of this rapid growth, but local companies are also growing quickly, notably in e-commerce and financial technology (fintech). For its part, the government has applied new policies and regulations to encourage this development.

The growth of the digital economy provides new opportunities for knowledge-intensive employment. The net revenue of firms offering software, digital content, and ICT services increased from $7.7 billion in 2015 to $11.5 billion in 2018 (Figure 3.32.11). Their combined contribution is 11.1% of net revenue in the ICT industry, an important employer. The number of jobs in ICT manufacturing grew from 533,000 in 2015 to 718,000 in 2018. In the same period, employment in the software industry, digital content, and ICT services grew by 36% to reach 255,000 jobs.

Viet Nam ranked 42 among 129 countries in the Global Innovation Index 2019, rubbing shoulders with top economies classified as upper-middle income. This ranking reflected high ICT exports and imports. Viet Nam has other advantages that should enable it to move up in the index. It has strong primary and lower-secondary education, a young population, abundant labor, and ample credit, with bank loans outstanding estimated to equal 135% of GDP in 2019.

Some factors nevertheless hold back the national innovation system. First, gross domestic expenditure on research and development, both public and private, equaled only 0.53% of GDP in 2017, far below 1.44% in Malaysia and 0.78% in Thailand a year earlier, which clearly illustrates that Viet Nam needs to step up its spending on it. Second, universities in Viet Nam rank lower than in upper-middle-income countries in Southeast Asia in quality and quantity, as measured by gross enrollment ratio. Although Viet Nam compares favorably in the number of students in tertiary education overseas and has 55,000 students enrolled domestically each year in tertiary ICT programs, these future graduate numbers may be insufficient to meet growing demand from rapidly growing ICT industries. Ensuring more and better fresh graduates is critical for Viet Nam to leap ahead in technological innovation. Third, while the financial sector has grown steadily and innovative fintech is being adopted, the current legal framework has not kept pace with the development of fintech products and services. An enabling regulatory framework to nurture the application of fintech would help Viet Nam to expand and deepen its financial services.

Figure 3.32.11 Net revenues of software industry, digital content, and ICT services

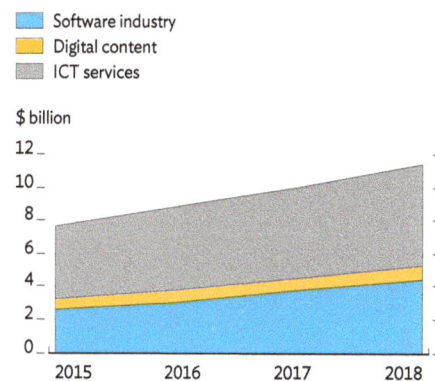

ICT = information and communication technology.
Source: Viet Nam Ministry of Information and Communications.

THE PACIFIC

Fiji

The economy performed below trend in 2019 as trade partners stagnated, the government reined in spending, and business confidence dwindled, initially because of tight liquidity early in the year. Inflation slowed by more than half. Lower imports in late 2019 and increased tourism and remittance inflows narrowed the current account deficit, reversing previous trends and allowing improved liquidity heading into 2020 and beyond. COVID-19 will significantly hit the economy as tourist arrivals decline.

Economic performance

After uninterrupted growth for the past 9 years, growth is estimated to have slowed from more than 3% in the previous 2 years to only 0.7% in 2019 (Figure 3.33.1). Weaker economic activity in major trade partners than in 2018 slowed growth in visitor arrivals to 2.8%, the lowest since 2013 (Figure 3.33.2). Growth in tourism earnings slowed from 4.5% in 2018 to 2.7%. In the first half of 2019, the current account deficit expanded notably as the primary income account saw significant outflow from profit and dividend repatriation. Foreign reserves and commercial bank liquidity consequently fell, triggering rises in deposit and lending rates.

Constrained by its debt ceiling and less buoyant revenue streams, the government announced a tighter budget for fiscal year 2019 (FY2019, ended 31 July 2019) than in FY2018. Collectively, these developments affected business confidence. A business survey conducted in June 2019 by the Reserve Bank of Fiji, the central bank, found that the number of respondents expecting improved business conditions in the next 6 months had dropped from 51% in December 2018 to 24%. Similarly, positive sentiment for the next 12 months slumped to 33% of respondents, one of the lowest percentages in recent years.

Growth in private sector credit decelerated from 7.3% in 2018 to 4.6% in 2019. New lending by commercial banks declined. Tax collections on goods and services slowed from 6.1% growth in 2018 to only 1.9%, while cement sales fell by 6.2%. New and second-hand vehicle registrations declined by more than 20%.

The sugar industry improved, with cane production growth accelerating from 4.0% in 2018 to 6.5% in 2019, and sugar production reversing an 11.2% decline to grow by 5.3%.

Figure 3.33.1 GDP growth

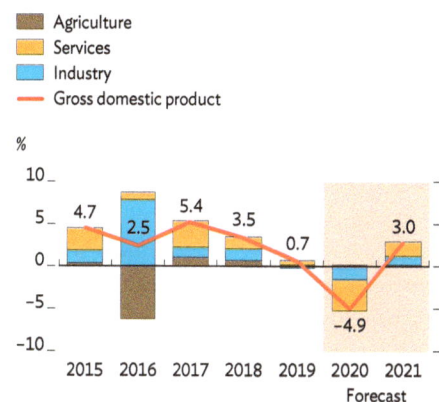

Sources: Fiji Bureau of Statistics; ADB estimates.

Figure 3.33.2 Visitor arrivals

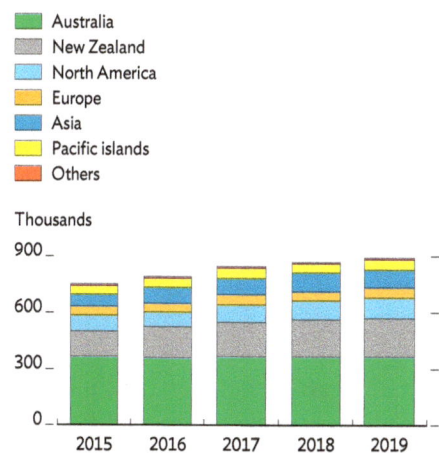

Source: Fiji Bureau of Statistics.

This chapter was written by Isoa Wainiqolo of the Pacific Subregional Office, ADB, Suva.

The fiscal deficit narrowed from the equivalent of 4.4% of GDP in FY2018 to 3.4% as expenditure fell and revenue remained broadly stable. Public debt expanded as a ratio of GDP from 45.8% at the end of 2018 to 48.0% a year later.

The current account deficit widened in the third quarter of 2019. Despite this, tourism receipts expanded by 2.7% year on year, and personal remittances rose by 4.4% in the whole year, helping to ease pressure on the external position. The current account deficit equaled an estimated 4.2% of GDP in 2019 (Figure 3.33.3).

In response to weak demand, monetary policy remained accommodative throughout the year with the official policy rate maintained at 0.5%. Reserves coverage rose from 4.2 months of retained imports of goods and nonfactor services at the end of March 2019 to 5.1 months at the end of the year. Annual inflation was down from 4.1% in 2018 to 1.8% on account of benign imported inflation and weak domestic demand, especially toward the end of the year.

Economic prospects

The economy is projected to decline by 4.9% in 2020 under COVID-19. The impact is expected to extend to supply chains, government revenue, and business and consumer confidence. The government announced a supplementary budget in late March to support containment and provide relief for affected industries and workers. The central bank reduced its policy rate on 18 March to stimulate economic activity. However, stringent containment measures undertaken by Fiji's main tourist markets are likely to dampen economic activity in the first half of 2020. If the pandemic is thus contained in its impact, the economy should rebound by 3.0% in 2021, led by the private sector.

Tourism and air transport are expected to be the worst hit during this global downturn. On 20 March, Fiji Airways suspended 95% of its international flights until the end of May in response to travel restrictions and low demand. Other businesses that feed off tourism and transport, such as wholesale and retail trade, will also struggle.

Inflation is expected to be low in 2020 at 1.5%, rising in 2021 to 3.5% (Figure 3.33.4). Spare capacity vacated in 2019 will likely persist into 2020, moderating expected international supply disruption, with domestic inflationary pressure returning toward the end of the year. Higher projected consumer prices in 2021 are in line with domestic growth, higher capacity utilization, and improved conditions in Fiji's major trade partners.

The external position is likely to take a hit in 2020 from lower tourism earnings, with the current account deficit projected to equal 7.1% of GDP in 2020. The current account deficit is expected to narrow to 3.6% of GDP in 2021 through gains in remittances and tourism receipts.

Figure 3.33.3 Current account balance

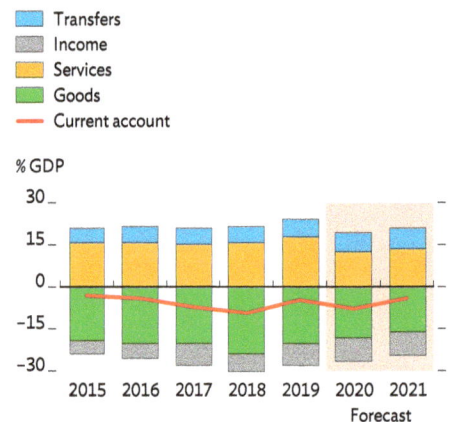

Sources: Fiji Bureau of Statistics; ADB estimates.

Table 3.33.1 Selected economic indicators (%)

	2018	2019	2020	2021
GDP growth	3.5	0.7	-4.9	3.0
Inflation	4.1	1.8	1.5	3.5
Current acct. bal. (share of GDP)	-8.9	-4.2	-7.1	-3.6

Sources: Fiji Bureau of Statistics; ADB estimates.

Figure 3.33.4 Inflation

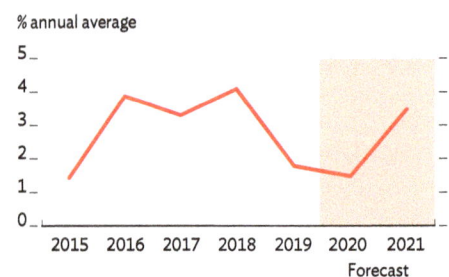

Sources: Fiji Bureau of Statistics; ADB estimates.

The government targets in its medium-term framework a fiscal deficit equal to 2.7% of GDP in FY2020 and 2.0% in FY2021 (Figure 3.33.5). However, lower government revenue as the economy contracts and higher expenditure to counter COVID-19 impacts are projected to widen the fiscal deficit to equal 4.2% of GDP in FY2020 and 3.5% in FY2021.

Risks to forecasts center on Fiji's worsening vulnerability to natural hazards and climate change, which could nullify development efforts, and on COVID-19 and its potential damage to tourism. The contraction could be greater than forecast if travel bans in key tourist markets persist until the second half of the year.

Policy challenge—strengthening domestic drivers of growth

The government needs to strengthen and empower the private sector to innovate, diversify, and drive economic recovery after COVID-19, while finding the right balance between investing in climate resilient infrastructure, limiting debt exposure, and building fiscal buffers.

To start, Fiji needs to improve its business and investment climate and encourage business innovation. Steps have been taken in this direction. In December 2019, the government announced business licensing reform with the aim of reducing maximum licensing time to 2 days. It launched its bizFIJI portal in July 2019 to provide a centralized online platform for starting a business and obtaining construction permits. The government's new Research and Innovation Scheme for Enterprises initiative has initial funding of F$500,000 to provide financial support to enterprises undertaking research and development in new or improved products, processes, or services. The central bank launched guidelines for a fintech regulatory sandbox, which aims to encourage innovation in finance.

The success of these initiatives will be short lived, however, without other enablers for business growth. The Fiji National Productivity Masterplan, 2021–2036 noted that government price controls on a wide range of goods reduces incentives for producers to improve their quality or expand productive capacity. The International Monetary Fund has advocated a review of price controls. When new firms are able to operate in a stable regulatory environment, innovation and economies of scale are encouraged, costs reduced, and productivity enhanced. If not, new initiatives are unlikely to flourish, and growth will continue to depend on fiscal stimulus, casting doubt on government debt sustainability.

Figure 3.33.5 Fiscal deficit

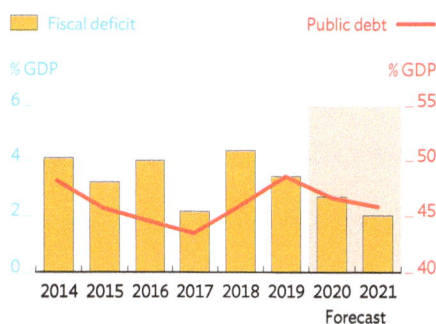

Note: Calendar year data for 2014; new fiscal year (July–August) data for 2015 onward. 2020 and 2021 reflect government forecasts before COVID-19.
Source: Fiji Ministry of Economy.

Papua New Guinea

A rebound in petroleum and mineral production supported growth and widened the current account surplus in 2019, but the economic picture deteriorated with the distraction of politics and the deferral of large investment projects. Inflation trended lower, yet an over-valued local currency and associated foreign exchange shortages continued to hold back economic activity. As the fiscal balance worsens, the government faces important challenges in managing public debt, including arrears, contingent liabilities, and state-owned enterprise debt.

Economic performance

Growth in 2019 was driven by a rebound in extractive industries following an earthquake in 2018 (Figure 3.34.1). Liquefied natural gas (LNG) bounced back to grow by about 16% in 2019, and crude oil production also jumped. Mining and quarrying, which provide some 10% of GDP, also rebounded, notably on account of increased production at the Porgera gold mine and, to a lesser extent, the Ok Tedi gold and copper mine. The Lihir gold mine, which was not affected by the earthquake, saw volumes fall. Combined, these three mines contribute most mining production. Capital expenditure at a number of mining sites, including advanced exploration works, also stimulated growth. Meanwhile, though, a legal dispute caused advanced works to be scaled down at the Wafi Golpu site in 2019.

Growth apart from minerals was weak. The resignation in May of the Prime Minister, who was facing a vote of no confidence, prompted a complete change in the coalition government and leadership. This caused some loss of economic momentum, with people distracted by politics and the altered government taking time to become established. While the economic policy of the new leadership does not significantly differ from that of the old, there are some important differences, in particular new priorities on reforming state-owned enterprises (SOEs) and increasing domestic ownership of mining and petroleum assets. In accordance with the second of these goals, the new leadership sought to renegotiate two new LNG investment projects, Papua LNG and the Papua New Guinea (PNG) LNG expansion project in the P'nyang gas field. Together, these two projects are set to drive the economy with projected capital expenditure of over $10 billion.

Figure 3.34.1 GDP growth

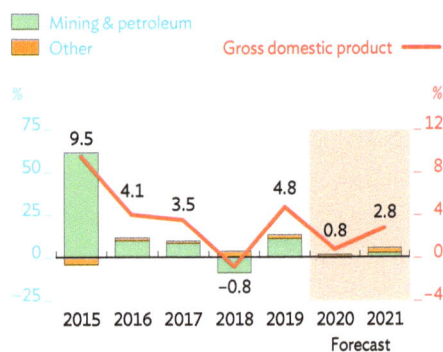

Source: ADB estimates using data from Papua New Guinea National Statistical Office.

This chapter was written by Edward Faber of the Papua New Guinea Resident Mission, ADB, Port Moresby.

However, negotiations were stalled, causing the projects to be deferred and dampening business confidence.

Growth was also tempered by the exchange rate mechanism, which continued to limit the availability of foreign currency in ways that affected businesses and investment decisions. Power outages were a frequent occurrence as well, further affecting business conditions. Government cashflow remained tight during most of the year, delaying payments to contractors and the private sector. Government revenue collection from companies in 2019 was lower than in 2018, confirming a subdued business environment. The employment index to September 2019 registered a small decline in the number of jobs in the formal sector, with declines in construction, transport, and financial services. Private sector credit growth was 6.1% in the year to December 2019, implying some growth in banks' loan books, but this was not significantly above inflation.

Agriculture, forestry, and fisheries continued to expand, by an estimated 2.5% in 2019. However, the production of export crops including palm oil, coffee, and cocoa probably declined slightly from 2018.

Construction is estimated to have declined. With the government's tight cashflow situation during 2019, many projects could not be delivered as envisaged. Weak performance in construction was highlighted by the construction employment index, which registered a 7% decline in the number of jobs from December 2018 to September 2019.

Average annual inflation dropped to an estimated 3.6% in 2019, reflecting slow growth and a strict policy maintained by the Bank of Papua New Guinea, the central bank, to limit its purchases of government securities (Figure 3.34.2). System liquidity contracted further as the central bank bought local currency with the proceeds of external loans. The inflationary impact from exchange rate movement was negligible, as the PNG kina depreciated by only about 1% against the US dollar and appreciated against the Australian dollar by 2.7%. Communications and health care were two sectors that saw prices fall in 2019.

The central bank responded to falling inflation by reducing the kina facility rate during the year from 6.25% to 5.00% (Figure 3.34.3). However, this policy instrument remains largely ineffective for stimulating the economy for lack of transmission to commercial bank lending rates. This is because banks can source cheap deposits and enjoy wide lending spreads.

The current account posted a significant surplus again, driven higher by increased LNG and gold exports, as well as a rising gold price (Figure 3.34.4).

The weak economy caused government finances to deteriorate in 2019 as revenue trended lower and expenditure control was poor (Figure 3.34.5). Revenue, as estimated in the

Figure 3.34.2 Inflation

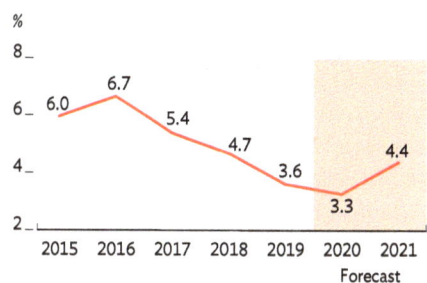

Sources: Papua New Guinea National Statistical Office (2014–2018); ADB estimates.

Figure 3.34.3 Kina facility rate

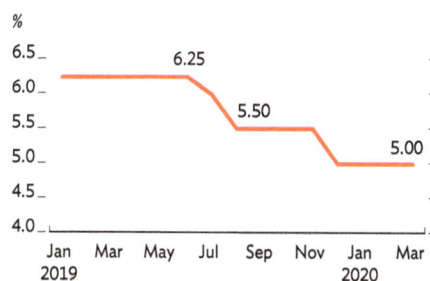

Source: Bank of Papua New Guinea.

supplementary budget released in November, was K12,079 million in 2019, equal to 14.3% of GDP in 2019, or 15.4% of GDP including grants. This was K1,200 million, or 9.1%, below expectations and also below the 2018 outcome of K12,250 million. Expenditure maintained its upward trend, however, reaching K16,526 million, equal to 19.5% of GDP. The public sector wage bill trended higher as new hires in health care and education continued. The resultant deficit, equal to 4.1% of GDP, was a significant departure from an earlier fiscal consolidation strategy. Multilateral and bilateral development partners were the main sources of deficit financing, through budget support loans.

Economic prospects

In the absence of major new investments in extractive industry commencing in the short term, growth will remain lackluster. Negotiations are expected to revive on the Wafi Goplu gold and copper mine, but progress will depend on reaching satisfactory agreements on the share of ownership and profits. The project has a capital investment value of about $3 billion, with production expected to begin 5 years after the start of investment. Great uncertainty surrounds Papua LNG and P'ynang as negotiations between the project developers and the government are stalemated over the flow of project benefits.

Gas production is expected to plateau but could fall in 2020 in response to reduced demand from the People's Republic of China (PRC) because of COVID-19. PNG sells about a quarter of its gas to the PRC, mostly on long term contracts. However, media reported in February 2020 that some buyers there were unable to take delivery of international gas purchases and claiming force majeure.

Oil production may expand slightly in 2020 as some oil fields return to normal production following the 2018 earthquake. However, output will likely fall thereafter in line with an overall declining trend in oil production as oil fields mature. In 2020, exploration and capital investment in the oil industry will likely scale down in response to lower oil prices. Meanwhile, gold and copper production is expected to expand, though some mining operations could suffer setbacks as COVID-19 crimps supply chains and staff movement to and from mine sites. The Ok Tedi gold and copper mine and the Lihir gold mine are both expected to increase production in 2020 and 2021 thanks to recent and ongoing capital investment. Gold production is also forecast to expand at medium-sized mining operations, including the Hidden Valley and Kainantu mines.

Apart from extractive industries, growth is forecast to remain weak in 2020. Unless kina depreciation is undertaken, an over-valued local currency and associated foreign currency shortages will persist, deterring investment.

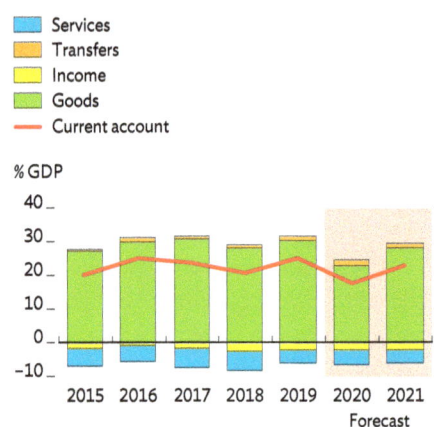

Figure 3.34.4 Current account balance

Legend: Services, Transfers, Income, Goods, Current account

Sources: Bank of Papua New Guinea; ADB estimates.

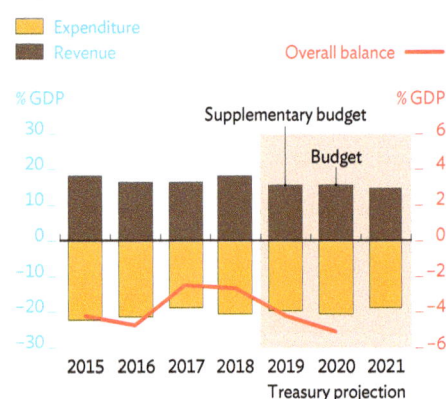

Figure 3.34.5 Fiscal balance

Legend: Expenditure, Revenue, Overall balance

Source: Papua New Guinea Department of Treasury.

Other structural bottlenecks—such as weak law and order, poor governance, and the limited availability of titled land for investment—are not expected to improve. COVID-19 is expected to have wide impact in 2020, with manufacturing struggling under disruption to supply chains; transportation, accommodation, and food services hit by restricted international travel by air and sea; and wholesale and retail trade hampered if imports of goods from the PRC and elsewhere are delayed. The public sector may also be affected if weaker commodity prices reduce revenue and force budget cuts. PNG reported no COVID-19 cases to mid-March, but if the virus reaches PNG and expands there, growth would be slowed beyond current projections.

Government capital expenditure is budgeted to grow by 18.8% in 2020, which could provide some stimulus, especially for construction (Figure 3.34.6). However, realizing such expenditure may prove difficult as the 2020 budget depends on securing significant external financing, not all of which is yet certain. In addition, in the first quarter of 2020, infrastructure projects being built by contractors from the PRC were slowed or suspended in response to COVID-19.

Agriculture is forecast to expand in 2020. New palm oil plantations may start to bear fruit within the forecast period, and new cocoa plantations should also begin to produce. However, COVID-19 could dent production as overseas demand weakens. Meanwhile, the government has increased its production tax on log exports from 30% to 50%, which is expected to push log production lower. In any case, demand for logs is another victim of COVID-19, with some ports in the PRC experiencing inventory buildup and unable to take delivery.

Inflation is forecast to maintain its downward trend in the short term as the economy outside of extractive industries remains weak. Communication costs, which have a weighting of 4.5% in the consumer price index, may fall further with the installation of a new fiberoptic cable to connect PNG to Australia and bring faster and cheaper internet. Inflation is seen to rise in 2021 in line with an anticipated recovery in economic growth but could pick up much faster if the authorities adopt a policy of kina depreciation. Limited domestic appetite for purchasing government treasuries may increase pressure on the central bank to finance domestic securities, which could add further inflationary pressures, but any such financing is not expected to be significant in light of the central bank's own strict approach.

The current account will continue to post significant surpluses despite declining in 2020 with a lower oil price. LNG exports should remain steady but could decline in 2020 with falling global demand. About 90% of gas is sold under long-term contracts linked to the oil price, and only 10% on the spot market. Gold exports should expand with increased

Table 3.34.1 Selected economic indicators (%)

	2018	2019	2020	2021
GDP growth	−0.8	4.8	0.8	2.8
Inflation	4.7	3.6	3.3	4.4
Current acct. bal. (share of GDP)	22.8	24.9	17.5	22.6

Source: ADB estimates.

Figure 3.34.6 Real capital expenditure

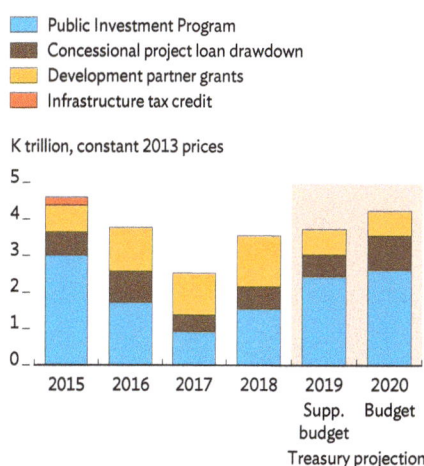

Public Investment Program
Concessional project loan drawdown
Development partner grants
Infrastructure tax credit

K trillion, constant 2013 prices

Source: Papua New Guinea Department of Treasury.

production, especially if the gold price stays elevated. Imports are not expected to pick up significantly, though they could increase to supply the Wafi Golpu project if it proceeds. A loosening of the exchange rate may not significantly reduce imports, which have already fallen under foreign currency rationing.

The new leadership is planning to pursue an expansionary fiscal policy in 2020, targeting a budget deficit equal to 5.0% of GDP. This deficit will have to be financed almost entirely externally for lack of domestic financing sources. The recent fall in oil and copper prices will lower government revenue, probably requiring a supplementary budget with expenditure cuts.

Policy challenge—debt management

Central government debt at the end of 2019 stood at K32,535 million, equal to 38.1% of GDP. It had increased from K29,759 million, or 36.2% of GDP, in 2018 mainly through "extraordinary" budget support loans from multilateral creditors and drawdowns from the proceeds of the government's inaugural 10-year sovereign bond, which was issued toward the end of 2018. The share of external debt in total government debt increased from 39% at the end of 2018 to 43% a year later (Figure 3.34.7). This was consistent with the government's medium-term debt strategy for 2018–2022 to lower domestic interest costs and restructure its domestic debt portfolio with a view to reducing refinancing risk from domestic sources (Figure 3.34.8).

The government faces important challenges in managing its public debt related to arrears, contingent liabilities, SOE debt, and the risks entailed in rolling over external commercial loans and domestic borrowings. Regarding arrears, during the last quarter of 2019, the government said it discovered relatively large amounts of public sector arrears in the form of unpaid bills, mainly wages, allowances, and unpaid invoices for its purchase of goods and services. The challenge has been and continues to be how to find, verify, and measure the whole of these arrears, currently estimated to be K2,623 million in 2019, or 14% of total domestic debt last year. An equally daunting challenge is to manage the fiscal impact of these arrears and efficiently pay them down. In its 2020 budget, the government committed itself to a substantial paydown of arrears, adding K1,050 million to its 2020 budget deficit. The plan is to pay down the balance of arrears in the next two budget cycles.

Figure 3.34.7 Public debt

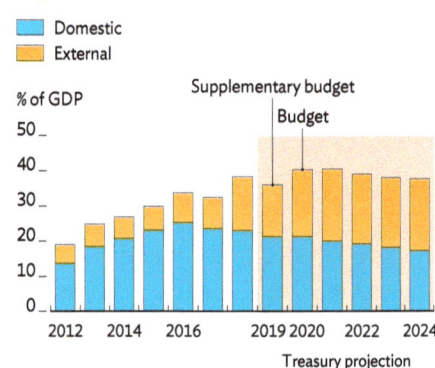

Source: Papua New Guinea Department of Treasury.

Figure 3.34.8 Debt service cost

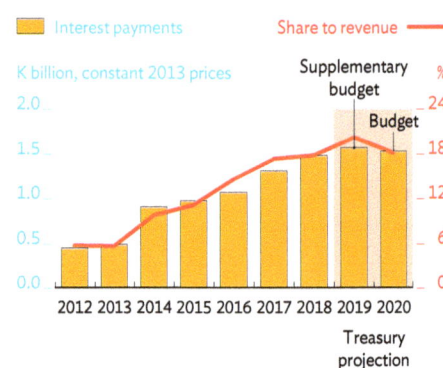

Source: Papua New Guinea Department of Treasury.

Regarding SOE debts, neither the Treasury nor any other department is actively monitoring them, leaving exact amounts unknown. In his budget speech, the minister of the Treasury rightly pointed out that "the financial challenges facing many of these SOEs will only worsen next year when expensive debt repayments fall due."

Contingent liabilities remain high, but exactly how high is another unknown. Last year the Treasury estimated these liabilities to be K14,134 million, with 91% of them being guarantees extended to external creditors. In the past, the servicing of both principal and interest costs of some guaranteed loans has become a burden on the government budget. With the absence of any procedures to manage risk, such risks can only get worse, and indeed these contingent commitments may haunt the budget this year and next. Following an October 2019 amendment to the Fiscal Responsibility Act that raised the permissible ratio of debt to GDP to 45%, there is room to include some of these guaranteed debts in the government's reporting of public debt. This would enhance transparency in government reporting and go some way toward allaying concern about how complete debt data are, which could eventually improve the government's credit rating. The government has now acknowledged this deficiency and plans to include elements of the debt that were previously unreported. Technical assistance in progress to help the government manage its debt management will provide support in these areas.

Solomon Islands

Growth slowed last year as exports and public investment fell. Inflation eased, and the current account deficit widened. Growth is expected to weaken significantly as construction only partly offsets a decline in logging, which will deepen under COVID-19, intensifying fiscal pressure. As the growth contribution from logging shrinks over the longer term, reforming the tax system becomes critically important to ensure that it supports broad-based growth in other areas.

Economic performance

Economic growth is estimated to have slowed sharply from 3.9% in 2018 to 2.6% in 2019, mainly from reduced logging and weaker construction. From a peak in 2018, log output fell by 4% in 2019 (Figure 3.35.1). Major crops such as palm oil, copra, and coconut oil were also down from the previous year. Growth in the fish catch slowed from 27% in 2018 to 8% in 2019. Weakness or contraction in agriculture had follow-on effects on services and manufacturing, which includes the processing of logs, fish, and other food.

Industry subtracted from growth in 2019 as construction slowed. Growth in electricity consumption slowed as well, while imports of machinery and transport equipment dropped by 20% and mining exports contracted by almost 10%.

Services, which contribute 60% of GDP, are dominated by wholesale and retail trade, transportation, and public administration. Weakening trade caused growth in revenue from consumption taxes, comprising goods and sales tax and import duties, to slow sharply from an average of 14.1% in 2017 and 2018 to only 1.6% in 2019.

Growth in public administration slowed with a decline in government expenditure following constraint early in the year. After a general election and the formation of a new government in April, spending increased but was still down for the whole year by an estimated 2.9% (Figure 3.35.2). Total revenue and grants fell by 9.0%, largely because lower log exports reduced revenue derived from duties. The fiscal deficit was estimated to equal 2.0% of GDP.

Figure 3.35.1 Logging output and exports

Sources: Central Bank of Solomon Islands; Solomon Islands National Statistics Office; ADB estimates.

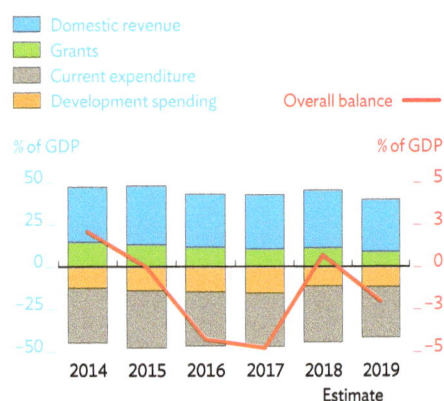

Figure 3.35.2 Fiscal accounts

Source: ADB estimates using data from the Ministry of Finance and Treasury and the International Monetary Fund.

This chapter was written by Jacqueline Connell of the Pacific Liaison and Coordination Office, ADB, Sydney, and Prince Cruz, consultant, Pacific Department, ADB, Manila.

Inflation pressures eased as economic conditions became less favorable and global commodity prices softened. Lower prices for food and household items more than offset higher prices for utilities, alcoholic beverages, and tobacco. This prompted the Central Bank of Solomon Islands to adopt an accommodative monetary stance in September and ease the moderate tightening adopted in March. Growth in private sector credit slowed in line with a weaker economy.

The current account deficit widened to the equivalent of 8.5% of GDP in 2019 (Figure 3.35.3). Exports of goods fell, dragged down by lower exports of logs, agricultural products, fish, and minerals, while lower service exports tracked visitor arrivals. Imports of goods rose despite lower imports of fuel and of machinery and transport equipment. Imports of services jumped on higher payments for telecommunication and construction services incurred to complete the Coral Sea Cable for internet connection. Gross official foreign reserves were 5% lower in December than a year earlier but sufficient to cover 11.8 months of imports.

Economic prospects

Economic growth is expected to slow again in 2020, as exports fall under COVID-19, before recovering in 2021 as construction on large infrastructure projects offsets a continuing decline in logging (Figure 3.35.4). Trade and travel disruption caused by COVID-19 is expected to delay construction on some infrastructure projects that rely on imports and foreign labor, contracting industry. Public administration services will remain the main contributor to growth. Expenditure on health care and COVID-19 preparedness are expected to expand.

Agriculture, logging, and fisheries—a third of GDP—will weaken in 2020. Logging output routinely surprises on the upside, but gradual reduction seen in 2019 will likely deepen in 2020 with reduced demand from the People's Republic of China, the main market. As logging supplies more than two-thirds of exports, this will weigh heavily on growth and have follow-on effects in other areas, including manufacturing, transport, and trade.

Once the disruptions pass, construction in 2021 should strengthen on a significant project pipeline including roads, water supply and sanitation upgrades, airport rehabilitation, and preparations for the Tina River hydroelectricity project and the 2023 Pacific Games. The Coral Sea Cable will improve internet connectivity and create opportunities for business and government e-services.

Figure 3.35.3 Current account balance

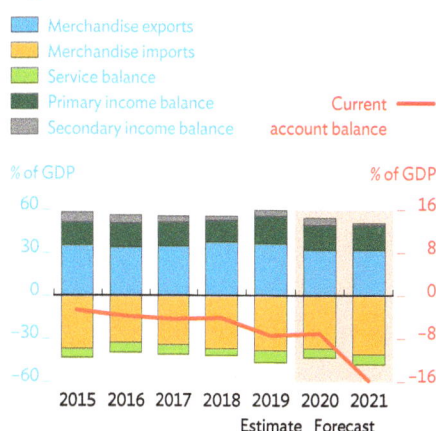

Source: ADB estimates using data from the Central Bank of Solomon Islands and the International Monetary Fund.

Figure 3.35.4 Supply-side contributions to growth

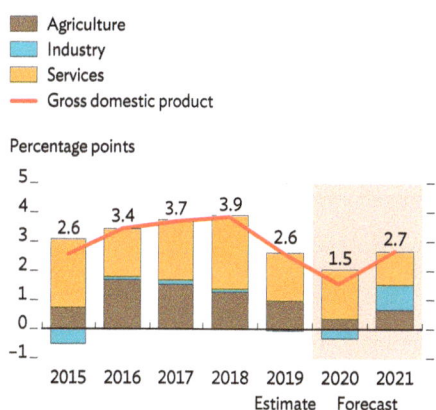

Source: ADB estimates using data from the Ministry of Finance and Treasury, Solomon Islands National Statistics Office, and International Monetary Fund.

Table 3.35.1 Selected economic indicators (%)

	2018	2019	2020	2021
GDP growth	3.9	2.6	1.5	2.7
Inflation	3.5	1.6	2.0	2.3
Current acct. bal. (share of GDP)	-3.5	-8.5	-8.7	-12.3

Sources: Ministry of Finance and Treasury, Solomon Islands National Statistics Office; International Monetary Fund; ADB estimates.

While the 2020 budget targets a balanced budget, fiscal pressures will intensify with higher government spending, particularly on health care in response to COVID-19, combined with lower revenue in line with economic weakening. The original budget assumed revenue falling by 6.7% from the 2019 revised budget because of reduced grants, export duties tracking lower log exports, and tax collection following a doubling of the tax-free threshold for personal income in January.

External debt has risen in recent years with increased lending from development partners to finance large infrastructure projects. It was estimated to equal 7.8% of GDP in 2019.

Inflation is expected to accelerate slightly in both 2020 and 2021 (Figure 3.35.5). Fuel and other commodity price are expected to remain soft. Domestic food price inflation is set to accelerate with higher import duties and goods taxes on white rice, intended to promote brown rice, and the expected implementation of higher taxes and import duties on sugar, salt, and sugary drinks. Extended COVID-19 constraint on trade could drive inflation higher. The central bank adopted an expansionary monetary policy in March in response to the subdued economic outlook.

The current account deficit is expected to widen, especially in 2021 as log exports decline and imports rise to supply construction.

Significant downside risk stems from COVID-19, mainly through reduced demand for Solomon Islands merchandise exports. A global economic slowdown sharper than currently assumed would severely undermine log exports and growth, intensifying pressure on the budget and current account.

Policy challenge—reforming consumption taxes

About 40% of domestic revenue comes from consumption taxes, including a goods tax, a sales tax, and import duties. As a percentage of GDP, revenue from consumption taxes peaked at 13.3% in 2012 and has remained below 12% since 2015 (Figure 3.35.6). A narrow base necessitates a high tax rate. This discourages compliance and creates incentives for smaller businesses to avoid formal registration and multiple taxes on their inputs and outputs.

The government has agreed to introduce a value-added tax (VAT), which over time will replace various consumption taxes. While this change is intended to be revenue neutral, it can generate revenue more efficiently, equitably, and transparently. To this end, the new VAT will need to be carefully designed, not least in its choice of tax base and rate structure.

Figure 3.35.5 Inflation

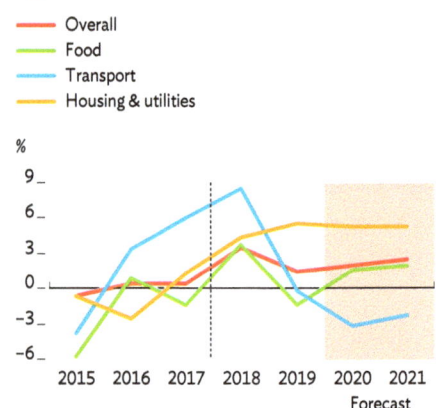

Note: A new consumer basket was introduced in 2018.
Source: ADB estimates using data from Solomon Islands National Statistics Office and the Central Bank of Solomon Islands.

Figure 3.35.6 Government revenue

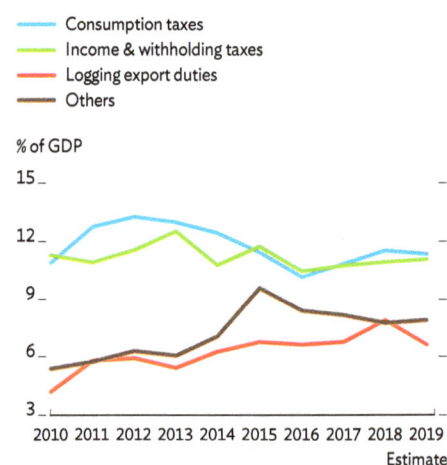

Source: ADB estimates using data from Solomon Islands National Statistics Office and the Central Bank of Solomon Islands.

It will be important to ensure adequate funding for and capacity in the Inland Revenue Division and the Customs Division of the Ministry of Finance and Treasury. At the same time, a continued focus on recovering tax arrears and improving compliance is needed to sustain the fiscal position. Sequencing reforms while strengthening revenue administration and using appropriate technology solutions will help to address some of the challenges.

VAT has been introduced in several Pacific countries and has proved to be a stable revenue source. Any expansion of the tax base can permit lower effective tax rates, and the resulting lower input prices can improve the business environment. Reform success crucially depends on engaging the private sector and considering the administrative costs that tax changes may entail.

Vanuatu

Economic growth was sustained in 2019 with public administration offsetting slowdowns in construction and tourism. Inflation was little changed but is forecast to dip briefly in 2020, when the current account will likely fall into deficit. The economy is forecast to contract in 2020 as travel restrictions arising from COVID-19 undermine tourism, which should recover in 2021. As more workers access labor mobility schemes, policies must ensure that benefits are broadly enjoyed and sustainable.

Economic performance

Strong growth in public administration, financed by higher spending, helped to sustain economic growth in 2019 despite weakness in other sectors. Setting aside kava, agriculture production declined by more than 10%. Low international prices and a rhinoceros beetle infestation caused copra output to drop.

While tourist arrivals by air reached their highest ever in 2019, tourism growth decelerated from 6% in 2018 to 4%. Australia and New Zealand, which supply more than 60% of air arrivals, sent fewer than in 2014, before Cyclone Pam (Figure 3.36.1). Arrivals on cruise ships, which contribute less to tourism earnings than air arrivals because of their short stay and onboard amenities, plummeted by almost half.

Construction slowed as government capital expenditure fell along with imports of cement and of machinery and transport equipment as several infrastructure projects reached completion.

Recurrent public expenditure jumped from a 3% increase in 2018 to almost 15% growth in 2019 on increases for goods and services, and for the public wage bill. This was financed mainly by higher revenue from honorary citizenship programs and value-added tax. Established to mobilize resources for reconstruction following Cyclone Pam, honorary citizenship provided about a third of revenue in 2019, or more than value-added tax (Figure 3.36.2).

With expenditure growth outpacing revenue, the fiscal surplus narrowed slightly to equal 6.7% of GDP. Some of the budget surplus was used to repay debt, including early repayment. Despite this, loan drawdowns drove external debt up to the equivalent of 39.5% of GDP in 2019.

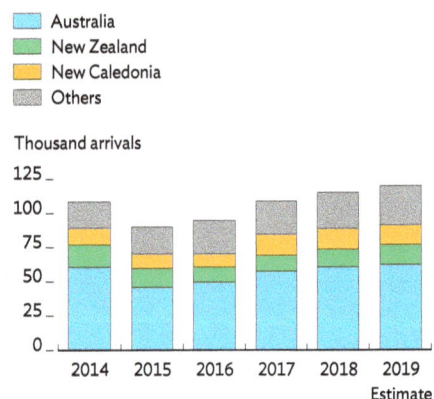

Figure 3.36.1 Vanuatu arrivals by air, by usual country of residence

- Australia
- New Zealand
- New Caledonia
- Others

Thousand arrivals

Sources: Vanuatu National Statistics Office; ADB estimates.

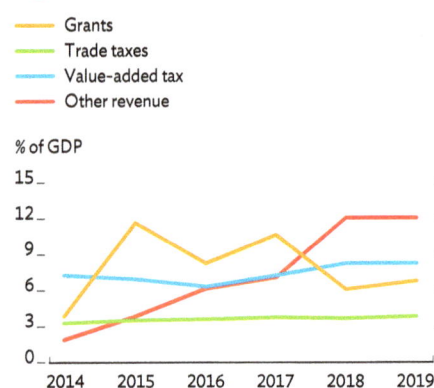

Figure 3.36.2 Government revenue

- Grants
- Trade taxes
- Value-added tax
- Other revenue

% of GDP

Note: Other revenue is mainly from honorary citizenship programs.
Source: ADB estimates using data from Ministry of Finance and Economic Management budget documents.

This chapter was written by Jacqueline Connell of the Pacific Liaison and Coordination Office, ADB, Sydney, and Prince Cruz, consultant, Pacific Department, ADB, Manila.

The Council of Ministers approved a revised debt-management strategy in 2019 that caps the ratio of nominal external debt to GDP at 40%.

Inflation was almost unchanged from 2018. The index for food and nonalcoholic beverages, which account for 40% of the basket, rose by 4.8% in 2019, but indexes were substantially lower for transport, alcohol and tobacco, and home utilities including water, electricity, and gas.

The current account surplus fell from the equivalent of 3.5% of GDP in 2018 to 2.7% in 2019 as agriculture exports weakened, though revenue from honorary citizenships remained strong. Increases in the export value of cocoa, beef, and especially kava were insufficient to offset large drops for copra and coconut oil (Figure 3.36.3).

Economic prospects

Economic contraction is forecast in 2020 as tourism declines steeply before recovering in 2021 (Figure 3.36.4). Public administration growth will accelerate with increased spending, in particular on health care and COVID-19 preparedness. However, growth in agriculture and industry are expected to decelerate in 2020 and 2021.

Travel restrictions to contain COVID-19 and the global economic slowdown will significantly reduce inbound tourism, including from Australia and New Zealand, the largest source markets. Further, last year's decline in arrivals aboard cruise ships is expected to continue as current COVID-19 restrictions prevent cruise ships from docking.

Agriculture is expected to remain weak as rhinoceros beetle continues to damage copra production. Meanwhile, industry is expected to slow as trade and travel disruption stemming from COVID-19 hamper construction on some infrastructure projects that rely on imports and foreign labor.

Government spending, which slowed in the first quarter of 2020 as a caretaker period preceded parliamentary elections held in March, is set to accelerate. The government projects a fiscal deficit equal to 4.6% of GDP with higher current and capital spending (Figure 3.36.5). The budget assumes that "other revenues," mainly from honorary citizenship programs, will be lower than in 2019. About 15% of domestic revenue is allocated to debt repayment, 45% of that for repaying external debt ahead of schedule.

Inflation is expected to slow in 2020 in line with economic weakening and softer global prices for fuel and other commodities, before rising in 2021 (Figure 3.36.6). If domestic and foreign trade are constrained by COVID-19, inflation may be driven higher. The current account balance is expected to fall into deficit in 2020 with lower tourism receipts.

Figure 3.36.3 Vanuatu merchandise exports

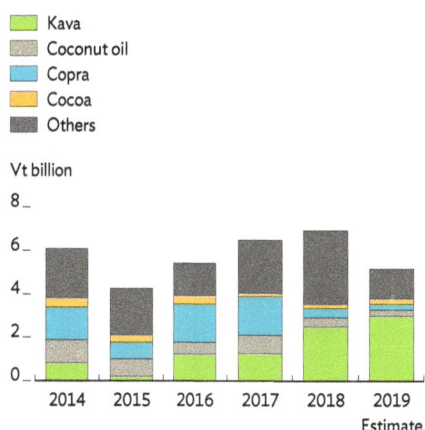

Sources: Vanuatu National Statistics Office; ADB estimates.

Figure 3.36.4 Supply-side contributions to growth

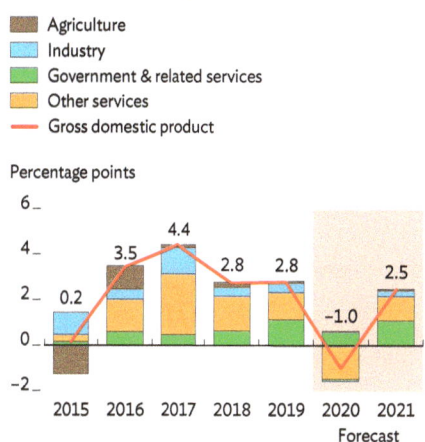

Source: ADB estimates using data from the Vanuatu National Statistics Office and the International Monetary Fund.

Figure 3.36.5 Fiscal balance

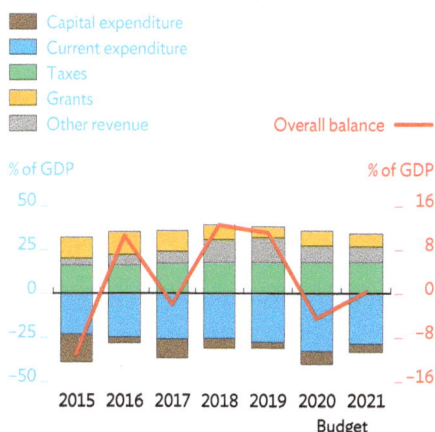

Source: ADB estimates using data from Vanuatu Ministry of Finance and Economic Management budget documents and the International Monetary Fund.

Planned aircraft purchases in line with a strategy to increase visitor arrivals would apply further pressure on the current account. The current account deficit is expected to narrow in 2021 as tourism gradually recovers.

Following 15 years of unbroken growth, a rarity in the Pacific, Vanuatu now faces significant downside risks from COVID-19. Uncertainty stems from the duration and severity of travel restrictions affecting tourism, a key generator of employment, income, and foreign exchange. Extended disruption to travel and trade would mean sharper economic contraction. They would put significant pressure on the current account as tourism receipts fell, and deteriorate the fiscal position, though this might be offset by increased grants.

Policy challenge—maximizing benefits from seasonal worker schemes

In 2018, Vanuatu contributed 40% of workers in Australia's Seasonal Worker Program and New Zealand's Recognized Seasonal Employer scheme (Figure 3.36.7). The country has successfully leveraged its early participation, and employers' preference to hire return workers, to become one of the biggest senders to both programs.

To contain COVID-19, the Government of Vanuatu suspended new workers' participation in both schemes in March 2020, even as job prospects in tourism weaken in Vanuatu. When travel restrictions ease, however, Vanuatu is likely to continue participating in both programs.

Labor mobility has enabled Vanuatu workers to earn higher incomes overseas while broadening their skills and experiences. Remittances, though much smaller than tourism and other export receipts, have grown significantly. The challenge is to maximize the development benefits labor mobility can offer to individuals, communities, and the economy of Vanuatu.

Vanuatu has lower financial penetration than do Fiji, Samoa, or Tonga, in terms of both ownership of bank accounts and access to formal credit. The cost of sending remittances is high, constraining people's ability to channel their earnings into savings and investments. In addition, workers often struggle to access the superannuation they accumulate overseas or are unable to transfer it to their local retirement accounts.

Recognizing these challenges, the government developed a financial inclusion strategy for 2018–2023. In 2019, the National Financial Inclusion Council launched digital financial products and services, including mobile money services for remittances. Improving financial literacy also promises to help seasonal workers use their earnings and experiences to build a more sustainable future when they return.

Table 3.36.1 Selected economic indicators (%)

	2018	2019	2020	2021
GDP growth	2.8	2.8	-1.0	2.5
Inflation	2.3	2.4	1.5	2.0
Current acct. bal. (share of GDP)	3.5	2.7	-8.7	-8.6

Sources: National Statistics Office; International Monetary Fund; ADB estimates.

Figure 3.36.6 Inflation

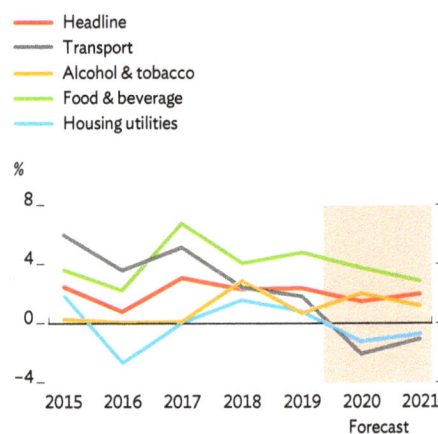

— Headline
— Transport
— Alcohol & tobacco
— Food & beverage
— Housing utilities

Sources: Vanuatu National Statistics Office; ADB estimates.

Figure 3.36.7 Vanuatu seasonal workers, by destination

% of all seasonal workers in Australia
% of all seasonal workers in New Zealand
Australia
New Zealand

Note: Years are fiscal years ending on 30 June of that year.
Sources: Australian Department of Home Affairs; Immigration New Zealand.

Central Pacific economies

Performance varied in 2019. Growth slowed in Nauru and Tuvalu but quickened in Kiribati. Inflation accelerated in Nauru and Tuvalu, while Kiribati fell into deflation. Fiscal balances deteriorated in both Kiribati and Tuvalu. Growth is expected to slow in all three economies in 2020 before recovering in 2021. Weak fiscal frameworks and reliance on external revenue make sustainable trust funds vital to a secure future, especially under recent financial market volatility.

Economic performance

The Central Pacific economies are Kiribati, Nauru, and Tuvalu, previously referred to in *Asian Development Outlook* as small island economies. None depends heavily on tourism, which may enable them to escape the worst direct impacts of COVID-19.

In Kiribati, the economy improved slightly over 2018 to grow by 2.4% in 2019 (Figure 3.37.1). The improvement came largely from government spending on wages and subsidies, which reversed a fiscal surplus equal to 27.2% of GDP in 2018 to a deficit of 8.0%. The deficit also reflected less budgetary support from development partners. Lower prices for food, beverages, and tobacco brought 1.8% deflation in 2019, and the current account surplus narrowed from the equivalent of 13.4% of GDP in 2018 to 7.6% as imports expanded.

Growth in Nauru slowed to 1.0% in fiscal year 2019 (FY2019, ended 30 June 2019) as phosphate output fell and activity slowed at the Regional Processing Centre (RPC) for asylum seekers. Recent national account estimates suggest that growth in FY2018 was significantly higher than previously estimated. The fiscal surplus narrowed to equal 16.0% of GDP in FY2019 despite a 44.8% increase in fishing license revenue and higher revenue derived from the RPC (Figure 3.37.2). Inflation jumped from 0.5% in FY2018 to 3.9% on higher alcohol and tobacco tariffs and with shipping disrupted in the port mooring system.

Tuvalu nearly matched 2018 growth with 4.1% expansion in 2019, aided by increased capital spending connected with the Pacific Islands Forum meeting in August.

Figure 3.37.1 GDP growth

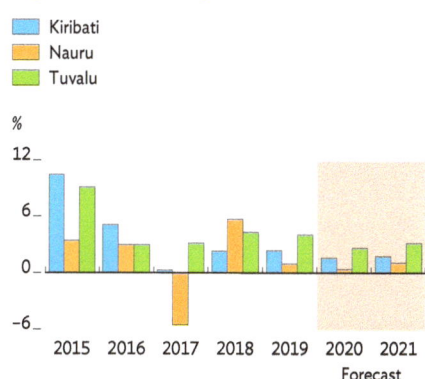

Note: Years are fiscal years ending on 30 June of that year in Nauru and coinciding with the calendar year in Kiribati and Tuvalu.

Sources: Kiribati budget documents; Nauru budget documents; Tuvalu budget documents; *Asian Development Outlook* database; International Monetary Fund Article IV Reports.

Figure 3.37.2 Fishing license revenue

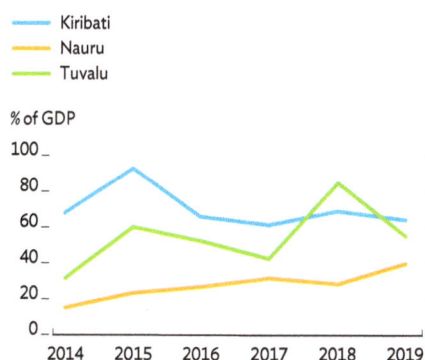

Note: Years are fiscal years ending on 30 June of that year in Nauru and coinciding with the calendar year in Kiribati and Tuvalu.

Sources: Kiribati budget documents; Nauru budget documents; Tuvalu budget documents; *Asian Development Outlook* database; International Monetary Fund Article IV Reports.

This chapter was written by Lily Anne Homasi and Isoa Wainiqolo of the Pacific Subregional Office, ADB, Suva; Jacqueline Renee Connell of the Pacific Liaison and Coordination Office, ADB, Sydney; and Prince Cruz and Noel Del Castillo, consultants, Pacific Department, ADB, Manila.

Higher spending and a steep decline in fishing receipts spelled a fiscal deficit equal to 9.8% of GDP in 2019, reversing a 34.2% surplus in 2018 (Figure 3.37.3). Inflation at 3.3% in 2019 reflected new taxes on alcohol and tobacco, as well as demand pressures heightened by infrastructure investment. The current account reversed a surplus equal to 4.8% of GDP in 2018 with a deficit estimated at 6.9%, mainly from higher imports and lower fishing revenue (Figure 3.37.4).

Economic prospects

Kiribati will likely see growth decelerate to 1.6% in 2020 before recovering to 1.8% in 2021. The economy is expected to be sluggish in the first half of 2020 because the government was unable to get approval for the 2020 budget with general elections coming in April 2020. COVID-19 restrictions will also be a drag on construction. Work on the South Tarawa Water Supply Project, Outer Islands Infrastructure Project, and South Tarawa Renewable Energy Project should support growth in 2021, assuming construction can resume.

The fiscal deficit is projected to narrow in 2020 to equal 0.8% of GDP because of delayed budget approval but then widen to 4.2% of GDP in 2021, driven by the high cost of infrastructure projects and of operating subsidies for newly purchased aircraft for Air Kiribati. The current account surplus is expected to narrow to 4.0% in 2020 as fishing revenue stabilizes and imports expand (Figure 3.37.4). It is forecast to narrow further in 2021 as domestic demand rises, driven by large infrastructure projects and related consumption spending.

Growth in Nauru is forecast to slow to 0.4% in FY2020 and recover to 1.1% in FY2021. This forecast assumes that RPC activity continues to moderate and that phosphate exports remain weak, while construction on a new seaport provides follow-on benefits to local services. Travel and trade disruption stemming from COVID-19 will drag on growth in the second half of FY2020. A downside risk to the outlook would be extended travel restrictions that delay infrastructure projects.

The fiscal surplus is expected to grow to the equivalent of 22.7% of GDP in 2020. Although spending is budgeted to remain elevated, revenue from fishing license fees and the RPC is projected to increase. The surplus will finance contributions to the national trust fund and a cash buffer, as well as arrears reduction. With RPC revenues uncertain, fiscal discipline will be critical in FY2021.

Tuvalu can expect growth to be affected by Tropical Cyclone Tino, which struck in January 2020. Rehabilitation largely financed by contingent budget support from multilateral organizations should, joined by a renewable energy project in the latter half of 2020, provide some stimulus, but growth is still projected lower at 2.7% in 2020 and 3.2% in 2021. COVID-19 is likely to drag on construction growth.

Figure 3.37.3 Fiscal balance

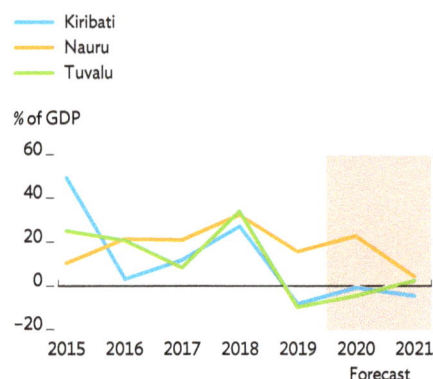

Note: Years are fiscal years ending on 30 June of that year in Nauru and coinciding with the calendar year in Kiribati and Tuvalu.

Sources: Kiribati budget documents; Nauru budget documents; Tuvalu budget documents; *Asian Development Outlook* database; International Monetary Fund Article IV Reports.

Figure 3.37.4 Current account balance

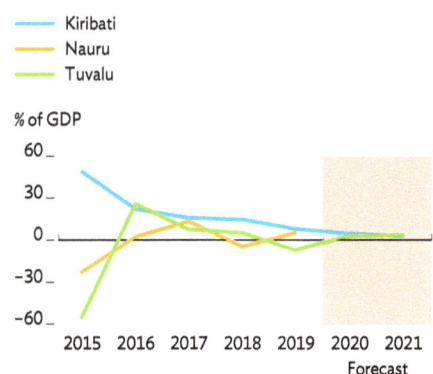

Note: Years are fiscal years ending on 30 June of that year in Nauru and coinciding with the calendar year in Kiribati and Tuvalu.

Sources: *Asian Development Outlook* database; International Monetary Fund Article IV Reports.

The government is projecting a lower fiscal deficit in 2020, equal to 4.3% of GDP. Expenditure is expected to be 5.1% lower than the outturn in 2019, and revenue 1.5% lower. Expenditure is forecast to fall further by 0.6% in 2021 as revenue grows by 4.8%, leaving a surplus equal to 2.5% of GDP. Current account surpluses equal to 2.8% of GDP in 2020 and 3.4% in 2021 are forecast in light of a stable outlook for fishing revenue and a trade balance projected to improve as capital imports ebb to a pre-2018 level.

Inflation in Nauru is forecast to decelerate in line with subdued global fuel prices in 2020 and 2021, but domestic price pressures are seen to result in a reversal of previous deflation in Kiribati and a slight acceleration in Tuvalu (Figure 3.37.5). A risk to the inflation outlook is possibly higher transport costs and supply disruption caused by COVID-19.

Policy challenge—ensuring the sustainability of public trust funds

If well managed, public trust funds can support the financial needs of developing countries. This is particularly useful in the Pacific, where narrow economic bases typically pose long-term fiscal risk. Kiribati, Nauru, and Tuvalu each has a sovereign wealth fund designed to provide long-term fiscal sustainability (Figure 3.37.6). With rising expenditure and heavy dependence on foreign sources of revenue, these economies use trust funds as fiscal buffers and their returns on investment as supplementary sources of financing. However, currently weak fiscal frameworks can tempt governments to draw down trust funds for short-term needs.

While investment returns have been broadly favorable in recent years, COVID-19 is expected to make them less so as global financial conditions tighten further. This could threaten trust fund sustainability over the longer term, rendering all three economies more vulnerable.

Kiribati established its Revenue Equalization Reserve Fund in 1956, funding it with phosphate mining revenue to smooth income from this volatile source and prepare against its inevitable depletion. Since 2012, most funding comes from windfall fishing license fees. In December 2019, the fund was worth $1.14 billion, but COVID-19 effects on financial markets drove down its nominal value in February 2020 by $27 million, or 2.3%. Meanwhile, with Kiribati at elevated risk of debt distress, continued high spending or a fishery decline could force more frequent withdrawals from the fund to finance fiscal deficits. The government may want to consider setting clear guidelines on fund use that balance explicitly permitted allotments for regular budget support with upholding intergenerational objectives.

Figure 3.37.5 Inflation

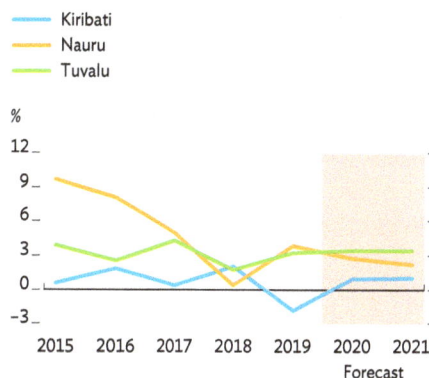

Note: Years are fiscal years ending on 30 June of that year in Nauru and coinciding with the calendar year in Kiribati and Tuvalu.

Sources: Asian Development Outlook database; International Monetary Fund Article IV Reports.

Figure 3.37.6 Trust fund balances

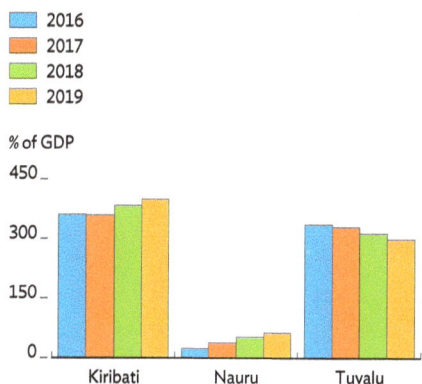

Notes: Years are fiscal years ending on 30 June of that year for Nauru and coinciding with the calendar year for Kiribati and Tuvalu. Tuvalu's 2018 and 2019 figures are projections.

Sources: Kiribati budget documents; Nauru Trust Fund Annual Reports; International Monetary Fund Article IV documents for Tuvalu.

The Intergenerational Trust Fund for the People of the Republic of Nauru was established in 2015, capitalized by the government and development partners. Its objective is to accumulate sufficient principal value to generate a revenue stream for future budget financing, replacing less sustainable sources. Since fund establishment, windfalls from fishing license fees and the RPC have flowed in as domestic revenue, about 10% of which has usually been put into the fund. However, Nauru's economy is vulnerable to fiscal shocks, most immediately a scaling-down of the RPC that could severely curtail revenue. Improving expenditure management and prioritizing critical expenditure would help ensure continued government contributions to the fund even if revenue falls over time, thereby securing the fund's longevity and ability to sustain future generations.

The Tuvalu Trust Fund (TTF) is a sovereign wealth fund established in 1987 through an international agreement with Australia, New Zealand, and the United Kingdom and designed to ensure long-term financial viability. Proceeds lend the government financial autonomy in the management of its budget. Recent market movements threaten to reduce TTF transfers to the Consolidated Investment Fund (CIF), from which the government can draw fiscal support, speeding CIF depletion in the medium term. Faster fiscal consolidation would maintain buffers in the CIF and alleviate uncertainty regarding TTF transfers. Higher taxation is an option worth considering to lessen short-term reliance on the TTF. Ensuring TTF sustainability may require the government to adopt a strategic intergeneration policy that provides a broad framework for pursuing long-term TTF objectives and ensuring its role in support of national development objectives.

Table 3.37.1 Selected economic indicators (%)

Kiribati	2018	2019	2020	2021
GDP growth	2.3	2.4	1.6	1.8
Inflation	2.1	-1.8	1.0	1.1
Current acct. bal. (share of GDP)	13.4	7.6	4.0	2.8
Nauru				
GDP growth	5.7	1.0	0.4	1.1
Inflation	0.5	3.9	2.8	2.3
Current acct. bal. (share of GDP)	-4.5	5.0	...	...
Tuvalu				
GDP growth	4.3	4.1	2.7	3.2
Inflation	1.8	3.3	3.5	3.5
Current acct. bal. (share of GDP)	4.8	-6.9	2.8	3.4

... = not available.
Source: ADB estimates.

North Pacific economies

Much higher growth last year in the Federated States of Micronesia was fueled largely by strong construction funded by development partners, as was slightly higher growth in the Marshall Islands. Meanwhile, Palau returned to contraction as visitor arrivals fell for various reasons. Economic performance is seen to weaken in all three economies this fiscal year from COVID-19 impacts, with cautious recovery anticipated next year. Over the longer term, pension fund reform is critical to contain fiscal risks.

Economic performance

Fortunes diverged in the North Pacific in fiscal year 2019 (FY2019, ended 30 September 2019) with acceleration in the Federated States of Micronesia (FSM), stable growth in the Republic of the Marshall Islands, and contraction in Palau (Figure 3.38.1).

The FSM saw growth recover on increased public investment and private sector activity following severe flooding in FY2018. The implementation of projects supported by multilateral development partners in energy and information and communications technology boosted capital spending and offset lingering management issues that hobble infrastructure projects funded through the Compact of Free Association with the US. Economic activity was buoyed as well by public spending ahead of national elections in March 2019, after which greater policy certainty bolstered business sentiment.

FSM fishing license revenues remained high at over $70 million for a third consecutive year, equaling 17% of GDP (Figure 3.38.2). Further, corporate income tax collection from foreign insurance and investment companies domiciled in the FSM remained elevated at over $50 million thanks to another large payment. The continued strong performance of these revenue sources allowed another substantial deposit into the FSM Trust Fund, which at the end of FY2019 stood at $267 million, including $43 million contributed during the year and $12 million in investment returns.

In the Marshall Islands, growth increased only slightly in FY2019 on higher construction, fishing, and public administration. Several health and sanitation projects were fast-tracked in response to a dengue outbreak in June, contributing to growth in construction and related services.

Figure 3.38.1 GDP growth in the North Pacific economies

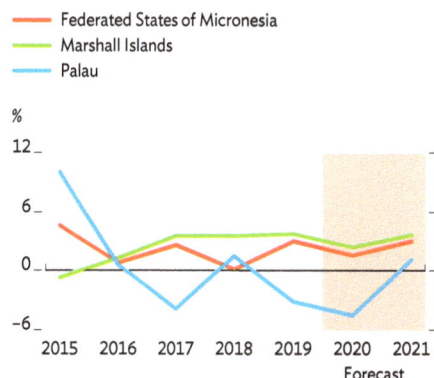

Note: Years are fiscal years ending on 30 September of that year.
Sources: ADB estimates using data from the Republic of the Marshall Islands, Federated States of Micronesia, and Republic of Palau FY2018 *Economic Briefs*.

Figure 3.38.2 Fishing license revenues in the Federated States of Micronesia

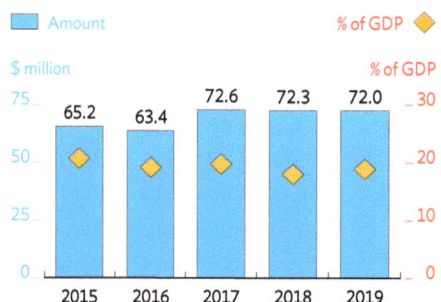

Note: Years are fiscal years ending on 30 September of that year.
Source: ADB estimates using data from the FSM Department of Finance and Administration Economic and Fiscal Update 2019.

This chapter was written by Rommel Rabanal of the Pacific Department, ADB, Manila, and Prince Cruz, consultant, Pacific Department, ADB, Manila.

Other projects are to support education and sports and to build sea walls in Ebeye and Majuro to enhance climate change resilience.

After several years of sputtering growth, agriculture expanded for a third consecutive year. The fish catch rebounded from a slowdown in FY2018, and this was reflected in double-digit growth in exports to Japan and Taipei,China. Copra production was also up, by 18%.

Higher grants and nontax revenues, mainly fishing license and ship registry fees, financed debt servicing, trust fund contributions, and higher current expenditure on health care, public administration, and subsidies to state-owned enterprises. A fiscal surplus, which rose from the equivalent of 2.5% of GDP in FY2018 to 3.0% in FY2019, was needed to finance higher debt servicing and to finally deliver on a commitment to contribute $3 million to the state trust fund. Government debt has fallen from the equivalent of 70% of GDP in FY2009 to 35% in FY2018 (Figure 3.38.3).

In Palau, economic recovery in FY2018 proved to be short-lived as GDP contracted again in FY2019 in tandem with tourism. Visitor arrivals dropped by 22.6% in FY2019, with all major markets falling except Taipei,China.

Arrivals from the PRC; Hong Kong, China; and Macau, China fell by almost half—reflecting policies aiming to limit travel to Palau and disruption from political unrest in Hong Kong, China—but this combined market remained the biggest, providing a third of all arrivals (Figure 3.38.4). Japan, which was the largest market until FY2014, remained the second biggest at 22%, despite a decline of almost 20%. Arrivals from Taipei,China rose by 23.9% in FY2019, on top of a 19.6% increase in FY2018.

Continued contraction in tourism took its toll on the labor market. For the first time in a decade, employment fell in FY2019, mainly in hotels and restaurants, transportation, and retail trade.

Economic contraction would have been worse if not for infrastructure projects funded by development partners, including under Palau's Compact of Free Association with the US. These included a rural housing project, sanitation projects to build a sewer in Koror-Airai and a landfill in Babeldaob, and transport projects to expand and upgrade the international airport in Airai, construct road connections in Babeldaob, and renovate the port in Angaur.

The fiscal surplus narrowed sharply as revenue fell, mainly with a decline in arrival tax receipts, while current expenditure increased. A portion of increased capital spending was matched by increased grants, mainly from the US and Taipei,China.

Figure 3.38.3 Marshall Islands external debt

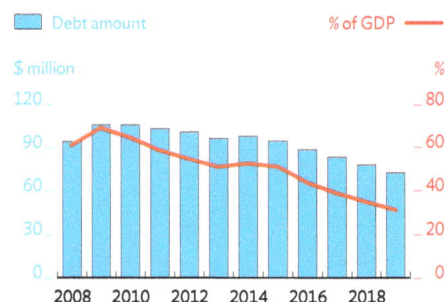

Note: Years are fiscal years ending on 30 September of that year. Value for 2019 is an estimate.
Source: ADB estimates using data Republic of the Marshall Islands FY2018 Statistical Appendices.

Figure 3.38.4 Visitor arrivals in Palau, by source

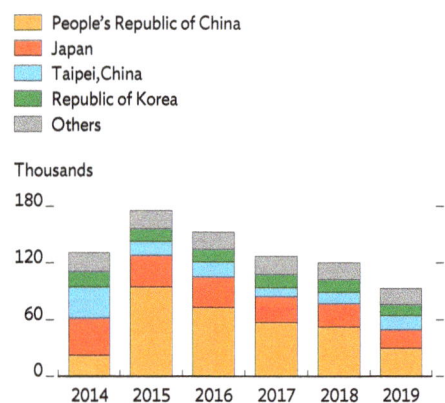

Notes: Years are fiscal years ending on 30 September of that year. Data presented for the People's Republic of China includes Hong Kong, China and Macau, China.
Source: Palau Bureau of Labor and Immigration.

Inflation eased in all three economies in FY2019 as prices for imported food and fuel declined. In Palau, the opening of a national slaughterhouse in 2018 may have helped lower domestic prices by making locally produced pork more available.

Economic prospects

Near-term prospects for the FSM and the Marshall Islands are linked to sustaining infrastructure investment, which is now likely to experience lengthy delays because of restricted mobility for labor and imported capital equipment under the COVID-19 pandemic. Palau, however, is expected to contract again in FY2020 before recovering in FY2021. Although all three North Pacific economies have restricted flights because of COVID-19, the impact will be strongest in tourist-dependent Palau.

In the FSM, GDP growth is projected to slow in FY2020 with the waning of election-related stimulus and construction delays affecting ongoing projects (Figure 3.38.5). The start of new capital projects supported by multilateral development partners—including renewable energy investments in Kosrae and Yap and a maritime project to upgrade infrastructure and improve the safety and efficiency of ports in all four FSM states—will now also be largely pushed back, supporting higher growth in FY2021 as construction ramps up.

A further upside to the FY2021 growth forecast is the potential resolution of project management issues, which would unlock $200 million in unspent Compact infrastructure grants. The government appears optimistic that the FSM and the US will agree soon on an arrangement—a strong incentive being the expiration of economic provisions under the current Compact in 2023.

In the Marshall Islands, economic growth is likely to decelerate in FY2020 as travel and transport restrictions caused by COVID-19 depress growth, notably in construction, agriculture and fishing, and trade. The continuing dengue epidemic will, along with measles, influenza, and COVID-19, further strain the public health system. Growth is seen to rebound in FY2021 as most restrictions are gradually eased.

Higher current expenditure, financed by grants, would allow the Marshall Islands to further fast-track projects such as water supply and sewerage systems and health-care facilities (Figure 3.38.6). Although capital expenditure in the FY2020 budget is 70% higher than a year earlier, resources are likely to be diverted to health care.

With dengue cases falling at the start of the fiscal year, travel restrictions were eased during the holiday season. Reported dengue cases started rising again in January, overwhelming the country's two hospitals. A measles outbreak in other Pacific countries raised an alarm to boost immunization.

Figure 3.38.5 Supply-side contributions to growth in the Federated States of Micronesia

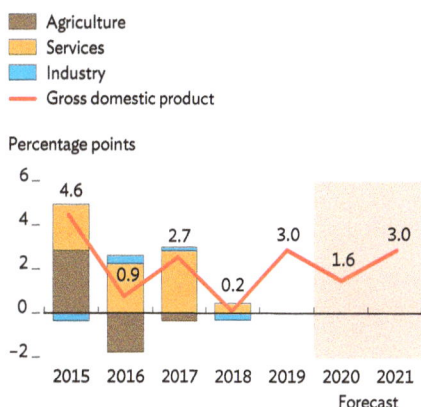

Note: Years are fiscal years ending on 30 September of that year.
Source: ADB estimates using data from the Federated States of Micronesia FY2018 *Economic Review.*

Figure 3.38.6 Grants and current expenditures in the Marshall Islands

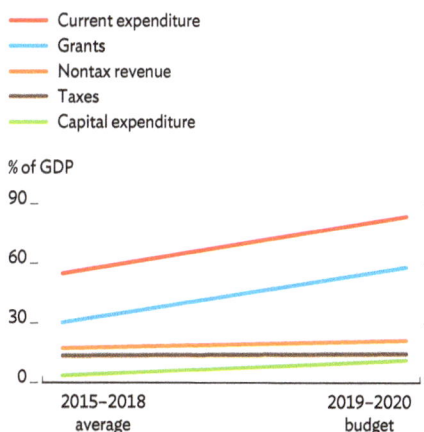

Note: Years are fiscal years ending on 30 September of that year.
Sources: ADB estimates using data from the Republic of the Marshall Islands *Economic Reviews* (various years) and FY2019–2020 national budget.

Overstretched fiscal resources in the Marshall Islands are further strained by a continuing need to service debt. Development partners are helping to restructure old loans to bring down debt-servicing costs from the equivalent of 3.3% of GDP in FY2020.

In Palau, economic contraction is expected to continue in FY2020 with visitor arrivals falling further because of COVID-19. Charter flights from the PRC were suspended in January, while flights from other countries were discontinued or significantly reduced in March. Preliminary figures indicate a 44% drop in visitor arrivals in February.

Palau's economy is expected to recover in FY2021 as travel restrictions are gradually lifted. Construction is expected to contract, however, as some projects reach completion. Visitors from Japan are expected to increase with the resumption of twice-weekly direct Skymark charter flights, launched in February. Skymark was set to start scheduled flights by July 2020, but this was deferred as COVID-19 restrictions came into force.

Arrivals from other major markets are also expected to increase with the completion of airport terminal rehabilitation in the second half of FY2020, though this may also be delayed. The renovation should improve services, expand passenger capacity, and increase revenue from concessionaires.

In response to COVID-19, Palau added $900,000 to the Hospital Trust Fund and released $6.0 million from the emergency fund, to cover an anticipated revenue shortfall. Despite the increase in spending, Palau is projected to maintain fiscal balance to the forecast horizon (Figure 3.38.7). Spending on public wages, transfers to the pension fund, and subsidies to state-owned enterprises will likely be maintained. As some infrastructure projects are financed by loans, rising debt-servicing costs may require lower current expenditure in FY2021.

Inflation in the North Pacific is likely to remain low in FY2020, with declines in the international price of crude oil offset by slight increases in food prices (Figure 3.38.8). In FY2021, low oil prices are seen to contain fuel and transport costs, but steady increases in imported food prices are forecast to lift consumer price inflation marginally.

Table 3.38.1 Selected economic indicators (%)

Federated States of Micronesia	2018	2019	2020	2021
GDP growth	0.2	3.0	1.6	3.0
Inflation	1.4	1.0	0.5	1.0
Current acct. bal. (share of GDP)	21.0	3.3	8.8	1.3
Marshall Islands				
GDP growth	3.6	3.8	2.5	3.7
Inflation	0.8	0.1	0.3	0.5
Current acct. bal. (share of GDP)	6.5	7.7	6.1	5.1
Palau				
GDP growth	1.5	-3.1	-4.5	1.2
Inflation	2.0	0.6	0.4	0.8
Current acct. bal. (share of GDP)	-9.5	-11.8	-13.5	-13.3

Source: ADB estimates.

Figure 3.38.7 Fiscal surpluses in North Pacific economies

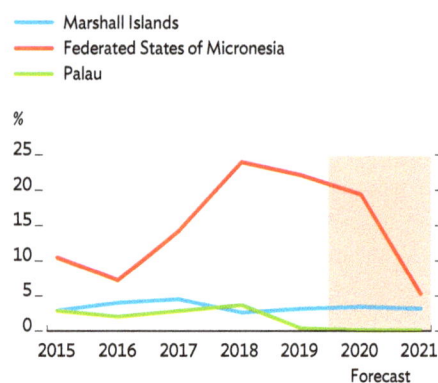

Note: Years are fiscal years ending on 30 September of that year.

Sources: ADB estimates using data from the Republic of the Marshall Islands, Federated States of Micronesia, and Republic of Palau FY2018 *Economic Briefs*.

Policy challenge—pension fund reform

Significant progress has been made in expanding social protection in the Pacific. This has often been funded by pension funds, however, which poses threats to their sustainability.

The FSM and Marshall Islands social security administrations cover formal employees in both the public and the private sector, while Palau's Civil Service Pension Plan (CSPP) covers public employees and its Social Security Retirement Fund (SSRF) covers private workers. The latest actuarial assessments show these pension funds having built up substantial unfunded liabilities as benefit payments have historically outstripped contributions. Unfunded liabilities are the most severe in the Marshall Islands, but the funded ratio is lowest for Palau's CSPP (Figure 3.38.9).

Social security administrations have implemented various measures toward improving fund sustainability: raising ceilings for taxable earnings, gradually increasing the retirement age, raising contribution rates, and cutting benefit entitlements. The FSM and Palau's SSRF were the first to implement reform, in 2013, and have achieved some immediate gains. Unfunded liabilities in the FSM fell from $259 million in 2014 to $235 million in 2017, with a corresponding increase in the funded ratio from 16% to 18%. Thanks to reform, Palau's SSRF has both the lowest unfunded liabilities, at $177 million, and the highest funded ratio, at 34%. After some years of delay, the Marshall Islands implemented similar reform in 2017, fending off an imminent collapse of its fund, which is now deemed able to remain afloat beyond 2030.

However, reform for Palau's CSPP remains stalled, and the recommendations of a 2018 actuarial study largely unimplemented. An audit of FY2018 concluded that the CSPP could be drained as early as FY2022, making immediate reform of paramount importance. The 2018 actuarial study recommended a balanced approach to increase contribution rates without sudden cuts in benefits, which can be achieved by introducing a defined contribution scheme to complement the current defined benefit plan and gradually close the gap between contributions and benefits.

Other North Pacific social security administrations can consider phasing in similar defined contribution schemes to shore up their pension funds. More broadly, reinvigorating employment growth—which has been slow or stagnant in the North Pacific over the past 2 decades—will be critical to pension fund sustainability over the longer-term. Strengthened private sector development and the steady creation of formal employment can accelerate contributions to catch up with benefit payments to retirees.

Figure 3.38.8 Inflation in the North Pacific economies

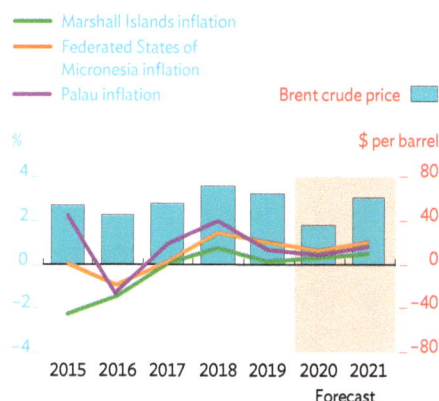

Note: Years are fiscal years ending on 30 September of that year.
Sources: ADB estimates using data from the Republic of the Marshall Islands, the Federated States of Micronesia, and the Republic of Palau FY2018 *Economic Briefs*.

Figure 3.38.9 Unfunded liabilities of North Pacific pension funds, latest available year

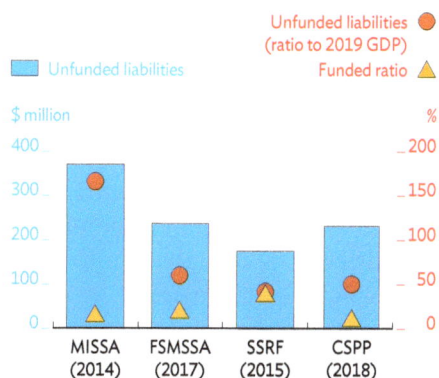

CSPP = Civil Service Pension Plan of Palau, FSMSSA = Federated States of Micronesia Social Security Administration, MISSA = Marshall Islands Social Security Administration, SSRF = Social Security Retirement Fund of Palau.

Sources: ADB estimates using data from the Republic of the Marshall Islands, Federated States of Micronesia, and Republic of Palau FY2018 *Economic Briefs*; and latest available pension fund actuarial reports.

South Pacific economies

Tonga recovered from a cyclone in 2019 as growth rebounded in Samoa and stayed strong in the Cook Islands. Lower global food prices slowed inflation in Samoa and Tonga and kept it low in the Cook Islands. The COVID-19 pandemic will severely hit tourism, undermining growth and fiscal outcomes, with significant downside risks. In the longer term, urbanization challenges must be addressed by upgrading infrastructure and ensuring better maintenance and timely repair.

Economic performance

Cook Islands economic growth slowed to 5.3% in fiscal year 2019 (FY2019, ended 30 June 2019) from 8.9% a year earlier (Figure 3.39.1). Government spending on infrastructure projects fell by 20% in FY2019 as implementation was delayed, but construction elsewhere continued to support growth. While arrivals rose by only 1.2% from FY2018, tourism receipts and domestic demand for tourism retail services continued to perform well, contributing 4.1 percentage points to GDP growth (Figure 3.39.2).

Inflation picked up from 0.1% in FY2018 to an estimated 0.8%. High demand for imports to support tourism drove price increases for food, apparel, alcohol, and tobacco.

The fiscal surplus expanded from the equivalent of 1.4% of GDP in FY2018 to an estimated 3.4% in FY2019 as revenue rose and government spending on infrastructure projects declined, mainly because of delayed implementation. Net debt at the end of June 2019 equaled 17.3% of GDP, below the government target of 30%.

The current account remained in surplus equal to 3.6% of GDP in FY2019 as growth in tourism receipts continued to outpace increases in imports of goods and services for domestic consumption and public infrastructure projects.

Samoa rebounded to 3.5% growth in FY2019 with large gains in general commerce and smaller contributions from construction, food and beverage manufacturing, hotels, and restaurants. Visitor arrivals had another strong year, growing by 9.3%. Business services and the "other services" category declined, as did fishing.

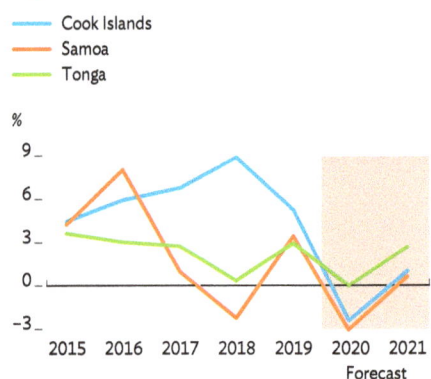

Figure 3.39.1 GDP growth

Note: Years are fiscal years ending on 30 June of that year.
Sources: Cook Islands Ministry of Finance and Economic Management; Samoa Bureau of Statistics; Tonga Department of Statistics; ADB estimates.

This chapter was written by James Webb and Lily Anne Homasi of the Pacific Subregional Office, ADB, Suva; Rommel Rabanal of the Pacific Department, ADB, Manila; and Noel Del Castillo, consultant, Pacific Department, ADB, Manila.

Inflation decelerated to 2.2% with lower imported inflation and despite higher pressure on prices from local sources, particularly food, nonalcoholic beverages, and, to a lesser extent, transport. Alcohol and tobacco made significant contributions, while most other price categories were flat.

The fiscal surplus expanded substantially to the equivalent of 2.7% of GDP in FY2019 on strong revenue growth and capital expenditure below expectations (Figure 3.39.3). Year-end external debt fell from the equivalent of 52.0% in FY2018 to 46.9% in FY2019, bringing it below the debt target of 50% as GDP grew and Samoa paid down existing debt. The current account surplus expanded from the equivalent of 0.8% of GDP in FY2018 to 2.3%, thanks largely to higher visitor arrivals and continued strength in remittances.

Tonga continued to focus on rehabilitation and recovery from Cyclone Gita. With delays affecting the rollout of major construction projects, however, gradual recovery to 3.0% growth in FY2019 drew support from stronger consumption supported by credit expansion. Fishing and agriculture were both weak, but tourism continued to post strong growth.

Inflation slowed from 7.0% in FY2018 to 4.1% as declines in commodity prices more than offset increased demand tied to government construction projects (Figure 3.39.4). The fiscal surplus narrowed from the equivalent of 3.2% of GDP in FY2018 to 2.7% in FY2019 as growth in expenditure outpaced revenue. External debt fell from 37.7% of GDP in FY2018 to 34.1% in FY2019, well below the external debt target of 50%.

The current account posted a deficit equal to 6.8% of GDP in FY2019. While remittance inflow increased by 6.7%, the merchandise trade deficit widened by 15.7% with higher payments for such imported goods as oil, motor vehicles, construction materials, and general goods for wholesale and retail trade.

Economic prospects

The Cook Islands economy is expected to be severely affected by a collapse in tourist arrivals from March 2020, with economic activity projected to contract by 2.2% in FY2020. Visitor arrivals will likely remain minimal in the peak travel period of June–October, with limited recovery beginning in December. Growth in FY2021 is projected at 1.0% as the government continues to implement its economic recovery plan. Downside risks pertain to the length of containment and speed of recovery in New Zealand.

Despite a projection for subdued global fuel prices, inflation is forecast to accelerate to 1.5% in 2020 and 1.7% in 2021, driven by price increases for other imported goods—particularly food, tobacco, alcoholic beverages, and construction materials—most of which are imported from New Zealand and will be subject to significant supply disruption in the short term (Figure 3.39.4).

Figure 3.39.2 Visitor arrivals from Australia and New Zealand to the Cook Islands and Samoa

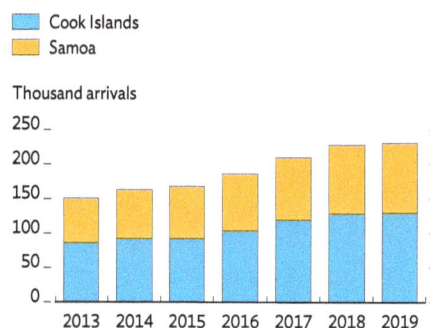

Note: Years are fiscal years ending on 30 June of that year.
Sources: Australian Bureau of Statistics; Statistics New Zealand; Cook Islands Ministry of Finance and Economic Management.

Figure 3.39.3 Fiscal balance

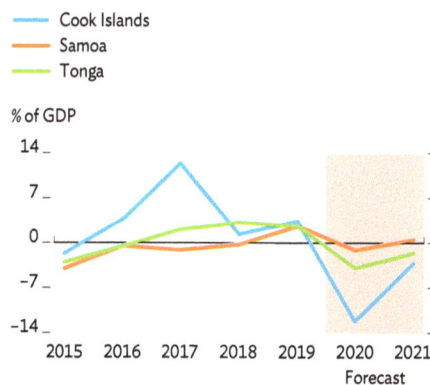

Note: Years are fiscal years ending on 30 June of that year.
Sources: Cook Islands Ministry of Finance & Economic Management; Samoa Ministry of Finance; Tonga Ministry of Finance and National Planning.

Figure 3.39.4 Inflation

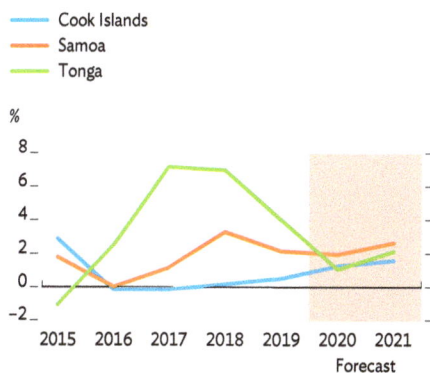

Note: Years are fiscal years ending on 30 June of that year.
Sources: Cook Islands Ministry of Finance and Economic Management; Samoa Bureau of Statistics; Tonga Department of Statistics; ADB estimates.

A fiscal deficit equal to 12.1% of GDP is projected for FY2020 to finance government responses to COVID-19. A 3.1% fiscal deficit is projected for FY2021 as tax revenue collapses, especially company and value-added tax. Debt is expected to remain below the government benchmark, at about 17.5% in FY2020 and FY2021, but it could increase if the government borrows to support additional response measures. The current account deficit is projected to equal 1.2% of GDP in FY2020, reflecting both higher imports and lower tourism receipts. Expected tourism recovery in the second half of FY2021 should leave a 1.1% surplus in the current account that year.

Samoa saw visitor arrivals and economic activity boosted by the Pacific Games in July, but the economy is expected to contract by 3.0% in FY2020 from the combined effects of measles and COVID-19 on tourism from the second quarter of FY2020. FY2021 will be similarly affected, with GDP expected to grow by only 0.8% as tourism recovers only slowly but with positive contributions from communications and agriculture.

Inflation is expected to slow to 2.0% in FY2020 as oil price declines mitigate local price pressures and disrupted supply. Recovery in local demand and from supply disruption are projected to accelerate inflation to 2.5% in FY2021.

Government finances are expected to fall into deficit equal to 5.0% of GDP in FY2020 as revenue from commerce and tourism declines and response measures are enacted. The fiscal deficit is projected to narrow to 3.5% in FY2021 with slow recovery.

The current account surplus will likely slip to deficit equal to 1.1% of GDP in FY2020 as reduced tourism more than offsets any reduction in domestic demand. Remittances fell toward the end of 2019 but are expected to recover in the remainder of FY2020 and offset some losses. The current account is expected to return to surplus in FY2021, at 0.5% of GDP, as visitor arrivals recover (Figure 3.39.5).

In Tonga, a significant decline in visitor arrivals will allow no economic growth in FY2020. However, tourism recovery and faster government implementation of rehabilitation and recovery from Cyclone Gita will provide vital support in FY2021, with the economy projected to rebound with 2.5% growth.

Inflation is forecast lower in FY2020, then rising slightly in FY2021. A gradual rollout of infrastructure projects and anticipated disruption to regional supply in FY2021 will put upward pressure on prices despite lower global oil prices.

The fiscal surplus in FY2019 will likely turn to a deficit equal to 3.8% of GDP in FY2020 as revenue falls and expenditure rises, but the deficit is expected to narrow to 1.5% in FY2021 with revenue recovery. Higher imports of capital goods and construction materials, combined with falling tourism and remittance receipts, will likely widen the current account deficit in FY2020 and FY2021, despite steady exports of food products to Australia and New Zealand.

Table 3.39.1 Selected economic indicators (%)

Cook Islands	2018	2019	2020	2021
GDP growth	8.9	5.3	-2.2	1.0
Inflation	0.1	0.8	1.5	1.7
Current acct. bal. (share of GDP)	7.1	3.6	-1.2	1.1
Samoa				
GDP growth	-2.2	3.5	-3.0	0.8
Inflation	3.6	2.2	2.0	2.5
Current acct. bal. (share of GDP)	0.8	2.3	-1.1	0.5
Tonga				
GDP growth	0.2	3.0	0.0	2.5
Inflation	7.0	4.1	1.3	2.2
Current acct. bal. (share of GDP)	-5.9	-6.8	-12.6	-13.4

Sources: Cook Islands Ministry of Finance and Economic Management; Samoa Bureau of Statistics; Tonga Department of Statistics; ADB estimates.

Figure 3.39.5 Current account balance

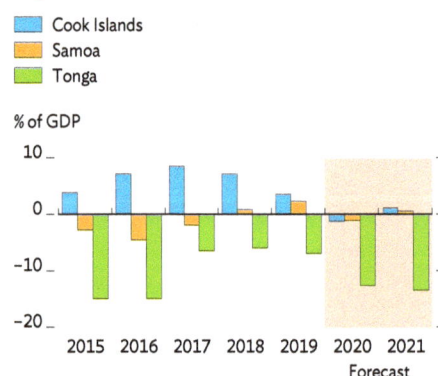

Note: Years are fiscal years ending on 30 June of that year.
Sources: Cook Islands Ministry of Finance and Economic Management; Samoa Bureau of Statistics; Tonga Department of Statistics; ADB estimates.

Box 3.39.1 **Introducing Niue, the newest member of ADB**

On 11 March 2019, Niue officially became the 68th member country of ADB. With a population of only 1,700 and a land area of 259 square kilometers, Niue is one of the smallest countries in the world. Access to basic services is relatively high in Niue, and so is gross national income per capita, at $16,500 in 2016. However, Niue has outsized vulnerabilities and development challenges stemming from its very narrow economic base, cost structures elevated by extreme remoteness, and disaster risks.

As in other South Pacific economies, tourism is a main driver of economic growth, with some 10,000 visitor arrivals annually and tourism receipts equal to about a third of annual GDP. Visitor arrivals have increased by fivefold since 2005, boosted by improved flight connections, investment in accommodation, and a coordinated marketing campaign. New Zealand is the main source market, providing up to 80% of arrivals.

A small agriculture sector produces honey and noni juice, but exports are constrained by extreme distance from major markets and limited transport infrastructure. Niue is 2,800 kilometers from New Zealand and 5,800 kilometers from Australia, the two primary export destinations.

On the demand side, the public sector provides 42% of GDP and directly employs a quarter of the population. Public spending is supported by large and stable annual inflows of official development assistance equal to three-quarters of GDP. The bulk of this assistance is received as an independent state in free association with New Zealand.

As are most of its Pacific peers, Niue is exposed to natural hazards, particularly cyclones. The most severe cyclone in its history, Cyclone Heta in 2004, wrought widespread damage valued at five times national GDP.

Most recently, Cyclone Tino in January 2020 damaged Alofi wharf, leaving the country's only maritime transportation hub temporarily out of commission and disrupting fishing and business activity for several weeks.

GDP growth averaged 4.0% in 2013–2017 on solid expansion in tourism (box figure). Growth accelerated to 6.5% in 2018 when government expenditure ramped up to resume the implementation of development partner-supported capital projects after some years of stagnation. Reflecting robust economic activity, inflation rose sharply in 2018, especially for alcoholic beverages and transportation. Fiscal stimulus has remained substantial despite easing slightly in 2019. GDP growth is estimated to have slowed consequently in 2019, with some moderation in visitor arrival growth cited as a contributing factor. The outlook for 2020 and 2021 will continue to depend heavily on the performance of Niue's tourism industry and the pace of infrastructure construction.

Niue economic indicators

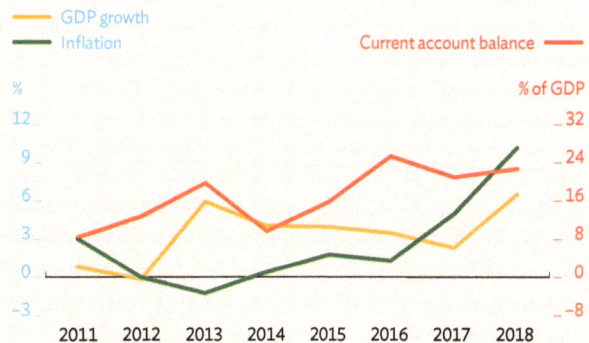

Source: Statistics Niue.

Policy challenge—addressing challenges to urbanization

A notable feature of South Pacific development is greater concentration of economic activity and population in central areas. Migration and concentrated development have strained urban infrastructure and public services. They render recent economic gains fragile, especially as climate risks mount and, if unaddressed, pose challenges to future economic growth and social equity. Formulating appropriate responses is now especially important to support long-term economic recovery from COVID-19.

Across the board, there has been a dramatic shift from rural areas to urban centers. The population of the Samoan capital Apia and its surrounding administrative areas has increased by 41% over the past 3 decades, greatly outpacing 15% growth in the rest of the country. Similarly, the population on Tongatapu, Tonga's main island, has increased by 17% as other islands suffered a 16% decline, and the population of Rarotonga, the largest of the Cook Islands, has increased by 16%, compared with a 44% decline elsewhere. The economies of these countries have similarly become increasingly dominated by capital islands, with the service sector, which exists predominantly in urban areas, contributing in the past 10 years 64% of growth in the Cook Islands, 41% in Tonga, and 100% in Samoa (as growth and contraction in smaller sectors net out). While this has improved incomes for increasingly urban populations, it has also put economies at greater risk to natural hazards, with a large portion of economic activity now concentrated along the waterfront in Apia and Nuku'alofa, and tourist developments crowded around Muri lagoon in Rarotonga.

Many of these areas have developed with little or no urban planning. This has commonly made it difficult and expensive to install adequate support infrastructure. Poor maintenance has raised costs further, with many critical utilities now requiring wholesale replacement to meet public demand for services.

While institutional changes are making progress toward better planning and management, gaps in infrastructure and public service delivery jeopardize the already fragile economic growth enjoyed by South Pacific economies in recent years. Regular flooding in the Apia urban area limits investment and imposes a cost burden on businesses. Sanitation issues in Rarotonga risk spoiling the pristine beaches and lagoons that have driven tourism growth. And Nuku'alofa faces an extreme risk of inundation under even modest sea-level rise. Economic losses and opportunity costs may be substantial if these infrastructure gaps go unaddressed. Fiscal resources will be needed to ensure that investment goes ahead, but this priority competes with others in national budgets, including education, health care, and public administration.

The most cost-effective approach would be to focus on ensuring better maintenance and timely repair. One way to do this is to develop infrastructure and maintenance frameworks to guide resourcing and sequencing efforts. It is widely shown that early intervention to sustain current infrastructure is far cheaper than replacing irreparably damaged infrastructure once it fails. Improved maintenance would reduce the cost of ensuring that existing infrastructure delivers the required services, as well as mean less service disruption.

With a large pipeline of investment already under way, a focus on preemptive maintenance would limit the maintenance overhang built up in the past, limiting the risk that infrastructure cannot be maintained without significant refurbishment. While this would avoid the capital cost of replacing current infrastructure stock, prudent fiscal management would still be required to ensure the availability of funds for initial investments. Careful project selection is key in ensuring that investments leverage the largest possible growth dividends, facilitating further revenue growth. Close coordination with development partners will be essential to ensure that investments can go ahead without sacrificing debt sustainability, especially in light of the fiscal and economic challenges posed by COVID-19.

4

STATISTICAL APPENDIX

Statistical notes and tables

The statistical appendix presents selected economic indicators for the 46 developing member economies of the Asian Development Bank (ADB) in 18 tables. The economies are grouped into five subregions: Central Asia, East Asia, South Asia, Southeast Asia, and the Pacific. Most of the tables contain historical data from 2015 to 2019; some have forecasts for 2020 and 2021.

The data were standardized to the degree possible to allow comparability over time and across economies, but differences in statistical methodology, definitions, coverage, and practices make full comparability impossible. The national income accounts section is based on the United Nations System of National Accounts, while the data on balance of payments use International Monetary Fund (IMF) accounting standards. Historical data were obtained from official sources, statistical publications, and databases, as well as the documents of ADB, the IMF, and the World Bank. For some economies, data for 2019 were estimated from the latest available information. Projections for 2020 and 2021 are generally ADB estimates made on the bases of available quarterly or monthly data, though some projections are from governments.

Most economies report by calendar year. The following record their government finance data by fiscal year: Brunei Darussalam; Fiji; Hong Kong, China; the Kyrgyz Republic; Singapore; Tajikistan; Thailand; and Uzbekistan. Reporting all variables by fiscal year are South Asian countries (except for Maldives and Sri Lanka), the Cook Islands, the Federated States of Micronesia, Myanmar, Nauru, Palau, the Republic of Marshall Islands, Samoa, and Tonga.

Regional and subregional averages or totals are provided for seven tables: A1, A2, A6, A11, A12, A13, and A14. For tables A1, A2, A6, A11, A12, and A14, averages were computed using weights derived from gross national income (GNI) in current US dollars following the World Bank Atlas method. The GNI data for 2015–2018 were obtained from the World Bank's World Development Indicators online. Weights for 2018 were carried over through 2021. The GNI data for the Cook Islands and Taipei,China were estimated using the Atlas conversion factor. For Table A13, the regional and subregional totals were computed using a consistent sum, which means that if country data were missing for a given year, the sum excluded that country.

Tables A1, A2, A3, A4, and A5. These tables show data on output growth, production, and demand. Changes to the national income accounts series for some countries were made to accommodate a change in source, methodology, and/or base year. The series for Afghanistan, Bhutan, India, Myanmar, and Pakistan reflects fiscal year data, rather than calendar year data, and those for Timor-Leste reflect GDP excluding the offshore petroleum sector.

Table A1: Growth rate of GDP (% per year). The table shows annual growth rates of GDP valued at constant market prices, factor costs, or basic prices. GDP at market prices is the aggregation of value added by all resident producers at producers' prices including taxes less subsidies on imports plus all nondeductible value-added or similar taxes. Constant factor cost measures differ from market price measures in that they exclude taxes on production and include subsidies. Basic price valuation is the factor cost plus some taxes on production, such as property and payroll taxes, and less some subsidies, such as for labor but not for products. Most economies use constant market price valuation. Pakistan uses constant factor costs, and Fiji and Maldives use basic prices.

Table A2: Growth rate of GDP per capita (% per year). The table provides the growth rates of real per capita GDP, which is defined as GDP at constant prices divided by the population. Nepal uses GDP at constant factor cost. Also shown are data on gross national income per capita in US dollar terms (Atlas method) for 2017, sourced from the World Bank's World Development Indicators online. Data for the Cook Islands and Taipei,China were estimated using the Atlas conversion factor.

Table A3: Growth rate of value added in agriculture (% per year). The table shows the growth rates of value added in agriculture at constant prices and agriculture's share of GDP in 2017 at current prices. The agriculture sector comprises plant crops, livestock, poultry, fisheries, and forestry.

Table A4: Growth rate of value added in industry (% per year). The table provides the growth rates of value added in industry at constant prices and industry's share of GDP in 2017 at current prices. This sector comprises manufacturing, mining and quarrying, and, generally, construction and utilities.

Table A5: Growth rate of value added in services (% per year). The table gives the growth rates of value added in services at constant prices and services' share of GDP in 2017 at current prices. Subsectors generally include trade, banking, finance, real estate, and similar businesses, as well as public administration. For Malaysia, electricity, gas, water supply, and waste management are included under services.

Table A6: Inflation (% per year). Data on inflation rates are period averages. Inflation rates are based on consumer price indexes. The consumer price indexes of the following economies are for a given city only: Cambodia is for Phnom Penh, the Marshall Islands for Majuro, Sri Lanka for Colombo, and Solomon Islands for Honiara. For Uzbekistan, data from 2016 onward reflect the IMF fixed weight method of estimating the consumer price index, as adopted by the government, which has not revised annual average inflation data for 2014–2016; for this period, IMF average consumer price data are used. For Brunei Darussalam, there is a series break starting 2016 because of the change in base year from 2010 to 2015 and for Indonesia, starting 2019 because of the change in base year from 2012 to 2018.

Table A7: Change in money supply (% per year). This table tracks annual percentage change in the end-of-period supply of broad money, M2 for most economies. M2 is defined as the sum of currency in circulation plus demand deposits (M1) plus quasi-money, which consists of time and savings deposits including foreign currency deposits. For Georgia and India, broad money is M3, which adds longer-term time deposits.

Tables A8, A9, and A10: Government finance. These tables give the revenue and expenditure transactions and the fiscal balance of the central government expressed as a percentage of GDP in nominal terms. Where full year data are not yet available, the shares to GDP are estimated using available monthly or quarterly data. For Cambodia, Georgia, India, Kazakhstan, the Kyrgyz Republic, Mongolia, the People's Republic of China, and Tajikistan, transactions are those reported by the general government. Starting from 2015, the series for Cambodia is based on the IMF *Government Finance Statistics Manual 2014* format.

Table A8: Central government revenue (% of GDP). Central government revenue comprises all nonrepayable receipts, both current and capital, plus grants. These amounts are computed as a percentage of GDP at current prices. For the Republic of Korea, revenue excludes social security contributions. For Kazakhstan, revenue includes transfers from the national fund. Grants are excluded for Cambodia, Malaysia, and Thailand; revenue from disinvestment is included for India; and only current revenue is included for Bangladesh.

Table A9: Central government expenditure (% of GDP). Central government expenditure comprises all nonrepayable payments to meet both current and capital expenses, plus net lending. These amounts are computed as a share of GDP at current prices. For Thailand, expenditure refers to budgetary expenditure excluding externally financed expenditure and borrowing. For Tajikistan, expenditure includes externally financed public investment programs. One-time expenditures are excluded for Pakistan.

Table A10: Fiscal balance of central government (% of GDP). Fiscal balance is the difference between central government revenue and expenditure. The difference is computed as a share of GDP at current prices. Data variation may arise from statistical discrepancy when, for example, balancing items for general governments (central plus selected subnational governments), and from differences between coverage used in individual revenue and expenditure calculations and in fiscal balance calculations. For Fiji, the fiscal balance excludes loan repayment. For Georgia, fiscal balance is calculated according to the *Government Finance Statistics Manual 2001* of the IMF. For Thailand, the fiscal balance is the cash balance of the combined budgetary and nonbudgetary balances. For Uzbekistan, the augmented fiscal balance includes the Fund for Reconstruction and Development. Some off-budget accounts are included in the computation of the fiscal balance for Turkmenistan. For Singapore, fiscal balance excludes special transfers (top-ups to endowment and trust funds) and contributions from net investment returns, while for the Republic of Korea it excludes social security-related funds.

Tables A11, A12, A13, and A14: Balance of payments. These tables show annual flows of selected international economic transactions of countries as recorded in the balance of payments.

Tables A11 and A12: Growth rates of merchandise exports and imports (% per year). These tables show the annual growth rates of exports and imports of goods. Data are in million US dollars, primarily obtained from the balance-of-payments accounts of each economy. Export data are reported free on board. Import data are reported free on board except for the following economies, which value them based on cost, insurance, and freight: Afghanistan; Hong Kong, China; Georgia; India; the Lao People's Democratic Republic; Myanmar; Singapore; and Thailand.

Table A13: Trade balance ($ million). The trade balance is the difference between merchandise exports and merchandise imports. Figures in this table are based on the export and import amounts used to generate tables A11 and A12.

Table A14: Current account balance (% of GDP). The current account balance is the sum of the balance of trade for merchandise, net trade in services and factor income, and net transfers. The values reported are divided by GDP at current prices in US dollars. For Cambodia, official transfers are excluded from the current account balance.

Table A15: Exchange rates to the US dollar (annual average). Annual average exchange rates are quoted as the local currency per US dollar.

Table A16: Gross international reserves ($ million). Gross international reserves are defined as the US dollar value of holdings of foreign exchange, special drawing rights, reserve position in the IMF, and gold at the end of a given period. For Taipei,China, this heading refers to foreign exchange reserves only. In some economies, the rubric is foreign assets plus reserves of national monetary authorities (the net foreign reserves of, for example, the State Bank of Pakistan) plus national funds for earnings from oil or other natural resources. The data for India are as of 10 March 2020.

Table A17: External debt outstanding ($ million). For most economies, external debt outstanding includes short-, medium-, and long-term debt, public and private, as well as IMF credit. For Cambodia, only public external debt is reported. Intercompany lending is excluded for Georgia. For the Kyrgyz Republic, Singapore, Sri Lanka, and Thailand, the figures for 2019 are as of the end of September.

Table A18: Debt service ratio (% of exports of goods and services). This table generally presents the total debt service payments of each economy, which comprise principal repayments (excluding on short-term debt) and interest payments on outstanding external debt, as a percentage of exports of goods and services. For Cambodia, debt service refers to external public debt only. For the Philippines, exports of goods, services, and income are used as the denominator. For Bangladesh, the ratio represents debt service payments on medium- and long-term loans as a percentage of exports of goods, nonfactor services, and overseas workers' remittances. For Azerbaijan, the ratio represents public and publicly guaranteed external debt service payments as a percentage of exports of goods and nonfactor services.

Table A1 Growth rate of GDP (% per year)

	2015	2016	2017	2018	2019	2020	2021
Central Asia	3.1	2.5	4.2	4.4	4.9	2.8	4.2
Armenia	3.2	0.2	7.5	5.2	7.6	2.2	4.5
Azerbaijan	1.1	−3.1	0.2	1.4	2.2	0.5	1.5
Georgia	3.0	2.9	4.8	4.8	5.1	0.0	4.5
Kazakhstan	1.2	1.1	4.1	4.1	4.5	1.8	3.6
Kyrgyz Republic	3.9	4.3	4.7	3.8	4.5	4.0	4.5
Tajikistan	6.0	6.9	7.1	7.3	7.5	5.5	5.0
Turkmenistan	6.5	6.2	6.5	6.2	6.3	6.0	5.8
Uzbekistan	7.4	6.1	4.5	5.4	5.6	4.7	5.8
East Asia	6.2	6.1	6.3	6.1	5.4	2.0	6.5
Hong Kong, China	2.4	2.2	3.8	2.9	−1.2	−3.3	3.5
Mongolia	2.4	1.2	5.3	7.2	5.1	2.1	4.6
People's Republic of China	7.0	6.8	6.9	6.7	6.1	2.3	7.3
Republic of Korea	2.8	2.9	3.2	2.7	2.0	1.3	2.3
Taipei,China	1.5	2.2	3.3	2.7	2.7	1.8	2.5
South Asia	7.3	7.6	6.8	6.1	5.1	4.1	6.0
Afghanistan	1.5	2.3	2.7	2.7	3.0	3.0	4.0
Bangladesh	6.6	7.1	7.3	7.9	8.2	7.8	8.0
Bhutan	6.2	7.4	6.3	3.8	4.4	5.2	5.8
India	8.0	8.3	7.0	6.1	5.0	4.0	6.2
Maldives	2.9	6.3	6.8	6.9	5.7	−3.0	7.5
Nepal	3.3	0.6	8.2	6.7	7.1	5.3	6.4
Pakistan	4.1	4.6	5.2	5.5	3.3	2.6	3.2
Sri Lanka	5.0	4.5	3.4	3.2	2.6	2.2	3.5
Southeast Asia	4.7	4.9	5.3	5.1	4.4	1.0	4.7
Brunei Darussalam	−0.4	−2.5	1.3	0.1	3.9	2.0	3.0
Cambodia	7.0	6.9	7.0	7.5	7.1	2.3	5.7
Indonesia	4.9	5.0	5.1	5.2	5.0	2.5	5.0
Lao People's Dem. Rep.	7.3	7.0	6.9	6.2	5.0	3.5	6.0
Malaysia	5.1	4.4	5.7	4.7	4.3	0.5	5.5
Myanmar	7.0	5.9	5.8	6.4	6.8	4.2	6.8
Philippines	6.1	6.9	6.7	6.2	5.9	2.0	6.5
Singapore	2.9	3.2	4.3	3.4	0.7	0.2	2.0
Thailand	3.1	3.4	4.1	4.2	2.4	−4.8	2.5
Timor-Leste	3.1	3.6	−3.8	−0.6	3.4	−2.0	4.0
Viet Nam	6.7	6.2	6.8	7.1	7.0	4.8	6.8
The Pacific	8.0	3.8	3.7	0.4	3.8	−0.3	2.7
Cook Islands	4.5	6.0	6.8	8.9	5.3	−2.2	1.0
Federated States of Micronesia	4.6	0.9	2.7	0.2	3.0	1.6	3.0
Fiji	4.7	2.5	5.4	3.5	0.7	−4.9	3.0
Kiribati	10.4	5.1	0.3	2.3	2.4	1.6	1.8
Marshall Islands	−0.6	1.3	3.6	3.6	3.8	2.5	3.7
Nauru	3.4	3.0	−5.5	5.7	1.0	0.4	1.1
Niue	4.0	3.5	2.4	6.5	...	...	...
Palau	10.1	0.6	−3.8	1.5	−3.1	−4.5	1.2
Papua New Guinea	9.5	4.1	3.5	−0.8	4.8	0.8	2.8
Samoa	4.3	8.1	1.0	−2.2	3.5	−3.0	0.8
Solomon Islands	2.6	3.4	3.7	3.9	2.6	1.5	2.7
Tonga	3.7	3.4	5.4	0.2	3.0	0.0	2.5
Tuvalu	9.1	3.0	3.2	4.3	4.1	2.7	3.2
Vanuatu	0.2	3.5	4.4	2.8	2.8	−1.0	2.5
Developing Asia	6.1	6.1	6.2	5.9	5.2	2.2	6.2
Developing Asia excluding the NIEs	6.7	6.6	6.6	6.4	5.7	2.4	6.7

... = data not available.

Note: The newly industrialized economies (NIEs) are Hong Kong, China; the Republic of Korea; Singapore; and Taipei,China.

Table A2 Growth rate of GDP per capita (% per year)

	2015	2016	2017	2018	2019	2020	2021	Per capita GNI, $, 2018
Central Asia	1.8	1.1	2.5	3.2	3.3	1.5	2.7	
Armenia	3.5	0.6	8.0	5.6	7.6	2.2	4.5	4,230
Azerbaijan	−0.1	−4.3	−1.0	0.6	1.4	−0.3	0.1	4,050
Georgia	2.6	2.7	4.9	4.8	5.3	−0.2	4.5	4,440
Kazakhstan	−0.3	−0.3	2.7	2.8	3.1	0.4	2.0	8,070
Kyrgyz Republic	1.8	2.2	2.7	1.9	2.8	2.2	2.7	1,220
Tajikistan	4.2	4.5	4.8	5.1	3.1	3.3	2.8	1,010
Turkmenistan	5.0	4.8	1.9	5.1	2.8	5.0	4.8	6,740
Uzbekistan	5.8	4.4	2.6	3.6	3.8	2.9	4.0	2,020
East Asia	5.7	5.6	5.8	5.6	5.0	1.6	6.0	
Hong Kong, China	1.5	1.5	3.0	2.0	−1.9	−3.9	2.8	50,300
Mongolia	0.2	−0.9	3.3	5.3	3.1	0.2	2.6	3,660
People's Republic of China	6.5	6.2	6.3	6.2	5.7	1.8	6.8	9,460
Republic of Korea	2.2	2.5	2.7	2.3	1.6	0.8	1.9	30,600
Taipei,China	1.2	1.9	3.1	2.6	2.6	1.6	2.4	26,250
South Asia	5.9	6.2	4.1	4.8	4.1	3.2	5.1	
Afghanistan	−1.5	−0.5	0.2	1.3	0.6	0.7	1.6	550
Bangladesh	5.1	5.7	6.0	6.6	6.9	6.5	6.6	1,750
Bhutan	4.6	5.8	4.9	4.0	4.3	5.5	6.4	3,080
India	6.7	6.9	4.1	4.8	4.3	3.3	5.5	2,020
Maldives	−0.9	2.3	2.6	2.6	1.3	−7.1	5.4	9,280
Nepal	1.5	−1.2	6.4	4.8	5.3	3.7	4.8	970
Pakistan	2.0	3.3	3.7	3.5	1.2	0.6	1.2	1,590
Sri Lanka	4.0	3.3	2.5	1.9	1.6	1.1	2.4	4,060
Southeast Asia	3.8	3.6	4.2	4.0	3.2	0.0	3.6	
Brunei Darussalam	−1.6	−3.6	−1.6	−2.9	2.8	1.1	2.0	29,660
Cambodia	5.7	5.6	4.5	6.0	5.6	0.9	4.3	1,390
Indonesia	4.5	3.7	3.8	3.9	3.8	1.4	3.8	3,840
Lao People's Dem. Rep.	2.9	5.2	5.2	4.5	2.7	1.1	3.9	2,450
Malaysia	3.5	3.0	4.5	3.6	3.7	−0.7	4.3	10,590
Myanmar	6.1	4.9	4.8	5.5	5.8	3.3	5.9	1,310
Philippines	4.9	5.3	5.0	4.7	4.4	0.6	5.1	3,830
Singapore	1.7	1.9	4.2	3.0	−0.4	−0.3	1.3	58,770
Thailand	2.5	2.9	3.3	3.5	1.8	−5.4	1.9	6,610
Timor-Leste	1.2	1.7	−5.5	−2.5	1.6	−3.7	2.2	1,820
Viet Nam	5.5	5.1	5.8	5.9	5.0	3.7	5.7	2,360
The Pacific	5.3	1.3	1.3	−1.9	1.4	−2.6	0.3	
Cook Islands	3.9	1.7	7.3	9.5	5.8	−1.7	1.5	18,538
Federated States of Micronesia	4.7	1.0	2.9	0.5	3.2	1.8	3.2	3,400
Fiji	4.1	1.9	5.0	2.9	0.1	−5.5	2.4	5,860
Kiribati	8.9	3.9	−0.9	1.1	1.2	0.4	0.6	3,140
Marshall Islands	−1.0	0.9	3.2	3.2	3.4	2.1	3.3	4,860
Nauru	−12.0	−1.6	−8.4	7.4	4.8	−1.2	0.4	12,060
Niue	2.8	2.3	1.3	5.3	...	...	...	...
Palau	9.0	−0.4	−4.8	0.5	−4.0	−5.4	0.2	17,280
Papua New Guinea	6.2	0.9	0.4	−3.8	1.6	−2.2	−0.3	2,570
Samoa	3.4	7.1	0.2	−3.0	2.6	−3.8	0.0	4,020
Solomon Islands	0.3	1.2	1.3	1.5	0.3	−0.7	0.4	2,020
Tonga	3.5	3.2	5.1	0.0	2.7	−0.3	2.2	4,300
Tuvalu	10.4	4.3	−0.8	−4.8	3.2	1.9	2.4	5,430
Vanuatu	−2.1	2.0	2.2	0.6	0.8	−2.9	0.5	3,130
Developing Asia	5.4	5.3	5.2	5.2	4.6	1.6	5.5	
Developing Asia excluding NIEs	5.9	5.8	5.6	5.6	5.1	1.8	6.0	

GNI = gross national income.

Note: The newly industrialized economies (NIEs) are Hong Kong, China; the Republic of Korea; Singapore; and Taipei,China.

Table A3 Growth rate of value added in agriculture (% per year)

	2015	2016	2017	2018	2019	Sector share, 2018, %
Central Asia						
Armenia	13.2	–5.0	–5.1	–8.5	–4.0	15.0
Azerbaijan	6.6	2.6	4.2	4.6	7.3	5.7
Georgia	–0.1	–2.7	–7.7	14.0	–1.0	7.8
Kazakhstan	3.5	5.4	3.2	3.8	0.9	4.7
Kyrgyz Republic	6.2	2.9	2.2	2.6	2.6	13.6
Tajikistan	3.2	5.2	6.8	4.0	7.1	20.9
Turkmenistan	7.9	9.0	5.9	3.5	4.0	11.0
Uzbekistan	6.1	6.2	1.2	0.3	2.5	33.5
East Asia						
Hong Kong, China	–6.8	–2.0	–5.1	–1.4	0.2	0.1
Mongolia	10.7	6.2	1.8	4.5	8.4	10.8
People's Republic of China	3.9	3.3	4.0	3.5	3.1	7.1
Republic of Korea	–0.2	–5.6	2.3	1.5	2.4	2.0
Taipei,China	49.6	–9.7	8.3	4.5	–1.6	1.7
South Asia						
Afghanistan	–5.7	6.0	3.8	–0.9	7.5	18.7
Bangladesh	3.3	2.8	3.0	4.2	3.9	13.8
Bhutan	3.4	4.4	3.6	3.7	3.8	16.4
India	0.6	6.8	5.9	2.4	3.7	17.1
Maldives	–0.4	1.5	8.3	4.8	1.6	6.5
Nepal	1.1	0.2	5.2	2.8	5.0	28.1
Pakistan	2.1	0.2	2.2	3.9	0.8	24.4
Sri Lanka	4.7	–3.7	–0.4	4.8	1.7	8.6
Southeast Asia						
Brunei Darussalam	6.4	–3.6	–1.7	–1.4	–1.4	1.0
Cambodia	0.2	1.3	1.7	1.1	–0.5	23.5
Indonesia	3.8	3.4	3.9	3.9	3.6	13.4
Lao People's Dem. Rep.	3.6	2.8	2.9	1.3	–0.2	17.8
Malaysia	1.4	–3.7	5.8	0.1	1.8	7.6
Myanmar	3.4	–0.5	–0.4	0.1	1.6	23.0
Philippines	0.1	–1.2	4.0	0.9	1.5	9.3
Singapore	–0.5	1.7	–0.9	–0.1	5.1	0.0
Thailand	–6.5	–1.2	4.7	5.5	0.1	8.1
Timor-Leste	–4.7	–0.9	–3.3	4.4	–1.7	17.2
Viet Nam	2.4	1.4	2.9	3.8	2.0	16.2
The Pacific						
Cook Islands	–1.5	–4.5	2.5	0.0	–1.9	3.8
Federated States of Micronesia	9.5	–4.8	–0.9	0.1	...	23.9
Fiji	2.9	–10.9	10.8	4.2	3.6	9.8
Kiribati	–0.8	...	...	...	...	...
Marshall Islands	6.1	–1.6	1.8	4.2	6.2	15.4
Nauru	5.2	...	...	...	...	...
Niue	2.0	1.2	3.5	1.7	...	19.1
Palau	–3.7	7.8	8.4	–5.2	–4.2	0.0
Papua New Guinea	–2.6	2.7	2.4	2.9	2.5	18.1
Samoa	–1.5	1.9	16.0	–7.9	–6.3	9.8
Solomon Islands	2.4	5.8	3.6	3.8	3.0	26.8
Tonga	–2.7	2.1	...	...	...	...
Tuvalu	...	...	...	...	...	...
Vanuatu	–15.8	5.1	0.4	1.0	0.5	23.0

... = data not available.

Table A4 Growth rate of value added in industry (% per year)

	2015	2016	2017	2018	2019	Sector share, 2018, %
Central Asia						
Armenia	2.8	−0.3	9.0	4.4	8.6	27.4
Azerbaijan	−1.9	−5.9	−3.6	−0.4	0.7	56.6
Georgia	2.6	6.7	4.4	−0.3	2.7	22.9
Kazakhstan	−0.4	1.1	6.8	4.4	5.3	35.9
Kyrgyz Republic	2.9	7.1	8.6	5.9	8.1	32.0
Tajikistan	11.2	16.0	21.3	11.8	13.6	19.4
Turkmenistan	3.1	2.5	5.4	6.0	6.9	44.8
Uzbekistan	5.3	5.4	5.2	10.8	6.6	28.3
East Asia						
Hong Kong, China	2.8	3.2	−0.7	0.3	−3.5	6.8
Mongolia	9.9	−0.4	0.7	7.9	2.9	39.1
People's Republic of China	5.9	6.0	5.9	5.8	5.7	45.6
Republic of Korea	2.3	3.1	4.2	2.1	0.9	37.3
Taipei,China	17.5	3.7	4.7	3.2	0.6	37.5
South Asia						
Afghanistan	4.2	−0.8	0.4	7.6	2.0	26.2
Bangladesh	9.7	11.1	10.2	12.1	12.7	30.2
Bhutan	6.0	7.6	4.7	−1.2	0.4	42.4
India	9.6	7.7	6.3	4.9	1.8	28.9
Maldives	18.1	8.9	10.7	10.5	4.8	15.0
Nepal	1.4	−6.4	12.4	9.6	8.1	14.9
Pakistan	5.2	5.7	4.6	4.9	1.4	19.2
Sri Lanka	2.2	5.7	4.1	0.9	2.6	29.4
Southeast Asia						
Brunei Darussalam	0.0	−2.9	1.5	−0.4	4.2	62.2
Cambodia	11.5	10.6	9.7	11.6	11.3	34.4
Indonesia	3.0	3.8	4.1	4.3	3.8	41.4
Lao People's Dem. Rep.	7.0	12.0	11.6	7.3	4.1	35.6
Malaysia	5.4	4.3	4.8	3.1	2.1	36.1
Myanmar	8.3	8.9	3.0	8.3	8.4	36.7
Philippines	6.4	8.1	7.1	6.7	4.9	30.7
Singapore	−2.5	2.6	6.8	4.9	−0.8	26.7
Thailand	3.0	2.7	1.7	2.7	0.1	34.8
Timor-Leste	22.4	7.7	−26.6	5.3	−3.6	16.2
Viet Nam	9.6	7.6	8.0	8.9	8.9	40.1
The Pacific						
Cook Islands	19.6	−13.6	11.1	11.7	25.6	8.2
Federated States of Micronesia	−6.2	6.4	2.9	−7.3	...	5.2
Fiji	6.9	7.2	4.2	4.4	−0.5	21.4
Kiribati	13.7	...	...	...	...	...
Marshall Islands	−12.9	−5.6	2.7	13.0	5.6	12.9
Nauru	−17.1	...	...	...	...	...
Niue	0.9	2.3	−4.7	90.4	...	3.7
Palau	30.3	13.1	−8.4	3.0	11.0	6.9
Papua New Guinea	35.3	8.1	4.7	−7.0	8.5	38.6
Samoa	−0.6	10.9	−6.2	−13.0	9.6	15.1
Solomon Islands	−5.0	0.9	1.2	1.1	−0.2	14.9
Tonga	10.8	7.8	...	...	...	...
Tuvalu	...	...	...	...	...	...
Vanuatu	35.4	4.2	7.1	3.7	3.3	11.0

... = data not available.

Table A5 Growth rate of value added in services (% per year)

	2015	2016	2017	2018	2019	Sector share, 2018, %
Central Asia						
Armenia	1.0	3.4	10.4	9.4	10.1	57.6
Azerbaijan	4.5	−0.7	3.5	3.5	3.7	37.7
Georgia	4.0	2.8	6.4	5.6	6.8	69.3
Kazakhstan	3.1	0.9	2.5	3.9	4.4	59.4
Kyrgyz Republic	3.7	3.4	3.3	2.8	2.9	54.4
Tajikistan	−7.1	−0.3	1.8	2.1	2.9	59.7
Turkmenistan	10.0	10.8	7.9	7.0	7.0	44.1
Uzbekistan	8.3	6.3	6.4	5.5	5.1	38.2
East Asia						
Hong Kong, China	1.7	2.3	3.6	3.4	0.4	93.1
Mongolia	0.6	1.1	7.7	4.7	5.8	39.3
People's Republic of China	8.8	8.1	8.3	8.0	6.9	47.3
Republic of Korea	3.1	2.9	2.6	3.2	2.7	60.7
Taipei,China	6.7	1.2	2.9	2.9	2.7	60.7
South Asia						
Afghanistan	2.1	2.0	2.5	1.8	1.8	55.0
Bangladesh	5.8	6.2	6.7	6.4	6.8	56.0
Bhutan	8.4	9.2	8.2	7.9	9.1	41.3
India	9.4	8.5	6.9	7.7	7.0	54.0
Maldives	2.4	6.7	6.0	6.5	5.7	78.6
Nepal	4.6	2.4	8.1	7.2	7.3	57.0
Pakistan	4.4	5.7	6.5	6.2	4.7	56.3
Sri Lanka	6.0	4.8	3.6	4.7	2.9	62.0
Southeast Asia						
Brunei Darussalam	−1.2	−1.6	1.1	0.8	3.4	36.7
Cambodia	7.1	6.8	7.0	6.8	6.2	42.1
Indonesia	5.5	5.7	5.7	5.8	6.4	45.2
Lao People's Dem. Rep.	8.0	4.7	4.5	7.0	7.2	46.6
Malaysia	5.3	5.7	6.2	6.8	6.1	56.2
Myanmar	8.7	8.1	3.2	8.7	8.3	40.4
Philippines	6.9	7.5	6.8	6.8	7.1	60.0
Singapore	4.1	2.5	3.3	3.4	1.1	68.7
Thailand	5.0	4.7	5.5	4.8	4.0	57.1
Timor-Leste	4.6	5.7	3.2	−2.6	5.4	66.6
Viet Nam	6.3	7.0	7.4	7.0	7.3	43.7
The Pacific						
Cook Islands	3.7	7.9	9.5	7.0	4.4	88.0
Federated States of Micronesia	3.0	2.8	2.9	0.9	...	70.9
Fiji	3.3	0.2	3.8	1.2	0.8	68.9
Kiribati	6.5	...	...	...	...	...
Marshall Islands	4.2	2.3	5.4	2.8	3.6	71.7
Nauru	11.6	...	...	...	...	...
Niue	4.6	4.2	2.4	4.7	...	77.2
Palau	8.6	−0.7	−2.8	2.9	−5.3	93.1
Papua New Guinea	−2.3	2.3	1.4	3.9	1.9	43.3
Samoa	6.4	8.2	0.8	1.2	3.6	75.1
Solomon Islands	5.0	3.3	2.9	4.7	3.0	58.2
Tonga	2.7	3.6	...	...	...	...
Tuvalu	...	...	...	...	...	...
Vanuatu	2.0	2.9	2.9	3.1	3.4	66.0

... = data not available.

Table A6 Inflation (% per year)

	2015	2016	2017	2018	2019	2020	2021
Central Asia	6.5	10.4	9.2	8.2	7.5	7.6	6.3
Armenia	3.7	−1.4	1.0	2.5	1.4	2.8	2.2
Azerbaijan	4.0	12.4	12.9	2.3	2.6	2.5	3.5
Georgia	4.0	2.1	6.0	2.6	4.9	4.5	3.0
Kazakhstan	6.7	14.6	7.4	6.0	5.3	6.0	5.7
Kyrgyz Republic	6.5	0.4	3.2	1.5	1.1	3.5	3.0
Tajikistan	5.1	6.1	6.7	5.4	8.0	9.0	8.0
Turkmenistan	7.4	3.6	8.0	13.2	13.4	13.0	8.0
Uzbekistan	8.4	8.8	13.7	17.5	14.6	13.0	10.0
East Asia	1.3	1.9	1.6	2.0	2.6	3.2	1.8
Hong Kong, China	3.0	2.4	1.5	2.4	2.9	2.0	2.5
Mongolia	3.3	1.1	4.3	6.8	7.3	6.6	7.9
People's Republic of China	1.4	2.0	1.6	2.1	2.9	3.6	1.9
Republic of Korea	0.7	1.0	1.9	1.5	0.4	0.9	1.3
Taipei,China	−0.3	1.4	0.6	1.3	0.6	0.4	0.8
South Asia	4.9	4.5	3.9	3.7	4.9	4.1	4.4
Afghanistan	−0.7	4.4	5.0	0.6	2.3	2.3	3.5
Bangladesh	6.4	5.9	5.4	5.8	5.5	5.6	5.5
Bhutan	6.6	3.3	4.3	3.7	2.8	3.8	4.0
India	4.9	4.5	3.6	3.4	4.7	3.0	3.8
Maldives	1.0	0.5	2.8	−0.1	0.2	1.0	1.2
Nepal	7.2	9.9	4.5	4.2	4.6	6.0	5.5
Pakistan	4.5	2.9	4.8	4.7	6.8	11.5	8.3
Sri Lanka	3.8	4.0	6.6	4.3	4.3	5.0	4.8
Southeast Asia	2.7	2.0	2.8	2.6	2.1	1.9	2.2
Brunei Darussalam	−0.4	−0.3	−1.3	1.0	−0.4	−0.2	0.1
Cambodia	1.2	3.0	2.9	2.5	1.9	2.1	1.8
Indonesia	6.4	3.5	3.8	3.2	2.8	3.0	2.8
Lao People's Dem. Rep.	1.3	1.6	0.8	2.0	3.3	4.0	4.5
Malaysia	2.1	2.1	3.8	1.0	0.7	1.0	1.3
Myanmar	10.0	6.8	4.0	5.9	8.6	7.5	7.5
Philippines	0.7	1.3	2.9	5.2	2.5	2.2	2.4
Singapore	−0.5	−0.5	0.6	0.4	0.6	0.7	1.3
Thailand	−0.9	0.2	0.7	1.1	0.7	−0.9	0.4
Timor-Leste	0.6	−1.5	0.5	2.3	0.9	1.3	1.8
Viet Nam	0.6	2.7	3.5	3.5	2.8	3.3	3.5
The Pacific	4.7	5.3	4.5	4.3	3.0	2.7	3.8
Cook Islands	3.0	−0.1	−0.1	0.1	0.8	1.5	1.7
Federated States of Micronesia	0.0	−0.9	0.1	1.4	1.0	0.5	1.0
Fiji	1.4	3.8	3.3	4.1	1.8	1.5	3.5
Kiribati	0.6	1.9	0.4	2.1	−1.8	1.0	1.1
Marshall Islands	−2.3	−1.5	0.0	0.8	0.1	0.3	0.5
Nauru	9.8	8.2	5.1	0.5	3.9	2.8	2.3
Niue	1.8	1.3	5.0	10.1	...	...	...
Palau	2.2	−1.3	0.9	2.0	0.6	0.4	0.8
Papua New Guinea	6.0	6.7	5.4	4.7	3.6	3.3	4.4
Samoa	1.9	0.1	1.3	3.6	2.2	2.0	2.5
Solomon Islands	−0.6	0.5	0.5	3.5	1.6	2.0	2.3
Tonga	−1.0	2.6	7.2	7.0	4.1	1.3	2.2
Tuvalu	4.0	2.6	4.4	1.8	3.3	3.5	3.5
Vanuatu	2.5	0.8	3.1	2.3	2.4	1.5	2.0
Developing Asia	2.1	2.4	2.2	2.5	2.9	3.2	2.3
Developing Asia excluding the NIEs	2.4	2.7	2.3	2.6	3.3	3.6	2.5

Note: The newly industrialized economies (NIEs) are Hong Kong, China; the Republic of Korea; Singapore; and Taipei,China.

Table A7 Change in money supply (% per year)

	2015	2016	2017	2018	2019
Central Asia					
Armenia	10.8	17.5	18.5	7.4	11.2
Azerbaijan	–1.1	–2.0	9.0	5.7	11.1
Georgia	19.3	20.2	14.8	14.7	16.7
Kazakhstan	33.8	15.6	–1.7	7.0	2.4
Kyrgyz Republic	14.9	14.6	17.9	5.5	12.8
Tajikistan	18.7	27.9	21.8	5.1	16.9
Turkmenistan	16.1	9.4	11.4	8.4	8.6
Uzbekistan	25.2	23.1	36.1	13.2	13.8
East Asia					
Hong Kong, China	5.5	7.7	10.0	4.3	2.8
Mongolia	–1.3	10.5	24.2	26.5	16.8
People's Republic of China	13.3	11.3	9.0	8.1	8.7
Republic of Korea	8.2	7.1	5.1	6.7	7.9
Taipei,China	5.8	3.6	3.6	2.7	4.5
South Asia					
Afghanistan	3.1	5.6	5.9	2.6	5.7
Bangladesh	12.4	16.3	10.9	9.2	9.9
Bhutan	3.8	23.0	17.4	6.5	–2.4
India	10.1	10.1	9.2	10.5	6.4
Maldives	12.1	–0.2	5.2	3.4	9.6
Nepal	19.9	19.5	15.5	19.4	15.8
Pakistan	13.2	13.7	13.7	9.7	11.3
Sri Lanka	17.8	18.4	16.7	13.0	7.0
Southeast Asia					
Brunei Darussalam	–1.8	1.5	–0.4	2.8	4.3
Cambodia	14.7	17.9	23.8	24.0	18.0
Indonesia	9.0	10.0	8.3	6.3	6.5
Lao People's Dem. Rep.	14.7	10.9	12.2	8.4	18.9
Malaysia	3.0	3.2	4.9	9.1	3.5
Myanmar	26.3	19.4	18.0	18.6	18.0
Philippines	9.4	12.8	11.9	9.5	11.3
Singapore	1.5	8.0	3.2	3.9	5.0
Thailand	4.4	4.2	5.0	4.7	3.6
Timor-Leste	7.1	14.2	12.1	3.1	–13.1
Viet Nam	16.2	18.4	15.0	11.3	12.1
The Pacific					
Cook Islands	9.6	–2.7	12.3	14.8	7.3
Federated States of Micronesia	...	...	...	...	...
Fiji	14.3	4.6	8.5	3.1	...
Kiribati	...	...	...	...	...
Marshall Islands	...	...	...	...	...
Nauru	...	...	...	...	...
Niue	...	...	...	...	...
Palau	...	...	...	...	...
Papua New Guinea	8.1	10.9	–0.7	–4.0	0.0
Samoa	0.6	7.1	7.8	16.5	9.9
Solomon Islands	15.0	13.4	3.5	6.8	2.1
Tonga	2.4	12.6	11.3	10.6	3.5
Tuvalu	...	...	...	...	...
Vanuatu	11.4	10.6	9.3	13.1	7.0

... = data not available.

Table A8 Central government revenue (% of GDP)

	2015	2016	2017	2018	2019
Central Asia					
Armenia	23.2	23.1	22.2	22.3	23.8
Azerbaijan	31.5	29.0	23.5	28.1	29.6
Georgia	26.4	27.0	26.8	26.5	25.8
Kazakhstan	18.7	19.8	21.3	17.5	18.6
Kyrgyz Republic	23.6	27.4	28.2	26.6	28.3
Tajikistan	31.0	30.4	30.6	29.1	26.7
Turkmenistan	16.6	11.7	14.9	13.5	13.1
Uzbekistan	25.1	24.4	23.7	26.7	26.1
East Asia					
Hong Kong, China	18.6	22.6	22.8	20.9	19.8
Mongolia	25.8	24.4	28.5	31.0	32.4
People's Republic of China	22.1	21.4	20.7	19.9	19.2
Republic of Korea	16.3	17.1	17.7	18.7	18.8
Taipei,China	11.3	10.8	10.8	11.0	10.6
South Asia					
Afghanistan	24.6	26.1	25.7	28.5	27.0
Bangladesh	9.6	10.0	10.2	9.6	9.9
Bhutan	29.6	30.7	28.0	31.9	24.5
India	9.1	9.4	9.1	8.7	9.4
Maldives	27.4	27.6	27.8	27.1	27.4
Nepal	20.8	23.1	24.0	25.3	22.5
Pakistan	14.3	15.3	15.5	15.1	12.7
Sri Lanka	13.3	14.1	13.7	13.4	12.2
Southeast Asia					
Brunei Darussalam	21.7	19.5	22.5	32.7	27.4
Cambodia	16.8	20.8	21.6	23.7	25.1
Indonesia	13.1	12.5	12.3	13.1	12.4
Lao People's Dem. Rep.	20.2	16.4	16.1	16.3	15.7
Malaysia	18.6	17.0	16.1	16.3	17.3
Myanmar	21.5	20.3	18.5	19.4	18.4
Philippines	15.8	15.2	15.6	16.4	16.9
Singapore	15.3	15.7	16.1	14.6	14.7
Thailand	16.2	16.8	15.4	15.6	15.1
Timor-Leste	108.4	60.8	67.5	79.5	93.5
Viet Nam	23.8	24.6	25.8	24.5	24.1
The Pacific					
Cook Islands	39.0	39.1	47.9	44.8	42.4
Federated States of Micronesia	66.0	68.9	78.2	79.7	81.9
Fiji	27.9	27.7	25.3	27.7	27.0
Kiribati	151.1	118.2	130.9	124.4	123.9
Marshall Islands	58.8	61.0	68.4	62.6	66.0
Nauru	93.6	114.9	121.8	129.3	141.6
Niue	73.8	69.9	58.0	69.3	82.6
Palau	23.5	23.6	22.9	25.5	26.0
Papua New Guinea	18.3	16.1	15.9	17.8	15.4
Samoa	28.0	28.5	29.3	30.6	31.8
Solomon Islands	47.9	42.8	42.8	45.3	39.6
Tonga	26.2	40.6	42.5	47.4	44.2
Tuvalu	147.2	176.5	127.3	182.8	133.3
Vanuatu	31.9	35.4	35.6	39.1	38.2

... = data not available.

Table A9 Central government expenditure (% of GDP)

	2015	2016	2017	2018	2019
Central Asia					
Armenia	27.9	28.6	27.0	24.1	24.8
Azerbaijan	32.7	29.4	25.1	28.5	29.9
Georgia	27.4	28.3	27.6	27.2	27.9
Kazakhstan	20.9	21.4	23.9	18.8	20.5
Kyrgyz Republic	24.0	30.2	28.8	27.7	28.4
Tajikistan	32.9	32.7	35.7	31.9	30.4
Turkmenistan	17.3	14.1	17.8	13.7	13.2
Uzbekistan	25.2	24.3	23.0	26.1	27.6
East Asia					
Hong Kong, China	18.0	18.2	17.3	18.5	21.3
Mongolia	30.8	39.8	32.3	28.5	31.0
People's Republic of China	25.5	25.2	24.4	24.0	24.1
Republic of Korea	18.6	18.4	18.7	19.3	21.4
Taipei,China	11.4	11.1	10.9	11.0	11.2
South Asia					
Afghanistan	25.9	26.0	26.3	26.9	26.9
Bangladesh	13.5	13.8	13.6	14.3	15.4
Bhutan	28.0	31.9	31.5	32.2	27.4
India	13.0	12.9	12.5	12.1	13.2
Maldives	34.0	37.6	30.9	32.3	33.1
Nepal	21.8	23.6	28.9	33.8	30.5
Pakistan	19.6	19.9	21.3	21.6	21.6
Sri Lanka	20.6	19.5	19.1	18.6	18.7
Southeast Asia					
Brunei Darussalam	37.1	37.8	35.7	32.5	29.0
Cambodia	19.4	21.1	22.4	23.1	19.8
Indonesia	15.7	15.0	14.8	14.9	14.5
Lao People's Dem. Rep.	26.1	21.5	21.6	21.0	20.7
Malaysia	21.8	20.1	19.0	20.0	20.8
Myanmar	25.7	22.9	21.1	24.0	23.4
Philippines	16.7	17.6	17.9	19.6	20.4
Singapore	15.9	16.1	15.6	15.5	15.4
Thailand	18.5	19.1	18.3	17.8	17.7
Timor-Leste	97.7	110.1	84.9	85.4	85.5
Viet Nam	28.2	26.8	27.1	28.2	27.6
The Pacific					
Cook Islands	40.5	35.4	35.4	43.4	38.9
Federated States of Micronesia	55.7	61.7	64.0	55.5	59.6
Fiji	29.8	31.4	27.3	32.1	30.5
Kiribati	102.1	114.8	119.0	97.2	131.9
Marshall Islands	56.0	57.1	64.0	60.1	63.0
Nauru	83.1	93.4	100.6	96.8	125.6
Niue	73.8	69.7	62.6	69.7	83.8
Palau	20.6	21.6	20.2	21.8	25.6
Papua New Guinea	22.9	20.9	18.4	20.4	19.5
Samoa	31.9	28.9	30.3	30.9	29.1
Solomon Islands	47.9	47.1	47.5	44.6	41.7
Tonga	29.1	41.1	40.4	44.2	41.5
Tuvalu	121.9	155.9	118.9	148.5	143.1
Vanuatu	39.3	28.5	36.8	31.5	31.4

... = data not available.

Table A10 Fiscal balance of central government (% of GDP)

	2015	2016	2017	2018	2019
Central Asia					
Armenia	−4.8	−5.5	−4.8	−1.8	−1.0
Azerbaijan	−1.2	−0.4	−1.6	−0.4	−0.3
Georgia	−1.0	−1.3	−0.8	−0.7	−2.1
Kazakhstan	−2.2	−1.6	−2.7	−1.3	−1.9
Kyrgyz Republic	−0.4	−2.8	−0.6	−1.1	−0.1
Tajikistan	−1.9	−2.3	−5.1	−2.8	−3.8
Turkmenistan	−0.7	−2.4	−2.8	−0.2	−0.1
Uzbekistan	−0.1	0.1	0.7	0.5	−1.5
East Asia					
Hong Kong, China	0.6	4.4	5.5	2.4	−1.3
Mongolia	−5.0	−15.4	−3.8	2.6	1.4
People's Republic of China	−3.4	−3.8	−3.7	−4.1	−4.9
Republic of Korea	−2.3	−1.3	−1.0	−0.6	−2.6
Taipei,China	−0.1	−0.3	−0.1	0.1	−0.6
South Asia					
Afghanistan	−1.3	0.1	−0.6	1.6	0.1
Bangladesh	−3.9	−3.8	−3.5	−4.7	−5.5
Bhutan	1.5	−1.1	−3.5	−0.3	−2.9
India	−3.9	−3.5	−3.5	−3.4	−3.8
Maldives	−6.5	−10.0	−3.1	−5.2	−5.7
Nepal	0.8	1.3	−3.2	−6.7	−5.1
Pakistan	−5.3	−4.6	−5.8	−6.5	−8.9
Sri Lanka	−7.2	−5.4	−5.4	−5.3	−6.5
Southeast Asia					
Brunei Darussalam	−15.4	−18.3	−13.2	0.2	−1.6
Cambodia	−2.6	−0.3	−0.8	0.6	5.3
Indonesia	−2.6	−2.5	−2.5	−1.8	−2.2
Lao People's Dem. Rep.	−5.9	−5.2	−5.6	−4.7	−5.0
Malaysia	−3.2	−3.1	−2.9	−3.7	−3.4
Myanmar	−4.3	−2.6	−2.5	−4.5	−5.0
Philippines	−0.9	−2.4	−2.2	−3.2	−3.5
Singapore	−0.6	−0.5	0.5	−0.8	−0.7
Thailand	−2.5	−2.7	−2.7	−2.5	−1.8
Timor-Leste	10.7	−49.3	−17.4	−5.9	8.0
Viet Nam	−4.4	−2.2	−1.2	−3.7	−3.5
The Pacific					
Cook Islands	−1.6	3.7	12.5	1.4	3.4
Federated States of Micronesia	10.3	7.3	14.2	24.2	22.3
Fiji	−1.8	−3.8	−2.0	−4.3	−3.4
Kiribati	49.0	3.4	11.9	27.2	−8.0
Marshall Islands	2.8	3.9	4.4	2.5	3.0
Nauru	10.5	21.5	21.3	32.6	16.0
Niue	0.0	0.3	−4.6	−0.5	−1.2
Palau	2.9	2.0	2.8	3.7	0.4
Papua New Guinea	−4.6	−4.7	−2.5	−2.6	−4.1
Samoa	−4.0	−0.4	−1.1	−0.2	2.7
Solomon Islands	0.0	−4.3	−4.8	0.7	−2.0
Tonga	−2.9	−0.4	2.1	3.2	2.7
Tuvalu	25.3	20.6	8.4	34.2	−9.8
Vanuatu	−7.3	7.0	−1.2	7.6	6.8

Table A11 Growth rate of merchandise exports (% per year)

	2015	2016	2017	2018	2019	2020	2021
Central Asia	−33.9	−15.6	21.5	25.1	5.5	−15.4	28.3
Armenia	−4.4	16.4	26.2	10.3	9.7	2.5	7.5
Azerbaijan	−44.8	−15.2	14.7	37.2	−6.4	−32.7	24.4
Georgia	−23.9	−5.4	24.0	22.4	13.5	3.6	11.9
Kazakhstan	−43.3	−20.8	33.3	26.4	−4.0	−35.4	42.2
Kyrgyz Republic	−34.8	−0.7	14.4	4.2	7.5	7.0	7.0
Tajikistan	−8.9	0.8	9.4	−10.4	9.3	10.0	10.0
Turkmenistan	−37.1	−38.2	3.6	49.6	8.1	7.0	7.9
Uzbekistan	−10.1	−5.0	12.3	11.4	28.6	12.0	25.0
East Asia	−5.5	−6.9	11.5	8.9	−0.3	−7.9	9.9
Hong Kong, China	−2.4	0.0	7.8	5.1	−4.1	−6.7	3.5
Mongolia	−18.7	8.0	21.4	12.4	9.1	−8.6	15.3
People's Republic of China	−4.5	−7.2	11.4	9.1	0.5	−8.5	9.8
Republic of Korea	−11.5	−5.7	13.4	7.9	−10.3	−7.8	15.2
Taipei,China	−11.1	−9.0	10.8	10.2	10.2	2.8	2.8
South Asia	−12.8	3.6	8.7	9.2	−0.5	−3.8	8.1
Afghanistan	−9.8	6.3	27.7	11.6	8.3	8.3	9.3
Bangladesh	3.1	8.9	1.7	6.7	10.1	0.0	10.0
Bhutan	8.4	−14.7	12.3	8.6	−10.3	12.4	4.4
India	−15.9	5.2	10.3	9.1	−1.6	−4.7	7.9
Maldives	−20.3	6.8	24.3	6.6	7.4	−1.5	9.0
Nepal	−3.9	−28.7	9.8	16.2	11.6	5.1	15.0
Pakistan	−3.9	−8.8	0.1	12.6	−2.1	6.0	6.7
Sri Lanka	−5.2	−2.2	10.2	4.7	0.4	−20.0	10.0
Southeast Asia	−11.2	−1.8	15.2	7.8	−2.4	−2.9	6.9
Brunei Darussalam	−44.9	−21.4	13.8	18.2	12.0	7.5	17.1
Cambodia	14.3	10.0	9.3	15.5	13.5	12.3	13.5
Indonesia	−14.9	−3.1	16.9	7.0	−6.8	−10.0	7.0
Lao People's Dem. Rep.	−12.9	9.7	15.3	18.7	4.5	4.0	7.0
Malaysia	−15.9	−5.1	12.5	10.7	−4.3	−8.5	9.6
Myanmar	−8.5	−0.4	10.5	7.4	10.0	8.5	12.0
Philippines	−13.3	−1.1	21.2	0.3	2.7	0.8	6.3
Singapore	−12.1	−5.5	10.5	11.2	−4.3	−1.3	4.1
Thailand	−5.9	0.1	9.5	7.5	−3.2	−8.3	10.0
Timor-Leste	16.4	11.1	−17.4	48.6	5.5	−3.7	12.0
Viet Nam	7.9	8.9	21.2	13.9	8.4	5.3	7.8
The Pacific	−7.8	−2.4	15.4	7.0	6.8	−5.1	18.4
Cook Islands	−17.0	−0.4	−16.4	91.7	−56.8	...	...
Federated States of Micronesia	4.4	24.7	11.2	−14.7	−0.3	2.1	4.0
Fiji	−19.4	−4.6	6.1	5.8	−7.1	−1.3	5.0
Kiribati	−21.6	15.8	−11.6	21.3	−6.9	...	...
Marshall Islands	−15.2	−12.6	16.9	5.1	−0.9	−2.8	3.8
Nauru	−54.6	68.1	−45.5	−35.2	−65.2	...	...
Niue	6.1	−6.1	26.4	−2.8	...	...	...
Palau	−17.9	2.1	5.5	−1.9	−4.4	−33.4	23.4
Papua New Guinea	−4.7	−6.0	19.4	8.0	11.1	−6.9	24.2
Samoa	12.2	32.3	2.9	−6.3	40.5	2.2	2.0
Solomon Islands	−7.5	2.6	8.6	14.0	−2.9	−13.1	1.1
Tonga	4.5	3.2	24.9	−63.7	95.6	42.2	10.5
Tuvalu	−4.3	3.5	11.5	4.9	1.7	...	...
Vanuatu	−39.3	34.5	21.5	5.6	−23.5	4.9	7.2
Developing Asia	−8.0	−4.8	11.7	9.1	−0.5	−6.8	9.5
Developing Asia excluding the NIEs	−7.6	−4.7	11.7	9.2	0.1	−7.1	9.5

... = data not available.

Note: The newly industrialized economies (NIEs) are Hong Kong, China; the Republic of Korea; Singapore; and Taipei,China.

Table A12 Growth rate of merchandise imports (% per year)

	2015	2016	2017	2018	2019	2020	2021
Central Asia	−14.2	−11.5	7.6	13.1	11.3	−5.0	12.0
Armenia	−25.1	0.9	32.6	17.5	8.5	7.5	6.5
Azerbaijan	4.7	−7.9	0.4	21.2	24.8	−37.8	23.5
Georgia	−10.8	−8.8	9.3	15.1	0.8	1.1	7.0
Kazakhstan	−21.8	−21.0	16.5	12.0	10.6	−11.7	11.5
Kyrgyz Republic	−27.0	−3.0	11.4	26.9	−6.3	−7.0	−5.0
Tajikistan	−20.1	−11.5	−8.5	13.5	6.3	0.0	5.0
Turkmenistan	−7.5	−6.2	−22.7	−47.8	1.6	5.4	7.0
Uzbekistan	−10.9	−1.2	6.2	43.8	16.3	20.0	14.0
East Asia	−14.0	−4.6	15.6	15.1	−2.7	−7.3	10.2
Hong Kong, China	−4.0	−1.2	8.7	6.6	−6.0	−7.0	5.0
Mongolia	−26.6	−10.8	−225.3	35.4	2.1	−4.2	8.3
People's Republic of China	−13.4	−4.2	16.0	16.2	−2.7	−7.8	10.2
Republic of Korea	−19.8	−6.5	18.0	10.6	−6.0	−6.6	14.3
Taipei,China	−17.2	−10.6	9.7	9.1	9.1	1.8	1.8
South Asia	−10.7	−0.4	18.2	12.1	−5.3	−5.5	10.4
Afghanistan	17.4	−14.2	7.6	−2.1	3.4	1.4	2.1
Bangladesh	3.0	5.9	9.0	25.2	1.8	−0.5	7.0
Bhutan	8.8	2.0	−0.3	0.5	−6.6	5.8	2.8
India	−14.1	−1.0	19.5	10.3	−5.9	−6.9	11.7
Maldives	−3.4	10.6	6.3	24.2	−4.0	−2.2	14.8
Nepal	8.0	−7.1	29.4	28.1	6.7	−5.0	9.4
Pakistan	−0.7	−0.2	18.0	16.2	−6.8	4.0	3.9
Sri Lanka	−2.5	1.3	9.4	6.0	−10.3	−15.0	9.4
Southeast Asia	−11.4	−0.5	15.2	15.2	−4.5	−2.0	8.5
Brunei Darussalam	−12.3	−17.3	15.5	33.7	24.2	25.0	12.3
Cambodia	10.5	6.3	9.8	21.3	19.5	8.2	11.0
Indonesia	−19.7	−4.4	16.2	20.6	−8.8	−9.0	9.0
Lao People's Dem. Rep.	−5.8	−11.4	8.0	6.0	0.5	1.0	4.0
Malaysia	−15.2	−3.7	12.9	11.1	−5.5	−8.2	9.3
Myanmar	10.6	2.4	9.3	2.9	7.3	7.0	10.0
Philippines	−1.0	17.7	17.6	11.9	−3.0	1.2	10.3
Singapore	−16.6	−6.6	11.6	12.6	−3.8	−1.0	4.4
Thailand	−10.6	−5.1	13.2	13.7	−5.4	−10.0	11.9
Timor-Leste	5.7	−13.3	11.4	−2.9	−3.4	−1.8	4.0
Viet Nam	12.0	7.0	22.3	12.2	6.8	4.7	6.8
The Pacific	−28.0	−13.5	34.8	6.7	4.4	6.9	10.4
Cook Islands	−5.8	−4.9	11.4	15.2	−5.0	...	...
Federated States of Micronesia	7.8	−4.6	9.6	0.1	8.2	−10.8	22.1
Fiji	−15.7	2.1	8.0	13.7	−11.5	−8.0	0.0
Kiribati	−1.0	7.5	9.5	3.4	−0.7	...	...
Marshall Islands	−10.8	−9.8	13.7	10.4	2.3	6.2	4.5
Nauru	−10.8	−18.4	−6.0	19.4	−4.8	1.0	0.1
Niue	−0.3	−7.4	27.3	10.6	...	...	...
Palau	−10.6	−1.5	4.0	−1.0	−4.8	−15.5	8.5
Papua New Guinea	−36.6	−19.2	48.0	4.4	8.3	12.0	10.1
Samoa	−3.5	−4.8	0.5	4.6	8.2	−4.8	2.1
Solomon Islands	−4.8	−4.4	10.4	14.7	4.7	−5.7	21.9
Tonga	10.7	−2.4	−21.1	9.1	44.1	10.6	6.7
Tuvalu	141.2	−47.0	11.5	16.7	−10.1	...	...
Vanuatu	13.3	8.2	−0.3	12.1	−13.6	9.0	8.5
Developing Asia	−13.2	−3.6	15.8	14.6	−3.1	−6.3	10.0
Developing Asia excluding the NIEs	−12.6	−3.1	16.1	15.3	−3.2	−6.6	10.1

... = data not available.

Note: The newly industrialized economies (NIEs) are Hong Kong, China; the Republic of Korea; Singapore; and Taipei,China.

Table A13 Trade balance ($ million)

	2015	2016	2017	2018	2019	2020	2021
Central Asia	3,942	–4,737	7,794	22,001	13,877	9,660	14,775
Armenia	–1,186	–945	–1,376	–1,789	–1,910	–2,125	–2,183
Azerbaijan	5,812	4,206	6,115	9,841	5,804	4,603	5,803
Georgia	–5,096	–5,181	–5,208	–5,780	–5,292	–5,252	–5,425
Kazakhstan	11,627	9,253	16,728	25,532	19,547	12,944	15,834
Kyrgyz Republic	–2,241	–2,137	–2,332	–3,376	–2,882	–2,397	–2,017
Tajikistan	–2,290	–1,885	–1,517	–1,888	–1,981	–1,886	–1,927
Turkmenistan	–1,887	–5,657	–2,401	6,328	7,186	7,773	8,440
Uzbekistan	–797	–2,392	–2,215	–6,867	–6,596	–4,000	–3,750
East Asia	747,297	660,934	649,370	565,939	623,330	567,696	612,782
Hong Kong, China	–22,871	–16,708	–22,912	–32,416	–22,461	–19,235	–27,913
Mongolia	563	1,338	1,490	676	1,149	781	1,306
People's Republic of China	576,191	488,883	475,941	395,171	462,800	409,691	442,585
Republic of Korea	120,275	116,462	113,593	110,087	76,856	65,265	79,171
Taipei,China	73,139	70,960	81,258	92,422	104,987	111,194	117,632
South Asia	–178,539	–161,490	–222,575	–260,097	–226,888	–207,959	–238,269
Afghanistan	–7,086	–5,649	–5,953	–5,721	–5,869	–5,887	–5,935
Bangladesh	–6,965	–6,460	–9,472	–18,178	–15,494	–15,217	–15,084
Bhutan	–430	–536	–472	–430	–423	–413	–414
India	–130,079	–112,442	–160,036	–180,282	–154,925	–136,934	–164,973
Maldives	–1,655	–1,839	–1,908	–2,425	–2,290	–2,237	–2,589
Nepal	–6,669	–6,409	–8,434	–10,895	–11,372	–10,704	–11,651
Pakistan	–17,267	–19,283	–26,680	–31,824	–28,517	–29,173	–29,590
Sri Lanka	–8,389	–8,873	–9,619	–10,343	–7,998	–7,395	–8,033
Southeast Asia	135,668	133,110	138,299	110,844	123,462	114,862	113,116
Brunei Darussalam	2,910	2,153	2,403	2,365	2,147	1,416	1,960
Cambodia	–3,949	–3,846	–4,278	–5,844	–7,761	–7,799	–8,244
Indonesia	14,049	15,318	18,814	–431	3,513	1,512	–1,384
Lao People's Dem. Rep.	–3,414	–2,235	–1,919	–1,788	–1,384	–1,218	–1,080
Malaysia	27,967	24,599	27,233	29,536	30,304	27,367	30,549
Myanmar	–4,048	–4,409	–4,696	–4,362	–2,463	–2,473	–2,486
Philippines	–23,309	–35,549	–40,215	–50,972	–46,466	–47,237	–54,255
Singapore	92,585	90,807	97,421	104,001	98,014	95,711	98,617
Thailand	26,116	35,776	32,581	22,388	26,630	28,154	27,213
Timor-Leste	–635	–546	–615	–589	–566	–557	–577
Viet Nam	7,396	11,042	11,570	16,540	21,494	24,089	28,509
The Pacific	3,600	3,620	4,059	4,325	5,305	4,480	6,489
Cook Islands	–98	–92	–107	–114	–121	...	...
Federated States of Micronesia	–128	–110	–120	–129	–143	–122	–157
Fiji	–912	–996	–1,093	–1,320	–1,122	–967	–920
Kiribati	–91	–97	–108	–110	–110	...	...
Marshall Islands	–53	–49	–54	–63	–67	–76	–80
Nauru	–48	–21	–34	–51	–56	–56	–56
Niue	–14	–13	–16	–18	...	...	...
Palau	–137	–134	–139	–138	–132	–114	–122
Papua New Guinea	5,876	5,861	6,408	7,032	7,904	6,701	8,866
Samoa	–295	–270	–271	–287	–299	–281	–287
Solomon Islands	–17	13	7	5	–36	–72	–181
Tonga	–189	–184	–136	–166	–234	–254	–270
Tuvalu	–42	–22	–25	–29	–26	...	...
Vanuatu	–253	–265	–253	–287	–255	–279	–304
Developing Asia	711,968	631,437	576,948	443,011	539,086	488,739	508,892
Developing Asia dexcluding NIEs	448,839	369,917	307,587	168,917	281,691	235,804	241,385

... = data not available.

Note: The newly industrialized economies (NIEs) are Hong Kong, China; the Republic of Korea; Singapore; and Taipei,China.

Table A14 Current account balance (% of GDP)

	2015	2016	2017	2018	2019	2020	2021
Central Asia	–3.8	–5.9	–1.9	–0.4	–2.2	–3.8	–2.4
Armenia	–2.7	–2.1	–3.0	–9.4	–8.0	–8.6	–8.2
Azerbaijan	–0.4	–3.6	4.1	12.9	7.3	4.4	6.3
Georgia	–11.8	–12.5	–8.1	–6.8	–4.5	–4.4	–4.2
Kazakhstan	–3.3	–5.9	–3.1	–0.2	–3.1	–5.3	–2.4
Kyrgyz Republic	–15.9	–11.6	–4.8	–12.3	–10.0	–12.0	–10.0
Tajikistan	–5.9	–4.8	2.1	–5.0	–4.5	–4.5	–4.2
Turkmenistan	–15.6	–19.9	–10.3	5.7	–0.6	–3.0	–4.7
Uzbekistan	0.6	0.4	2.5	–7.1	–4.2	–4.0	–3.5
East Asia	3.7	2.8	2.5	1.3	2.0	2.2	1.9
Hong Kong, China	3.3	4.0	4.6	3.7	6.4	7.0	5.0
Mongolia	–8.1	–6.3	–10.1	–16.8	–13.1	–13.9	–7.8
People's Republic of China	2.8	1.8	1.6	0.4	1.3	1.6	1.2
Republic of Korea	7.2	6.5	4.6	4.5	3.7	2.8	3.5
Taipei,China	13.9	13.1	14.1	11.6	10.5	10.0	12.0
South Asia	–0.8	–0.5	–2.0	–2.7	–1.5	–0.7	–1.3
Afghanistan	2.9	8.4	5.9	9.6	2.0	1.0	0.5
Bangladesh	1.8	1.9	–0.5	–3.5	–1.7	–0.8	–0.3
Bhutan	–27.9	–30.3	–23.9	–19.1	–22.6	–19.1	–18.4
India	–1.0	–0.6	–1.8	–2.1	–0.9	–0.3	–1.2
Maldives	–7.4	–23.5	–21.7	–26.1	–21.5	–23.0	–22.0
Nepal	5.1	6.2	–0.4	–8.2	–7.7	–5.0	–5.6
Pakistan	–1.0	–1.7	–4.1	–6.3	–4.9	–2.8	–2.4
Sri Lanka	–2.3	–2.1	–2.6	–3.2	–2.1	–2.8	–2.6
Southeast Asia	3.1	3.2	3.0	1.6	2.5	1.9	1.9
Brunei Darussalam	16.7	12.9	16.4	7.9	9.0	5.5	9.5
Cambodia	–8.8	–8.6	–8.3	–12.2	–17.6	–19.0	–16.9
Indonesia	–2.0	–1.8	–1.6	–2.9	–2.7	–2.9	–2.9
Lao People's Dem. Rep.	–25.4	–15.7	–14.0	–13.0	–9.5	–9.4	–8.1
Malaysia	3.0	2.4	2.8	2.1	3.3	2.3	2.9
Myanmar	–5.2	–4.3	–4.7	–3.7	–3.5	–4.5	–4.5
Philippines	2.5	–0.4	–0.7	–2.7	–0.1	–0.3	–1.4
Singapore	18.7	17.6	16.3	17.2	17.0	17.0	17.0
Thailand	6.9	10.5	9.6	5.6	6.7	7.1	6.7
Timor-Leste	14.8	–34.6	–17.7	–12.2	8.1	–10.5	–30.4
Viet Nam	0.5	2.9	2.9	2.4	5.0	–0.2	1.0
The Pacific	14.4	15.9	13.6	14.3	16.0	10.1	13.9
Cook Islands	3.9	7.1	8.4	7.1	3.6	–1.2	1.1
Federated States of Micronesia	4.5	7.2	10.3	21.0	3.3	8.8	1.3
Fiji	–2.5	–3.9	–7.0	–8.9	–4.2	–7.1	–3.6
Kiribati	45.6	20.4	14.5	13.4	7.6	4.0	2.8
Marshall Islands	17.2	16.1	7.5	6.5	7.7	6.1	5.1
Nauru	–21.3	2.1	12.7	–4.5	5.0	...	...
Niue	15.9	25.2	21.0	22.7	...	...	...
Palau	–5.0	–7.7	–10.9	–9.5	–11.8	–13.5	–13.3
Papua New Guinea	20.5	23.5	21.5	22.8	24.9	17.5	22.6
Samoa	–2.8	–4.5	–2.0	0.8	2.3	–1.1	0.5
Solomon Islands	–3.0	–3.9	–4.6	–3.5	–8.5	–8.7	–12.3
Tonga	–15.0	–15.0	–6.5	–5.9	–6.8	–12.6	–13.4
Tuvalu	–52.0	24.0	7.0	4.8	–6.9	2.8	3.4
Vanuatu	–1.5	0.8	–6.4	3.5	2.7	–8.7	–8.6
Developing Asia	2.8	2.2	1.8	0.7	1.5	1.6	1.4
Developing Asia excluding the NIEs	1.8	1.2	0.9	–0.3	0.7	0.9	0.5

Note: The newly industrialized economies (NIEs) are Hong Kong, China; the Republic of Korea; Singapore; and Taipei,China.

Table A15 Exchange rates to the United States dollar (annual average)

	Currency	Symbol	2015	2016	2017	2018	2019
Central Asia							
Armenia	dram	AMD	477.9	480.5	482.7	483.0	480.5
Azerbaijan	Azerbaijan new manat	AZN	1.0	1.6	1.7	1.7	1.7
Georgia	lari	GEL	2.3	2.4	2.5	2.5	2.8
Kazakhstan	tenge	T	221.7	342.1	326.0	344.7	382.7
Kyrgyz Republic	som	Som	64.5	69.9	68.9	68.8	69.8
Tajikistan	somoni	TJS	6.2	7.8	8.6	9.2	9.6
Turkmenistan	Turkmen manat	TMT	3.5	3.5	3.5	3.5	3.5
Uzbekistan	sum	SUM	2,573.5	2,968.9	5,140.3	8,069.0	8,851.4
East Asia							
Hong Kong, China	Hong Kong dollar	HK$	7.8	7.8	7.8	7.8	7.8
Mongolia	togrog	MNT	1,970.3	2,145.5	2,439.8	2,467.5	2,663.5
People's Republic of China	yuan	CNY	6.2	6.7	6.7	6.6	7.0
Republic of Korea	won	W	1,133.1	1,163.3	1,122.3	1,100.6	1,165.4
Taipei,China	NT dollar	NT$	31.9	32.3	30.4	30.2	30.9
South Asia							
Afghanistan	afghani	AF	61.2	67.9	68.0	72.4	77.8
Bangladesh	taka	Tk	77.7	78.3	79.1	82.1	84.0
Bhutan	ngultrum	Nu	62.1	66.3	66.4	65.1	70.6
India	Indian rupee-	₹	65.5	67.1	64.5	69.9	70.7
Maldives	rufiyaa	Rf	15.4	15.4	15.4	15.4	15.4
Nepal	Nepalese rupee/s	NRe/NRs	99.5	106.4	106.2	104.4	112.9
Pakistan	Pakistan rupee/s	PRe/PRs	101.3	104.2	104.8	109.8	136.1
Sri Lanka	Sri Lanka rupee/s	SLRe/SLRs	135.9	145.6	152.0	162.5	178.8
Southeast Asia							
Brunei Darussalam	Brunei dollar	B$	1.4	1.4	1.4	1.3	1.4
Cambodia	riel	KR	4,063.0	4,051.3	4,045.0	4,044.1	4,062.7
Indonesia	rupiah	Rp	13,389.4	13,308.7	13,380.8	14,238.0	14,148.2
Lao People's Dem. Rep.	kip	KN	8,127.7	8,124.3	8,245.3	8,401.4	8,679.9
Malaysia	ringgit	RM	3.9	4.1	4.3	4.0	4.1
Myanmar	kyat	MK	1,218.9	1,259.2	1,355.7	1,381.9	1,525.8
Philippines	peso	P	45.5	47.5	50.4	52.7	51.8
Singapore	Singapore dollar	S$	1.4	1.4	1.4	1.3	1.4
Thailand	baht	B	34.2	35.3	33.9	32.3	31.0
Timor-Leste	US dollar	$	1.0	1.0	1.0	1.0	1.0
Viet Nam	dong	D	21,675.6	21,931.0	22,370.3	22,602.9	23,050.5
The Pacific							
Cook Islands	New Zealand dollar	NZ$	1.3	1.5	1.4	1.4	1.5
Federated States of Micronesia	US dollar	$	1.0	1.0	1.0	1.0	1.0
Fiji	Fiji dollar	F$	2.1	2.1	2.1	2.1	2.2
Kiribati	Australian dollar	A$	1.3	1.3	1.3	1.3	1.4
Marshall Islands	US dollar	$	1.0	1.0	1.0	1.0	1.0
Nauru	Australian dollar	A$	1.2	1.4	1.3	1.3	1.4
Niue	New Zealand dollar	NZ$	1.4	1.4	1.4	1.4	...
Palau	US dollar	$	1.0	1.0	1.0	1.0	1.0
Papua New Guinea	kina	K	2.8	3.1	3.2	3.3	3.4
Samoa	tala	ST	2.4	2.6	2.5	2.6	2.6
Solomon Islands	Sol. Islands dollar	SI$	7.9	7.9	7.9	8.0	8.2
Tonga	pa'anga	T$	1.9	2.2	2.2	2.3	2.3
Tuvalu	Australian dollar	A$	1.3	1.3	1.3	1.3	1.4
Vanuatu	vatu	Vt	116.3	110.8	109.0	110.1	114.0

Table A16 Gross international reserves ($ million)

	2015	2016	2017	2018	2019
Central Asia					
Armenia	1,775	2,204	2,314	2,259	2,840
Azerbaijan	5,017	3,974	5,335	...	...
Georgia	2,500	2,800	3,100	3,300	3,300
Kazakhstan	27,871	29,713	30,997	30,927	28,958
Kyrgyz Republic	1,778	1,969	2,177	2,155	2,369
Tajikistan	494	745	1,272	1,211	1,385
Turkmenistan	...	...	...	...	...
Uzbekistan	24,300	26,428	28,076	27,081	29,172
East Asia					
Hong Kong, China	358,812	386,040	431,896	424,716	439,206
Mongolia	1,323	1,296	3,008	3,549	4,349
People's Republic of China	3,406,112	3,097,845	3,235,895	3,167,992	3,323,292
Republic of Korea	367,944	371,103	389,267	403,694	408,816
Taipei,China	426,031	434,204	451,500	461,784	478,126
South Asia					
Afghanistan	6,808	7,357	8,139	8,273	8,298
Bangladesh	25,025	30,168	33,407	32,916	32,717
Bhutan	1,103	1,127	1,104	1,111	1,065
India	360,176	369,955	424,545	412,871	471,300
Maldives	564	467	587	712	753
Nepal	8,148	9,736	10,494	10,084	9,500
Pakistan	13,525	18,143	16,145	9,765	7,280
Sri Lanka	7,304	6,019	7,959	6,919	...
Southeast Asia					
Brunei Darussalam	3,367	3,489	3,488	3,407	4,273
Cambodia	7,377	9,123	12,201	14,629	18,763
Indonesia	105,931	116,362	130,196	120,654	129,183
Lao People's Dem. Rep.	1,058	884	1,016	873	997
Malaysia	95,288	94,501	96,421	103,978	102,384
Myanmar	4,764	5,134	5,370	6,307	7,244
Philippines	80,667	80,692	81,570	79,193	87,840
Singapore	247,747	246,575	279,900	287,673	279,450
Thailand	156,514	171,853	202,562	205,641	224,327
Timor-Leste	16,655	16,125	17,344	16,614	18,348
Viet Nam	28,298	36,688	49,233	55,263	78,518
The Pacific					
Cook Islands	...	...	...	...	...
Federated States of Micronesia	...	...	...	...	...
Fiji	927	917	1,100	1,192	1,296
Kiribati	...	...	...	...	...
Marshall Islands	...	...	...	...	...
Nauru	...	...	...	...	...
Niue	...	...	...	...	...
Palau	...	...	...	...	...
Papua New Guinea	1,865	1,677	1,736	2,477	2,426
Samoa	132	111	122	163	193
Solomon Islands	534	526	577	613	598
Tonga	143	166	192	215	213
Tuvalu	...	...	...	...	...
Vanuatu	269	267	396	502	552

... = data not available.

Table A17 External debt outstanding ($ million)

	2015	2016	2017	2018	2019
Central Asia					
Armenia	4,316	4,806	5,495	5,536	5,790
Azerbaijan	6,894	6,913	9,398	...	...
Georgia	11,768	13,083	14,363	15,009	15,855
Kazakhstan	153,007	163,309	167,218	158,776	157,180
Kyrgyz Republic	6,670	6,830	6,998	6,828	6,966
Tajikistan	2,183	2,276	2,833	2,924	...
Turkmenistan	8,354	...	...	...	...
Uzbekistan	11,800	15,200	20,050	17,400	23,350
East Asia					
Hong Kong, China	1,300,365	1,356,411	1,576,560	1,696,008	1,649,317
Mongolia	22,718	24,625	27,493	28,715	30,678
People's Republic of China	1,382,980	1,415,801	1,757,958	1,965,214	...
Republic of Korea	396,058	382,162	412,028	440,599	466,979
Taipei,China	158,954	172,238	181,938	191,161	184,659
South Asia					
Afghanistan	1,231	1,199	1,168	1,213	1,321
Bangladesh	23,901	26,306	28,337	33,512	37,836
Bhutan	1,855	2,316	2,505	2,642	2,728
India	485,081	471,308	529,290	543,189	557,519
Maldives	696	849	1,190	1,389	1,418
Nepal	3,391	3,642	4,025	4,805	5,381
Pakistan	65,169	73,945	83,477	95,237	106,348
Sri Lanka	44,839	46,418	51,604	52,310	...
Southeast Asia					
Brunei Darussalam	...	...	...	...	...
Cambodia	5,648	5,860	6,669	7,022	7,606
Indonesia	310,730	320,006	352,469	375,430	404,282
Lao People's Dem. Rep.	13,537	14,134	15,766	16,732	17,073
Malaysia	195,010	203,848	217,927	223,484	231,226
Myanmar	9,500	9,100	9,600	11,000	11,000
Philippines	77,474	74,763	73,098	78,960	76,415
Singapore	1,321,952	1,380,146	1,422,849	1,516,851	1,543,928
Thailand	131,078	132,158	155,225	162,376	166,220
Timor-Leste	45	76	104	146	228
Viet Nam	...	...	...	...	...
The Pacific					
Cook Islands	74	77	56	68	79
Federated States of Micronesia	81	80	80	76	..
Fiji	660	603	663	698	693
Kiribati	33	42	43	42	47
Marshall Islands	95	88	83	78	73
Nauru	40	34	37	38	34
Niue	...	...	...	...	...
Palau	64	79	85	91	87
Papua New Guinea	1,449	1,776	1,995	3,642	3,642
Samoa	446	391	401	426	399
Solomon Islands	81	77	95	94	98
Tonga	195	176	179	188	172
Tuvalu	19	16	15	12	9
Vanuatu	183	241	310	350	366

... = data not available.

Table A18 Debt service ratio (% of exports of goods and services)

	2015	2016	2017	2018	2019
Central Asia					
Armenia	4.4	4.7	5.2	6.5	7.1
Azerbaijan	...	...	...	...	...
Georgia	21.4	20.7	18.8	19.3	18.8
Kazakhstan	74.9	75.4	69.0	53.4	60.1
Kyrgyz Republic	42.2	32.1	35.1	32.8	30.2
Tajikistan	7.6	17.3	...	...	...
Turkmenistan	...	...	...	...	...
Uzbekistan	10.0	12.8	15.3	19.5	15.2
East Asia					
Hong Kong, China	...	...	...	...	...
Mongolia	41.6	88.5	21.2	22.5	...
People's Republic of China	5.0	6.1	5.5	5.5	...
Republic of Korea	9.0	9.3	8.2	8.8	9.8
Taipei,China	1.6	2.1	1.9	2.3	4.7
South Asia					
Afghanistan	...	...	...	...	...
Bangladesh	3.2	2.8	3.0	3.5	3.4
Bhutan	19.8	14.5	24.8	23.4	15.8
India	8.8	8.3	7.5	6.4	5.8
Maldives	2.3	2.6	2.7	3.1	6.0
Nepal	8.1	9.9	10.8	8.3	8.2
Pakistan	18.0	19.4	29.6	24.9	39.3
Sri Lanka	28.2	25.6	23.9	28.9	...
Southeast Asia					
Brunei Darussalam	...	...	...	...	...
Cambodia	1.0	1.3	1.3	1.4	1.5
Indonesia	30.6	35.3	25.5	25.1	26.0
Lao People's Dem. Rep.	13.6	21.6	22.6	21.9	24.4
Malaysia	14.3	14.7	6.8	5.2	6.6
Myanmar	4.7	4.7	4.1	4.0	4.0
Philippines	5.6	7.0	6.2	6.6	6.6
Singapore	...	...	...	...	...
Thailand	6.4	5.9	5.8	6.2	6.1
Timor-Leste	0.2	0.6	1.2	2.6	6.4
Viet Nam	...	...	...	...	...
The Pacific					
Cook Islands	7.2	6.6	6.4	5.8	6.8
Federated States of Micronesia	7.8	7.0	6.1	4.5	..
Fiji	1.8	13.5	1.8	1.7	...
Kiribati	6.0	5.0	5.0	4.5	9.3
Marshall Islands	9.4	9.4	9.5	8.0	8.5
Nauru	3.7	3.0	0.0	5.0	28.5
Niue	...	...	...	...	...
Palau	4.8	6.0	5.4	6.2	9.0
Papua New Guinea	0.4	0.3	0.5	0.6	1.1
Samoa	10.2	8.2	8.2	9.6	8.6
Solomon Islands	10.0	9.4	8.4	7.0	7.4
Tonga	9.8	8.0	6.5	6.7	8.3
Tuvalu	12.2	12.0	11.6	12.4	...
Vanuatu	6.7	7.2	5.2	9.7	4.3

... = data not available.